Private Enforcement of European Competition and State Aid Law

International Competition Law Series

VOLUME 82

Editor

In its series editor, Alastair Sutton, Kluwer is fortunate to engage and benefit from the experience and expertise of one of the world's outstanding authorities on European Union and international economic law.

Introduction

In their efforts to regulate competition in an increasingly complex business environment, competition authorities face a daunting task. The European Commission and Courts, as well as national courts and legislatures, policymakers, and regulators, are constantly proposing, enacting, reviewing, and enforcing new legal measures, often addressing novel situations. Every industry and service is affected.

Contents/Subjects

With many titles currently available and new ones appearing regularly, the series' coverage includes detailed analyses of relevant legislation and case law in major global trading jurisdictions, defences used in cases involving the digital network economy, state aid cases, enforcement methodologies and a great deal more.

Objective & Readership

The purpose of Kluwer's International Competition Law Series is to follow the ever-changing contours of this dynamic area of the law, keeping the practice in sharp focus so that practising lawyers (including in-house counsel) and academics can be assured of the most up-to-date guidance and sources, in the widest possible range of applications.

The titles published in this series are listed at the end of this volume.

Private Enforcement of European Competition and State Aid Law

Current Challenges and the Way Forward

Edited by

Ferdinand Wollenschläger
Wolfgang Wurmnest
Thomas M.J. Möllers

Co-funded by the Erasmus+ Programme of the European Union

Wolters Kluwer

Published by:
Kluwer Law International B.V.
PO Box 316
2400 AH Alphen aan den Rijn
The Netherlands
E-mail: international-sales@wolterskluwer.com
Website: lrus.wolterskluwer.com

Sold and distributed in North, Central and South America by:
Wolters Kluwer Legal & Regulatory U.S.
7201 McKinney Circle
Frederick, MD 21704
United States of America
Email: customer.service@wolterskluwer.com

Sold and distributed in all other countries by:
Air Business Subscriptions
Rockwood House
Haywards Heath
West Sussex
RH16 3DH
United Kingdom
Email: international-customerservice@wolterskluwer.com

ISBN 978-94-035-0281-6

e-Book: ISBN 978-94-035-0210-6
web-PDF: ISBN 978-94-035-0233-5

List of Contributors

Prof Dr Rafael Amaro, Université de Caen Normandie
Prof Dr Luis Arroyo Jiménez, Universidad de Castilla-La Mancha
Benedetta Biancardi, Università degli Studi di Torino
Prof Christopher Bovis, University of Hull
Prof Dr Enrico Camilleri, Università degli Studi di Palermo
Prof Roberto Caranta, Università degli Studi di Torino
Prof Dr Willemien den Ouden, Universiteit Leiden
Simone Donzelli, LL.M. (Queen Mary, University of London), Policy Officer, European Commission, DG Competition
Prof Dr Jens-Uwe Franck, LL.M. (Yale), Universität Mannheim
Dr Johannes Holzwarth, LL.M. (Chicago), Policy Officer, European Commission, DG Competition
David Hug, Ruhr-Universität Bochum
Johannes Laitenberger, Director General, European Commission, DG Competition (now: Judge, General Court of the European Union)
Prof Dr François Lichère, Université Jean Moulin Lyon III
Dr Rogier Meijer, Partner, Zippro Meijer Advocaten, Amsterdam
Prof Dr Thomas M.J. Möllers, Universität Augsburg
Prof Dr Fernando Pastor-Merchante, LL.M. (Columbia), IE University
Dr Patricia Pérez Fernández, Principal Associate, Cuatrecasas, Madrid
Prof em Dr Wulf-Henning Roth, LL.M. (Harvard), Universität Bonn
Prof Dr Sebastian Unger, Ruhr-Universität Bochum
Prof Dr Jacobine E. van den Brink, Universiteit van Amsterdam
Prof Dr Florian Wagner-von Papp, LL.M. (Columbia), Helmut Schmidt Universität/Universität der Bundeswehr Hamburg
Prof Dr Ferdinand Wollenschläger, Universität Augsburg
Prof Dr Wolfgang Wurmnest, LL.M. (Berkeley), Universität Augsburg
Dr Erik-Jan Zippro, Partner, Zippro Meijer Advocaten, Amsterdam

Summary of Contents

List of Contributors v

Foreword xxiii

List of Abbreviations xxvii

Chapter 1
Introduction
Ferdinand Wollenschläger, Wolfgang Wurmnest & Thomas M.J. Möllers 1

Part I
Private Enforcement of EU Competition Law after Directive 2014/104/EU 11

Chapter 2
The European Perspective
Wulf-Henning Roth 13

Chapter 3
The European Commission's View
Johannes Holzwarth 39

Chapter 4
Private Enforcement in France
Rafael Amaro 55

Chapter 5
Private Enforcement in Germany
Jens-Uwe Franck 77

Chapter 6
Private Enforcement in Italy
Enrico Camilleri 117

Chapter 7
Private Enforcement in the Netherlands
Rogier Meijer & Erik-Jan Zippro 143

Chapter 8
Private Enforcement in the United Kingdom
Florian Wagner-von Papp 161

Part II
Private Enforcement of EU State Aid Law 195

Chapter 9
The European Perspective
Fernando Pastor-Merchante 197

Chapter 10
The Role of the European Commission and the Cooperation with National Courts
Simone Donzelli 215

Chapter 11
Private Enforcement in France
François Lichère 235

Chapter 12
Private Enforcement in Germany
Sebastian Unger & David Hug 249

Chapter 13
Private Enforcement in Italy
Roberto Caranta & Benedetta Biancardi 267

Chapter 14
Private Enforcement in the Netherlands
Jacobine E. van den Brink & Willemien den Ouden 289

Chapter 15
Private Enforcement in Spain
Luis Arroyo Jiménez & Patricia Pérez Fernández 319

Chapter 16
Private Enforcement in the UK
Christopher Bovis 339

Part III
Analysis and Outlook 353

CHAPTER 17
Private Enforcement of EU Competition and State Aid Law: Comparative Analysis and the Way Forward
Ferdinand Wollenschläger & Wolfgang Wurmnest 355

Index 387

Table of Contents

List of Contributors v

Foreword xxiii

List of Abbreviations xxvii

CHAPTER 1
Introduction
Ferdinand Wollenschläger, Wolfgang Wurmnest & Thomas M.J. Möllers 1
I. Private enforcement of EU competition and state aid law in the European Union 2
A. Private enforcement of EU competition and state aid law is on the rise 2
B. Private enforcement of EU competition law after Directive 2014/104/EU 3
C. Private enforcement of EU state aid law 6
II. The book as an effort of the Jean-Monnet Centre of Excellence INspiRE 8
A. People 8
B. Methodology 8
C. The project in context 9
III. Acknowledgements 10

PART I
Private Enforcement of EU Competition Law after Directive 2014/104/EU 11

CHAPTER 2
The European Perspective
Wulf-Henning Roth 13
I. Introduction 14
II. The case law of the Court of Justice 15
A. *Courage* 16

B. *Manfredi* 17
C. *Kone* 18
D. Observations 18
III. Directive 2014/104/EU 20
A. Transposition of case law 20
B. No clarifications 21
C. Problems addressed 21
1. Compensation, not deterrence 22
2. Passing-on 22
a) Offensive use 22
b) Defensive use 23
c) Collective redress 23
3. Effectiveness of private enforcement 23
a) Decisions of national competition authorities 23
b) Disclosure provisions 24
c) Proof of harm 24
d) Guidelines for courts 25
4. Private and public enforcement 25
5. Final observations 25
IV. The relationship between public and private enforcement 26
A. The problem 26
B. Disclosure 27
C. Follow-on actions 29
D. Limited liability of immunity recipients 29
V. The relationship between primary Union law and Directive 2014/104/EU 30
A. General principles of interpretation 30
B. Is the Directive in conformity with the case law of the Court? 31
1. The problem 31
2. Examples 31
3. Framework of analysis 32
4. Limits to legislative competence? 35
VI. Summary 36

CHAPTER 3
The European Commission's View
Johannes Holzwarth 39
I. Overview 40
II. The Commission's private enforcement policy and its effects 40
III. New rules: new (and old) questions 42
A. Limitation periods and effects of infringement decisions (*Cogeco v Sport TV Portugal*) 42
1. The relevant facts: a complaint, a decision, a claim 42
2. Questions on pre-Directive rules 43
3. Kokott on the effective application of Article 102 TFEU in damages actions 44

4. Four observations 45
B. The EU concept of undertakings in the context of private enforcement (*Vantaan v Skanska/NCC/Asfaltmix*) 46
1. An invitation to comment more broadly 46
2. An initial reaction based on established case law and the Damages Directive 47
3. Wahl on the necessary adoption of the rules on economic succession 48
C. Further guidance on causation necessary (*Otis v Land Oberösterreich*) 49
1. Potential limits on a rather complex chain of causation 49
2. Further thoughts on the relevance of Kone 50
D. EFTA Court cases: *Fjarskipti v Síminn & Nye Kystlink v Color Line* 51
IV. Passing-on of overcharges and the upcoming guidelines 52
V. Summary and conclusions 53

CHAPTER 4
Private Enforcement in France
Rafael Amaro 55
I. Introduction 56
II. The development of private enforcement 58
A. The French judicial system 58
B. Overview of the French legal framework 58
1. Transposition rules: the brand-new Title VIII of Book IV of the Commercial Code 59
2. Pre-transposition rules: four codes and a rich jurisprudence 59
III. What is effective and what are the impediments to private enforcement? 59
A. Preliminary remarks about the concept of 'effectiveness' 59
1. The 'effectiveness' of domestic rules: a matter of viewpoint? 59
2. The ECJ's definition of effectiveness 60
B. The origins of the French bad reputation: the 'magnifying effect' of the ineffectiveness of cartel damages actions? 61
1. Empirical evidence 61
a) Cartels 61
b) Abuses of a dominant position 62
c) Settlements? 63
2. The X factor behind this empirical evidence: the Directive and/or a change of attitude? 63
IV. Particular topics 64
A. Which entity is liable for damages? 64
1. Overview of the transposition rules 64
2. Persistent issue as regards the fault requirement 65
B. Binding effect of the decisions of competition authorities 66
1. Overview of the transposition rules 66

2. The *'final decision'* in the meaning of the transposition provisions 67
3. Critical appraisal 67
C. Limitation 68
1. A frequent issue in French courts 68
2. The (mind-blowing) problem of the *ratione temporis* application of the French limitation rules 69
3. Uncertainties with regard to the interaction between public and private enforcement 70
4. Overview of the transposition rules 71
5. Critical appraisal 72
D. Collective actions/pooling of claims 72
1. A long-running story ... 72
2. Main features of the action en représentation conjointe 73
3. Main features of the *action de groupe* 73
4. Critical appraisal 74

CHAPTER 5
Private Enforcement in Germany
Jens-Uwe Franck 77
I. Introduction and outline 78
II. The development of private enforcement 79
III. What does 'effectiveness' require and what are the impediments to private enforcement? 82
A. Preliminary remarks 82
1. Defining a yardstick of 'effectiveness' 82
a) Legal perspective 82
b) Theoretical perspective(s) 85
(1) Overarching regulatory purposes: deterrence and corrective justice 85
(2) On the various cost factors 87
2. (Lack of) empirical findings 88
B. Favourable developments 90
1. Clarifying legal standards: German courts appear to be on the right track (though it is not a fast track) 90
a) The right to interest in 'old' cases 90
b) Rules of proof and evidence 92
(1) Applicability of the lowered standard of proof pursuant to section 287 of the German Code of Civil Procedure 93
(2) Cartelisation as prima facie evidence or as basis for a positive presumption for a generally increased price level 94
(3) Cartelisation as prima facie evidence of an effect on the individual transaction 95

(4) Preliminary conclusions 96
2. Taking 'effectiveness' seriously: the German legislature as 'repairer' 97
C. Unsolved issues: the lack of collective redress as a major flaw 98
D. Some ambiguous findings: is the glass half full or half empty? 99
1. Costs 99
2. Expertise of the judiciary 101
3. Efficiency of court proceedings 101
IV. Particular topics 102
A. Which entity is liable for damages? 102
B. Binding effect of decisions by competition authorities 106
1. Decisions by 'foreign' NCAs ('cross-border binding effect') 107
2. Scope of the binding effect 109
3. The competition authorities as key players 111
a) Access to the decisions 111
b) Content of the decisions 112
C. Statutes of limitation 112
1. The regular period of limitation following a subjective system 113
2. Two objective periods of limitation 113
3. Enforcement actions by competition authorities 114
4. Effect of limitation 115
D. Collective action and pooling of claims 115

CHAPTER 6
Private Enforcement in Italy
Enrico Camilleri 117
I. Introduction 117
II. The development of private enforcement 118
III. What is effective and what are the impediments to private enforcement? 122
IV. Some key issues in light of Directive 2014/104 EU and its implementation 125
A. Which entity is liable for damages? 125
B. Binding effects of decisions of competition authorities 128
C. Limitation of actions 131
D. Collective actions/pooling of claims 133
V. The (further) missing pieces of the puzzle: causation and quantification of damages: some concluding remarks 136

CHAPTER 7
Private Enforcement in the Netherlands
Rogier Meijer & Erik-Jan Zippro 143
I. Introduction 143
II. The development of private enforcement 144
A. Introduction 144

B. Jurisdiction over international competition infringements 145
C. Masterfoods Defence 146
D. Applicable law 147
E. Passing-on 148
F. Implementation of Damages Directive 149
III. What is effective and what are the impediments to private enforcement? 151
IV. Which entity is liable for damages? 152
V. Binding effect of decisions of competition authorities 153
VI. Limitation of actions 153
VII. Collective actions/pooling of claims 155
A. Introduction 155
B. Assignment model 155
C. Mass settlements 156
D. Collective damages actions 157
VIII. Conclusion 159

CHAPTER 8
Private Enforcement in the United Kingdom
Florian Wagner-von Papp 161
I. Introduction and outline 162
II. The development of private enforcement 163
III. What is effective and what are the impediments to private enforcement? 167
A. What is effective? 167
1. Disclosure of evidence 167
a) Disclosure under the Civil Procedure Rules in the High Court of England & Wales 168
b) Disclosure under the CAT Rules 170
c) Confidential information 171
2. Specialised tribunal and commercially minded judges 172
3. Further advantages of the UK as a venue 173
4. Collective proceedings 174
B. What are the impediments to effective enforcement? 174
IV. Which entity is liable for damages 176
V. Binding effect of decisions of competition authorities 179
VI. Limitation of actions 181
VII. Collective actions/pooling of claims 182
A. Collective redress in the European discussion 182
B. Collective redress in the United Kingdom 183
1. First stage: Representative actions and Group Litigation Orders 183
2. Collective Proceedings Orders after the CRA 2015 184
a) The legislative scheme 184
b) Dorothy Gibson v Pride Mobility Products 185
c) Merricks v Mastercard 187
VIII. Brexit 189

A. No deal 189
1. Jurisdiction and Enforcement: Brussels I Recast Regulation 190
2. Taking of Evidence 190
3. 2019 Regulations and follow-on actions 191
4. Brexit implications for the implementation of the Damages Directive 192
B. Withdrawal Agreement 192
IX. Conclusion 193

PART II
Private Enforcement of EU State Aid Law 195

CHAPTER 9
The European Perspective
Fernando Pastor-Merchante 197
I. Introduction 197
II. The public enforcement of State aid law 199
III. The role of national courts in the enforcement of State aid law 202
IV. Stand-alone actions based on the direct effect of the standstill clause 204
V. Follow-on actions based on the direct effect of Commission decisions 209
VI. The interplay between the public and the private enforcement of State aid law 211
VII. Conclusion 213

CHAPTER 10
The Role of the European Commission and the Cooperation with National Courts
Simone Donzelli 215
I. Introduction 215
II. Legal framework: the roles of the Commission and the national courts in supervising State aid 216
III. The cooperation tools 220
A. From their origins to their codification 220
B. The cooperation tools in practice 223
C. The use of cooperation tools 226
IV. The enforcement of State aid rules by national courts in relation to the cooperation tools 229
V. Gathering information and outlook on enforcement: the 2019 Study 232
VI. Concluding remarks 233

CHAPTER 11
Private Enforcement in France
François Lichère 235
I. Figures and presentation of the French framework for private enforcement of state aid rules 236

A. Figures 236
II. Presentation of the French private enforcement system and its framework 238
III. Efficiency of the French private enforcement system 239
A. Efficient remedies 239
1. Standing 239
2. Timing of actions 241
3. Legal arguments which can be invoked 241
4. Power of the courts 242
5. Efficiency of recovery actions 242
6. Recovery of illegal state aid 243
B. Inefficient remedies 244
1. Interim measures: conditions and pitfalls 244
2. Damages: conditions and practical difficulties 245
IV. Conclusion 247

Chapter 12
Private Enforcement in Germany
Sebastian Unger & David Hug 249
I. Introduction: Germany as a late developer in private enforcement 249
II. Private enforcement of the standstill obligation in Germany 251
A. Private enforcement and the dualistic court system 251
B. Violation of a subjective right as the procedural bottleneck 252
C. Claims for recovery of state aid in typical constellations 252
1. State aid granted by administrative acts 253
2. State aid granted by private or public law contracts 254
3. State aid granted in two stages 255
D. Interim measures to safeguard competitors' rights 256
III. The competitors' information deficit 257
A. Transparency obligations under EU law 257
B. Rights to information under national law 258
IV. Competitors' claims for damages 259
A. Legal basis under national law 260
B. Burden of proof on the claimant 260
C. Potential facilitation of evidence 261
V. Cooperation between the National Courts and the Commission 262
A. Deutsche Lufthansa and its general reception in Germany 262
B. Coming to terms with Deutsche Lufthansa: the German courts 263
VI. Conclusion 265

Chapter 13
Private Enforcement in Italy
Roberto Caranta & Benedetta Biancardi 267
I. Introduction: the development of private enforcement in Italy 267
II. Legal framework 268

A. An asymmetric dual jurisdiction system 268
B. Standing 270
III. Substantive prohibition of state aid (Article 107 TFEU) 272
IV. Enforcement of the standstill obligation (Article 108(3) section 3 TFEU) and interim relief 275
V. Transparency and right of access 276
VI. Damages 279
VII. Cooperation and coordination between national courts and the European Commission and the CJEU 283
VIII. A digression on public procurement and concessions 285
IX. Private enforcement of EU competition and state aid law: the way forward 287

CHAPTER 14
Private Enforcement in the Netherlands
Jacobine E. van den Brink & Willemien den Ouden 289
I. Introduction 290
II. Illegal state aid: which court has jurisdiction? 291
III. The Dutch administrative courts and state aid claims 293
A. Spatial planning 293
B. Unlawful advantage for the competitor 296
C. Levy decisions 299
D. Decisions to reject a request for aid and revocation decisions 300
E. Recovery decisions 300
IV. The Dutch tax courts and state aid claims 301
V. The Dutch civil courts and state aid claims 302
A. Introduction 302
B. Types of disputes before the civil courts 302
1. Disputes where the government is accused of having granted an advantage to a competitor 303
2. Disputes between the alleged beneficiary and another private party 304
3. Disputes about levies intended to finance state aid 304
4. Disputes concerning expropriation 305
5. Disputes on the enforcement of a recovery decision taken by the European Commission 305
6. Disputes where the government has revoked a granted benefit or refuses to grant an advantage 305
C. Available judgment options for the civil courts 306
D. Bottlenecks in state aid cases before the civil courts 307
1. Interest requirements and the Schutznorm 307
a) Competitors 307
b) Other private parties that invoke state aid law 308
c) Government interest in bringing proceedings in the civil courts 310

2. Qualification of state aid 310
3. Compensation for damages in state aid cases 312
4. A ray of light: the alleged support conflicts with general principles of sound administration 313
VI. Taking stock of the private enforcement of state aid law in the Netherlands 315
VII. Dutch State Aid Recovery Act 316

Chapter 15
Private Enforcement in Spain
Luis Arroyo Jiménez & Patricia Pérez Fernández 319
I. The enforcement of the standstill obligation 319
A. General issues 319
B. Legal framework 320
C. Public law remedies 322
1. Preventing the payment of unlawful aid 322
2. Recovery of unlawful aid and illegality interest 323
3. Damages for competitors and other third parties 326
4. Interim measures against unlawful aid 328
5. Procedural issues 330
D. Private law remedies 331
II. Cooperation and coordination between national courts and the European Commission 332
III. The enforcement of European Commission decisions 333
A. Recovery of subsidies 334
B. Recovery of fiscal state aids 335
IV. Conclusions 336

Chapter 16
Private Enforcement in the UK
Christopher Bovis 339
I. Introduction 339
II. The structure of the UK's competition regime 341
III. The UK state aid compliance system 343
IV. The UK remedial system of state aid 344
A. Locus standi 344
B. Judicial review in state aid 346
C. Damages in state aid 346
D. Recovery of illegal state aid 347
E. Private enforcement of state aid rules in the UK 350
V. Conclusions 351

Part III
Analysis and Outlook 353

CHAPTER 17
Private Enforcement of EU Competition and State Aid Law: Comparative Analysis and the Way Forward
Ferdinand Wollenschläger & Wolfgang Wurmnest 355
I. Private enforcement of EU competition law after Directive 2014/104/EU 356
A. The Damages Directive: standard setting, frictions and (potential) impact 356
1. General standards 356
2. Frictions with primary law 357
3. Fostering private enforcement? 358
B. Harmonising the law of private enforcement 359
1. Entity liable for damages 359
2. Binding effect of national decisions 362
3. Prescription (limitation of actions) 365
C. The role of national courts and legislatures 366
II. Private enforcement of EU state aid law 367
A. Background: EU law framework for state aid 367
B. Key issues of private enforcement 369
1. Enforcement of EU state aid law 370
a) EU law background 370
aa) Standstill obligation (Article 108(3) TFEU) 370
bb) Substantive prohibition of state aid (Article 107 TFEU) 373
b) Enforcement at the national level 374
aa) General remarks 374
bb) Remedies 376
cc) Information deficits 378
2. Cooperation and coordination between national courts and the European Commission 379
a) EU law background 379
b) Enforcement at the national level 381
III. The way forward 382
A. Spill-over effects 382
B. Strengthening private enforcement of EU competition law 382
1. Guidance for courts 382
2. Improving the law at the national level 383
3. Closing gaps at the European level 384
C. Constructing a proper framework for private enforcement of EU state aid law 385

Index 387

Foreword

The conference on 'Private Enforcement of European Competition and State Aid Law' offered an extremely valuable forum for discussion. Not only did it allow speakers, as well as participants, to discuss the achievements that we have already reached in the emerging field of private enforcement of EU law, this conference also specifically addressed the challenges we need to tackle in the future to safeguard that any EU citizen can effectively exercise the right to compensation for harm suffered due to infringements of competition or State aid law. I would like to congratulate Professor Dr Ferdinand Wollenschläger, Professor Dr Wolfgang Wurmnest and Professor Dr Thomas M.J. Möllers for having organised this conference. It is a great pleasure and honour for me to contribute to the lasting outcome of the conference by sharing some thoughts in this foreword.

While private enforcement of EU competition law has been on top of the political agenda for some years, one can readily argue that private enforcement of EU State aid law has still much to accomplish.

As regards private enforcement of EU competition law, the adoption of the Damages Directive 2014/104/EU marked, without doubt, a first peak of a policy project that was essentially triggered by the Court of Justice of the EU in two judgments that probably any competition lawyer has heard of: *Courage v Crehan* and *Manfredi*. These judgements also triggered a broad public debate which the Commission stimulated with a Green Paper in 2005, a White Paper in 2008 and the legislative proposal in 2013. In this debate, academic discussions have not only accompanied legislative developments but also essentially paved the paths for future rules at EU and national level.

The policy project in the area of private enforcement of EU competition law reached its second peak when all of the Member States implemented the Damages Directive 2014/104/EU. It means that throughout the EU there are now harmonised rules in place that strike the right balance between public and private enforcement and that allow victims to seek compensation for infringements of Articles 101 and 102 TFEU effectively. It comes with a degree of contentment that recent studies show an increasing number of damages actions for competition law infringements. This proves that the legislative efforts are bearing fruits already. However, the Commission should not lean back and take a rest.

Speaking for the Directorate General for Competition of the European Commission, this means that we must attentively monitor how the new provisions are applied in practice and, if necessary, evaluate whether intervention might be opportune.

Further, a core task of the Commission in the field of private enforcement of EU competition law has been to support and give guidance to the national courts and judges who are facing increasingly complex proceedings. Indeed, damages actions for competition law infringements are often challenging not only with respect to the legal questions but also especially in relation to the economic assessment. It is exactly for this reason why the European Commission already issued a practical guide on quantifying antitrust overcharges (in 2013) and is now finalising guidelines on the passing-on of overcharges (to be adopted in 2019).

When it comes to the supervision of State aid, private enforcement is also an inherent feature of the system established under the TFEU. The direct effect of Article 108(3) TFEU, in fact, gives national courts the responsibility to prevent the unlawful payment of aid that needs approval by the European Commission.

The role of private enforcement and its complementarity with the public enforcement of State aid rules, as recognised by the Court of Justice of the EU, is an axiom for the functioning of the internal market. In particular, the European Commission openly acknowledged the importance of private litigation in its 2005 State aid action plan. The 2012 State aid modernisation, by which almost all of the new aid measures are exempted from notification to the European Commission, amplifies the role of private enforcement. To support their role, national courts have at their disposal a series of communications and guidelines by the European Commission, on both substantive and procedural matters. In addition, since 1995, the European Commission has streamlined tools to improve cooperation with national courts.

However, the studies carried out in 1999, 2006 and 2009 demonstrated that private enforcement was still in its infancy. At the same time, in light of the complementarity between the role of the European Commission and that of national courts, it is difficult for the European Commission to gain a privileged view over the private enforcement of State aid rules and study ways to make it more effective. Against this background, the European Commission tendered in 2018 a study on the enforcement of State aid rules and decisions by national courts. The study should present the current state of play of private enforcement in all its aspects. From that standpoint, the European Commission may consider whether and how to foster recourse to private enforcement and cooperation with national courts.

To conclude, I wish to emphasise that promoting private enforcement as a complement to public enforcement is not only a means to strengthen the European internal market as a whole but also notably a means from which every company and every citizen of the European Union as a consumer directly benefits.

The proceedings of the conference that are put together in this book contribute to this goal.

Many thanks for this contribution.

Johannes Laitenberger
Former Director General, European Commission and
now Judge at the General Court of the European Union

List of Abbreviations

a.M.	am Main
AC	Appeal Cases
AG	Advocate General
AGCM	Autorità garante della concorrenza e del mercato
AIDA	Annali Italiani del Diritto d'Autore
AJCA	Actualité Juridique des Contrats d'Affaires
AJDA	Actualité Juridique Droit Administratif
Ariz. Law Review	Arizona Law Review
Art.	Article
B2B	Business-to-Business
B2C	Business-to-Costumer
BB	Betriebs-Berater
BeckRS	Beck online Rechtsprechung
BEIS	Department for Business, Energy & Industrial Strategy (UK)
BGH	Bundesgerichtshof
BGHZ	Entscheidungen des Bundesgerichtshofs in Zivilsachen
BJCL	Bulletin Juridique des Collectivités Locales
Bull. Joly Sociétés	Bulletin Joly Sociétés
BVerfG	Bundesverfassungsgericht
BVerwG	Bundesverwaltungsgericht
c.	chapter number
CA	Competition Act, Court of Appeal
CAA	Cour administrative d'appel

Cass.	Corte di Cassazione
Cass. civ. 1	Cour de Cassation, première chambre civile
Cass. com.	Cour de Cassation, chambre commerciale
CAT	Competition Appeal Tribunal
CBb	College van Beroep voor het Bedrijfsleven
CC	Civil Code
CE	Conseil d'Etat, Constitución Española de 1978
CE Ass.	Conseil d'Etat, assemblée du contentieux
CEPS	Erasmus Centre for European Policy Studies
cf.	confer
CFR	Charter of Fundamental Rights of the EU
Ch	Chancery
chron.	chronique
CISG	United Nations Convention on Contracts for the International Sale of Goods
CJEU	Court of Justice of the European Union
CLC	Commercial Law Cases
CMA	Competition and Markets Authority
CML Rev.	Common Market Law Review
CMLR	Common Market Law Reports
CNMC	Comisión Nacional de la Competencia
COM	European Commission
Comm	Commercial Court
Comm.	Commentaires
concl.	conclusions
Cons. conc.	Conseil de la concurrence
Cons. Giustizia Amm. Reg. Sicilia	Consiglio di giustizia amministrativa per la Regione siciliana
Cons. Stato	Consiglio di Stato
Contrats conc. consom.	Contrats Concurrence Consommation
CPI	Competition Policy International
CPO	Collective Proceedings Order
CPR	Civil Procedure Rules
CRA	Consumer Rights Act
CRvB	Centrale Raad van Beroep
CSOH	Court of Sessions, Outer House
D.	Recueil Dalloz
D.lgs	Decreto legislativo

DCFR	Draft Common Frame of Reference
déc.	décision
DG	Directorate General
DG Comp	Directorate General for Competition
DGIP	Directorate General for Internal Policies
Dir. Comm. Int.	Il Diritto commerciale internazionale
Dir. e Prat. Tributaria	Diritto e pratica tributaria
Div Ct	Divisional Court
Dr. adm.	Droit administratif
e.g.	exempli gratia
E.L. Rev.	European Law Review
EA	Enterprise Act
EBOR	European Business Organization Law Review
EC	European Commission, European Communities
ECA	European Communities Act
ECHR	European Convention on Human Rights
ECJ	European Court of Justice
ECLR	European Competition Law Review
ECR	European Courts Report
ECtHR	European Court of Human Rights
ed.	editor, edition
eds	editors
EEA Agreement	Agreement on the European Economic Area
EEC	European Economic Community
EFTA Court	Court of Justice of the European Free Trade Association
EGC	General Court
EIS	Enterprise Investment Scheme
EPPPL	European Procurement & Public Private Partnership Law Review
ERA Forum	Journal of the Academy of European Law
ERPL	European Review of Public Law
EStAL	European State Aid Law Quarterly
et al.	et alii
et seq.	et sequens
etc.	et cetera
EU	European Union
EuLR	European Law Reports

EUR	Erasmus University Rotterdam, Euro
EuR	Europarecht
EuZW	Europäische Zeitschrift für Wirtschaftsrecht
EWCA Civ	England and Wales Court of Appeal (Civil Division)
EWHC	England and Wales High Court
EWS	Europäisches Wirtschafts- und Steuerrecht
GALA	General Administrative Law Act (Netherlands)
GBER	General Block Exemption Regulation
GC	General Court
GDP	Gross Domestic Product
Giur. Ital.	Giurisprudenza Italiana
GRUR	Gewerblicher Rechtsschutz und Urheberrecht
GWB	Gesetz gegen Wettbewerbsbeschränkungen
Hof	Gerechtshof
HR	Hoge Raad
i.e.	id est
ibid.	ibidem
ICR	Irish Circuit Reports
Iowa L.Rev.	Iowa Law Review
IRJS	Institut de Recherche de la Sorbonne
Italian ConsumerC	Italian Consumer Code
Italian CPC	Italian Civil Procedure Code
ItalianCC	Italian Civil Code
J. Comp. L. & Econ.	Journal of Competition Law & Economics
J.L. Econ. & Org.	Journal of Law, Economics, & Organization
J.Law. & Econ.	Journal of Law & Economics
JCP	Semaine juridique
JECLAP	Journal of European Competition Law & Practice
JOR	Jurisprudentie Onderneming & Recht
JORF	Journal Officiel de la République Française
KG	Kammergericht
KommJur	Kommunaljurist
L	Legge
LCD	Ley de Competencia Desleal
LDC	Ley de Defensa de la Competencia
Lfg.	Lieferung
LG	Landgericht

LGDJ	Librairie Générale de Droit et de Jurisprudence
LGS	Ley General de Subvenciones
LGT	Ley General Tributaria
LJCA	Ley de la Jurisdicción Contencioso-Administrativa
LPAC	Ley de Procedimiento Administrativo Común
LRJSP	Ley de Régimen Jurídico del Sector Público
Ltd	Limited
m	million
MEP	Milieukwaliteit van de Elektriciteitsproductie
MIF	Multilateral Exchange Fees
MJ	Maastricht Journal of European and Comparative Law
n.	note
NCA	National Competition Authority
NIQB	Northern Ireland Queens Bench of High Court of Justice
NJ	Nederlandse Jurisprudentie
NJOZ	Neue Juristische Online-Zeitschrift
NJW	Neue Juristische Wochenschrift
NJW-RR	NJW-Rechtsprechungs-Report Zivilrecht
no.	number
NPC	National Pensioners Convention
NVwZ	Neue Zeitschrift für Verwaltungsrecht
NZKart	Neue Zeitschrift für Kartellrecht
obs.	observations, commentaires doctrinaux
OFT	Office of Fair Trading
OJ	Official Journal of the European Union
OLG	Oberlandesgericht
ord.	ordinanza
OVG	Oberverwaltungsgericht
para., paras	paragraph, paragraphs
QBD	Queen's Bench Division
Rb.	Rechtbank
Rec. Leb.	Recueil Lebon (Recueil des décisions du Conseil d'État, statuant au contentieux)
Rev. Sociétés	Revue des Sociétés
RFDA	Revue Française de Droit Administratif
Riv. Trim. Dir. e Proc. Civ.	Rivista Trimestrale di Diritto e Proceduria Civile
RJDA	Revue de Jurisprudence de Droit des Affaires

RLC	Revue Lamy de la Concurrence
RLDA	Revue Lamy Droit des Affaires
RLDC	Revue Lamy Droit Civil
RPC	Reports of Patent Cases
RRP	Recommended Retail Price
RSC	Rules of the Supreme Court
RTD civ.	Revue Trimestrielle de Droit civil
RTD com.	Revue Trimestrielle de Droit commercial et de droit économique
s.r.l.	Società a responsabilità limitata
SAAP	State Aid Action Plan
SAM	EU State Aid Modernisation
SEW	Tijdschrift voor Europees en economisch recht
sez.	sezione
Sez. Un.	Corte di cassazione, Sezioni Unite
SGEI	Services of General Economic Interest
SMEs	Small and Medium-Sized Enterprises
Stan. L. Rev.	Stanford Law Review
Stb.	Staatsblad van het Koninkrijk der Nederlanden
sub	subchapter
SWD	Staff and Joint Staff Working Documents
T. com.	Tribunal de Commerce
T.A.R.	Tribunale Amministrativo Regionale
tbl.	table
TEU	Treaty on European Union
TFEU	Treaty of the Functioning of the EU
TGI	Tribunal de Grande Instance
Trib.	Tribunal
TTIP	Transatlantic Trade and Investment Partnership
U.Chic.L.Rev.	University of Chicago Law Review
UK	United Kingdom
UKCLR	UK Competition Law Reports
UKHL	House of Lords
UKSC	Supreme Court
US	United States of America
v	versus
VCT	Venture Capital Trusts Scheme
Verg	Vergabesache(n)

VG	Verwaltungsgericht
vol.	volume
wbl	Wirtschaftsrechtliche Blätter
WiVerw	Wirtschaft und Verwaltung
WL	Westlaw
WLR	Weekly Law Reports
WTO	World Trade Organization
WuW	Wirtschaft und Wettbewerb
WuW/E	Wirtschaft und Wettbewerb – Entscheidungssammlung
ZfPW	Zeitschrift für die gesamte Privatrechtswissenschaft
ZHR	Zeitschrift für das gesamte Handelsrecht und Wirtschaftsrecht
ZWeR	Zeitschrift für Wettbewerbsrecht

CHAPTER 1

Introduction

Ferdinand Wollenschläger, Wolfgang Wurmnest & Thomas M.J. Möllers

I. Private enforcement of EU competition and state aid law in the European Union
   A. Private enforcement of EU competition and state aid law is on the rise
   B. Private enforcement of EU competition law after Directive 2014/104/EU
   C. Private enforcement of EU state aid law
II. The book as an effort of the Jean-Monnet Centre of Excellence INspiRE
   A. People
   B. Methodology
   C. The project in context
III. Acknowledgements

This book explores private enforcement of EU competition and state aid law in the European Union (section I.). It is an effort of the INspiRE project (European Integration – Rule of Law and Enforcement), a Jean-Monnet Centre of Excellence at the University of Augsburg (section II.), and it would not have seen the light of day without the support of many helping hands (section III.).

I. PRIVATE ENFORCEMENT OF EU COMPETITION AND STATE AID LAW IN THE EUROPEAN UNION

A. Private enforcement of EU competition and state aid law is on the rise

This book is the fruit of an international conference that took place in Augsburg on 22 and 23 November 2018.[1] It addresses two key areas of EU law in which private law enforcement has become increasingly important over the last years, albeit to a different extent: EU competition law and EU state aid law. Both areas are examined from the EU perspective and from the perspective of the national law of selected Member States. In a concluding section, the country reports are evaluated from a comparative perspective to identify enforcement deficits and to discuss how the existing legal framework can be improved. In addition, it is evaluated to what extent the strengthening of private enforcement of competition law has a spill-over effect on the area of state aid law, a field in which the private enforcement of the EU law prohibition of unlawful state aids is ripe for being strengthened and possibly harmonised through a European instrument. Also taken into consideration is whether the private enforcement of state aid law projects its own spill-over effect in the field of competition law.

The section on competition law enforcement has the following background: The EU Member States have recently finished implementation of the so-called *Damages Directive* (Directive 2014/104/EU),[2] which covers important issues – but not all areas – of private enforcement of competition law. Furthermore, the Damages Directive provides full harmonisation in relation to many, albeit not all issues. The legal framework is therefore not completely harmonised in Europe, leaving room for forum shopping.[3] In view of this new legal framework, the 'law in action' for the enforcement of the European competition rules in various Member States is examined, in the process focusing on damages claims against cartels, which are currently the most common form of private law enforcement. This compilation is one of the first to be published after the transposition of the Damages Directive.[4]

The background of the section on state aid law is the following: In view of limited administrative capacities at the European level, the trend towards decentralising the review of state aid systems and the structural deficits associated with state aid law being enforced by national authorities (themselves responsible for breaches of state aid

1. On the conference *see* Cornelia Kibler and Simon Zechmann, *Private Enforcement of European Competition and State Aid Law: Current Challenges and the Way Forward* [2019] EuZW 73–75; Johannes Stapf and Benedikt Wössner, *Private Enforcement of European Competition and State Aid Law: Current Challenges and the Way Forward – Konferenz in Augsburg am 22. und 23.11.2018* [2019] NZKart 96–98.
2. Directive 2014/104/EU of the European Parliament and of the Council of 26 November 2014 on certain rules governing actions for damages under national law for infringements of the competition law provisions of the Member States and of the European Union [2014], OJ L349/1.
3. Jürgen Basedow, *Die kartellrechtliche Schadensersatzhaftung und der Wettbewerb der Justizstandorte* [2016] Basler Juristische Mitteilungen 217, 239; Wolfgang Wurmnest, *Forum Shopping bei Kartellschadensersatzklagen und die Kartellschadensersatzrichtlinie* [2017] NZKart 2, 10.
4. For a similar study *see* Barry Rodger, Miguel Sousa Ferro and Francisco Marcos (eds), *The EU Antitrust Damages Directive: Transposition in the Member States* (OUP 2018).

law), the importance of private enforcement for an effective enforcement of EU state aid law has been continuously stressed and the number of cases before national courts has increased. Nonetheless, there is room for improvement both in terms of numbers and the efficiency of private enforcement. The main challenge results from the fact that, despite its importance, private enforcement has not been harmonised. Hence, the obligations resulting from EU law have to be enforced according to rules of national law which diverge greatly and do not provide for specific remedies. Against this background, a first step to strengthening private enforcement of state aid law is to analyse the mechanisms of enforcement available within the national legal orders. This allows identifying not only key obstacles to private enforcement in the relevant procedural and substantive rules but also best practices. On this basis and with regard to the experiences gained in the area of competition law, the need for a harmonisation on the EU level is explored, notably with regard to claims for damages, which form the basis of the recently adopted Directive 2014/104/EU in competition law. Such an analysis – which also includes the current case law, particularly in view of recent developments on both the EU and national levels – is at present not available in book form.

The book has a tripartite structure: The first part takes a closer look at the law of private enforcement of EU competition law after the implementation of the Directive 2014/104/EU. The second part deals with the European foundations of private enforcement of state aid law. The final part draws the strings together and evaluates the tool of private enforcement from a European and comparative perspective.

B. Private enforcement of EU competition law after Directive 2014/104/EU

1. The part on private enforcement of EU competition law starts with a chapter on the European perspective written by *Wulf-Henning Roth* (Universität Bonn). *Inter alia*, this chapter explains the European concept of private enforcement of competition law as it is manifested in the Damages Directive. In addition, the relationship between public and private enforcement is highlighted, and tensions between the older case law (based on EU primary law) and the Damages Directive are evaluated. The European perspective is completed by a comment from *Johannes Holzwarth* (European Commission). He explains the European Commission's private enforcement policy and takes a look at proceedings pending before the European Court of Justice to evaluate their impact on private enforcement; further, he touches upon the draft guidelines on the passing-on of cartel overcharges.
2. The subsequent chapters contain national reports for five selected countries, thereby exploring the law in action following the implementation of the Damages Directive. The book first considers three legal systems of EU Member States which have considerable experience with the private enforcement of competition law. These jurisdictions are Germany, the United Kingdom and the Netherlands.

The German report is written by *Jens-Uwe Franck* (Universität Mannheim). *Germany* transposed the Damages Directive by amending the Act against Restraints of

Competition in June 2017.[5] As Germany has a relatively long tradition of competition law, it had already implemented reforms several years earlier to foster the enforcement of competition law by private plaintiffs. As a result, there is a significant body of case law in Germany on claims for damages arising from competition law infringements which are only in part affected by the transposition of the Damages Directive.

The *United Kingdom* is one of the leading European jurisdictions for claims in respect of damages arising from competition law infringements. There is a considerable amount of case law, and the UK has also attracted many foreign plaintiffs harmed by international cartels. The Damages Directive was transposed in March 2017.[6] As the UK has maintained more favourable rules for plaintiffs as far as this was compatible with the Directive and has also introduced measures of collective redress, its rules may serve as model for other states wishing to improve their legal framework for actions for damages. The UK report, which also tries to assess the impact of Brexit on private enforcement (based on a 'no-deal' scenario and based on the Withdrawal Agreement) is written by *Florian Wagner-von Papp* (Helmut Schmidt Universität/Universität der Bundeswehr Hamburg).

The Dutch report is a joint effort by *Rogier Meijer* and *Erik-Jan Zippro* (Zippro Meijer Advocaten). *The Netherlands* transposed Directive 2014/104/EU in January 2017.[7] Even before the transposition of the Directive, this country was an attractive forum for plaintiffs seeking compensation for competition law infringements. Not only national but also many international cases were litigated before Dutch courts. In addition, the Netherlands introduced measures for collective remedies.

In addition to these jurisdictions, the book takes into account the national systems of two states where such private enforcement actions have – at least from the view of the outsider – only recently emerged in greater numbers. In *France*, the private enforcement of competition law was on the rise even before the transposition of the Damages Directive in March 2017.[8] In addition, France is a very important civil law jurisdiction whose tort law system has influenced many other codifications in southern Europe. The French report was written by *Rafael Amaro* (Université de Caen Normandie).

In *Italy*, Directive 2014/104/EU was implemented by Legislative Decree no. 3/2017.[9] Given that prior to this point the system of private enforcement of competition

5. Neuntes Gesetz zur Änderung des Gesetzes gegen Wettbewerbsbeschränkungen of 1 June 2017, BGBl. 2017 I, 1416.
6. The Claims in respect of Loss or Damage arising from Competition Infringements (Competition Act 1998 and Other Enactments (Amendment)) Regulations 2017, Statutory Instruments 2017 no. 385 of 8 March 2017.
7. Implementatiewet richtlijn privaatrechtelijke handhaving mededingingsrecht of 25 January 2017, Staatsblad van het Koninkrijk der Nederlanden 2017, 28.
8. Ordonnance no. 2017-303 of 9 March 2017 and Décret no. 2017-305 of 9 March 2017 relative aux actions en dommages et intérêts du fait des pratiques anticoncurrentielles, JORF no. 59 of 10 March 2017, no. 29 and no. 31.
9. Decreto Legislativo 3/2017, Attuazione della direttiva 2014/104/UE del Parlamento europeo e del Consiglio, del 26 novembre 2014, relativa a determinate norme che regolano le azioni per il risarcimento del danno ai sensi del diritto nazionale per violazioni delle disposizioni del diritto della concorrenza degli Stati membri e dell'Unione europea, Gazetta Ufficiale no. 15 of 19 January 2017.

law seemed to be underdeveloped, the Italian contribution, written by *Enrico Camilleri* (Università degli Studi di Palermo) focuses on the changes and evaluates whether and to what extent they will foster private enforcement.

3. Since it would go beyond the scope of the publication to deal with all legal issues related to private enforcement, the editors have predefined four sets of questions that all the rapporteurs have addressed. These questions concern key issues of private enforcement.

The first issue concerns the question of the entity liable for competition law infringements. It was – at least before the *Skanska* judgment[10] of the European Court of Justice – hotly debated whether the liable party is exclusively the economic entity directly involved in the cartel or, in accordance with the principles applicable to infringement decisions of the EU Commission, also, for example, the parent company behind the cartel member where it exercises a decisive influence over its subsidiary. In this regard, there is a dispute not only as to whether the 'economic entity doctrine' should apply to damages claims, but also whether this transferal flows from the Damages Directive or from primary EU law.

The second issue concerns the binding effect of decisions of national competition authorities. Article 9 Damages Directive sets forth general rules. The reporters explain the scope and effects of the national implementation of these rules, which might reveal differences.

The third issue concerns the law of prescription (limitation of actions), which is of great concern in practice. The Damages Directive partly sets forth a minimum harmonisation, thus giving the Member States some leeway to structure the law. In light of these different regimes, limitation issues are of great practical importance and can incentivise 'forum shopping'.

Finally, the national reporters should address the possibilities of plaintiffs having recourse to collective actions or (in case there are no collective-action mechanisms) pooling their claims by assignment. The Damages Directive does not touch upon collective redress mechanisms since the Member States could not reach an agreement on the specific structure of such a mechanism. However, the Commission has issued a recommendation to the Member States asking them to implement collective-action mechanisms. Some states (e.g., France, the Netherlands and Italy) have created collective actions whose effectiveness for the enforcement of competition law remains to be evaluated. In other states, such as Germany, assignment models have been emerged in legal practice allowing the pooling of claims. Both models are analysed.

In addition to these issues, all country reporters address specific issues which they believe that their respective Member State handles particularly well and also issues that raise potential impediments to the private enforcement of competition law. Each country report therefore follows the following general structure, but the reporters were of course free to adapt it to their needs:

10. ECJ, Case C-724/17 *Vantaan kaupunki v Skanska Industrial Solutions* [2019] ECLI:EU:C:2019:204.

- Introduction.
- The development of private enforcement.
- What is effective and what are the impediments to private enforcement?
- Which entity is liable for damages.
- The binding effect of decisions of competition authorities.
- Prescription (limitation of actions).
- Collective actions/pooling of claims.

C. Private enforcement of EU state aid law

1. The part on private enforcement of EU state aid law first introduces the general EU law framework (*Fernando Pastor-Merchante*, IE University), while a second contribution specifically focuses on the role of the European Commission as well as its cooperation with national courts (*Simone Donzelli*, European Commission). The concept of private enforcement of state aid law as well as its relationship with public enforcement is explored. Moreover, its development and the EU legal framework as established particularly in the European Court of Justice's case law - but also in the practice of the EU Commission - is sketched. A particular focus lies on the different functions that national courts play in the area of state aid law.
2. Since private enforcement in EU state aid law has, unlike in competition law, not been harmonised, the (national) implementation of the general EU law requirement of effective (private) enforcement of EU state aid law is of great interest. Insofar, the subsequent chapters found in this part will analyse different legal systems of EU Member States which have substantial experience with private enforcement: France (*François Lichère*, Université Jean Moulin Lyon), Germany (*Sebastian Unger/David Hug*, Ruhr-Universität Bochum), Italy (*Roberto Caranta/Benedetta Biancardi*, Università degli Studi di Torino), the Netherlands (*Jacobine E. van den Brink*, Universiteit van Amsterdam, and *Willemien den Ouden*, Universiteit Leiden), Spain (*Luis Arroyo Jiménez*, Universidad de Castilla-La Mancha, and *Patricia Pérez*, Cuatrecasas) and the United Kingdom (*Christopher Bovis*, University of Hull).

The editors have predefined key issues of private enforcement that all the rapporteurs have addressed. These are:

First, apart from an overview on the general legal framework, the contributions analyse which remedies are available under which conditions, asking further which specific obstacles in the relevant procedural and substantive as well as which best practices may be identified. Notably, the issue of damages is explored in more detail since, on the one hand, the availability of damages constitutes a strong incentive for competitors to embark on the route of private enforcement, but on the other hand their practical role seems to be limited in view of the difficulties in establishing causation and the existence of a damage. A further potential obstacle to effective private enforcement seems to be information deficits, which is why their relevance and possible countermeasures, such as competitors' claims seeking access to information, have to be

addressed. Moreover, it is asked whether specific difficulties in cross-border cases have become manifest.
A second key issue concerns the cooperation and coordination between national courts and the European Commission, since private and public enforcement may overlap, especially in view of assessing the existence of state aid: To what extent does a decision of the European Commission to initiate a formal examination procedure produce a binding effect? Such effect is, in principle, required by EU law, but it has been qualified by national courts such as the German Supreme Civil Court (Bundesgerichtshof). Moreover, how do national courts establish the existence of state aid and to what extent do they cooperate with the European Commission in this regard; in particular, what is the relevance of requests for information/observations and of amicus curiae interventions under Article 29 Regulation 2015/1589?

Ultimately, the aforementioned aspects should lead to general findings on private enforcement within the national legal orders, thereby including observations on: its development (is there any reluctance to be observed, like in Germany?); any influence of competition law; its relevance and effectiveness, this including a discussion of possible improvements (key obstacles to private enforcement in the relevant procedural and substantive rules, best practices, a need for codification); and its role in the context of enforcing (EU) law, notably with respect to its relationship with public enforcement (what is the appropriateness of allocating enforcement tasks to the judiciary, also in view of the binding effect of executive decisions?).

In addition to these issues, all country reporters address specific issues which they believe their Member State handle particularly well and also those issues raising potential obstacles in their country. Each country report in the state aid part, therefore, follows the following general structure, but the reporters were, of course, free to adapt this structure to their needs:

- Introduction.
- The development of private enforcement.
- Legal framework.
- Enforcement of the standstill obligation (Article 108(3) TFEU) and of the EU Commission's final decision (remedies and information deficits).
- Cooperation and coordination between national courts and the European Commission.
- Overall assessment in view of key obstacles, best practices and the need for codification.

II. THE BOOK AS AN EFFORT OF THE JEAN-MONNET CENTRE OF EXCELLENCE INspiRE

A. People

The Jean-Monnet Centre of Excellence INspiRE (European Integration - Rule of Law and Enforcement) at the University of Augsburg for research on legal enforcement aims to combine several legal spheres and to collaborate across the various legal areas because similar questions arise in multiple Member States of the European Union as well. Its mission is to conduct research on European law from the perspective of legal enforcement ('law in action'). The people behind INspiRE are *Thomas M.J. Möllers, Ferdinand Wollenschläger, Wolfgang Wurmnest* (all Augsburg), *Beate Gsell* (Munich), *Frédérique Ferrand* (Lyon), *Enrico Camilleri* (Palermo) and *Tong Zhan* (Beijing). It is funded by the Erasmus + Programme of the European Union.

B. Methodology

The research project is based on three pillars.

First, the 'intra-disciplinary-pillar' is of particular importance; through this approach, the problem is taken into account by treating a general topic from the viewpoint of different fields of law. This allows an in-depth depiction of the underlying difficulties within the framework of legal enforcement, and it enriches research with synergistic effects vis-à-vis innovative solutions existing at the macro level. The first INspiRE conference in November 2018 discussed the issue of private enforcement of EU competition and state aid law; the second conference in May 2019 dealt with issues surrounding the enforcement of consumer and capital market law.[11]

The second pillar is the comparative perspective. In Europe, a purely national perspective makes little sense, even though many approaches in research are still oriented towards this standard. By contrast, the Centre of Excellence involves the participation of, for example, researchers from Germany, France and Italy so as to acquire a broader perspective. A horizontal comparison of law can serve to optimally depict the strengths and weaknesses of an individual solution and thus mutually enrich the legal systems involved. Various other national legal systems, including those of the Netherlands, Great Britain and Spain, are also taken into account.

Finally, the research is based on an inductive approach. The idea is to start with the specifics of different legal areas (competition law, state aid law, consumer law, capital market law etc.) and to progress to general principles. In which legal fields do civil damage claims and class-action claims already exist? Are there requirements which can be generalised, a standard of comparison, the *tertium comparationis*? Subsequently, a conclusion is drawn deductively, moving from general to specific. At this point, it is not yet possible to present the final results of the INspiRE research

11. Beate Gsell and Thomas M.J. Möllers (eds), *Enforcing Consumer and Capital Market Law – The Diesel Emissions Scandal,* forthcoming.

project. Competition law will certainly also affect other areas of law. Accordingly, legal scholars are already discussing the transferability of selected legal instruments from one field of law to another.[12]

C. The project in context

Apart from the two international academic conferences already mentioned, the project tries to reach a broader public by organising panel discussions on the enforcement of EU law. The objective is to raise the insight among citizens as to the relationships between national and European law. In 2015, an event regarding TTIP, the then planned Free Trade Agreement between the EU and the USA, attracted about 250 persons.[13] Another event organised in summer 2017, in cooperation with the Europa-Union and the city of Augsburg, dealt with mechanisms of collective redress.[14] Finally, in November 2018 a panel discussion on the issue of data protection took place.[15]

Moreover, INspiRE aims at ameliorating the access to law. The established database on German and European Economic Law 'CAPLAW'[16] is constantly being expanded with national court decisions relating to European law. Decisions of national courts that have been enacted after a preliminary ruling procedure before the European Court of Justice are translated into English and published online in the database. These

12. *See* Thomas M.J. Möllers and Bernhard Pregler, *Zivilrechtliche Rechtsdurchsetzung und kollektiver Rechtsschutz im Wirtschaftsrecht – Ein Vergleich der kollektiven Rechtsdurchsetzung im Wettbewerbs-, Kartell-, Gesellschafts- und Kapitalmarkrecht* [2012] ZHR 144, translated in: *Civil Law Enforcement and Collective Redress in Economic Law – A comparison between collective redress actions in competition, antitrust, company and capital markets law* [2013] Europa e diritto privato 27. Also contributing to the discussion: Philipp Maume, *Staatliche Rechtsdurchsetzung im deutschen Kapitalmarktrecht* [2016] ZHR 358, 365; Caroline Geiger, *Kollektiver Rechtsschutz im Zivilprozess* 205 et seq. (Mohr Siebeck 2015); Thomas M.J. Möllers, '*Private Enforcement of Competition Law in Europe*' in: Henning Rosenau and Nghia Tang Van (eds), *Economic Competition Regime: Raising Issues and Lessons from Germany* 43, 51 (Nomos 2014).
13. *TTIP Chance oder Risiko? – Transatlantic Trade and Investment Partnership* [Chances and Risks of TTIP] (5 May 2015). Participants of the panel discussion: Joachim E. Menze, European Commission, Head of the Regional Office in Munich; Linus Förster, Member of the Bavarian Landtag; Christine Kamm, Member of the Bavarian Landtag; Bruno Marcon, Attac Germany; William E. Moeller, U.S. Consulate General, Consulate Munich; Thomas M.J. Möllers, University of Augsburg; Thorsten Frank, Europa-Union District Association Augsburg.
14. *Sammelklagen in der EU – Fluch oder Segen für den Verbraucherschutz?* [Class actions in the EU – A curse or blessing for consumer protection?] (18 July 2018). Participants of the panel discussion: Beate Czerwenka, Federal Ministry of Justice and Consumer Protection; Florian Popella, Bavarian Industry Association; Astrid Stadler, University of Konstanz; Ottmar Lell, Federation of German Consumer Organisations; Thomas M.J. Möllers, University of Augsburg; Thorsten Frank, Europa-Union District Association Augsburg.
15. *Google, Amazon, Facebook – Wer hat ein Recht auf meine Daten?* [Google, Amazon, Facebook – Who has a right to my data?] (13 November 2018). Participants of the panel discussion: Michael Schmidl, Attorney-at-law in Munich/University of Augsburg; Volker Ullrich, Member of the German Bundestag; Werner Hülsmann, German Association for Data Protection; Werner Stengg, European Commission; Michael Will, Bavarian State Ministry of the Interior; Rita Bottler, Bavarian Chamber of Commerce and Industry; Thomas M.J. Möllers, University of Augsburg; Thorsten Frank, Europa-Union District Association Augsburg.
16. www.caplaw.eu/inspire (accessed 20 August 2019). The database is (partly) available in several languages, such as German, English, French and Chinese. The database is publicly accessible and generates around two million hits annually.

judgments provide information on how the national judges methodologically adapt and apply the rulings of the European Court of Justice to national law. Until now, such judgments existed only in the respective national language, not in other languages of other Member States. Decision collected in the CAPLAW database can also be those that - despite European relevance - have not led to preliminary rulings. The collection of such important national decisions allows other scholars, judges, lawyers and the interested public (including journalists) to make horizontal legal comparisons, and it will thus ultimately serve the enforcement of European law.

III. ACKNOWLEDGEMENTS

The editors want to warmly thank *Dominic Merk* for organising and managing the INspiRE conference that resulted in this publication. He was supported by *Benita Bentlage, Petra Eberl, Niklas Gronemann, Curtis Haug, Patricia Jauch, Laura Mähle, Maximilian Merwald, Tamara Mohrhart, Sandra Paulson, Julia Ranzinger, Antonia Ruck, Aline Seggelke, Alexander Streif, Fabian Wallner, Jonathan Wehrstein* and *Helga Weidenhammer.*

We owe further thanks to *Lena Franke, Cornelia Kibler, Julian Kimmerle, Ingeborg Stahl* and *Aneesa Chaudhry* for editorial assistance, and to *Michael Friedman* for carrying out the linguistic revision of the manuscripts.

Finally we are indebted to *Simon Bellamy* from Wolters Kluwer for his support and patience throughout the project.

Part I Private Enforcement of EU Competition Law after Directive 2014/104/EU

CHAPTER 2

The European Perspective

Wulf-Henning Roth

I. Introduction
II. The case law of the Court of Justice
  A. *Courage*
  B. *Manfredi*
  C. *Kone*
  D. Observations
III. Directive 2014/104/EU
  A. Transposition of case law
  B. No clarifications
  C. Problems addressed
    1. Compensation, not deterrence
    2. Passing-on
    3. Effectiveness of private enforcement
    4. Private and public enforcement
    5. Final observations
IV. The relationship between public and private enforcement
  A. The problem
  B. Disclosure
  C. Follow-on actions
  D. Limited liability of immunity recipients
V. The relationship between primary Union law and Directive 2014/104/EU
  A. General principles of interpretation
  B. Is the Directive in conformity with the case law of the Court?
    1. The problem
    2. Examples

3. Framework of analysis
4. Limits to legislative competence?
VI. Summary

I. INTRODUCTION

The issue of private enforcement of competition law has been with us for many years. In Germany, an intensive debate had started already in the 1970s on the question of whether and how far the public enforcement of economic law, and competition law in particular, could be transferred to or complemented by civil law remedies.[1] To be sure, for quite a long time, civil law remedies have also been applied by the courts of the Member States with regard to violations of European competition law as well.[2] However, with regard to actions for damages, the so-called Ashurst-Report, in 2004, described the substantive and procedural law of the Member States to be in a state of total underdevelopment.[3] The EU Commission, in 1993 and 2004 respectively, published two notices to stimulate and promote a cooperation between the Commission and the courts of the EU Member States.[4] And the *Courage* judgment of the Court of Justice in 2001[5] finally exerted a strong push towards private enforcement, calling for a right to demand damages for anyone who has suffered from a violation of EC competition law. Finally, since the enactment of Regulation 1/2003, which has opened the way for a direct application of ex Article 81(3) EC by national courts, the topic of strengthening private enforcement has been intensively pursued by the EU

1. For example, Ernst Steindorff, *Gesetzgeberische Möglichkeit zu verbesserter Durchsetzung des Gesetzes gegen Wettbewerbsbeschränkungen* (1974) 138 ZHR 504; Karsten Schmidt, *Aufgaben und Leistungsgrenzen der Gesetzgebung im Kartelldeliktsrecht: Eine rechtspolitische Studie zu den außerstrafrechtlichen Sanktionen im GWB* (Nomos 1978); starting the discussion in the 1960s: K. Peter Mailänder, *Privatrechtliche Folgen unerlaubter Kartellpraxis* (Verlag Versicherungswirtschaft 1964).
2. For an early study *see* Ernst Steindorff, *Zur Entwicklung des europäischen Kartellrechts (Teil I)* (1973) 137 ZHR 203; Ernst Steindorff, *Europäisches Kartellrecht und Staatenpraxis (Teil II)* (1978) 142 ZHR 525; Ernst Steindorff, *Europäisches Kartellrecht vor staatlichen Gerichten 1971–1978 (Teil III)* (1982) 146 ZHR 140; Ernst Steindorff, '*Europäisches Kartellrecht vor staatlichen Gerichten, Teil I: 1958–1970*' in Wilhelm G. Grewe, Hans Rupp & Hans Schneider (eds), *Europäische Gerichtsbarkeit und nationale Verfassungsgerichtsbarkeit: Festschrift zum 70. Geburtstag von Hans Kutscher* 437 (Nomos 1981). *See also* August Braakman, *The Application of Articles 85 and 86 of the EC Treaty by National Courts in the Member States* (Office for Official Publications of the European Communities 1997).
3. Denis Waelbroeck, Donald Slater & Gil Even-Shoshan, *Study on the conditions of claims for damages in case of infringement of EC competition rules: comparative report* (Ashurst 2004).
4. European Commission, Notice on cooperation between national courts and the Commission in applying Articles 85 and 86 of the EEC Treaty, OJ 1993 C 39/6; European Commission, Commission Notice on the co-operation between the Commission and the courts of the EU Member States in the application of Articles 81 and 82 EC, OJ 2004 C 101/54.
5. ECJ, Case C-453/99 *Courage Ltd v Bernard Crehan and Bernard Crehan v Courage Ltd and Others* [2001] ECR I-6297.

Commission,[6] accompanied by conferences,[7] comparative reports,[8] and in-depth analyses by academics.[9] This endeavour to develop private enforcement as an effective instrument alongside public enforcement of EU competition law by the EU Commission and the national competition authorities finally led to the enactment of Directive 2014/104/EU of 26 November 2014, setting forth the basic standards for the pursuit of damage actions for infringements of EU competition law and the competition law of the Member States.[10]

The topic of this chapter shall be dealt with in four steps: First, I will recall the relevant case law of the Court of Justice concerning damage claims with regard to the violation of competition law (*see* II, *infra*). In a second step, the question of whether and to what extent Directive 2014/104/EU has changed the picture shall be dealt with, especially whether and how far the Directive contributes to a more effective private enforcement (*see* III, *infra*). Third, we will look to the relationship between private and public enforcement, as envisaged by the Directive (*see* IV, *infra*). And fourth, and finally, I would like to discuss the relationship between the case law of the Court of Justice, especially relating to the effectiveness principle, and some of the provisions in the Directive that may be regarded as being in conflict with this principle (*see* V, *infra*). A summary concludes the chapter (*see* VI, *infra*).

II. THE CASE LAW OF THE COURT OF JUSTICE

A right to seek compensation by a person who has suffered harm caused by an infringement of European competition law is foreseen neither by the original Treaty on the European Economic Community nor by its latest version, the Treaty on the Functioning of the European Union (TFEU). This is, of course, in obvious contrast to

6. European Commission, Green Paper on Damages actions for breach of the EC antitrust rules, COM(2005) 672 final; European Commission, White Paper on Damages actions for breach of EC antitrust rules, COM(2008) 165 final. *See also* the study commissioned by the EC Commission: CEPS, EUR & LUISS, *Making antitrust damage actions more effective in the EU: welfare impact and potential scenarios: Final Report*, 21 December 2007.
7. For example, Claus-Dieter Ehlermann and Isabela Atanasiu (eds), *European Competition Law Annual 2001: Effective Private Enforcement of EC Antitrust Law* (Hart Publishing 2003); Jürgen Basedow (ed.), *Private Enforcement of EC Competition Law* (Kluwer 2007); Jürgen Basedow, Jörg Terhechte & Lubos Tichý, *Private Enforcement of Competition Law* (Nomos 2011).
8. Gerhard Dannecker and Oswald Jansen (eds), *Competition Law Sanctioning in the European Union* (Kluwer 2004); Barry Rodger (ed.), *Competition Law: Comparative Private Enforcement and Collective Redress across the EU* (Kluwer 2014).
9. For example, Assimakis Komninos, *EC Private Antitrust Enforcement* (Hart Publishing 2008); Hans Philip Logemann, *Der kartellrechtliche Schadensersatz* (Duncker & Humblot 2009); Christian Alexander, *Schadensersatz und Abschöpfung im Lauterkeits-und Kartellrecht* (Mohr Siebeck 2010); Veljko Milutinovic, *The 'Right to Damages' under EU Competition Law: from Courage v Crehan to the White Paper and Beyond* (Kluwer 2010); Gero Meeßen, *Der Anspruch auf Schadensersatz bei Verstößen gegen EU-Kartellrecht* (Mohr Siebeck 2011); Roman Inderst and Stefan Thomas, *Schadensersatz bei Kartellverstößen* (Handelsblatt Fachmedien GmbH 2015; 2nd ed. 2019); Folkert Wilman, *Private Enforcement of EU Law before National Courts* (Edward Elgar Publishing 2015).
10. Directive 2014/104/EU of the European Parliament and of the Council of 26 November 2014 on certain rules governing actions for damages under national law for infringements of the competition law provisions of the Member States and of the European Union [2014], OJ L 349/1.

Article 340(2) TFEU, a provision dealing with the non-contractual liability of the Union, a contrast that may be explained to some extent by the fact that Article 103 TFEU provides a competence for the Union legislature to deal with the enforcement of competition law. The private law dimension of European competition law is, indeed, touched upon by Article 101(2) TFEU, which says that 'any agreements or decisions prohibited by this Article shall be automatically void' – a provision that amounts to an important, and sometimes undervalued, instrument (used in a defensive fashion as a 'shield'[11]) to enforce European competition law in the sphere of contractual relations. But, of course, there is no reference to a right to seek compensation. As is well known, such a right to seek compensation for harm, caused by anticompetitive conduct, has been developed by the Court of Justice in its case law, starting with the *Courage* judgment in 2001[12] and, in the years to follow, confirmed by *Manfredi*[13] and *Kone*[14] as well as further judgments.[15] In a nutshell, the case law has developed in the following manner.

A. *Courage*

In *Courage*, the main issue to be decided was whether the English *in pari delicto* doctrine could be applied vis-à-vis an action for damages, based on English law, concerning a tying contract violating the European competition rules. Despite the fact that the claim was (and undisputedly could be) based on English law, the Court of Justice, in paragraphs 26 and 27 of its judgment, took the chance to make some very general observations on the right to seek compensation with regard to the underlying legal principle – the full effectiveness of the competition provisions – and the policy reasons for developing such a right. In paragraph 26 of the *Courage* judgment the Court holds: 'The full effectiveness of [as it then was] Article 85 of the Treaty and, in particular, the practical effect of the prohibition laid down in Article 85(1) would be put at risk if it were not open to any individual to claim damages for loss caused to him by a contract or by conduct liable to restrict or distort competition.' And the Court added in paragraph 27: 'Indeed, the existence of such a right strengthens the working of the Community competition rules and discourages agreements or practices, which are frequently covert, which are liable to restrict or distort competition. From that point of view, actions for damages before the national courts can make a significant contribution to the maintenance of effective competition in the Community.'

11. Komninos, *supra* n. 9, at 149; Milutinovic, *supra* n. 9, at 144.
12. Case C-453/99 *Courage and Crehan*, *supra* n. 5.
13. ECJ, Joined Cases C-295/04 to C-298/04 *Vincenzo Manfredi and Others v Lloyd Adriatico Assicurazioni SpA and Others* [2006] ECR I-6619.
14. ECJ, Case C-557/12 *Kone and Others v ÖBB-Infrastruktur AG* [2014] ECLI:EU:C:2014:1317.
15. ECJ, Case C-199/11 *Europese Gemeenschap v Otis and Others* [2012] ECLI:EU:C:2012:684; ECJ, Case C-536/11 *Bundeswettbewerbsbehörde v Donau Chemie AG and Others* [2013] ECLI:EU:C:2013:366; ECJ, Case C-724/17 *Vantaan kaupunki v Skanska Industrial Solutions Oy and Others* [2019] ECLI:EU:C:2019:204.

These statements have been repeated (in a 'copy and paste' fashion) in one way or another in the subsequent case law of the Court.[16] It may be worth adding three observations regarding *Courage*. First: *Courage* is a case in which the Court stressed the importance of private damage actions (based on national law) for the *effective enforcement* of the competition rules. The emphasis is on the instrumental function[17] of such a private law remedy,[18] with the vigilance of the private actor strengthening the working of competition law.[19] Second: The well-known reference to 'any individual' that should have a right to claim damages for loss caused by anticompetitive conduct underlines the instrumental approach of the Court with regard to private law remedies.[20] Though, in the context of the *Courage* proceedings, the reference may be understood to clarify the issue that even partners to an anticompetitive contract (who are *in pari delicto*) should have the right to claim damages, the terminology of 'any individual' turned out to be the basis for a *broad concept of legal standing* in the ensuing case law. Third: In paragraph 29 of the *Courage* judgment, there is a reference to the fact that no Community provisions as yet dealt with the matter. The implications of such reference to the non-existence of Community rules (which appears in later judgments as well) will be discussed later on (*see* V, *infra*). It certainly has been a decisive stimulus for the Commission to initiate legislation on actions for damages, leading to Directive 2014/104/EU.

B. *Manfredi*

In *Manfredi*, the Court again underlines the instrumental function of the right to claim damages concerning the effective enforcement of competition law, and it unequivocally states that such a remedy has to be available in national law (paragraphs 60, 91), circumscribing this remedy in three directions: (1) the 'any individual' formula is extended to downstream market partners, including consumers (paragraph 60); (2) the damages claim is to be dependent on a causal relationship between the harm and the anticompetitive conduct of the infringer (paragraph 61); and (3) the claim for compensation should embrace actual loss (*damnum emergens*), lost profit (*lucrum cessans*), and interest (paragraph 95).

Apart from these requirements set forth by Union law, the relevant details of such a damage claim have to be considered as a matter of national law, however, restrained by the principles of equivalence and effectiveness (paragraphs 62, 71, 77, 92).

---

16. Case C-557/12 *Kone and Others*, *supra* n. 14, at para. 23 with further references.
17. This is in some contrast to the reasoning in *Francovich*, in which the Court also stressed the effective enforcement of Community law but, moreover, characterised the principle of State liability as being 'inherent in the system of the Treaty'; *see* ECJ, Joined Cases C-6/90 and C-9/90 *Francovich and Others v Italian Republic* [1991] ECR I-5357, para. 35.
18. Though not mentioned in the judgment, the apparent emphasis on the private enforcement of European competition law goes hand in hand with the ongoing discussion on the decentralisation of the public enforcement of competition law, leading to Regulation No. 1/2003.
19. This, of course, comes close to the *private attorney general* in the US (legal) discourse; e.g., Dörte Poelzig, *Normdurchsetzung durch Privatrecht* 54 (Mohr Siebeck 2012).
20. *See*, e.g., Poelzig, *supra* n. 19, at 140; Jens-Uwe Franck, *Marktordnung durch Haftung* 198 (Mohr Siebeck 2016).

C. *Kone*

The *Kone* judgment (in paragraphs 21–23) builds on the just-cited statements in *Courage* and *Manfredi*. The notion of 'any individual' who may claim compensation caused by anticompetitive conduct is extended to market participants who are not in a contractual relationship with the infringers, but who suffer harm from the so-called umbrella pricing strategy of competitors of cartel participants. The gist of the judgment is that national law does infringe the principle of effectiveness if, as a categorical matter, it forecloses causation of the harm in cases where the injured persons are not in a contractual relationship with the injurer (paragraph 33). Rather, the issue of causation has to be analysed in every individual case with regard to the special features of the relevant market, whereby, as a liability-limiting factor, it might become relevant whether the injurer could foresee the causation and circumstances of remote damages (paragraph 34).

D. Observations

Wrapping up the case law of the Court of Justice, the following elements seem to be of importance: (1) The full effectiveness of Union competition law requires, as a matter of primary law, the existence of a right to claim damages in the law of the Member States.[21] (2) It is in the competence of the Member States to provide for detailed rules relating to such a claim, including the notion of causality, whereby national law has to be in conformity with the principles of equivalence and effectiveness. (3) The notion of 'any individual' that may claim damages for harm caused by anticompetitive conduct has, again as a matter of primary law, to be broadly conceived.

Viewed in a somewhat broader perspective of Union law, the case law of the Court concerning the private enforcement of EU competition law gives reason for two more general observations.

As for the notion of *full effectiveness* of EU competition law, the case law stands in an apparent *contrast* to the legal remedies available and required with regard to *secondary Union law*. As a general matter, the Member States are obliged to enforce the objectives of a directive by sanctions that are to be considered as dissuasive, effective, and proportionate,[22] whereby the Member States are left with the choice between criminal, administrative, and private law sanctions. To put it in a somewhat different

21. Whether the claim is derived from Union law or based on an applicable law of a Member State (which is under the obligation to instal such a claim in its legal order) is still in dispute; in favour of the former position: Komninos, *supra* n. 9, at 171; Milutinovic, *supra* n. 9, at 69 and 91; in favour of the latter position: Meeßen, *supra* n. 9, at 40; Franck, *supra* n. 20, at 620.
22. For example, Directive 2006/54/EC of the European Parliament and of the Council of 5 July 2006 on the implementation of the principle of equal opportunities and equal treatment of men and women in matters of employment and occupation (recast) [2006], OJ L 204/23, Article 25; Council Directive 2000/78/EC of 27 November 2000 establishing a general framework for equal treatment in employment and occupation [2000], OJ L 303/16, Article 17; Directive 2005/29/EC of the European Parliament and of the Council of 11 May 2005 concerning unfair business-to-consumer commercial practices in the internal market and amending Council Directive 84/450/EEC, Directives 97/7/EC, 98/27/EC and 2002/65/EC of the European Parliament and of

light: Private law remedies are (perhaps with the exception of the *Munoz* judgment[23] dealing with civil law injunctive relief) not regarded as essential for the enforcement of (secondary) Union law, except in cases in which the legislative explicitly calls for such a sanction.[24]

This point may be exemplified by one of the more recent judgments of the Court, the *Schmitt* case,[25] dealing with Directive 93/42/EEC on medical devices.[26] The Directive provides for an obligation of the competent national administrative unit to supervise the production process of medical devices. In one of the recitals of the Directive, it is expressly stated that the control of medical devices is aimed at a high level of protection of public safety and health. Nevertheless, when it comes to a violation of the surveillance duties by the competent administrative unit, the Court, despite the protective *telos* of the Directive, does not call on the notion of effectiveness in order to attribute injured persons standing to sue for their harm incurred. Rather, the Court argues that as long as the Directive does not expressly provide for specific compensation, the injured person will not have such a remedy.[27] Obviously, the Court is inclined to leave it to the discretion of the Member States how to achieve the effectiveness of the relevant provisions: Though individuals are to be protected and certainly might be in a good position to enforce their rights, it is in the autonomy of the Member States to decide which instruments they use to enforce Union law.

Given this as background and given the fact that European competition law is enforced by the EU Commission, and the national competition authorities as well, it seems all the more remarkable that, without any indication in the Treaty, the Court, since *Courage*, has nevertheless based its case law on the simple notion of effectiveness, thereby creating a right to compensation based on Article 101(1) TFEU.

A second observation is in order: From the very beginning with *Courage* (in its paragraph 29), the Court has, with regard to a number of legal issues, made an express reference to the *absence* of Community rules governing the matter. In *Manfredi*, we find no less than five such references, dealing with such issues as jurisdiction and procedural rules governing actions for damages (paragraphs 62, 71, 77, 92), rules as to the right to claim compensation and the issue of causation (paragraph 64), and the

the Council and Regulation (EC) No. 2006/2004 of the European Parliament and of the Council [2005], OJ L 149/22, Article 13 sentence 2.

23. ECJ, Case C-253/00 *Antonio Muñoz y Cia SA and Others v Frumar Ltd. and Others* [2002] ECR I-7289, paras 30–31. For a discussion of this judgment *see*, e.g., Franck, *supra* n. 20, at 200.
24. For example, Council Directive 2004/113/EC of 13 December 2004 implementing the principle of equal treatment between men and women in the access to and supply of goods and services [2004], OJ L 373/37, Article 8(2); Directive 2006/54/EC, *supra* n. 22, at Article 18; Directive 2010/41/EU of the European Parliament and of the Council of 7 July 2010 on the application of the principle of equal treatment between men and women engaged in an activity in a self-employed capacity and repealing Council Directive 86/613/EEC [2010], OJ L 180/1, Article 18; Directive 2003/71/EC of the European Parliament and of the Council of 4 November 2003 on the prospectus to be published when securities are offered to the public or admitted to trading and amending Directive 2001/34/EC [2003], OJ L 345/64, Article 6.
25. ECJ, Case C-219/15 *Elisabeth Schmitt v TÜV Rheinland LGA Products GmbH* [2017] ECLI: EU:C:2017:128.
26. Council Directive 93/42/EEC of 14 June 1993 concerning medical devices [1993], OJ L 169/1.
27. Case C-219/15 *Schmitt*, *supra* n. 25, at para. 55; cf. also ECJ, Case C-222/02 *Peter Paul and Others v Bundesrepublik Deutschland* [2004] ECR I-9425, paras 38–40.

criteria for determining the extent of the damages for the harm caused by anticompetitive conduct (paragraph 98). These references were surely meant and had to be understood, as a strong hint by the Court that the Community organs should, within the boundaries of their competence,[28] legislate on this matter. Moreover, it may also be viewed as an implicit indication that the Court regarded these issues as matters in which the Union legislature should have the say – a perspective to which we turn in section V of this chapter.

III. DIRECTIVE 2014/104/EU

Directive 2014/104/EU is the result of a long-ongoing discussion on the principles and the details of private enforcement as an effective instrument for claimants to seek compensation. In what follows, a short overview shall be given on some major points dealt with by the Directive, without going into the details.

A. Transposition of case law

To some extent, the Directive, as indicated in recital 12 of the preamble, may be regarded as an instrument simply transposing the then-existing case law of the Court of Justice into secondary law: The Directive reaffirms 'the *acquis communautaire* on the right to compensation for harm caused by infringements of Union competition law, particularly regarding standing and the definition of damage, as stated in the case-law of the Court of Justice, and does not pre-empt any further development thereof. Anyone who has suffered harm caused by such an infringement can claim compensation for actual loss (*damnum emergens*), for gain of which that person has been deprived (loss of profit or *lucrum cessans*), plus interest, irrespective of whether those categories are established separately or in combination in national law'.

First: The *principles of equivalence* and *effectiveness*, as developed by the Court, are referred to in Article 4 (and recital 11 of the preamble) as guiding principles for the transposition of the Directive and the application of the domestic substantive and procedural law of the Member States.

Second: Article 3(1) attributes the right to claim compensation to '*any* natural or legal person who has suffered harm ...'. Thereby, Article 3(1) refers to a notion in the case law of the Court, starting with *Courage* ('*any* individual') and referred to ever since, without any further definition or explanation.[29]

Third: The right to seek *full compensation*, as set forth in Article 3(1) (and recital 12), is defined in the same way as set forth, for instance, in the *Manfredi* (paragraph 95) and *Donau-Chemie* (paragraph 24) judgments as covering compensation for actual loss, loss of profit, and the payment of interest.

Fourth: The clarification set forth in *Kone* (paragraphs 30–34) that the claim for compensation does not presuppose a contractual relationship between the injured

28. *See* Article 103 TFEU.
29. *See also* the use of 'anyone' in Directive 2014/104/EU Article 12(1) and recital 12.

person and the infringing undertaking is taken up in recital 13 of the preamble of the Directive, however, without going into the specifics of the consequences of umbrella pricing.

B. No clarifications

With regard to some issues, the Directive has (deliberately) refrained from reaching a clarification. Take, as an example, the notion of an '*undertaking*' that in the case law of the Court (dealing with fines) has been defined as an 'economic entity' potentially comprising more than one enterprise.[30] The Directive uses the term 'undertaking' in various provisions (e.g., Article 1(1), Article 2(2), and Article 11(1)). However, it refrains, in the catalogue of definitions set forth in Article 2, from giving a specific definition, neither an autonomous one nor by reference to the case law of the Court. However, there is much to be said for the contention that the notion of 'undertaking' in the Directive should be interpreted in the light of the case law of the Court.[31]

As for standing to sue, the Directive has not even attempted to give the notion of '*any*' person who may bring an action for damages any further concreteness. It has, of course, to be taken into account that Article 14, dealing with the claims of *indirect* purchasers, gives proof of the fact that the term 'any person' goes beyond the persons that stand in a direct contractual relationship with the infringing party. Nevertheless, the Directive does not give any indication whether, and according to which criteria, the personal scope of the right to full compensation might be restricted.[32]

C. Problems addressed

The Directive goes beyond the *Courage* case law insofar as it covers not only infringements of Articles 101 and 102 TFEU but also violations of provisions of competition law of the Member States that predominantly pursue the same objectives as Articles 101 and 102 TFEU (Article 2 No. 1 and No. 3). The Directive is, moreover, addressed to some important issues of private enforcement, and it has taken some steps devoted to a more effective pursuit of claims for damages.

30. ECJ, Case C-516/15 P *Akzo Nobel and Others v Commission* [2017] ECLI:EU:C:2017:314, para. 49; GC, Case T-419/14 *Goldman Sachs Group Inc. v European Commission* [2018] ECLI: EU:T:2018:445. For a closer analysis of the case law *see*, e.g., Wulf-Henning Roth, in Wolfgang Jaeger, Juliane Kokott, Petra Pohlmann & Dirk Schroeder (eds), *Frankfurter Kommentar zum Kartellrecht* § 33a GWB paras 42–45 (Ergänzungslieferung 92, Otto Schmidt 2018). Most recently Case C-724/17 *Skanska Industrial Solutions and Others, supra* n. 15, para. 47.
31. *See* V.B, *infra*; e.g., Roth, *supra* n. 30, at § 33 GWB paras 7, 95, 99; at § 33a GWB paras 46–56. *See also* Directive 2019/1 of the European Parliament and of the Council of 11 December 2018 to empower the competition authorities of the Member States to be more effective enforcers and to ensure the proper functioning of the internal market [2019], OJ L 11/1, Article 2 No. 10 and Article 13(5).
32. Cf. Roth, *supra* n. 30, at § 33a paras 25–29.

1. *Compensation, not deterrence*

First of all, the Directive has ended the discussion on the question of whether and to what extent private law claims should be shaped in such a way as to exert a *deterrent effect* towards anticompetitive conduct of the market participants. Such notion of a deterrent effect of private law claims is not only familiar with regard to the US experience with treble damage claims but also has been discussed with regard to the carefully drawn paragraph 26[33] of the *Courage* judgment (and repeated in a number of later judgments[34]), in which the Court stresses the *instrumental function* of the right to claim damages to discourage anticompetitive behaviour, thereby maintaining effective competition in the Community.[35] However, Article 3(1) of the Directive opts against deterrence as a self-standing aim and in favour of a mere right of the injured individual to seek *full compensation* of the relevant harm, expressly excluding overcompensation, 'whether by means of punitive, multiple or other types of damages', as stated in Article 3(3). The Union legislature insofar seems to deliberately deviate from the *Manfredi* judgment, which had left the door open to the Member States to introduce an action for punitive damages. Actions for compensation may therefore be considered as exerting a deterrent effect only in so far as a claim for compensatory damages turns out to be a de facto credible threat for potential infringers of competition law.

2. *Passing-on*

a) *Offensive use*

The issue of passing-on has received detailed treatment in the Directive. With the principle of full compensation in mind, Article 12(1), dealing with the *offensive use* of the passing-on formula (as a 'sword'), extends the right to seek compensation beyond the group of direct purchasers and providers (*see* Article 12(4)) to 'anyone who suffered harm' from anticompetitive conduct, embracing – among others – all persons to whom the overcharge has been passed on. The claimant may reasonably require disclosure from the defendant and third parties as to the existence and the scope of passing-on (Article 14(1)). Moreover, the Directive calls for a rebuttable presumption for the existence of passing-on where the conditions set forth in Article 14(2) are met.

33. Case C-453/99 *Courage and Crehan, supra* n. 5, at para. 26: '... the existence of such a right strengthens the working of the Community competition rules and discourages agreements or practices ... which are liable to restrict ... competition. From that point of view, actions for damages before the national courts can make a significant contribution to the maintenance of effective competition in the Community'.
34. Case C-557/12 *Kone and Others, supra* n. 14, at para. 23 with further references.
35. This is not undisputed; e.g., Martin Ebers, *Rechte, Rechtsbehelfe und Sanktionen im Unionsprivatrecht* 573 (Mohr Siebeck 2016).

b) *Defensive use*

Passing-on may also be used as a *defence* ('shield') *against* a claim for damages if the defendant/injurer proves that the relevant overcharge was passed on by the claimant to third parties (Article 13). It is the explicit purpose of the Directive to *avoid overcompensation* at any level of the supply chain (Article 12(2)).

c) *Collective redress*

To be sure, the *offensive use* of passing-on may go down the supply chain to the very end-consumers. It may be considered as a matter of 'justice' that those end-consumers who, ultimately, carry the harm of anticompetitive conduct do have a right to claim their damages. However, as we all know, the harm caused to individual end-consumers may often be truly negligible, leaving the consumers without any incentive to individually go to court and bring an action for damages. This, of course, will lead to the much-discussed[36] enforcement vacuum (and a de facto shield for the infringing enterprise) that could only be overcome by effective redress by way of collective actions in one form or another.

Unfortunately, the Directive deliberately does not provide for such a redress,[37] thereby neglecting the intimate relationship between private law remedies on the one hand and the procedural counterparts for an effective enforcement of those remedies on the other.

3. *Effectiveness of private enforcement*

The effectiveness of private enforcement is meant to be promoted by a number of instruments set forth in the Directive. The most important are the following.

a) *Decisions of national competition authorities*

Proof of an infringement of competition law amounts to a sometimes unsurmountable barrier for the claimant. Effective assistance may be at hand if the claims may be

36. *See* Franziska Weber, *'A chain reaction' or the necessity of collective actions for consumers in cartel cases* (2018) 25 MJ 208; Roger Van den Bergh, *Private Enforcement of European Competition Law and the Persisting Collective Action Problem* (2013) 20 MJ 12. An overview of collective redress in the Member States is presented in Rodger, *supra* n. 8.

37. *See* recital 13 of the preamble of the Directive 2014/104/EU. But *see* Commission Recommendation 2013/396/EU of 11 June 2013 on common principles for injunctive and compensatory collective redress mechanisms in the Member States concerning violations of rights granted under Union Law [2013], OJ L 201/60; European Commission, Communication from the Commission to the European Parliament, the Council, the European Economic and Social Committee and the Committee of the Regions 'Towards a European Horizontal Framework for Collective Redress', COM(2013) 401 final; European Commission, Proposal of 11 April 2018 for a Directive on representative actions for the protection of the collective interests of consumers, and repealing Directive 2009/22/EC, COM(2018) 184 final (however not dealing with claims for damages relating to anticompetitive conduct).

brought forward by way of a *follow-on action*. Similar to Article 16(1) of Regulation 1/2003[38] dealing with the binding nature of a Commission decision for national civil proceedings, Article 9(1) of the Directive demands that a final decision of a national competition authority (or a review court) on an infringement of competition law will irrefutably establish the infringement for the purposes of an action for damages before the relevant national court. Moreover, final decisions of the authorities of other Member States are to be taken at least as prima facie *evidence* with respect to such an infringement (Article 9(2)). It may be assumed that these provisions will further stimulate follow-on actions by injured parties, who in the future will no longer carry the full burden of proof for an infringement of competition law, instead needing only to prove the existence and scope of their harm.

b) *Disclosure provisions*

Beyond the assistance pursued with regard to follow-on actions, the Directive calls for *procedural devices* in favour of claimants to compensate for the *information asymmetry* regarding the potential infringements of competition law vis-à-vis the defendant/ injurer. National courts are to have, under certain conditions, the power to order the defendant or a third party to disclose evidence within their control that is relevant to the claim set forth in the action (Article 5(1)). This power of the courts to ask for disclosure extends to confidential information (Article 5(4)) and, in a somewhat restrictive fashion (Article 6(4)-(6)), to the evidence included in the file of a competition authority (Article 6(1)). Whether and to what extent these provisions on disclosure will strengthen private enforcement will depend on their effective transposition in national law and remains to be seen. Most probably, claims for damages will later be pursued as follow-on claims, as mentioned beforehand.

c) *Proof of harm*

Beyond the proof of an infringement of competition law, private claimants have a hard time establishing the existence and the scope of their harm. The Directive addresses this issue in two ways:

(1) As far as cartels are concerned, Article 17(2) introduces a *presumption* that a cartel causes harm. This presumption (as for causation and for the existence of harm) is, however, rebuttable by the defendant.
(2) With regard to the *quantification of harm*, the Member States are obligated to enable their courts to estimate the amount of harm if the burden of proving the extent of the harm turns out to be excessively heavy for the injured claimant (Article 17(1)).

38. Council Regulation (EC) No. 1/2003 of 16 December 2002 on the implementation of the rules on competition laid down in Articles 81 and 82 of the Treaty [2003], OJ L 1/1.

d) Guidelines for courts

Claims for damages will be pursued in an effective manner only if the courts have an *adequate understanding* of the economic implications relating to the determination of harm, caused by anticompetitive conduct, and of the calculation of the extent of damages. To this end, Article 16 of the Directive requires the Commission to issue *guidelines* for national courts on how to estimate the share of the overcharge which was 'passed on' to an indirect purchaser. The Commission has recently published such draft guidelines ('Draft Passing-On Guidelines') and has asked for comments and contributions from interested parties.[39] Moreover, with regard to quantifying harm caused by anticompetitive conduct, the Commission, already before the enactment of the Directive, published a Communication on quantifying harm, in 2013,[40] accompanied by a Practical Guide that is meant to inform the national courts on economic methods and techniques, with special emphasis on harm caused by a rise in prices and by exclusionary practices.[41] It is to be expected that the national courts which may not be wholly familiar with the standard methods and techniques for analysing the economic issues involved will closely follow the recommendations set forth in these (non-binding[42]) guidelines.

4. *Private and public enforcement*

Beyond these regulations designed to make private enforcement more effective, the Directive addresses also the relationship between public and private enforcement, an issue which will be dealt with in section IV.

5. *Final observations*

Three final observations concerning the effectiveness of private enforcement as pursued by the Directive are in order:

(1) As the Directive, in most parts, is directed towards full harmonisation,[43] it is important to note that not all legal problems, relevant for the right to compensation, are within the scope of the Directive. In its recital 11, the

39. European Commission, Draft Guidelines for national courts on how to estimate the share of cartel overcharges passed on to indirect purchasers and final consumers, http://ec.europa.eu/competition/consultations/2018_cartel_overcharges/index_en.html (accessed 20 May 2019).
40. European Commission, Communication from the Commission on quantifying harm in actions for damages based on breaches of Article 101 or 102 of the Treaty on the Functioning of the European Union, OJ 2013 C 167/19.
41. European Commission, Commission Staff Working Document: Practical Guide on Quantifying Harm in Actions for damages based on breaches of Article 101 and 102 of the treaty on the Functioning of the European Union, SWD(2013) 205.
42. Cf. ECJ, Case C-360/09 *Pfleiderer AG v Bundeskartellamt* [2011] ECR I-5161, para. 21; ECJ, Case C-226/11 *Expedia Inc. v Autorité de la concurrence and Others* [2012] ECLI:EU:C:2012:795, paras 29–31.
43. Only minimum harmonisation is pursued in Directive 2014/104/EU Article 9(2) and Article 10.

preamble makes it clear that certain issues have been deliberately left to the law of the Member States. The recital refers to the issues of *imputability*, *adequacy*, and *culpability*. The application of these principles in national law may, to some extent, still work as a restriction on a successful full compensation of the relevant harm.

(2) As has already been mentioned, the Directive does not set forth any provisions on *collective redress*. It is therefore to be expected that consumers, to whom the overcharge has been passed on by way of higher prices, will, also in the foreseeable future, abstain from pursuing their claims. This omission has to be regarded as a *major defect* of the Directive.

(3) One provision in the Directive that runs counter to the principle of full effectiveness is Article 11(2), providing for the *protection of small and medium-sized enterprises*[44] against claims for damages pursued by persons other than their direct and indirect purchasers. This much-criticised[45] provision – like some other provisions of the Directive – raises the issue of whether it may be regarded as compatible with the principle of full effectiveness of Articles 101 and 102 TFEU on which the Court has heavily relied in its case law ever since *Courage*. We will return to this problem in section V *infra*.

IV. THE RELATIONSHIP BETWEEN PUBLIC AND PRIVATE ENFORCEMENT

A. The problem

In the last decade, the discussion on a more effective private enforcement of competition law has been accompanied by a growing awareness that effective private and public enforcement may, at least with regard to the harm caused by cartels, be regarded as being in tension, if not in a potential conflict, with one another.[46] On the one hand, there is the great and undisputable success of the leniency programmes of the Union and the Member States in uncovering cartels of long duration and broad geographic scope. And, on the other hand, there has always been the fear that this success might be threatened and the leniency programmes put into jeopardy if the leniency statements (as well as settlement submissions) will have to be disclosed by the competition

44. As defined in Commission Recommendation 2003/361/EC of 6 May 2003 concerning the definition of micro, small and medium-sized enterprises [2003], OJ L 124/36.
45. For example, Mark-Oliver Mackenrodt, in Christian Kersting and Rupprecht Podszun (eds), *Die 9. GWB-Novelle* ch. 8 paras 131–140 (C.H. Beck 2017); Carsten Krüger, *Gesamtschuld, Gesamtschuldnerausgleich und Vergleiche im neuen Kartellschadensersatzrecht* [2017] WuW 229, 231 ('absurd').
46. *See*, e.g., Komninos, *supra* n. 9, at 7; Erling Hjelmeng, *Competition law remedies: Striving for coherence or finding new ways?* (2013) 50 CML Rev. 1007, 1030; Philip Lowe and Mel Marquis (eds), *European Competition Law Annual 2011: Integrating Public and Private Enforcement of Competition Law – Implications for Courts and Agencies* (Hart Publishing 2014); Christopher Hodges, *Law and Corporate Behaviour: Integrating Theories of Regulation, Enforcement, Compliance and Ethics* 118 (Hart Publishing, C.H. Beck and Nomos 2015).

authorities to potentially injured parties seeking compensation from the infringing cartel members.

The Union legislature was aware of this inherent conflict. Recital 6 of the preamble of the Directive calls for effective private as well as public enforcement, as 'both tools are required to interact to ensure maximum effectiveness of the competition rules'. The Directive therefore describes it as its task to 'regulate the coordination of those two forms of enforcement in a coherent manner …'. The provisions on disclosure reflect this endeavour.

B. Disclosure

Given the *asymmetry of information* between the infringing and the injured party as to the existence of an infringement of competition law, and given the difficulties for the injured party in proving the existence and the quantity of harm, effective disclosure of evidence by the defendant as well as by third parties seems to be of utmost importance. The Directive, in its Article 5, demands that national courts are to have the power *to order disclosure* of specified items of evidence, thereby recognising the principle of proportionality and the protection of confidential information.

The power to order disclosure of evidence is extended by Article 6 of the Directive to the *files of a competition authority* (including the Commission; recital 15); however, this occurs in a somewhat restricted fashion:

(1) The request for disclosure is to be limited by a principle of subsidiarity insofar as such disclosure is to be made only if such evidence is not available from the defendant or third parties (Article 6(10)).
(2) Moreover, national courts will have to assess the *proportionality* of the order for disclosure with regard to, among other considerations, the need to safeguard the effectiveness of the public enforcement of competition law (Article 6(4)).
(3) In order to *protect ongoing proceedings* initiated by the competition authorities, national courts must not order the disclosure of certain categories of evidence in the file as long as the proceedings have not been closed by the competition authority (Article 6(5)).
(4) And finally, in its Article 6(6), the Directive contains an *absolute prohibition* against national courts addressing an order to any party, including national competition authorities, *to disclose leniency statements* and *settlement submissions*.

These provisions markedly reflect the endeavour of the Union legislature to protect the effectiveness of public enforcement of competition law against the negative consequences and implications resulting from a disclosure of evidence as pursued in civil proceedings. To some extent, the provisions take heed of the case law of the Court of Justice, set forth in *Pfleiderer*[47] and *Donau-Chemie*,[48] in which the Court has established that the right to seek full compensation calls for national procedural rules on the disclosure of evidence that enable the (potentially) injured parties to have access to documents relating to national proceedings (*Pfleiderer*, paragraph 23; *Donau-Chemie* paragraph 26), at least on a subsidiary basis (*Donau-Chemie* paragraphs 32, 44). Thereby, the Court of Justice requires the national courts to weigh the respective interests of the parties involved with regard to the individual case (*Pfleiderer* paragraph 30; *Donau-Chemie* paragraph 30): (i) the interests in favour of a disclosure of the information, (ii) interests for the protection of professional and business secrecy and the protection of personal data by the concerned parties, and also (iii) the harmful consequences which may result for the public enforcement of competition law (*Donau-Chemie* paragraphs 33, 45). Therefore, as a general matter, *neither* a rigid rule, providing for an absolute refusal to grant access to the relevant documents forming part of the competition proceeding (*Donau-Chemie* paragraph 31), *nor* a rule of generalised access to those documents should be viewed as being acceptable (*Donau-Chemie* paragraph 33).

It is submitted that the Union legislature has attempted to stick to these principles as far as Article 6(4) (with its reference to the proportionality principle) is concerned, whereas Article 6(5) (protecting information in the files prepared for proceedings of the competition authority) provides for a rigid rule in as far as disclosure may only be ordered after the proceedings have been closed, which does not allow for a weighing of interests.

Moreover, the rigid prohibition laid down in Article 6(6) against ordering a disclosure of leniency statements and settlement submissions 'at any time' (which means: also after a decision has been adopted) seems to run counter to the statements in *Pfleiderer* (paragraph 30) and *Donau-Chemie* (paragraph 46) that the just-described *weighing approach* has also to be applied with regard to statements relating to a *leniency programme*. In *Donau-Chemie* (paragraph 48) the Court states that it is only where an order for disclosure of a *specific* document (and not: general access to leniency statements) would *actually* (that is to say: in the specific case) undermine the effectiveness of the leniency programme that non-disclosure of that document could be regarded as justified. It is evident that the Union legislature expressly deviates from this balancing approach of the Court, preferring a rigid rule of non-disclosure in order to safeguard the effectiveness of the public enforcement of competition law by national authorities and protect against any weakening of national leniency programmes.[49]

To put the case law of the Court into a somewhat broader perspective, it should, however, be mentioned that the relevant leniency programmes have not been based on legislative acts - neither in the Union nor in the Member States - but rather on guidelines set forth by the competition authorities. This may, to some extent, account for the fact that the Court has declined to accept a rigid rule of non-disclosure,

47. Case C-360/09 *Pfleiderer, supra* n. 42.
48. Case C-536/11 *Donau Chemie and Others, supra* n. 15.
49. *See also* recital 26 of the preamble of Directive 2014/104/EU.

preferring instead its weighing approach with regard to the circumstances in the individual case.

C. Follow-on actions

It should be conceded that by protecting the *effectiveness of leniency programmes*, Article 6(6) of the Directive *weakens* the right of potentially injured persons to seek compensation in an individual case. However, at the same time, this approach *strengthens* the effective and efficient pursuit of such claims by way of *follow-on actions*: In recital 26 of the preamble, reference is made to the fact that many decisions of national competition authorities are based on proof connected to leniency statements. As many damage actions in cartel cases follow from those decisions, the protection of leniency programmes thus works as a *prerequisite* for the effective pursuit of damage claims with regard to the harm caused by cartels. Article 9(1) of the Directive, introducing the *binding effect* of a final decision of a national competition authority for the purposes of an action for damages, has still enhanced the importance of effective public enforcement of competition law in relation to the right to seek compensation, pursued by follow-on actions. Recent case law in Germany reflects the fact that – at least with regard to cartels – actions to seek compensation are for the most part pursued as follow-on actions,[50] with the claimants then left to establish the existence of harm and quantify damages (the latter admittedly being a sometimes very difficult task).[51]

D. Limited liability of immunity recipients

The intention of the Union legislature to protect leniency programmes (of the Union and of the Member States) against a weakening influence by actions to seek damages has also inspired the regulation in Article 11(4) of the Directive providing for only limited civil liability of an *immunity recipient* (i.e., a person that has been granted immunity by the Commission or a national competition authority under a leniency programme; Article 2 No. 19): The immunity recipient is to be jointly and severally liable to its direct and indirect purchasers and providers, but to all other injured parties it incurs such liability *only* if full compensation cannot be obtained from other undertakings involved in the same infringement of competition law. The purpose of this provision is to forestall the danger that the immunity recipient becomes a preferred target of damage claims as a result of the fact that the decision of the competition authority may become final for the immunity recipient at an earlier stage than for the other infringers involved that do not receive immunity.[52] Again, the Union legislature

50. For example, Bundesgerichtshof (BGH), 12 June 2018, KZR 56/16, [2018] WuW 405; Landgericht (LG) Stuttgart, 19 July 2018, 30 O 33/17, [2018] WuW 2018, 593.
51. *See*, e.g., BGH, 11 December 2018, KZR 26/17.
52. These provisions are accompanied by provisions limiting the liability of the immunity recipient as far as recourse among the infringing parties is concerned; Directive 2014/104/EU Article 11(5) and (6).

seems to have opted against the approach taken by the Court to give 'any individual' an unrestrained right to seek compensation, as set forth in paragraph 26 of *Courage*.[53] This leads to the more general question, already more than once touched upon, regarding the relationship between the Directive and the case law of the Court dealing with primary Union law.

V. THE RELATIONSHIP BETWEEN PRIMARY UNION LAW AND DIRECTIVE 2014/104/EU

In what follows, a closer look shall be taken towards two issues that touch on the relationship between primary Union law and Directive 2014/104/EU: (1) The Directive is – to some extent – based on the *acquis communautaire* as developed in the case law of the Court of Justice. This should have implications for the interpretation of some of its provisions. (2) Some of the provisions of the Directive seem to explicitly or implicitly deviate from the case law of the Court. This leads to the question of how we should deal with these provisions.

A. General principles of interpretation

Union law, in general, is subject to an *autonomous interpretation*, based on the wording, the context, and the objective of the very provision in question.[54] This interpretation of Union law notions and terms is independent of the law of the Member States. This goes without saying with regard to the terms of the Directive as listed in its Article 2, where we find definitions of terms such as 'claim for damages', 'injured party', 'overcharge', 'cartel', 'leniency statement', 'direct' and 'indirect purchaser', and the like.

Other terms do not appear in the list of definitions, the most prominent example being the notion of an 'undertaking'. According to the case law of the Court, terms used in Union legislation are, even without being defined, nevertheless to be treated as a Union law concept and also interpreted in an autonomous fashion.[55] A vertical reference to a national concept should be assumed only in the event of an express reference to national law regarding its meaning and its scope.[56] Given this jurisprudence of the Court, it has to be assumed that the term 'undertaking' in the Directive is to be given a Union law meaning.[57] At this point, primary Union law comes into play. As the Directive has forgone a concrete and self-standing definition of its own, it seems

53. *See* II.A, *supra*.
54. For example, ECJ, Case C-467/08 *Padawan SL v Sociedad General de Autores y Editores de España (SGAE)* [2010] ECR I-10055, para. 32; ECJ, Case C-201/13 *Deckmyn and Vrijheidsfonds v Vandersteen and Others* [2014] ECLI:EU:C:2014:2132, para. 14.
55. ECJ, Case C-14/08 *Roda Golf & Beach Resort SL* [2009] ECR I-5439, paras 46–50; Case C-201/13 *Deckmyn and Vrijheidsfonds*, *supra* n. 54, at para. 15.
56. ECJ, Case C-149/15 *Sabrina Wathelet v Garage Bietheres & Fils SPRL* [2016] ECLI:EU:C:2016:840, para. 28; ECJ, Case C-388/13 *Nemzeti Fogyasztóvédelmi Hatóság v UPC Magyarország Kft.* [2015] ECLI:EU:C:2015:225, para. 33.
57. Cf. now Directive 2019/1 Article 2 No. 10 and Article 13(5).

to be highly plausible that the term 'undertaking' has to be interpreted in the light of the case law that has been developed by the Court with regard to the term as used in Articles 101 and 102 TFEU.[58] This is all the more true as the Directive – according to its recital 3 in the preamble – is explicitly meant to protect the subjective rights of private individuals, as derived from Articles 101 and 102 TFEU, vis-à-vis the infringing parties named therein.

It is submitted that the same approach will have to be taken with regard to Article 3(1) of the Directive, in which standing to sue for full compensation is attributed to 'any person ... who has suffered harm'. As there are no indications whatsoever that the Union legislature has proceeded on a diverging concept, the term 'any person' in the Directive should be interpreted in the light of the case law of the Court developed since *Courage*.

B. Is the Directive in conformity with the case law of the Court?

1. *The problem*

The Court, more than once, has held that the right of an individual to seek full compensation for harm caused by an infringement of Article 101(1) TFEU is derived from the principle of effective protection against the adverse effects of such infringement,[59] thereby giving the individual's right to full compensation and its effective protection *a constitutional standing*. Viewed from this perspective, three provisions of the Directive that may be regarded as restricting the effective exercise of this right (and therefore putting its practical effect 'at risk'[60]) may appear to have a somewhat problematic status.

2. *Examples*

(a) Take as the most prominent and most-discussed issue the *disclosure of evidence* as to leniency statements (and settlement submissions): As mentioned earlier (*see*, IV.B, *supra*), the Court, referring to the constitutionally based right to full compensation, has (in *Pfleiderer* and *Donau-Chemie*) called for a weighing-of-interests approach with regard to each individual case: A refusal to order a disclosure of a leniency document has to be based on overriding reasons relating to the effectiveness of the national leniency programme with regard to each specific document to which access is refused (*Donau-Chemie* paragraphs 47–48). It seems obvious that Article 6(6) of the

58. *See* III.B, *supra*, and most recently ECJ, Case C-724/17 *Skanska Industrial Solutions and Others*, *supra* n. 15, para. 47.
59. For example, Case C-536/11 *Donau Chemie and Others*, *supra* n. 15, at para. 24.
60. *See* the language used in Case C-453/99 *Courage and Crehan*, *supra* n. 5, at para. 26.

Directive, with its outright and absolute prohibition against disclosing leniency statements (as defined by Article 2 No. 16), stands in marked contrast to this case law.[61]

(b) The right to full compensation afforded an injured party other than a direct or indirect purchaser is restricted *in favour of small and medium-sized enterprises* (SMEs) as infringers under the conditions set forth in Article 11(2) and (3) of the Directive. This provision obviously is meant to protect an infringing SME at the expense of the injured party's right to full compensation.

(c) Last but not least, the shield put up *in favour* of an *immunity recipient* according to Article 11(4) may raise doubts: Direct liability of the immunity recipient is restricted to the recipient's own direct and indirect purchasers and providers, whereas all other injured persons will have a right to compensation only if full compensation cannot be obtained from the other parties involved in the same infringement of competition law (a case of only subsidiary liability).

3. *Framework of analysis*

What are the consequences of this apparent deviation of some of the provisions of the Directive from the principles set forth by the Court in its case law regarding the right of any injured individual to seek full compensation? In the following discussion, it is argued that the Union legislature should be attributed a *broad discretion* to shape the instruments of substantive and procedural law, with regard to the right to compensation, and to coordinate private and public enforcement in a coherent and (in its view) effective manner, notwithstanding some outer limits that may restrict this discretion.[62] The following considerations may be advanced for such a contention:

(1) The case law of the Court has been developed so as to set guidelines for and limitations to the substantive and procedural law *of the Member States*, on the one hand, and, with regard to the leniency programmes, to set parameters for the *executive branch* of the Union and the Member States on the other. The Court, since *Courage*, has time and again emphasised that its case law applies with regard to Member State law 'in the absence of binding regulation under

61. *See also* recital 26 of the preamble of Directive 2014/104/EU. As for the discussion in academic literature *see*, e.g., Thomas Kapp, *Comment* [2013] BB 1551, 1555; Peter Gussone and Lars Maritzen, *Comment* [2013] EWS 288, 293; Christoph Palzer, *Unvereinbarkeit der österreichischen Regelung zur Akteneinsicht Kartellgeschädigter mit EU-Recht* [2013] NZKart 324, 326; Lilly Fiedler, *Der aktuelle Richtlinienvorschlag der Kommission – der große Wurf für den kartellrechtlichen Schadensersatz?* [2013] BB 2179, 2184; Corinna Potocnik-Manzouri, *Das Offenlegungsverbot für Kronzeugenerklärungen – (K)ein Problem?* (2017) 31 wbl 131.

62. *See* for what follows Wulf-Henning Roth, *Privatrechtliche Kartellrechtsdurchsetzung zwischen primärem und sekundärem Unionsrecht* (2015) 179 ZHR 668; Roth, *supra* n. 30, at Vor §§ 33-33h GWB paras 12–16; Franck, *supra* n. 20, at 624.

European Union law on the subject' (*Courage* paragraph 29; *Manfredi* paragraphs 62, 64, 71, 77, 92; *Kone* paragraph 24; *Pfleiderer* paragraph 23; *Donau-Chemie* paragraph 25). This repeated reference to missing Union legislation may (at first sight) be understood as a concealed message directed at the Union organs to legislate on the issue. Beyond this message, however, it has primarily to be taken as an indication that the case law of the Court may be viewed in a somewhat different light when it comes to Union legislation: The relevant case law may be understood as being addressed to the law of the Member States in the absence of Union legislation and not as a limitation on Union legislation as such.

(2) The constitutional status of the case law regarding the right to seek compensation for harm caused by anticompetitive conduct has been derived by the Court from a basis that remarkably differs from the basis of *State liability* as developed by the *Francovich* case law.[63] On the one hand, it is, indeed, remarkable that in *Courage* some of the paragraphs read like a word-by-word offprint from the *Francovich* judgment (paragraphs 31–34), e.g., referring to the direct effect of Union law and, foremost, the principle of full effectiveness. On the other hand, a close reading of the two judgments shows that they depart from one another in one important point: Whereas, in *Francovich* the Court holds that State liability for damages caused to individuals by breach of Community law should be regarded as 'inherent in the system of the Treaty' (paragraph 35), such a statement is missing in the *Courage* judgment. *Courage* (in paragraph 26) contends that the principle of effectiveness demands that individuals be able to claim damages, but this argument goes to the law of torts of the *Member States*. This, of course, may also be taken as a reference to Article 103(2) TFEU, which empowers the Union legislature to deal with important matters with regard to European competition law, such as fines, the relationship between national laws and the provisions of European competition law, and, here most important, the right to compensation – this by implication[64] and perhaps in conjunction with Article 114 TFEU.[65]

(3) It is submitted that issues regarding the right to claim damages are less a matter of constitutional law[66] than a matter for the Union legislature to deal with (on the basis of Articles 103, 114 TFEU). Take the question of standing

63. Joined Cases C-6/90 and C 9/90 *Francovich and Bonifaci v Italy, supra* n. 17.
64. *See* Axel Reidlinger, in Rudolf Streinz (ed.), *EUV/AEUV* Article 103 AEUV para. 19 (3rd ed., C.H. Beck 2018); Werner Berg, in Werner Berg and Gerald Mäsch (eds), *Deutsches und Europäisches Kartellrecht* Article 103 AEUV para. 4 (3rd ed., Luchterhand 2018).
65. Helmut Schröter, in Helmut Schröter, Thinam Jakob, Robert Klotz & Wolfgang Mederer (eds), *Europäisches Wettbewerbsrecht* Article 103 AEUV para. 29 (2nd ed., Nomos 2014); Carsten Nowak, in Matthias Pechstein, Carsten Nowak & Ulrich Häde (eds), *Frankfurter Kommentar zu EUV, GRC und AEUV* vol. III, Article 103 AEUV para. 38 (Mohr Siebeck 2017). In favour of Article 114 TFEU as the exclusive basis for competence when it comes to harmonisation of Member State laws, *see* Stefan Korte, in Joachim Bornkamm, Frank Montag & Franz Jürgen Säcker (eds), *Münchener Kommentar Europäisches und Deutsches Wettbewerbsrecht, Band 1 – Europäisches Wettbewerbsrecht* Article 103 AEUV para. 28 (2nd ed., C.H. Beck 2015).
66. *See* for this topic in a more generalised analysis, Dieter Grimm, *Europa ja – aber welches?* 27, 40, 131 (3rd ed., C.H. Beck 2016).

for an action for damages: There is no indication whatsoever in Articles 101 and 102 TFEU as to the personal scope of standing, especially whether and to what extent indirect purchasers (and providers) should be afforded such a claim. Moreover, the same arguments relating to the principle of effectiveness that may be brought forward for the existence of damage claims may also be advanced in favour of claims for injunctive relief, but it is less than convincing that indirect purchasers should have the standing to sue in a parallel fashion.[67]

(4) *Institutional balance* is a normative principle[68] not only with regard to the relationship between the EU Parliament and the other EU organs[69] (and between the Commission and the Court[70]) but also between the Court and the Union legislature. It should be admitted that Articles 101 and 102 TFEU do not offer any intrinsic standards for the development of principles that a right to compensation should follow. And the Court – as compared to the EU legislature – seems to be without the institutional competence to decide on the manifold aspects that relate to the delictual liability of undertakings accused of anticompetitive conduct.

(5) Moreover, private enforcement has to be coordinated with the instruments of public enforcement. This involves questions of an empirical and factual nature that should be left to and resolved by the legislature. From a functional point of view, the Court does not appear to be an institution that follows procedures that are appropriate for dealing with such questions. Moreover, the *coordination of public and private enforcement* involves *complex questions* as to their relative value, their effectiveness and coherence (with potential side effects), and the institutional prerequisites that come into play. Just to give two examples: Should the legal setting for antitrust enforcement favour follow-on actions at the (potential) expense of stand-alone actions or should it be the other way around? Should private enforcement be preferred to public enforcement and, if so, to what extent? The same holds true, of course, with regard to the protection of leniency statements and settlement submissions and the protection of the leniency recipient against damage claims.

It is therefore submitted that issues of effective enforcement should be analysed and resolved by the legislature, *effectiveness* being to a large extent a *matter of appreciation* of the ways and means of promoting one objective or the other. Seen from this perspective, it basically appears to be a matter of *legislative* appreciation whether

67. Wulf-Henning Roth, '*Zur Aktivlegitimation im deutschen Kartelldeliktsrecht*' in Juliane Kokott, Petra Pohlmann & Romina Polley (eds), *Europäisches, deutsches und internationales Kartellrecht: Festschrift für Dirk Schroeder* 709 (Otto Schmidt 2018); Roth, *supra* n. 30, at § 33 GWB paras 55–59.
68. *See* Rudolf Streinz, in Streinz (ed.), *supra* n. 64, at Article 13 EUV paras 23–24.
69. ECJ, Case C-70/88 *European Parliament v Council of the European Communities* [1990] ECR I-2041, para. 21; ECJ, Case C-21/94 *European Parliament v Council of the European Union* [1995] ECR I-1827, para. 17.
70. Cf. Alexander Fritzsche, *Ermessen und institutionelles Gleichgewicht* (Heymann 2008).

and to what extent disclosure of leniency statements should or should not be ordered and to what extent small and medium-sized undertakings should be shielded against delictual liability in order to keep and protect them as viable competitors in the relevant market. It is suggested that the case law of the Court dealing with the compensation issue should be attributed solely a *gap-filling* role. In the absence of Union legislation dealing with the matter, it may, from a functional point of view, be characterised less as constitutional case law and more as *quasi-legislative pronouncements* directed towards the Member States that may be supplemented and qualified by Union legislation based on Articles 103(2), 114 TFEU.[71]

4. *Limits to legislative competence?*

In the end, this leaves us with the question of whether and to what extent there are any *discernible limits* on the competence of the Union legislature to deal with this matter – or to put it more concretely, whether Directive 2014/104/EU may be regarded as overstepping such limits in one aspect or another.

To be sure, the Union legislator, when acting on the basis of Articles 103(2) and 114 TFEU, is bound to enforce the principles set forth in Articles 101 and 102 TFEU: Article 103(1) empowers the legislature only to enact 'appropriate' acts (regulations and directives). The legislature will therefore have to treat the right of any individual to claim damages as a right flowing from Articles 101 and 102 TFEU. As the Treaty does not give any concrete standards on how – with regard to private enforcement – the legislature should achieve this objective, it is to be assumed that the legislature, as already pointed out, enjoys *broad discretion*: (i) in the way how, to what extent, and by which instruments competition law is to be enforced; and (ii) in which ways and by what means public and private enforcement is to be coordinated, as long as the right of the injured person to claim damages is not abrogated or restricted in an unreasonable fashion.

The right of injured persons to compensation is to be considered as so fundamental (in the light of *Courage* paragraph 26) that the Union legislature is obligated to protect and enforce this right in an effective manner. It is, however, another and a different question whether truly *any* person who has suffered harm should have a right to claim damages.[72] Though the Union legislature has enacted Directive 2014/104/EU exactly based on this assumption, it is contended that it has the competence to specify and to restrict the personal scope of standing to bring damage claims, as it has the competence to limit injunctions of injured persons to certain groups of persons. The legislature should not be regarded as being bound by the approach advocated in *Kone* of dealing with *umbrella claims* on a case-by-case basis.[73]

71. Roth, *supra* n. 30, at Vor §§ 33-33h GWB para. 13.
72. Perhaps deviating from this position, Case C-724/17 *Skanska Industrial Solutions and Others*, *supra* n. 15, para. 27 (solely referring to the 'modalities' exercising the right to claim damages); ECJ, Case C-637/17 *Cogeco Communications v Sport TV Portugal and Others* [2019] ECLI:EU:C:2019:263 para. 42.
73. Case C-557/12 *Kone and Others*, *supra* n. 14, at paras 32–33.

Turning to the somewhat restrictive role that the leniency programmes of the Member States are attributed in the case law of the Court,[74] it is submitted that this case law will need a re-evaluation. To be sure, leniency programmes may be regarded simply as executive guidelines, but with Article 6(6) of Directive 2014/104/EU – and all the more with Articles 17–23 of Directive 2019/1/EU[75] – they have become accepted by the legislature as an important instrument of public enforcement. Moreover, the protection of leniency statements is no longer a matter of autonomous procedural law of the Member States; rather, it has, by way of Directive 2014/104/EU, also become a policy pursued by the Union legislature. The case law of the Court should therefore not be applied to the provisions of the Directive with the same strictness as it was vis-à-vis the legislation of the Member States prior to the enactment of the Directive.

Such a double-standard approach to primary Union law – strict standards towards Member State law, loose standards with regard to secondary Union law – as is thereby advocated would not be unknown to Union law: In its case law regarding the fundamental freedoms, the Court has applied the proportionality test in an apparently differentiated manner. Whereas Member States have to justify their restrictive measures on the basis of a strictly applied proportionality test, the Court applies the proportionality standard in a rather loose manner when Union legislative measures are at stake.[76] It is submitted that the provisions in Directive 2014/104/EU, as discussed in this chapter, should be evaluated on the basis of a test whether the Union legislature, acting with broad discretion on the basis of Article 103(2) TFEU (and Article 114(1) TFEU, respectively), has made a plausible effort to use its competence to set reasonable standards for the private enforcement of competition law. If we accept such a test, it seems likely that the relevant provisions in the Directive should stand up to this test.[77]

VI. SUMMARY

(1) The Union legislature has, to some extent, transposed the case law of the Court of Justice into Directive 2014/104/EU (*see* III.A, *supra*), regarding it as *acquis communautaire*. Some issues, like the notion of 'undertaking', have not been clarified.

(2) The Directive has addressed a number of issues in a somewhat autonomous fashion: It has opted for full compensation but against deterrence going beyond compensation. Issues addressed include, among others, passing-on, the relevance of decisions of national competition authorities, procedural devices for seeking disclosure, and proof of harm.

74. *See* IV.B, *supra*.
75. Directive 2019/1.
76. For an analysis of the case law *see* Werner Schroeder, in Streinz (ed.), *supra* n. 64, at Article 34 AEUV para. 29; Thorsten Kingreen, in Christian Calliess and Matthias Ruffert, *EUV/AEUV* Articles 34–36 AEUV paras 109–110 (5th ed., C.H. Beck 2016).
77. For further issues *see* Roth, *supra* n. 30, at Vor §§ 33-33h GWB para. 16.

(3) The Directive deals with the effectiveness of public enforcement by limiting the disclosure of leniency statements and settlement submissions and by restricting the liability of leniency recipients.
(4) The provisions limiting disclosure as to leniency statements and restricting the liability of immunity recipients may be considered as contravening the case law of the Court with regard to the principle of effectiveness. It is, however, submitted that this case law has developed in the absence of Union legislation and that it is addressed solely to the law of the Member States.
(5) The Union legislature has the competence to deal with the relevant issues on the basis of Articles 103(2) and 114 TFEU. When addressing these issues, the Union legislator should, as a matter of institutional balance, be attributed broad discretion. Insofar, the relevant provisions of the Directive should be regarded as being in conformity with the TFEU.

CHAPTER 3

The European Commission's View

Johannes Holzwarth

I. Overview
II. The Commission's private enforcement policy and its effects
III. New rules: new (and old) questions
  A. Limitation periods and effects of infringement decisions (*Cogeco v Sport TV Portugal*)
    1. The relevant facts: a complaint, a decision, a claim
    2. Questions on pre-Directive rules
    3. Kokott on the effective application of Article 102 TFEU in damages actions
    4. Four observations
  B. The EU concept of undertakings in the context of private enforcement (*Vantaan v Skanska/NCC/Asfaltmix*)
    1. An invitation to comment more broadly
    2. An initial reaction based on established case law and the Damages Directive
    3. Wahl on the necessary adoption of the rules on economic succession
  C. Further guidance on causation necessary (*Otis v Land Oberösterreich*)
    1. Potential limits on a rather complex chain of causation
    2. Further thoughts on the relevance of Kone
  D. EFTA Court cases: *Fjarskipti v Síminn* & *Nye Kystlink v Color Line*
IV. Passing-on of overcharges and the upcoming guidelines
V. Summary and conclusions

I. OVERVIEW

This[1] chapter will focus on the European Commission's perspective after the implementation of the Damages Directive 2014/104/EU[2] by the Member States. It is structured in three parts. The first part will outline the private enforcement policy that the Commission currently pursues and will address its potential as well as its already perceivable effects (II.). The second part will cover preliminary references of major importance for the private enforcement of competition law that are currently pending before the Court of Justice of the European Union (CJEU). In this main part, the facts of the cases as well as questions raised by the national courts will be set out briefly and discussed (III.). The last part will deal with the passing-on of overcharges and the upcoming guidelines in this respect (IV.).

II. THE COMMISSION'S PRIVATE ENFORCEMENT POLICY AND ITS EFFECTS

To fully comprehend the Damages Directive, it is necessary to take a step back to understand its underlying policy. Most importantly, this Directive pursues two complementary goals:[3] first, it aims at providing victims of competition law infringements effective instruments to claim compensation for the harm suffered. Second, it intends to strike the right balance and optimise the interplay between public and private enforcement. Since the Damages Directive has been implemented by the Member States, the Commission has started to look into how exactly the rules of the Damages Directive have been transposed into national law and whether the rules' spirit is being respected or not.[4] However, to comment on whether the Commission's policies are taking the intended effect, it is also necessary to analyse the application in practice.[5]

Some promising studies already suggest an appreciable impact of the Damages Directive. For instance, a recent study conducted by the French economist Jean-Francois Laborde provides a good overview of the increasing relevance of private enforcement of competition law.[6] *Laborde* collected and analysed recent judgments rendered by national courts of EU Member States. The scope of his study covers damages claims featuring one or several plaintiffs alleging that a cartel caused an

1. All views expressed in this chapter are strictly personal and should not be construed as statement of the European Commission or its Directorate General for Competition.
2. Directive 2014/104/EU of the European Parliament and of the Council of 26 November 2014 on certain rules governing actions for damages under national law for infringements of the competition law provisions of the Member States and of the European Union [2014] OJ L 349/1 (Damages Directive).
3. *See* Commission, *The Damages Directive – Towards more effective enforcement of EU competition rules*, Competition policy brief, Issue 2015-1.
4. *See* Commission, press release of 24 January 2019, MEMO/19/462, https://europa.eu/rapid/press-release_MEMO-19-462_EN.htm (accessed 20 August 2019).
5. Article 20(1) of the Damages Directive also requires the Commission to review the Damages Directive and submit a report thereon to the European Parliament and the Council by 27 December 2020.
6. Jean-François Laborde, *Cartel damages actions in Europe: How courts have assessed overcharges (2018 ed.)* (2019) 1 Concurrences 1 et seq.

overcharge, and in which a court handed down a judgment on the merits, i.e. cases in which the courts have actually reached a conclusion on the substantive damages claims.[7] On the basis of this overview, it seems to be very difficult to argue that the Damages Directive has had hardly any impact.

Figure 3.1 Cartel Damages Actions in Europe: How Courts Have Assessed Overcharge

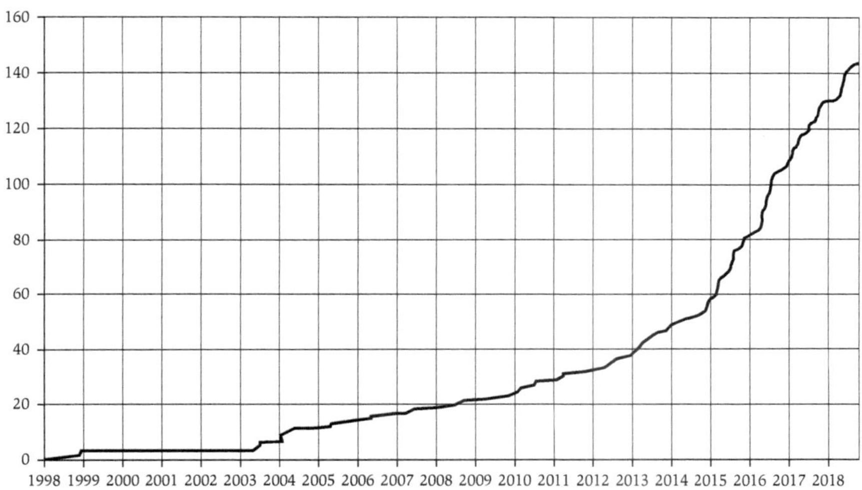

Source: Jean-François Laborde, *Cartel damages actions in Europe: How courts have assessed overcharges (2018 ed.)* (2019) 1 Concurrences 1.

Laborde's study on *Cartel damages actions in Europe: How courts have assessed overcharge* shows the rising number of judgments on the merits (*see* Figure 3.1). In 2014, the year in which the Damages Directive was adopted, an increase in the amount of such judgments can be noted, which could give a good indication as to where we are going. With the implementing national laws now in place, this trend is likely to continue in the future. However, the Directive's full impact can probably only be measured in a few years' time. This is particularly due to Article 22(1) of the Damages Directive, which provides that the Directive's substantive provisions do not apply retroactively and which thereby limits its scope of application *ratione temporis*. Further, the conformity and completeness checks currently conducted by the Commission seem to reveal that the vast majority of Member States did not opt for a retroactive application of the Directive's procedural rules either.

7. In particular, the study included three sets of judgments: judgments awarding damages, judgments establishing liability but setting no amount of damages and judgments dismissing claims for a lack of merit. It excluded cases in which the harm was not an overcharge (e.g., exclusion), cases in which there was an out-of-court settlement before any judgment on the merits was rendered and claims that were dismissed on strictly formal grounds (e.g., jurisdiction or limitation). With regard to the geographical scope, the study covered the twenty-eight EU Member States as well as Switzerland and Norway.

III. NEW RULES: NEW (AND OLD) QUESTIONS

With regard to the effects of the Damages Directive, these impact statistics are however only one side of the coin, with the other side being the legal one. The creation of new rules by the Directive has inevitably raised some new and maybe even refreshed some older questions. For the sake of legal certainty, it seems important that these questions are to be comprehensively answered by the CJEU, making requests for preliminary rulings by the Member State courts a crucial link. Fortunately, the national courts seem to have acknowledged their relevance and have already submitted a number of cases to the CJEU in which it can rule on the disputed issues at European level. Out of these preliminary references, three cases of particular interest for the private enforcement of EU competition law that are currently pending before the CJEU shall be presented in further detail below. In addition, two important decisions by the Court of Justice of the European Free Trade Association (EFTA Court) shall be briefly presented.

A. Limitation periods and effects of infringement decisions (*Cogeco v Sport TV Portugal*)

The first request for a preliminary ruling requiring an in-depth presentation is *Cogeco*.[8] On the one hand, this case raises more fundamental questions, such as which effects does the Damages Directive have prior to its implementation into national law and which conclusions can be drawn directly from Article 102 of the Treaty of the Functioning of the EU (TFEU) and the principle of effectiveness in relation to private enforcement. On the other hand, it deals with more specific questions concerning the application of limitation periods – which is why the dates of the main events matter in this case – and the relevance of decisions that have been issued by national competition authorities for damages actions.

1. The relevant facts: a complaint, a decision, a claim

In this case, the Portuguese national competition authority issued an infringement decision for the abuse of a dominant position against Sport TV Portugal in 2013. The relevant behaviour had allegedly taken place between 2006 and 2011. Cogeco, a competitor of Sport TV Portugal, had filed a complaint with the Portuguese competition authority in July 2009, which later sanctioned the dominant player for its assumed abusive behaviour. However, the infringement decision was challenged before the competent courts, which partially annulled and partially upheld the decision. More specifically, the Portuguese Court of First Instance held that there had only been a violation of Portuguese national law corresponding to Article 102 TFEU and found that Article 102 TFEU was not applicable due to an alleged lack of effect on trade. This judgment was rendered in June 2014, i.e. before the Damages Directive was adopted at

8. ECJ, Case C-637/17 *Cogeco Communications Inc v Sport TV Portugal and Others* [2018] OJ C 32/14.

the end of 2014, and it was later confirmed by the appellate court. In February 2015, Cogeco lodged the relevant damages action in Portugal, i.e. before the deadline to implement the Damages Directive expired at the end of 2016 and before Portugal actually transposed the Directive in 2018.

In the damages action that Cogeco had filed, the defendant argued that the claim was time-barred under pre-Directive Portuguese law which established a three-year limitation period beginning to run when the injured party became aware of the claim, even without knowing the infringer and the extent of the harm. This law did not foresee any suspension or interruption of the limitation period when a competition authority had started to investigate the alleged competition law infringement.

The defendant's argument would be valid if Portuguese limitation law remained unaffected by the adoption and entry into force of the Damages Directive in 2014. However, it is unclear if the claim would also be time-barred if either the provisions of the Damages Directive or the principle of effectiveness were to effect the application of Portuguese law before the expiration of the deadline to implement the Damages Directive.

2. *Questions on pre-Directive rules*

Against this background, the Portuguese civil court was required to precisely determine the limitation period applicable to the damages claim, and it thus filed a preliminary reference to the CJEU. First, the query concerns the direct application of the Directive and hence primary law. It reframes the question of whether certain provisions of a directive can apply horizontally even before the deadline for its transposition has expired. However, as the CJEU has already decided in *Ratti*,[9] the horizontal application of a directive before the expiration of the deadline for transposition would interfere with the Member States' right to freely regulate the issue within this time frame and will therefore most likely be rejected by the court.

The second question regarding a possible impact of either the Damages Directive's provisions or Article 102 TFEU in connection with the principle of effectiveness on the Portuguese limitation law seems much harder to answer. It is true that, in comparison with the Portuguese law prior to the implementation of the Damages Directive, the Directive's limitation period is longer (five instead of three years), and it explicitly requires that limitation periods must be suspended or interrupted when a competition authority investigates the alleged infringement of EU competition law. Furthermore, the limitation period begins to run under more restrictive conditions compared to Portuguese law. However, before the implementation of the Damages Directive across the Member States, a limitation period of three years for damages actions before national courts was not unusual.

Moreover, any finding of when such a subjective limitation period starts may seem to depend on which event is assumed to be the relevant point in time, i.e. the date on which the injured party became aware of its right. At first sight, it seems compelling

9. ECJ, Case 148/78 *Pubblico Ministero v Ratti* [1979] ECR 1629 = [1979] NJW 1764, paras 43 et seq.

that, in the case at hand, the relevant knowledge points to the filing of the complaint by the claimant in 2009 – which certainly is the position the defendant would assume. However, in line with Article 102 TFEU in connection with the principle of effectiveness, the relevant date could also be defined as the day when the Portuguese competition authority issued its infringement decision. In this case, the limitation period of three years would still have been ongoing at the time of the proceedings, even without a suspension for the time of investigation by the competition authority. While the assessment of the underlying facts and the application of national law to those facts are core tasks of the national court, the legal questions under EU law may remain. In this respect, the opinion recently given by Advocate General Kokott might allow a certain outlook into the decision of the CJEU.[10]

3. *Kokott on the effective application of Article 102 TFEU in damages actions*

By reference to Article 22(1) of the Damages Directive, which precludes the retroactive application of national law implementing the substantive provisions of the Damages Directive, and with reference to the general rule that directives do not have horizontal effects, Advocate General Kokott stated that the Damages Directive would not apply in the case at hand.[11] While she left it open whether the rules on limitation periods set out in the Damages Directive are substantive or procedural because they could not 'resurrect' a claim that is time-barred in any case, Advocate General Kokott nevertheless referred to the qualification of limitation periods as being substantive under Portuguese law prior to the implementation of the Damages Directive.[12] This reference is interesting since an autonomous interpretation of the Damages Directive could well lead to the qualification of its limitation periods as procedural law. As a consequence, there may be a tension between the qualification of national rules that existed prior to the implementation of the Damages Directive and those that implement the rules of the Directive. In any case, the clear wording of Article 22(1) of the Damages Directive ('national measures adopted ... to comply with substantive provisions of this Directive') and the harmonisation purpose of the Damages Directive seem to run counter an interpretation which takes into account the qualification of national implementing law as substantive or procedural.[13]

Considering the pre-Directive Portuguese limitation periods 'as a whole', Kokott concluded that they contradict Article 102 TFEU as regards the principle of effectiveness.[14] This was essentially not due to the duration of three years but rather because,

10. Case C-637/17 *Cogeco Communications Inc v Sport TV Portugal and Others* [2019] ECLI: EU:C:2019:32, Opinion of AG Kokott.
11. *Ibid.*, paras 68–70.
12. *Ibid.*, para. 63.
13. This argument, which seems to be rather difficult to reconcile with the autonomous interpretation of the Damages Directive, was made in Oberlandesgericht (OLG) Düsseldorf, 3 April 2018, VI-W (Kart) 2/18, paras 30–41 = [2018] NZKart 228, 229–230, but later qualified in OLG Düsseldorf, 7 May 2018, VI-W (Kart) 2/18, para. 27.
14. Case C-637/17 *Cogeco Communications*, Opinion of AG Kokott, *supra* n. 10, at paras 81, 86.

first, these limitation periods started to run even if the victim did not know the infringer and the extent of the harm and, second, they were not interrupted or suspended when the national authority investigated the alleged competition law infringement.[15]

As regards the question on the effects of such decisions rendered by national competition authorities, Kokott concluded that Article 102 TFEU in connection with the principle of effectiveness precludes the application of national law according to which such a decision has no effect in subsequent damages actions for the infringement of Article 102 TFEU.[16] However, if this law could be interpreted as to ensure prima facie evidence of an infringement decision in such actions, this interpretation would be a sufficiently effective application of Article 102 TFEU.[17]

4. Four observations

Four additional aspects of Kokott's conclusions should be highlighted. First, while she draws inspiration from the rules of the Damages Directive when giving rather detailed guidance on the basis of Article 102 TFEU in light of the principle of effectiveness, Kokott stresses that the Damages Directive does not merely codify what would have already (indirectly) followed from Article 102 TFEU and the principle of effectiveness. Rather, she seems to promote the added value of the Damages Directive for private enforcement of EU competition law in relation to both limitation periods and the effects of infringement decisions.

Second, it is interesting that Kokott takes issue particularly with the Portuguese rule according to which the limitation period starts to run even if the victim does not know the *infringer*.[18] Such a rule may be crucial where Article 101 TFEU is concerned, e.g. when it is unclear who exactly participated in a secret cartel. In cases of alleged infringements of Article 102 TFEU, like the case at hand, this knowledge may typically not be an issue since the alleged abuse often occurs in the course of business between a particular supplier and its customer.

Third, by making reference to the recent judgment of the CJEU in *Tele 2 Polska*[19] and Article 5 of Regulation 1/2003,[20] Kokott seems to confirm that the finding of non-applicability of Article 102 TFEU – found in the case at hand by the first instance court partially annulling the infringement decision – cannot have ('negative') binding effects, in neither follow-on nor stand-alone damages actions.[21] For the case at hand, this notion means that the court deciding on Cogeco's damages action can decide whether Article 102 TFEU is applicable, irrespective of the appellate court's finding that there was no effect on trade.[22]

15. *Ibid.*, paras 78–86.
16. *Ibid.*, para. 97.
17. *Ibid.*
18. *Ibid.*, paras 82–84.
19. ECJ, Case C-375/09 *Tele 2 Polska* [2011] ECR I-3055, paras 21–30.
20. Council Regulation (EC) No 1/2003 of 16 December 2002 on the implementation of the rules on competition laid down in Articles 81 and 82 of the Treaty [2002] OJ L 001.
21. Case C-637/17 *Cogeco Communications*, Opinion of AG Kokott, *supra* n. 10, at paras 49–52.
22. *Ibid.*, para. 53.

Fourth, at the very end of her opinion and by reference to the fundamental case law of the CJEU, Kokott reasons that national courts are required to interpret national law in light of Article 102 TFEU and the principle of effectiveness, but without having to reach an interpretation *contra legem*.[23] This reasoning seems crucial in the case at hand since it would be for the Portuguese court to carefully analyse any room for interpretation of the applicable rules in Portugal.

Whatever the result turns out to be for the concrete case, it remains important to underscore that in rendering its judgment the CJEU might interpret only EU primary law, namely Article 102 TFEU with regard to the principle of effectiveness. Since the new rules of the Damages Directive will most probably not be found directly applicable in this case, the CJEU's decision will consequently only guide and influence the interpretation of the respective national rules by the Portuguese court.

B. The EU concept of undertakings in the context of private enforcement (*Vantaan v Skanska/NCC/Asfaltmix*)

The second pending preliminary reference of major relevance for private enforcement of EU competition law is *Skanska*.[24] This case deals with the EU concept of 'undertakings'. While this concept has been well established by Union courts in the context of public enforcement of EU competition law, its application in the context of private enforcement has not yet been addressed by the CJEU and, indeed, courts in the Member States have taken different approaches. Some of them have applied the EU concept of undertakings in the context of private enforcement;[25] others have rejected its application.[26]

1. An invitation to comment more broadly

The *Skanska* preliminary reference essentially concerns the question of whether a legal entity having acquired assets of a dissolved legal entity is liable for the damages that have resulted from an infringement of EU competition law committed by that dissolved legal entity or its predecessors. However, the preliminary ruling is likely to answer other questions in relation to the application of the EU concept of undertakings in damages actions as well. One of these other questions concerns the civil liability of parent companies for competition law infringements perpetrated by their subsidiaries. In fact, in its second question, the referring court indicates that 'liability may be founded in particular on belonging to the same economic unit'. This indication

23. *Ibid.*, paras 105–106.
24. ECJ, Case C-724/17 *Vantaan kaupunki v Skanska Industrial Solutions Oy and Others* [2018] OJ C 83/14.
25. *See* Oberster Gerichtshof (OGH), 2 August 2012, 4 Ob 46/12m, paras 7.3 et seq.; Competition Appeal Tribunal (CAT), *Sainsbury's Supermarkets Ltd. v Mastercard Inc.* [2016] CAT 11, para. 363 with further references; Landgericht (LG) Nürnberg-Fürth, 11 October 2018, 19 O 8786/15, [2018] NZKart 593.
26. *See* LG Düsseldorf, 8 September 2016, 37 O 27/11 (Kart.); LG Berlin, 6 August 2013, 16 O 193/11 (Kart).

basically invites the CJEU to comment on parental liability in the context of private enforcement.

The case itself concerns legal entities that had been involved in the Finnish asphalt cartel. The restructuring of the legal entities involved in this cartel was rather complex. However, put simply, at a given point in time they were dissolved and their assets were transferred to other legal entities, including Skanska, which continued the relevant economic activities. Hence, the question arose as to whether these other entities could be held liable for the harm that resulted from the competition infringement in which the dissolved entities had taken part. This question was decisive because, according to Finnish law, a legal entity is generally only liable for the loss it itself has caused to others, and only in very exceptional circumstances is it liable for the damage caused by another legal entity.

Following the claimant's argument, the question arose as to *whether* the EU concept of undertakings adopted for public enforcement under Article 101 TFEU must be extended to apply also in damages actions. And if this result is to be adopted, the follow-up question arises as to *how* it applies, i.e. whether the application of the European concept flows directly from Article 101 TFEU or whether national law in principle still determines under which circumstances a legal entity is liable for harm caused by others, influenced by the principle of effectiveness. Both questions ('whether' and 'how') are subject to the preliminary reference in *Skanska*.

2. *An initial reaction based on established case law and the Damages Directive*

It seems fair to argue that the application of the EU concept of undertakings in damages actions before national courts follows directly from Article 101 TFEU. This is first of all due to the case law of the CJEU on Article 101 TFEU, according to which any individual may invoke this Article 'to claim damages for loss caused to him by a contract or by conduct liable to restrict or distort competition'.[27] One could argue that because Article 101 TFEU is already understood to set out *who is able to claim* compensation, it should consequently also govern the question of *who is liable* for the harm caused, all the more since Article 101 TFEU explicitly uses the term 'undertakings'. This interpretation also squares well with the fundamental case law of the CJEU according to which Articles 101 and 102 TFEU 'tend by their very nature to produce direct effects in relations between individuals'.[28] Second, as mentioned above, there is extensive case law on the EU concept of undertakings in the context of the public enforcement of Article 101 TFEU. If nothing else, it would simply be consistent to apply this case law also in the

27. ECJ, Case C-453/99 *Courage Ltd v Bernard Crehan and Bernard Crehan v Courage Ltd and Others* [2001] ECR I-6297 = [2002] EuR, 216, para. 26 and ECJ, Joined Cases C-295/04 to C-298/04 *Vincenzo Manfredi and Others v Lloyd Adriatico Assicurazioni SpA and Others* [2006] ECR I-6619 = [2006] EuZW 529, para. 60.
28. ECJ, Case 127/73 *Belgische Radio en Televisie and société belge des auteurs, compositeurs et éditeurs v SV SABAM and NV Fonior* [1974] ECR 313, para. 16.

context of private enforcement, and, moreover, such an application would not least serve the purpose of realising a level playing field across the EU.[29]

It is true that the Damages Directive does not include detailed rules on the EU concept of undertakings. However, the first sentence of Article 1 of the Damages Directive links 'an infringement of competition law by an undertaking' with 'the right to claim full compensation for that harm *from that undertaking*' (emphasis added), and Article 2 of the Damages Directive also refers to an 'undertaking' for the purpose of defining 'infringer'. When EU legislators used the term 'undertaking', it is difficult to imagine that the underlying concept was not the one established by the CJEU in the context of public enforcement.

Even if one disregarded the Damages Directive and considered the Member States to be competent to govern the matter of who is liable for the harm caused by a competition law infringement, the arguments in relation to the purpose of Article 101 TFEU would remain. In this case, it would be Article 101 TFEU in connection with the principle of effectiveness that essentially required national courts to interpret the applicable national law in accordance with the EU concept of undertakings. The case at hand seems to illustrate quite well why this interpretation is necessary since without the application of the EU concept of undertaking it would be impossible or at least excessively difficult for the claimant to receive compensation from the dissolved company.

3. *Wahl on the necessary adoption of the rules on economic succession*

The opinion recently delivered by Advocate General Wahl goes in the same direction. This is particularly true since, in the context of private enforcement, he supports the application of 'a broad concept of "undertaking" along with its corollary, the principle of economic continuity'.[30] Wahl also concludes that the persons liable to pay compensation for harm caused by conduct contrary to Article 101 TFEU should be determined on the basis of EU law and not on the basis of the national domestic law.[31] His arguments are similar to those made above.[32] For example, he reasons that 'a solution whereby the interpretation of "undertaking" would be different depending on the mechanism employed to enforce EU competition law [i.e. public or private enforcement] would simply be *untenable*'[33] (emphasis added).

However, Wahl's opinion seems to be quite distinct in at least two respects. First, by reference to the *Kone*[34] judgment of the CJEU, Wahl picks up on a distinction between, on the one hand, 'constitutive conditions' of the right to claim compensation,

29. In the context of public enforcement, this argument can be found in Case C-501/11 P *Schindler Holding and Others v Commission* [2013] ECLI:EU:C:2013:248, Opinion of AG Kokott, para. 76.
30. Case C-724/17 *Vantaan kaupunki v Skanska Industrial Solutions Oy and Others* [2019] ECLI:EU:C:2019:100, Opinion of AG Wahl, para. 76.
31. *Ibid.*, paras 56–58.
32. *Ibid.*, paras 61–67 with reference to case law and the Damages Directive.
33. *Ibid.*, para. 80.
34. ECJ, Case C-557/12 *Kone and Others v ÖBB-Infrastruktur AG* [2014] ECLI:EU:C:2014:1317 = [2014] EuZW 586.

which could be drawn directly from Article 101 TFEU so as to guarantee its effective application and, on the other hand, 'detailed rules governing the exercise of the right to claim compensation', notably the rules laid down in the Member States, to which the 'classic tests' of equivalence and effectiveness would apply.[35] Second, Wahl puts great emphasis on the deterrent effects of Article 101 TFEU and even argues that 'the compensatory function of an action for damages for an infringement of competition law remains ... *subordinate* to that of its deterrent function' (emphasis added).[36] If deterrence was indeed perceived as a main goal of private enforcement of Article 101 TFEU, this would be a strong argument for the application of the EU concept of an undertaking not only in the context of the public enforcement of Article 101 TFEU.[37] However, this perception contradicts the compensatory nature of private enforcement of EU competition law, as enshrined in the Damages Directive, which frequently highlights the right to full compensation and not once mentions the deterrence of damages actions for competition law violations. It will be interesting to see if the CJEU will comment on the goals of private enforcement of EU competition law and, of course, whether it promotes the application of the EU concept of undertaking with all its consequences for the question of civil liability in damages actions for competition law infringements.

C. Further guidance on causation necessary (*Otis v Land Oberösterreich*)

The last case to be discussed here is the case *Otis v Land Oberösterreich*.[38] Unlike what its designation may suggest, it is in substance not really a follow-up to the *Otis I* case,[39] in which also the EU Commission claimed damages, but more a follow-up to the *Kone*[40] decision. This is because the case deals with particular questions on causation.

1. *Potential limits on a rather complex chain of causation*

The case concerns rather complex facts on the basis of which a public body (the Land Oberösterreich) filed a damages action against a cartel member (Otis). As part of its housing development policy, the Land Oberösterreich had granted loans to construction companies and homeowners for the construction of new homes. These loans were granted at a discounted interest rate, i.e. a rate below market conditions, and for a certain percentage of the total costs of the construction. In one of the transactions, a construction company received funding through such a loan to buy cartelised elevators and escalators. On the premise that, absent the cartel, its own costs for granting the subsidised loan would have been lower, the Land Oberösterreich claimed damages

35. Case C-724/17 *Vantaan kaupunki and Others*, Opinion of AG Wahl, *supra* n. 30, at paras 40–41.
36. *Ibid.*, para. 50.
37. *Ibid.*, para. 80.
38. Case C-435/18, *Otis Gesellschaft m.b.H. and Others v Land Oberösterreich and Others* [2018] OJ C 352/19.
39. ECJ, Case C-494/11 P *Europese Gemeenschap v Otis NV and Others* [2012] ECLI:EU:C:2012:684.
40. Case C-557/12 *Kone and Others*, *supra* n. 34.

from Otis. It argued that the additional funding that it had granted could instead have been invested profitably at least at the average interest rate of federal bonds. This argument led to the question of whether such harm was caused by Otis.

While this question is currently pending before the CJEU, the referring court has indicated that national law may lead it to find that there is no causation. The court indicated that this finding could be based on the lack of a sufficient link of unlawfulness (*Rechtswidrigkeitszusammenhang*) between the infringement of Article 101 TFEU and the alleged harm because the harm may fall outside of the protective purpose of the provision (*Schutzzweck der Norm*).[41] In its preliminary reference, the national court also seems to assume that the protective purpose of Article 101 TFEU covers only harm suffered by participants acting on the very market affected by the cartel. On the basis of this assumption, the court seems to have doubts as to whether the alleged loss in the case at hand is covered.

The national court's assumption, according to which the Land Oberösterreich is 'not active as supplier or customer on the relevant product and geographic market affected by a cartel', may be inconsistent from an economic point of view. This is because the Land Oberösterreich could be seen as a supplier of capital to the purchaser of the cartelised product. Further, it may not square well with the rules of the Damages Directive, which explicitly mention public authorities and suppliers as well as even more remotely affected victims, such as consumers, as those having the right to claim damages for infringements of Article 101 TFEU.[42] Moreover, as regards the protective scope of Article 101 TFEU, the CJEU explicitly stated in *Kone* that 'the objective pursued by Article 101 TFEU [is] to guarantee effective and undistorted competition in the internal market, and, accordingly, prices set on the basis of free competition'.[43]

2. *Further thoughts on the relevance of Kone*

When analysing the questions raised by the referring court, it is necessary to recall that the case law of the CJEU is relatively clear on the question of standing, i.e. any individual's right to seek compensation for the harm suffered as a result of an infringement of Article 101 TFEU. On the basis of this notion, the CJEU essentially held in *Kone* that nobody can be excluded a priori from seeking such compensation.[44]

This does not mean, however, that there are no limits to the liability of an infringer, and the rules on causation may certainly establish those.[45] In fact, in *Kone*, the CJEU confirmed the requirement of a 'causal relationship' in damages actions for

41. The Austrian rules on the link of unlawfulness (*Rechtswidrigkeitszusammenhang*) between the infringement of a statutory duty and the alleged harm and the theory on the protective purpose of the provision (*Schutzzweck der Norm*) were mentioned already in Case C-557/12 *Kone and Others*, *supra* n. 34, *see* paras 13–15.
42. *See* Recitals 13 and 43 of the Damages Directive.
43. Case C-557/12 *Kone and Others*, *supra* n. 34, at para. 32.
44. *See* Case C-557/12 *Kone and Others*, *supra* n. 34, at para. 21.
45. For an overview of the national rules on causation that establish such limits *see* Ioannis Lianos, *Causal Uncertainty and Damages Claims for the Infringement of Competition Law in Europe* (2015) 34 Yearbook of European Law 170.

infringements of Article 101 TFEU and stated that, in the absence of detailed Union rules governing this requirement, the relevant national rules apply, provided they comply with the principles of equivalence and effectiveness.[46]

It seems that in *Kone* the CJEU deliberately decided not to set out detailed conditions. This was despite Advocate General Kokott's more far-reaching suggestions that drew upon the case law addressing the non-contractual liability of European Union institutions pursuant to Article 340 TFEU[47] and even the protective purpose of the provision (*Schutzzweck der Norm*).[48]

However, the CJEU arguably endorsed at least Kokott's foreseeability criterion[49] when it highlighted that the circumstances of the case that were liable to have the effect of umbrella pricing 'could not have been ignored by the members of that cartel'.[50] Indeed, it seems that such a criterion may not be fulfilled in a case like the one at hand, in which the claimant actually did not act as a profit-maximising firm (e.g., granting loans under preferential terms) but alleges that it would have acted like a profit-maximising firm in the absence of the cartel (e.g., investing the amount profitably). This was different in *Kone*, in which the umbrella pricing was found to be foreseeable.[51] In any event, it must be stressed that it is ultimately up to the national court to assess the circumstances of a given case.

Irrespective of whether the CJEU has established a foreseeability criterion in *Kone*, that judgment arguably does not prevent the courts of Member States from applying national rules on causation provided they comply with Article 101 TFEU and the principle of effectiveness. More specifically, these rules may not be applied so as to a priori deny certain types of claimants standing because their harm allegedly falls outside of the protective purpose of the provision.[52]

D. EFTA Court cases: *Fjarskipti v Síminn & Nye Kystlink v Color Line*

Finally, two cases of the EFTA Court ought to be mentioned briefly since they seem to pave the way for private enforcement under the Agreement on the European Economic Area (EEA Agreement). The first case is *Fjarskipti v Síminn*.[53] The judgment following the referral from an Icelandic court seems to be as fundamental in relation to Articles 53 and 54 EEA Agreement as the CJEU's preliminary ruling in *Courage v Crehan* was for the counterparts of Articles 101 TFEU and 102 TFEU in the sense that the judgment of

46. *Ibid.*
47. ECJ, Joined Cases C-46/93 and C-48/93 *Brasserie du Pêcheur SA v Bundesrepublik Deutschland and The Queen v Secretary of State for Transport* [1996] ECR I-1029, para. 51.
48. Case C-557/12 *Kone and Others* [2014] ECLI:EU:C:2014:45, Opinion AG Kokott, paras 31 et seq.
49. *Ibid.*, paras 41–52.
50. Case C-557/12 *Kone and Others*, *supra* n. 34, at para. 34.
51. Case C-557/12 *Kone and Others*, *supra* n. 34, at para. 29.
52. The *Telegate* judgment of the Oberlandesgericht Düsseldorf could potentially be seen as an example of such a scenario, *see* OLG Düsseldorf, 8 June 2014, VI – U (Kart) 2/11.
53. The case, which also concerned questions on margin squeeze, is summarised in EFTA court, *Press Release 04/18 – Case E-6/17 – Fjarskipti hf. v Síminn hf.*, https://eftacourt.int/wp-content/uploads/2019/01/6_17_PR_EN.pdf (accessed 13 May 2019).

the EFTA Court establishes any individual's right to claim damages.[54] The second case was referred to the EFTA Court by a Norwegian court and concerns – like the *Cogeco* case mentioned above – limitation periods.[55] Although the ruling primarily deals with the principle of effectiveness, it also includes a very interesting side note on the principle of equivalence discussed in relation to a specific rule on limitation.

IV. PASSING-ON OF OVERCHARGES AND THE UPCOMING GUIDELINES

The EU Commission has recently published draft guidelines on the passing-on of cartel overcharges[56] and has invited stakeholders to comment. The guidelines aim at supporting the business community with practical guidance on how to apply the rather abstract rules on passing-on in practice, as foreseen in Article 16 of the Damages Directive. What is more, they are intended to help national courts confronted with passing-on issues, e.g. when having to quantify and take into account the overcharges passed on to indirect purchasers and final consumers to measure the remaining damage incurred by a direct purchaser.

While the guidelines are being finalised, one important aspect needs to be stressed from the outset. Whereas some stakeholders would find it useful if the Commission supported new rules that are in line with an emerging tendency in the case law of national courts to limit the passing-on defence, this including the case law of lower courts in Germany, the EU Commission could decide to only provide guidance and not create new rules.[57] A striking example of such a rule-making decision by a lower German court is a recent judgment of the Landgericht Hannover.[58] In a scenario with allegedly no competitive downstream market, the court ruled that there had not been any passing-on to indirect purchasers nor consumers, thereby restricting the passing-on defence as a shield. Another limitation of the passing-on defence was adopted by the Landgericht Stuttgart,[59] holding that it applies only where the purchaser simply resells the cartelised product.

This case law seems to take up a tendency already adopted in the UK.[60] There, limits to allegedly excessive findings of causality are debated with reference to the discussion of whether there is a difference between economic and legal causation. For example, if a postal company had bought cartelised trucks to provide its postal services

54. EFTA court, Case E-6/17 *Fjarskipti v Síminn*, 30 May 2018 = [2018] NZKart 325.
55. EFTA court, Case E-10/17 *Nye Kystlink v Color Line*, 17 September 2018 = [2018] NZKart 495.
56. European Commission, Draft guidelines for national courts on how to estimate the share of cartel overcharges passed on to indirect purchasers and final consumers, available at http://ec.europa.eu/competition/consultations/2018_cartel_overcharges/index_en.html (accessed 5 June 2019).
57. *See* Hans-Petter H. Hanson and Johannes Holzwarth, *Discovering New Spheres of Antitrust Damages Quantification: The European Commission, National Courts, and Guidelines on Passing-On* 3, https://www.competitionpolicyinternational.com/discovering-new-spheres-of-antitrust-damages-quantification-the-european-commission-national-courts-and-guidelines-on-passing-on/ (accessed 13 May 2019).
58. LG Hannover, 16 April 2018, 18 O 21/17 [2018] BeckRS 7910.
59. LG Stuttgart, 19 July 2018, 30 O 33/17 [2018] NZKart 484.
60. As done most explicitly by the Landgericht Dortmund, which refers to UK and Dutch case law, *see* LG Dortmund, 27 June 2018, 8 O 13/17 (Kart).

and later raised the prices for stamps, an economist may very well come to the conclusion that there is a causal link between the cartel agreement and the price increase for stamps. However, lawyers might argue that the rules on causation limit the liability of the cartelists for the harm that the end customer has suffered due to the price increase for stamps as well as the loss of profit stemming from the volume effect because end customers purchase fewer stamps. On the basis of the CJEU's judgment in *Kone*, and potentially its new preliminary ruling in the matter of Land *Oberösterreich v Otis*, lawyers may have good arguments. However, to respect the compensatory nature of EU private enforcement, more caution might be necessary so as not to dismiss passing-on arguments too quickly. A more nuanced approach to passing-on in damages actions for competition law infringements seems to be more advisable. The upcoming passing-on guidelines will hopefully assist in this respect.

V. SUMMARY AND CONCLUSIONS

Private enforcement of EU competition law is on the rise. It is difficult to dispute that the Commission's policy and its major piece of legislation – the Damages Directive – have not contributed to this development. However, while the two goals of the Damages Directive are clear – helping victims of infringements of EU competition to effectively seek compensation and striking the right balance between public and private enforcement – the real impact of these new rules remains to be seen.

The new rules that are now in place in all of the Member States will most likely lead to questions of interpretation. However, as the preliminary references currently pending before the CJEU show, there are fundamental questions of private enforcement of EU competition law which have not yet been comprehensively addressed. All of these preliminary references are governed by rules that existed before the implementation of the Damages Directive and thus are to be analysed by reference to the principle of effectiveness. The Advocate General opinions delivered so far reveal a certain tendency to infer rather detailed rules from Articles 101 and 102 TFEU. However, at least the opinion in *Cogeco* highlights the added value of the Damages Directive, and the opinion in *Skanska, inter alia*, raises the fundamental question of the purpose of private enforcement. It remains to be seen if the CJEU will address these aspects as well when it answers the national courts' questions.

In addition to these legal clarifications, it seems to have become clear that more practical guidance may be needed in damages actions for competition law infringements. As foreseen in Article 16 of the Damages Directive, such guidance may be particularly useful when national courts have to deal with passing-on. The guidelines that are planned to be adopted this year will hopefully contribute towards this end.

CHAPTER 4

Private Enforcement in France

Rafael Amaro

I. Introduction
II. The development of private enforcement
  A. The French judicial system
  B. Overview of the French legal framework
    1. Transposition rules: the brand-new Title VIII of Book IV of the Commercial Code
    2. Pre-transposition rules: four codes and a rich jurisprudence
III. What is effective and what are the impediments to private enforcement?
  A. Preliminary remarks about the concept of 'effectiveness'
    1. The 'effectiveness' of domestic rules: a matter of viewpoint?
    2. The ECJ's definition of effectiveness
  B. The origins of the French bad reputation: the 'magnifying effect' of the ineffectiveness of cartel damages actions?
    1. Empirical evidence
    2. The X factor behind this empirical evidence: the Directive and/or a change of attitude?
IV. Particular topics
  A. Which entity is liable for damages?
    1. Overview of the transposition rules
    2. Persistent issue as regards the fault requirement
  B. Binding effect of the decisions of competition authorities
    1. Overview of the transposition rules
    2. The '*final decision*' in the meaning of the transposition provisions
    3. Critical appraisal
  C. Limitation

1. A frequent issue in French courts
2. The (mind-blowing) problem of the *ratione temporis* application of the French limitation rules
3. Uncertainties with regard to the interaction between public and private enforcement
4. Overview of the transposition rules
5. Critical appraisal

D. Collective actions/pooling of claims
1. A long-running story …
2. Main features of the action en représentation conjointe
3. Main features of the *action de groupe*
4. Critical appraisal

I. INTRODUCTION

According to a widespread opinion, French law does not offer an 'effective' legal framework for the private enforcement of competition law. The French scholar who tours conferences in France and abroad on this inspiring topic will always have the pleasure to meet eminent lawyers from international law firms or from companies specialising in the purchase of damage claims that will explain to him how the French system is unable to handle this complex litigation. In general, the scholar will silently endure this lecture in comparative law, which usually ends with a vibrant plea to litigate such actions in the United Kingdom or the Netherlands.

It would be interesting someday in the future to carry out a sociological or ethnographic enquiry about the origins of this bad reputation and the biases introduced by the sudden arrival of a certain type of private antitrust enforcement advocates.[1] But let sociologists take care of that. My task is to present a thoroughly written and (if possible) unbiased report on the legal situation in France.

In France, as elsewhere in Europe, the private enforcement of competition law is not a new subject.[2] Since the 1960s, the nullity of anticompetitive contracts and the compensation of the damage caused by cartels and abuses of dominant position have given rise to a steady flow of cases before French courts. For instance, thirty-five years ago, a little-known decision of the French Supreme Court (*Cour de cassation*) approved in very clear terms a judgment of the Court of Appeal that had on the basis of the general clause of tort law (then Article 1382 (today: Article 1240) of the French Civil Code (*Code civil*)) awarded damages resulting from an anticompetitive agreement in

1. There is already such a field of 'legal' ethnography, *see*, e.g., Bruno Latour, *La fabrique du droit. Une ethnographie du Conseil d'Etat* (La Découverte 2004).
2. For an overview on the topic *see* Martine Béhar-Touchais, Catherine Prieto & David Bosco (eds), *L'intensification du private enforcement* (IRJS Editions 2016); Rafael Amaro, *Le contentieux privé des pratiques anticoncurrentielles. Étude des contentieux privés autonome et complémentaire devant les juridictions judiciaires* (Bruylant 2014); Marie Dumarçay, *La situation de l'entreprise victime dans les procédures de sanction des pratiques anticoncurrentielles* (Litec 2010); Silvia Pietrini, *L'action collective en droit des pratiques anticoncurrentielles* (Bruylant 2010).

the vegetable sector.[3] Thus private enforcement in France is not a new phenomenon,[4] even though it has to be conceded that it was necessary to wait until the beginning of the 2000s and the famous *Courage* case[5] before the French lawyers became really aware of the potential of this area of law. We know what happened next: Directive 2014/104 (hereinafter 'Damages Directive') was negotiated for more than nine years until it was finally enacted in November 2014.[6]

The Damages Directive was transposed into French law by two statutory instruments: an *ordonnance*[7] and a *décret*,[8] both of 9 March 2017.[9] These two instruments created a new Title VIII in Book IV of the French Commercial Code (*Code de commerce*) entitled *Des actions en dommages et intérêts du fait des pratiques anticoncurrentielles*. Over the past decade, most academic contributions have focused on these transposition instruments and the Directive itself.

But despite this understandable interest, the new provisions have had little practical impact in France so far. This is so for at least three reasons.

First, the transitional rule of Article 12 of the 2017 *ordonnance* provides that the procedural rules apply to proceedings commenced on or after 26 December 2014, while the substantive rules apply to facts that occurred after 11 March 2017. In other words, for infringements committed before 11 March 2017, the old rules (liability under Articles 1240 et seq.) of the Civil Code continue to apply. This explains why the substantive rules of the new regime have so far never been applied in significant cases by French courts. It is very likely that it will take ten to fifteen years before the new law will play a major role when one takes into account the time it takes from the detection of a cartel until the bringing of an action for damages.

Second, it is important to keep in mind that the transposition instruments do not solve every legal issue. Actually, many burning questions will remain governed by the general rules of the Civil Code and the Code of Civil Procedure.

Third, the Damages Directive does not seem to have radically changed the French state of play.[10] Much of the case law preceding the Directive therefore remains relevant.

3. Cour de Cassation, Chambre commerciale (Cass. com.), 1 March 1982, 80-15.834, *Bull. civ.* IV, No. 76.
4. *See*, e.g., for a pioneering work, Roger Houin, *Les conséquences civiles d'une infraction aux règles de la concurrence* [1963] Annales de la Faculté de droit de Liège 27 et seq.
5. ECJ, Case C-453/99 *Courage Ltd v Bernard Crehan and Bernard Crehan v Courage Ltd* [2001] ECR I-6297.
6. Directive 2014/104/EU of the European Parliament and of the Council of 26 November 2014 on certain rules governing actions for damages under national law for infringements of the competition law provisions of the Member States and of the European Union [2014] OJ L 349/1.
7. An *ordonnance* is a legal instrument issued by the Government to rule on matters which are usually reserved to the parliament, i.e. legislative activity usually reserved to the two chambers of the French Parliament.
8. Usual instrument issued by the Government in its own field of legislative activity. In the French hierarchy of norms, *ordonnances* and *lois* prevail over *décrets*.
9. Ordonnance No. 2017-303 du 9 mars 2017 and Décret No. 2017-305 du 9 mars 2017 relative aux actions en dommages et intérêts du fait des pratiques anticoncurrentielles, JORF No. 0059 du 10 mars 2017, Nos 29 and 31.
10. *See* the analysis of the present author, Rafael Amaro, *Transposition de la directive Dommages en France: Regards sur le nouveau titre VIII du livre IV du Code de commerce* (2017) 2 Concurrences 70 et seq.

Therefore, it seems premature to assess the impact of the Damages Directive in detail, but it is possible to give an outline of the French law as it stands and the problems it creates.

II. THE DEVELOPMENT OF PRIVATE ENFORCEMENT

A. The French judicial system

Concerning the court judicial system, it is useful to recall that the French national competition authority (*Autorité de la concurrence*) is responsible for the public enforcement of competition law. Its decisions may only be challenged in Chamber 5-7 of the Paris Court of Appeal (*Cour d'appel de Paris*).

As for private enforcement, at the first-instance level, where the litigation involves only private bodies, actions for damages must be brought before the civil courts (*tribunaux de grande instance*) or to the commercial courts (*tribunaux de commerce*). These courts belong to the so-called judicial order (*ordre judiciaire*), as opposed to the administrative courts of the 'administrative order' (*ordre administratif*) that are competent for litigation between public bodies and private parties. Sixteen civil and commercial courts[11] have exclusive jurisdiction to adjudicate stand-alone and follow-on actions for damages.[12] As they frequently involve only businesses, most first-instance private actions are brought before commercial courts, and especially the Paris Commercial Court. The Paris Court of Appeal also has exclusive jurisdiction to decide on appeals against private enforcement judgments from all first-instance courts in France.

It is noteworthy that if the claimant is a public body, the action for damages is brought before the administrative courts (*tribunaux administratifs*) and the administrative courts of appeal (*cours administratives d'appel*). Unlike litigation before the judicial courts, no special rule of exclusive jurisdiction applies to administrative proceedings.

B. Overview of the French legal framework

The law on private enforcement is a mix of codified rules and judge-made law. But to have a clear view of the current state of play, it is important to answer a first key question: which rules apply *ratione temporis*? The transposition rules of the Directive (1) or the rules in force before their enactment (2)?

11. There are eight commercial courts and eight civil courts located in Marseille, Bordeaux, Lille, Fort-de-France, Lyon, Nancy, Paris and Rennes.
12. Articles L. 420-7 and R. 420-3 to R. 420-5 of the Commercial Code.

1. *Transposition rules: the brand-new Title VIII of Book IV of the Commercial Code*

The French legislature has transposed the Damages Directive in the new Title VIII of Book IV of the Commercial Code (Articles L. 481-1 and R. 481-1 et seq.).

The new regime applies from 26 December 2014 as to procedural rules and from 11 March 2017 as to the substantive rules. As explained above (*see* IV.C, *infra*), the new regime has hardly applied *ratione temporae*.

2. *Pre-transposition rules: four codes and a rich jurisprudence*

If the pre-transposition provisions apply, things are more complicated. Claimants have to find their way through a tangle of various sets of rules drawn from different sources.

Rules from at least four different codes may apply to private actions: the substantive rules from the Civil Code for issues like fault, causation, damages and limitation; and the general procedural rules of the Code of Civil Procedure (*Code de procédure civile*), coupled with specific procedural rules from the Commercial Code and the Consumer Code (*Code de la consommation*). According to the principle *specialia generalibus derogant*, if no specific rule from the Commercial Code or the Consumer Code provides for a solution, then the general rules from the Civil Code and the Code of Civil Procedure will apply.[13]

In addition, the Code of Administrative Justice (*Code de justice administrative*) will apply to procedural aspects of actions for damages brought by public bodies.

To these statutory rules, it is necessary to add the case law developed in the past decades (or even centuries when it comes to the Civil Code) by the *Cour de cassation* and the leading courts of appeal, such as the one in Paris. Some examples will be mentioned later (*see* IV, *infra*, dealing with limitation).

III. WHAT IS EFFECTIVE AND WHAT ARE THE IMPEDIMENTS TO PRIVATE ENFORCEMENT?

A. Preliminary remarks about the concept of 'effectiveness'

1. *The 'effectiveness' of domestic rules: a matter of viewpoint?*

Answering the question of what is effective and what is not in the French system raises an obvious methodological difficulty: what is meant by an 'effective' legal framework?[14] Are we talking about the length of time taken to reach a final judgment? The

13. Soraya Amrani-Mekki, *Inciter les actions en dommages et intérêts en droit de la concurrence: le point de vue d'un processualiste* (2008) 2 Concurrences 11 et seq.
14. This question has been addressed by French scholars, *see*, e.g., Philippe Conte, '*"Effectivité", "inefficacité", "sous-effectivité", "surefficacité" ... : "variations pour droit penal"*' in *Le droit privé français à la fin du XXe siècle, Etudes offertes à Pierre Catala* (Litec 2001) 125 et seq.; Marie-Anne Frison-Roche, '*Efficient and/or Effective Enforcement*' in Josef Drexl, Laurence Idot & Joël

quality of the judgments issued by domestic courts? Do we discuss the rate of application of a rule to disputes? Are we talking about 'efficiency' in the sense that rules should ease the claimant's burden to bring and win an action for damages? If so, what about the procedural rights of the defendant? Obviously, a legal framework considered as 'effective' for claimants can be seen as 'ineffective' for the defendants if it results in their systematic liability! Reasoning in terms of 'effectiveness' therefore remains highly debatable and could be just a matter of viewpoint.

In the German report (*see* Chapter 3), Jens-Uwe Franck wisely addresses the question of the 'appropriate yardstick to measure effectiveness'. He shows that the effectiveness could be measured by different approaches. I fully adhere to his conclusions, especially with regard to what could be called the 'official' definition of effectiveness, i.e. the approach voiced by the ECJ. In the *Rewe* and *San Giorgio* cases, the court developed its own understanding of this notion by shaping the now unavoidable principle of effectiveness.

2. *The ECJ's definition of effectiveness*

Article 4 of the Damages Directive provides a definition of the principle of effectiveness in the following terms:

> In accordance with the principle of effectiveness, Member States shall ensure that all national rules and procedures relating to the exercise of claims for damages are designed and applied in such a way that they do not render practically impossible or excessively difficult the exercise of the Union right to full compensation for harm caused by an infringement of competition law.

This principle was already applied in the context of competition damages actions in *Kone*[15] and more recently in *Cogeco*.[16] In both cases, it resulted from its application that the domestic rules at stake were considered as incompatible with the principle. More precisely, the application of the Austrian rules governing causation and standing (in *Kone*) and the application of the Portuguese rules governing limitation (in *Cogeco*) made any successful damages action of the victims almost impossible in practice.

In the light of this case law, two conclusions may be drawn. First, it can be assumed that the concept of 'effectiveness' is to be understood from the perspective of the victims of anticompetitive conduct. Second, it appears from a closer examination of the rules at stake in *Kone* and *Cogeco* that the requirement to be met by the domestic rules – in terms of compliance with the principle of effectiveness – is high. This

Monéger (eds), *Economic Theory and Competition Law* (Edward Elgar Publishing 2009) 211 et seq.; Marie-Anne Frison-Roche, *'L'idée de mesurer l'efficacité économique du droit'* in Guy Canivet, Marie-Anne Frison-Roche & Michael Klein (eds), *Mesurer l'efficacité économique du droit* (LGDJ 2005) 19 et seq.

15. ECJ, Case C-557/12 *Kone AG v ÖBB-Infrastruktur AG* [2014] ECLI:EU:C:2014:1317. *See* on this case Susanne Carval, *La responsabilité civile des membres d'une entente peut être engagée du fait du dommage causé par un effet d'ombrelle sur les prix* [2014] D. 1525 et seq.
16. ECJ, Case C-637/17 *Cogeco Communications Inc v Sport TV Portugal SA and Others* [2019] ECLI:EU:C:2019:263.

benchmark allows a conclusion: the ECJ's interpretation set forth a protective standard for claimants.

Following this path, it will be considered that the effectiveness of the French legal system will be defined as the ability of French procedural and substantive rules to grant the victims of anticompetitive a swift and satisfactory solution.

The answer to the question of whether French law is effective depends on the type of litigation, the type of infringement and the type of litigants.

In our opinion, there are no clear-cut answers, but some empirical evidence may help to draw (temporary) conclusions.

B. The origins of the French bad reputation: the 'magnifying effect' of the ineffectiveness of cartel damages actions?

A look at the empirical evidence on actions for damages for competition law infringements reveals a striking fact: no significant infringement decision issued by the European Commission or the French Competition Authority has been followed by a successful private action for damages in a commercial or civil court. This finding is indisputable for cartels that affect consumers.[17] The reason for this is the worrying inefficiency of collective redress mechanisms (*see* IV.D.4, *infra*). To a lesser extent, this also applies to B2B litigation.

In addition to certain explanations mentioned in the introduction, the bad reputation of the French system could be explained by the 'magnifying effect' of cartel litigation.

1. *Empirical evidence*

a) *Cartels*

In France, an empirical study[18] showed that thirty-three cartel damages actions were brought before the administrative courts and thirteen cases before judicial courts. These thirty-three cases followed five decisions of competition authorities (four from the French Competition Authority and one from the European Commission). The decision of the French Authority sanctioning a cartel in the field of road signs has been followed by at least twenty-eight cases, mainly initiated by *Départements* (a French administrative division corresponding to a median population of 500,000 inhabitants). These public claimants obtained damages in twelve of the thirty-three cases (which is a success rate of almost 36%) before administrative courts.[19] In fourteen cases, an

17. *See* for a complete fiasco, Tribunal de Grande Instance (TGI) Lille, 6 June 2017, 15/10938 *Mme V. c/ sociétés Colgate Palmolive, Henkel et al.* (2017) 4 Concurrences 218, with a case note by Rafael Amaro.
18. Jean-François Laborde, *Cartel damages actions in Europe: How courts have assessed cartel overcharges* (2018) 1 Concurrences Art. No. 88879.
19. *See*, e.g., sous Cour administrative d'appel (CAA) Nantes, 15 June 2017, 16NT02222, *Département des Côtes-d'Armor c/ Signalisation France* and 10 May 2017, 16NT01778; *Département du*

expert had been appointed, and the defendants were held liable in interlocutory judgments. Only in seven of thirty-three cases were the claims rejected (which is a rate of almost 20%). As compared to litigation before judicial courts, the outcomes seen in the administrative courts are relatively favourable for the claimants: before civil and commercial courts, damages were awarded in only five of the thirteen cases, and eight actions were rejected (a non-success rate of 62%).

This difference can be explained with the special features of the litigation in the administrative courts.[20] First, this type of litigation involves horizontal agreements entered during the bidding process for public contracts. This means that these agreements are intended to increase prices. The causal link between the overcharge supported by the public entity and the agreement is therefore beyond doubt.

Second, in these cases, there is no possibility of a passing-on of the overcharge since the direct purchaser – the public entity – is also the final purchaser.

Third, the assessment of overcharge is, in this type of case, rather simple. Usually, similar public contracts have been concluded over the years, which allows a comparison of the prices with and absent the cartel in a manner that is usually robust enough to convince administrative courts as to the amount of damages to be awarded. Litigation in civil and commercial jurisdictions is often more complex, which explains the lower success rate (and the bad reputation of the French legal system).

b) *Abuses of a dominant position*

To the best of our knowledge, there are no statistical studies concerning abuse-of-dominant-position litigation in France,[21] but remarkable cases may be reported.

For instance, in 2017 the Paris Commercial Court ruled on a stand-alone action introduced by *Digicel* (now owned by Bouygues) against *France Telecom* (now Orange) for different abuses committed in the telephone sector in the 2000s.[22] The appeal is still pending, but we can recall from the court's first-instance judgment of 18 December 2017 that Orange has been sentenced to pay EUR 179.4 million in damages (plus interest in an amount which is debated[23] and thus fluctuates between approx. EUR 167 and 250 million). The calculation rate for interest is impressive: 10.4% per year over

Morbihan c/ Signalisation France; CAA Nancy, 21 March 2017, 15NC02367, *Département de la Meuse c/ Signaux Girod*; CAA Douai, 15 June 2017, 17DA00538, *Signalisation France c/ Département de l'Eure* (2017) 4 Concurrences 219, with a case note by Rafael Amaro.

20. For an overview *see* Joëlle Adda, Rafael Amaro & Jean-François Laborde, *Réparation du dommage causé par les ententes devant le juge administratif* (2019) 6 AJDA 320 et seq.
21. Suzanne Carval and Jean-François Laborde, *La réparation des préjudices causés par les abus de position dominante* (2018) 1 Concurrences 214 et seq.
22. Tribunal de Commerce (T. com.) Paris, 18 December 2017, 2009016849, *SAS Digicel Antilles Française Guyane c/ SA Orange Caraïbe et SA Orange (anciennement SA France Telecom).*
23. *See* the interlocutory judgment of the Court of Appeal (CA) Paris, 10 October 2018, 18/08088, *SA Digicel Antilles Françaises Guyane c/ SA Orange Caraïbe et SA Orange* (2019) D. 747 with a case note by Rafael Amaro.

eight years. This case is significant, but other ongoing proceedings in the telecommunications sector or the digital economy[24] are of about the same dimension, and it can be noted that in some previous abuse litigations, claimants were awarded from one to EUR 7 million.[25]

c) *Settlements?*

Of course, these figures should not obscure the fact that in the Netherlands or in the UK;[26] for example, there are a considerable number of disputes ended by settlement. But this is also the case in France, although it is obviously impossible to provide any reliable data.

2. *The X factor behind this empirical evidence: the Directive and/or a change of attitude?*

The empirical evidence presented here leads to a first observation. The French legal framework is obviously in need of improvement. For B2B or B2C cartel damages actions, the law as it stands is far from being effective. Yet, the picture in other areas of private enforcement (cases involving stand-alone vertical agreements, cases involving stand-alone abuses of a dominant position and follow-on actions before administrative courts) is much brighter. Why is this so?

At first sight, this evolution could be seen as the consequence of recent legal reforms favouring the plaintiffs. However, this would be to forget a fundamental fact already pointed out: the transposition rules of the Damages Directive have never been applied to significant cases! How then could it be assumed that it had any effect in practice?

Our opinion – and this will be our second observation – is that the Directive has had a psychological impact. It made practitioners (in-house lawyers, attorneys and judges) aware of the potential of this type of litigation. In-house lawyers, whose corporations had been the victims of anticompetitive practices, therefore began to more systematically alert their management as to the possibilities of obtaining very substantial amounts of damages. Attorneys have gradually trained in this area to master its subtleties and to be able to measure more accurately the risks and

---

24. *See*, e.g., CA Paris, 18 September 2018, 18/04914, *G.I.E. Pari Mutuel Urbain c/ Société Betclic Enterprises Limited* and the first-instance judgment: TGI Paris, 22 February 2018, 15/09129 *Société Betclic Enterprises Limited c/ G.I.E. Pari Mutuel Urbain* (2018) 2 Concurrences 229, with a case note by Rafael Amaro.
25. CA Paris, 10 May 2017, 15/05918, *SA Orange Caraïbe et SA Orange c/ SAS Outremer Télécom* (2017) 4 Concurrences 215, with a case note by Rafael Amaro; CA Paris, 14 December 2016, 13/08975, *SNCF c/ Switch* (2017) 2 Concurrences 218, with a case note by Rafael Amaro; CA Paris, 2 October 2015, 14/15779, *SAS Cowes c/ Orange* (2016) AJCA 152, with a case note by Rafael Amaro.
26. Barry J. Rodger, *Private Enforcement of Competition Law, The Hidden Story: Competition Litigation Settlements in the United Kingdom, 2000–2005* (2008) 29 ECLR 96 et seq.

opportunities for their clients. Judges as well have steadily gained a deeper understanding of the economic aspects of this type of litigation and have been able to hand down better judgments. This becomes apparent when one compares some decisions issued ten years ago with those issued recently. Today, the courts' assessment of fault and the quantification of losses are consistent. It was not uncommon a few years ago that French courts, faced with complex and uncertain counterfactuals, decided that the damage was uncertain and refused, sometimes against common sense, to award damages to the victim. This type of misguidance, however, is tending to become rare as French judges rely more and more on economic expertise.

In the end, the following conclusion may be drawn: it is not the new legal framework that explains the advances of private competition law litigation in France but, as often, the human factor. This factor is difficult to quantify. It is much less visible than the legislative changes and yet, it is what seems to be decisive.

IV. PARTICULAR TOPICS

The rules on the conditions of liability open the new Title VIII of Book IV (Articles L. 481-1 to L. 481-14 of the Commercial Code). They transpose Articles 3, 9, 11 to 15 and 17 of the Damages Directive (general principles, binding effect, joint and several liability, passing-on of overcharge and quantification of harm). Article 10 of the Damages Directive is transposed in Article L. 482-1 of the Commercial Code. Its rules apply to three of the four questions addressed in this section: which entity is liable? How far does the binding effect go? What are the rules on limitations? Regarding the fourth question dealing with collective redresses, the Damages Directive did not address it. Thus it remains governed only by French provisions in the Consumer Code and the Code of Civil Procedure.

A. Which entity is liable for damages?

1. *Overview of the transposition rules*

In French law, the rules on civil liability prior to the Directive are those of the Civil Code. Their application has given rise to certain developments mentioned below (*see* IV.A.2, *infra*).

The new Article L. 481-1 of the Commercial Code states that:

> Any natural or legal person forming an undertaking or an organisation referred to in Article L. 464-2 is liable for the damage it has caused as a result of the commission of an anti-competitive practice defined in Articles ... as well as Articles 101 and 102 of the Treaty on the Functioning of the European Union.[27]

27. Free translation of Article L. 481-1 of the Commercial Code, stating: 'Toute personne physique ou morale formant une entreprise ou un organisme mentionné à l'article L. 464-2 est responsable du dommage qu'elle a causé du fait de la commission d'une pratique anticoncurrentielle définie aux articles L. 420-1, L. 420-2, L. 420-2-1, L. 420-2-2 et L. 420-5 ainsi qu'aux articles 101 et 102 du traité sur le fonctionnement de l'Union européenne'.

In other words, Article L. 481-1 provides a useful clarification that removes the doubts that could have arisen from the preliminary draft (*avant-projet*) of the transposition rules.[28] It provides that 'any natural or legal person *forming* an undertaking or an organisation – *within the meaning of competition law may be added* – is liable for the harm caused by the anticompetitive practice attributed to the undertaking'. This circumlocution helps one to fully understand the link between the notion of an 'undertaking' (subject of competition law) and that of a 'legal person' (subject of tort law). The legal persons liable *in the meaning of tort law* are the same as those who constitute the undertaking to which an anticompetitive practice is attributed.[29] The identification of the undertaking by the competition authorities or by the courts must therefore be the subject of particular care because of its crucial consequences for the field of tort law.

2. *Persistent issue as regards the fault requirement*

Article L. 481-1, however, leaves open an important question in practice: must the claimant prove the existence of misconduct imputable to each legal person that constitutes 'the undertaking' in the meaning of competition law? Or is the proof of a misconduct by one of these entities sufficient to hold responsible the other legal persons as part of the same undertaking?

This question is not only a textbook scenario. In the *JCB Service* case, the *Cour de cassation* ruled that even if the European Commission referred to the 'group' of companies in the *motifs* (the reasoning) of its decision – *including* parent and subsidiaries – this is not enough to hold the subsidiaries liable where only the parent company was identified in the *dispositif* (the formal court/ authority order) as the infringer.[30] This does not mean that a claimant cannot sue the subsidiaries, but to succeed this, claimant will need to establish that such subsidiaries *participated* in the infringement, as the *Cour de cassation* added in a further judgment of 6 October 2015.[31] According to this judgment, this 'participation' may be proved by the fact that the subsidiaries took part in the commercial policy of the parent. The *Cour de cassation* approved the ruling of the Paris Court of Appeal with these words:

28. The draft version stated that 'Any undertaking or body is liable for the damage caused by the commission of a prohibited practice in Articles L. 420-1, L. 420-2, L. 420-2-1 and L. 420-5 and Articles 101 and 102 of the Treaty on the Functioning of the European Union.' ('Toute entreprise ou tout organisme est responsable du dommage causé par la commission d'une pratique prohibée aux articles L. 420-1, L. 420-2, L. 420-2-1 et L. 420-5 ainsi qu'aux articles 101 et 102 du traité sur le fonctionnement de l'Union européenne.').
29. *See* for a deeper analysis Martine Behar-Touchais, Suzanne Carval, *Le débiteur des dommages et intérêts dus en cas de pratique anticoncurrentielle* (2015) 4 Concurrences 84 et seq.
30. Cass. com., 15 November 2011, 10-21701 (2012) Contrats conc. consom., comm. 66, with a case note by Marie Malaurie-Vignal; *Bull. Joly Sociétés* 395, with a case note by Catherine Prieto (2012); Rev. Sociétés 37, with a case note by Sylvain Prévost.
31. Cass. com., 6 October 2015, 13-24.854, ECLI:FR:CCASS:2015:CO00871; (2015) AJCA 526, with a case note by Robert Saint-Esteben; (2016) 1 Concurrences 253, with a case note by Rafael Amaro.

> These two companies [the subsidiaries] inform distributors [the victims] about the anti-competitive distribution agreements on the order of JCB SERVICE [the parent] ... apply the instructions of the commercial policy of JCB SERVICE and contribute to the achievement of the violations reported; ... they have thus committed a fault under French law; the claim to be dismissed from the lawsuit is not justified and in this regard, the fact that they [the subsidiaries] were not found to have committed a violation in the European Commission's decision does not prevent the national court from determining in the light of those elements, including the European Commission's decision, the part of their behaviour that constituted a fault.[32]

Nevertheless, the subsidiaries are not automatically held responsible. Practically, this solution could make the claimant's demonstration much more complicated in situations where the participation of subsidiaries is not easy to prove. Indeed, proving the involvement of the subsidiaries may sometimes assume that the claimants will produce confidential documents that are difficult to access. For this reason, one could question the compatibility of these solutions with the principle of effectiveness. It is even more likely, in line with the recent solution adopted in *Skanska* on the neighbouring question of the economic unit test,[33] that the ECJ will decide that the scope of liability is governed by the direct effect of Articles 101, 102 TFEU. Thus, the principle of effectiveness (and the principle of procedural autonomy) will not apply. In these circumstances, it seems very possible in light of the *Skanska* case that the ECJ will align the rules of imputation for civil liability within a group of companies with those of competition law.

B. Binding effect of the decisions of competition authorities

1. Overview of the transposition rules

As regards the binding effect of the decisions of competition authorities, Article 9 of the Directive is transposed in Article L. 481-2 of the Commercial Code. This Article sets forth three rules: one for the decisions rendered by the French Competition Authority (paragraph 1), another for the decisions rendered by the national competition authorities of another Member State (paragraph 2), the last one for the decisions rendered by

32. Author translation of CA Paris, 26 June 2013, 12/04441, *Sté JCB Sales Ltd, Sté JC Bamford Excavators Ltd et Sté JCB Service c/ SA Central Parts*; (2013) Lettre Creda-Concurrence, 15–19 July, with a case note by Alain Ronzano. *See also* the *Arkopharma* case, one of the '*Vitamins cartel*' follow-on litigations, where the Nanterre Commercial Court of First Instance ruled that a subsidiary was liable as it had: '... obviously carried out the instructions of the authors of the cartel and participated in the commission of the offense'; T. com. Nanterre, 11 May 2006, 2004F02643, *SA Les Laboratoires pharmaceutiques Arkopharma c/ sté Roche et sté F. Hoffmann La Roche AG* (2007) 10 RLC 62, with a case note by Muriel Chagny.
33. ECJ, Case C-724/17 *Skanska Industrial Solutions and Others* [2019] ECLI:EU:C:2019:204 para. 51: '... Article 101 TFEU must be interpreted as meaning that, in a case such as that in the main proceedings, in which all the shares in the companies which participated in a cartel prohibited by that article were acquired by other companies which have dissolved the former companies and continued their commercial activities, the acquiring companies may be held liable for the damage caused by the cartel in question.'

the European Commission (paragraph 3). In the first situation, an infringement of competition law found by a final decision of the French Competition Authority has the probative value of an irrebuttable presumption of fault. In the second situation, an infringement found by a decision of another national competition authority is only a *mode de prevue* of this fault. It means that it is nothing more than an evidence, conclusive or not. In both situations, paragraphs 1 and 2 of Article L. 481-2 add that the decision of the competition authority that has such a probative value is the one 'which can no longer be the subject of an ordinary means of review for the part relating to that finding'.[34] Concerning the decisions issued by the European Commission, paragraph 3 only states that Article 16 of Regulation 1/2003 applies.

2. *The* 'final decision' *in the meaning of the transposition provisions*

Compared to the first draft of this text in the *avant-projet*, which referred only to the *final decision* (as Article 9 of the Damages Directive does), two modifications deserve to be noted in the first paragraphs of Article L. 481-2 of the Commercial Code.

The first is the addition of this precision: 'for the part relating to this finding'. Taken literally, it means that the new text allows the claimants to bring their action for damages even though the decision of the authority is being challenged in a review procedure for a finding *other than that of the infringement* (e.g., the finding concerning the sanction). In practice, this situation is frequent.

The second important change is the addition of the adjective 'ordinary' to qualify the reviewing procedures (*voies de recours ordinaires*). In the meaning of Article 527 of the Code of Civil Procedure, these ordinary means of review are the ordinary appeal in the French Courts of Appeal (*appel*) and the so-called *opposition* ('motion to set aside' in the official translation of the French Code of Civil Procedure).[35] Nonetheless, the appeal in cassation (*pourvoi en cassation*) is qualified as an extraordinary means of review. Following an *a contrario* interpretation of this provision, the new text could therefore allow the claimants to bring the action for damages before a court even though the decision is subject to an appeal in cassation, as is always the situation in significant cartel or abuse cases. If this is the interpretation taken by French courts, the time saved for the claimants could be considerable (at least one year and sometimes more than three years).

3. *Critical appraisal*

Are these new provisions 'effective' as regards the objective of the Directive? So far, no empirical evidence supports a positive or a negative answer. That is why we will limit our critical appraisal here to three cautious remarks.

---

34. Final version: 'Une décision qui ne peut plus faire l'objet d'une voie de recours ordinaire pour la partie relative au constat de l'existence et de l'imputation d'une pratique anticoncurrentielles'.
35. According to the official translation of Article 567 of the Code of Civil Procedure, this is a means that 'aims at retracting a judgement rendered by default. It is available only in favour of the defaulting party'.

First, it should be noted that an irrebuttable presumption is limited to infringements found by the French Competition Authority, not to those found by other NCAs.

Second, Article L. 481-2 fails to specify whether only the findings established in the *dispositif* (the order) of the competition authorities' decisions have a probative force or whether this effect extends to the *motifs* (the reasoning). This question has already arisen in French courts in the *JCB Service* cases mentioned above (*see* IV.A.2, *supra*).

Finally, one may wonder whether this new binding effect is really useful. In practice, in the overwhelming majority of follow-on litigation, French courts follow precisely the decisions of the competition authorities even without these decisions being attributed any legally binding effect.[36] It is therefore possible to argue that there is already a 'de facto presumption' of fault. In some cases, this presumption even appears almost irrebuttable because of the credibility that the French Competition Authority enjoys before the courts.[37]

C. Limitation

1. *A frequent issue in French courts*

Questions on the topic of limitation are subject to a lively debate in France. A crucial question, for example, is whether the limitation period runs from:

- the date of the competition authority's decision;
- the date of the possible hearing of a victim in the course of a procedure before the competition authority; or even earlier
- the date of entry into the market of the victim.

Given the economic stakes that these different starting points may represent, the question is very relevant for claimants, which is a first explanation for this discussion. Two other reasons can explain it.

First, a factual explanation: infringements are often committed more than ten years before the actions for damages are brought to court. The defendants are therefore encouraged to plead that the claimant's action is time-barred.

36. *See* Cass. com., 26 April 2017, 15-28.197, ECLI:FR:CCASS:2017:CO00611 (2017) 4 Concurrences 221, with a case note by Rafael Amaro. The *Cour de cassation* clearly states that: '… if the court cannot decide on a case by reference to extraneous decisions, it is not forbidden for the court to assess, in the light of the evidence submitted by the litigants, in particular decisions and opinions rendered by a competition authority, the behaviour of the defendant' (free translation). French version: '… si le juge ne peut statuer par voie de référence à des décisions étrangères au litige, il ne lui est pas interdit d'apprécier, au regard des pièces qui lui sont soumises, notamment des décisions et avis rendus par une autorité de régulation, les éléments du comportement de la partie poursuivie constitutifs d'une faute'.

37. *See*, e.g., CAA Nantes, 27 April 2018, 17NT01719, 17NT01740, 17NT01741 and 17NT01770 *Département de l'Orne c/ Société Signalisation France et al.* and 17NT02571 *Département du Calvados c/ Société Signalisation France* (2018) 4 Concurrences 231, with a case note by Rafael Amaro.

Second, a legal explanation: the uncertainties of French law regarding issues of limitation give defendants much room to argue. It may be surprising that French law still inadequately regulates such a crucial question as limitation. However, these uncertainties can be explained by the 'chaos'[38] of the legal rules on limitation.

For competition litigation, two important instruments have recently changed the state of play: the Act of June 2008 that completely reshaped the general rules of the French Civil Code[39] and the *Loi Hamon* of March 2014[40] that introduced a new ground of interruption (*cause interruptive – see* IV.C.2, *infra*).

These recent changes raise a first difficulty related to their application *ratione temporis*. They also raise a second issue regarding the interaction between public and private enforcement.

2. *The (mind-blowing) problem of the* **ratione temporis** *application of the French limitation rules*

The fact that competition law infringements will have been committed long before an action for damages is launched and the continuing nature of anticompetitive practices raise complex temporal conflicts of laws issues.[41] For example, as to the starting point of the limitation period, no less than three different provisions may still apply *ratione temporis*:

(1) Former Article 2270-1, paragraph 1 of the Civil Code for cases whose facts predate the entry into force of the law of 18 June 2008;
(2) Article 2224 of the Civil Code for cases whose facts are subsequent to the entry into force of the law of 18 June 2008 and prior to the transposition instrument of 9 March 2017;
(3) Article L. 482-1 of the Commercial Code for cases whose facts are subsequent to the said instrument.

As for the grounds for an interruption of the limitation period, here again different regimes remain applicable (presented in further detail below):

38. Alain Bénabent, '*Le chaos du droit de la prescription*' in *Mélanges Louis Boyer* (Presses de l'Université Toulouse 1 1996) 123 et seq.
39. Loi n° 2008-561 du 17 juin 2008, *portant réforme de la prescription en matière civile*; *See* among many comments on this major reform, Philippe Casson and Philippe Pierre (eds), *La réforme de la prescription en matière civile, Le chaos enfin régulé?* (Dalloz 2010) 111 et seq.; Bénédicte Fauvarque-Cosson and Jérôme François, *Commentaire de la loi du 17 juin 2008 portant réforme de la prescription en matière civile* [2008] D. 2512 et seq. *See also* for a comparative analysis, Denis Mazeaud, Robert Wintgen, *La prescription extinctive dans les codifications savantes* [2008] D. 2523 et seq.
40. Loi n° 2014-344 du 14 Mars 2014 relative à la consommation ('Loi Hamon').
41. For a general approach, *see* Georges Wiederkehr, *Conflits de lois dans le temps et dans l'espace en matière de prescription* [2009] RLDA 89 et seq.

- the case-law-based rule laid down in the cases *Lycées d'Ile de France* and *JCB Service*, issued on the basis of the general rules of the Civil Code, for cases prior to the entry into force of the *Loi Hamon* of March 2014;
- Article L. 462-7 of the Commercial Code in the wording resulting from the *Loi Hamon* for cases whose facts are subsequent to the entry into force of this Act and prior to the transposition instrument of 2017;
- Article L. 462-7 of the Commercial Code in the wording resulting from the transposition instrument of 2017 and as applicable from its entry into force.

In such circumstances, it is easy for the inexperienced lawyer (or judge) to lose the overview. Certainly, there are provisions to resolve these temporal conflicts, such as the transitional law provisions of Article 26 of the Act of June 2008.[42] But this Article is very insufficient for competition litigation. Indeed, no further provisions intended to facilitate the articulation of the general rules stemming from this Act of 2008 with the special provisions of the *Loi Hamon* of 2014, and those of the transposition instrument of 2017 completed it later. It is therefore necessary to lean on the general principles of intertemporal law, whose application always leaves room for debate.[43]

3. *Uncertainties with regard to the interaction between public and private enforcement*

The second difficulty flows from the unclear interplay of public and private enforcement. This issue is centred around the question of whether the competition authorities' proceedings have an interruptive effect on the limitation period of the action for damages. As it has been said above, the answer varies according to the applicable law *ratione temporis*. The *Cour de cassation* has held in *Lycées Ile de France*[44] and *JCB Service*[45] that a public enforcement proceeding does not interrupt the limitation period applicable to the action for damages. In turn, Article L. 462-7 of the Commercial Code as resulting from the *Loi Hamon* (and as confirmed by the transposition instrument) lays down the opposite solution.

The claimant whose damage occurred before the enactment of the *Loi Hamon* and who did not take the precaution of bringing an action for damages before a court while the competition authority was dealing with the case will face high risks of being

42. Point II of this Article states that: 'The provisions of this Act which reduce the duration of the limitation period shall apply to the prescriptions from the day of the entry into force of this Act, without the total duration exceeding the duration provided for by the previous law' (free translation). French version: 'Les dispositions de la présente loi qui réduisent la durée de la prescription s'appliquent aux prescriptions à compter du jour de l'entrée en vigueur de la présente loi, sans que la durée totale puisse excéder la durée prévue par la loi antérieure'.
43. *See*, e.g., CA Paris, 5-4, 6 March 2019, 17/21261, SARL Arkeos et al. c/ SA EDF, SASU EDF Énergies Nouvelles Réparties et SASU EDF ENR Solaire, (2019) 3 Concurrences 233, with a case note by Rafael Amaro.
44. TGI Paris, 15 January 2009, 08/55030, 08/59948, 08/59949, *Conseil régional d'Île-de-France et Région Île-de-France* (2009) 19 RLC 97, with a case note by Muriel Chagny.
45. CA Paris, 26 June 2013, 12/04441, *Sté JCB Sales Ltd, Sté JC Bamford Excavators Ltd et Sté JCB Service c/ SA Central Parts.*

time-barred,[46] unlike the claimant whose damage occurred after the *Loi Hamon*. This discrepancy will fade over time, but not in the next years.

It has to be noted that recently, the Paris Court of Appeal (in *Arkeos*)[47] ruled that the starting point of the limitation period is to be settled at a time where the claimant has a sufficient knowledge of its damage, i.e.:

> the date on which the claimant knew or could have known that he had been a victim of the offense, and know the consistency of the offense, its accountability and its duration[48]

As this new case law will apply to litigations ruled by the pre-transposition rules, it will counterbalance the defendant-friendly solution adopted as to the cause of interruption on the field of the starting point.

4. *Overview of the transposition rules*

The new rules relating to limitation are the subject of Chapter II of the new Title VIII. They are codified in a single article of the legislative part: Article L. 482-1. This Article transposes Article 10 of the Damages Directive.

Its first paragraph lays down a five-year limitation period which begins to run if the claimant knows or ought to have known:

> (1) The acts or facts constituting a prohibited practice, and the fact that they constitute such a practice ... (2) A damage caused by the practice, (3) The identity of one of the authors of the prohibited practice.[49]

The following paragraph adds what appears to be a fourth cumulative condition: the practice must have ceased.[50]

It should be noted that in the draft version of the *avant-projet*, a provision explicitly excluded the application of Article 2232 of the Civil Code, which provides for a twenty-year limitation period running from the date of the occurrence of the facts

46. *See*, e.g., CA Fort-de-France, 24 January 2017, RG 15/00486 *C. c/ SARL Cinésogar SARL Filmdis, SAS Mediagestion* (2017) 4 Concurrences 213, with a case note by Rafael Amaro.
47. CA Paris, 5-4, 6 March 2019, 17/21261, *SARL Arkeos et al. c/ SA EDF, SASU EDF Énergies Nouvelles Réparties et SASU EDF ENR Solaire*, (2019) 3 Concurrences 233, with a case note by Rafael Amaro.
48. Author translation for: '*la date à laquelle (la demanderesse) savait ou aurait pu savoir qu'elle avait été victime de l'infraction, et connaître la consistance de celle-ci, son imputabilité et sa durée*'.
49. Article L. 482-1 states: 'L'action en dommages et intérêts fondée sur l'article L. 481-1 se prescrit à l'expiration d'un délai de cinq ans. Ce délai commence à courir du jour où le demandeur a connu ou aurait dû connaître de façon cumulative:
    (1) Les actes ou faits imputés à l'une des personnes physiques ou morales mentionnées à l'article L. 481-1 et le fait qu'ils constituent une pratique anticoncurrentielle.
    (2) Le fait que cette pratique lui cause un dommage.
    (3) L'identité de l'un des auteurs de cette pratique'.
50. 'Toutefois, la prescription ne court pas tant que la pratique anticoncurrentielle n'a pas cessé'.

which is not subject to interruption (*délai butoir*).[51] This provision was ultimately removed. It must therefore be concluded that Article 2232 of the Civil Code applies to competition damages actions.

5. *Critical appraisal*

While the new rules may be close to the general rules on the law of limitation as found in Article 2224 of the Civil Code,[52] they have the advantage of being more precise as to the identification of the starting point of the five-year period. That being said, they will be inadequate to solve most of the current difficulties, which are essentially related to transitional law issues as mentioned above (*see* IV.C.2, *supra*).

It will be observed as well that the application of Article 2232 paragraph 1 of the Civil Code could in some cases seriously jeopardise the claimant's chances of success. It is therefore very doubtful whether this rule is compatible with the principle of effectiveness.

D. Collective actions/pooling of claims

1. *A long-running story ...*

The history of collective actions in France is full of unexpected twists. After almost four decades of fierce discussions, two kinds of collective redress mechanism have been set up in French law: the *action en representation conjointe* (introduced in 1992) and the *action de groupe* (introduced in 2014). Both the *action en representation conjointe* and the *action de groupe* follow an opt-in scheme under which only associations have the standing to bring the collective action. In the French system, as elsewhere, the 'official' objective pursued by collective redress mechanisms is to facilitate compensation and access to justice. This aim cannot be attained, however, in reality.

In the context of competition litigation, it should be noted that the Consumer Code governs the *action en representation conjointe*[53] and the *action de groupe*.[54] As such, their scopes are limited to harm suffered by consumers. It means that only B2C litigation is eligible for collective actions, not B2B litigation. When considering the fact that almost 100% of the private enforcement in France is initiated by businesses, it seems obvious that there is something wrong in the French collective redress system.

Without going into details, it has to be noted that the minimal impact of collective redress in France is attributable to the main features of these mechanisms.

51. Article 2232 states: 'The deferral of the starting point, the suspension or the interruption of the prescription cannot have the effect of extending the period of the extinctive prescription beyond twenty years from the day of the birth of the right. ...' (official translation).
52. 'Personal actions or movable rights of action prescribe in five years from the day the holder of a right knew or should have known the facts enabling him to exercise his right' (official translation).
53. Articles L. 622-1 et seq.
54. Articles L. 623-1 et seq.

2. *Main features of the action en représentation conjointe*

Concerning the *action en representation conjointe*, Article L. 622-1 paragraph 1 enables consumers associations to represent consumers in private litigation, provided that they obtain a mandate (*mandat*) of at least two consumers. Paragraph 2 of this Article prohibits associations from making use of publicity measures.[55] These two requirements are the main cause for the complete failure of this legal device.

This can be demonstrated by a closer look at the 'mobile phones' cartel case. This case involved the three major operators in the French mobile phone market. In 2005, the French Competition Authority fined them up to EUR 534 million for price-fixing and market sharing.[56] One year later, the leading French consumer association *UFC-Que Choisir?* brought an action for damages to obtain compensation for the overcharge paid by the 20 million consumers harmed by this cartel. The value of the claim was significant: between EUR 1.2 and 1.6 billion.[57] Of these 20 million consumers, the association gathered only 12,500 mandates, representing not more than 0.06% of the victims.[58] The trial was time-consuming for the association and monopolised the efforts of its legal service division for years. After a short-lived success, the association's action was deemed illegal by the *Cour de cassation* because *UFC-Que Choisir?* used prohibited means of public appeal to inform consumers.[59] Since then, no further *action en representation conjointe* has been brought to French courts in the field of competition litigation.

At the time of the preparation of the *Loi Hamon* (*see* IV.C.1, *supra*), the mobile phone cartel case was in all minds and the *action de groupe* was seen as a way to address the weaknesses of the *action en representation conjointe*.

3. *Main features of the* action de groupe

The *action de groupe* created by the *Loi Hamon* has been applicable in competition litigation since October 2014 (it has been extended since then to other sectors).[60]

55. It states: 'The mandate may not be solicited by means of a public appeal on radio or television, nor by means of posting of information, by tract or personalised letter. Authorisation must be given in writing by each consumer.'
56. Cons. conc., 30 November 2005, 05-D-65 *relative à des pratiques constatées dans le secteur de la téléphonie mobile.*
57. According to the association's quantification.
58. Que choisir, *Action de groupe: 99.94% des victimes de l'entente entre les opérateurs mobiles ne seront pas indemnisées!*, Press release of 13 October 2006, https://www.quechoisir.org/action-ufc-que-choisir-action-de-groupe-99-94-des-victimes-de-l-entente-entre-les-operateurs-mobiles-ne-seront-pas-indemnisees-n12565/ (accessed 25 June 2019).
59. Cass. civ. 1, 26 May 2011, 10-15676 [2011] D. 1884, with a case note by Nicolas Dupont [2011] RTD com. 627, with a case note by Bernard Bouloc. *See also* on this case Gaëlle Patetta, *Une illustration flagrante des limites du système judiciaire français* (2010) 70 RLDC. 59 et seq.
60. *See* among many contributions on the topic, Sylvia Pietrini, *L'action collective en droit des pratiques anticoncurrentielles* (Bruylant, 2012); Mireille Bacache, *Action de groupe et responsabilité civile* [2014] RTD civ. 450 et seq.; Martine Béhar-Touchais, '*L'action de groupe à la française, voie prometteuse ou (trop) Limitée?*' in Muriel Chagny (ed.), *La réparation des dommages concurrentiels en France et en Europe: État des lieux et changements à venir* (2014) 3

The structure of this legal device differs greatly from most of the existing collective redress mechanisms in the Western world.[61] For this reason, it has been described as a 'procedural monster'.[62]

As with the *action en representation conjointe*, only associations are entitled to bring actions. They must be representative at the national level, have existed for at least one year and have proof of performing an effective and public activity with a view to the protection of consumer interests. Very few associations meet these requirements (around fifteen in France).

The action itself follows an (awkward) two-stage procedure.

In the first stage - the liability phase (*jugement sur la responsabilité*) - the court decides on the liability of the defendant on the basis of individual 'model' cases brought by the association. The court will hand down an interlocutory judgment where it will rule on the scope of the defendant's liability, the damage, the remedies, the criteria that claimants must meet to be part of the group, the conditions of its advertisement and the period to opt in. The group is therefore constituted *after* the judgment on the merits and not before.

In the second stage - the enforcement phase (*mise en oeuvre du jugement*) - the claimants who meet the criteria can opt in and join the group and obtain compensation via the association (who will receive the money from the defendant) or by asking the defendant itself. During this phase, the court may still address any disputes related to the damages distribution.

It is important to note that Article L. 623-23 of the Consumer Code prohibits stand-alone *action de groupe*. Only follow-on *actions de groupe* may be brought in French courts.

4. *Critical appraisal*

So far, it is impossible to assess accurately the effectiveness of such a system for a simple reason: no *action de groupe* has ever been initiated in the area of competition litigation.

Nevertheless, a sceptical view seems to be in order for at least three reasons.
First, the opt-in system has proven its ineffectiveness for litigation involving consumers. The mobile phone cartel case is the best proof.
Second, the exclusion of lawyers 'from the game' paralyses a business-oriented approach towards collective redress. The political reasons for this exclusion are very clear: a mixture of hostility to the legal-business world and the well-conducted lobbying done by the associations defending the interests of major French companies.

Concurrences 51 et seq.; Emmanuelle Claudel, *Action de groupe et autres dispositions concurrence de la loi consommation: un dispositif singulier* [2014] RTD com. 339 et seq.; Camille Marechal, *Le volet « concurrence » de la loi n°2014-344 du 17 mars 2014 relative à la consommation* [2014] Contrats conc. consom. dossier 4.

61. Soraya Amrani-Mekki, *Action de groupe, mode d'emploi* (2014) 12 Procédure, étude 16; Hervé Croze, *Action de groupe de droit commun. – schéma procedural* (2014) 12 Procédure, étude 17.
62. *See*, e.g., Nicolas Molfessis, *L'exorbitance de l'action de groupe à la française* [2014] D. 947 et seq.

But this political choice could eventually condemn the French model to never being applied. An *action de groupe* requires time, expertise and ultimately a lot of money. Associations are ill equipped for this task. Who other than lawyers, possibly funded by third parties, can efficiently bring an action of collective redress?

Lastly, as the market abhors vacuums, private initiatives may supplant official *action de groupe* far more effectively. Obviously, we are thinking of companies whose business model is to pool claims. Such companies are capable of bringing the claims of thousands of small businesses together in a single trial. No French legal device can compete. Unless the French rulers initiate a U-turn, the bad reputation of French law is likely to persist. For mass litigation, this reputation will be deserved. For the rest, it is more questionable.

CHAPTER 5

Private Enforcement in Germany

Jens-Uwe Franck

I. Introduction and outline
II. The development of private enforcement
III. What does 'effectiveness' require and what are the impediments to private enforcement?
    A. Preliminary remarks
        1. Defining a yardstick of 'effectiveness'
        2. (Lack of) empirical findings
    B. Favourable developments
        1. Clarifying legal standards: German courts appear to be on the right track (though it is not a fast track)
        2. Taking 'effectiveness' seriously: the German legislature as 'repairer'
    C. Unsolved issues: the lack of collective redress as a major flaw
    D. Some ambiguous findings: is the glass half full or half empty?
        1. Costs
        2. Expertise of the judiciary
        3. Efficiency of court proceedings
IV. Particular topics
    A. Which entity is liable for damages?
    B. Binding effect of decisions by competition authorities
        1. Decisions by 'foreign' NCAs ('cross-border binding effect')
        2. Scope of the binding effect
        3. The competition authorities as key players
    C. Statutes of limitation
        1. The regular period of limitation following a subjective system
        2. Two objective periods of limitation

3. Enforcement actions by competition authorities
4. Effect of limitation
D. Collective action and pooling of claims

I. INTRODUCTION AND OUTLINE

Private competition litigation is not a recent phenomenon in Germany. Yet, for a long time, infringements of competition law were for the most part invoked solely either to challenge the validity of agreements or to tackle abusive and discriminatory practices, such as refusals to supply. It has only been in the aftermath of the ECJ's seminal judgment in *Courage v Crehan* in 2001[1] and the subsequent reform of the Gesetz gegen Wettbewerbsbeschränkungen ('Act against Restraints of Competition', hereinafter 'Competition Act') in 2005 that competition damages litigation has achieved its breakthrough in cartel cases.[2] Since then, a considerable body of case law has been generated. A recent study lists sixty-nine judgments handed down between 2003 and 2017.[3] A significant number of damages actions are currently pending before the courts. Alongside the UK and the Netherlands, Germany is considered to be one of the three European jurisdictions where plaintiffs are most active in bringing damages claims,[4] attracting a substantial part of the damages actions following on from the European Commission's discovery and fining of cartels.[5] It appears that, particularly in the aftermath of the Commission's decision to impose fines in the truck cartel case,[6] a considerable number of foreign plaintiffs have also filed suit before German courts.

With a focus on damages actions against cartels, this report analyses the legal and institutional framework in three parts. In the first part, some essential facts regarding the development of the law up to the transposition of the Directive on Actions for

1. ECJ, Case C-453/99 *Courage Ltd v Bernard Crehan* and *Bernard Crehan v Courage Ltd* [2001] ECR I-6297.
2. Ulf Böge and Konrad Ost, *Up and Running, or Is It? Private Enforcement–the Situation in Germany and Policy Perspectives* [2006] ECLR 197, 198 ('Claims for damages by victims of hardcore cartels, however, so far have only been successfully asserted once').
3. Lukas Rengier, *Kartellschadensersatz in Deutschland – die ersten 15 Jahre in Zahlen und Lehren für die Zukunft* [2018] WuW 613, 619, n. 48. The numbers include declaratory judgments and preliminary decisions on the merits.
4. An overview of court practice in these three jurisdictions is provided by Matthijs Kuijpers, Tommi Palumbo, Elaine Whiteford & Thomas B. Paul, *Actions for Damages in the Netherlands, the United Kingdom and Germany* (2018) 9 JECLAP 55–73 (relating to the period July 2016–September 2017); Matthijs Kuijpers, Stefan Tuinenga, Elaine Whiteford & Thomas B. Paul, *Actions for Damages in the Netherlands, the United Kingdom and Germany* (2017) 8 JECLAP 47–65 (relating to the period July 2014–July 2016); Matthijs Kuijpers, Stefan Tuinenga, Stephen Wisking, Kim Dietzel, Suzy Campbell & Alexander Fritzsche, *Actions for Damages in the Netherlands, the United Kingdom and Germany* (2015) 6 JECLAP 129–142 (relating to the period July 2013–July 2014).
5. Follow-on actions have been filed in Germany in the aftermath of the Commission's decisions in several cartel cases, including vitamins, car glass, carbonless paper, elevators and escalators, and trucks; Rengier, *supra* n. 3, at 614.
6. COM, Case AT.39824 *Trucks* [2016] C(2016) 4673.

Competition Damages 2014/104/EU[7] will be outlined (section II). In the second part, a general appraisal of the status quo will be given. We will identify developments that can be regarded as favourable (section III.A) but also flaws in the framework (section III.B) and findings where the proverbial glass could be considered half full or half empty (section III.C). Finally, in the third part, four specific issues that are widely discussed in the context of the transposition of the Directive will be taken up: the application of the single economic unit doctrine (section IV.A); the binding effect of decisions by competition authorities (section IV.B); the statute of limitations (section IV.C); and collective actions and the bundling of claims through assignments (section IV.D).

II. THE DEVELOPMENT OF PRIVATE ENFORCEMENT

After World War II, the military governments introduced for the first time a prohibition of cartels in (West) Germany. The virtually identical U.S. and British decartelisation laws came into effect in 1947 as occupation laws and remained in force as laws of the Federal Republic of Germany until their replacement by the Competition Act (Gesetz gegen Wettbewerbsbeschränkungen/Act against Restraints of Competition) in 1958.[8] While the decartelisation laws did not contain specific rules on private enforcement, the German courts[9] recognised that an infringement of these statutes could trigger civil liability based on section 823(2) of the Civil Code (Bürgerliches Gesetzbuch),[10] a provision that is equivalent to the common law tort of breach of a statutory duty.

When the Competition Act came into force on 1 January 1958, it contained an explicit legal basis – initially laid down in section 35 and, since the 6th amendment of the Competition Act in 1999, in section 33 – for private rights of action. The provision was modelled on section 823(2) of the Civil Code and, therefore, only the infringement of those rules of competition law for which the intention was to protect another person could trigger civil liability (the so-called protective purpose requirement). This statutory basis embodied in the Competition Act did not apply if EU competition law had been infringed. In those cases, the plaintiffs could, however, still invoke section 823(2)

7. Directive 2014/104/EU of the European Parliament and of the Council of 26 November 2014 on certain rules governing actions for damages under national law for infringements of the competition law provisions of the Member States and of the European Union [2014], OJ L 349/1 (hereinafter referred to as 'the Directive' or 'the Directive on Actions for Competition Damages').
8. For an overview of the impact of the allied decartelisation laws *see* David J. Gerber, *Law and Competition in Twentieth Century Europe* 268–270 (Oxford University Press 1998, reprinted 2003); Stefan A. Riesenfeld, '*The Protection of Competition*' in Eric Stein and Thomas L. Nicholson (eds), *American Enterprise in the European Common Market: A Legal Profile* 213–215 (University of Michigan Law School 1960).
9. Bundesgerichtshof (BGH), 21 November 1953, VI ZR 91/52, [1954] NJW 147–148 (*Innungsboykott*); Oberlandesgericht (OLG) Düsseldorf, 9 February 1954, 4 U 349/52, WuW/E OLG 71, 72 (*Arztrechnungen*). Both cases concerned the decartelisation laws enacted by the British Control Commission for Germany.
10. Section 823(2) of the Civil Code reads: 'The same duty [to make compensation to the other party for the damage arising] is held by a person who commits a breach of a statute that is intended to protect another person.' Throughout this article, translations of German legislation are taken from https://www.gesetze-im-internet.de.

of the Civil Code. Consequently, civil liability following a breach of both German competition law and EU competition law was subject to the 'protective purpose' requirement.

Though the explanatory memorandum that accompanied the draft bill of the Competition Act indicated that the legislature had envisaged a rather broad tortious liability[11] and that private enforcement would play an important role alongside public enforcement,[12] the courts adopted in the following years a rather restrictive approach towards private rights of action. Only those firms that had been specifically targeted by an infringer were considered to be in a position to apply for an injunction or to claim damages. Cases in point included, for instance, boycotts[13] and discriminatory behaviour that violated competition law.[14] An infringement of the cartel prohibition of (what is now) Article 101 TFEU and section 1 of the Competition Act could only trigger liability under those rather exceptional circumstances where the anticompetitive coordination was aimed at specific customers or suppliers, for example in the case of a coordinated refusal to supply a firm[15] or a collusion among customers to force a certain supplier to offer better conditions.[16] In contrast, those customers that simply paid an inflated price because of cartelisation were not considered eligible for competition damages. This restrictive approach remained the prevailing position among the German courts until 2004.[17]

After the judgment in *Courage v Crehan* and the ECJ's famous statement according to which '[t]he full effectiveness of Article 85 of the Treaty [now Article 101 TFEU] ... would be put at risk if it were not open to any individual to claim damages for loss caused to him by ... conduct liable to restrict or distort competition',[18] it became clear that such a narrow reading of the 'protective purpose' requirement did not comply with EU law. Consequently, through the 7th amendment of the Competition Act in 2005, the German legislature abolished the 'protective purpose' requirement. Section 33 of the Competition Act 2005 was converted into a uniform legal basis for private rights of action in case of an infringement of both German and EU competition law. With the same reform the legislature introduced several other measures to facilitate competition damages actions: a binding effect of final decisions of the German

11. *See* Deutscher Bundestag, Drucksache 2/1158, 22 January 1955, Entwurf eines Gesetzes gegen Wettbewerbsbeschränkungen, 44 (draft of the bill stating that numerous provisions of this Act including the prohibition of cartels must be regarded as having a protective purpose).
12. *Ibid.*, 25 ('*Vom wirtschaftstheoretischen Ausgangspunkt des Gesetzes ist also jede Kartellvereinbarung als solche ... zu mißbilligen. Sie ist zivilrechtlich für unwirksam zu erklären; wer sich darüber hinwegsetzt, wird mit einer Geldstrafe bedroht und hat Schadensersatz zu leisten*' ['Starting from the economic premise of this Act, any cartel agreement has to be disapproved as such. It has to be declared as null and void; whoever does not abide by it will be threatened with a fine and has to pay damages']).
13. BGH, 2 July 1996, KZR 20/91, WuW/E BGH 3067, 3072–3073 (*Fremdleasingboykott*).
14. BGH, 2 July 1996, KZR 31/95, WuW/E BGH 3074 (*Kraft-Wärme-Kopplung*).
15. OLG Düsseldorf, 14 March 1989, U Kart 1/86, WuW/E OLG 4481, 4483 (*Schmiedeeisenwaren*).
16. OLG Koblenz, 5 November 1998, U 596/98 - Kart, WuW/E Verg 184–185 (*Feuerlöschgeräte*).
17. *See*, e.g., Landgericht (LG) Mainz, 15 January 2004, 12 HK O 52/02, [2004] NJW-RR 478, 480–481 (*Vitaminpreise*); LG Mannheim, 11 July 2003, 7 O 326/02, [2004] GRUR 182.
18. Case C-453/99 *Courage and Crehan*, *supra* n. 1, at para. 26.

competition authorities,[19] of the EU Commission, and of the national competition authorities (hereinafter 'NCAs') of other Member States if based on Articles 101 and 102 TFEU;[20] a duty imposed on infringers to pay interest from the time the damage occurred;[21] and a suspension of limitation periods if a competition authority institutes proceedings for infringement of competition law.[22]

The 2005 reform package turned out to be a milestone - not only because of its actual amendments but also because the German legislature clearly signalled to the courts and to the aggrieved parties that formerly established and widely accepted restrictions on damages actions were not to be maintained. As a result, the number of cartel damages actions began to rise steadily, and the courts got the chance to reconsider their approach towards competition damages actions and to gradually clarify outstanding legal issues. In its first landmark judgment handed down after the reform, the Bundesgerichtshof (Federal Court of Justice) adopted in *ORWI* this fundamental change without hesitation and applied it to damages actions that had to be assessed according to the legal situation before the reform, i.e., with the 'protective purpose' requirement still in place.[23] More particularly, the court granted a cause of action based on the 'protective purpose' requirement to those parties that had paid a cartel-induced overcharge, even if these firms had not been specifically 'targeted' by the cartel. It is quite remarkable that the Federal Court of Justice changed its jurisprudence without reference to *Courage v Crehan* or the EU law principle of effectiveness, feigning an intrinsically motivated reconsideration of the 'protective purpose' requirement.

With the 9th amendment of the Competition Act in 2017, the legislature transposed the Competition Damages Directive[24] into German law.[25] This reform changed, first of all, the outer structure of the German law on competition damages claims. While before the reform the rules specifically related to competition damages had been concentrated in section 33 of the Competition Act 2005, the rules were now split up essentially[26] into eight provisions, namely section 33a to 33h of the Competition Act. In regard to substantive damages law, the changes, while certainly not insignificant, were

19. Note that this reference to 'German competition authorities' encompasses the Bundeskartellamt, i.e., the Federal Cartel Office in Bonn, and - due to Germany's federal structure - the sixteen competition authorities in each *Land* (state); *see* sections 48 and 49 of the Competition Act.
20. Section 33(4) of the Competition Act 2005, now section 33b of the Competition Act 2017.
21. Section 33(3) sentence 4 of the Competition Act 2005, now section 33a(4) sentence 1 of the Competition Act 2017.
22. Section 33(5) of the Competition Act 2005, now section 33h(6) of the Competition Act 2017.
23. BGH, 28 June 2011, KZR 75/10, BGHZ 190, 145, para. 13 (*ORWI*).
24. Directive 2014/104/EU, 1.
25. For details of the implementation process *see* Christian Kersting, '*Transposition of the Antitrust Damages Directive into German Law*' in Barry Rodger, Miguel Sousa Ferro & Francisco Marcos (eds), *The EU Antitrust Damages Directive: Transposition in the Member States* 124-127 (Oxford University Press 2018).
26. Since the 9th amendment, section 33 of the Competition Act now provides the law on injunctive relieve but it is also of relevance to cartel damages claims owing to a reference in section 33a of the Competition Act. Sections 89a to 89e of the Competition Act comprise certain procedural rules.

far from revolutionary.[27] Most notably, the amendment resulted in a certain revitalisation of the passing-on defence,[28] a prolongation of periods of limitation,[29] and detailed rules on joint and several liability, including modifications for small and medium-sized firms and immunity recipients.[30] The prohibition of overcompensatory damages pursuant to Article 3(3) of the Directive did not require an amendment as German competition damages law – as indeed German law in general – does not provide for multiple, exemplary, or punitive damages.[31] A more fundamental change, however, has been brought about by the new disclosure regime[32] as the German courts traditionally make only sparse use of their competence to order defendants or third parties to produce documents or other material that could assist a plaintiff in substantiating her cause of action.

III. WHAT DOES 'EFFECTIVENESS' REQUIRE AND WHAT ARE THE IMPEDIMENTS TO PRIVATE ENFORCEMENT?

A. Preliminary remarks

1. *Defining a yardstick of 'effectiveness'*

As it is the ambition of the comparative study in this book not only to outline the status quo of domestic legal systems but also to appraise its 'effectiveness' in practical terms – bearing in mind potential options to amend the legal framework at the level of the EU and/or the Member States – we have to reflect on the appropriate yardstick to measure effectiveness.

a) *Legal perspective*

The first response that comes to mind is that domestic law on competition damages is 'effective' if it is consistent with EU law. The trouble with this statement is, however, that it can answer the question only in part. This is, first of all, because EU law does not provide standards in respect of all issues that are relevant for an effective enforcement of competition law via damages actions.

The Directive on Actions for Competition Damages covers only some aspects, and even those are often not regulated exhaustively. To give but one example, Article 3(1)

27. In a recent statistical evaluation, the author relates the sharp increase in the number of judgments in cartel damages cases in the years 2015 and 2016 with the adoption of the Directive. Rengier, *supra* n. 3, at 615. Yet the author does not give any reason why such a (causal) connection – which seems not very plausible – could be presumed.
28. Section 33c of the Competition Act 2017.
29. Section 33h of the Competition Act 2017.
30. Sections 33d and 33e of the Competition Act 2017.
31. But note that in the run-up to the 7th amendment of the Competition Act, the German Monopoly Commission had proposed that successful plaintiffs should receive damages set at double the actual damage. Monopolkommission, *Das allgemeine Wettbewerbsrecht in der Siebten GWB-Novelle*, para. 83 (2004).
32. Section 33g of the Competition Act 2017.

of the Directive states, 'Member States shall ensure that any ... person who has suffered harm caused by an infringement of competition law is able to claim and to obtain full compensation of that harm.' While the Directive, thus, grants standing rights to those suffering 'harm *caused* by an infringement', it leaves open the door for Member States to make use of doctrines such as remoteness, proximate causation, directness of injury, causation in law, adequacy, and the like to restrict the availability of damages claims to certain classes of aggrieved parties. This is confirmed in recital 11 of the Directive.[33] We can recall that the Austrian Oberster Gerichtshof in *Kone* initially assumed that those firms that suffered harm due to an umbrella effect were not entitled to claim damages under Austrian law because no sufficient causal link could be established between infringement and harm:[34] would the Oberster Gerichtshof have understood from Article 3 of the Directive that umbrella damages must be compensated? In the light of the aforesaid, certainly not. Member States may maintain conditions for compensation such as, for instance, imputability or adequacy. This illustrates nicely that the principle of full compensation as enshrined in particular in Articles 1(1) and 3(1) of the Directive *as such* does not provide an answer to the question of whether or not umbrella damages must be compensated. The answer to that question lies (only) in the principle of effectiveness and the ECJ's jurisprudence, which is based thereon.

The ECJ sees itself as entitled to verify whether the domestic laws of Member States are designed so that they can fulfil the objectives that are associated with the establishment of the right to competition damages in *Courage v Crehan*. The court bases such a review on the principle of effectiveness from *Rewe* and *San Giorgio*,[35] and on the principle of effective judicial protection as established in the case law starting from *Johnston*[36] and now embodied in Article 47 of the EU Charter of Fundamental Rights and Article 19(1) TEU. These legal doctrines are in part (functionally) interchangeable. Moreover, the court does not always distinguish clearly whether it derives a standard from an *effet utile* interpretation of EU competition law or from *Rewe* effectiveness.[37] In any case, it is important to see that those standards are an integral part of EU primary law, and thus, as long as the court respects the institutional balance and does not inappropriately interfere with the EU legislature's competence under

33. Recital 11 of the Directive 2014/104/EU states: 'All national rules governing the exercise of the right to compensation for harm resulting from an infringement of Article 101 or 102 TFEU, *including those concerning aspects not dealt with in this Directive such as the notion of causal relationship between the infringement and the harm*, must observe the principles of effectiveness and equivalence. ... Where Member States provide *other conditions for compensation under national law, such as imputability, adequacy or culpability*, they should be able to maintain such conditions in so far as they comply with the case-law of the Court of Justice, the principles of effectiveness and equivalence, and this Directive' (emphasis added).
34. The court essentially argued that, first, no adequate causal link between infringement and harm could be established as the pricing of the cartel's competitors must be regarded an independent business decision and, second, because the cartelists aimed only at obtaining a higher surplus at the expense of its customers and, therefore, harm due to umbrella pricing must be considered a mere side effect. *See* Oberster Gerichtshof, 17 October 2012, 7 Ob 48/12b, para. 5.
35. Case C-453/99 *Courage and Crehan*, *supra* n. 1, at para. 29.
36. ECJ, Case C-222/84 *Johnston v Chief Constable of the Royal Ulster Constabulary* [1986] ECR 1651.
37. *See*, e.g., ECJ, Case C-557/12 *Kone AG v ÖBB-Infrastruktur AG* [2014] ECLI:EU:C:2014:1317, para. 33.

Article 103 TFEU, they are binding not only on Member States but also on the EU legislature.[38] The rules set by the EU legislature must, therefore, comply with the ECJ's jurisprudence; this is, however, not always the case – the access to leniency material is an obvious example.[39]

The principle of effectiveness found in *Rewe* and *San Giorgio* and the principle of effective judicial protection concern *any* rule of domestic law that has an impact on the enforcement of competition damages claims. But as long as an issue has not been taken up by the ECJ, it is often not more than tapping around in the dark to predict whether a certain domestic rule is sufficiently 'effective' or not. It is only after the ECJ has judged on a particular aspect, as, for example, in *Kone* on the compensation of umbrella damages, that a standard has been established.[40]

It is apparent from the foregoing that EU law provides only partially for standards that domestic law has to comply with. Therefore, to evaluate the 'effectiveness' of Member States' laws, one cannot avoid considering the policy objectives that are associated with the ECJ's fundamental decision to posit an implicit right to competition damages, or the theoretical concepts that may be useful to develop legal standards based on the general principles enshrined in EU law. What is more, it is only on this basis that one can obtain a yardstick that allows one to critically evaluate the standards established by the adjudication of the ECJ or the EU legislature.

Ultimately, a yardstick that allows specific requirements to be deduced from the principle of effectiveness beyond the existing case law of the ECJ is relevant for the interpretation of the rules of domestic law that implement the Directive. It is noteworthy that Article 4 of the Directive stipulates:

> In accordance with the principle of effectiveness, Member States shall ensure that all national rules and procedures relating to the exercise of claims for damages are designed and applied in such a way that they do not render practically impossible or excessively difficult the exercise of the Union right to full compensation for harm caused by an infringement of competition law.

The importance of this codification of the principle of effectiveness as stated by the ECJ in *Rewe* and *San Giorgio* lies not so much in the fact that it ascertains that regulatory gaps left by the EU legislature must be closed by domestic law considering the principle of effectiveness; its importance is that the wording of the provision makes it clear that Article 4 of the Directive applies to any kind of national law that relates to actions for competition damages and, therefore, also clarifies that the rules of domestic law that transpose the Directive have to be construed in the light of the principle of effectiveness – which is only logical given that the EU legislature is bound by the principle of effectiveness, too.

---

38. Jens-Uwe Franck, *Striking a Balance of Power between the Court of Justice and the EU Legislature: The Law on Competition Damages as a Paradigm* (2018) 43 E.L. Rev. 837, 842–843, 849–852.
39. *Ibid.*, 853–856 (arguing that the court's statements in *Pfleiderer* and *Donau Chemie* are not binding on the EU legislature as they disregard the principle of institutional balance).
40. Though one might doubt whether the ECJ should have better left the decision to the legislature – be it the EU legislature or the domestic legislature, *ibid.*, 852.

b) *Theoretical perspective(s)*

Though this is not the place to develop a comprehensive theory of effective and efficient enforcement via damages actions, it is useful to outline at least some considerations that one should bear in mind when engaging in a policy discussion in this respect and which are apt to flesh out 'effectiveness' as a legal concept.

(1) Overarching regulatory purposes: deterrence and corrective justice

In *Courage v Crehan*, the ECJ above all stressed that a right to damages will have a deterrent effect on competition law infringements.[41] Subsequently, in *Donau Chemie*, the court extended its reading of the desired 'practical effect' of the competition law rules by a reference to corrective justice as an additional objective associated with the availability of damages claims.[42] These objectives provide a starting point to derive a regulatory yardstick against which 'effectiveness' might be measured. Yet, things are by no means trivial.

First, optimal deterrence theory suggests that competition law infringers should be forced to pay damages that equal the amount of the profits they generate from the wrongdoing at the expense of other players in the market plus the harm they inflict beyond that on social welfare.[43] Most importantly, in the case of a cartel, this means that the cartel should disgorge the entire overcharge, which is the amount of the price increase times the volume of sales at the cartel price, as well as the deadweight loss, which is represented by the value that the units that were not produced because of the rise in prices would have had to consumers had they been able to buy those units at the low pre-cartel prices, and by the lost profits to the cartel's customers on units that they did not produce or resell because of the cartel-induced reduction in consumer demand. Taking up again the example of umbrella pricing, this approach reveals that the compensation for umbrella damages entails risks of systematic overdeterrence because

41. C-453/99, *Courage and Crehan*, *supra* n. 1, at para. 27 ('Indeed, the existence of such a right … discourages agreements or practices, which are frequently covert, which are liable to restrict or distort competition'). ECJ, Case C-724/17 *Skanska Industrial Solutions and Others* [2019] ECLI:EU:C:2019:204, para. 45 ('… actions for damages for infringement of EU competition rules are an integral part of the system for enforcement of those rules, which are intended to punish anticompetitive behaviour on the part of undertakings and to deter them from engaging in such conduct').
42. ECJ, Case C-536/11 *Bundeswettbewerbsbehörde v Donau Chemie AG* [2013] ECLI:EU:C:2013:366 para. 24 ('Secondly, that right constitutes effective protection against the adverse effects that any infringement of Article 101(1) TFEU is liable to cause to individuals, as it allows persons who have suffered harm due to that infringement to seek full compensation not only for actual loss (*damnum emergens*) but also for loss of profit (*lucrum cessans*) plus interest …') (references omitted).
43. *See*, e.g., Richard A. Posner & Frank H. Easterbrook, *Antitrust* 550 (8th ed., West 1981); William M. Landes, *Optimal Sanctions for Antitrust Violations* (1983) 50 U. Chi. L. Rev. 652, 656; William Breit and Kenneth G. Elzinga, *Private Antitrust Enforcement: The New Learning* (1985) 28 J. Law & Econ. 405, 410–412; William H. Page, *The Scope of Liability for Antitrust Violations* (1985) 37 Stan. L. Rev. 1445, 1455; Richard A. Posner, *Economic Analysis of Law* §10.14, 394 (9th ed., Wolters Kluwer 2014); John M. Connor & Robert H. Lande, *Cartels as Rational Business Strategy: Crime Pays* (2012) 34 Cardozo Law Review 427, 431–435, 468.

this kind of damage reflects neither the deadweight loss nor a transfer to the infringer but a mere transfer of wealth between innocent parties. Thus, in an ideal world of deterrence through damages liability, losses resulting from umbrella pricing should not figure in the damages.[44] There may be, however, good reasons to award compensation for damages caused by umbrella pricing as a second-best solution.[45]

Second, a severe enforcement gap is entailed because it is (far) less than 100% certain that, first, a competition infringement will be detected[46] and that, second, all the aggrieved parties will successfully claim adequate compensation. This shortcoming could be remedied through the award of multiple damages. Yet the EU legislature has taken this option off the table: Article 3(3) of the Directive excludes an upward adjustment of the actual damages awarded to cope with this risk of underdeterrence. What is more, the enforcement challenge due to the secret character of cartels, which was also highlighted by the ECJ in *Courage v Crehan*,[47] reminds us that, in order to exploit the potential of damages actions to contribute to an effective enforcement, standing rights[48] should be given primarily to those who have the highest likelihood of being informed about infringements. This encourages market players to act upon their private information on infringements either by directly filing a suit for damages or by informing the competition authorities, waiting for the fining of a cartel, and then using a (binding) decision as the basis for bringing a damages suit.

Third, given that a cartel is not a single entity but consists of a group of individual actors, the issue of deterrence cannot be fully addressed by focusing merely on the overall level of damages or fines that a cartelist has to reckon with if caught. Coordinated illegal activities such as cartels can be effectively deterred by making sure that cartelists cannot sufficiently trust their partners in this illegal activity.[49] Consequently, if firms that are granted leniency have to pay damages in private lawsuits, deterrence might well be more difficult, as a cartel may be sustained more easily when the overall payment is increased. This is an intriguing example of how the interdependency between public and private enforcement adds considerable complexity to policy discussions on the effectiveness of private enforcement. This explains why it is so contentious, first, to what extent or whether at all potential plaintiffs should have a right to access leniency materials, and, second, to what extent or whether at all immunity recipients should be exempted from the liability to compensate aggrieved

44. Posner, *supra* n. 43, at 395.
45. Jens-Uwe Franck, *Umbrella Pricing and Cartel Damages Under EU Competition Law* (2015) 11 European Competition Journal 135, 140–148.
46. The detection rate of cartels is estimated to be in the 10% to 25% range. *See* Connor and Lande, *supra* n. 43, at 486–490, tbl. 3.
47. *See supra* n. 41.
48. The term 'standing right' is used here in a non-technical sense, embracing a plurality of rules that may effectively delimit the class of potential plaintiffs such as 'remoteness of damage', 'causation in law', and the like.
49. *See* for a clear exposition of this point Maria Bigoni, Sven-Olof Fridolfsson, Chloé Le Coq & Giancarlo Spagnolo, *Trust Leniency, and Deterrence* (2015) 31 J. L. Econ. & Org. 663, 663–666.

parties. On the latter aspect, one may expect a reopening of the debate should the recent trend of a decreasing number of leniency applications[50] continue.

Fourth, there can be no doubt that, as a matter of principle, it serves the pursuit of corrective justice that cartelists have to compensate the damage they cause to their customers and other market players. But even a rigorous implementation of corrective justice does not require that *any* individual loss, however remote it is related to an infringement, has to be compensated.[51] Therefore, the crucial question is where to draw the line between damage for which compensation is cogent in terms of corrective justice and damage for which compensation may be excluded under legal doctrines such as remoteness, proximate causation, directness of injury, and the like.[52] Coherence with existing doctrine under domestic jurisprudence often appears to be the most that courts and commentators can reasonably strive for. This is, on the one hand, a solid basis for the development of a consistent body of competition damages law, in particular within the framework of domestic law. Yet, on the other hand, it provides at best little guidance for an observer who wants to critically evaluate the 'effectiveness' of domestic law as an instrument of corrective justice.

(2) On the various cost factors

Private enforcement is a socially costly commodity. It is, therefore, in the interest of society to ensure that competition damages litigation contributes to the effective enforcement of competition law at a reasonable cost, or, to put it bluntly: there is no good reason to believe that private competition enforcement is not subject to declining marginal utility and increasing marginal cost.[53] This regards, first of all, the (direct) costs that come along with keeping the machinery of justice going, and which are borne partly by society as a whole via taxpayers' money (e.g., for the maintenance of courthouses and the salaries of judges) and partly by the parties to the litigation, which have to contribute to those costs in the form of court and lawyers' fees.

The costs to society in a strict sense (i.e., understood as a loss to social welfare) include, in particular, *error costs* that occur due to mistakes by the courts and costs due

50. In 2017, the Bundeskartellamt received thirty-seven applications for leniency, *see* Press Release of 27 August 2018, available at https://www.bundeskartellamt.de > Über uns > Presse > Pressemitteilungen (accessed 8 April 2019). In the seven preceding years, the numbers were consistently higher (59 in 2016, 76 in 2015, 72 in 2014, 66 in 2013, 51 in 2012, 41 in 2011, and 56 in 2010), *see* https://www.bundeskartellamt.de > Kartellverbot > Bonusregelung (accessed 16 April 2019). While the European Commission does not officially disclose the number of leniency applications, two senior officials of DG Comp have personally confirmed to me that there has been a decrease during recent years.
51. *See*, e.g., in regard to umbrella damage, Case C-557/12 *Kone and Others* [2014] ECLI: EU:C:2014:45, Opinion of AG Kokott, para. 33 ('it is perfectly legitimate, for the purposes of examining the existence of a causal link, to lay down criteria which ensure that cartel members are not subject to unlimited liability to provide compensation for any losses, however remote, for which their anti-competitive behaviour may have been the cause in the sense of a "conditio sine qua non" (also known as an equivalent causal link or a but-for causal link)').
52. One may therefore doubt whether ideas of corrective justice can meaningfully be employed to define the limits of damages liability; *see* Franck, *supra* n. 45, at 152.
53. Herbert Hovenkamp, *Federal Antitrust Policy* §17.1, 871 (5th ed., West 2016).

to *entry barriers* to the justice system. From a social point of view, the latter may be either too low and, thus, result in too many unmeritorious actions, or too high and consequently bring about too little litigation and an inefficiently low level of private enforcement. There are a great number of legal and institutional factors that are relevant in this regard, including:

- rules that define the level of reimbursable court fees and lawyers' fees as well as their allocation (loser-pays rule, one-way fee-shifting, etc.);
- rules that influence the courts' and judges' expertise as they determine, for instance, the number of judges that sit in actions for damages cases or whether certain judges or panels may specialise in competition damages law;
- rules governing the recourse to experts by courts and parties;
- rules that define the role of competition authorities in private litigation (e.g., their right or duty to intervene as an amicus curiae);
- factors influencing the typical length of proceedings (e.g., the availability of 'fast-track' procedures or 'summary judgments');
- rules on the disclosure of evidence by defendants and third parties;
- standards of proof, in particular in regard to demonstrating that a cartel affected a certain transaction and the estimation of a cartel-induced damage.

2. *(Lack of) empirical findings*

If we seek to evaluate the effectiveness of competition enforcement via damages actions, the question is: what do we actually know about the effectiveness of actions for competition damages in Germany? For a start, we can study the 'law in the books' – the legal texts and scholarly writings. Court judgments provide us with an insight into a significant part of the 'law in action'.[54] Decisions by the Federal Court of Justice are published in a database available on the court's website.[55] A major part of the decisions of the Higher Regional Courts and a certain number of the decisions by Regional Courts are published in legal databases.[56] The courts are in general not obliged to make judgments publicly available but will provide a non-confidential version of a decision on request. A comprehensive compilation of private competition litigation is at the disposal of the Bundeskartellamt (Federal Cartel Office). This is because section 90(1) of the Competition Act requires all German courts to inform the Bundeskartellamt

54. The German Federal Cartel Office (*Bundeskartellamt*) has an overview of all private litigation that involves competition law; *see* section 90(1) of the Competition Act, which states, 'The German courts shall inform the Bundeskartellamt about all legal actions in which the decision depends in whole or in part on the application of the provisions of this Act, on decisions made pursuant to these provisions, or on the application of Articles 101 or 102 of the Treaty on the Functioning of the European Union …'.
55. Available at http://www.bundesgerichtshof.de > Entscheidungen.
56. The most important legal databases are Juris, available at http://www.juris.de, and Beck-online, available at https://beck-online.beck.de.

about all decisions that 'depend in whole or in part' on the application of EU or German competition law.[57]

Moreover, if systematically surveyed, judgments can provide a basis for an empirical assessment of cartel damages litigation.[58] Based on a data set of sixty-nine judgments that were handed down between 2003 and 2017, *Rengier* explores the development of cartel damages litigation over time and presents findings on the outcome of the litigation, the number of judgments, the amount of damages and interests awarded, and the length of the proceedings.[59]

While the facts revealed in in this study are certainly relevant in respect of the effectiveness of actions on cartel damages, its significance in regard to the policy objectives associated with those actions – deterrence and corrective justice – is fairly restricted. For one thing, since the compiled judgments are for the most part declaratory judgments and interim judgments on the merits, the study includes only seven observations on the amount of damages awarded.[60] Moreover, the obvious blind spot of such a study is the missing insight into the practice of settlements. Background talks with lawyers and press releases give us a glimpse of the substantial number of settlements and reveal that there are indeed high figures involved. Thus, newspapers reported in 2016 that the German steelmaker ThyssenKrupp reached an out-of-court settlement with the national railway operator Deutsche Bahn and agreed to pay about EUR 150 million to compensate for damage caused through price-fixing of railway tracks.[61] As parties settle in the shadow of the law, the (relative) success of settlements mirrors the quality of the legal and institutional framework for damages actions. Yet, without sound data in particular on the amount of compensation that is paid as a result of settlements, it is difficult to engage in any kind of empirical analysis on the costs and results of the whole machinery of cartel damages actions, let alone in more sophisticated studies on their effectiveness and efficiency as an instrument of deterrence.

57. Based on this data set, a study by *Peyer* provides certain empirical insights into private competition litigation from 2005 to 2007. Of 338 identified cases only 11 cases were based on an allegation of horizontal price-fixing and in only 40 cases did plaintiffs apply for damages. This reflects the fact that the study focuses on a time period where follow-on cartel damages actions were still underdeveloped in Germany. *See* Sebastian Peyer, *Private Antitrust Litigation in Germany from 2005 to 2007: Empirical Evidence* (2012) 8 J. Comp. L. & Econ. 331–359.
58. Empirical data on private competition litigation (including damages actions) in the EU is provided in Barry Rodger (ed.), *Competition Law Comparative Private Enforcement and Collective Redress across the EU* Chapters 3 and 4, 73–156 (Wolters Kluwer 2014).
59. Rengier, *supra* n. 3, at 613–619.
60. *Ibid.*, 616.
61. *See* Markus Balser, *Schienenkartell: Deutsche Bahn treibt Hunderte Millionen Euro Schadenersatz ein*, https://www.sueddeutsche.de/wirtschaft/illegale-preisabsprachen-schienenkartell-deutsche-bahn-treibt-hunderte-millionen-euro-schadenersatz-ein-1.2915565 (accessed 8 April 2019).

B. Favourable developments

1. *Clarifying legal standards: German courts appear to be on the right track (though it is not a fast track)*

Competition damages litigation is a risky business. It requires considerable upfront investment by plaintiffs, which is to a large part case-specific, in particular investment in the gathering and processing of information and data and on economic surveys. Against this background, it appears particularly problematic if the legal standards applicable to actions for competition damages are not sufficiently clarified.

Given that now more than seventeen years have passed since *Courage v Crehan* (2001) and more than thirteen years since the subsequent reform of the German Competition Act (2005), one may well regard it as somewhat unsatisfactory that some issues that are crucial to the 'plain vanilla' follow-on cartel damages action – in particular certain questions with regard to proof and evidence – have still not yet been comprehensively addressed by the Federal Court of Justice.

Yet there is a significant body of case law that has been developed, partly through four important judgments by the Federal Court of Justice but for the most part by the Higher Regional Courts, which act as courts of appeal. The judgments of the latter have, on the one hand, already contributed substantially to a certain clarification of the law and, on the other hand, if challenged, provide the Federal Court of Justice with the opportunity to further clarify the law. At the moment, there are quite a few cases pending before the Federal Court of Justice. Therefore, it seems fair to consider that we are now in the middle of a process that will lead to more legal certainty.

While the efficiency of the court proceedings and, consequently, the pace in which the jurisprudence develops, leave something to be desired – at least from the plaintiffs' point of view[62] – actual findings in present court practice give cause for optimism, as will be illustrated by the two following examples.

a) *The right to interest in 'old' cases*

Through the 7th amendment of the Competition Act, the German legislature imposed an obligation on competition law infringers to pay interest from the time the damage occurred.[63] The provision came into force on 1 July 2005. In a recent decision, the Federal Court of Justice clarified that the provision was not applicable to claims for damages that had arisen before, i.e., with regard to competition infringements and inflicted damage that had occurred before 1 July 2005.[64] Those 'old' cases were considered to be subject to the law as it stood before the reform.

62. *See also* text accompanying *infra* n. 125.
63. Article 33(3) of the Competition Act 2005, now Article 33a(4) of the German Competition Act 2017.
64. BGH, 12 June 2018, KZR 56/16, para. 49 (*Grauzementkartell II*).

The Federal Court of Justice realised, however, that such a result might conflict with the EU law principle of effectiveness. Quoting the ECJ's judgment in *Manfredi*,[65] the court ascertained that the award of interest in accordance with national law constitutes 'an essential component of compensation'.[66] Furthermore, the court emphasised that the ECJ was referring in *Manfredi* to its judgment in *Marshall*, which did not concern infringements of competition law but a discriminatory dismissal of an employee.[67] Based on this reference and the ECJ's statement in *Marshall*, according to which 'full compensation for the loss and damage sustained as a result of discriminatory dismissal cannot leave out of account factors, such as the effluxion of time, which may in fact reduce its value',[68] the Federal Court of Justice concluded that EU law required a payment of interest right from the time that a (competition) damage occurred.[69]

To bring German law in line with this standard derived from the EU principle of 'effectiveness', the court established in the *Cement Cartel Case* that section 849 of the Civil Code (Bürgerliches Gesetzbuch) should be applicable to competition damages claims. This provision of the Civil Code's section on 'Torts' states:

> If compensation is to be paid for the value of a thing of which a person has been deprived, or if compensation is to be paid for the decrease in value of a thing as a result of damage, then the injured person may demand interest on the amount to be paid in compensation from the date on which the determination of the value is based.[70]

The court argued that as the provision had been held to be applicable if a person has been deprived of a certain sum of money as a consequence of a tortious act,[71] it may also cover (at any rate by way of analogy) a case where customers had to pay prices that were inflated because of an anticompetitive conspiracy.[72]

The Federal Court of Justice's judgment, though at this point arguably not contentious from a policy perspective, shows in its reasoning a degree of loyalty towards the EU law principle of 'effectiveness' that is remarkable for three reasons.

First, while the court's reading of the ECJ's case law is convincing and in line with the Commission's view,[73] it was by no means straightforward to assume that general

65. ECJ, Case C-295/04 *Vincenzo Manfredi v Lloyd Adriatico Assicurazioni SpA* [2006] ECR I-6619, para. 97.
66. BGH, KZR 56/16, *supra* n. 64, at para. 46 ('*unerlässlicher Bestandteil einer Entschädigung wegen eines Kartellrechtsverstoßes*' ['indispensable element of a compensation for a competition infringement']).
67. *Ibid.*
68. ECJ, Case C-271/91 *Marshall v Southampton and South West Hampshire Area Health Authority* [1993] ECR I-4367, para. 31.
69. BGH, KZR 56/16, *supra* n. 64, at para. 46.
70. Section 849 of the Civil Code (Bürgerliches Gesetzbuch) reads: 'Verzinsung der Ersatzsumme. Ist wegen der Entziehung einer Sache der Wert oder wegen der Beschädigung einer Sache die Wertminderung zu ersetzen, so kann der Verletzte Zinsen des zu ersetzenden Betrags von dem Zeitpunkt an verlangen, welcher der Bestimmung des Wertes zugrunde gelegt wird'.
71. BGH, 26 November 2007, II ZR 167/06, [2008] NJW 1084.
72. BGH, KZR 56/16, *supra* n. 64, at para. 46.
73. *See* European Commission, Staff Working Paper accompanying the White Paper on Damages action for breach of the EC antitrust rules, 2 April 2008, SEC(2008) 404, para. 187 ('With regard

principles of EU law prescribe a right to interest from the moment harm has been inflicted upon a cartel victim. In *Manfredi*, the ECJ itself had left it at a general reference to its statements related to the right to interest in *Marshall* without explicitly clarifying whether it had indeed such a consequence in mind.[74]

Second, the judgment in the *Cement Cartel Case* was solely based on an infringement of the German Competition Act but not of Article 101 or 102 TFEU.[75] Therefore, the Federal Court of Justice acted under no EU law obligation to achieve compliance with the standards the ECJ had derived from the principle of effectiveness, and it thus autonomously aligned German competition damages law with EU standards.[76]

Finally, the Federal Court of Justice implemented the standard it derived from EU law based on an analogy or at least a very broad understanding of section 849 of the Civil Code, which certainly is on the one hand well defensible on the basis of its previous jurisprudence and which had been suggested in academic literature,[77] but which on the other hand certainly did not appear to be an evident solution. This shows the court's willingness to make a certain 'methodological effort' to bring about a consistency of the German law on competition damages with the EU law principle of 'effectiveness'.

b) *Rules of proof and evidence*

One of the essential challenges of any plaintiff in a follow-on damages action is to show that the cartel inflicted harm on her. Such proof of actual damage can be provided through two steps. First, the plaintiff shows that the cartel had an actual impact on market parameters, in particular on prices. Second, the plaintiff demonstrates that the cartel affected her transaction with a cartelist (or with a competitor if a claim is based on alleged 'umbrella pricing'), in other words that she purchased at the inflated market price. The rules of proof that apply in this regard are crucial as to the effectiveness of competition damages actions as an enforcement mechanism.

---

to the payment of interest, the Court refers to its earlier judgment in the 1993 Marshall case. … The Court's objective is thus clearly to ensure that the victim is given the real value of the loss suffered. The reference in *Manfredi* to the payment of interest should therefore be understood as covering the whole period from the time the damage occurred until the capital sum awarded is actually paid' (references omitted)).

74. Note that, while Article 3(2) of the Directive 2014/104/EU mentions merely the right to payment of interest as an integral part of the principle of full compensation, it requires in recital 12 that payment of interest 'should be due from the time when the harm occurred' (with an implicit reference to the ECJ's statement in *Marshall* as quoted in the text accompanying supra n. 68).
75. BGH, KZR 56/16, *supra* n. 64, at para. 46.
76. Such a uniform interpretation is, however, certainly in line with the legislature's intention.
77. Eckart Bueren, *Zinsen ab Schadenseintritt schon vor der 7. GWB-Novelle!* [2012] WuW 1056, 1059–1061.

(1) Applicability of the lowered standard of proof pursuant to section 287 of the German Code of Civil Procedure

In *Lottoblock II*, a judgment rendered in 2016, the Federal Court of Justice held that, instead of the regular standard of proof pursuant to section 286 of the Code of Civil Procedure,[78] the relaxed standard pursuant to section 287 of the Code[79] should apply as to whether a plaintiff suffered actual damage due to an established competition infringement.[80] It is sufficient, therefore, that the judge finds 'on a reliable basis *a clear probability*' of an infliction of harm on the plaintiff.[81]

The Federal Court of Justice explicitly referred to the EU law principle of effectiveness as an essential reason for this lowered standard of proof. The court stipulated that an application of the regular standard would have entailed a risk for the effective enforcement of EU competition law. It stressed that, given the plurality of factors that may have an impact on market parameters, there would otherwise be a considerable number of cases where the infliction of harm could not be demonstrated to the full conviction of the court as required under section 286 of the Code of Civil Procedure.[82]

According to the adjudication of the Federal Court of Justice, the latter (stricter) standard applies, however, as to the question of whether a cartel affected the price or other parameters of the individual transaction between the plaintiff and the defendant cartelist or – in the case of alleged umbrella damages – between the plaintiff and a firm outside the circle of cartel participants.[83] Consequently, the court does distinguish between 'Schadensentstehung' ('occurrence of damage') and 'Kartellbetroffenheit' ('being affected by a cartel').[84]

---

78. Section 286(1) of the German Code of Civil Procedure reads as follows: 'The court is to decide, at its discretion and conviction, and taking account of the entire content of the hearings and the results obtained by evidence being taken, if any, whether an allegation as to fact is to be deemed true or untrue. The judgment is to set out the reasons informing the conviction of the judges.'
79. Section 287(1) of the German Code of Civil Procedure reads as follows: 'Should the issue of whether or not damages have occurred, and the amount of the damage or of the equivalent in money to be reimbursed, be in dispute among the parties, the court shall rule on this issue at its discretion and conviction, based on its evaluation of all circumstances. The court may decide at its discretion whether or not – and if so, in which scope – any taking of evidence should be ordered as applied for, or whether or not any experts should be involved to prepare a report. The court may examine the party tendering evidence on the damage or the equivalent in money thereof ... .'
80. BGH, 12 July 2016, KZR 25/14, BGHZ 211, 146, paras 42–44 (*Lottoblock II*).
81. BGH, KZR 25/14, *supra* n. 80, at para. 41 ('*Für die richterliche Überzeugungsbildung reicht daher eine deutlich überwiegende, auf gesicherter Grundlage beruhende Wahrscheinlichkeit aus, dass ein Schaden entstanden ist* ...') (emphasis added).
82. BGH, KZR 25/14, *supra* n. 80, at para. 45 ('*Würde bei der Frage, ob durch einen Kartellrechtsverstoß ein Schaden entstanden ist, statt § 287 Abs. 1 ZPO die Vorschrift des § 286 ZPO angewendet, so bestünde die Gefahr, dass die effektive Durchsetzung des Kartellrechts der Union verhindert würde, weil im Hinblick auf die Vielzahl auf dem Markt wirksamer Einflüsse häufig nicht zur vollen Überzeugung des Gerichts feststehen wird, dass ein durch einen Kartellrechtsverstoß betroffener Marktteilnehmer auch tatsächlich einen Schaden erlitten hat*').
83. BGH, KZR 25/14, *supra* n. 80, at para. 47; BGH, 11 December 2018, KZR 26/17, [2019] WuW, 91, 94, para. 59 (*Schienenkartell*).
84. BGH, KZR 26/17, *supra* n. 83, at para. 47.

(2) Cartelisation as prima facie evidence or as basis for a positive presumption for a generally increased price level

Based on section 33a(2) of the Competition Act – which transposes Article 17(2) of the Directive into German law – plaintiffs who lodge claims for damages that have arisen since 26 December 2016 may benefit from a rebuttable presumption that 'a cartel results in harm'.

With regard to 'older' cases, i.e., effectively concerning all cases that are currently pending, the courts have also applied rules to ease the burden of proof on the plaintiffs, which are, however, not as far-reaching as section 33a(2) of the Competition Act. Beginning with a judgment of the Kammergericht Berlin in 2009,[85] a considerable number of Higher Regional Courts had accepted the existence of a cartel as prima facie evidence of price-increasing effects ('*allgemein preissteigernde Wirkung*').[86] Nevertheless, in a recent judgment, the Federal Court of Justice rejected this approach, arguing that a prima facie evidence rule could only apply if there was a 'very high' probability that a cartel would result in a generally increased price level – which the court declined to accept given the plurality of factors that influence price formation.[87] Instead, the court argued that there remains a 'positive presumption' ('*tatsächliche Vermutung*') that cartelisation will result in higher prices. That means that if the existence of a cartel can be demonstrated, this has to be considered strong circumstantial evidence ('*starke indizielle Bedeutung*') for a generally increased price level.[88] As a consequence, the position of plaintiffs is weakened, as the courts will have to consider all the facts pleaded by the defendant party (and not only those facts that are capable of rebutting the prima facie evidence) as part of an overall assessment.[89]

Remarkably, in a judgment handed down shortly after, the Higher Regional Court in Düsseldorf explicitly rebutted the standard established by the Federal Court of Justice and indicated that it would not follow the precedent. The Higher Regional Court argued that the Federal Court Justice had for no good reason deviated from its previous jurisprudence. Moreover, though the presumption of damage pursuant to section 33(2) of the Competition Act was not yet applicable in the case, the court considered that the intention of the legislature should have been taken into account already in the interpretation of the applicable law.[90] Nonetheless, as the Higher Regional Court assumed that the plaintiff had provided sufficient evidence to meet also the higher standard of proof, it considered the controversy not decisive for the dispute at hand.[91]

85. Kammergericht (KG), 1 October 2009, 2 U 10/03 Kart, WuW/E DE-R 2773, 2777 (*Berliner Transportbeton*).
86. OLG Karlsruhe, 31 July 2013, 6 U 51/12 Kart, [2014] NZKart, 366, 367 (*Feuerwehrfahrzeuge*); OLG Frankfurt, 17 November 2015, 11 U 73/11 Kart, [2016] WuW 312, 312 et seq. (*Grauzementkartell*); OLG Karlsruhe, 9 November 2016, 6 U 204/15 Kart (2), [2017] WuW 43, 44 et seq. (*Grauzementkartell*); Thüringer OLG, 22 February 2017, 2 U 583/15 Kart, [2017] WuW 203, 205 et seq. (*Schienenkartell*).
87. BGH, KZR 26/17, *supra* n. 83, at paras 50–57.
88. BGH, KZR 26/17, *supra* n. 83, at paras 55–56.
89. BGH, KZR 26/17, *supra* n. 83, at para. 58.
90. OLG Düsseldorf, 23 January 2019, VI-U Kart 18/17, [2019] WuW 158, 161 (*Schienenkartell II*).
91. OLG Düsseldorf, VI-U Kart 18/17, *supra* n. 90, at 160.

This indicates that, even though the Federal Court of Justice's rejection of a prima facie evidence rule has increased the burden of proof for plaintiffs, this might in practice not yield different results as cartelisation still has to be considered strong circumstantial evidence of a generally increased price level.

In addition, it is worth noting that Article 17(2) of the Directive and section 33a(2) of the Competition Act do not relate to the existence of umbrella effects. In this respect, the general domestic rules of proof continue to apply after the transposition of the Directive. Several Higher Regional Courts have already assumed a 'general experience' according to which a cartel has caused an umbrella effect.[92] This was effectively accepted by the Federal Court of Justice in a case where the cartel had a market share of 71.3 % and where the pricing by the cartelists was transparent to their competitors, though it must be noted that the court had to review in this case (only) a declaratory judgment and, thus, assumed a rather low standard of proof in regard to the question of whether damage had been inflicted on the plaintiff.[93]

(3) Cartelisation as prima facie evidence of an effect on the individual transaction

Pursuant to Article 17(2) of the Directive, transposed in section 33a(2) sentence 1 of the Competition Act, there is a presumption that 'a cartel results in harm'. But even this newly introduced rebuttable presumption does not release the plaintiff from the burden of showing that her individual transaction had been affected by a cartel.

During the last years, various Higher Regional Courts had adopted a prima facie evidence rule whereby an individual transaction is deemed to have been affected by a cartel if it can be established that the transaction falls in the objective, geographical, and temporal scope of the cartel agreement.[94]

While many observers had reckoned that the Federal Court of Justice would dwell on this issue in the *Cement Cartel Case*, the court stressed that the standard of proof had to be regarded as significantly relaxed as the appeal concerned an action for declaratory relief. Thus, the plaintiff had to demonstrate only a 'certain probability' of a damage,[95] or, in other words, it suffices to show that the possibility of harm actually having been inflicted upon the plaintiff is greater than merely 'remote'.[96] On this basis, the court, first, confirmed that there is a 'general economic experience' that firms cartelise in order to achieve higher profits and, consequently, that there is 'a high probability' that a cartel has been formed and maintained because it achieves higher

92. OLG Karlsruhe, 6 U 51/12 Kart, *supra* n. 86, at 367; OLG Karlsruhe, 6 U 204/15 Kart (2), *supra* n. 86, at 45 et seq.; Thüringer OLG, 2 U 583/15, *supra* n. 86, at 206.
93. BGH, KZR 56/16, *supra* n. 64, at paras 38–40.
94. *See*, e.g., OLG Karlsruhe, 6 U 51/12 Kart, *supra* n. 86, at 367; Thüringer OLG, 2 U 583/15 Kart, *supra* n. 86, at 206.
95. BGH, KZR 56/16, *supra* n. 64, at para. 34 ('gewisse Wahrscheinlichkeit für den Eintritt eines Schadens').
96. BGH, KZR 56/16, *supra* n. 64, at para. 3 ('Insoweit genügt die nicht entfernt liegende Möglichkeit eines Schadens').

prices than under competitive market conditions.[97] Second, based on the relaxed standard of proof applicable in actions for declaratory relief, the court assumed without hesitation that it is in the same way sufficiently probable that the cartel's customers suffered damages caused by the inflated market price.[98] Consequently, the court confirmed the appealed judgment without explicitly addressing the issue of prima facie evidence.

However, in its recent judgment on a follow-on damages action concerning the 'railway track cartel', the Federal Court of Justice emphasised that the implementation of a cartel agreement might in practice face various difficulties, and therefore the court refused to accept the prima facie evidence rule as it had been developed by the lower courts.[99] Instead – in a similar way as with the question of whether a cartel inflated prices – the court assumed that there is nevertheless strong circumstantial evidence that the terms of a contract are affected if it falls within the objective, geographical, and temporal scope of the cartel agreement.[100] Thus, while it is true that the Federal Court of Justice has insisted on a stricter standard of proof, the practical consequences of this remain to be seen when it is applied by the lower courts. A subsequent judgment handed down by the Higher Regional Court in Düsseldorf[101] indicates that it may presumably still be difficult for defendant cartelists to overcome the 'positive presumption' ('*tatsächliche Vermutung*') so as to allow the conclusion that an individual contract that came within the ambit of a cartel agreement was nevertheless not affected.

(4) Preliminary conclusions

The rules on the standard of proof as to the question of whether a cartel has inflicted harm on a plaintiff are rather fragmented. Yet, in all probability, we will see even more nuanced doctrines developed by the courts in the future. The law is in flux, and we are still awaiting clarifying statements by the Federal Court of Justice on important issues. But the adjudication of the German courts gives rise to positive expectations as it indicates their readiness to establish reasonable standards that do not ask too much of the plaintiffs and that, thus, do not obstruct the role of actions for competition damages as an enforcement mechanism. In further waves of cases that will reach the Federal Court of Justice at some point in the future, the courts will have the chance to clarify the still somewhat open issue of what the reduced standard of proof pursuant to Article 287 of the Code of Civil Procedure means for the estimation of the amount of harm inflicted upon a plaintiff. In particular, the courts will have to address what the minimum standards are that plaintiffs have to meet in order to provide the court with sufficient basis for an estimation of the actual damage.

97. BGH, KZR 56/16, *supra* n. 64, at para. 35.
98. *Ibid.*
99. BGH, KZR 26/17, *supra* n. 83, at para. 62. Note that the judgment concerned an appeal against a preliminary decision on the merits but not a declaratory judgment. Thus, the court did apply the normal standard of proof pursuant to section 286 of the Code of Civil Procedure.
100. BGH, KZR 26/17, *supra* n. 83, at para. 61.
101. OLG Düsseldorf, VI-U Kart 18/17, *supra* n. 90, at 158–160.

2. *Taking 'effectiveness' seriously: the German legislature as 'repairer'*

Even beyond the transposition of the Directive, the German legislature has proven loyal to the principle of 'effectiveness'. An illustrative example concerns plaintiffs' cost risks due to third-party interventions. Where a plaintiff sues one or several of the cartelists, the fellow cartelists receiving a third-party notice will typically intervene in support of the defendant cartelist(s). The possibility of such third-party interventions generates significant cost risks because it is the general rule under German law that plaintiffs who do not prevail in a dispute have to bear not only the costs of the opposing party but also the intervenors' costs.[102] These cost risks are, for one thing, difficult to calculate because a plaintiff cannot foresee the number of intervenors. For another thing, in particular, a judgment by the Higher Regional Court in Düsseldorf made it apparent that the involved cost risks were quite substantial. In contrast to earlier decisions by other Higher Regional Courts,[103] the court in Düsseldorf held that each third-party intervenor was entitled to compensation of its legal costs calculated on the basis of the full amount in dispute.[104]

The German legislature recognised that this situation created a real risk that potential plaintiffs might be deterred from bringing suit because of unpredictable and inappropriately high trial costs due to third-party interventions.[105] Consequently, the legislature introduced section 89a(3) of the Competition Act, which states:

> the reimbursement of costs shall only cover the intervener's legal assistance costs on the basis of the value in dispute which the court determines at its own discretion. In the case of several intervenors, the total amount of the values in dispute of all individual interventions shall not exceed the value in dispute in the main action.[106]

Thus, the legislature has, first, granted courts discretion to determine the value in dispute (based on which the refundable costs of an intervenor have to be calculated) and, second, reduced significantly the maximum cost risk due to third-party interventions.

102. *See* section 101(1) of the Code of Civil Procedure in conjunction with sections 91 et seq. of the Code of Civil Procedure.
103. *See*, e.g., OLG Köln, 30 March 2012, 16 W 30/11, paras 6–8.
104. OLG Düsseldorf, 18 February 2015, VI-W Kart 1/15, paras 3–5 (*CDC Zement*).
105. Deutscher Bundestag, Drucksache 18/10207, 7 November 2016, Gesetzentwurf der Bundesregierung, Entwurf eines Neunten Gesetzes zur Änderung des Gesetzes gegen Wettbewerbsbeschränkungen, 100.
106. Section 89a(3) of the Competition Act reads: 'Ist in einer Rechtsstreitigkeit, in der ein Anspruch nach § 33a Absatz 1 geltend gemacht wird, ein Nebenintervenient einer Hauptpartei beigetreten, hat der Gegner, soweit ihm Kosten des Rechtsstreits auferlegt werden oder soweit er sie übernimmt, die Rechtsanwaltskosten der Nebenintervention nur nach dem Gegenstandswert zu erstatten, den das Gericht nach freiem Ermessen festsetzt. Bei mehreren Nebeninterventionen darf die Summe der Gegenstandswerte der einzelnen Nebeninterventionen den Streitwert der Hauptsache nicht übersteigen'.

C. Unsolved issues: the lack of collective redress as a major flaw

There can be little doubt that the biggest flaw of the German legal framework is the lack of any mechanism of collective redress. Certainly, competition damage claims can be bundled through assignments. But this option involves considerable barriers which, though not unsurmountable, make bundling cumbersome and costly.[107] Hence, particularly in regard to scattered and low-value damage, there remains a significant enforcement gap. At most a modest improvement has been achieved through the new law on model case proceedings in business-to-consumer disputes, which came into force on 1 November 2018.[108] This instrument will probably only be of minor significance for competition damages actions as it applies only to claims by final consumers and as standing rights are restricted to consumer protection associations which may apply for declaratory relief.[109]

Given that the legal framework as established by the Directive foresees a passing-on defence and, in fact, facilitates such a defence compared to the status quo under German law after the Federal Court of Justice's judgment in *ORWI*, there is a realistic probability that we will see cases where the courts ascertain a passing-on of cartel-induced costs to final consumers. It is especially in those scenarios that an efficient mechanism of collective redress is indispensable to safeguard the role of competition damages actions as an effective enforcement instrument. It is highly significant, and indeed intriguing, that when the EU Commission prepared the Directive on Actions for Competition Damages and considered whether a passing-on defence should be available or not, it argued the other way around: because the Commission had in mind an approach that was intended to enable even those claimants 'who find themselves towards the end of the distribution chain', and thus typically suffer only 'relatively small and scattered damage', to seek compensation, it was considered incoherent to refuse the passing-on defence 'on the basis of the assumption that these claimants do not bring a damages claim'.[110] Therefore, as we are now in a situation

107. *See* sub. IV.D, *infra*.
108. Sections 606 et seq. of the Code on Civil Procedure.
109. *See* on the various shortcomings of this instrument and its presumably only marginal role for competition damages actions, Jürgen Basedow, *Trippelschritte zum kollektiven Rechtsschutz. Aktionismus in Berlin und Brüssel* [2018] EuZW 609, 610–611; Martin Mengden, *David gegen Goliath im Kartellschadensersatzrecht – Lassen sich Musterfeststellungsklagen bzw. EU-Verbandsklagen als kollektive Folgeklagen einsetzen?* [2018] NZKart 398–405; Roman A. Mallmann & Sarah Erne, *Musterfeststellungsklage und Kartellschadensersatz* [2019] NZKart 77–83; Wolfgang Wurmnest, '*Mehr Freiheit wagen im Kartell- und Marktregulierungsrecht*' in Anatol Dutta & Christian Heinze (eds), '*Mehr Freiheit wagen' – Beiträge zur Emeritierung von Jürgen Basedow*, 240–243 (Mohr Siebeck 2018); Joachim Bornkamm and Jan Tolkmitt in Eugen Langen and Hermann-Josef Bunte (eds), *Kartellrecht* Vol. 1, §33b GWB para. 17, 1036–1037 (13th ed., Luchterhand 2018).
110. *See* European Commission, SEC(2008) 404, *supra* n. 73, at para. 212 ('Moreover, since the Commission considers it appropriate to address the obstacles faced by claimants who find themselves towards the end of the distribution chain (thus more likely to have relatively small and scattered damage and a long causation line to the infringement), it would be incoherent to devise a policy on the basis of the assumption that these claimants do not bring a damages claim. As a result, the defendant in an antitrust damages case would have to be entitled to raise the passing-on defence against the claimant who is not a final consumer').

where EU law, on the one hand, stipulates the availability of the passing-on defence and, on the other hand, merely recommends the introduction of mechanisms of collective redress,[111] it is the responsibility of Member States to bring about consistency and, consequently, to introduce effective mechanisms that also allow for compensation in case of mass and dispersed damage.

Finally, it should be noted that, in light of the dispersion of damages actions as we currently observe in Germany, the availability of effective mechanisms of collective redress might also seem to be in the interest of alleged competition law infringers. Currently, a number of cartelists have been sued based on the same competition infringement before a multitude of courts. This means a sharp rise in litigation costs not only for the defendant cartelists but also for their fellow cartelists, who will typically intervene in support of the defendant(s).

D. Some ambiguous findings: is the glass half full or half empty?

The institutional framework for competition damages actions in Germany is by and large characterised by a fair number of features, the quality of which very much lies in the eye of the beholder: while there is certainly considerable room for improvement, the conditions are for the most part neither specifically obstructive nor specifically facilitative of actions for competition damages. Whether the proverbial glass should be considered half full or half empty very much depends on the perspective that one adopts.[112] This will be illustrated below by some features with respect to costs, the expertise of the judiciary, and the efficiency of court proceedings.

1. Costs

Court fees are calculated based on the value in dispute and do not depend on the actual length and complexity of the litigation. There is a cap for the value in dispute at EUR 30 million. Consequently, when plaintiffs sue for damages at an amount of EUR 30 million or more, they have to pay upfront a court fee that amounts to approximately EUR 330,000.[113]

The 'loser-pays' rule applies. The losing party has to pay the court fees and her opponent's litigation costs, including the costs of third parties who have intervened. The reimbursement of lawyers' fees is limited by statute. In addition, pursuant to section 89a(1) of the Competition Act, the court may order that the value of the dispute is reduced in support of a party who demonstrates that:

111. Commission Recommendation 2013/396/EU of 11 June 2013 on common principles for injunctive and compensatory collective redress mechanisms in the Member States concerning violations of rights granted under Union Law [2013], OJ L 201/60.
112. A comparative overview on institutional aspects of private enforcement is provided in Barry Rodger, '*Institutions and Mechanism to Facilitate Private Enforcement*' in Barry Rodger (ed.), *Competition Law Comparative Private Enforcement and Collective Redress across the EU* Chapter 2, 23–71 (Wolters Kluwer 2014).
113. In fact, EUR 329,208. *See* section 34 of the Court Fees Act (Gerichtskostengesetz) and No. 1210 of the Cost Catalogue of the Court Fees Act.

> its economic situation would be seriously jeopardised if it had to bear the costs of litigation calculated on the basis of the full value in dispute. ... The court may make its order contingent on the party credibly demonstrating that the costs of litigation to be borne by it are not directly or indirectly assumed by a third party.[114]

This effectively means that both the court fees and the lawyers' fees this party may have to bear in the event she loses the litigation are reduced. Whether this newly introduced rule will have some practical effect remains to be seen. As already mentioned and, indeed, very significant from a practical point of view, in section 89a(3) of the Competition Act, the legislature introduced a ceiling to limit cost risks due to third-party interventions.[115]

'No-win-no-fee' agreements (contingency fees or conditional fees) are permitted only:

> for an individual case and only if the client, upon reasonable consideration, would be deterred from taking legal proceedings without the agreement of quota litis on account of his economic situation.[116]

These conditions are presumably not often fulfilled in competition damages cases.

---

114. Section 89a(1) of the Competition Act reads: 'Ist (1) Macht in einer Rechtsstreitigkeit, in der ein Anspruch nach den §§ 33, 33a Absatz 1 oder § 34a geltend gemacht wird, eine Partei glaubhaft, dass die Belastung mit den Prozesskosten nach dem vollen Streitwert ihre wirtschaftliche Lage erheblich gefährden würde, so kann das Gericht auf ihren Antrag anordnen, dass die Verpflichtung dieser Partei zur Zahlung von Gerichtskosten sich nach einem ihrer Wirtschaftslage angepassten Teil des Streitwerts bemisst. Das Gericht kann die Anordnung davon abhängig machen, dass die Partei glaubhaft macht, dass die von ihr zu tragenden Kosten des Rechtsstreits weder unmittelbar noch mittelbar von einem Dritten übernommen werden ...'.
115. *See* sub. III.B.2, *supra.*
116. Section 4a(1) of the Law on the Remuneration of Attorneys (*Rechtsanwaltsvergütungsgesetz*) reads: 'Ein Erfolgshonorar (§ 49b Abs. 2 Satz 1 der Bundesrechtsanwaltsordnung) darf nur für den Einzelfall und nur dann vereinbart werden, wenn der Auftraggeber aufgrund seiner wirtschaftlichen Verhältnisse bei verständiger Betrachtung ohne die Vereinbarung eines Erfolgshonorars von der Rechtsverfolgung abgehalten würde. In einem gerichtlichen Verfahren darf dabei für den Fall des Misserfolgs vereinbart werden, dass keine oder eine geringere als die gesetzliche Vergütung zu zahlen ist, wenn für den Erfolgsfall ein angemessener Zuschlag auf die gesetzliche Vergütung vereinbart wird. Für die Beurteilung nach Satz 1 bleibt die Möglichkeit, Beratungs- oder Prozesskostenhilfe in Anspruch zu nehmen, außer Betracht.' Section 49b(2) of the Federal Lawyers Act (Bundesrechtsanwaltsordnung) reads: 'Vereinbarungen, durch die eine Vergütung oder ihre Höhe vom Ausgang der Sache oder vom Erfolg der anwaltlichen Tätigkeit abhängig gemacht wird oder nach denen der Rechtsanwalt einen Teil des erstrittenen Betrages als Honorar erhält (Erfolgshonorar), sind unzulässig, soweit das Rechtsanwaltsvergütungsgesetz nichts anderes bestimmt. Vereinbarungen, durch die der Rechtsanwalt sich verpflichtet, Gerichtskosten, Verwaltungskosten oder Kosten anderer Beteiligter zu tragen, sind unzulässig. Ein Erfolgshonorar im Sinne des Satzes 1 liegt nicht vor, wenn lediglich vereinbart wird, dass sich die gesetzlichen Gebühren ohne weitere Bedingungen erhöhen'.

2. *Expertise of the judiciary*

Competition damages actions must be filed with a Regional Court (Landgericht).[117] All but one of the sixteen German states (*Länder*) have made use of the option to refer private law actions that involve issues of competition law to one specific Regional Court for the districts of several Regional Courts.[118] Thus, there are twenty-four Regional Courts[119] where a competition damages action may be filed. These actions will be heard by divisions which consist of three professional judges.[120] Within a Regional Court, these actions may be assigned to one or several specialised divisions. At the Regional Court of Mannheim, for example, which has rendered the most judgments in cartel damages cases of all Regional Courts between 2003 and 2017[121] and where a considerable number of competition damages actions are pending, these actions have been exclusively assigned to one specialised division.[122]

Thus, the institutional framework allows for a reasonable degree of specialisation of those chambers and judges, respectively, that have to deal with competition damages actions. Yet, where a specialised court, such as the Competition Appeals Tribunal (CAT) in the UK, is competent to hear cases from across the country, this naturally entails still greater opportunities for judges to acquire special expertise.

3. *Efficiency of court proceedings*

Documents can be submitted electronically to the courts. But it seems fair to say that the electronic administration of documents does not yet operate smoothly everywhere. Moreover, it should not come as a surprise that section 184 of the Courts Constitution Act (*Gerichtsverfassungsgesetz*) provides that '[t]he language of the court shall be German'. Consequently, not only the decisions by the courts but also the parties'

117. *See* section 87 of the Competition Act: 'Für bürgerliche Rechtsstreitigkeiten, die die Anwendung von Vorschriften des Teils 1, des Artikels 101 oder 102 des Vertrages über die Arbeitsweise der Europäischen Union ... betreffen, sind ohne Rücksicht auf den Wert des Streitgegenstands die Landgerichte ausschließlich zuständig. ...' ('Regardless of the value of the matter in dispute, the Regional Courts [Landgerichte] shall have exclusive jurisdiction in civil actions concerning the application of provisions of Part 1, of Articles 101 or 102 of the Treaty on the Functioning of the European Union ...').
118. *See* section 89 of the Competition Act.
119. *See* for a list of those Regional Courts Bornkamm & Tolkmitt, *supra* n. 109, at Vol. 1 § 89 GWB para. 4, 1777-1778 (13th ed., Luchterhand 2018).
120. *See* section 75 of the Courts Constitution Act (*Gerichtsverfassungsgesetz*).
121. Rengier, *supra* n. 3, at 619.
122. The competent '*Zivilkammer 14*' ('Division for Civil Law No. 14') has been recently established at the Regional Court in Mannheim as a specialised division because of the particular importance of and the increasing workload due to competition damages litigation. The chamber is competent to hear not only competition damages cases but any case that involves private competition litigation (with the notable exception of cases that also concern IP law, in particular patent rights, which are assigned to chambers that are specialised in IP law). In cases that involve competition law *but not claims for competition damages*, parties have a choice to file suit either with the '*Zivilkammer 14*' or with a '*Kammer für Handelssachen*', i.e., a division that is specialised in commercial law matters. *See* section 95(2) No. 1 of the Courts Constitution Act (Gerichtsverfassungsgesetz).

submissions, applications, and requests must be written in German. However, records or documents produced as evidence need not necessarily be translated. Section 142(3) of the German Code of Civil Procedure provides that '[t]he court may direct that records or documents prepared in a foreign language be translated by a translator ...'. Thus, it lies in the discretion of the court to accept written pieces of evidence without translation.[123]

In regard to the timing and length of proceedings, anecdotal evidence of knowledgeable observers suggests a somewhat mixed bag. On the one hand, lawyers complain that, when it comes to the scheduling of hearings and the issuing of decisions, some courts are proceeding 'at a snail's pace' and their approach comes close to a 'denial of justice'.[124] On the other hand, it appears that the judges at certain Regional Courts have developed a genuine interest in actions for competition damages. Therefore, plaintiffs are advised to consider carefully the court at which they should file suit.[125]

A glance at available data reveals that the length of the median proceedings at the Regional Courts between 2003 and 2017 was one year and six months. In the same period, the median appeal proceedings at the Higher Regional Courts took one year and eight months and at the Federal Court of Justice one year; the latter result, however, was based on only two observations.[126] As the vast majority of the decisions in the data set are (only) declaratory judgments or preliminary judgments on the merits, it should be emphasised, however, that the figures do not reflect the true period a plaintiff has to reckon with until a court ultimately finds that the defendant cartelists owe him a certain amount of damages. Furthermore, it should be noted that the survey covers only court decisions (over a relatively short period of time) and not the number of actions brought before the courts or the appeals filed over time or the total number of pending cases. Thus, it seems plausible that the data set produces somewhat distorted results as cases with relatively lengthy proceedings – whether that is because the involved issues are particularly complex or because the courts work inefficiently – are underrepresented at all three instances.

IV. PARTICULAR TOPICS

A. Which entity is liable for damages?

Articles 101 and 102 TFEU, as well as the equivalent provisions under German competition law,[127] address 'undertakings'. The term defines, first of all, the substantive reach of the provisions, i.e., the category of actors to which EU competition law

123. For further details *see* Christian Armbrüster, *Fremdsprachen im Gerichtsverfahren* [2011] NJW 812, 813–814.
124. Andreas Weitbrecht, *Kartellschadensersatz 2017* [2018] NZKart 106, 111.
125. *Ibid.*
126. Rengier, *supra* n. 3, at 618.
127. This includes, first of all, sections 1 and 2 as well as section 19 of the Competition Act but also certain provisions that are particular to German competition law such as sections 20 and 29 of the Competition Act.

applies. According to the European court's case law, it encompasses 'every entity engaged in an economic activity, regardless of the legal status of the entity and the way in which it is financed'.[128] The competition law rules are 'aimed at economic units which consist of a unitary organization of personal, tangible, and intangible elements which pursues a specific economic aim on a long-term basis'.[129]

This functional (economic) approach means that the term 'undertaking' is not (necessarily) identical with concepts of natural or legal personality as enshrined in domestic laws. An 'economic unit' in the aforementioned sense may, in fact, be comprised of several natural or legal persons. Thus, it is in particular settled case law in regard to parent–subsidiary relationships that the entities constitute an 'economic unit' if the subsidiary 'has no real freedom to determine its course of action on the market'.[130]

This doctrine has, on the one hand, the consequence that coordination between those entities that form a single economic unit falls outside the scope of application of Article 101(1) TFEU.[131] On the other hand, the doctrine entails crucial and, indeed, controversial[132] consequences in respect of the sanctioning of infringements. Because sanctions cannot be addressed to the 'undertaking' as defined under Articles 101 and 102 TFEU, it is necessary to identify one or several persons, natural or legal, who can be held responsible for the infringement of the 'undertaking' and to whom, thus, a sanction can be addressed. In the light of the above, the ECJ has consistently held that, where a subsidiary that participates in a cartel and its parent company form a single economic unit, the parent may be held liable for an infringement on the ground that it forms part of the same undertaking. Consequently, the Commission may also impose the fine on the parent company 'without having to establish the personal involvement of the latter in the infringement'.[133]

What counts in our context is that the ECJ derives the single economic unit doctrine, including its consequences for the sanctioning of infringements, directly from Articles 101 and 102 TFEU.[134] From the court's perspective, the question of whether or

128. ECJ, Case C-41/90 *Höfner and Elser v Macrotron* [1991] ECR I-1979, para. 21.
129. GC, Case T-11/89 *Shell International Chemical Company v Commission* [1992] ECR II-757, para. 311.
130. ECJ, Case C-15/74 *Centrafarm BV and Adriaan De Peijper v Sterling Drug Inc* [1974] ECR 1147, para. 41.
131. ECJ, Case C-48/69 *ICI v Commission* [1972] ECR 619, para. 134.
132. Critics stress in particular that the concept is at odds with the principles of personal responsibility, the presumption of innocence, and limited liability, *see*, e.g., Marco Bronckers & Anne Vallery, *No Longer Presumed Guilty: The Impact of Fundamental Rights on Certain Dogmas of EU Competition Law* (2011) 34 World Competition 535; Karl Hofstetter & Melanie Ludescher, *Fines against Parent Companies in EU Antitrust Law: Setting Incentives for 'Best Practice Compliance'* (2010) 33 World Competition 55; Stefan Thomas, *Guilty of a Fault That One Has Not Committed. The Limits of the Group-Based Sanction Policy Carried Out by the Commission and the European Courts in EU Antitrust Law* (2012) 3 JECLAP 11–28.
133. ECJ, Case C-97/08 P *Akzo Nobel NV and Others v Commission of the European Communities* [2009] ECR I-8237, paras 58–59.
134. Note that in academic literature, the same result is justified partly with an application of the principle of effectiveness. *See*, e.g., Wolfgang Wurmnest, '*Schadensersatz wegen Verletzung des EU-Kartellrechts. Grundfragen und Entwicklungslinien*' in Oliver Remien (ed.), *Schadensersatz im europäischen Privat- und Wirtschaftsrecht* 48 (Mohr Siebeck 2012).

under which circumstances a parent company may be fined on the ground of a subsidiary's participation in a cartel is an issue not of the correct interpretation of Article 23 of Regulation 1/2003 but of the single economic unit doctrine as established under Article 101(1) TFEU.[135] Accordingly, the ECJ concluded its judgment on a cartelist's liability for umbrella damages by formulating that:

> Article 101 TFEU must be interpreted as meaning that it precludes the interpretation and application of domestic legislation enacted by a Member State which categorically excludes, for legal reasons, any *civil liability of undertakings belonging to a cartel* for loss resulting from the fact that an undertaking not party to the cartel, having regard to the practices of the cartel, set its prices higher than would otherwise have been expected under competitive conditions.[136]

This was explicitly confirmed by the ECJ in the recently handed down judgment in *Skanska*:

> the determination of the entity which is required to provide compensation for damage caused by an infringement of Article 101 TFEU is directly governed by EU law. ...
>
> Since the liability for damage caused by infringements of EU competition rules is personal in nature, the undertaking which infringes those rules must answer for the damage caused by the infringement.
>
> It follows from the foregoing consideration that the entities which are required to compensate for the damage caused by a cartel or practice prohibited by Article 101 TFEU are the undertakings, within the meaning of that provision, which have participated in that cartel or that practice.[137]

Thus, it is the court's position that the concept of a single economic unit should uniformly apply with a view to effective sanctioning of EU competition law, be it by way of fines, of cease and desist orders, or of damages actions.

Moreover, it seems evident that the European Commission shares this view on the single economic unit doctrine. In the Commission's fining decisions that concern a parent-subsidiary relationship, the Commission constantly discusses the issue of which legal person may be held liable for the infringement as part of its explanations on Article 101 TFEU under the rubric of 'addressees'. Just like the ECJ, the Commission derives the liability of a parent company for the participation of its subsidiary in a cartel directly from the concept of a single economic unit as established under Article 101

135. Case C-97/08 *Akzo Nobel and Others v Commission*, *supra* n. 133, at paras 54–66, in particular at para. 59.
136. *See* Case C-557/12 *Kone and Others*, *supra* n. 37, at para. 37 (emphasis added).
137. Case C-724/17 *Skanska Industrial Solutions and Others*, *supra* n. 41, at paras 28, 31–32. Note that the case concerned the application of the doctrine of economic continuity, which is, however, much in the same manner as the liability of parent companies, based on the single economic unit doctrine. *See supra* n. 41, at paras 36–40.

TFEU.[138] The Commission has consistently found that parent companies have 'infringed' Article 101 TFEU,[139] and thus held parent companies jointly and severally liable along with their wholly owned subsidiaries, assuming that the former had effectively exerted a decisive influence on their subsidiaries during the infringement.

In light of the foregoing, it seems clear that the Commission's view, when it prepared a proposal for a Directive on Actions for Competition Damages, was that there was simply no alternative other than to adopt the concept of an 'undertaking' understood as a single economic unit as established by the court. This explains why the EU legislature had no reason to engage in a political discussion about this issue during the legislative process, and why it stipulated without hesitation in Article 1(1) of the Directive that parties harmed 'by an infringement of competition law by an undertaking ... can effectively exercise the right to claim full compensation ... from that undertaking ...'.[140]

This means that EU law prescribes that the concept of an 'undertaking' understood as a single economic unit is applicable in competition damages cases. Therefore, the German legislature got it exactly right when it simply stipulated in section 33a (in conjunction with section 33) of the Competition Act that '[w]hoever intentionally or negligently commits an infringement' of Article 101 or 102 TFEU or of German competition law 'shall be liable for any damages arising from the infringement'. The statement that it is the 'infringer' who is liable for damages must be read as a reference to the substantive reach of competition law, which in turn makes it clear that the concept of an 'undertaking' as a single economic unit applies equally in regard to both substantive competition law and competition damages law. Consequently, the identification of the persons who can be held responsible for the infringement and who ultimately may be sued for damages must follow the same rules as established by the ECJ in regard to the Commission's fining decisions.[141]

The transposition of the Directive has been criticised on the grounds that the legal position was not sufficiently precise and clear,[142] such that potential plaintiffs could not be fully aware of the applicability of the single economic unit doctrine.[143] Certainly, on the one hand, the continuing disagreement and debate surrounding this aspect is disadvantageous to potential plaintiffs. Therefore, it would have been appropriate if the legislature had made an explicit statement in this regard during the legislative process that led to the 9th amendment of the Competition Act. On the other hand, as

138. *See*, e.g., COM, Case COMP/E-1/38.823 *PO/Elevators and Escalators* [2007] OJ C 75/19 paras 603–605; COM, Case COMP/F/38.899 *Gas Insulated Switchgear* [2007] OJ C 5/7 paras 333–339.
139. *See*, e.g., Case Comp/E-1/38.823, *supra* n. 138, at Article 1 (144); Case Comp/F/38.899, *supra* n. 138, at Article 1 (116).
140. *See* Case C-724/17 *Skanska Industrial Solutions and Others*, *supra* n. 41, at paras 33–35.
141. This is disputed in academic literature. *See* for the opposite view, e.g., Stefan Thomas and Sarah Legner, *Die wirtschaftliche Einheit im Kartellzivilrecht* [2016] NZKart 155, 156–159; Philipp von Hülsen and Boris Kasten, *Passivlegitimation von Konzernen im Kartell-Schadensersatzprozess? – Gedanken zur Umsetzung der Richtlinie 2014/104/EU* [2015] NZKart 296, 299–306.
142. This standard for a correct transposition into national law has been established by the ECJ; *see*, e.g., ECJ, Case C-144/99 *Commission v Netherlands* [2001] ECR I-3541, para. 17.
143. Kersting, *supra* n. 25, at 134.

the German legislature has established that it is the 'infringer' against whom a damages action may be brought, it has implemented a clear reference to the concept of 'undertaking' and consequently also to the notion of a single economic unit. Given that the EU legislature made it clear both in Article 1 of the Directive and by the statement that it is the 'undertaking' that is responsible for compensating for the harm caused by an infringement, the German law meets the standard for a correct transposition pursuant to Article 288(3) TFEU and Article 4(3) TEU.

While, thus, the legal situation under German law should be considered sufficiently clarified, the applicability of the single economic unit doctrine was initially not recognised by the judiciary. There were at least two final judgments by Regional Courts that rejected its application in actions for cartel damages.[144] Though these judgments concerned claims for damages that had to be assessed according to the legal situation before the transposition of the Directive, both cases involved an infringement of Article 101 TFEU and, therefore, the single economic unit doctrine ought to have been applied as required by EU law. However, after the ECJ's clarifying judgment in *Skanska*, this has now been correctly recognised at least by one Regional Court.[145]

B. *Binding effect of decisions by competition authorities*[146]

Pursuant to section 33b of the Competition Act, in competition damages actions the courts are bound:

> by a finding that an infringement has occurred, as made in a final decision by the competition authority, the European Commission, or the competition authority – or court acting as such – in another Member State of the European Union. The same applies to such findings in final court judgements on appeals against decisions pursuant to sentence 1.

The binding effect of decisions was introduced by the 7th amendment of the Competition Act in 2005. The rationale of the binding effect is essentially twofold: consistency in the application of competition law, in particular of Articles 101 and 102 TFEU, and facilitating follow-on actions for damages.[147] First, civil court judgments that run counter to (final) decisions of competition authorities should be avoided. Second, plaintiffs that bring a follow-on action for damages should be relieved of the difficulties of establishing an infringement of competition law. Thus, private plaintiffs will benefit from the investigatory powers of public authorities.

144. LG Berlin, 16 August 2013, 16 O 193/11 Kart, WuW/E DE-R 4456, 4466–4467 (*Fahrtreppen*); LG Düsseldorf, 8 September 2016, 37 O 27/11 Kart (*Aufzugskartell*).
145. LG Mannheim, 24 April 2019, 14 O 117/18 Kart, [2019] NZKart 389–390 (LKW-Kartell).
146. This section is in part based on Jens-Uwe Franck, '*Binding Effect of Decisions of National Authorities: I. Introduction with Some Comparative Remarks from a German Perspective*' in *Implementation of the EU Damages Directive into Member State law*, Conference (2017) 3 Concurrences 37–40.
147. *See* recital 34 of the Directive 2014/104/EU. This is consistent with the general purpose of 'regulat[ing] the coordination of [private and public] enforcement in a coherent manner': recital 6 of the Directive.

Insofar as a binding effect of the Commission's decisions is stipulated by the ECJ's jurisprudence in *Masterfoods* and by Article 16(1) of Regulation 1/2003, respectively,[148] section 33b of the Competition Act is of a declaratory nature only. This can be considered problematic as it risks disguising that the binding effect of the European Commission's decisions is a result of directly applicable EU law. Insofar as section 33b of the Competition Act stipulates a binding effect on decisions of national competition authorities, it transposes Article 9 of the Directive.

1. Decisions by 'foreign' NCAs ('cross-border binding effect')

The binding effect under German law goes further than Article 9 of the Directive as it also stipulates a cross-border binding effect of decisions of national NCAs, while the Directive requires only that such decisions can be presented as 'prima facie evidence'. It is noteworthy that in its initial proposal the European Commission, inspired by German law, had suggested a binding cross-border effect.[149] It appears, however, that this idea did not prevail because of doubts as to whether the administrative and court proceedings within all of the Member States would sufficiently guarantee the fundamental rights of the defendants, as safeguarded in particular by Article 47 of the Charter of Fundamental Rights of the EU.[150]

It is essentially for this reason that the binding effect of decisions of NCAs from other Member States as embodied in the Competition Act since 2005 has also not been

148. The ECJ held in *Masterfoods* 'that the national courts must refrain from rendering a judgment that conflicts either with a prior decision or with a decision contemplated by the European Commission'. ECJ, Case C-344/98 *Masterfoods Ltd v HB Ice Cream Ltd* [2000] ECR I-11369, paras 51–52. This rule has subsequently been codified in Article 16(1) of Council Regulation (EC) No 1/2003 of 16 December 2002 on the implementation of the rules on competition laid down in Articles 81 and 82 of the Treaty [2003], OJ L 1/1. In *Otis* the ECJ confirmed that the rule applied 'when national courts are hearing an action for damages for loss sustained as a result of an agreement or practice which has been found by a decision of the Commission to infringe Article 101 TFEU'. ECJ, Case C-199/11 *Europese Gemeenschap v Otis NV and Others* [2012] ECLI:EU:C:2012:684, para. 51.

149. *See* European Commission, Proposal for a Directive of the European Parliament and of the Council on certain rules governing actions for damages under national law for infringements of the competition law provisions of the Member States and of the European Union, COM(2013) 404, 36, Article 9 ('Member States shall ensure that, where national courts rule, in actions for damages under Article 101 or 102 of the Treaty or under national competition law, on agreements, decisions or practices which are already the subject of a final infringement decision by a national competition authority or by a review court, those courts cannot take decisions running counter to such finding of an infringement').

150. *See* Committee on Economic and Monetary Affairs, Rapporteur: Andreas Schwab, Report on the proposal for a Directive of the European Parliament and of the Council on certain rules governing actions for damages under national law for infringements of the competition law provisions of the Member States and of the European Union (COM(2013)0404 – C7-0170/2013 – 2013/0185(COD)), 89, where the following amendment to the Commission's initial draft had been proposed: 'This obligation is without prejudice ... to the right to an effective remedy and a fair trial, and the right of defence, pursuant to Articles 47 and 48 of the Charter, and to the right to a fair hearing pursuant to Article 6 of the ECHR. Accordingly, decisions of national competition authorities and competition courts shall be binding provided that there were no manifest errors in the investigation and provided that the rights of the defence were complied with.'

without its critics. It must not simply be (irrebuttably) presumed that the rights of defence and a fair trial as enshrined in EU law, though of course mandatory if NCAs enforce EU competition law, are sufficiently complied with throughout the Union. Therefore, courts have the prerogative to refuse the recognition of decisions of NCAs from other Member States on the ground of public policy if the right to a fair legal process was not sufficiently guaranteed during the proceedings.[151] The legal basis for this reservation can be established by way of an analogy to public-policy clauses as enshrined, for example, in section 343(1) of the German Insolvency Statute (Insolvenzordnung)[152] or Article 45(1)(a) of the Brussels Ia Regulation.[153]

The cross-border binding effect as stipulated in Article 9 of the Directive covers infringements of both Articles 101 and 102 TFEU and national competition law, i.e., of:

> provisions ... that predominantly pursue the same objective as Articles 101 and 102 TFEU and that are applied to the same case and in parallel to Union competition law pursuant to Article 3(1) of Regulation (EC) No 1/2003.[154]

This latter aspect is not reflected in the text of section 33b of the Competition Act, according to which the cross-border binding effect applies only to a finding of an infringement of Articles 101 and 102 TFEU. A glance at the legislative materials reveals that the German legislature had recognised that the finding of an infringement of national competition law by a competition authority of another Member State must be considered prima facie evidence of the existence of such an infringement. Nevertheless, the legislature assumed that no legislative amendment was necessary in this regard.[155] On the one hand, it is true that the concept of prima facie evidence as such is well established under German law, and, thus, the courts should indeed have less of a problem construing German law in compliance with Article 9 of the Directive. Yet, on the other hand, the ECJ has consistently held that, while a proper implementation of a

151. *See* European Commission, Staff Working Paper accompanying the White Paper on Damages action, *supra* n. 73, at para. 162 ('The rights of defence and fair trial are guaranteed by the European Convention on Human Rights and the EU Charter on Fundamental Rights and all Member States' instances are held to fully respect them in the proceedings that lead to an NCA decision and in subsequent review court proceedings. The Commission would nonetheless see no objection if Member States were to introduce an additional safeguard ensuring the protection of the rights of defence, and to make the binding effect of an NCA decision from another Member State subject to an exception analogous to that contained in Article 34(1) of Council Regulation (EC) No 44/2001 of 22 December 2000 on jurisdiction and the recognition and enforcement of judgments in civil and commercial matters [2000], OJ L 12/1 as regards fair legal process').
152. Section 343(1) of the German Insolvency Statute reads: 'Anerkennung. (1) Die Eröffnung eines ausländischen Insolvenzverfahrens wird anerkannt. Dies gilt nicht, ... soweit die Anerkennung zu einem Ergebnis führt, das mit wesentlichen Grundsätzen des deutschen Rechts offensichtlich unvereinbar ist, insbesondere soweit sie mit den Grundrechten unvereinbar ist.' ('Recognition. (1) The opening of foreign insolvency proceedings shall be recognized. This shall not apply ... where recognition leads to a result which is manifestly incompatible with major principles of German law, in particular where it is incompatible with basic rights.').
153. Regulation (EU) No 1215/2012 of the European Parliament and of the Council of 12 December 2012 on jurisdiction and the recognition and enforcement of judgments in civil and commercial matters (recast) [2012], OJ L 351/1.
154. *See* Article 2(1) and (3) of the Directive 2014/104/EU.
155. Deutscher Bundestag, Drucksache 18/10207, *supra* n. 105, at 56.

directive does not necessarily require legislative action, Member States have to ensure that 'the legal position under national law should be sufficiently precise and clear and that individuals are made fully aware of their rights'.[156] It is, however, not beyond doubt that the conditions of the doctrine of prima facie evidence as conventionally understood under German law are met with regard to the findings of competition authorities of another Member State. Thus, while the German courts have sufficient leeway to implement the Directive properly, it is in particular the ECJ's last-mentioned condition that is not fulfilled under the law as it currently stands in Germany.

2. Scope of the binding effect

Recital 34 of the Directive provides some guidance on the reach of the binding effect, stipulating that it 'cover[s] only the nature of the infringement and its material, personal, temporal and territorial scope as determined by the competition authority … in the exercise of its jurisdiction'. This statement seems to be very much consistent with the current practice in Germany, though there are still some aspects that need clarifying. It was only two years ago that the Federal Court of Justice held that the binding effect relates to all findings in law and fact on which an authority's decision that an infringement has occurred is based.[157]

As the establishment of an infringement as such does not require findings on a causal relationship between the infringement and the harm done to others or on the amount of damage caused, the binding effect does not cover these aspects, which are, however, essential for a successful follow-on action.[158] Thus, any firm that has been unescapably identified as an infringer may maintain that its illegal conduct did not cause any harm to any plaintiff. In particular, where a national cartel authority includes findings on the inflicted harm in order to justify the amount of a fine imposed on a cartelist, these considerations are not binding in a follow-on action.[159] Nonetheless, where a decision contains, for example, findings on the appropriate market definition, these findings are binding on a civil court where a plaintiff relies thereon to establish that certain categories of products or customers, etc. were affected by an infringement. This was explicitly clarified by the German legislature in course of the 9th amendment of the Competition Act[160] as there had been a diverging judgment by the Higher Regional Court in Munich. The latter court had not considered itself bound by the market definition adopted by the Bundeskartellamt (Federal Cartel Office) in a decision

156. Case C-144/99 *Commission v Netherlands*, *supra* n. 142, at para. 17.
157. BGH, KZR 25/14, *supra* n. 80, at paras 18–19.
158. *See* Deutscher Bundestag, Drucksache 15/3640, 12 August 2004, Gesetzentwurf der Bundesregierung, Entwurf eines Siebten Gesetzes zur Änderung des Gesetzes gegen Wettbewerbsbeschränkungen, 54.
159. OLG München, 21 February 2013, U 5006/11 Kart, para. 90 (*Fernsehvermarktung*).
160. *See* Deutscher Bundestag, Drucksache 18/10207, *supra* n. 105, at 56 ('*Von der Bindungswirkung erfasst sind die Feststellungen zu sämtlichen Tatbestandsmerkmalen, deren Verwirklichung den Verstoß begründet und zu denen die Behörde oder das Gericht in seiner Entscheidung Feststellungen getroffen hat. Dazu gehören insbesondere auch die räumliche und sachliche Marktabgrenzung sowie das zeitliche Ausmaß des Verstoßes, soweit die Entscheidung hierzu Feststellungen enthält …*' (references omitted)).

to fine a firm because of vertical restraint of competition.[161] Rather, the court had adopted a different market definition and, thus, had denied standing to a firm that alleged to have sustained damage due to market foreclosure even though, according to the Bundeskartellamt's market definition, the firm should have have had been regarded as an actor on the foreclosed market.

Since the binding effect is limited to the establishment of an infringement of competition law, it does not include the establishment of fault in a fining decision. Therefore, the binding effect does not concern the establishment of fault, as required for a damages claim pursuant to section 33a(1) of the Competition Act. Nevertheless, the Higher Regional Court in Karlsruhe has indeed assumed a binding effect in this regard.[162]

As we have seen in the previous section, the single economic unit doctrine uniformly applies both to substantive competition law and to cartel damages law.[163] Therefore, any findings of the authorities in this regard, e.g., a finding that a parent company exerted a decisive influence on its subsidiary during the infringement and therefore has to be considered as part of the infringing undertaking, will have a binding effect in a follow-on damages litigation.

The right of due process, in particular the rights of defence and a fair hearing, requires that the binding effect of a decision can only be invoked against its addressees. If, for example, in a case of an illegal distribution system the competition authority addresses a decision against a manufacturer, the binding effect cannot be invoked against the distributors if a damages action is later brought against them.[164] This restriction of the personal scope concerns those firms that have been granted full immunity from fines if the competition authority – as is the common practice of the Bundeskartellamt – simply ends the proceedings against those immunity recipients without finding that an infringement has been committed.[165] Certainly, this does not mean that immunity recipients could escape damages liability. Even if they are not reached by the binding effect of the fining decisions addressed to their fellow cartelists, plaintiffs can submit these decisions as (prima facie) evidence to substantiate an infringement by an immunity recipient.[166]

161. OLG München, U 5006/11 Kart, *supra* n. 159, at para. 101.
162. OLG Karlsruhe, 6 U 51/12 Kart, *supra* n. 86, at para. 46.
163. *See supra* nn 135–137 and accompanying text.
164. Example borrowed from Bornkamm and Tolkmitt, *supra* n. 109, at Vol. 1, §33b GWB para. 17, 1036–1037.
165. By contrast, the European Commission finds that there was an infringement by the immunity recipient but imposes a fine of 'EUR 0'. *See*, e.g., Case Comp/F/38.899 *Gas Insulated Switchgear*, *supra* n. 138, at Article 1 (116) and Article 2 (117).
166. *See* KG, 2 U 10/03 Kart, *supra* n. 85, at 2775.

3. *The competition authorities as key players*

a) *Access to the decisions*

Plaintiffs may only benefit from the binding effect if they obtain access to the relevant decisions by the competition authority. The European Commission has to publish a non-confidential version,[167] which must include 'the main content of the decision'.[168] Usually, the Commission will promptly publish a summary of its decision in the Official Journal and aims to also publish a full (non-confidential) version of the decision swiftly on its website. However, in many cases, such a publication is severely delayed by disputes with the infringers about which information must be left out on grounds of confidentiality.[169]

With the 9th amendment of the Competition Act in 2017, the German legislature imposed the duty on the Bundeskartellamt to inform the public about a fining decision on its website.[170] This notification must contain *inter alia* information on the facts of the case, the type and time frame of the infringement, the firms that participated in the infringement, and the goods and services concerned. This information should be sufficient to attract the attention of possible victims of a competition infringement. But, to prepare a damages action, potential plaintiffs will have to get hold of the actual decision, which typically will be a fining decision.

To get hold of a fining decision *before* an action has been brought, potential plaintiffs basically have two options. First, section 89c(5) sentence 2 of the Competition Act clarifies that potential plaintiffs have a 'right to request access to the fining decisions of a competition authority' on the basis of section 406e of the German Code of Criminal Procedure (Strafprozessordnung).[171] Thus, a (non-confidential) version of a fining decision can be directly requested from the Bundeskartellamt. Second, potential plaintiffs may request from the alleged infringer access to a fining decision – which may be a decision by the European Commission or by an NCA – pursuant to section 33g of the Competition Act. To enforce such a right, potential plaintiffs can apply for a preliminary injunction under section 89b(5) of the Competition Act.[172]

After a plaintiff has filed suit, she may ask the court to request that the respective competition authority disclose documents, including, for example, a fining decision.[173]

167. *See* Article 30(2) sentence 2 of Regulation 1/2003 ('It shall have regard to the legitimate interest of undertakings in the protection of their business secrets').
168. Article 30 of Regulation 1/2003.
169. *See*, e.g., ECJ, Case C-162/15 P *Evonik Degussa GmbH v European Commission* [2017] ECLI:EU:C:2017:205.
170. Section 53(5) of the Competition Act.
171. In conjunction with section 46 of the Act on Regulatory Offences (Ordnungswidrigkeitengesetz).
172. *See* OLG Düsseldorf, 3 April 2018, VI-W Kart 2/18, [2018] NZKart 228 (*Herausgabe von Beweismitteln*).
173. *See* section 89c(1) of the Competition Act.

b) *Content of the decisions*

Ultimately, the *effet utile* of the binding effect will to a considerable extent depend on the way the competition authorities substantiate and publish their decisions. From the perspective of the cartel victims, it is particularly important whether the decisions contain useful information on the kind of products that have been affected by the cartel[174] or whether they reveal facts that are helpful in calculating damages.

Certainly, the binding effect is restricted to the finding of an infringement, and there is a considerable difference between the facts an authority needs to show an infringement and the facts a cartel victim needs in order to substantiate an action for cartel damages. Nevertheless, an authority may to a greater or lesser extent be ambitious in supporting potential plaintiffs by including in a decision as precise and detailed information as possible about the affected sales, customers, or the time frame of the cartel infringement. In particular, there is a concern that competition authorities might be inclined to describe infringements only in a fairly general manner if such a 'sweetener' facilitates a settlement.[175]

C. Statutes of limitation

The rules on limitation periods as embodied in Article 10 of the Directive deviate from the general approach insofar as they leave considerable regulatory leeway to the domestic legislatures. First of all, Article 10(1) of the Directive assigns merely a responsibility to Member States to lay down rules that determine 'when the limitation period begins to run, the duration thereof, and the circumstances under which it is interrupted or suspended'.

Pursuant to Article 10(2) of the Directive, Member States have to provide for a limitation period that follows a subjective system, i.e., its beginning depends on what the claimant knows or can reasonably be expected to know. The wording ('shall not begin to run *before*', emphasis added) makes it clear that the EU legislature at this point defines only the minimum conditions. Article 10(3) of the Directive requires that the limitation period must run for at least five years. Thus, Member States remain free to add further conditions for the start of the limitation period as well as to extend the limitation period. Further, recital 36 sentence 5 of the Directive explicitly allows Member States 'to maintain or introduce absolute limitation periods' provided that they comply with the principle of effectiveness. Finally, Member States have a choice over whether certain enforcement actions taken by the competition authorities will result in a suspension or an interruption of the limitation period. Against this background, the following notes will focus on how this regulatory leeway has been used by the German legislature.

---

174. *See* on the standard of proof in this regard sub. III.B.1.b), *supra*.
175. *See* Albrecht Bach and Christoph Wolf, *Germany: Private Antitrust Litigation* [2019] The European, Middle Eastern and African Antitrust Review 112, 114.

1. *The regular period of limitation following a subjective system*

Regarding the regular period of limitation, it is remarkable that the German legislature opted for a limitation period of five years[176] and, thus, for the shortest duration possible pursuant to the Directive. However, the German legislature modified the framework as envisaged in the Directive in several respects.

First of all, pursuant to section 33h(2) No. 1 of the Competition Act, the limitation period will only begin to run when the 'claim arose'. This requires that an infringement has inflicted harm on the claimant. It suffices that the latter has, for example, agreed to purchase a cartelised good (at an inflated price).[177] The condition is mainly of a clarifying nature. Article 10(2)(b) of the Directive requires that the infringement caused harm to the claimant.

Second, the German legislature has arguably tightened the subjective conditions that must be fulfilled for a start of the limitation period. While it is sufficient pursuant to Article 10(2) of the Directive to show that a claimant 'can reasonably be expected to know' certain facts, pursuant to section 33h(2) No. 2 of the Competition Act, the defendant needs to show that the claimant's ignorance of those facts is the result of 'gross negligence'.

Third, pursuant to section 33h(2) of the Competition Act, the limitation period does not immediately begin to run when the listed conditions are fulfilled but only 'with the end of the year'.[178] The provision discharges the parties and the courts from the burden of determining an exact date when the requirements for a start of the limitation period are met. It suffices, instead, to ascertain whether this was before or after New Year. Hence, the duration of the regular limitation period under German law is, strictly speaking, not five years but 'five years plus the rest of the year'.

2. *Two objective periods of limitation*

The German legislature has introduced two objective periods of limitation. Section 33h(3) of the Competition Act provides for a limitation period of ten years, which starts running when the claim for competition damages arose and the infringement that gives rise to the claim has ceased. The latter requirement is taken from Article 10(2) of the Directive and aims at preventing a limitation period from starting to run before the day on which a continuous or repeated infringement[179] ceases.

Commentators have questioned whether this rule is compatible with the principle of effectiveness, pointing to the scenario where the aggrieved party learns of the infringement only more than ten years after the infringement has ceased.[180]

---

176. Section 33h(1) of the Competition Act.
177. OLG München, 8 March 2018, U 3497/16, para. 178 (*Schienenkartell*).
178. This is in line with the general regime on limitation periods. *See* section 199(1) of the Civil Code.
179. *See* Article 25(2) sentence 2 of Regulation 1/2003.
180. Oliver Remien, '*Limitation Periods: III. Germany*' in *Implementation of the EU Damages Directive into Member State law*, Conference (2017) 3 Concurrences 47, para. 28.

The ECJ has commented in its *Manfredi* judgment on the issue of objective periods of limitation:

> A national rule under which the limitation period begins to run from the day on which the agreement or concerted practice was adopted could make it practically impossible to exercise the right to seek compensation for the harm caused by that prohibited agreement or practice, particularly if that national rule also imposes a short limitation period which is not capable of being suspended.
>
> In such a situation, where there are continuous or repeated infringements, it is possible that the limitation period expires even before the infringement is brought to an end. ...[181]

It appears that section 33h(3) of the German Competition Act is much less restrictive compared to the type of limitation rule the ECJ described as possibly infringing the principle of effectiveness. First, the commencement of the limitation period presupposes not only an infringement but also the occurrence of damage. Second, a period of ten years can hardly be regarded as 'short'. In the *Ashurst* study, which was published two years before the judgment in *Manfredi*, the authors noted that the limitation periods applicable in the Member States varied considerably. They ranged from one year to thirty years or – if one considered only objective limitation periods – from five years to thirty years.[182] Against this background, it makes sense to regard a ten-year period not as 'short'[183] but at any rate as 'medium-long', irrespective of whether or not its commencement presupposes the termination of the infringement. Third, the scenario of a limitation period in a case of a persistent (secret) infringement, which the ECJ apparently regards as particularly problematic, is excluded because the limitation period begins only after the infringement has ended. Against this background and given that the ECJ does not consider objective limitation periods as unacceptable per se, section 33h(3) of the German Competition Act should be viewed as compatible with the principle of effectiveness.

Finally, pursuant to section 33h(4) of the Competition Act, a claim for competition damages 'shall become statute-barred 30 years from the date when the infringement ... occurred'. Thus, the limitation period of thirty years depends neither on the infliction of harm nor on a termination of the infringement. Therefore, in case of continuous infringements, it may well be that the thirty-year limitation period expires earlier than the ten-year limitation period.

3. *Enforcement actions by competition authorities*

Section 33h(6) of the Competition Act transposes Article 10(4) of the Directive and provides for a suspension of limitation periods if competition authorities 'take action

181. ECJ, Case C-295/04 *Manfredi, supra* n. 65, at paras 78–79.
182. Study on the conditions of claims for damages in case of infringement of EC competition rules, Comparative Report, Prepared by Denis Waelbrock, Donald Slater and Gil Even-Shoshan, 31 August 2004, 88.
183. *See* ECJ, Case C-637/17 *Cogeco Communications Inc.* [2019] ECLI:EU:C:2019:263, paras 49, 51 and 53, where the court considers a limitation period of three years as being 'short'.

for the purpose of the investigation of its proceedings' in respect of an infringement of competition law. It is remarkable that the provision is also applicable if a foreign competition authority takes enforcement measures based on the assumption that there is an infringement of (only) domestic competition law.

4. *Effect of limitation*

When a limitation period expires, a defendant party may refuse to pay compensation and can invoke limitation as a defence.[184]

D. Collective action and pooling of claims

The German law of civil procedure does not provide for an instrument of collective redress that would allow for the consolidation of claims of different aggrieved parties into one action. Plaintiffs may, however, jointly sue an infringer if their actions are based on the same or at least an essentially similar factual and legal cause.[185] This may enhance procedural efficiency, in particular as it allows for joint hearings. Such a joinder of parties does not alter, however, the legal separation of the various actions against the defendant.

If plaintiffs want to bundle claims, they can do so via assignments. In practice, schemes have been established according to which the aggrieved parties assign their claims to 'special purpose vehicles'. Typically, parties must agree on a commission in the range of 20% to 50% of the damages the assignee is ultimately able to collect from the infringer.[186] While, thus, the risk of default remains essentially with the assignor, it is established case law that the assignee is entitled to bring an action against the infringer.[187]

The assignment must be carefully structured, however, as disregarding certain requirements will render an assignment void. First, a special purpose vehicle that has been established to enforce competition damages claims offers a legal service within the meaning of section 2(1) of the Act on Out-of-Court Legal Services and therefore needs special authorisation pursuant to section 3 of that Act. Without authorisation, it is illegal to provide this service and any assignment that is part of such an illegal service will be considered null and void. In a typical case, however, there should be no obstacles to a registration.[188] In particular, it should be stressed that combining the services of litigation and financing litigation is not incompatible.[189] It triggers a financial interest of the assignee in the litigation and, thus, helps to align its interests

184. Section 214(1) of the Civil Code.
185. *See* sections 59 and 60 of the Code of Civil Procedure.
186. Timo Fest, *Rechtsverfolgungsgesellschaften: Hindernisse bei der zivilrechtlichen Lösung eines prozessualen Problems* [2016] ZfPW 173, 178.
187. OLG Düsseldorf, 14 May 2008, VI-U (Kart) 14/07, WuW/E DE-R 2311, 2316–2317.
188. *See* sections 10 et seq. of the Act on Out-of-Court Legal Service (*Gesetz über außergerichtliche Rechtsdienstleistungen*).
189. *See ibid.*, section 4.

with those of the aggrieved parties.[190] Nevertheless, anecdotal evidence from practitioners suggests that at least some courts have refused the registration of special purpose vehicles. If this turns out to be a widespread phenomenon, the German legislature should consider clarifying the issue in the Act on Out-of-Court Legal Services.

Second, it must be noted that under German law contingency fees or conditional fees are permitted only in very exceptional circumstances[191] and that lawyers are barred from any engagement in financing litigation.[192] These provisions, that are intended to safeguard the independence of lawyers, must not be circumvented through the establishment of special purpose vehicles. Thus, while the commission-based model as such is not prohibited, those lawyers who ultimately represent the special purpose vehicle before court must not hold a share in that vehicle. Otherwise, the contracts that underlie the financing of the litigation and, consequently, the assignments will be void.

Third, assignments will be considered null and void when they are agreed upon for the purpose of shifting the financial risks of litigation to the defendant. In an overly strict application of this principle,[193] the Higher Regional Court in Düsseldorf considered assignments of competition damages claims null and void because the assignee was at the time of the agreement not in a financial position to reimburse its opponent's costs as potentially required pursuant to the 'loser-pays rule'.[194] Thus, for the time being, parties of an assignment should make sure that they meet the strict standard as stipulated by the Higher Regional Court and provide the specific purpose vehicle with sufficient assets to cover any court fees and claims for reimbursement of costs as may arise in the course of litigation, which includes appeal proceedings at a Higher Regional Court and revision proceedings at the Federal Court of Justice.[195] Legal intervention to establish a clear standard on this matter seems to be desirable.

In sum, the conditions for a valid assignment of competition damages claims are not entirely clarified, but they do not appear to be insurmountable. In any event, they make the bundling of claims cumbersome and costly.

---

190. Markus Hartung, *Noch mal: Klagen ohne Risiko – Prozessfinanzierung und Inkassodienstleistungaus einer Hand als unzulässige Rechtsdienstleistung?* [2017] BB 2825, 2827–2828.
191. Section 4a(1) of the Law on the Remuneration of Attorneys (*Rechtsanwaltsvergütungsgesetz*) and section 49b(2) of the Federal Lawyers Act (*Bundesrechtsanwaltsordnung*).
192. Section 49b(2) of the Federal Lawyers Act.
193. It is in particular unconvincing that the court assumed the main purpose of the assignments was shifting the risk of litigation costs to the defendant. *See*, e.g., Christoph Thole, *Die Prozessfinanzierung bei Kartellschadensersatzklagen – Lehren aus dem Fall CDC/Zementkartell* [2015] ZWeR 93, 106 and 116.
194. OLG Düsseldorf, 18 February 2015, VI-U (Kart) 3/14, paras 61–118.
195. *Ibid.*, para. 67.

CHAPTER 6

Private Enforcement in Italy

Enrico Camilleri

I. Introduction
II. The development of private enforcement
III. What is effective and what are the impediments to private enforcement?
IV. Some key issues in light of Directive 2014/104 EU and its implementation
  A. Which entity is liable for damages?
  B. Binding effects of decisions of competition authorities
  C. Limitation of actions
  D. Collective actions/pooling of claims
V. The (further) missing pieces of the puzzle: causation and quantification of damages: some concluding remarks

I. INTRODUCTION

Directive 2014/104/EU on certain rules governing actions for damages under national law for infringements of the competition law provisions of the Member States and of the European Union[1] (hereinafter 'Damages Directive') has been transposed in Italy by

1. Directive 2014/104/EU of the European Parliament and of the Council of 26 November 2014 on certain rules governing actions for damages under national law for infringements of the competition law provisions of the Member States and of the European Union [2014], OJ L349/1.

means of Legislative Decree no. 3 of 2017 (hereinafter 'Decree 3/2017'),[2] which largely reproduces the Directive not only with regard to the structure but also in respect of the wording of the provisions.

As with other Member States, for example France,[3] Italian lawmakers opted to enact a *lex specialis* for antitrust damages actions and limited the implementation to what was necessary, without any amendment to the codes of Italy, neither to the Code of Civil Procedure nor to the Civil Code, the latter of which contains the general rules of tort law.

Although pragmatic at a first glance, such a choice makes the interplay between general rules and principles, on the one hand, and the 'special regime' for antitrust damages actions, on the other, somehow harsh. Moreover, from a systematic point of view, that interplay could even turn into a clash where the new set of rules, while having a relevant incidence on the private law remedy concerned (i.e., civil liability), fails to fully overlap with it. This will undermine the interpretative argument 'rule-exception' and potentially convert what was meant to be a form of a practical solution into an increasing theoretical problem.

II. THE DEVELOPMENT OF PRIVATE ENFORCEMENT

The enactment of the Damages Directive, while urged by the ECJ's *Pfleiderer* decision and the resulting threats to the strength of leniency programmes,[4] marked the reaching of an important intersection along the 'winding road' towards the establishment of an effective antitrust private enforcement mechanism in Europe, complementary to the public one and to its best functioning.[5]

However, while concededly remarkable in many aspects, it will likely prove to be a sort of intermediate destination more than *the* landing place, an approach stage more than an epiphany itself of (US-style) regulation achieved through private litigation,

2. Decreto legislativo 19 gennaio 2017, n. 3, https://www.gazzettaufficiale.it/archivioCompleto > 2017 > no. 15 del 19-01-2017 > Decreto Legislativo 19 gennaio 2017, no. 3 (accessed 6 June 2019).
3. *See*, e.g., Laurence Idot, '*Private damages actions before and after the Implementation of the Directive: I. France*' in *Implementation of the EU Damages Directive into Member State law*, Conference (2017) 3 Concurrences 4 et seq.
4. *See* ECJ, Case C-360/09 *Pfleiderer AG v Bundeskartellamt* [2011] ECR I-5161. Cf. Sven B. Völcker's note (2012) 49 CML Rev., 695, 716.
5. *See*, e.g., Mario Libertini, '*Il ruolo necessariamente complementare di "private" it e "public enforcement" in materia di antitrust*' in Marisaria Maugeri and Andrea Zoppini (eds), *Funzioni del diritto privato e tecniche di regolazione del mercato*, 171, 174 (Il Mulino 2009).

sketched out by the modernisation package[6] in the wake of the ECJ's case law on the direct effect of EU primary law and the so-called *Community-based right to damages.*[7]

The reason for such a cautious evaluation involves the nature of the opted-for source of law and its contents; put briefly: what it is and what it says. The following parts of the analysis will focus on both aspects from mainly an Italian law perspective, but some broader preliminary remarks will be offered as well.

The adoption of a Directive was certainly not an obvious choice when one takes into account where we come from. To that point, there was Regulation 1/2003, which had a fully binding effect and already contained, among others, a specific norm (Article 6) conferring competence upon national courts in relation to Articles 101 and 102 TFEU,[8] not to mention its Recital 7, stressing the role played by national courts as regards the protection of subjective rights under Community law, 'for example by awarding damages to the victims of infringements'.

That being said, opting for a Directive tells us even more than the switching towards a soft harmonisation strategy, since it reveals a background of ambitious plans that remained largely frustrated by the proof of facts,[9] and it also induces some pessimism regarding the near future.

6. *See* Regulation 1/2003/EC of the Council of 16 December 2002 on the implementation of the rules on competition laid down in Articles 81 and 82 of the Treaty [2002], OJ L 001, Recital 6, assessing as crucial the role played by national courts 'in applying the Community competition rule', by deciding disputes between private individuals, 'for example by awarding damages to the victims of infringements'; *see* furthermore Article 6 of the cited Regulation: 'National courts shall have the power to apply Articles 81 and 82 of the Treaty.' As regards the 'modernization' of EU competition law *see* David J. Gerber, *Two forms of modernization in European Competition Law* (2008) 31 Fordham International Law Journal, 1235. *See* also Claus Dieter Ehlermann, *The modernization of EC antitrust policy: a legal and cultural revolution* (2000) 37 CML Rev., 537; Barry Rodger and Angus MacCulloch, *Competition Law and Policy in the EC and UK* 52 (3rd ed., Cavendish Pub. Ltd, 2004).
7. The expression 'Community law based right to damages' is used by Assimakis P. Komninos, *New prospects for private enforcement of EC competition laws* (2002) 39 CML Rev. 447, 449. As to the case law on the direct effect of the EC Treaty norms cf. ECJ, Case 26/62 *NV Algemene Transport en Expeditie Onderneming van Gend & Loos v NederlandseAdministratie der Belastingen* [1963] ECR 1; ECJ, Case C-127/63 *BRT v SABAM* [1974] ECR 313; ECJ, Joined Cases C-6/90 and C-9/90 *Francovich v Repubblica italiana* [1991] ECR I-5357, [1993] 2 CML Rev. 66; ECJ, Case C-128/92 *Banks & Co Ltd v British Cool Co* [1994] ECR I-1209, paras 36–45: 'the principle established in Francovich can also be applied to the case of breach of a right which an individual derives from an obligation imposed by Community law on another individual.' The statement about the importance of (private) actions for damages before national courts, related to infringements of EU competition law, has also become a sort of *leit motif* in the ECJ's jurisprudence concerning the issue: *see* the landmark decisions of the ECJ, Case C-453/99 *Courage Ltd v Bernard Crehan and Bernard Crehan v Courge Ltd and Others* [2001] ECR I-6297 and ECJ, Joined Cases C-295/04 to C-298/04 *Vincenzo Manfredi and Others v Lloyd Adriatico Assicurazioni SpA and Others* [2006] ECR I-6619. The direct effect of EU competition law rules as well as 'the right in Union law to compensation for harm resulting from infringements of Union and national competition law' are clearly emphasised by Recitals 3 and 4 of the Damages Directive.
8. Whenever to be applied in combination with or in parallel to national antitrust rules.
9. *See*, e.g., Brien, Idot et al., *supra* n. 3, at 7, noting that 'The Damages Directive is an exercise in frustration and a glaring example of how EU competition policy may lose its legitimacy in the eyes of the "European citizen".' *See* also the Editorial Comments *'One bird in the hand ...' The Directive on damages actions for breach of the competition rules* (2014) 51 CML Rev., 1333, 1334.

The reasons why the modernisation package[10] was unable to promote private damages actions and overcome the situation of both an astonishing diversity between national legislation and an underdevelopment of available remedies – as remarked by the *Ashurst Report* in 2004[11] and as repeatedly stressed six years later by Advocate General *Mazak* in his Opinion on the *Pfleiderer* case[12] – are well known and have been accurately analysed by scholarly opinion,[13] reasons beginning with a series of obstacles concerning procedural rules at national level.[14]

As a Directive is binding just as to the ends, and given that the EU legislature did not opt for a strong 'full harmonisation approach' similar to that one recently adopted by the EU legislation in the field of consumer rights,[15] the Damages Directive comes along with a high risk of leaving room for persisting differences between national legislation, in spite of its main goal of promoting a level playing field for undertakings and consumers[16] and notwithstanding the duty of consistent interpretation.[17] More remarkably, while mainly dealing with tortious liability,[18] it shows a range of action

10. Beginning with its preparatory document as represented by the European Commission's Green Paper on Damages actions for breach of the EC antitrust rules, COM (2005) 672 final and the European Commission's White Paper on Damages Actions for breach of the EC antitrust rules, COM (2008) 165 final.
11. *See* Denis Waelbroeck, Donald Slater & Gil Even-Shoshan, *Study on the conditions of claims for damages in case of infringement of EC competition rules: comparative report* (Ashurst 2004).
12. Case C-360/09 *Pfleiderer, supra* n. 4, Opinion of AG Mazák, at para. 40: 'Regulation No 1/2003 and the case-law of the Court have not established any de jure hierarchy or order of priority between public enforcement of EU competition law and private actions for damages. While no de jure hierarchy has been established, at present the role of the Commission and national competition authorities is, in my view, of far greater importance than private actions for damages in ensuring compliance with Articles 101 and 101 TFEU. Indeed so reduced is the current role of private actions for damages in that regard that I would hesitate in overly using the term "private enforcement".' The lack of uniformity in national legislation has been underlined by ECJ in its *Manfredi* decision: *see* Joined Cases C-295/04 to C-298/04 *Manfredi, supra* n. 7, para. 72.
13. *See*, e.g., Andreas Heinemann, '*Remedies in Antitrust Law*' in Thomas M.J. Möllers and Andreas Heinemann (eds), *The Enforcement of Competition Law in Europe* 450 (Cambridge University Press 2009).
14. *See*, e.g., Enrico Camilleri, *A decade of EU antitrust private enforcement: chronicle of a failure foretold?* (2014) 10 ECLR 531, 537.
15. Cf. Directive 2011/83/EU of the European Parliament and of the Council of 25 October 2011 on consumer rights, amending Council Directive 93/13/EEC and Directive 1999/44/EC of the European Parliament and of the Council and repealing Council Directive 85/577/EEC and Directive 97/7/EC of the European Parliament and of the Council [2011], OJ L 304/64, Article 4. Pursuant to Damages Directive Article 5, para. 8: 'Without prejudice to paragraphs 4 and 7 and to Article 6, this article shall not prevent Member States from maintaining or introducing rules which would lead to wider disclosure of evidence.'
16. *See* Damages Directive Recitals 7–10.
17. *See* ECJ, Case C-106/89 *Marleasing SA v La Comercial Internacional de Alimentación SA* [1990] ECR I-4135.
18. Which is supposed to be the most versatile among the private law remedies for achieving the pursued goals and which is at least in part recalled by Damages Directive Recital 5, pursuant to which 'Actions for damages are only one element of an effective system of private enforcement of infringements of competition law and are complemented by alternative avenues of redress, such as consensual dispute resolution and public enforcement decisions that give parties an incentive to provide compensation.'

narrower than that which is necessary by simply introducing 'certain rules governing' antitrust damage claims.

As a consequence, the Directive is based on a non-exhaustive, even sketchy, soft harmonisation approach, one whose key feature may be synthesised as 'I'd like to, but I can't.' Caught between policy and actual facts (i.e., normative data), it searches for an advanced equilibrium between the principles of effectiveness and equivalence, on the one hand, and of national autonomy, on the other; as Recital 11 makes quite clear: 'In the absence of Union law, actions for damages are governed by the national rules and procedures of the Member States' but in compliance with the 'principles of effectiveness and equivalence.'

To sum up, although ultimately in line with the norms of the Treaties (particularly Article 5 TEU and Articles 103 and 114 TFEU, which provide the Directive's legal basis[19]) and despite the introduction of somehow useful measures, the Directive's deficiencies – although in part unavoidable at the present stage – threaten to affect the effectiveness of private enforcement considerably.

It is certainly true that a softly harmonised regime – one made up of principles and rules such as the exclusion of any overcompensation for private claims, the assessment of binding effects of NCAs decisions, immunity measures for leniency applicants, a series of rebuttable presumptions softening the burden of proof on claimants, the law of limitation, basic rules on joint and several liability and, lastly, an opening up of both defensive and offensive recourse to a passing-on argument – represents something new, needed and, in the end, positive.[20] Nonetheless, the Directive remains to a large extent uncompleted.

It is uncomplete from the antitrust law viewpoint since, beyond any declaration of principle, it deals with certain kinds of violations only, mainly cartels and to some extent exploitative conduct in general.

Uncomplete from the private law viewpoint since, as noted above, it flattens (better: impoverishes) private antitrust enforcement to just tortious liability, without taking into account other tailor-made remedies such as injunctions or interim relief.[21]

Last but not least, even uncomplete from the tort law viewpoint since crucial issues remain sometimes untouched despite being evoked (as is the case for causation), sometimes addressed obliquely (as is the case for the proof of harm suffered by individuals and for quantification of damages) and sometimes unmentioned although impending as a stone guest (as is the case for collective redress mechanisms).

---

19. *See* Damages Directive Recital 54.
20. *See*, e.g., Pier Luigi Porcu, Giorgio Monti & Marco Botta (eds), *Private Enforcement of EU Competition Law: The Impact of the Damages Directive* (Edward Elgar Publishing 2018).
21. *See* for critical remarks, F.G. Wilman, *The end of the absence? The growing body of EU legislation on private enforcement and the main remedies it provides for* (2016) 53 CML Rev. 887, 909.

III. WHAT IS EFFECTIVE AND WHAT ARE THE IMPEDIMENTS TO PRIVATE ENFORCEMENT?

Since the most probative test aimed at verifying the aforementioned critical remarks cannot help but being the field of national legislation, the Italian one offers useful food for thought.

Despite the fact that one of the ECJ's leading decisions on private antitrust enforcement (the *Manfredi* case[22]) originated as a follow-on action filed before an Italian court which subsequently submitted it to the ECJ for a preliminary ruling, and notwithstanding a (sort of) class action regime already being in force, the number of private actions registered to date in Italy, even if rising in recent years, has proven to be very limited both in absolute terms and on a comparative basis with other jurisdictions, such as Germany, UK and the Netherlands.[23]

The reasons for the minimal amount of actions are manifold and involve either civil procedure or substantive law rules, as well as the main features of the harm that a victim may suffer from third parties' infringement of competition law rules, irrespective of the fact whether he/she is a competitor or not, a direct or an indirect purchaser, a business or a consumer.[24] The combination of these factors has made the Italian jurisdiction less plaintiff-friendly and attractive than other jurisdictions in Europe, with the side effect of deterring private parties from bringing actions for antitrust damages, if not even triggering a forum shopping phenomenon.

As unanimously recognised, antitrust cases are fact-intensive.[25] Therefore, as soon as we think about the ideal dialectic between the subjects who may be potentially involved in a downstream damage claim, the emergence of an informative asymmetry soon throws a shadow over the chances for the injured party to sue.

The occurrence of anticompetitive behaviour, which is to say the main source of the harm suffered, does in fact represent the very first element to be proved for access to the remedy in tort. It should also be noted that besides not being easily detectable as to its material dimension – at least whenever hidden by the conspiracy of silence between the co-infringers in cases of collusive misconduct – that behaviour counts as a violation of competition law rules insofar as a series of other conditions are fulfilled, most of which are based on economic data.

Such premise is now clearly pointed out by Recital 14 of the Damages Directive, stating that whereas the assessment of any antitrust infringement rests on 'a complex factual and economic analysis ... [t]he evidence necessary to prove a claim ... is often

22. Joined Cases C-295/04 to C-298/04 *Manfredi*, *supra* n. 7.
23. *See*, e.g., Roberto Chieppa, *Il recepimento in Italia della Dir. 2014/104/UE e la prospettiva dell'AGCM* (2016) 24 Il Diritto Industriale 314, 321; Massimo Scuffi, *Riflessioni a margine della Dir. 104/2014 (e del D.lgs 3/2017) sull'azione di classe* (2017) 25 Il Diritto Industriale 5, 8.
24. *See*, e.g., Alexander Italianer, *Competition Law within a framework of rights and the Commission's proposal for a Directive on antitrust damage actions* (12th Annual conference of the Association of European Competition Law Judges (AECLJ), Luxembourg, 14 June 2013) http://ec.europa.eu/competition/speeches/text/sp2013_06_en.pdf (accessed 23 April 2019).
25. *See*, e.g., Alexander Bruns, '*Private Enforcement of Competition Law: Evidence*' in Jürgen Basedow, Jörg Philipp Terhechte and Ludos Tichý (eds), *Private Enforcement of Competition Law* 127, 130 (Nomos 2011). *See* also Damages Directive Recital 45.

held exclusively by the opposing party or by third parties, and is not sufficiently known by, or accessible to, the claimant'.

That being said, the Italian legislation made - and to some extent still makes - things even worse off for a plaintiff by imposing on him a heavy burden of proof and by making it difficult to access the specific and necessary information for bringing an action in tort.

Pursuant to Article 2697 of the Italian Civil Code (hereinafter 'Italian CC'), the party who claims a right has the burden to prove the facts supporting his or her claim ('*onus probandi incumbit ei qui dicit*'); therefore, in the absence of specific norms[26] - like those recently adopted by the Damages Directive, introducing some rebuttable legal presumptions - the injured party has to prove the defendant's (illegal) conduct, the qualified harm suffered ('*danno ingiusto*') and the existence of a causal link between the conduct and the harm: in other words, the injured party has to prove the existence of the whole set of conditions required for the remedy in tort to be invoked, pursuant to Article 2043 Italian CC.

However, according to the Civil Procedure Code (hereinafter 'Italian CPC'), neither does the claimant have a comprehensive right to demand disclosure nor can the judge order it without any limit. Pursuant to Articles 210 Italian CPC and 94 of the provisions for the implementation of the Italian CPC (*region decreto No. 1368/1941*), a disclosure may be granted upon application of a party only for a precisely identified document and only to the extent that it is necessary. Disclosure remains in any case precluded when it may cause a serious harm to the party that has to disclose the document.[27]

Further elements, mostly pertaining to the main features of domestic tort law, have also concurred to interfere with private antitrust claims, beginning with the rules on causation and quantification of damages. Since, however, they remained untouched by the Damages Directive, the assessment as to whether they still remain problematic in the cases at issue should be postponed behind to the analysis of those provisions recently introduced (or at least of some of them).

For now, it suffices to say that the combined effect of the typical informative asymmetry between the potentially involved parties and the strict regime on proof has led to a 'claimant-adverse environment' for antitrust damages actions in Italy, a situation at high risk of even 'imped[ing] the effective exercise of the right to compensation guaranteed by the TFEU'.[28]

It is however worth noting that the Italian courts, mainly the *Corte di Cassazione*, have tried to soften such a posture and strengthen the alignment of, on the one hand,

26. *See*, e.g., Marco De Cristofaro, *Innovazioni e prospettive nella dimensione processuale che sta al cuore del private antitrust enforcement* [2018] Le Nuove Leggi Civili Commentate 523, 531, 533.
27. *See* Marcella Negri, '*Disclosure of documents that lie in the control of the parties: IV. Italy*' in *Implementation of the EU Damages Directive into Member State law*, Conference (2017) 3 Concurrences 18.
28. As feared by Damages Directive Recital 14: 'strict legal requirements for claimants to assert in detail all the facts of their case at the beginning of an action and to proffer precisely specified items of supporting evidence can unduly impede the effective exercise of the right to compensation guaranteed by the TFEU'.

substantive/procedural rules and, on the other, the push towards the availability of tort remedies in antitrust cases as have emerged at the European level.

Two decisions especially deserve to be mentioned in this regard. In the first one, which dates back to 2005, the Court of *Cassazione* abandoned its restrictive attitude and recognised the existence of a legally qualified interest in the competitive structure of the market, thereby entitling, for the very first time, all market players – either consumers or rival undertakings – to enforce the remedy in tort for the protection of that interest, once violated by specific monopolistic conduct.[29] In the second one, from 2015, the Court favoured in a stand-alone action an extensive interpretation of the Italian rules on proof in order to be consistent with the Damages Directive, although not yet implemented at that time, and simply required that the plaintiff provided serious, plausible circumstantial evidence of the alleged anticompetitive conduct of the defendant.[30]

Though positive, the emergence of such a posture from the courts was however surrounded by the uncertainties that are typical of 'judge-made law'. Decree 3/2017 should therefore provide for a much more stable framework.

As aptly observed by scholarly opinion, within the Directive, and therefore within the implementing norms, the procedural dimension occupies centre stage.[31] And in fact, just moving from those obstacles to the private antitrust enforcement that I have emphasised above as emblematic under Italian law, useful new legal provisions quickly come to one's attention.

First, there is the introduction of a series of rebuttable presumptions in favour of the plaintiff. Pursuant to Article 12(2) Decree 3/2017 (in conformity with Article 14 of the Damages Directive), the passing-on of the overcharge from the defendant to the plaintiff (i.e., the indirect purchaser) is presumed whenever certain detailed conditions are fulfilled; even more remarkably, pursuant to Article 14(2) of the same provision (in conformity with Article 17 of the Damages Directive), the existence of a harm caused by a cartel is presumed as well. In both cases the presumptions are rebuttable.[32]

Second, as regards the disclosure of evidence, the measures enshrined in Article 5 of the EU Damages Directive, implemented through Article 3 Decree 3/2017, have had the result that antitrust damages actions are governed by a less strict rule than Article 210 Italian CPC, mentioned above: to mention just the main features of the (new) special regime, the party seeking disclosure is no longer requested to provide an *ex ante* precise description of the sought document/evidence, and the judge's order of disclosure, even if limited by a proportionality test, may nevertheless extend to concern even 'relevant categories of evidence' once the plausibility of the claim is verified.[33]

29. *See* Corte di Cassazione, no. 2207, 4 February 2005, [2005] Giurisprudenza italiana 1675, later confirmed also by Corte di Cassazione, no. 2305, 2 February 2007, [2007] Foro italiano 1097.
30. *See* Corte di Cassazione, no. 11564, 4 June 2015.
31. Cf. De Cristofaro, *supra* n. 26, at 529.
32. *See* Enrico Camilleri, *Il risarcimento del danno per violazioni del diritto della concorrenza: ambito di applicazione e valutazione del danno* [2018] Le Nuove Leggi Civili Commentate 143, 159; Mario Todino, *Il danno risarcibile* [2015] AIDA 15, 23.
33. In order to prevent 'fishing expeditions'. *See*, e.g., Giuseppe Finocchiaro, *La disciplina dell'-esibizione delle prove nei giudizi risarcitori per violazione delle norme antitrust in attuazione della Dir. 2014/104 UE* [2018] Le Nuove Leggi Civili Commentate 415; Paolo Comoglio, *Note a*

IV. SOME KEY ISSUES IN LIGHT OF DIRECTIVE 2014/104 EU AND ITS IMPLEMENTATION

A. Which entity is liable for damages?

Following the methodological indications provided by the editors, I will now focus on a list of selected issues that are pivotal for the best promotion of private antitrust enforcement and arguably critical in terms of their potential impact on domestic legislation.

The first issue to be dealt with concerns the identification of the entity liable for competition law infringements.

Article 2(2) Damages Directive states: 'infringer means an undertaking or association of undertakings which has committed an infringement of competition law'. This definition was carried over verbatim by Italian lawmakers in Article 2(1) (a) Decree 3/2017.

On first reading, the aforementioned definition simply echoes the cartel prohibition (Article 101 TFEU) and its typical subjective profile (namely: 'agreements between undertakings, decisions by associations of undertakings'), so that one may argue that the liable legal entity cannot be anything but the cartelist, as such and along with the co-infringers, within the mechanism of joint and several liability recently introduced.[34]

An in-depth analysis, however, reveals also a secondary, hidden meaning so as to take into account the economic unit doctrine as elaborated in the wake of some leading cases.

As it is well known, according to the ECJ's interpretation, the application of Article 101 TFUE should be excluded for intra-corporate group agreements, to the extent that the companies at issue have such an intense and close economic relationship as to form a single economic entity.[35]

At the same time, in the *Akzo Nobel* judgment, the Court made it clear that the meaning of 'undertakings', for the application of administrative fines in relation to Article 101 TFEU, 'must be understood as designating an economic unit even if in law

---

una prima lettura del d.lgs n. 3 del 2017. Novità processuali e parziali inadeguatezze in tema di danno antitrust [2017] *Riv. Trim. Dir. e Proc. Civ.* 991; *see* Negri, *supra* n. 27, at 18; Marco De Cristofaro, *Onere probatorio e disciplina delle prove quale presidio di efficienza del private antitrust enforcement* [2015] AIDA 100; Andrea Giussani, *Direttiva e principi del processo civile italiano* [2015] AIDA 251.

34. *See* Damages Directive Article 11 and, as for Italy, Article 9 Decree 3/2017. It should be noticed that the ECJ has adopted a functional approach in the context of competition law such that, first, 'the concept of an undertaking encompasses every entity engaged in an economic activity, regardless of the legal status of the entity and the way in which it is financed' and, second, 'employment procurement is an economic activity'.
    See ECJ, Case C-41/90 *Klaus Höfner and Fritz Elser and Macrotron GmbH* [1991] ECJ I-1979, para. 21.
35. *See*, in the sense of the autonomy between the companies of a group maintaining complete economic independence ECJ, Case C-22/71 *Béguelin Import Co. and Others And S.A.G.L. Import Export, Nice and Others* [1971] ECR 949. *See*, for the opposite, ECJ, Case C-97/08 P *Akzo Nobel NV and Others v Commission of the European Communities* [2009] ECR I-8237, paras 55–58. As for the doctrine *see*, e.g., Richard Whish and David Bailey, *Competition Law*, 93 (ninth ed., Oxford University Press 2018).

that economic unit consists of several persons, natural or legal'. Moreover, the Court stated that whenever 'such an economic entity infringes the competition rules, it falls, according to the principle of personal responsibility, to that entity to answer for that infringement' while 'the conduct of a subsidiary may be imputed to the parent company in particular where, although having a separate legal personality, that subsidiary does not decide independently (...) but carries out, in all material respects, the instructions given to it by the parent company'.[36]

Against this background, different scenarios need to be distinguished.

It could be that, notwithstanding the existence of a parent company, the subsidiary has definite economic autonomy; under these circumstances, the latter is, when participating in a cartel, the infringer to be sued.

It may also happen that where a cartel involves just those companies whose relationship embodies a single economic unit, the cartel itself indeed disappears, sometimes being superseded by a different kind of infringement consisting of an abuse of dominant position, as discussed in the *Viho* decision.[37]

Finally, the situation may arise where a cartel does involve two or more undertakings, one of them being part of an economic unit in which the subsidiary acted. In such a case, the conduct of the subsidiary can be imputed to the parent company so that both companies are jointly and severally liable.

As mentioned above, the last scenario does frequently occur in connection with the application of administrative fines, thus in cases pertaining to the sphere of public enforcement.[38]

That being said, the question to answer now is whether such an 'economic unit' doctrine also applies in cases of civil liability for harm caused by anticompetitive

36. *See* ECJ, Case 48/69 *Imperial Chemical Industries v Commission of the European Communities* [1972] ECR 619; *see* also Case no. C-97/08 *Akzo Nobel and Others v Commission, supra* n. 35, paras 55–58; ECJ, Case C-217/05 *Confederación Española de Empresarios de Estaciones de Servicio v Compañía Española de Petróleos SA* [2006] ECR I-11987. The ECJ has declared that the autonomous parent company's responsibility exists whenever is proved that it exercised a decisive influence over the subsidiary: *see* also ECJ, Joined cases C-293/13 and C-294/13 *Fresh Del Monte Produce Inc v European Commission* [2015] ECLI:EU:C:2015:416, para. 75. It is, furthermore, worth highlighting the judicial tendency towards an extensive application of the economic unit doctrine, up to covering situations where the 'direction and control' of an undertaking over another is exercised by means of contract services, as in cases of 'hub and spoke' cartels: *see*, e.g., ECJ, Case C-542/14 *SIA 'VM Remonts' (formerly SIA 'DIV un KO') and Others v Konkurences padome* [2016] ECLI:EU:C:2016:578. Cf. Ioannis Apostolakis, *Antitrust liability in cases of indirect contacts between competitors: VM Remonts* [2017] 54 CML Rev., 605–630.
37. ECJ, Case C-73/95 P *Viho Europe BV v Commission* [1996] ECR I-5457, paras 15–17.
38. The situation referred to in the text typically produces consequences in the quantification of fines applicable since, according to Article 23, second paragraph, Regulation 1/2013, the threshold of 10% of an undertaking's worldwide turnover needs to be applied to the entire group's turnover: *see*, e.g., Whish and Bailey, *supra* n. 35, at 99; Ivo Van Bael and Jean-François Bellis, *Il diritto comunitario della concorrenza* 991 (Giappichelli 2009). As to recourse to the economic unit doctrine for the application of administrative fines in Italy *see*, e.g., Federico Ghezzi and Mariateresa Maggiolino, *L'imputazione delle sanzioni antitrust nei gruppi di imprese, tra responsabilità personale e finalità dissuasive* [2014] Rivista delle società, 1060; Federico Ghezzi, *Impresa e sanzioni nella prassi applicativa dell'Autorità garante della concorrenza: qualche problema teorico* [2016] Giur. comm. I 812.

conduct. In other words, it is to be clarified whether the claimant is able to sue also the parent company of a cartelist (subsidiary) by invoking the existence of a legal unit between them, it is being alleged or presumed[39] that the latter did not decide independently upon its own conduct on the market but strictly carried out the instructions received by the parent company.

The arguments in favour of the application of the economic unit doctrine to antitrust damages actions – in order to identify the liable person – have been part of an intense doctrinal debate since even before the enactment of the Directive. It has been argued that, consistent with the application of administrative fines, an action for damages could be brought either against a parent company or against the subsidiary, with both however being jointly and severally liable.[40]

An explicit and authoritative endorsement of this approach comes now from the very recent ECJ case of *Vantaan v Skanska*.[41] The Court, in fact, made it once more clear that the concept of an 'undertaking', within the meaning of Article 101 TFEU, 'must be understood as designating an economic unit even if in law that economic unit consists of several persons, natural or legal', and also that 'when an entity that has committed an infringement of the competition rules is subject to a legal or organisational change, this change does not necessarily create a new undertaking free of liability for the conduct of its predecessor that infringed the competition rules, when, from an economic point of view, the two are identical'.[42] Furthermore, and with a greater importance for our discussion, the ECJ has stressed that 'the concept of "undertaking", within the meaning of Article 101 TFEU, which constitutes an autonomous concept of EU law, cannot have a different scope with regard to the imposition of fines by the Commission under Article 23(2) of Regulation No 1/2003 as compared with actions for damages for infringement of EU competition rules'.[43]

Now, looking at the issue at hand from the Italian perspective, it seems that particularly in the aftermath of the implementation process of the Damages Directive, the favourable arguments for an extension of the economic unit doctrine to antitrust damages claims have in fact been strengthened by the wordings of the rules – either European or Italian ('undertaking or association of undertakings') – in connection with along with the principle of coherent interpretation of EU law.[44]

To the extent that, for the application of an administrative fine, the existence of an economic unit between two or more (natural or legal) persons implies that unit

39. *See* Case C-97/08 *Akzo Nobel and Others v Commission*, *supra* n. 35, at para. 60: 'in the specific case where a parent company has a 100% shareholding in a subsidiary which has infringed the Community competition rules, first, the parent company can exercise a decisive influence over the conduct of the subsidiary and, second, there is a rebuttable presumption that the parent company does in fact exercise a decisive influence over the conduct of its subsidiary'.
40. *See* Wish and Bailey, *supra* n. 35, at 94.
41. *See* ECJ, Case C-724/17 *Vantaan kaupunki v Skanska Industrial Solutions Oy and Others* [2019] ECLI:EU:C:2019:204.
42. *See ibid.*, paras 37–38.
43. *See ibid.*, para. 47.
44. As argued persuasively by Giorgio Afferni, *Il risarcimento dei danni per violazioni del diritto della concorrenza: prescrizione e responsabilità solidale* [2018] Le Nuove Leggi Civili Commentate 171, 190.

being held responsible for the infringement - which is to say that the parent is (also, jointly and severally) responsible whenever its control over the subsidiary that participated in the anticompetitive conduct was strict and pervasive - the same should hold true as to the duty to compensate damages for harms caused to third parties.

No special proof concerning the parent company's fault should be required, since its responsibility arises from the mere exercise of a decisive influence over the subsidiary, so that the *thema probandum* will be the existence of that influence, at least whenever it could not be presumed.

B. Binding effects of decisions of competition authorities

The potential impact of administrative decisions on subsequent claims for damages is a great theme of the debate as regards private antitrust enforcement, in Europe as well as overseas.[45]

The rule on the binding effect of an infringement decision of a competition authority has its roots in the information asymmetry between the harmed party (the potential claimant) and the infringer (the potential defendant), and it promises to be the most effective instrument for overcoming this asymmetry, at least in follow-on actions. However, while already in force in respect of the Commission's infringement decisions, pursuant to Article 16(1) Regulation 1/2003,[46] it has remained a controversial issue in terms of a full extension to NCA decisions finding strong obstacles in national law, including the relevant Italian legislation.

Already within its White Paper, the EU Commission expressed some critical remarks regarding the widespread reluctance to ascribe a binding effect to decisions having a final character; therefore, it suggested to adopt a rule according to which national courts, whenever having to take decisions on damage claims, subsequent to an NCA's final decision finding an infringement of Articles 101 and 102 TFEU 'cannot take decisions running counter to any such decision or ruling'.[47]

Almost ten years later, that rule has been finally adopted as part of a soft harmonisation regime. Article 9 Damages Directive reads that: 'Member States shall ensure that an infringement of competition law found by a final decision of a national competition authority or by a review court is deemed to be irrefutably established for the purposes of an action for damages brought before their national courts under Article 101 or 102 TFEU or under national competition law.' A narrower effect is then promoted for cross-border decisions, since national legislation should allow the claimant to produce such decisions as 'prima facie evidence', this being a compromise between the first draft of the Directive - in favour of the attribution of a full binding effect - and the widespread concerns that are raised by the (not undisputed) conformity of administrative decisions and court proceedings vis-a-vis the principles of a fair

45. *See* section 5(a) of Clayton Antitrust Act of 1914, Pub. L. no. 63-212, 38 Stat. 730 (codified at 15 U.S.C. §§ 12-27, 29 U.S.C. §§ 52-53).
46. In the wake of the decision of the ECJ in Case C-344/98 *Masterfoods Ltd v HB Ice Cream Ltd.* [2000] ECR I-11369, paras 51 et seq.
47. *See* European Commission, White Paper on Damages Actions, *supra* n. 10.

trial and a right of defence pursuant to Article 47 European Charter of Fundamental Rights and Article 6(1) ECHR.[48]

Looking at this rule from the Italian law perspective, it can be said that its underlying principle is not entirely novel, although it is disputed.

Beginning with a leading decision of the Court of *Cassazione* from 2009,[49] Italian courts have already recognised NCA infringement decisions as strong evidence in subsequent damage claims, referring to a '*prova privilegiata*', this being in-between 'merely admissible evidence subject to judicial appreciation and something less than conclusive evidence, owing to the fact that the defendant could theoretically adduce evidence in rebuttal'.[50] Furthermore, the courts have also grounded some presumptions based on this 'evidence', these concerning other elements of tortious liability, such as the existence of the harm and the causal link between the anticompetitive misconduct and the harm itself.[51]

Without dealing with the inconsistencies between such a broad use of presumptions for assessing crucial elements of a tort law remedy, it should be noted that the main concerns have been expressed with regard to basic principles of the Italian legal system: the rigid separation between administrative and judicial power, on the one hand, and the full autonomy that is granted to the latter, on the other (grounded on either Article 24(2) or Article 101(2) Italian Constitution). And this is not to mention those concerns related to Articles 47 European Charter of Fundamental Rights and 6(1) ECHR, particularly in the wake of the ECtHR cases *Menarini* and *Grande Stevens*.[52]

In general terms, the judge - being subject to the law only, pursuant to Article 101(2) Italian Constitution - should be totally free to evaluate the relevant facts, or at least not bound to a specific reconstruction of them provided by an administrative decision.[53]

This premise is of paramount importance in understanding the rationale behind the way how Italian lawmakers have implemented Article 9 Damages Directive.

48. *See* European Commission, Proposal for a Directive of the EU Parliament and of the Council on certain rules governing actions for damages under national law for infringements of the competition law provisions of the Member States and of the European Union, COM(2013) 404 final, Article 9. *See* the comments by Jens-Uwe Frank, '*Binding effects of decisions of national authorities: I. Introduction with some comparative remarks from a German perspective*' in *Implementation of the EU Damages Directive into Member State law*, Conference (2017) 3 Concurrences 37-38; Marcella Negri, *L'efficacia delle decisioni amministrative nel processo civile* [2018] *Le Nuove Leggi Civili Commentate* 476, 518.
49. Cf. Corte di Cassazione, no. 3640, 13 February 2009.
50. Oliver Remien, '*Limitation Periods: I. Introduction*' in *Implementation of the EU Damages Directive into Member State law*, Conference (2017) 3 Concurrences 47, 48. A critical position towards the referenced approach is expressed by Aldo Frignani, *La difesa disarmatanelle cause follow-on per danno antitrust. La Cassazione in Guerra con se stessa* [2013] Mercato Concorrenza e Regole 429.
51. Among others *see* Corte di Cassazione, no. 10211, 10 May 2011.
52. *See* ECtHR, no. 43509/08, *Menarini Diagnostics v Italia*, 27 October 2011; ECtHR, no. 18640/10, *Grande Stevens and Others v Italy*, 4 March 2014. *See* also the critical remarks expressed by Gianroberto Villa, *La Direttiva europea sul risarcimento del danno antitrust: riflessioni in vista dell'attuazione* [2015] Il Corriere giuridico 301, 306; Giuseppe Guizzi, *La sentenza CEDU 4 marzo 2014 e il sistema delle potestà sanzionatorie delle Autorità amministrative indipendenti: sensazioni di un civilista* [2014] Il Corriere giuridico 1321; Giussani, *supra* n. 33, at 251 et seq.
53. For insightful remarks *see* Giussani, *supra* n. 33, at 252 and footnote 3.

Article 7(1) Decree 3/2017, at least in its first part, provides an almost faithful translation of its European counterpart, by declaring as binding - in subsequent damages actions - an NCA infringement decision, provided that it is final, that it was confirmed by the reviewing court or that it was not challenged in due time.

Continuing on with our reading of the article, we then find a compromise - or an attempt at one - which was caused by the uncertainties that have been identified above: pursuant to Article 7(1) second part, the binding effect of an administrative decision rests on the fact that - before becoming final - it can be challenged before a court having full jurisdiction over the matter; the administrative court's judicial review covers either the facts upon which the challenged decision is grounded or the 'technical assessments which are not characterized by a substantial margin of appreciation'.[54]

Such a formulation is, however, not fully persuasive and does not dispel all doubts since it seems to exempt from a full review those economic assessments that are at the basis of competition law enforcement;[55] that is why, although the last paragraph of the Italian transposition states (as does Article 9 Damages Directive) that the 'binding effect rule' comes 'without prejudice to the rights and obligations of national courts under Article 267 TFEU', some scholars argue that the courts may also exercise a *refusal to apply*-power, whenever they find that the concerned decision is manifestly illegal.[56]

Moreover, some remarks are needed as to the borders, either objective or subjective, set on the binding effect of NCA decisions.

First, the Directive and its implementation rule refer to infringement decisions only; this means that no binding effect can be ascribed to other kinds of decisions, such as commitment decisions.

Second, according to the indications contained in Recital 34 Damages Directive, the Italian legislature has circumscribed the binding effect to the nature of the infringement and its material, personal, temporal and territorial scope, as determined by the competition authority or the review court. It follows that other crucial issues for the damages claim, like causation and the determination of an individual harm having been suffered by the plaintiff, are left to the regular rules on the burden of proof, as integrated by the special regime of rebuttable presumptions that is traced by Articles 14(2) and 17(2) Damage Directive (Articles 12(2) and 14(2) Decree 3/2017).

Third, as to the subjective boundaries, the Italian provision is clear in restricting the binding effect of the infringement decision to the infringer only. The rationale behind this rule is quite clear: it ensures that the binding effect is limited to the person that has been involved in the prior administrative proceeding.

54. *See* Negri, *supra* n. 48, at 494 et seq.
55. *See* Gianroberto Villa, *L'attuazione della Direttiva sul risarcimento del danno per violazione delle norme sulla concorrenza* [2017] Il Corriere giuridico 441, 445-446. For the opposing view *see* Nicoletta Rangone, *D.lgs 19 gennaio 2017, n. 3: profili amministrativistici* [2018] Le Nuove Leggi Civili Commentate, 255, 265-266.
56. *See* Negri, *supra* n. 48, at 494 et seq., 499; Marcella Negri, '*Binding effect of decisions of national authorities: III. Italy*' in *Implementation of the EU Damages Directive into Member State law*, Conference (2017) 3 Concurrences para. 26.

Some interpretative tensions are easily foreseeable in the wake of the ECJ's *Kone* decision:[57] in cases of umbrella pricing, while the ECJ has affirmed the liability of the cartelists, it has not excluded that the cartelist(s) could, after being held liable for the damages suffered by the rival undertaking's contractual counterpart who paid an umbrella price, later bring an action against that competitor for its conduct. In this event, such an action will be a sort of stand-alone action in the sense that the cartelist(s) will not benefit from any NCA infringement decision concerning the umbrella pricing conduct perpetrated by the rival.[58]

A final remark deserves to be made with regard to decisions of foreign NCAs: they have no binding effect and the European legislature refers to them as constituting 'prima facie evidence'. This concept is unknown to the Italian law of evidence; therefore, and wisely, Italian lawmakers opted for the term 'proof'. Cross-border decisions are thus an admissible (simple) means of proof among other means and are subject to the free judge's persuasion.[59]

C. Limitation of actions

The issue of limitation is a sensitive subject matter since it is capable of impeding the exercise of the right to compensation or significantly jeopardising the level playing field between market participants from State to State, even triggering forum shopping.

It shall suffice here to mention the concerns expressed by the ECJ in its *Manfredi* judgment,[60] which nevertheless recalled the Member States' competence on the issue, 'provided that the principles of equivalence and effectiveness are observed', and suffice it also to mention the suggestions contained in the Commission's White Paper[61] on achieving the proper balance between legal certainty and the effectiveness of the right to sue.

As clearly stressed in the *Manfredi* case, having the limitation period commence from the day on which the agreement or concerted practice is adopted could make it impossible to exercise the right to seek compensation for the harm caused, and such a risk becomes greater as the length of the limitation period becomes shorter, particularly when it is not capable of being suspended.[62] These were precisely the main features of the Italian law in force at the time that decision was handed down.

Pursuant to Article 2947 Italian CC, the right to compensation in a tort liability case had a limitation period of five years, starting from the day when the *fact* occurred. This wording traditionally gave rise to a strict interpretation, according to which the limitation period should be understood as running from the day when the harm was provoked.

---

57. ECJ, Case C-510/11 P *Kone AG and Others v European Commission* [2013] ECLI:EU:C:2013:696.
58. *See* Giussani, *supra* n. 33, at 253.
59. *See*, e.g., Chieppa, *supra* n. 23, at 316; Rangone, *supra* n. 55, at 268.
60. *See* Joined Cases C-295/04 to C-298/04 *Manfredi*, *supra* n. 7, at paras 77–82.
61. *See* European Commission, White Paper on Damages Actions, *supra* n. 10.
62. *See* Joined Cases C-295/04 to C-298/04 *Manfredi*, *supra* n. 7, at para. 78.

However, just a few years after the *Manfredi* case, the Italian Court of *Cassazione* adopted a less rigid reading of the prescription rule, done by emphasising a coordination between Article 2947 Italian CC and the general legal provision, contained in Article 2935 Italian CC.

Pursuant to the latter article, the limitation period begins to run from 'the day when the right can be exercised'; a *dies a quo* that the Court held to be the moment when the person having the right to sue has a concrete chance, if acting diligently, to learn about the occurrence of the *harm*, its relevance in legal terms[63] and the identity of the tortfeasor.[64]

That being said, and apart for a couple of explicit provisions - concerning the express relevance of an ongoing or terminated administrative investigation/proceeding, on the one hand, and the prerequisite that the violation causing the harm has ended before a right to sue is enforceable, on the other - it can be observed that the Italian law in force prior to the Damages Directive seemed to be already quite in line with the cornerstones of the harmonised regime laid down in this European instrument.

Pursuant to Article 10 Damages Directive, the European text requires Member States to adopt legislation prescribing that the commencement of the limitation period is fixed 'not before the infringement of competition law has ceased and the claimant knows, or can reasonably be expected to know' specific circumstances regarding the behaviour (and the fact that it constitutes an infringement of competition law), the fact that the infringement caused harm and the identity of the infringer.

Furthermore, the Directive fixes a minimum length of five years, and there are also specific legal provisions for suspending the limitation period once the competition authority takes action for the purpose of the investigation.

Moving back to Italy, Article 8 Decree 3/2017 provides a faithful translation of the Directive's provision, along with an exercise 'at the minimum level allowed' of the only discretionary power conferred upon the States: the length of the limitation period. That is because Italian lawmakers fixed it at five years - in conformity with the general provision on tortious liability - and decided moreover not to fix any 'absolute limitation period', although this is encouraged in Recital 36 Damages Directive.[65]

Yet appearances are sometimes deceiving, and as soon as we go beyond such a minimal approach and the general overall coherence, a concern arises in the wake of the implementation process. Specifically, while Article 10 Damages Directive simply lists facts and the circumstances that the entitled person need to know - or should be aware of - before having the chance to exercise the right to claim damages, the Italian transposition (Article 8 Decree 3/2017) requires that these facts be fulfilled in a cumulative manner; the resulting undesirable outcome - undeniably undermining the certainty of law - is that, especially in cases of stand-alone actions, the full discovery of these elements (i.e., the *dies a quo* for limitation) could even occur a considerable

63. Which is to say, about its being a *danno ingiusto* under Article 2043 CC.
64. Cf. Corte di Cassazione, no. 2305, 2 February 2007 regarding an antitrust claim for damages following the detection of a horizontal prohibited cartel between car insurance undertakings.
65. *See*, e.g., Villa, *supra* n. 55, at 441.

time after the violation at issue was committed, a risk that is all the greater because Italy has not adopted an 'absolute limitation period'.[66]

D. Collective actions/pooling of claims

The Damages Directive lacks any provisions on collective redress. It contains rules neither on class actions nor on representative actions. Along with the exclusion of any overcompensation laid down in Article 3(3) Damages Directive, this gap deepens the rift between the emerging European model of private antitrust enforcement and the overseas benchmark, i.e. the US system,[67] where a combination of treble damages[68] and the availability of an opt-out class action[69] creates a positive combination of (optimal) deterrence and adequate incentives to sue.[70]

While the adoption of a merely compensatory regime is a deliberate, final choice, coherent with the function (compensatory) and characteristics of the tort remedy in Europe,[71] the current reference made by the newly harmonised rules to individual actions - or at least their silence on aggregate litigation - mainly hides the difficulties of an ongoing planning stage.[72]

The importance of collective redress as a sort of flywheel for private antitrust enforcement has been stressed many times by the European Commission, through a

66. *See* Afferni, *supra* n. 44, at 171-178; *see* also Vincenzo Meli, *Introduzione al D.lgs 19 gennaio 2017 n. 3, di attuazione della Dir. 2014/104/UE sul risarcimento dei danni per violazione della normativa antitrust* [2018] *Le Nuove Leggi Civili Commentate* 119, 138.
67. *See* Clifford A. Jones, *Private Enforcement of Antitrust Law in the EU, UK and USA*, 210 (Hart Publishing 1999).
68. Pursuant to section 4, Clayton Antitrust Act of 1914, *supra* n. 45.
69. Rule 23, para. a) to b), Federal Rule of Civil Procedure, as amended in particular by the *Class Action Fairness Act* (2005), aimed at preventing some abuses and correcting some distortions. An insightful analysis on the main differences between the US and European models as regards a decentralised antitrust enforcement is given by David J Gerber, '*Competition Law and the Institutional Embeddedness of Competition*' in Josef Drexl, Laurence Idot, Joël Monéger (eds), *Economic Theory and Competition Law*, 20 (Edward Elgar Publishing 2009).
70. *See*, e.g., William M. Landes, *Optimal Sanctions for Antitrust Violations* (1983) 50 U. Chic. L. Rev. 652, 678; Richard A. Posner, *Antitrust Law* 267 (2nd ed., University of Chicago Press 2001); Herbert Hovenkamp, *Federal Antitrust Policy. The Law of Competition and its Practice* 52 (2nd ed., Thomson West 1999); William H. Page, *The Scope of Liability for Antitrust Violations* (1985) 37 Stan. L. Rev. 1445, 1453. It deserves to be noted, however, that in the current overseas debate, as well as in the light of many US Supreme Court decisions, there is a growing criticism about the use of class actions: *see*, e.g., Spencer Weber Waller and Olivia Popal, *The Fall and Rise of the Antitrust Class Action* (2016) 39 World Competition 29: 'The irony is that while the Supreme Court continues to narrow the doorway to class actions, the rest of the world is increasingly interested in creating new mechanisms for aggregate litigation to better support effective private damage litigation in competition cases, and in particular the large number of small claims cases that led to the class action boom in the U.S. in the first place.'Back to Europe, the absence of adequate incentives to sue, within the Directive, is clearly underlined by Andrea Nervi, *Directive 2014/104/EU on Antitrust Damages Actions. Some Considerations from the Perspective of Italian Law* [2016] The Italian Law Journal 131, 155-156.
71. *See* Heinemann, *supra* n. 13, at 637.
72. On the issue in general terms, *see*, e.g., Christopher Hoodges, *The Reform of Class and Representative Actions in European Legal Systems* (Hart Publishing 2008); *See* also Thomas M. J. Möllers and Bernahrd Pregler, *Civil law enforcement and collective redress in economic law* [2013] Europa e Diritto Privato, 27, 55.

series of documents and initiatives: the Green and White Papers *on Damages actions for breach of the EC antitrust rules*, the Green Paper of 2008 on *consumer collective redress*, not to mention the public consultation of 2011 *'Towards a more coherent European approach to collective redress'*.

Particularly in the White Paper on Damages Actions, the Commission stressed how '[i]ndividual consumers, but also small businesses, especially those who have suffered scattered and relatively low-value damage, are often deterred from bringing an individual action for damages by the costs, delays, uncertainties, risks and burdens involved'; a remark whose importance is even greater today in light of the option, chosen by the Directive, in favour of an offensive use of passing-on and also the explicit extension of standing requirements to indirect purchasers.[73]

Given, however, that collective redress mechanisms can play a pivotal role for the entire enforcement of individual rights conferred by the EU law, the European Parliament, in 2012, adopted the resolution '*Towards a Coherent European Approach to Collective Redress*' and argued for a wider harmonisation process, one to be achieved through a 'horizontal framework including a common set of principles providing uniform access to justice via collective redress within the Union and specifically but not exclusively dealing with the infringement of consumer rights'. Undeniably an ambitious goal, one whose result has at least in the short run been the weakening of any harmonisation process on collective redress, as shown by the mere adoption of a Commission Recommendation (the Commission Recommendation 2013/396 'on common principles for injunctive and compensatory collective redress mechanisms') – thus, while waiting to take two steps forward, one step back – or aside – has been taken instead.[74]

Notwithstanding the lack of a harmonised regime at EU level, some countries have already adopted some sort of collective redress mechanisms, and Italy is one of them.

73. The choice on passing-on that is made by the Damages Directive is, as known, dissonant with the US model, where, in the wake of two leading Supreme Court decisions, indirect purchasers have no standing to bring (individual/class) damages actions: *Hanover Shoe Inc v United Shoe Machinery Corp.*, 392 US. 481 (1968); *Illinois Brick Co. V State of Illinois*, 431 US 720 (1977). *See*, e.g., William M. Landes and Richard Posner, *Should Indirect Purchasers Have Standing to Sue under the Antitrust Laws? An Economic Analysis of the Rule of Illinois Brick* [1979] 46 Univ. Chic. L. Rev. 602, 608; Gregory J. Werden and Marius Schwartz, *Illinois Brick and the Deterrence of Antitrust Violations – An Economic Analysis* [1984] 35 Hastings Law Journal 629 et seq.; Herbert Hoverkamp, *Federal Antitrust Policy: The Law of Competition and its Practice* 615 et seq. (2nd ed., West Group 1999). For critical remarks *see*, however, Stephens Calkins, *An Enforcement Official's Reflections on Antitrust Class Action* [1997] 39 Ariz. Law Rev. 413, 424; Adam Thimmesch, *Beyond Treble Damages: Hanover Shoe and Direct Purchaser Suits After Cames v Microsoft Corp.* [2005] 90 Iowa Law Rev. 1649 et seq.

74. For critical remarks about the choice made *see*, e.g., Josef Drexl, '*Private and Public Enforcement of EU Competition Law*' in Hans-W. Micklitz and Andrea Wechsler (eds), *The Transformation of Enforcement. European Economic Law in a Global Perspective* 135, 156 (Hart Publishing 2016). *See* also the comments contained within Directorate-General for International Policies, *Collective Redress in Antitrust: study*, IP/A/ECON/ ST/2011-19 – PE 75.120, 12, http://ec.europa.eu/competition/antitrust/actionsdamages/index.html > Collective redress > Study on legislative action in the area of collective redress in the field of antitrust (accessed 24 April 2019).

Pursuant to Article 140 bis of the Italian Consumer Code (Legislative Decree n. 206 of 2015) (hereinafter 'Italian ConsumerC'), an opt-in class action is in fact available for granting damages (or restitution) in cases where consumers' homogeneous rights are violated by a series of conduct, including anticompetitive conduct.[75] Accordingly, the domestic implementation of the Damages Directive, pursuant to Article 1 Decree 3/2017, explicitly extends its range of application to antitrust damages claims brought in the form of aggregate litigation.

Meanwhile, on 3 April 2019, the Italian Parliament approved (Ddl 844/19) a new comprehensive regulation on class actions whose entry into force is postponed until twelve months after the date of publication in the *Gazzetta Ufficiale*. The new regime consists of several articles amending the Italian CPC (Article 840 bis–840 sexiesdecies) and is intended to replace the still valid Article 140 bis of the Italian ConsumerC). The new class action abandons its exclusive reference to consumers, becoming instead a general technique of aggregate litigation for damages or restitution claims arising from any violation (including antitrust violations) of homogeneous individual rights of the class members, and it is available against undertakings, either private and public, the latter as entrusted with the operation of public services.

Of course, it is impossible at this point to say anything as regards the practical impact that the new rules will have on antitrust private enforcement. In any event, since most of the new rules share many of their main features with the regime laid down in Article 140 bis of Italian ConsumerC, several critical remarks already valid for the latter will apply to the former too, strengthening the argument that the Italian model is not – as of now – an efficient substitute for the missing EU class action.

As clearly pointed out by the DGIP's Study on Collective Redress in Antitrust, we should first note that an opt-in mechanism, even though it has the advantage of limiting the risks of unmeritorious actions, entails a low participation rate. Low rates are a significant drawback to effective antitrust law enforcement, being no less problematic than the absence of economic incentives to sue (i.e., punitive damages) combined with the typical occurrence of parcelled and low-value damages.[76] Moreover, along with legal standing being restricted to individual consumers,[77] a further bottleneck stems from the need for homogeneity of claimants' rights, this being a premise for recognising the existence of the class and, thus, the admissibility of the action brought.

The 'homogeneity' prerequisite – still required by the amendments of 2019 – in fact gives rise to judicial uncertainty between: (i) a rigid interpretation, according to which the same kind of individual consequences (types of harms), originating from an

75. *See*, e.g., Enrico Camilleri, *Azione di classe a tutela dei consumatori e comportamenti anticoncorrenziali: criticità (e velleità) di un tentativo di trade-off* [2010] AIDA 415 et seq.
76. Directorate-General for International policies, *supra* n. 74, at 13. By contrast, the Commission Recommendation 2013/396/EU of 11 June 2013 on common principles for injunctive and compensatory collective redress mechanisms in the Member States concerning violations of rights granted under Union Law [2013], OJ L201/60, Articles 21–24, is in favour of the 'opt-in' method.
77. Such a circumscription of the legitimate claimants to consumers implies, of course, the exclusion of intermediate buyers/sellers.

antitrust violation,[78] are needed; and (ii) a more recent, open approach, according to which homogeneity should be conceived simply in relation to the same origin of individual harm, without thereby precluding a differentiation into subclasses as regards nature and amount.[79]

Further drawbacks refer to the damages awarded. Pursuant to Article 140 bis(12) Italian ConsumerC, in the event of success, claimants may obtain a judge's equitable estimation of the damages or the establishment of a homogeneous criterion to be applied for quantification. In both cases, even if with different *nuances*, the outcome of the lawsuit is a 'ballpark figure' evaluation, at high risk of yielding under-compensation and therefore at risk of dissuading more than incentivising individual adhesion, especially given that it implies relinquishing the right to bring individual actions (for either damages or restitution) that are grounded on the same facts as the collective claim. The same critical remark seems also valid with reference to the new mechanism introduced by the Italian CPC, at least when reading the vague formulation of Article 840 sexies (sub letters a and h).

If these elements are not disheartening enough, the overall picture on Italian class actions for antitrust infringement is worsened even further by the implementation of the Damages Directive: pursuant to Article 18 Decree 3/2017, actions for damages, either individual or collective, can be brought only before the specialised sections ('*sezione specializzata in materia di impresa*') of three Tribunals: Milan, Rome and Naples. The rationale behind this provision is to ensure a high expertise from the courts, given the complicated legal and economic issues involved in these type of claims. The negative, and practical, side effect of this choice of lawmakers is, however, to make the existing bottleneck even narrower.

V. THE (FURTHER) MISSING PIECES OF THE PUZZLE: CAUSATION AND QUANTIFICATION OF DAMAGES: SOME CONCLUDING REMARKS

There are two more missing pieces to the puzzle of EU antitrust private enforcement, two pieces that have been disregarded or are least not adequately dealt with by the new harmonised regime on damage claims, despite being pivotal for its optimal functioning in practice: causation and quantification of damages.

Causation is a structural constituent element of tortious liability, an element whose role within the framework of the remedy is to ensure that the tortfeasor is liable only for the harm that is the immediate and direct outcome of his/her conduct.[80]

78. *See*, e.g., Tribunale di Milano, ord. 8 November 2013, *Altro consumo-Bianchi (e altri) c/Trenord s.r.l.*
79. *See* Corte d'Appello di Milano, no. 2828, 25 August 2017, overruling Tribunale di Milano, ord. 8 November 2013; Corte d'Appello di Torino, 30 June 2016; Corte d'Appello di Milano, ord. 3 March 2014.
80. *See* Simon Deakin, Angus Johnston & Basil Markesinis, *Markesinis and Deakin's Tort Law* 185 (Oxford University Press, fifth ed., 2005); Isabelle C. Durant, '*Causation*' in Helmut Koziol and Reiner Schulze (eds), *Tort Law of the European Community* 63 (Springer 2008).

In terms of antitrust damages actions, the importance of the causation nexus becomes even greater than in traditional tort actions since – as is common in cases of pure economic loss – there is a typical dispersion of losses through the market and 'the victims are not only competitors, but also rivals, suppliers and firms operating in complementary markets'.[81]

Moreover, the wider the range of interests that the violated norm is meant to protect, the more crucial the need will be to use the causation requirement as a tool to control the floodgates and access to the remedy. This dynamic is even stronger in competition law since it is meant to protect general interests (such as a competitive structure or the competition on a given market) within which a set of more specific interests are represented.

The distortion of a competitive market is often an event causing multiple injuries. One anticompetitive action may simultaneously cause damages to competitors, to companies operating at different market levels and to final consumers. Therefore, in order to prevent that a violation of such a general interest also implies an unmanageable number of follow-on damages actions, the link between a specific anticompetitive conduct and the harm that can be described as directly related to this conduct needs to be stringent.

The ECJ has many times stressed the pivotal role played by the causation requirement for antitrust damages claims, despite pointing out that this issue is governed by national law, given the lack of a common European doctrine on the issue.[82] However, notwithstanding this awareness, or perhaps exactly because of it, the Damages Directive does not introduce any specific provision on causation, while the Italian implementation only indirectly refers to it in the context of the quantification of damages; pursuant to Article 14 Decree 3/17: 'Compensation for damages caused by a violation of the law of competition [that are] due to the injured person must be determined according to the provisions of Articles 1223 … of the Italian CC.'[83]

That being said, causation is commonly conceived as having a twofold meaning: on the one hand there is 'causation-in-fact', which is used in order to establish a link between the wrongful conduct of the tortfeasor and the harm suffered by the victim (the standard usually applied to determine this link is the 'but-for' test). On the other hand, there is 'legal causation', which is used in order to limit the extent of an

81. *See*, e.g., Pedro Caro de Sousa, *EU and national approaches to passing on and causation in competition damages cases: a doctrine in search of balance* (2018) 55 CML Rev. 1751, 1780; *see* also Ioannis Lianos, Peter Davis & Paolisa Nebbia, *Damages Claims for the Infringement of EU Competition Law* 103 (Oxford University Press 2015).
82. *See*, as leading cases on the issue, Joined Cases C-295/04 to C-298/04 *Manfredi*, *supra* n. 7, at paras 61–64; Case C-510/11 *Kone and Others v Commission*, *supra* n. 57, at paras 22–24; Case C-360/09 *Pfleiderer*, *supra* n. 4, at para. 28; ECJ, Case C-199/11 *Europese Gemeenschap v Otis NV and Others* [2012] ECLI:EU:C:2012:684, para. 43. *See* also ECJ, Case 48/72 *Brasserie de Haecht v Wilkin II* [1973] ECR 77. For a wider analysis of the ECJ's posture on the theme *see* Caroline Cauffman, *The DCFR and the Attempts to Increase the Private Enforcement of Competition Law: Convergences and Divergences* (2010) 18 ERPL, 1079–1105.
83. Article 1223 of the Italian Civil Code is a norm explicitly provided for a breach of contract, but it is also applicable to tort law; it reads as follows: 'The compensation for damage … must therefore include the loss suffered by the creditor as loss of income, as it is an immediate and direct consequence thereof.'

attributable harm for which the tortfeasor can be held liable[84] and which is oriented on two main functions: the explanatory and the attributive functions,[85] the fulfilment of which rest on the use of several tests and formulas that express concepts regarding proximity, foreseeability, scope of the rule, etc.

The combined effect of both these meanings makes clear the distance between the scientific and the legal discourse on causation, the former aiming at the prediction of future events, given specific antecedents, and therefore mainly pertaining to an *ex ante* evaluation; the latter aiming at the attribution of responsibility to an agent in light of his/her actions or omissions, which is to say a typical *ex post*, counterfactual analysis.

This usual interplay between causation in fact and legal causation proves, however, to be much more complex in antitrust cases as the more removed the harm (pecuniary loss) suffered in the supply chain is, the weaker the causal link between that harm and the wrongful conduct (antitrust infringement) that is supposed to be its direct cause, to the point of the link disappearing entirely, especially whenever a contract works as a diaphragm between the conduct and the event.

The latter situation typically occurs in the context of cartels and downstream contracts, where the tension – if not the divergences – between an economic approach and a legal approach to causation can be easily described.

And in fact, even if from an economic point of view the harm suffered by a contractual counterpart – independent of whether a direct counterpart or even an indirect purchaser, supplier or client – is directly linked to the upstream restrictive agreement, from a private law viewpoint that harm, consisting, for example, of an inflated price, is but the direct effect of the contract itself. And the contract will not only be the result of a meeting of minds involving the counterpart's will; rather, it is the only 'fact' capable, as such, of causing the harmful event. More precisely, while the contract can be described as the sole proximate cause of the harm (i.e., the cause in the absence of which the effect would not have happened), upstream antitrust infringement is but a secondary one (i.e., an event in the absence of which the effect would not have been prevented).

Italian jurisprudence has, particularly in more recent years, tried to handle this critical issue by embracing a wide use of rebuttable presumptions: according to some decisions taken by the Court of *Cassazione*,[86] mainstream economic analyses provide a reliable ground for presuming that a cartel is the direct cause of a damage to the whole market, once its existence has been proved. This is a rebuttable presumption, of

84. *See*, e.g., Ioannis Lianos, *Causal Uncertainty and Damages Claims for Infringement of Competition Law in Europe*, CLES Research Paper Series 2/2015, https://www.ucl.ac.uk/cles/sites/cles/files/cles-2-2015.pdf (accessed 24 April 2019); Lianos, Davis & Nebbia, *supra* n. 81, at 75. As for the Italian law of torts *see*, e.g., Massimo Franzoni, '*Dei fatti illeciti: artt. 2043-2059*' in Francesco Galgano (ed.), *Commentario del Codice Civile* Scialoja-Branca, 84 (Zanichelli 1993).
85. *See*, Antony Honoré, '*Causation in the Law*' in Edward n. Zalta (ed.), *The Stanford Encyclopedia of Philosophy* (Winter 2010 edn).
86. *See*, among the others, Corte di Cassazione, no. 11904, 28 May 2014; Corte di Cassazione, no. 9116, 23 April 2014.

course, in the sense that the defendant can prove the interruption of any causal link between the antitrust infringement and the harm.

It should be noted that such an interpretation is quite disputed in Italy since it subverts the general rule about the burden of proof and, above all, since it relies excessively on a probabilistic method - the 'more likely than not' rule -working better as regards causation in fact than for legal causation, the latter requiring a specific, individualised evaluation of the facts.[87]

These queries have now been even further sharpened by the Damages Directive and its implementing rules. It suffices to mention that Article 3 Damages Directive stresses - consistent with the case law of the ECJ - that 'any natural or legal person who has suffered harm caused by an infringement of competition law' has to be able to claim and obtain full compensation for that harm, a formula that, in light of the Directive, captures indirect purchasers of the infringers[88] as well as third parties that have been harmed by an 'umbrella price'.[89]

In any event, particularly in the latter cases, the antitrust violation really seems to be too remote from the harm, so that a finding of liability appears to heed a policy directive more than the main features of a tort remedy. In other words, the remedy in tort seems capable of intercepting the closest harm caused by the wrongful conduct, but it cannot encompass the whole perimeter within which the distorting wave propagates.

That being said, we may wonder which kind of damage it is that we are presuming. Which harm we are talking about? What is in fact 'more likely than not' is that an antitrust infringement, and more precisely a cartel, inflicts damage on the market as a whole and not a parcelled individual harm. And this is twice as true as soon as we refer to exclusionary practices.[90]

This remark introduces the last critical point that deserves to be underlined: the issue of quantification of damages.

In granting the right to a full compensation, the Directive evokes either the *damnum emergens* or the *lucrum cessans*. Pursuant to Article 3(2) Damages Directive: 'Full compensation shall place a person who has suffered harm in the position in which that person would have been had the infringement of competition law not been committed. It shall therefore cover the right to compensation for actual loss and for loss of profit, plus the payment of interest.'

87. Roberto Pardolesi, *Note minime in tema di nesso di causalità* [2014] *Concorrenza e mercato* 317, 321.
88. As regards the likelihood that damages claims could really be brought by indirect purchasers, it has been rightly observed that '[i]n the overwhelming majority of cases, damages actions are brought by direct purchasers' whereas it is 'extremely rare that they are introduced by indirect purchasers': *see* Lianos, Davis & Nebbia, *supra* n. 81, at 104. *See* Enrico Camilleri, *Il trasferimento del sovrapprezzo anticoncorrenziale nella Direttiva 2014/104/UE* [2015] AIDA 32; Francesco Mezzanotte, *Il trasferimento del sovrapprezzo anticoncorrenziale* [2018] Le Nuove Leggi Civili Commentate 215.
89. This in the wake of the Kone case: Case C-510/11 *Kone and Others v Commission*, *supra* n. 57.
90. *See*, e.g., Mario Libertini, *La determinazione del danno risarcibile nella proposta di Direttiva comunitaria sul risarcimento del danno antitrust. Alcune osservazioni preliminary* [2014] Concorrenza e Mercato 265.

This reading recalls Mommsen's *Differenztheorie*; a theory, however, whose application in antitrust cases proves to be highly inadequate since the quantification of damages (suffered by third parties) rests on complex, counterfactual analyses that are properly based on economic data.

As commendably observed overseas, '[t]he marriage between economics and ... antitrust policy becomes rocky when it reaches the law of damages ... the law of damages has the much more difficult task of quantifying injury; the difference between saying that a certain practice is harmful and quantifying the amount of harm can be significant'.[91]

Now, in order to soften this burden of proof for plaintiffs, the Directive introduces at least two rebuttable presumptions: that of Article 17(2), according to which '[i]t shall be presumed that cartel infringements cause harm' and that contained in Article 14, regarding the presumption of the passing-on of overcharges: 'In the situation referred to in paragraph 1, the indirect purchaser shall be deemed to have proven that a passing-on to that indirect purchaser occurred where that indirect purchaser has shown that: (a) the defendant has committed an infringement of competition law; (b) the infringement of competition law has resulted in an overcharge for the direct purchaser of the defendant; and (c) the indirect purchaser has purchased the goods or services that were the object of the infringement of competition law, or has purchased goods or services derived from or containing them.'

In any event, these presumptions apply to cartels only, whereas they are not capable of capturing other infringements, like exclusionary or exploitative conduct; moreover, they provide a provisional answer to the question of whether the harm does exist, without saying anything as to the main quantification of damages suffered. The plaintiff and the judge should therefore handle on their own this issue. They could of course refer to soft law texts like the Commission's Guidelines on the quantification of damages, but the complex economic assessments involved suggest that the Court requires specialised assistance, either from an NCA or from other institutions or persons.

The two likely outcomes are both negative: either an equitable estimation (with the implied risks of overestimation or underestimation) or a sort of *damnum in re ipsa*.[92] In any case, what results is something that is far from the proclaimed goal of full compensation, something that is instead, as stressed regarding the causality nexus, a forced application of tortious liability.

In conclusion, although paradoxical at a first glance, it seems that the Damages Directive on non-contractual liability even worsens the interplay between competition law (goals) and private law remedies. It is an interplay whose critical attributes have been clearly summarised in querying whether competition policy is 'a tool to protect the competitive process and to serve the public goals or ... primarily an instrument of

91. *See* Herbert Hovenkamp, *A Primer on Antitrust Damages*, University of Iowa Legal Studies Research Paper, https://papers.ssrn.com/sol3/papers.cfm?abstract_id=1685919 (accessed 24 April 2019).
92. Which is, in any event, strongly opposed by the Court of Cassazione: *see*, e.g., Corte di Cassazione, no. 1931, 25 January 2017; Corte di Cassazione, no. 207, 8 January 2019.

consumer protection'.[93] It is, as well, self-evident that agreement on the first alternative - thereby also following some hints from the ECJ itself[94] - would make clear the inconsistencies in the scope of private law tools (remedies) as assigned to solve conflicts between particular interests.

The fact is that the Damages Directive, beyond any apparent paradox, simply corroborates this thesis, by fashioning a sort of allotrope of the classical private law remedy in tort, an allotrope in relation to which what is written as 'private interest' should be regarded as general (public) interest:[95] an interest in the regulation of markets.

The time when antitrust private enforcement development was supposed to be a flywheel for a European private law - parallel to or at least harmonious with the most advanced projects for a 'codification' of the latter, such as seen with the DCFR[96] - really belong to a past phase in the process of European integration.

93. *See* Josef Drexl, Beatrix Conde Gallego et al., *Comments by the Max Planck Institute for Intellectual Property, Competition and Tax Law, on the White Paper by the Directorate-General of Competition on Damages Actions for Breach of EC Antitrust Rules* [2008] IIC 799. For critical remarks *see* also Jürgen Basedow, '*Recognition of Foreign Decisions within the European Competition Network*' in Jürgen Basedow, Jörg Philipp Terhechte and Ludos Tichý (eds), *Private Enforcement of Competition* Law 169, 171 (Nomos 2011). *See* also Heike Schweizer, '*Competition Law and Public Policy: Reconsidering an Uneasy Relationship – The Example of Article 81*' in Josef Drexl, Laurence Idot & Joël Monéger (eds), *Economic Theory and Competition Law* 134, 145 (Edward Edgar Publishing 2009).
94. *See* ECJ, Joined Cases C-468/06 and C-478/06 *Lélos kai Sia and Others v GlaxoSmithKline* [2008] ECR I-7139, paras 65–66.
95. *See*, e.g., Marie-Anne Frison-Roche, *Efficient and/or Effective Enforcement*, in Josef Drexl, Laurence Idot & Joël Monéger (eds), Economic Theory and Competition Law, 211 (Edward Edgar Publishing 2009).
96. *See*, e.g., Cauffman, *supra* n. 82.

CHAPTER 7

Private Enforcement in the Netherlands

Rogier Meijer & Erik-Jan Zippro

I. Introduction
II. The development of private enforcement
  A. Introduction
  B. Jurisdiction over international competition infringements
  C. Masterfoods Defence
  D. Applicable law
  E. Passing-on
  F. Implementation of Damages Directive
III. What is effective and what are the impediments to private enforcement?
IV. Which entity is liable for damages?
V. Binding effect of decisions of competition authorities
VI. Limitation of actions
VII. Collective actions/pooling of claims
  A. Introduction
  B. Assignment model
  C. Mass settlements
  D. Collective damages actions
VIII. Conclusion

I. INTRODUCTION

The Netherlands is generally considered to be a favourable jurisdiction for private enforcement of competition law. Over the last years, there have been many cases pending before the Dutch courts where parties filed a claim for damages in connection with an infringement of competition law. Most of these cases concern follow-on actions where a competition authority – in most cases the European Commission – issued a decision in which it established a cartel infringement.

II. THE DEVELOPMENT OF PRIVATE ENFORCEMENT

A. Introduction

Following the European Ashurst report, at the request of the Dutch Ministry of Economic Affairs, a study was conducted to assess the possibilities for private enforcement of competition law in the Netherlands.[1] This study was finished in 2005. One of the main conclusions was that the Dutch situation confirmed the conclusion from the Ashurst report. Although the number of judgments from civil law courts in competition cases showed an increase, the total number was still small. That was especially true for cases where damages were claimed and awarded. The report showed that only in few cases was the aim to receive damage compensation rather than filing a claim for an injunction of certain behaviour. The report identified also almost no claims in relation to hardcore infringements. As possible reasons for the low number of damage claims, the report mentioned *inter alia* difficulties in evidence, the passing-on defence, difficulties in damage calculation, the difficulties in bringing collective actions (e.g., procedural problems and financing issues) and the restriction at the time (this has changed, *see* VII.D, *infra*) that precluded collective damage actions.

Since this 2005 report, things have fundamentally changed. A substantial number of follow-on cartel damage actions have been brought before the Dutch courts. The cases concern, for example, damage claims following the *Elevator* cartel,[2] the *Bitumen* cartel,[3] the *Air Cargo* cartel,[4] the *Paraffin Wax* cartel,[5] the *Sodium Chlorate* cartel,[6] the *Prestressing Steel* cartel,[7] the *CRT* cartel,[8] the *Gas Insulated Switchgear*

1. Maarten F.J. Haak & Weyer VerLoren van Themaat, *De mogelijkheden voor civielrechtelijke handhaving van de mededingingsregels in Nederland* (een inventarisatie in opdracht van het Ministerie van Economische Zaken, 3 November 2005), https://docplayer.nl/16371173-De-mogelijkheden-voor-civielrechtelijke-handhaving-van-de-mededingingsregels-in-nederland.html (accessed 15 July 2019).
2. Rechtbank (Rb.) Rotterdam, 17 July 2013, ECLI:NL:RBROT:2013:5504 *Stichting Elevator Claim/Kone et al.*
3. Rb. Rotterdam, 9 February 2011, ECLI:NL:RBROT:20100:BP7518.
4. For example, Rb. Amsterdam, 12 April 2017, ECLI:NL:RBAMS:2017:2841 *SCC/KLM et al.* and Rb. Amsterdam, 13 September 2017, ECLI:NL:RBAMS:2017:6607 *Equilib/KLM et al.*
5. For example, Rb. Den Haag, 1 May 2013, ECLI:NL:RBDHA:2013:CA1870; Rb. Den Haag, 21 September 2016, ECLI:NL:RBDHA:2016:11305 *CDC/Shell et al.*
6. For example, Rb. Amsterdam, 4 June 2014, ECLI:NL:RBAMS:2014:3190 *CDC/Akzo et al.*; Gerechtshof (Hof) Amsterdam, 21 July 2015, ECLI:NL:GHAMS:2015:3006 *Kemira/CDC.*
7. Rb. Limburg, 16 November 2016, ECLI:NL:RBLIM:2016:9897 *Deutsche Bahn/Nedri et al.*
8. Rb. Oost-Brabant, 29 November 2017, ECLI:NL:RBOBR:2017:6331 *Cemaz/Philips et al.*; Rb. Oost-Brabant, 29 November 2017, ECLI:NL:RBOBR:2017:6333 *IGB/Philips et al.*; Rb. Oost-Brabant, 29 November 2017, ECLI:NL:RBOBR:2017:6332 *Itautec/Philips et al.*; Rb. Oost-Brabant, 27 June 2018, ECLI:NL:RBOBR:2018:3170 *Vestel/Philips et al.*

cartel[9] and more recently the *Truck* cartel.[10] In the follow-on proceedings in connection with the *Gas Insulated Switchgear* cartel, an amount of more than EUR 23 million was awarded.[11] Many of the other proceedings mentioned are still pending at first instance or on appeal.

Even though many of the aforementioned cases are still pending and have not yet resulted in final decisions, there have been numerous (interim) judgments in these cases that have given direction to the area of private enforcement of competition law. Below we discuss some of the main issues that have been addressed before the Dutch courts in this respect over the last years.

B. Jurisdiction over international competition infringements

Since many cartels are Europe-wide (or even global), most cases deal with defendants - i.e. the companies that participated in the cartel - from different jurisdictions. There are several possibilities to establish the jurisdiction of the Dutch courts. In most of the follow-on cartel damage proceedings, jurisdiction is founded through the use of a claim against a Netherlands-based defendant that serves as an anchor defendant with which the claims against the other cartel members are connected.[12] Dutch courts have a relatively liberal approach as to accepting that the judicial and factual circumstances of the claims against the various defendants are similar. When claims are based on the same competition infringement as established by the European Commission, a sufficient connection will in principle be assumed. In this respect, it is not necessary that it follows from the Commission decision that the anchor defendant was directly involved in the infringement. Also in the situation where the defendant was an addressee of the decision as the parent company - of a subsidiary directly involved in the infringement - this claim is considered to be a claim based on the same judicial and factual circumstance leading to the jurisdiction of the Dutch court.[13] The Dutch courts find it foreseeable for a defendant that it can be summoned before the courts of (one of) the other defendant(s) when the European Commission has established in a binding decision the existence of a single continuous infringement of competition law as a result of which each cartel participant is liable for the damage resulting from this cartel. In that situation, a cartel participant should reasonably take account of the fact that they could be summoned before the courts of the domicile of the other cartel

9. Rb. Gelderland, 16 January 2013, ECLI:NL:RBONE:2013:BZ0403; Hof Arnhem-Leeuwarden, 2 September 2014, ECLI:NL:GHARL:2014:6766; Hoge Raad (HR), 8 July 2016, ECLI:NL:HR:2016:1483; Rb. Gelderland, 29 March 2017, ECLI:NL:RBGEL:2017:1724 *TenneT cs/ABB et al.*; Rb. Gelderland, 16 June 2015, ECLI:RBGEL:2015:3713 *TenneT/Alstom*.
10. Rb. Amsterdam, 15 May 2019, ECLI:NL:RBAMS:2019:3574 *CDC et al./ DAF et al.*
11. Rb. Gelderland, 29 March 2017 *TenneT/ABB, supra* n. 9.
12. In the meaning of Article 8 Brussel I bis Regulation or Article 6 Dutch Code of Civil Procedure (in cases involving defendants outside the European Union).
13. Rb. Amsterdam, 4 June 2014 *CDC/Akzo et al., supra* n. 6; Rb. Den Haag, 1 May 2015, ECLI:NL:RBDHA:2013:CA1870 *CDC/Shell et al.*

participants.[14] This is not different because the cartel infringement is also connected to other jurisdictions.[15]

C. *Masterfoods* Defence

The defence that the civil damage proceedings should be stayed awaiting the outcome of the appeal proceedings before the EU courts against the relevant decision of the EU Commission - the so-called *Masterfoods* Defence[16] as now laid down in Article 16 of Regulation 1/2003[17] - is not likely to be successful before the Dutch courts.

The Court of Appeal of Amsterdam, for example, rejected this defence in follow-on proceedings in the *Air Cargo* cartel case.[18] The court reasoned that the *Masterfoods* Defence must be understood in the context of the division of tasks between the European Commission and the EU courts on the one hand and the national courts on the other hand. From this, it does not follow that in every situation where one of the parties has appealed against the decision of the EU Commission establishing the competition infringement, the civil proceeding must be suspended. According to the Court of Appeal, suspension is necessary only to the extent that in the national proceedings questions arise - of either a factual or legal nature - whose answers depend on the validity of the Commission's decision. In this respect, the court is of the opinion that suspension is justified only if there is a reasonable doubt as to the validity of the decision of the EU Commission.[19]

As a result, in the situation in which a party's claim relies on a decision to establish its cartel damage, it falls upon the defendant that is disputing the validity of that decision and requesting suspension of the civil proceedings: (i) to demonstrate that it invoked a timely appeal to nullify the decision, (ii) to make clear that it has reasonable grounds for objecting against the decision before the EU courts and (iii) to indicate which defences it wants to invoke such that the national court is able to assess if the validity of the decision is important for these defences.[20] On the basis of the foregoing, the national court will decide if it is necessary (and if so, to what extent) to suspend the civil proceedings. This approach does justice to the interest of the claimant to avoid unnecessary delays in pursuing its claim for compensation while at the same time meeting the interest of the defendant to limit costs for defending itself in civil proceedings before the Commission's decision has become final.

14. Hof Amsterdam, 21 July 2015 *Kemira/CDC, supra* n. 6.
15. Rb. Limburg, 25 February 2015, ECLI:NL:RBLIM:2015:1791 *Deutsche Bahn/Nedri Spanstaal et al.* and Rf. Amsterdam, 4 June 2014 *CDC/Akzo cs, supra* n. 6.
16. ECJ, Case C-344/98 *Masterfoods Ltd v HB Ice Cream Ltd* [2000] ECR I-11369.
17. Council Regulation (EC) No 1/2003 of 16 December 2002 on the implementation of the rules on competition laid down in Articles 81 and 82 of the Treaty [2003] OJ L 1/1.
18. Hof Amsterdam, 24 September 2013, ECLI:NL:GHAMS:2013:3013 *Equilib/KLM.*
19. The Court of Appeal (Hof) refers to Case C-199/11 *Europese Gemeenschap v Otis NV and Others* [2012] ECLI:EU:C:2012:388, Opinion of AG Cruz Villalón, para. 52.
20. *Ibid.*

D. Applicable law

As many competition infringements are multi-jurisdictional, pan-European or even worldwide, in most of the civil proceedings following on these infringements there will be questions about the applicable law. For harmful events occurring since 11 January 2009, the Rome II Regulation applies (hereinafter 'Rome II').[21] Under Article 6(3)(a) Rome II, the law applicable for claims arising from a restriction of competition is the law of the country where the market is, or is likely to be, affected, the so-called market rule. In the situation where the market is, or is likely to be, affected in more than one country, Article 6(3)(b) Rome II provides for the possibility for a claimant to base his claim on the law of the seized court, provided that the market in that Member State is among those directly and substantially affected by the restriction of competition. This last option is to avoid a fragmentation of different applicable law systems.

Many of the currently pending follow-on proceedings before the Dutch courts – at least partly – relate to claims from before 11 January 2009. These claims therefore fall outside the temporal scope of Rome II. For these claims, the question of the applicable law is governed by the Dutch Unlawful Acts (Conflict of Laws) Act (*Wet conflictenrecht onrechtmatige daad* (hereinafter 'WCOD')). As with Rome II, the WCOD provides for a market rule, but without the possibility of a claimant opting for the law of the court where there is more than one market involved. As a result, there may be a fragmentation of the applicable law systems if claims are brought that involve markets from different jurisdictions. It should be noted, however, that under the WCOD an *ex post* choice of law was possible, as a result of which parties could avoid such a fragmentation by agreeing on one applicable law system.

Also, it is not always clear what the result of the market rule should be. In several judgments, the place where supply and demand came together was used as a starting point. In proceedings relating to the *Paraffin Wax* cartel, this led The Hague District Court to the conclusion that the applicable law in the context of the market rule was the law of the country of the production site of the purchasers.[22] In civil proceedings regarding the *Sodium Chlorate* cartel, the Amsterdam court reached a similar decision.[23]

However, in follow-on proceedings regarding the *Air Cargo* cartel, the Amsterdam court reached a different conclusion.[24] According to the claimant (a claim vehicle), all claims should be decided under Dutch law since the worldwide cartel also affected the competition in the Dutch market. Defendants – the airlines providing the airfreight services – argued that the applicable law should be assessed per individual transaction between the airline and the customer, a transaction which is governed by the law of the country of the airport of departure of the airfreight. The District Court of Amsterdam decided to pose preliminary questions to the Dutch Supreme Court to

21. Regulation (EC) No 864/2007 of the European Parliament and of the Council of 11 July 2007 on the law applicable to non-contractual obligations (Rome II) [2007] OJ L 199/40.
22. Rb. Den Haag, 17 December 2014, ECLI:NL:RBDHA:2014:15722 *CDC/Shell cs.*
23. Rb. Amsterdam, 10 May 2017, ECLI:NL:RBAMS:2017:3166 *CDC/Kemira.*
24. Rb. Amsterdam, 1 May 2019, ECLI:NL:RBAMS:2019:3394 *Equilib/KLM cs.*

receive guidance on how to apply the market rule in this situation. However, the Supreme Court did not answer the questions asked by the district court because the questions were not permissible as preliminary questions since the Commission's decisions establishing the cartel infringement was not yet final due to appeal proceedings before the European Court of Justice. Also, the Supreme Court found that it was not clear that the question asked would also be relevant for other cases with similar issues, in part because this is a question under 'old' law (the WCOD).[25] We consider this a missed opportunity since in reality this is a question where guidance is needed in many pending cases (e.g., the pending damage proceedings following on the *Truck* cartel) and which is likely to be an issue for the coming years.

Without the requested guidance from the Supreme Court, the district court came to the decision that Dutch law applied to all claims since the market rule under the WCOD did not provide for a workable solution. The underlying reasoning for this was that the cartel had a worldwide impact such that the market rule could result in the applicability of practically every legal system of the world. In its ruling, the court noted that the legislature apparently did not consider a situation like this. The court reasoned that since also the Dutch market was affected, Dutch law arguably could be applied to all claims. The court considered this a practical solution, one which was also intended by the Dutch legislature (with regard to the WCOD) and one which was furthermore in line with the European principle of effectiveness as also expressed in Directive 2014/104/EU (hereinafter 'Damages Directive').[26] In this respect, the court observed that although the Damages Directive had not entered into effect at the moment the claims arose, the principle of effectiveness was already a principle of Union law that had to be taken into account before the Damages Directive.

E. Passing-on

Before the implementation of the Damages Directive, Dutch law did not provide for specific rules on passing-on. However, it was generally assumed that a passing-on defence was a valid defence under Dutch law. Another question was how the passing-on defence must be seen under Dutch law, i.e. as an element of (the existence of) damage or, alternatively, as a benefit that must be considered when assessing if the whole damage must be compensated. Such that the benefits resulting from any passing-on should be deducted from the damages to be awarded, to the extent this would be reasonable. To a large extent this is a doctrinal Dutch law discussion which was 'solved' by the Supreme Court by deciding that it can be seen as both (i.e., part of the damage or as benefit in the context of the deduction of collateral benefits)

25. Which is one of the formal requirements to raise a preliminary question with the Supreme Court (HR).
26. Directive 2014/104/EU of the European Parliament and of the Council of 26 November 2014 on certain rules governing actions for damages under national law for infringements of the competition law provisions of the Member States and of the European Union [2014], OJ L349/1.

depending on the manner the claim is brought forward and the debate between the parties.[27]

Following this judgment of the Supreme Court, the District Court of Gelderland in a follow-on case in the *Gas Insulated Switchgear* cartel had to assess the passing-on defence invoked by ABB against TenneT.[28] ABB argued that TenneT - a high-voltage electricity grid manager - passed on the overcharge resulting from the cartel to its customers by charging higher electricity prices. The court started with the consideration that the nature of the cartelised product (an installation/immovable object) was such that the overcharge would not be directly passed on to the customers of TenneT but would be gradually passed on through electricity prices. In principle, this would mean that the causal link between the overcharge on fixed assets and the passing-on by the depreciation of these assets in the prices was too remote for a passing-on defence to be based on. This is also true given the fact that it is a free choice to pass on the overcharge or not. However, the tariffs that can be charged by TenneT are set by the government such that TenneT did not have that choice. As a result, the court did accept the existence of a causal link in this situation, and it considered that ultimately the end-consumers would have paid most of the overcharge. Since the likelihood that consumers would claim these scattered damages from ABB was negligible, and in light of the expectation of the court that damage compensation made to TenneT - featuring 100% participation of the Dutch State - would be for the benefit of all Dutch residents and therefore broadly distributed to the same injured end users, the court did not accept the passing-on defence.

F. Implementation of Damages Directive

The Damages Directive was implemented into Dutch law on 10 February 2017.[29] The most important changes occasioned by the Damages Directive relate to issues regarding:

(1) the presumption of damage; although some Dutch courts already accepted that a cartel agreement could be assumed to cause damage,[30] this assumption has now been codified in Dutch law;[31]

27. HR, 8 July 2016, ECLI:HR:2016:1483 *ABB/TenneT*.
28. Rb. Gelderland, 29 March 2017 *TenneT/ABB*, *supra* n. 9.
29. Implementatiewet richtlijn privaatrechtelijke handhaving mededingingsrecht of 25 January 2017, Staatsblad van het Koninkrijk der Nederlanden (Stb.) 2017, 28.
30. *See*, e.g., Rb. Oost-Brabant 16 January 2013, ECLI:NL:RBONE:2013:BZ0403 *TenneT TSO/ABB*.
31. Article 6:193l Dutch Civil Code.

(2) the special position of SMEs[32] and recipients of immunity;[33]
(3) the implications of a settlement;[34]
(4) disclosure of documents;[35]
(5) the passing-on defence;[36] and
(6) suspension of proceedings[37] and (the extension of) limitation periods.[38]

For other parts of the Damages Directive, the Dutch legislature was of the opinion that Dutch law already was in conformity with the directive, such that changes in Dutch law were not necessary.

The Damages Directive may also be relevant for cases that strictly fall outside the temporal scope of the directive. In follow-on proceedings between ABB and TenneT in relation to the *Gas Insulated Switchgear* cartel, the Supreme Court indicated that also in out-of-scope situations it is desirable to apply and interpret Dutch law in a manner that leads to a result that is consistent with the Damages Directive.[39] The District Court of Rotterdam followed this reasoning in the *Bitumen* case.[40] It clarified that – other than as argued by defendant Shell – this would not constitute a *contra legem* interpretation since the discretionary room in interpreting existing Dutch law will in most cases be sufficient to prevent any *contra legem* interpretation. This will not mean, however, that it always will be accepted by Dutch courts to rely on the Damages Directive – by means of an EU-consistent interpretation of Dutch law – in situations where the claim is outside the temporal scope of the directive. The Court of Appeal at Arnhem-Leeuwarden, for example, rejected the argument of the claimant that on the basis of the Damages Directive the defendant as a cartel member was jointly and severally liable for the damage resulting from the cartel infringement, including the damage caused during the period in which defendant did not participate in the infringement. The Court of

32. Provided that full compensation can be collected from the other cartel member, SMEs with a market share of at least 5% on the relevant market will only be liable for the damage suffered by their direct and indirect customers if full liability would cause the company to become unviable (Article 6:193m (2), unless an executive of the company was involved in the infringement or induced the infringement or the company has been involved in a breach of competition law before (Article 6:193m (3) Dutch Civil Code)).
33. Provided that full compensation can be collected from the other cartel member, a recipient of immunity is only liable for the damage suffered by its direct and indirect customers and suppliers (Article 6:193m (4) Dutch Civil Code). A new Article 6:193n Dutch Civil Code provides for the implementation of the special position of the immunity recipient as regards the internal contribution to the damages awarded to claimants.
34. Article 6:193o Dutch Civil Code.
35. Implementation legislation into Dutch law (Article was mainly necessary to safeguard the disclosure of leniency documentation).
36. Article 6:193 and 6:193q Dutch Civil Code.
37. Article 6:193r Dutch Civil Code allows the court to suspend the damage proceedings following a competition infringement for one year if parties are involved in out-of-court dispute resolution. This is also a reason for extension of the limitation period pursuant to Article 6:193t Dutch Civil Code.
38. Article 6:193s Dutch Civil Code and 6:193t(2) Dutch Civil Code.
39. HR, 8 July 2016 *ABB/TenneT*, *supra* n. 27.
40. Rb. Rotterdam, 26 September 2018, ECLI:NL:RBROT:2018:8001.

Appeal here merely ruled that the Damages Directive did not apply due to its temporal scope.[41]

III. WHAT IS EFFECTIVE AND WHAT ARE THE IMPEDIMENTS TO PRIVATE ENFORCEMENT?

In general, the Dutch legal system is characterised by the high quality of its judicial system, its efficiency and the practical approach of its courts in complex cases. Further, the court fees are fixed and relatively modest.[42] Also, in the Netherlands, the litigation costs awarded to a prevailing party are usually limited to the court registry fee, the costs of witnesses and experts and a limited fixed amount for lawyers' fees.

The practical and efficient approach can, for example, be illustrated by the approach of the Dutch courts in relation to the *Masterfoods* Defence (as discussed II.C., *supra*). Also, the decision of the Amsterdam court in the *Air Cargo* case in relation to the applicable law (II.D., *supra*) is a good example of a court taking into account the function it has in safeguarding the possibility to claim for damages for an infringement of competition law.

Another feature of Dutch law which has proven to be effective is the possibility under the Collective Mass Claims Settlements Act ('Wet Collectieve Actie Massaschade') to have a settlement declared universally binding upon the class of those who have suffered damage (except for the parties that opt out from the settlement). This instrument is not limited in its material scope and therefore also applies to claims resulting from competition law infringements. In order for this settlement to be eligible to be declared binding, the settlement must be reached by defendant(s) with a foundation or association having full legal capacity that can institute legal proceedings for the protection of the interests of other persons, insofar as these interests are represented in accordance with its articles of association. These so-called 3:305a foundations or associations (named after Article §3:305a of the Dutch Civil Code) could until recently seek only a declaratory ruling and/or an order or injunction. It was not possible to claim for damages. However, a recent change in the law makes it possible to also bring a collective claim for damages (*see* in more detail VII.D, *infra*).

There are no clear substantial impediments to private enforcement in the Netherlands. Obviously, it may be that for some cases, another jurisdiction may be more attractive, such as when large-scale pretrial discovery is expected to be necessary. Although the Dutch regime provides for a rather sophisticated system of discovery, the possibilities are still limited compared to, for example, the UK legal system. Although there are no clear impediments, we see some potential risks for the Dutch legal system in terms of resources of the courts. Being an increasingly popular jurisdiction for mass

41. Hof Arnhem-Leeuwarden, 28 August 2018, ECLI:NL:GHARL:2018:7753 *Grid Solutions SAS/TenneT TSO*.
42. Although the amount of the fixed court fees is dependent on the monetary amount at stake, the highest category is the category from EUR 100,000 onwards. At the moment (2019 level), court fees for a claim of EUR 100,000 or more that is brought by a legal entity are EUR 4,030 (natural persons have to pay less: EUR 1,599).

claims, it is necessary to ensure that the courts are sufficiently staffed and financed. There are cautious signs that the courts are under an increasing pressure to maintain the current high quality. Also, the duration of proceedings may become an issue when sufficient resources are not ensured.

IV. WHICH ENTITY IS LIABLE FOR DAMAGES?

Under Dutch law, the starting point is that the only entities liable for damages are those that themselves acted unlawfully towards claimants who consequently suffered damage. As a result, it would need to be established which entities acted in breach of competition law and whether this breach caused any damage to claimants. Formally, another condition for liability is that the norms infringed must be aimed at protecting against the damage as suffered by the claimants (*Schutznorm*), but in view of the *Manfredi* judgment – where the European Court ruled that any person is entitled to damages resulting from infringements of (currently) Articles 101 and 102 TFEU[43] – this could be considered to be a non-issue in the context of damage claims for infringement of European competition law.

As to the question of whether every legal entity that was an addressee of the infringement decision of the EU Commission is automatically liable, there has been little case law to date. One example is a judgment in the *Elevator* cartel, where the court ruled that the parent companies could not be held liable for the infringements of their subsidiaries. The claimant did not bring forward facts indicating the involvement of the parent companies in the infringements that took part in the level of the subsidiary companies. The court did not accept the argument that Article 101 TFEU is aimed at companies understood as an economic unity instead of legal entities. In this regard, the court referred to the *Manfredi* judgment, where the European Court ruled that in the event of an infringement of Article 101 TFEU, any person can claim for damages under the internal rules of the Member State, where there is a causal connection between the infringement and the damage. According to the court, it follows from this that Dutch law must be applied to assess whether the claimant is entitled to damages. Under Dutch law, an undertaking is in principle not liable for damage caused by unlawful behaviour by another undertaking even if the two undertakings are part of the same concern structure. This would only be different in exceptional circumstances. It is clear that this judgment would no longer hold after the *Skanska* judgment, where the European Court of Justice made clear that the concept of an undertaking is an autonomous concept of EU law that must be applied similarly in the context of private enforcement of competition law.[44]

43. ECJ, Case C-295/04 *Vincenzo Manfredi v Lloyd Adriatico Assicurazioni SpA* [2006] ECR I-6619.
44. ECJ, Case C-724/17 *Skanska Industrial Solutions and Others* [2019] ECLI:EU:C:2019:204.

V. BINDING EFFECT OF DECISIONS OF COMPETITION AUTHORITIES

Under Dutch law decisions of national competition, authorities do not have any binding effect. Before the implementation of the Damages Directive, the same was true for decisions of the Dutch competition authority – the Netherlands Authority for Consumers and Markets (hereinafter 'ACM') – or at least this issue was subject of debate. The implementation of the Damages Directive resulted in a new Article in the Dutch Code of Civil Procedure, pursuant to which a final infringement decision of the ACM is now irrefutable evidence in damage proceedings.[45]

Dutch courts are not bound by the decisions of national competition authorities of other Member States. However, under the general Dutch rules on evidence, decisions of foreign competition authorities can be submitted as (rebuttable) evidence of the claimant's allegations of the infringement. In the view of the Dutch legislature, Article 9(2) of the Damages Directive thus does not require implementation into Dutch law since the courts already can use the decisions of foreign competition authorities as prima facie evidence. Although this is in principle correct, we feel that it would have been better if this provision of the Damages Directive had been explicitly implemented, as the mere fact that there is room for consistent interpretation by the courts is not the same as a clear statutory rule providing that the decisions of foreign competition authorities constitute prima facie evidence.

VI. LIMITATION OF ACTIONS

In the context of damage claims for competition law infringements, there are two relevant limitation periods: (1) the (objective) long-stop limitation period of twenty years and (2) the (subjective) short-stop limitation rule of five years.

In general, the short limitation period starts to run after the claimant has become aware of: (i) his damage and (ii) the identity of the party/parties responsible for this damage. In cartel cases – which are hidden by nature – in most cases, the short limitation period will not start to run before a competition authority has issued a decision establishing a cartel infringement. In a case before the District Court of Rotterdam, however, the court found that a cartel damage claim could become time-barred even before a competition authority issued its cartel infringement decision.[46] The exceptional circumstance here, however, was that the expiry of the limitation period was invoked against a claimant who had filed a complaint with the competition authority which ultimately resulted in the infringement decision upon which the claimant was relying in the civil proceedings. Apart from this type of exceptional circumstances, Dutch courts have accepted that the short-stop limitation period will not start running before the press release of the European Commission on the infringement decision.[47]

45. Article 161a Dutch Civil Code of Procedure.
46. Rb. Rotterdam, 7 March 2007, ECLI:NL:RBROT:2007:BA0926.
47. Hof Arnhem-Leeuwarden, 2 September 2014, ECLI:NL:GHARL:2014:6766 *TenneT/ABB*; Hof Arnhem-Leeuwarden, 28 August 2018, ECLI:NL:GHARL:2018:7753 *TenneT/Alstom*.

In various cases, Dutch courts have also had to apply foreign limitation rules. In the context of these proceedings, questions arose as to whether the application of some of these foreign law regimes having short limitation periods would be contrary to the principle of effectiveness. In the *Sodium Chlorate* case, the court tested limitation periods under Finish and Swedish law against the Union law principle of effectiveness.[48]

The Finish limitation period was ten years, commencing at the end of the cartel in February 2000. The claimant - a claim vehicle filing suit on the basis of assigned claims - only served the writ of summons in May 2011, thus after the expiry of the limitation date. The claimant argued that her assignors had only become aware of the cartel infringement with the publication of the summary decision of the European Commission in June 2009. As a result, the claims had already become time-barred six months after the summary decision, and this result would be in breach of the principle of effectiveness. The Amsterdam court rejected this argument for the reason that the European Commission had issued a press release on the existence of a cartel on the market for Sodium Chlorate already in June 2008. Also, the claimant did not make clear which essential information was not available in the press release that was available in the summary decision. And even if it were accepted that not all necessary essential information was available with the press release, this would still have left a small number of months to file a claim after the summary decision and before the claims became time-barred.

Under the Swedish limitation rules, the claims in this case became time-barred even before claimants could become aware of their claims.[49] Still, the court did not find this in breach of the principle of effectiveness. The reason was that it also took into account the time from when the claimant did become aware of the cartel infringement and the moment it actually filed a claim. In this case, the claimant did not serve a writ until almost three years after the press release and two years after the publication of the summary decision. The court ruled that it can be expected that a claimant - and its assignors - will make sufficient efforts to take prompt action after becoming aware of an infringement and file their claims accordingly. How much time in general can be considered reasonable for this depends on the circumstances of the case, but here the court found two or three years too long to be able to successfully invoke the principle of effectiveness.

As already indicated, the Dutch regime on limitation was amended in order to implement the Damages Directive. Pursuant to Article 10(2) of the directive, the limitation period for claims on the basis of cartel infringements will only start to run after: (i) the infringement of competition law has ceased; additionally, the claimant must know, or can reasonably be expected to know (ii) of the behaviour and the fact that it constitutes an infringement of competition law, (iii) that the infringement caused harm and (iv) the identity of the infringer. Dutch law has also been amended to ensure that a limitation period is suspended if a competition authority takes an action in the

48. Rb. Amsterdam, 19 May 2017, ECLI:RBAMS:2017:3166 *CDC/Kemira*.
49. In view of ECJ, Case C-637/17 *Cogeco Communications Inc. v Sport TV Portugal and Others* [2019] ECLI:EU:C:2019:263, this seems to be in breach of the principle of effectiveness.

context of an investigation or proceedings in respect of an infringement of competition law to which the claim for damages relates. Pursuant to the new Article 6:193t Dutch Civil Code, an investigation of a competition authority will extend a limitation period until one year after the investigation ended.

Furthermore, it is important to note that it is relatively easy to interrupt the limitation periods for damage claims under Dutch law. This can be done by sending a written notice to the defendant in which the claimant unequivocally reserves his right to claim damages (Article 3:317 Dutch Civil Code). An out-of-court suspension of the limitation period is therefore possible.

VII. COLLECTIVE ACTIONS/POOLING OF CLAIMS

A. Introduction

Both collective actions and pooling of claims are possible under Dutch law. Many of the currently pending follow-on actions have been initiated by 'claim vehicles' on the basis of assigned claims. This pooling of claims by litigation vehicles has been accepted by Dutch courts (VII.B.).

It is also possible to bring a collective claim, although up to this point such an action could not be a claim for damages, instead being limited to an injunction, an order or a legal declaration that the infringing party is liable towards claimants. Subsequently, individual proceedings have been necessary in order to collect individual damages unless a settlement could be reached, whereby the settlement could also be a collective settlement (*see* VII.C, *infra*). Recently, however, there has been a change in the legislation which makes it possible to also bring a collective claim for damages (VII.D.).

B. Assignment model

As already indicated, many of the currently pending cases have been brought on the basis of an assignment model under which parties that are harmed by a competition infringement assign their claims to a claim vehicle. There are no requirements as to the legal form of such a litigation entity – unlike, for example, the collective claim for damages as will be discussed below.

In several proceedings, the validity of the assignments to a claim vehicle has been subject to debate. Fundamental arguments in this respect were, for example, that these type of assignments would be contrary to the so-called *fiduciaverbod* (prohibition on ownership of collateral; fiduciary prohibition) and would be contrary to public policy or good morals. Both arguments have been rejected. In a judgment concerning Air Cargo follow-on proceedings, the Amsterdam District Court decided that a claim vehicle keeping a percentage of the collected damages as part of the purchase price and transferring the remainder of the collected damages to the assignors does not cause this assignment to breach the fiduciary prohibition. The court also made clear that cartel damage claims make a substantial contribution to the enforcement of competition law and that the pooling of cartel damage claims by means of assignments to a claim vehicle is a legitimate instrument for achieving an efficient settlement of cartel damages.[50]

C. Mass settlements

The Act on the Collective Settlement of Mass Damage (*Wet Collectieve Afwikkeling Massaschade*, hereinafter 'WCAM') provides for court-approved mass settlements that are binding on an entire class of injured parties, unless they opt out.[51] The WCAM has already given rise to several mass claims, though not in the field of competition law yet.[52]

Additionally, international settlements can be declared binding on all class members on an 'opt-out' basis. The Amsterdam Court of Appeal accepted jurisdiction both in the situation where only a portion of the claimants were residing in the Netherlands[53] and in the situation where none of the liable parties and only some of the potential claimants were domiciled in the Netherlands.[54]

The WCAM proceedings consist of four stages:

(1) *First Stage – Settlement Agreement:* a foundation or association which acts as representative of the injured class enters into a settlement agreement with the defendant. Under the settlement agreement, the defendant agrees to make settlement payments to the injured parties.
(2) *Second Stage – Petition:* parties request the Amsterdam Court of Appeal – a special chamber of the Amsterdam Court of Appeal has exclusively been appointed to these matters – to declare the settlement binding. In this respect the court will assess whether the settlement is reasonable, also taking into account the extent of the damages, the ease and speed with which the settlement payment can be obtained from the defendant, the costs and efforts which the injured parties would otherwise have to make to litigate the matter, the potential causes of the damage and other relevant circumstances.
(3) *Third Stage – Opting Out:* individual injured parties have a period of at least three months during which they can opt out of the settlement. In the absence of opting out, the settlement becomes binding on them. It can be agreed in the

50. Rb. Amsterdam, 13 September 2017 *Equilib/KLM et al, supra* n. 4.
51. Wet van 23 juni 2005 tot wijziging van het Burgerlijk Wetboek en het Wetboek van Burgerlijke Rechtsvordering teneinde de collectieve afwikkeling van massaschades te vergemakkelijken, Stb. 2005, 340. The WCAM entered into force on 27 July 2005 (Stb. 2005, 380).
52. *See*, e.g., Hof Amsterdam, 1 June 2006, ECLI:NL:GHAMS:AX6440 *Des* [2006] NJ 461; Hof Amsterdam, 25 January 2007, ECLI:NL:GHAMS:AZ7033 *Dexia* [2007] JOR 71; Hof Amsterdam, 29 May 2009, ECLI:NL:GHAMS:BI5744 *Shell* [2009] JOR 197; Hof Amsterdam, 17 January 2012, ECLI:NL:GHAMS:BV1026 *Converium* [2012] NJ 355; Hof Amsterdam, 29 April 2009, ECLI:NL:GHAMS:BI2717 *Vie d'Or* [2009] JOR 2009, 196; Hof Amsterdam, 15 July 2009, ECLI:NL:GHAMS:BJ2691 *Vedior* [2009] JOR 325; Hof Amsterdam, 13 July 2018, ECLI:NL:GHAMS:2018:2422 *Fortis*.
53. Hof Amsterdam, 29 May 2009, LJN: BI5744 *Shell* [2009] JOR 197.
54. Hof Amsterdam, 17 January 2012 *Converium, supra* n. 52.

settlement agreement that the defendant can withdraw from the settlement if too many injured parties opt out.

(4) *Fourth Stage – Distribution of Funds:* after the opt-out period, the settlement payments will be distributed to the injured parties, who must be given a period of at least one year to collect their settlement funds.

D. Collective damages actions

Currently, a collective action can be initiated in the Netherlands only to obtain a declaratory ruling. Damages cannot be claimed collectively; rather, persons suffering damages must initiate separate follow-on proceedings in order to claim financial compensation. The Act on the Resolution of Mass Damages in Collective Action (*Wet Afwikkeling Massaschade in Collectieve Actie*, hereinafter 'WAMCA') changes this and will introduce collective actions for damages under Article 3:305a of the Dutch Civil Code.[55] The Act will amend the existing provisions regarding collective actions to allow a claim vehicle (or representative entity) to file a claim for collective damages on an opt-out basis. The objective is to make it easier for aggrieved parties to recover damages through a collective action and to prevent multiple litigation proceedings from being initiated by different interest groups regarding the same event.

Exclusive Representative

Pursuant to Article 3:305a Dutch Civil Code, a claim vehicle may initiate a collective action which aims to promote 'similar interests'. A claim vehicle must be set up as a foundation (*stichting*) or as an association with full legal capacity (*vereniging*) which promotes these similar interests under the terms of its articles of association; further, the interests must be sufficiently safeguarded.[56]

A claim vehicle can only initiate a collective action if the claim has a sufficiently close connection with the Dutch legal sphere. A sufficiently close connection exists if:

---

55. On 1 April 2019, the Act on the Resolution of Mass Damages in Collective Action (Wet Afwikkeling Massaschade in Collectieve Actie) was published in the Bulletin of Acts and Decrees. The date of entry into force of the Act is still to be announced, but it is expected to be 1 January 2020.
56. A claim vehicle must meet certain requirements in order to have sufficient standing to initiate a collective action. An exception applies to certain cases where the imposition of these requirements would be disproportionate. These requirements include:

    (1) Requirements regarding governance, funding and transparency: a representative entity must be able to show that it has both the experience and the expertise to bring collective actions, it must have a proper governance structure (in most cases including a supervisory board), it must involve members of the class in the decision-making process, it must have sufficient financial means to fund a collective action and it must be transparent about certain matters, including its management structure, salaries paid to its officers, objectives and methods of operation and contributions claimed from class members (if any).
    (2) Non-profit: the representative entity must operate on a non-profit basis; the direct or indirect objective of its founders and their successors must not be to make a profit 'through the representative entity'.

(1) the majority of persons, whose interests the collective action aims to protect, have their habitual residence in the Netherlands; or (2) the party against whom the collective action is directed is domiciled in the Netherlands and additional circumstances suggest a sufficient connection with the Dutch legal sphere; or (3) the event or events to which the collective action relates took place in the Netherlands. If the claim is not sufficiently connected to the Netherlands, the claim vehicle has no standing and the collective action will not be admissible.

If more than one collective action based on the same event or events is entered into the register, the collective actions are consolidated and the court will appoint an exclusive representative.[57]

Opt-out (Dutch class members) and opt-in (foreign class members)

The court's decisions on the appointment of the exclusive representative, the scope of the collective action and the narrowly defined class represented by the exclusive representative must be published in one or more daily newspapers. Furthermore, notice must be given to all known members of the class by regular post. The notice should state how the members may 'opt out' of the collective action by giving notice to the court registrar. The court, with a minimum of one month, will set the 'opt-out' period. If there are members of the class residing outside of the Netherlands, the court may order notice to be given in other ways and/or other languages. A judgment in the collective proceedings will be binding on all members who have not opted out. Claim vehicles representing members that have opted out may continue separate proceedings. The court may, however, at the request of any interested party, suspend such proceedings for the period of one year or until a judgment has been rendered in the collective action (whichever comes first).

For members of the class residing outside of the Netherlands, a different procedure applies. They are only bound by the collective action if they expressly opt in by notifying the court registrar within the aforementioned 'opt-out' period.

Settlement agreement/Second opt-out

Following the appointment of an exclusive representative, the court may set a period for the parties to attempt to reach a collective settlement agreement. A collective settlement agreement must meet certain requirements set forth in Article 7:907 Dutch Civil Code and is subject to court approval. If a settlement agreement is reached and

(3) Reasonable attempt to settle: a collective action will only be admissible after the representative entity has made a reasonable attempt to settle the case. In this context, Article 3:305a Dutch Civil Code provides that a letter that gives the defendant two weeks to respond will in any case be sufficient.

57. In selecting the most suitable exclusive representative the court will consider the following circumstances: the number of claimants represented, the size of the financial interests represented by these claimants, other activities carried out by the representative entity in and out of court and prior activities and collective actions initiated by the representative entity. The court may appoint more than one exclusive representative if this is prompted by the nature of the collective action or the interests of the claimants involved.

approved by the court, there is a second opportunity for class members to 'opt out' of the collective settlement agreement by giving notice to the court registrar. The 'opt-out' period will be set by the court, with a minimum of one month. After expiry of the opt-out period, the settlement agreement will become binding upon all members of the class who have not opted out. If no settlement agreement is reached, the proceedings will continue. The court's decisions on a collective resolution scheme must be notified to all known members of the class. Furthermore, the decision must be published in one or more daily newspapers.[58]

Temporal scope

The new regime applies only to collective actions initiated on or after the date of entry into force of the Act and relating to events that occurred on or after 15 November 2016 (the day the draft legislative proposal was submitted to the Dutch House of Representatives).

VIII. CONCLUSION

The Dutch jurisdiction has proved to be an attractive forum for private enforcement of competition law over recent years. The currently existing case law on a broad variety of topics can be expected to provide predictability and efficient proceedings. Additionally, the new developments on the Dutch collective damage action may attract new claims. In any event, it seems safe to say that private enforcement is here to stay and will continue to give rise to interesting legal developments in the coming years.

58. The notices and newspaper publications should contain a short description of the collective resolution scheme, in particular how the members may obtain compensation from the defendant and, if the collective resolution scheme so provides, the period of time during which compensation may be claimed.

CHAPTER 8

Private Enforcement in the United Kingdom

Florian Wagner-von Papp

I. Introduction and outline
II. The development of private enforcement
III. What is effective and what are the impediments to private enforcement?
  A. What is effective?
    1. Disclosure of evidence
    2. Specialised tribunal and commercially minded judges
    3. Further advantages of the UK as a venue
    4. Collective proceedings
  B. What are the impediments to effective enforcement?
IV. Which entity is liable for damages
V. Binding effect of decisions of competition authorities
VI. Limitation of actions
VII. Collective actions/pooling of claims
  A. Collective redress in the European discussion
  B. Collective redress in the United Kingdom
    1. First stage: Representative actions and Group Litigation Orders
    2. Collective Proceedings Orders after the CRA 2015
VIII. Brexit
  A. No deal
    1. Jurisdiction and Enforcement: Brussels I Recast Regulation
    2. Taking of Evidence
    3. 2019 Regulations and follow-on actions
    4. Brexit implications for the implementation of the Damages

Directive
B. Withdrawal Agreement
IX. Conclusion

I. INTRODUCTION AND OUTLINE

The United Kingdom has been one of the favourite forum choices for claimants in antitrust damages actions in the EU. This is due to several features, many of which will be discussed in this contribution, such as a mature regime of disclosure of evidence with the concomitant safeguards for privileged and confidential information, a judiciary that has commercial expertise and is used to dealing with (few but) large cases, a specialised competition tribunal, a high concentration of specialised competition solicitors and barristers in London – including US American law firms with transferable expertise in private US antitrust enforcement – sophisticated approaches to expert evidence, venues for both litigation and arbitration, the use of the English language in the proceedings without need for any translations, and collective proceedings, including more recently introduced opt-out collective proceedings.

This is not to say that claimants have not faced difficulties in the UK in the past. Some of these difficulties have been resolved in the meantime. For example, the bifurcation of jurisdiction for the specialised Competition Appeal Tribunal (hereinafter 'CAT') and the general High Court in England and Wales[1] used to result in different regimes for limitation (or prescription) periods. The Consumer Rights Act 2015 (hereinafter 'CRA 2015') addressed the issue partially, and the implementation of the Damages Directive – in the 'Claims in respect of Loss or Damage arising from Competition Infringements (Competition Act 1998 and Other Enactments (Amendment)) Regulations 2017' (hereinafter '2017 Regulations')[2] – has finally resolved the issue in favour of a uniform limitation period of six years (or, in Scotland, a five-year prescription period), even though issues will continue for claims that arose before 1 October 2015.

Other difficulties for claimants and defendants persist, such as the high costs for the – by European standards very extensive – disclosure of evidence, as well as for legal representation by solicitors and barristers.

Finally, new difficulties are being created: Brexit will impede private enforcement, *inter alia*, by excluding the possibility of bringing follow-on actions based on Commission decisions and by removing the benefits of the rules on jurisdiction and enforcement in the Brussels I *Recast* Regulation.

Scottish and Northern Irish readers may have noticed, possibly with dismay, that I am primarily referring to the English and Welsh regime. To a large extent, private competition law enforcement is governed by uniform UK law. This is true in particular for substantive competition law, largely contained in the Competition Act 1998 and the

1. In Scotland: Sheriff or Court of Session; in Northern Ireland: High Court in Northern Ireland.
2. The Claims in respect of Loss or Damage arising from Competition Infringements (Competition Act 1998 and Other Enactments (Amendment)) Regulations 2017, Statutory Instruments 2017 No. 385, made on 8 March 2017.

Enterprise Act 2002. Even when it comes to procedural law, the rules are largely uniform across the UK: In practice, private competition law enforcement will in the future mostly be brought before (or transferred to) the CAT, which has UK-wide jurisdiction, and to the extent this is the case, the CAT Rules 2015[3] (or, in legacy cases, the CAT Rules 2003[4]) will govern the procedure.[5] The implementation of the Damages Directive in the 2017 Regulations has led to further harmonisation of the applicable rules. Nevertheless, there are remaining differences between England & Wales, Northern Ireland, and particularly Scotland, for example when it comes to limitation or prescription periods, to the application of substantive contract or tort/delict law, or to claims brought before the general courts, namely the High Court in England & Wales with an appeal to the Court of Appeal in England & Wales, the Sheriff in Scotland (with an appeal to the Sheriff Appeal Court or the Inner House of the Court of Session) or the Outer House of the Court of Session with an appeal to the Inner House or the UK Supreme Court, or the High Court in Northern Ireland with an appeal to the Court of Appeal in Northern Ireland. My primary focus on English and Welsh law in this contribution is primarily explicable by my greater familiarity with English law and the higher proportion of cases brought in English courts.[6]

II. THE DEVELOPMENT OF PRIVATE ENFORCEMENT

The 1983 decision in *Garden Cottage Foods v Milk Marketing Board* established that a party that has suffered loss caused by an infringement of competition law has a cause of action based on the breach of a statutory duty, with the statutory duty arising from section 2 of the European Communities Act 1972 in combination with (what is today) Article 101 or 102 TFEU.[7] In cases in which the infringement is not capable of affecting

3. CAT Rules 2015, Statutory Instruments 2015 No. 1648.
4. CAT Rules 2003, Statutory Instruments 2003 No. 1372.
5. In *Deutsche Bahn v Mastercard* [2016] CAT 13, the CAT noted in a decision of 27 July 2016 at para. 3 that: 'these proceedings are treated pursuant to the Tribunal Rules as proceedings in England and Wales. However, the Tribunal is a UK tribunal and the relevant provisions of the CA and the Tribunal Rules which fall to be construed apply equally to proceedings in Scotland and Northern Ireland. It is therefore both appropriate and necessary to consider the interpretation of those provisions also in the context of proceedings which would be treated as brought in those different jurisdictions in the United Kingdom'. For the reasons why transfers from the High Court to the CAT appear likely in the future *see Sainsbury Supermarkets v Mastercard* [2015] EWHC 3472 (Ch); *but see* Richard Whish & David Bailey, *Competition Law* 328 (9th ed., Oxford University Press 2018) (noting that the High Court continues to have advantages with respect to party autonomy and the combination with claims other than competition claims and that the High Court will not invariably transfer cases to the CAT, pointing to *Unwired Planet v Huawei* [2016] EWHC 958 (Pat)).
6. Scottish and Northern Irish readers can rest assured that, since 23 June 2016, my sympathy lies, if anything, more with them than with the majority in England & Wales. For greater depth on private enforcement in Scotland and Northern Ireland, *see* Mark Brealey & Kyla George (eds), *Competition Litigation – UK Practice and Procedure* Chapters 23 & 24 (2d ed., Oxford University Press 2019).
7. *Garden Cottage Foods v Milk Marketing Board* [1984] AC 130, 141. *See also*, e.g., *BritNed Development Ltd v ABB AB* [2019] EWCA Civ 1840 para. 20; *Roche v Provimi* [2003] EWHC 961 (Comm) para. 25; *Sempra Metals Ltd v IRC* (2007) 3 WLR 354, 377; *Devenish Nutrition v Sanofi-Aventis* [2007] EWHC 2394 (Ch) para. 18.

trade between Member States, the statutory duty to avoid substantive competition law infringements arises today under the Chapter I or Chapter II prohibitions of the Competition Act 1998 (hereinafter 'CA 1998'). In addition to a breach of a statutory duty, the claimant has to show that the breach caused a relevant loss in the individual case.[8]

Claims may also be based on other causes of actions,[9] such as the tort of interference with business by unlawful means, which requires that there was wrongful interference with the actions of a third party of economic interest to the claimant and that the interference was intended to cause loss to the claimant;[10] or the torts of deceit, conspiracy to use unlawful means to harm economic interests,[11] misrepresentation, or restitution. It is noteworthy that while most of these causes of action require for accrual the showing of 'gist damage', the judge in *BritNed v ABB* accepted that the loss of the chance to benefit from competitive conditions constituted in itself sufficient 'gist damage' for the cause of action in tort (here: breach of a statutory duty) to accrue.[12]

The standard remedy under English law is compensatory damages.[13] There is a recognition that the uncertainties of the quantification of damages should not be to the detriment of the victim, and that '[t]he restoration by way of compensation is therefore accomplished to a large extent by the exercise of a sound imagination and the practice of the broad axe'.[14] The *Devenish Nutrition* case tested whether available damages could include 'exemplary damages', that is, the English equivalent to punitive damages in the US, and whether restitutionary remedies were available. Restitutionary remedies were found to be available at best only under very restrictive conditions that generally are not fulfilled in competition cases.[15] Exemplary damages were said to be usually unavailable in competition cases because the deterrent function of exemplary damages is generally already served by the fines imposed by the competition authority in public enforcement actions.[16] Only where exceptionally the competition authority did not impose a fine (e.g., where the turnover in question was *de minimis*) was there said to

8. For an extensive discussion of causation and damages assessment *see* Ioannis Lianos, Peter Davis & Paolisa Nebbia, *Damages Claims for the Infringement of EU Competition Law* Chapters 4-6 (Oxford University Press 2015).
9. David Bailey & Laura Elizabeth John (eds.), *Bellamy & Child: European Union Law of Competition* §§ 16.055–16.059 (8th ed., Oxford University Press 2018).
10. *See*, e.g., *Air Canada v Emerald Supplies* [2015] EWCA Civ 1024 paras 159 et seq.
11. *See*, e.g., *W.H. Newson Holding v IMI* [2012] EWHC 3680 (Ch). This tort also requires - beside the combination of at least two persons to use illicit means - these persons' intention to cause loss, as well as harm suffered by the claimant.
12. *BritNed v ABB* [2018] EWHC 2616 (Ch) paras 422–429. However, the judge provided an alternative argument in case this assessment was wrong at para. 465, indicating that the level of confidence in the correctness of the primary approach was not infinite.
13. *See*, e.g., *Devenish Nutrition v Sanofi-Aventis* [2008] EWCA Civ 1086 para. 2; *Merricks v Mastercard* [2019] EWCA Civ 674 para. 19; *BritNed v ABB*, *supra* n. 7, at paras 27–43, 57, 234.
14. *Devenish Nutrition v Sanofi-Aventis*, *supra* n. 13, at paras 110, 159, quoting Lord Shaw in *Watson Laidlaw & Co Ltd v Pott, Cassells and Williamson* (1914) 31 RPC 104 at 117–118. *See* also *Merricks v Mastercard*, *supra* n. 13, at para. 18, and *BritNed v ABB*, *supra* n. 7, at paras 23, 24, 57.
15. *Devenish Nutrition v Sanofi-Aventis*, *supra* n. 13, at paras 33 et seq.
16. *Devenish Nutrition v Sanofi-Aventis*, *supra* n. 7, at paras 40–74 (this part was not appealed to the Court of Appeal).

be room for exemplary damages.[17] Even this exceptional availability of exemplary damages was laid to rest with the 2017 Regulations implementing the Damages Directive's prohibition of overcompensatory damages, which introduced paragraph 36 in Schedule 8A to the CA 1998, providing that exemplary damages may not be awarded.[18]

Despite the relatively early acknowledgement in *Garden Cottage Foods* that, in principle, harm caused by competition law infringements gives rise to a cause of action, published decisions on damages actions in the UK remained as rare as elsewhere in Europe for the next two decades. It is not entirely clear to what extent this is due to confidential settlements of claims, but it is arguably fair to say that competition damages actions remained largely dormant in the UK until the *Courage v Crehan* case and the European Court of Justice's decision,[19] an action that had originated in UK courts.[20] Since then, there has been a remarkable growth of damages actions in the UK.

The first major legislative intervention facilitating private enforcement was the establishment of the specialised CAT in the Enterprise Act 2002 (hereinafter 'EA 2002') and the simultaneous introduction of follow-on actions by inserting section 47A into the CA 1998,[21] making binding on the CAT, in actions for monetary claims, those decisions by the European Commission or the Competition and Markets Authority (hereinafter 'CMA') that are based on Article 101 or 102 TFEU or on the Chapter I or Chapter II prohibitions of the CA 1998.[22] The original version of section 47B CA 1998[23] provided for actions on behalf of consumers, but that provision was used only in one significant case, with limited success,[24] and has since been replaced by new provisions on collective proceedings in the Consumer Rights Act 2015 (*see* VII.B.2, *infra*). The EA 2002 also inserted section 58A into the CA 1998, which provides for a binding effect of Commission and OFT (now: CMA) decisions for monetary follow-on claims before the courts in the UK, similar to the binding effect in follow-on claims before the CAT in section 47A CA 1998. This binding effect for follow-on actions complemented the already existing provision in section 58 CA 1998. According to that latter provision (as

17. *2 Travel Group plc (in liquidation) v Cardiff City Transport Services Ltd* [2012] CAT 19 at paras 448–598, especially 496, 593–598; *Albion Water Ltd v Dŵr Cymru Cyfyngedig* [2010] CAT 30.
18. This resolves any uncertainty, such as it was, whether the Damages Directive prohibits exemplary damages (which was doubted in Renato Nazzini *Competition Enforcement and Procedure* § 3.44 (2nd ed., Oxford University Press 2016)).
19. ECJ, Case C-453/99 *Courage v Crehan* [2001] ECR I-6297.
20. *See* originally *Courage v Crehan* [1998] EWHC Ch 281. After the preliminary reference procedure, the case was eventually decided against the claimants, *Inntrepreneur Pub Company v Crehan* [2006] UKHL 38.
21. Section 18 EA 2002.
22. References (then to the Office of Fair Trading, and to Articles 81, 82 EC) have been changed to the current nomenclature and numbering, and the references to the European Coal and Steel Community Treaty have been omitted.
23. Inserted by section 19 EA 2002.
24. The *Consumers' Association v JJB Sports plc*, Case No. 1078/7/9/07. The case, brought in March 2007, concerned a follow-on claim on behalf of consumers following the OFT decision in *Replica Football Kits*. The Article 47B claim was settled. *See* https://www.catribunal.org.uk/cases/107 87907-consumers-association (accessed 22 July 2019). For the terms of the settlement and the assessment of the opt-in procedure under the old section 47B CA 1998 as unsatisfactory, *see*, e.g., Nazzini, *supra* n. 18, at § 3.70.

modified), certain findings of fact made by the CMA are binding on the court or tribunal.[25]

After the CAT had been established, claimants in the UK could bring follow-on actions either in the CAT or in the general courts (more particularly the High Court), while stand-alone actions could, until recently, be brought exclusively in the general courts. Even many actions that pursue *primarily* follow-on claims *also* contain stand-alone claims (so-called hybrid claims), for example, because the private action is also brought against undertakings that were not named in the decision of the competition authority, and these actions accordingly had to be brought in the general courts.[26] Furthermore, the limitation period in the High Court in England & Wales was sometimes more favourable to the claimant than that in the CAT Rules 2003. The result was that many damages actions continued to be brought in the general courts instead of the specialised CAT.

In anticipation of the Damages Directive, the UK initiated a more general review of the rules on the private enforcement of competition law. Even before the Damages Directive was finalised, Parliament discussed the bill that eventually became the CRA 2015. Schedule 8 to the CRA 2015 opened the possibility of stand-alone claims to be brought before the CAT (instead of exclusively before the High Court), harmonised the limitation periods before the CAT and the High Court, and introduced collective proceedings, including the possibility of opt-out collective proceedings, as well as collective settlements, CMA-approved consumer compensation schemes, and a fast-track procedure before the CAT.

Because the CRA 2015 had been passed before the Damages Directive was finalised, the entry into force of the Damages Directive required further amendments. These were implemented in the 2017 Regulations, which added a new Schedule 8A to the CA 1998.

This is the state of the applicable law at the proof stage in mid-November 2019. The implementation of the decision in the 2016 referendum to leave the European Union (hereinafter 'Brexit') will bring further changes in the near future. What these changes will be depends substantially on the form that Brexit will take. More than seven months after the originally envisaged Brexit date, it is still unclear what Brexit will look like (and, as Mark Brealey writes in the preface to his book (*see* note 6, *supra*): '[D]elaying publication of the book to await Brexit is akin to a never-ending story'). However, it seems likely that if there is a Brexit, it will take one of two forms: Either, it will be a Brexit with a 'deal', in which case it will be substantially the Withdrawal Agreement negotiated under former Prime Minister Theresa May with the modifications negotiated by Prime Minister Boris Johnson that governs during the transition period, or there will be a 'no-deal Brexit', in which case the Competition (Amendment, etc.) (EU Exit) Regulations 2019[27] (hereinafter '2019 Regulations') will come into effect on Exit Day. The implications for private enforcement will be considered below in section VIII.

---

25. *See* V, *infra*.
26. *Bellamy & Child*, *supra* n. 9, at § 16.064.
27. Statutory Instruments 2019 No. 93.

III. WHAT IS EFFECTIVE AND WHAT ARE THE IMPEDIMENTS TO PRIVATE ENFORCEMENT?

A. What is effective?

As mentioned in the introduction, the UK as a venue for competition actions has a number of attractive features, such as a mature regime for the disclosure of evidence, a specialised tribunal and commercially minded judges at the courts, a high concentration of specialised competition solicitors and barristers in London, venues for both litigation and arbitration, a sophisticated approach to expert evidence, the use of the English language in the proceedings, and collective proceedings, including more recently introduced opt-out proceedings.

1. Disclosure of evidence

One crucial aspect of bringing 'fact-intensive' damages actions is access to evidence.[28] While the Damages Directive has made some rudimentary provision for rules on access to evidence in all Member States, these provisions in themselves are unlikely to lead to effective disclosure regimes across the EU. In English courts and tribunals, however, disclosure has a long and established tradition, even though the rules have been modified over time.[29] Disclosure rules in England & Wales are contained in the Civil Procedure Rules (hereinafter 'CPR') if the action is initiated in the High Court, and in the CAT Rules 2015 if the action is brought before the CAT. Even though most actions will in the future likely be brought before the CAT, the description below will start with disclosure in the CPR, because the CAT, whose rules on disclosure are less detailed than those in the CPR but are 'based on the same philosophy',[30] will look to the practice of the courts applying the CPR for inspiration.

In Scotland, the power to order inspection of documents is provided for in section 1 of the Administration of Justice (Scotland) Act 1972 (c. 59), and in the Court of

28. This section is largely based on Florian Wagner-von Papp, *Access to Evidence and Leniency Materials*, https://ssrn.com/abstract=2733973 (accessed 22 July 2019) and idem in: Jochen Bernhard, Laurence Idot et al., *Disclosure of documents that lie in the control of the parties* (2017) 3, paras 56–78, and draws on material from these contributions. For greater depth, *see* David Ashton, *Competition Damages Actions in the EU – Law and Practice* Chapter 4 (2d ed., Edward Elgar 2018); Brealey & George, *supra* n. 6, at Chapter 9.
29. Both the *Woolf* review and the *Jackson* review sought to limit disclosure in order to reduce costs, but the impact on legal practice appears to have been limited. On the Jackson reform, *see* Rupert Jackson, *Review of Civil Litigation Costs: Final Report* (The Stationery Office 2010); *see also* Lord Justice Jackson's paper for the Civil Justice Council Conference on 21 March 2014, para. 3.13, https://www.judiciary.uk/publications/review-of-civil-litigation-costs/ (accessed 22 July 2019); Rupert Jackson, *Controlling the Costs of Disclosure, Seventh Lecture in the Implementation Programme, The Lexisnexis Conference on Avoiding and Resolving Construction Disputes*, para. 4.7, 4.8, http://www.judiciary.gov.uk/wp-content/uploads/JCO/Documents/Speeches/controlling-costs-disclosure.pdf (accessed 22 July 2019).
30. *AC Nielsen Company Ltd v Competition and Markets Authority and Information Resources, Inc* [2014] CAT 13 para. 16.

Session, the Court of Session Rules Chapter 35 on Recovery of Evidence and Chapter 86A on Applications in Competition Proceedings apply.

a) Disclosure under the Civil Procedure Rules in the High Court of England & Wales

Disclosure in England and Wales is covered in Part 31 of CPR. Practice Direction 31C contains specific amendments for competition claims, necessitated by, and implementing, the requirements of the Damages Directive.

'Standard disclosure' under CPR 31.6 provides for the disclosure of:

> (a) the documents on which [the party] relies; and
> (b) the documents which –
> (i) adversely affect his own case;
> (ii) adversely affect another party's case; or
> (iii) support another party's case; and
> (c) the documents which he is required to disclose by a relevant practice direction.[31]

Even where this test for standard disclosure is not satisfied, the court may order disclosure where the broader original *Peruvian Guano* ('train of enquiry') test applies,[32] or make any other order it deems appropriate.[33] The 'menu option', now contained in CPR 31.5(7),[34] provides that disclosure orders may range from no disclosure at all to the full *Peruvian Guano* disclosure or 'key to the warehouse orders', where the parties grant access to the other party to search for relevant documents themselves.[35]

In contrast to the American discovery procedure, under English law, disclosure usually takes place after, and on the basis of, fact-pleading. In principle, the court may allow pre-action disclosure, but such an application will be granted only in exceptional circumstances and is accordingly rare in practice.[36] The question of how specific the pleading of the factual allegations has to be before disclosure is granted presents difficulties in all legal regimes. English courts have been relatively generous to claimants, at least in cartel cases:

> In a case involving an allegation that a secret cartel has operated (...) there is an inevitable tension in domestic procedural law between the impulse to ensure that claims are fully and clearly pleaded so that a defendant can know with some exactitude what case he has to meet (and also so that disclosure obligations can be

31. CPR 31.6.
32. *Compagnie Financière du Pacifique v Peruvian Guano Co* (1882) 11 QBD 55, 63, interpreting the test under the Rules of the Supreme Court (hereinafter 'RSC') (1875) Order XXXI rule 12, subsequently RSC (1965) Order 24 (a predecessor of part 31 CPR).
33. CPR Rule 31.5(7).
34. Introduced by Rule 11 of the Civil Procedure (Amendment) Rules 2013, SI 2013/262, in force since 1 April 2013.
35. On the menu option *see* Rupert Jackson, *Review of Civil Litigation Costs: Final Report* (The Stationery Office 2010) 275–277.
36. CPR 31.16 (introduced by the Woolf Reforms). For the emphasis on exceptionality, *see* *Hutchinson 3G Ltd v O2 (UK) Ltd and Others* [2008] EWHC 55 (Comm), [2008] UKCLR 83.

> fully understood, expert witnesses given clear instructions and so on), on the one hand, and on the other the impulse to ensure that justice is done and a claimant is not prevented by overly strict and demanding rules of pleading from introducing a claim which may prove to be properly made out at trial, but which will be shut out by the law of limitation if the claimant is to be forced to wait until he has full particulars before launching a claim.[37]

The court in *Nokia* held that 'the balance is to be struck by allowing a measure of generosity in favour of a claimant'.[38] Nevertheless, there are limits. In *Hutchinson 3G Ltd v O2 (UK)*, the court refused disclosure for lack of sufficiently specific fact-pleading, albeit in the special setting of *pre-action* disclosure where standards may be stricter because of its exceptional nature.[39]

Where a parent company is a party to the proceedings, but the evidence is not in the hands of the parent but of a subsidiary, English courts apply the *Lonrho* test that requires a 'presently enforceable right to possession', which a parent may or may not have against its subsidiary, depending on the circumstances.[40] This question becomes relevant in particular if the subsidiary is outside the court's jurisdiction, so that enforcing a non-party disclosure order against the subsidiary is not feasible. In *Ardila Investments*, Mr Justice Males summarised the position as follows:

> First, it remains the position that a parent company does not merely by virtue of being a 100% parent have control over the documents of its subsidiaries. Second, an expectation that the subsidiary will in practice comply with requests made by the parent is not enough to amount to control. Third, in such circumstances (...) there is no obligation even to make the request, although it may, in some circumstances, be legitimate to draw inferences if the party to the litigation declines to make sensible requests. (...) Fourth, however, a party may have sufficient practical control (...) if there is evidence of the parent already having had unfettered access to the subsidiary's documents or if there is material from which the court can conclude that there is some understanding or arrangement by which the parent has the right to achieve such access.[41]

As implied above, disclosure orders may in principle also be addressed to non-parties,[42] although the court may afford greater weight to the interest of a

37. *Nokia Corporation v AU Optronics Corporation* [2012] EWHC 731 (Ch) para. 62, cited with approval in *Bord Na Mona Horticultural Ltd & Another v British Polythene Industries Plc* [2012] EWHC 3346 (Comm), para. 30, in turn cited with approval in *Emerald Supplies Ltd v British Airways plc and Others* [2014] EWHC 3514 (Ch) para. 50.
38. *Nokia Corporation v AU Optronics Corporation*, *supra* n. 37, at para. 67.
39. *Hutchinson 3G Ltd v O2 (UK) Ltd and Others*, *supra* n. 36.
40. *Lonrho v Shell Petroleum* (1980) 1 WLR 627, 633–7 (applying RSC Order 24). Today, control is defined as physical possession, a right to possession, or a right to inspect or take copies, in the past or present (CPR 31.8(2) and CAT Rules 2015, Rule 60(4)). *See also* the discussion in Brealey & George, *supra* n. 6, *at* paras 9.18–9.23.
41. *Ardila Investments NV v ENRC NV v Zamin Ferrous Ltd*, [2015] EWHC 3761 (Comm) paras 13, 14. For an example for the fourth point in the list, *see Schlumberger Holdings Ltd v Electromagnetic Geoservices* [2008] EWHC 56 (Pat) paras 8–21, where the parent had already obtained the subsidiaries' consent; *see also North Shore Ventures Ltd v Anstead Holdings Inc* [2012] EWCA Civ 11 paras 26–40.
42. CPR 31.17. For evidence that non-party disclosure may be more difficult to obtain (*see* text after this footnote), *cf. BritNed v ABB*, *supra* n. 7, at paras 36, 37.

non-party in avoiding business disruption than it would in the case of a disclosure order directed at a party to the dispute.

The *Woolf* and *Jackson* reviews have both attempted to rein in the costs of disclosure by strengthening the 'proportionality' criterion. However, the costs have remained high, with disclosure costs of a magnitude of GBP 1 million–GBP 2 million for larger cases not being unusual.[43] More recently, there are tentative moves by courts in competition cases to make use of the new powers to achieve more targeted disclosure, among other things by isolating trial issues through case management.[44]

In addition to the rules on disclosure, Part 18 of the CPR gives the court the power to require a party to clarify matters or provide further information. This power will usually be exercised after disclosure has taken place,[45] and where the disclosed documents are not self-explanatory, for example, because they use a code to conceal cartel activity.[46]

b) *Disclosure under the CAT Rules*

Where a stand-alone or follow-on claim is brought before the CAT under the amended section 47A of the Competition Act 1998, the CAT may 'at any point give directions as to how disclosure is to be given', including 'what searches are to be undertaken, of where, for what, in respect of which time periods (...) and the extent of any search for electronically stored documents'.[47] As the CAT has explained in its *Guide to Proceedings*,[48] this means that disclosure in the CAT is not automatic. It needs to be ordered by the tribunal, usually upon a request by a party to the proceedings. The tribunal must be satisfied that the disclosure sought is necessary, relevant, and proportionate to determine the issues before it.[49] The CAT generally 'shall seek to ensure that each case is dealt with justly and at proportionate cost',[50] and more specifically it shall have

43. Cf. *Infederation Ltd v Google Inc and Others* [2013] EWHC 2295 (Ch) para. 23 (party estimated costs for standard disclosure at more than GBP 2 million, although the judge considered this estimate too high); *Hutchinson 3G Ltd v O2 (UK) Ltd and Others, supra* n. 36, paras 36, 60, the court noting that the costs of the pre-action disclosure sought would be in the order of magnitude of GBP 1 million.
44. *Infederation Ltd v Google Inc and Others, supra* n. 43, paras 37–38 (limiting Google's disclosure to the material documents within the category of 35,000 documents already disclosed to the European Commission, and deferring disclosure on one of the five allegations; *see also* paras 33–36, achieving further efficiencies through case management, specifically by bi-/trifurcating the trial on the issues of abuse on the one hand and dominant position and quantum of damages on the other).
45. *National Grid v ABB and Others* [2012] EWHC 869 (Ch) paras 73–79.
46. *National Grid v ABB and Others* [2014] EWHC 1555 (Ch), [2014] WL 1220027 para. 40.
47. Rule 60(3) of the CAT Rules 2015.
48. Tribunal's Guide to Proceedings (2015), para. 5.86. *See also* Mr Justice Peter Roth, *Practice Direction Relating to Disclosure and Inspection of Evidence in Claims Made Pursuant to Parts 4 and 5 of the CAT Rules 2015 of 14 March 2017*, Introduction.
49. *Claymore Dairies Ltd and Others v OFT (Recovery and Inspection)* [2004] CAT 16 para. 113; followed in *Albion Water Ltd and another v Water Services Regulation Authority* [2008] CAT 3 paras 29, 42, 43.
50. Compare Rule 4 of the CAT Rules 2015 with CPR 1.1. (*see* already *HCA International Ltd v CMA* [2014] CAT 11 para. 16, a case decided under the CAT Rules 2003).

regard to 'the need to limit disclosure to that which is necessary to deal with the case justly'.[51] In considering proportionality, regard is to be had, among other things: '(i) to the amount of money involved; (ii) to the importance of the case; (iii) to the complexity of the issues; and (iv) to the financial position of each party'.[52] The CAT further decided that the 'object of a disclosure application is to obtain production of specified documents. Accordingly, the application must specifically identify the documents sought; it must not be of a fishing or speculative nature'.[53] However, the CAT Rules also provide for orders for classes of documents to be disclosed. Like the CPR, the CAT Rules 2015 provide for the possibility of disclosure even before proceedings start and for non-party disclosure,[54] and they also empower the CAT to seek clarifications of the disclosed materials.[55]

c) *Confidential information*

The long experience with disclosure of evidence also means that courts and tribunals are used to handling confidential information. In principle, confidential information has to be disclosed,[56] but the court or tribunal may order the protection of confidential information by redacting documents or confining the disclosure to a confidentiality ring.[57] However, even confidentiality rings have their limits: The Court of Appeal

51. Rule 60(2)(b) of the CAT Rules 2015. The CAT's duty is not particularly strict: Rule 60(2) makes this duty subject to the CAT's directions under Rule 60(3) and to the proviso '*unless the Tribunal otherwise thinks fit*'.
52. Rule 4(2)(c) of the CAT Rules 2015.
53. *Albion Water Ltd and another v Water Services Regulation Authority* [2008] CAT 3 para. 41 (applying the CAT Rules 2003). *See also* 2.2–2.4. of the CAT Practice Direction Relating to Disclosure and Inspection of Evidence in Claims Made Pursuant to Parts 4 and 5 of the CAT Rules 2015 of 14 March 2017 (implementing Article 5(3) of the Damages Directive).
54. Rules 62, 63 of the CAT Rules 2015; cf. CPR 31.16 and 31.17. For an application for non-party disclosure under the CAT Rules 2003 cf. *Deutsche Bahn and Others v Morgan Crucible Company and Others* [2014] CAT 15 (order of 9 September 2014).
55. CAT Rules 2015, Rule 53(2)(d).
56. *See* generally Lord Wilberforce in *Nassé v Science Research Council* [1979] UKHL 9, [1980] AC 1028. In the competition law context: *MTV Europe v BMG Records (UK) Ltd* [1998] EWCA Civ 430; for the CAT: *Albion Water Ltd and another v Water Services Regulation Authority* [2008] CAT 3 para. 61; *Aberdeen Journals v DGFT* [2003] CAT 14; *Umbro v OFT* [2004] CAT 3. For a more extensive discussion *see* Brealey & George, *supra* n. 6, at paras 9.47–9.66.
57. *See* CAT Rules 2015, Rule 53(2)(h) (CAT may give directions to create a confidentiality ring). In the High Court, *see*, e.g., *National Grid Electricity Transmission plc v ABB and Others* [2012] EWHC 869 (Ch) para. 58 (lifting the redaction of a 'number of, but by no means all' passages); *see also* the order of Mr Justice Peter Roth of 11 July 2011, establishing a confidentiality ring in this case; *see also IPCom GmbH & Co KG v HTC and Others* [2013] EWHC 2880 (Ch) paras 47–49, where Mr Justice Peter Roth imposed a 'particularly tight confidentiality club' (excluding, among others, a German lawyer) on the application of the non-parties Qualcomm and Intel, whose source code was in question, under CPR Rule 40.9. For the practice in the CAT in appeal proceedings, *see*, e.g., *National Grid plc v Gas and Electricity Market Authority*, CAT Order of 23 May 2008 in Case 1099/1/2/08 (the confidentiality ring was varied in several subsequent orders); *Talktalk Telecom Group plc v British Telecommunications plc, Ofcom v Sky UK Ltd* [2015] CAT 13 paras 9–17; *AC Nielsen Company Ltd v Competition and Markets Authority and Information Resources, Inc*, *supra* n. 30, at paras 14–22 (on the treatment of disclosed confidential information after proceedings have come to an end; noting, *inter alia*, that while

overturned Mr Justice Peter Smith's order to disclose a (minimally redacted) confidential version of a Commission decision into a confidentiality ring.[58]

2. *Specialised tribunal and commercially minded judges*

An additional general advantage of the English legal system has long been said to be that the judges, by virtue of their previous careers as barristers (which is de facto still the career path of choice for High Court judges), tend to be well acquainted with commercial practices and that a career judge in a civil law jurisdiction may lack this experience.[59] One has to be careful not to read too much into this perceived difference. By the time career judges in civil law jurisdictions reach the higher courts, it seems likely that they have gathered a similar level of experience as a former barrister-turned-judge, and depending on the respective areas of specialisation of the English barrister-turned-judge and the civil law career judge, the balance of relevant expertise need not necessarily be in the English judge's favour.

What is arguably more important in competition cases is whether or not the judges are practising at a *general* court or a *specialised* competition court or tribunal, or, to be more precise, whether the judges have sufficient experience with competition cases - which will be more likely where the court or tribunal is specialised, although specialisation is neither a necessary nor a sufficient condition for experience. While the need for engaging with economic concepts is not unique to competition law, it is arguably greater in competition cases.

There are High Court judges (and, I assume, in Scotland sheriffs) that happen to have specific competition law knowledge, but systematically and institutionally the expertise is concentrated in the CAT, which may include panel members with specialist economic knowledge, and which may also co-opt High Court judges with competition expertise.[60] Mr Justice Barling, a High Court judge who cannot be accused of lacking knowledge of competition law, summarised the advantages of the CAT as follows:

> One obvious feature of competition litigation is the almost ubiquitous presence of expert economic evidence, often of a complex and technical nature. Another common feature, related to the last one, is evidence as to the characteristics and dynamics of specific industries and markets. Mindful of these features, Parliament provided for the specialist competition tribunal to have a multidisciplinary constitution. In this way panels have the potential to include not just lawyers but also, for example, distinguished economists, accountants or industry experts, selected for each case from the members appointed to the CAT by reason of their knowledge and experience in these areas. Expertise of this kind is of considerable

'the CPR does not apply to proceedings in the Tribunal ... the Tribunal Rules are based on the same general philosophy as the CPR', *ibid.* para. 16; *see also* the confidentiality ring order of 15 May 2014 in that case).

58. *Air Canada and Others v Emerald Supplies* [2015] EWCA Civ 1024.
59. Cf., e.g., Joseph Dainow, *The Civil Law and the Common Law: Some Points of Comparison* (1967) 15 American Journal of Comparative Law 419, 431.
60. *Sainsbury Supermarkets v Mastercard, supra* n. 5, paras 13-18.

> assistance in understanding and resolving the difficult issues which are a common feature of competition litigation.[61]

Mr Justice Barling saw an additional attractive feature of the CAT in the availability of *referendaires*.[62]

3. *Further advantages of the UK as a venue*

There are further advantages of the UK, and more specifically London, as a venue for private competition enforcement.

The UK has the natural advantage that English as the lingua franca of business is used in proceedings (including before appeal courts) anyway; all participants are guaranteed to have a sufficient grasp of it, translations of documents in English are not necessary, and all applicable laws, rules, and guidelines are written in English as well. Discussions about the conceptual and practical difficulties of introducing English-language courts and tribunals that have taken place in some other jurisdictions (such as Germany,[63] France,[64] and the Netherlands[65]) are, therefore, unnecessary in the UK.

The fact that England is largely centralised, with the High Court, Competition Appeal Tribunal, Court of Appeal, and the UK Supreme Court (as well as the headquarters of the London Court of International Arbitration) all located in London, means that nearly all the large English commercial law firms and specialised competition barristers are clustered in London. Furthermore, the anglophone UK was the gateway into the EU for the big US American law firms, which all have a large presence in London as well. When private enforcement in the EU started to become an attractive business opportunity, London was the first choice for US American law firms on the plaintiffs' side.

The civil procedure before English courts and tribunals also provides for some elements beyond disclosure that may be considered particularly helpful in private competition law enforcement. Practices such as hot-tubbing of economic experts – essentially letting the expert witnesses fight it out among themselves in the litigation equivalent of cage fighting[66] – and, more generally, the cross-examination of witnesses and expert witnesses may facilitate fact-finding and understanding these facts in complex litigation.

61. *Ibid.*, para. 15 (transfer from High Court to CAT).
62. *Ibid.*, para. 16.
63. The Landgericht Frankfurt a.M. has introduced a Chamber for International Commercial Disputes in which English can be used by choice of the parties as of 1 January 2018, but the jurisdiction of this chamber explicitly excludes competition cases.
64. The Commercial Court and Cour d'appel introduced English-speaking chambers starting from 1 March 2018.
65. The anglophone Netherlands Commercial Court and the Netherland Commercial Court of Appeal launched on 1 January 2019.
66. CPR Rule 35.12. For more detail, *see* the Civil Justice Council, *Concurrent Expert Evidence and 'Hot-Tubbing' in English Litigation since the 'Jackson Reforms'*, https://www.judiciary.uk/wp-content/uploads/2011/03/cjc-civil-litigation-review-hot-tubbing-report-20160801.pdf (accessed 22 July 2019).

While the costs of competition litigation are high in the UK, and constitute a potential impediment to private enforcement (*see* III.B., *infra*), an advantage of the UK system is that access to litigation financing is comparatively easy, with established specialised litigation financing firms which identify competition law as a particular area of interest and cooperate with ('claimants') law firms,[67] and the possibility for law firms to use Alternative Business Structures,[68] or to employ in individual cases (collective) conditional fee arrangements ('no win, no fee') or damages-based agreements.

4. *Collective proceedings*

A newer attractive feature of private enforcement in the UK is the collective redress regime introduced in the CRA 2015, which goes far beyond the European Commission's recommendation and collective redress in practically all other EU Member States,[69] in that it includes opt-out collective proceedings and collective settlements in the available arsenal. While initial CAT decisions such as *Dorothy Gibson v Pride Mobility Scooters*[70] and *Merricks v Mastercard*[71] seemed to indicate that the criteria for a collective proceedings order (hereinafter 'CPO') are so difficult to satisfy as to make it nearly impossible to succeed in an application for opt-out collective proceedings,[72] the more recent decision by the Court of Appeal in *Merricks* has arguably breathed new life into this feature.[73] Details of collective redress in the UK will be discussed below in section VII.

B. What are the impediments to effective enforcement?

Access to evidence is possibly still the greatest hurdle for claimants in damages actions for competition law infringements, even with the comparatively extensive disclosure regime in place in the UK.[74]

---

67. *See*, e.g., Burford Capital, *A Guide to Financing Competition Litigation*, http://www.burfordcapital.com/blog/guide-financing-competition-litigation/ (22 July 2019); Craig Arnott, *Follow-on claims and litigation finance: Burford's view* (both, however, describing financing of Hausfeld's activities in *Germany*).
68. Part 5 of the Legal Services Act 2007 c. 29.
69. The Dutch regime of class settlements is arguably the closest competitor in the EU. For a comparative overview see Barry Rodger (ed.), *Competition Law: Comparative Private Enforcement and Collective Redress across the EU* (Wolters Kluwer 2014).
70. *Dorothy Gibson v Pride Mobility Products* [2017] CAT 9.
71. *Walter Hugh Merricks v Mastercard Inc and Others* [2017] CAT 16.
72. Even at that time not quite as pessimistic, but also critical of the CAT's restrictive stance: Peter Davis *Economic Analysis in Damages Actions: Insights from Recent Proceedings in the UK* (2017) 8 JECLAP 593, 603 ('While the CAT has rejected the CPO applications in both of these first two opt-out cases, it certainly does not mean that other cases will not survive scrutiny. Still, the CAT will need to continue to consider how high a burden it should place on the claimant before issuing a CPO when such decisions must be made on the basis of limited disclosure.').
73. *Merricks v Mastercard Inc and Others*, *supra* n. 13.
74. *See* III.A.1, *supra*.

Given the information asymmetry that is characteristic of cartel cases, the quantification of damages is a particular problem in the UK. While judges in the UK do not shy away from engaging with economic evidence, and if necessary use a 'broad axe' or a 'broad brush' to assess damages, this does not necessarily make the use of such evidence more predictable. The first follow-on damages action to reach a judgment and damages award, *BritNed v ABB*,[75] provides a cautionary tale.

The economic expert for the claimants in that case had performed a regression analysis comparing prices 'during' and 'after' the cartel period, using data on both submarine and underground cable projects as proxies, and she reached the conclusion that the estimated cartel overcharge was approximately 25%.[76] The economic expert for the defendant compared, primarily, the profit margin – using a cost-based approach with ABB's actual cost figures – for the BritNed project with the profit margins for other projects (during and after the cartel period); he concluded that while the profit margins during the cartel period had been generally higher, the profit margin in the BritNed project at issue was *lower* than the average profit margins in the *post*-cartel period.[77]

The judge considered the approach based on ABB's cost figures instead of proxies generally closer to the truth, at least in so far as direct costs were concerned, and also considered that BritNed had partially extracted concessions from persons within ABB who were not aware of the cartel and therefore overestimated the competitive pressures; however, the judge further considered that a cartel may lead to what the judge called '*baked-in inefficiencies*' and that a cartelist may save costs, for example, because it is unnecessary to invest into painstaking tenders that have internally been allocated to a different cartel participant ('*cartel savings*').[78] On the basis of tentative evidence that ABB had used more copper in its cables than competitors, the judge used 15% of the prices for copper components to estimate the 'baked-in inefficiencies', reaching an amount of EUR 7.5 million.[79] By estimating the number of projects that might be lost under competitive conditions and taking into account the average cartel overcharge for these projects, he estimated the 'cartel savings' as 1.9% of the overall price, or approximately EUR 5.5 million. Overall, the judge thus awarded some EUR 13 million (later reduced to some EUR 11.7 million in the supplementary judgment to take account of the possibility that the overcharge reduced the risk of breaching a regulatory cap on BritNed's profits); this amount was calculated on a basis that was not exhaustively discussed in the proceedings, and for which the evidential basis was accordingly thin. Conversely, the judge was not willing to draw adverse inferences against the defendant, despite some indications that it was less than forthcoming in providing evidence. BritNed appealed, and ABB cross-appealed, to the Court of Appeal.

---

75. *BritNed v ABB*, *supra* n. 12, at para. 423 (with amendments in a 'supplementary judgment', [2018] EWHC 2913 (Ch)), cross-appeal allowed by the Court of Appeal in relation to the 'cartel savings' described below, *BritNed v ABB*, *supra* n. 7.
76. *BritNed v ABB*, *supra* n. 12, paras 288 et seq.
77. *Ibid.*, paras 339 et seq.
78. *Ibid.*, paras 365 et seq., 414 et seq., 445 et seq. With regard to the cartel savings, it should be noted that these are not strictly speaking compensatory damages; they are at best restitutionary (gain-based) damages, an issue not discussed by the judge.
79. *Ibid.*, paras 451 et seq.

The Court of Appeal ([2019] EWCA Civ 1840) largely confirmed the trial judge's approach in a judgment dated 31 October 2019 and dismissed BritNed's appeal. However, the Court of Appeal allowed ABB's cross-appeal in so far as the High Court judge had awarded compensation for ABB's 'cartel savings'. The Court of Appeal considered these cartel savings to be a gains-based (not a loss-based) remedy, which is unavailable under *Devenish Nutrition* (paragraphs 21–26, 223–245 of the judgment, and *supra*, section II of this chapter).

Even though the information asymmetry often makes it difficult for claimants to find a solid basis for estimating and proving damages, there are no plans to broaden the UK disclosure regime, because the marginal benefits of further-reaching disclosure (perhaps along the lines of US discovery) have to be balanced against the incremental increase in costs. Instead of discussing a broadening of disclosure, the direction of recent reforms of UK civil procedure has generally been to *limit* disclosure so as to reduce costs.[80] This leads to a second impediment to effective enforcement in the UK: litigation costs.

From a theoretical perspective, disclosure costs should be less of a problem in the UK when compared to the US, because in the UK the general rule for cost allocation is the European (or, as the English like to call it, the 'English') 'loser pays all' rule. This is in contrast to the 'American' rule of cost allocation, where costs are generally borne by the party that incurs them, so that one party may make extensive discovery requests in the relatively safe knowledge that it will be the other party who will have to bear the costs of compliance with these discovery requests. In the US regime, each party has an incentive to leave no stone unturned. That should theoretically not be the case in the English system, where each party has to take into account the expected costs of losing the case. Nevertheless, disclosure tends to be extensive and expensive even in the UK. One explanation could be that the parties are overoptimistic, leading them to underestimate the probability of losing the case and bearing the costs. Another potential explanation for exorbitant disclosure costs is that there may be a principal-agent problem between lawyers and clients at work: Law firms can rack up many hours spent by junior associates and paralegals on disclosure requests, which can be profitable if hourly fees are agreed. Whatever the true reason, disclosure costs are high in the UK. Beside disclosure costs, another reason for the high litigation costs is the split between solicitors and barristers, which leads to an inflated number of professionals involved in the teams of each party.

IV. WHICH ENTITY IS LIABLE FOR DAMAGES

The issue which entity is liable for damages was addressed relatively early in the High Court for England & Wales, in the *Provimi* case, a case resulting from the *Vitamins* cartel.[81] In that case (and in a number of subsequent cases), the question of whether it is the legal entity or the undertaking as a single economic unit that is liable came up as

80. An exception was the introduction of third-party and pre-action disclosure, which were cautiously broadened in the Woolf Reforms.
81. *Roche v Provimi*, *supra* n. 7.

a jurisdictional question. The Commission decision on which the claimants relied had been addressed to the parent undertaking (F. Hoffmann-La Roche AG (Switzerland)). In order to establish jurisdiction of the English courts under the (then) Brussels I Regulation 44/2001 or the Lugano Convention, the claimants had included, among other Roche subsidiaries, the UK subsidiary, Roche Products Ltd, as an 'anchor defendant'. Mr Justice Aikens held on a strikeout application that:

> 31. It seems to me to be arguable that where two corporate entities are part of an 'undertaking' (call it 'Undertaking A') and one of those entities has entered into an infringing agreement with other, independent, 'undertakings', then if another corporate entity which is part of Undertaking A then implements that infringing agreement, it is also infringing Article [101 TFEU]. In my view it is arguable that it is not necessary to plead or prove any particular 'concurrence of wills' between the two legal entities within Undertaking A. The EU competition law concept of an 'undertaking' is that it is one economic unit. The legal entities that are a part of the one undertaking, by definition of the concept, have no independence of mind or action or will. They are to be regarded as all one. Therefore, so it seems to me, the mind and will of one legal entity is, for the purposes of Article [101 TFEU], to be treated as the mind and will of the other entity. There is no question of having to 'impute' the knowledge or will of one entity to another, because they are one and the same.[82]

This has led to the question of how to define 'the undertaking'. It can be considered settled in English law that the parent is liable for its subsidiary's infringements under the rules applied by the Commission and the Court of Justice when imposing fines on legal entities under EU law. In other words, the parent is liable where it exercises decisive influence, or where such exercise is presumed, such as with wholly or nearly wholly owned subsidiaries, and the presumption is not rebutted; the Commission's principles established in fining decisions are applicable to damages claims as well, as the *Skanska* decision clarified.[83]

More controversial is the converse situation: Are subsidiaries liable when the parent company that exercises decisive control over them infringes competition law, even when the subsidiaries did not knowingly implement the infringement?[84] It is settled under English law that not all legal entities that are members of the corporate group to which the infringer belongs are liable *ipso facto*. Instead, the case law agrees with *Provimi* that a first condition for liability of a legal entity is that it is part of 'the undertaking' and that the legal entity must have 'implemented' the infringement.[85] Courts have doubted that the 'single economic unit' concept should be applied to make

---

82. *Ibid.*, para. 31.
83. ECJ, Case C-724/17 *Vantaan kaupunki v Skanska Industrial Solutions Oy* [2019] ECLI: EU:C:2019:204, paras 28–37; *Media-Saturn Holding GmbH v Toshiba Information Systems UK Ltd* [2019] EWHC 1095 (Ch) at paras 84, 85.
84. *See* the discussion in *Media-Saturn Holding v Toshiba, supra* n. 83, paras 86 et seq. The *Skanska* decision, *supra* n. 83, implies that this question is also determined by EU law. According to a blog post on d-kart.de by Hans-Markus Wagener, dated 15 November 2019, a Spanish court has made a preliminary reference to the Court of Justice (APB sección 15a, Order of 24 October 2019, Rollo no 775/2019-2ª) on precisely this question.
85. *Media-Saturn Holding v Toshiba, supra* n. 83; *Vattenfall v Prysmian* [2018] EWHC 1694 (Ch) at paras 54–55; *Cooper Tire & Rubber v Dow Deutschland* [2009] EWHC 2609 (Comm), (2009) 2

liable subsidiaries of infringing parents if the subsidiaries have not 'knowingly implemented' an infringement, especially if the subsidiary is active in a completely unrelated market (known as the 'shoe polish subsidiary').[86]

The CAT summarised its view in *Mastercard v Sainsbury* as follows:

> (22) [A] legal person may be liable for breach of competition law:
>
> (i) Because he, she or it has in some way participated in that breach, as a part of the single economic unit or 'undertaking' that has infringed the law; and/or
> (ii) Because he, she or it has exercised a decisive influence over one or more of the persons within the 'undertaking' who have participated in the infringement.
>
> (23) On the other hand, in our view a person is not ipso facto liable for an infringement of Article 101 [TFEU] by reason only of the fact that he, she or it is a member of an undertaking responsible as a matter of EU law for the infringement, in circumstances where the person in question neither participated in the infringement nor had decisive influence over the conduct in the relevant market of other member(s) of the undertaking who did participate. We appreciate that in such circumstances it may well be unlikely that the person in question would in fact be held to be part of that 'undertaking'.[87]

Judges tend to be generous to claimants when it comes to establishing the 'knowing implementation', at least at the strikeout/summary judgment stage.[88] For the 'implementation' prong, it has been considered sufficient that the defendants sold products affected by the infringement, even where the volume of the products sold was very small, even where the sales were to customers *other than the claimants*, and even where the defendants were selling only as agents for another member of the corporate group.[89] The sale of transformed cartelised products is sufficient.[90] At the strikeout/summary judgment stage, even the subsidiary's provision of 'administrative support' to the infringer that fell short of actual sales was considered sufficient in *Vattenfall*.[91] When this was attacked by the parties in a subsequent case as going one step too far, Mr Justice Barling held that, more generally, the issue whether an infringement was implemented was a factual question that is generally not suitable to being decided at the strikeout/summary judgment stage of proceedings, 'except in very clear cases'.[92]

CLC 619 para. 56; *Toshiba Carrier v KME Yorkshire* [2011] EWHC 2665 (Ch) para. 49. *See* text below for the yardstick applied to whether or not the infringement was 'implemented'.

86. *Cooper Tire & Rubber v Dow Deutschland [2m]* [2010] EWCA Civ 864, (2010) 2 CLC 104 para. 45; *Vattenfall v Prysmian, supra* n. 85, at para. 53.
87. *Sainsbury's Supermarkets Ltd v Mastercard Incorporated & Others* [2016] CAT 11 para. 363; cited with approval in *Vattenfall v Prysmian, supra* n. 85, at para. 59.
88. For the standards applied to strikeout applications and summary judgment applications in competition cases, *see Media-Saturn Holding v Toshiba, supra* n. 83, at paras 73–79.
89. *See Vattenfall v Prysmian, supra* n. 85, at paras 54–55, 62–74, 77; *see also Media-Saturn Holding v Toshiba, supra* n. 83.
90. *Media-Saturn Holding v Toshiba, supra* n. 83 at paras 102–111, 117, 118 (where the English subsidiary had sold colour TVs manufactured using the cartelised cathode ray tubes).
91. *Vattenfall v Prysmian, supra* n. 85, at paras 77–82.
92. *Media-Saturn Holding v Toshiba, supra* n. 83, at paras 110–111.

Where the subsidiary has implemented the parent's infringement, the next question is whether it must do so 'knowingly'. Most English decisions to date have assumed that it is necessary for the subsidiary to implement the infringement knowingly, although they have given substantial latitude to claimants at the strikeout/summary judgment stage in the light of the difficulty of establishing this subjective criterion before disclosure has taken place, so that claimants often merely have to plead the defendant's knowledge with as much particularity as possible on the basis of the (often scant) available evidence.[93] It has been indicated, however, that where the knowledge of the infringement is 'mere speculation', it may be permissible to give summary judgment against the claimants before disclosure.[94] In a recent case, Judge Barling left for another day the question of whether a 'knowing' implementation would also be found if the defendants 'should have known' about the infringement, or at least where they 'shut [their] eyes to the obvious'.[95] In the same case, however, Mr Justice Barling also considered the General Court's decision in *Biogaran*, which had held that if parent and subsidiary belong to one and the same undertaking, it is unnecessary for the subsidiary to be aware of the parent's actions, as the concept of the single economic entity means that knowledge of one is knowledge of the other.[96] Yet another claim advanced by the claimants in the *Media-Saturn* case, and not rejected at the strikeout/summary judgment stage, was that the parent company or its directors may be acting as shadow or de facto directors, or both, of a subsidiary, so that their knowledge is attributable to that subsidiary.[97] It remains to be seen whether the 'knowing implementation' requirement is compatible with the (EU law) concept of undertaking in private actions in the light of the Court of Justice's *Skanska* decision.

V. BINDING EFFECT OF DECISIONS OF COMPETITION AUTHORITIES

First, decisions by the European Commission benefit from the directly applicable Article 16 of Regulation 1/2003, which provides that neither national courts nor NCAs may take decisions running counter to a Commission decision when ruling on agreements, decisions, or practices under Article 101 or 102 TFEU.

Second, under section 58A Competition Act 1998 in its currently applicable version, final decisions by the European Commission finding an infringement of Article 101 or 102 TFEU, and decisions by the CMA finding an infringement of these TFEU provisions or of the Chapter I or Chapter II prohibitions in the Competition Act 1998, as well as CAT decisions confirming such CMA infringement decisions, are binding on the High Courts in England and Wales and in Northern Ireland, as well as on the Sheriff and

93. *Vattenfall v Prysmian*, *supra* n. 85, at paras 75, 83–87.
94. *Toshiba Carrier UK Ltd v KME Yorkshire Ltd* [2012] EWCA Civ 169 at para. 30.
95. *Media-Saturn Holding v Toshiba*, *supra* n. 83 at paras 91–95.
96. *See* the discussion in *Media-Saturn Holding v Toshiba*, *supra* n. 83, at paras 146–157, discussing Judgment of the General Court of 12 December 2018 in GC, Case T-677/14 *Biogaran v Commission* ECLI:EU:T:2018:910. Mr Justice Gerald Barling did not ultimately decide whether this meant that in the relevant constellations there is no knowledge criterion any more, *Media-Saturn Holding v Toshiba*, *supra* n. 83; at paras 155–157.
97. *Media-Saturn Holding v Toshiba*; *supra* n. 83, at paras 158–173, 207–210.

Court of Session in Scotland, and the CAT in actions under section 47A or section 47B Competition Act 1998.

The exact extent of the binding effect under section 58A Competition Act 1998 may create controversy in individual cases, but the generally accepted formula is that binding is: (1) the operative part of the decision and (2) those recitals that constitute the essential basis for the operative part.[98]

Section 58 Competition Act 1998 goes further than section 58A in that section 58 additionally makes binding on the parties in the courts or tribunal certain findings of *fact* made by the CMA in the course of investigations in respect of an infringement decision or an alleged infringement of Article 101 or 102 TFEU or the Chapter I or Chapter II prohibitions, provided that the decision is no longer open to appeal or any appeal was unsuccessful. Unlike the binding effect in section 58A Competition Act 1998, however, the binding effect with regard to findings of fact under section 58 Competition Act 1998 is made subject to a proviso that the court or tribunal may 'direct otherwise'. The underlying reason for this proviso is that facts that do not form the essential basis for the infringement decision, but are 'peripheral or incidental', may not have been challenged by the infringer even if they misrepresent the true state of affairs.[99] Examples of a finding of fact that may, or may not, be made binding on the parties under section 58 Competition Act are findings in the CMA's infringement decision that specified purchasers or classes of purchasers have suffered a loss or findings as to a specific overcharge.[100]

Prior to the implementation of the Damages Directive, decisions by NCAs from other Member States did not have any binding or otherwise formal effect. While the Commission Proposal for a Damages Directive had envisaged in Article 9 the 'German approach' of introducing a binding effect of NCA decisions from any Member State, Article 9(2) of the eventual Damages Directive provides only that an NCA decision from another Member State should be considered 'at least prima facie evidence that an infringement of competition law has occurred and, as appropriate, may be assessed along with any other evidence adduced by the parties'. The UK has implemented this provision with the 2017 Regulations by introducing paragraph 35(1) in Schedule 8A to the CA 1998, which provides that '[f]or the purposes of competition proceedings, a final decision of a member State competition authority or review court that there has been an infringement of Article 101(1) or Article 102 [TFEU] by an undertaking is prima facie evidence of the infringement'.

At the time of writing, the form Brexit will take (if any) is yet unclear, and section VIII of this chapter will consider the implications of different forms of Brexit, *inter alia*,

98. *BritNed v ABB*, *supra* n. 12, at para. 67 under (6)(a) and (b), as distinguished from other recitals, *ibid.* (c).
99. *Enron Coal Services Ltd v English Welsh & Scottish Railway Ltd* [2011] EWCA Civ 2 para. 50; *Dorothy Gibson v Pride Mobility Products*, *supra* n. 70, at para. 117 (lit. c).
100. Cf. the (ultimately inconclusive) discussion in *Dorothy Gibson v Pride Mobility Products Ltd*, *supra* n. 70, at para. 117 lit. c., whether a finding made by the CMA that the agreement in question had a 'not insignificant impact' on the market for mobility scooters and that it was 'liable to lead to consumers paying higher prices' should be binding under section 58 Competition Act 1998.

for the binding effect of Commission decisions and the prima facie evidence effect of decisions by NCAs.

VI. LIMITATION OF ACTIONS

Despite recent attempts to resolve issues with the application of rules on limitation of actions, these will still pose problems for claimants for years to come. Problems have arisen primarily in the CAT. In the High Court, limitation has long been determined by the Limitation Act 1980, which provides for a six-year period from the time of accrual of the claim, but where the defendant had deliberately concealed facts from the plaintiff, the period did not begin to run before the plaintiff had detected the concealment or could have detected it with reasonable diligence. In contrast, the CAT Rules 2003 provided for a two-year limitation which started to run from the time the infringement decision became final.[101] In principle, the two-year rule was meant to be a boon to the claimant, by allowing the claimant to wait for a final decision before bringing a follow-on claim, regardless of the time passed since the harm or damage was suffered. However, subsequent cases have shown that for domestic actions the two-year-after-the-final-decision rule in the CAT Rules 2003 sometimes turned out to be more restrictive than the usual rules on limitations would have been and that the CAT Rules 2003 do not enable claimants to bring claims that are governed by foreign law where the limitation periods of the applicable foreign law have expired, even if the claim is brought before the CAT within two years of the underlying infringement decision becoming final.

The *Deutsche Bahn v Morgan Crucible* case highlighted the problematic issue of limitation periods in the CAT. The House of Lords decided that in follow-on cases under the CAT Rules 2003, the two-year limitation period started to run as soon as the infringement decision against the individual defendant – in particular, the non-appealing immunity recipient – had become final, even if co-infringers had appealed the competition authority's infringement decision.[102] This decision meant that if claimants wanted to bring follow-on claims against immunity recipients, they would usually have to do so before the decision against the other cartel participants had become final.

Subsequent legislative changes in the Consumer Rights Act 2015 and the CAT Rules 2015 removed this problem, but only prospectively. The two-year time limit in Rule 31 of the CAT Rules 2003 was removed in the 2015 version. However, the legislator appeared to give with one hand only to take away with the other: Rule 119 of the CAT Rules 2015 contains a savings clause under which the old two-year rule applies to all claims that 'arose' (not only: actions brought) before 1 October 2015. This ensured that the two-year rule will be applicable for many years to come.

101. CAT Rules 2003, Rule 31.
102. *Deutsche Bahn v Morgan Advanced Materials plc* [2014] UKSC 24.

The implementation of the Damages Directive in the 2017 Regulations has introduced uniform limitation (in Scotland: prescription) periods. The rules on limitation and prescription are now to be found in part 5 (sections 17 to 26) of Schedule 8A to the CA 1998. The limitation period is now a uniform six years, and the prescription period in Scotland is a uniform five years. The respective periods begin when the infringement that is the basis for the claim ceases, or on the claimant's day of knowledge, whichever comes later.[103] The limitation and prescription periods are suspended in cases of disability, during the investigation by a competition authority, during a consensual dispute resolution process, and during collective proceedings.[104] These provisions on limitation, however, also apply only prospectively to claims that relate to loss or harm suffered after the 2017 Regulations came into force on 9 March 2017.[105] The problems created by the transitional Rule 119 in the CAT Rules 2015 mentioned above were raised in the consultation preceding the implementation of the Damages Directive but were dismissed by the government.[106] This means that the old two-year time limit will continue to apply to claims that arose prior to 1 October 2015, which may continue to create problems in particular in collective proceedings that would otherwise be hybrid claims, but where the stand-alone claim is out of time.

VII. COLLECTIVE ACTIONS/POOLING OF CLAIMS

A. Collective redress in the European discussion

The dispersed harm of antitrust infringements, with the number of harmed individuals often rising exponentially with the number of distribution levels, frequently leads to 'rational apathy' of the harmed individuals; the costs of bringing a claim would exceed the expected recovery.[107] In the absence of forms of collective redress, the infringer retains part or all of the ill-gotten gains (to the extent public enforcement does not skim them off). In the United States, this reasoning has made antitrust claims for treble damages a prime example for opt-out class actions.

103. Paragraph 19 of Schedule 8A to the CA 1998. The 'claimant's day of knowledge' is defined in section 19(2) as the day on which the claimant has or should reasonably have known about the infringing conduct, that the conduct constituted an infringement, that the claimant suffered a loss or damage, and the identity of the infringer. Section 19(6) adds that references to knowledge mean that the person has to have 'sufficient knowledge … to bring competition proceedings'. Special provision is made for persons acquiring the right for a competition claim in section 19(3)-(5). For a discussion when the claimant 'should reasonably have known' about facts, *see Arcadia Group Brands v Visa* [2015] EWCA Civ 883.
104. Paragraphs 20 to 24 of Schedule 8A to the CA 1998.
105. Paragraphs 42(1), 44 of Schedule 8A.
106. Department for Business, Energy & Industrial Strategy, *Competition Policy: Damages for breaches of competition law – government response to consultation* (December 2016), paras 135-138.
107. For a discussion of the policy reasons and the development of collective redress in general and in the EU, *see*, e.g., Arianna Andreangeli, *Private Enforcement of Antitrust: Regulating Corporate Behaviour through Collective Claims in the EU and US* (Edward Elgar 2014); Barry Rodger (ed), *Competition Law: Comparative Private Enforcement and Collective Redress across the EU* (Wolters Kluwer 2014); Matthias Casper, André Janssen et al. (eds.), *Auf dem Weg zu einer europäischen Sammelklage?* (sellier 2009) (with contributions in English and German).

In the European discussion about strengthening private enforcement, the United States always served as the backdrop – be it as a positive example of a jurisdiction in which private enforcement works, constitutes a large percentage of all antitrust actions, and results in a deterrent effect against antitrust infringements, as well as compensation for the harmed individuals, or as a negative example of how the 'excesses' of private litigation can create costs for the legal system and the economic actors on the market, and enrich the lawyers involved while insufficiently compensating the harmed individuals. The discussion about collective redress was no exception. The reasoning that dispersed harm leads to rational apathy unless collective redress options are introduced became prominent in the European discussions about strengthening private enforcement,[108] as did the warnings about the excesses of opt-out class actions as a technique for abusive litigation.[109]

The first, unpublished, draft of a Damages Directive under the Kroes Commission still contained provisions on group and representative actions.[110] It was these provisions in particular that raised the hackles of the European Parliament, which insisted on a legislative procedure of co-decision for the introduction of collective redress and called for an integrated, horizontal approach to collective redress not restricted to competition claims. These objections resulted in the elimination of the respective provisions in the Damages Directive, and the transfer into the non-binding Recommendation on collective redress, which was quite conservative in recommending only collective opt-in procedures, going so far as to make any opt-out regime the exception requiring justification.[111]

B. Collective redress in the United Kingdom

1. First stage: Representative actions and Group Litigation Orders

It did not take long for claimants in the UK to test the scope of the existing collective redress options. In *Emerald Supplies v British Airways*, the claimants pursued a representative action under CPR 19.6, which provides that '[w]here more than one person has the same interest in a claim, the claim may be [begun or continued] by or against one or more of the persons who have the same interest as representatives of any other persons who have that interest', with the resulting judgments and orders being binding on the parties and the represented persons. The claimants, themselves importers of flowers, sought to represent all direct and indirect purchasers of air cargo services who paid prices inflated by restrictive agreements and concerted practices

108. *See*, e.g., European Parliament resolution of 26 March 2009 on the White Paper on damages actions for breach of the EC antitrust rules, A6-0123/2009, para. 9.
109. *Ibid.*
110. For a discussion of the Kroes draft, *see* Florian Wagner-von Papp, *Der Richtlinienentwurf zu kartellrechtlichen Schadensersatzklagen* [2009] Europäisches Wirtschafts- und Steuerrecht 445 (in German).
111. Commission Recommendation of 11 June 2013 on common principles for injunctive and compensatory collective redress mechanisms in the Member States concerning violations of rights granted under Union Law, [2013] OJ L 201/60, para. 21.

against the colluding airlines. At first instance, the Chancellor considered that the 'same interest' had been interpreted in the case law to mean that 'the claimants and the class they seek to represent must all have "a common interest and a common grievance" and "the relief sought [must] in its nature [be] beneficial to all" of them' at the time the representative claim was brought.[112] Neither the large number of individuals nor their geographic dispersion or fluctuations in the composition were necessarily bars to bringing a representative action.[113] However, he considered two factors to make the claim unsuitable for a representative action: First, the identity of the represented claimants depended on the decision on the substance of the claim; that is, only after the decision on the substance would it become clear if any given person did or did not belong to the circle of represented claimants with the 'same interest' as the representative.[114] Second, there were inherent conflicts between direct and indirect purchasers, because the latter would argue that the pass-on was high, while the former would argue that there was no, or only a low proportion of, pass-on.[115] The Chancellor indicated that the use of a Group Litigation Order under CPR 19.11, under which claimants interested in pooling their claims can opt into the action by entering themselves into the group register, would have been a possibly more appropriate way forward. The Court of Appeal refused permission to amend the pleadings and dismissed the appeal.[116] The 'bold attempt at keeping a procedural novelty alive'[117] had failed.

2. *Collective Proceedings Orders after the CRA 2015*

a) *The legislative scheme*

In order to overcome the rational apathy of individuals harmed by infringements,[118] the CRA 2015 inserted new sections 47B–47E into the CA 1998, which provide for the possibility of collective proceedings in the CAT.[119] To pursue collective proceedings, it is necessary for the tribunal to make a CPO,[120] which requires that the tribunal considers it 'just and reasonable' that the person – who may or may not be a class member – acts as the representative for the class and that the 'claims are eligible for inclusion', which is the case where they 'raise the same, similar or related issues of fact or law and are suitable to be brought in collective proceedings'.[121] If a CPO is made, the

112. *Emerald Supplies v British Airways* [2009] EWHC (Ch) 741 para. 33 with para. 31.
113. *Ibid.*, para. 30.
114. *Ibid.*, paras 34, 35.
115. *Ibid.*, paras 36, 37.
116. *Emerald Supplies v British Airways* [2010] EWCA Civ 1284, (2011) 2 WLR 203.
117. *Ibid.*, para. 1.
118. *See* VII.A, *supra*; Department of Business, Industry and Skills, *Private Actions in Competition Law: A consultation on options for reform – Government response* BIS/13/501 6; *Dorothy Gibson v Pride Mobility Products*, *supra* n. 70, at para. 22; *Merricks v Mastercard*, *supra* n. 13, at paras 59, 60.
119. Section 81 and Schedule 8 of the CRA 2015.
120. Section 47B(4).
121. Section 47B(5) with (6) and (8).

tribunal will specify the collective proceedings as 'opt-in' or 'opt-out' collective proceedings.[122]

Slightly more detailed rules on the procedural issues of collective proceedings are provided in Part 5 of the CAT Rules 2015,[123] sections 73 to 93.

The CRA 2015 also introduced provisions on collective settlements in section 49A and 49B CA 1998, with procedural provisions in Part 5 of the CAT Rules 2015, sections 94 to 98.

b) *Dorothy Gibson v Pride Mobility Products*

The first case in which a CPO was sought was *Dorothy Gibson v Pride Mobility Products*.[124] This concerned a follow-on action on the basis of a decision by the Office of Fair Trading (hereinafter 'OFT') of 27 March 2014, which had held that Pride and several independent dealers (hereinafter 'the Relevant Retailers') had agreed not to advertise online prices for certain Pride mobility scooter models (hereinafter 'Relevant Models') that were below the recommended retail price (hereinafter 'RRP') during a two-year period between February 2010 and February 2012 (hereinafter 'relevant time period'). Despite its simplicity in factual terms, the case can serve to demonstrate the differences between public and private enforcement. The public enforcement decision had been straightforward: This was, as a vertical resale price maintenance case, a restriction by object, so that any reference to effects was not strictly necessary, and the OFT's statement that the restriction had had a 'not insignificant' impact on the mobility scooter market in the UK was purely gratuitous (and, indeed, not even relevant for sanctioning purposes because no fines were imposed because of the *de minimis* turnover thresholds of the parties).

In contrast to the straightforward public enforcement case, the applicant in the private action faced the hurdle of showing that the proposed class members were harmed and by how much; the class was defined as everyone who had bought a new Pride mobility scooter – except in the course of a business – in the UK in the relevant time period, a definition that was estimated to comprise some 30,000 people. The applicant's own economic expert had already distinguished between four subgroups of class members: (1) those who had bought the Relevant Models online at RRP and who were directly affected by the infringement; (2) those who had bought Relevant Models in physical stores for prices that were higher because they were indirectly affected by the lower competitive pressure from online competition; (3) those who had bought other than Relevant Models online but had paid higher prices (e.g., because they compared them to the higher online prices for Relevant Models, or because of the general umbrella effect); and (4) those who had bought other than Relevant Models in physical stores, who had paid more because of the umbrella effect. The economic expert (using a 'before-and-after' econometric test) estimated the overcharge for the

122. Section 47B(7) with (10) and (11).
123. Statutory Instruments 2015 No. 1648, made on the 7 September 2015, in force since 1 October 2015.
124. *Dorothy Gibson v Pride Mobility Products*, *supra* n. 70.

Relevant Models at 16.2 % and the overcharge for other models at 4.6 %, resulting in an overall damage of about GBP 3 million before interest.[125]

Pride, however, argued that the OFT decision had only found an infringement by 8 Relevant Retailers of some 250–300 retailers who sold Pride scooters on a regular basis,[126] that only 7 of about 38 Pride models were affected, that even the Relevant Retailers could advertise that prices could be individually negotiated, that even the Relevant Retailers did not always adhere to the advertising prohibition during the relevant time, and that – because a mobility scooter was a major purchase for most customers – there was a significant amount of individual haggling.[127] Even customers buying from one of the Relevant Retailers would likely have seen (online or offline) prices by other retailers, possibly below RRP, so that there would have been significant competitive pressure making any price effect of the infringement unlikely, at least outside the very limited category of online sales of the Relevant Models by the Relevant Retailers (a category comprising only some 260 sales), and the individual search and negotiation behaviour of every single customer would have determined whether there was any overcharge at all, and if so, how high that overcharge would have been.[128]

Given that the case was the first CPO application, the CAT discussed the relevant standard for the issuance of a CPO, and the determination of the commonality issue, at some length. It noted that one could not simply transfer the US case law on class certification to the UK, among other things, because class certification in the US was preceded by substantial discovery and because common issues had to 'predominate', whereas in the UK disclosure would (usually) be subsequent to the CPO, and because there was no requirement in the CA 1998 that the common issues 'predominate'; it was sufficient that they 'raise the same, similar or related issues of fact or law'. Given the different statutory wording, the CAT considered the Canadian standard, established in *Pro-Sys Consultants Ltd v Microsoft Corp.* [2013] SCC 57 paragraph 113, to be more apposite. There, the court had considered that expert evidence could be used to establish the overcharge on a class-wide basis (and so constitute a 'common' issue) as long as the calculation was 'grounded on the facts of the particular case' and were not 'purely theoretical or hypothetical'. In principle, the CAT was sympathetic to the expert of the applicant. However, it noted that the claim was a pure follow-on claim, and the OFT decision had only found an infringement of those retailers that had communicated their assent to the policy back to Pride.[129] This meant that the subclasses for whom the effects would need to be estimated would have to be subdivided into the sales of Relevant Models from Relevant Retailers; the sales of other Pride models from Relevant

125. *Ibid.*, paras 92, 93.
126. The OFT had, however, left open the possibility that other retailers had been affected.
127. *Dorothy Gibson v Pride Mobility Products*, *supra* n. 70, at paras 94–98.
128. *Ibid.*, paras 100, 101.
129. As a matter of substantive competition law, that is questionable. Pride had adopted a market-wide policy. By continuing to sell Pride mobility scooters, the retailers arguably acquiesced into that policy. The CAT considered that the OFT 'chose the low hanging evidential fruit' (*Dorothy Gibson v Pride Mobility Products*, *supra* n. 70, at para. 109). It was not possible for the applicant to treat this as a hybrid follow-on/stand-alone claim, because the stand-alone part would have been out of time under the transitional rule in CAT Rule 119, because the claim had arisen more than two years prior to the application; *ibid.*, para. 110.

Retailers; and subclasses of buyers at other Pride retailers as 'umbrella' claims. The CAT was willing to be relatively generous to the applicant and granted an adjournment to allow for a revision of the expert evidence along these lines, partially because the OFT had found that the infringement had a 'not significant impact' on the UK market for mobility scooters. The CAT also indicated that on an amended application it would be willing to grant a CPO on an opt-out basis and that it would consider Ms Gibson (who was not herself a class member, but was the General Secretary of the National Pensioners Convention) to be a suitable representative, given that she had the logistical support of the NPC and was represented by a law firm with experience in group litigation.

However, eventually the applicant withdrew the application, possibly because it would have been difficult to show an umbrella effect of the very limited number of instances in which Relevant Models were bought specifically from the eight Relevant Retailers. The first application for a CPO on an opt-out basis had failed, even if only by a whisker.

c) *Merricks v Mastercard*

The second application for a CPO was made by Walter Hugh Merricks in a follow-on action based on the European Commission decision from 2007 finding Mastercard's system of multilateral exchange fees (hereinafter 'MIF') to infringe Article 101 TFEU. Mr Merricks proposed to represent 'all individuals over the age of 16 who had been resident in the UK for a continuous period of at least 3 months and who between 22 May 1992 and 21 June 2008 purchased goods or services from businesses in the UK which accepted Mastercard', whether or not they used a Mastercard for payment. The applicant's argument was that if Mastercard had behaved lawfully, there would either have been no interchange fees between the Acquirer and the Issuer at all or interchange fees would have been negotiated on a bilateral basis and would have been lower and that not only the savings would have been passed on from the acquiring banks to the merchants but also that all or nearly all of it would also have been passed on from the merchant to the consumers in the proposed class. However, the expert's report also allowed for the possibility that pass-on rates may be different in different sectors of the economy. Mastercard had seized on this statement and argued that, first, it would need to be shown that every class member suffered loss, and second, that it would be impossible to find sufficient evidence for different merchants in the time period from 1992 to 2008. Mastercard also objected to the class-wide damages calculation with a per capita distribution, which was said to contravene the compensatory principle.

The CAT interviewed the expert witness and refused a CPO because there was no sufficient data to determine pass-on rates of overcharges from different merchants to consumers, and these various pass-on rates to consumers were not considered 'common issues' in the meaning of section 47B(6).[130] Additionally, in the CAT's view,

130. *Merricks v Mastercard*, *supra* n. 71.

no plausible methodology to calculate the loss of the different class members existed so as to find a sufficient basis for a distribution of the aggregate award (if any).

The Court of Appeal allowed the appeal and set aside the CAT's decision.[131] The Court of Appeal considered that the CAT had applied too stringent a test in its scrutiny of the evidence underlying the application. In the Court of Appeal's view, all the applicant has to do in an application for a CPO is to 'demonstrate ... that he has a real prospect of success', whereas the CAT – in the Court of Appeal's view – had 'more or less' conducted a mini-trial when assessing whether the applicant would be able to adduce sufficient evidence for the pass-on.[132] The Court of Appeal derived the proper test in particular by referring to Canadian class actions, which were seen to be closely related to the UK system,[133] which – if the UK Supreme Court dismisses the appeal against the Court of Appeal's decision in *Merricks* – any future potential CPO applicant will do well to take into account when drafting the application. The Court of Appeal advised that any deficiencies in the available evidence should better be assessed after pleadings, disclosure, and expert evidence are complete, which is possible because CPOs may, under section 47B(9), be varied or revoked at any time.[134]

With regard to the question of whether it has to be shown that individual class members suffered a loss, and how much, the Court of Appeal pointed out that section 47C(2) allows for an aggregate award and therefore permits a top-down approach and that requiring a showing of individual loss would render this provision largely nugatory.[135] If such an aggregate award was made, the distribution among all class members would not have to follow the compensatory principle (although it was still an ideal to be aspired to if the actual loss was calculable without particular problems).[136]

The implications of the Court of Appeal decision in *Merricks v Mastercard* go far beyond the case itself (and the test established there would arguably also have resulted in a different outcome in the *Gibson v Pride* case). The decision makes clear that the standard for obtaining a CPO are not a high hurdle and that most issues are better postponed to the time after disclosure. When it comes to collective redress, there is always a tension between making private enforcement effective by overcoming the rational apathy of harmed individuals on the one hand, and on the other hand the danger that class actions are used either to enrich class representatives and/or the lawyers or used as means to extort settlements for unmeritorious claims. The European approach until now has laid more emphasis on the latter aspect, invoking the 'excesses of US American opt-out class actions' and restricting representative actions to a tightly controlled regime. The CAT appears to have followed a similar approach by closely scrutinising CPOs. In contrast, the Court of Appeal has now firmly put the emphasis on overcoming the rational apathy of consumers.

However, in July 2019, the UK Supreme Court granted leave to appeal the Court of Appeal's decision in *Merricks v Mastercard*. The decision of the UK Supreme Court,

131. *Merricks v Mastercard, supra* n. 13, at para. 19.
132. *Ibid.*, paras 52, 54.
133. *Ibid.*, paras 38 et seq.
134. *Ibid.*, para. 53.
135. *Ibid.*, para. 47; *see also* paras 58–62.
136. *Ibid.*, paras 56, 57.

expected at some point in the year 2020, will likely determine the standards to be applied to CPO applications.

Accordingly, hearings on new CPO applications before the CAT in the *Trucks* cases were adjourned to await the UK Supreme Court decision on the application to give leave to appeal,[137] and given that this application was granted in July 2019, it seems likely that the CAT will further adjourn the hearings until the UK Supreme Court has handed down its judgment in the *Merricks* case.

But before this happens, it is likely that the UK will leave the European Union, and the next section will turn to the question of how this is likely to affect private enforcement in the UK.

VIII. BREXIT

A lot of ink has been spilled on Brexit, even on the more specific topic of Brexit and competition law.[138] Here, there is space only for a few words with regard to the effects of Brexit on private enforcement. At proof stage, in mid-November 2019, more than seven months after the date originally planned for the UK's departure from the EU, it is still unclear what form Brexit will eventually take. Two scenarios will be considered below: Either there will be a 'no-deal Brexit' or the revised Withdrawal Agreement will be ratified.

A. No deal

If there is a no-deal Brexit, EU law will immediately cease to apply *as EU law*. However, the European Union (Withdrawal) Act 2018 seeks to transform most EU law into domestic UK law, subject only to necessary modifications through Statutory Instruments and to later amendments or repeals by Parliament. This approach of unilateral adoption of EU law as domestic law works for large swathes of EU law: In our context, for example, the provisions on applicable law in the Rome I and Rome II Regulations, and the provisions of the Damages Directive as implemented by the 2017 Regulations in Schedule 8A to the CA 1998 will continue to apply, unless explicitly modified or repealed.

However, this unilateral approach by 'domesticating' EU law fails to deliver the desired result where the relevant EU instruments require reciprocity or cooperation from other EU Member States.

137. *UK Trucks Claim Ltd v Fiat Chrysler Automobiles and Others*, and *Road Haulage Association Ltd v MAN SE and Others* [2019] CAT 15.

138. *See*, e.g., House of Lords EU Committee, *Brexit: competition and state aid*, HL Paper 67; Florian Wagner-von Papp, '*Brexit: Challenges and Regulatory Solutions in the field of Competition Policy and State Aid*' in Friedemann Kainer and René Repasi (eds) *Trade Relations After Brexit* (Nomos & Hart Publishing, forthcoming) 327 (the following paragraphs here draw on the parts on private enforcement of that chapter, *ibid.* 358–364); Brexit Competition Law Working Group, *Conclusions and Recommendations* (July 2017).

1. *Jurisdiction and Enforcement: Brussels I Recast Regulation*

In the area of private enforcement, one crucial instrument that cannot simply be replicated as domestic law is the Brussels I *Recast* Regulation 1215/2012, which will cease to apply on Exit Day. This means that as of Exit Day, issues of jurisdiction will become more complicated - for example, because the courts in the EU27 no longer have to recognise the *lis alibis pendens* rule where litigation has started in the UK[139] - and, even more crucially, that judgments by UK courts are no longer automatically enforceable across the area of the EU27.

It is unclear what the post-Brexit position will be. There is a debate whether or not the 1968 Brussels Convention will revive, or whether this Convention was completely and irretrievably replaced by the Brussels I Regulation (and then the Brussels I *Recast* Regulation). While private international lawyers tend to the view that the 1968 Convention will revive,[140] the UK government has indicated in a short notice in September 2018 that the UK will 'instead revert to the existing domestic common law and statutory rules, which currently apply in cross border cases concerning the rest of the world'.[141] The 1988 Lugano Convention was irretrievably replaced by the 2007 Lugano Convention, and in 2007 it was only the EU, not the UK, that acceded, so that the UK would be outside the Lugano Convention until it applies for readmission. While the UK plans to apply for readmission into Lugano, it has apparently not done so yet. While the UK has ratified the Hague Convention of 30 June 2005 on Choice of Court Agreements,[142] this Convention excludes competition matters from its scope.[143]

2. *Taking of Evidence*

Another Regulation that requires reciprocity is the Taking of Evidence Regulation 1206/2001. In a no-deal Brexit, UK courts and tribunals will no longer be able to rely on this regulation. However, the experience with that Regulation in competition cases had been mixed, as the *National Grid* case showed, and its loss is arguably by far not as problematic as the loss of the Brussels I *Recast* Regulation described above.

---

139. Regulation (EU) No 1215/2012 of the European Parliament and of the Council of 12 December 2012 on jurisdiction and the recognition and enforcement of judgments in civil and commercial matters [2012], OJ L 351/1, Article 29 would no longer apply; however, courts in the EU27 could stay proceedings if they chose to, Articles 33, 34 of the Regulation.
140. *See*, e.g., the discussion in Andrew Dickinson, *Back to the future: the UK's EU exit and the conflict of laws* (2016) 12 Journal of Private International Law 195, 204-206.
141. Department for Business, Energy & Industrial Strategy and Ministry of Justice, Guidance, *Handling civil legal cases that involve EU countries if there's no Brexit deal* (13 September 2018).
142. It ratified on 28 December 2018, requesting to accede from 1 April 2019, only to request extensions on 28 March 2019 and again on 12 April 2019. Depending on the developments in October 2019, this might develop into a regular pen friendship.
143. Article 2(2)(h) of the 2005 Hague Convention on Choice of Court Agreements.

3. *2019 Regulations and follow-on actions*

Another consequence of Brexit for the private enforcement of competition law is that the '2019 Regulations' will come into force.[144] In the consultations, competition lawyers had pleaded with the government that, while Article 16 of Regulation 1/2003 would no longer apply, the UK legislator should unilaterally replicate its effect in so far as it makes EU Commission decisions binding on UK courts and the tribunal, so that claimants can continue to bring follow-on actions based on EU Commission decisions.[145]

However, the 2019 Regulations eliminate nearly indiscriminately all references to 'Article 101 or 102' TFEU or EU institutions in competition legislation, including in sections 47A and 58A CA 1998.[146] Only for decisions the European Commission reached before Exit Day will the binding effect continue as before.[147] While this ensures that follow-on actions based on Commission decisions can still be brought for quite some time – there is usually a substantial time lag between the infringement decision and the initiation, and certainly the decision, of any private enforcement actions – it makes private follow-on actions based on Commission decisions a species whose extinction in the UK is nearly certain.

More optimistic observers would say that the CMA will adopt parallel decisions whenever there are Commission infringement decisions, so that follow-on actions can still be brought based on the resulting CMA decision. For reasons explained elsewhere in more detail, this seems unlikely: First, this is, under the current law, not even possible where an agreement or concerted practice has not been implemented in the UK, or a unilateral practice has not affected trade in the UK. Second, even where it would in principle be possible for the CMA to adopt parallel decisions, it is unlikely that the CMA will do so in all cases. The CMA has a traditional weakness when it comes to enforcement numbers anyway. And while the CMA has been addressing this weakness in recent years, Brexit will swamp the CMA with a host of new challenges, such as merger control decisions when the one-stop shop ends, and an entirely new domestic state aid regime. This will leave little spare capacity for parallel enforcement decisions replicating the work the Commission has done, especially because the UK will, in the case of a no-deal Brexit, not have the cooperation agreements with the EU, its Member States, or third countries in place to deal with the international cartel cases with which the Commission deals. For 'parallel decisions', it will not be enough to copy-paste the Commission's findings, and even with the increased CMA budget there will simply not

144. Statutory Instruments 2019 No. 93.
145. *See*, e.g., Brexit Competition Law Working Group, *Conclusions and Recommendations*, paras 2.18, 2.19 (suggesting that the current wording of sections 47A, 58A of the CA 1998 should be retained), 2.22–2.25 (noting considerable support for this recommendation, and rejecting objections raised by 'one or two respondents').
146. This is not a mere oversight; the Explanatory Memorandum to the 2019 Regulations notes specifically (under 7.2) that '[i]n particular, they [ie, the 2019 Regulations] … amend sections 47A and 58A of the Competition Act so that decisions of the European Commission reached after exit day are no longer binding on UK courts in follow-on claims …'.
147. This is the consequence of the savings provisions in Part 6 of Schedule 4 to the 2019 Regulations.

be enough resources for the CMA to reinvestigate all the cartel cases with which the Commission deals, and write the decisions that stand up to the UK courts' and the CAT's diligent scrutiny.

4. *Brexit implications for the implementation of the Damages Directive*

Otherwise, the Brexit-induced changes to the implementation of the Damages Directive in the 2019 Regulations are relatively minor. All references to European provisions and institutions are eliminated, but, otherwise, the content of Schedule 8A to the CA 1998, which implements the Damages Directive, will mostly stay unaffected. The only substantive change is that paragraph 35 of Schedule 8A, which stipulates that infringement decisions by EU Member States' competition authorities are prima facie evidence of the infringement, will be omitted.

B. Withdrawal Agreement

The current Prime Minister of the UK, Boris Johnson, has renegotiated former Prime Minister May's Withdrawal Agreement, substantially by taking up the original proposals of the European Union for a Customs Border in the Irish Sea (revised Withdrawal Agreement of 19 October 2019). Unless the Parliament reconstituted after the general election scheduled for December 2019 ratifies this revised Withdrawal Agreement, or the new government successfully applies for yet another extension (or, less likely, withdraws its Article 50 TEU notice), there will nevertheless be a no-deal departure on 31 January 2020 (*see* VIII.A, *supra*). The alternative is that either the revised Withdrawal Agreement is ratified after all or – for reasons of political arithmetic less likely – the Article 50 TEU notification is withdrawn.

If the Article 50 notification were withdrawn in accordance with the Court of Justice's *Wightman* decision, the legal position (in contrast to the political situation) would be clear.

If the revised Withdrawal Agreement is ratified, the immediate negative consequences of a no-deal Brexit on private competition enforcement described above would largely be averted, at least for the time of the transition period and, because of the transition rules of the Withdrawal Agreement which envisage continuity of jurisdiction for acts initiated during the transition period (which have not changed from Prime Minister May's deal), often beyond the transition period; eventually, the position will depend on what form of a future relationship between the EU and the UK will be negotiated (which could still end up in a no-deal Brexit at the end of the transition period).

Article 67 of the Withdrawal Agreement ensures that the rules on jurisdiction, enforcement, and recognition in the Brussels I *Recast* Regulation will largely apply for actions initiated during the transition period and that the Taking of Evidence Regulation will also continue to apply for requests received during transition.

Article 95 of the revised Withdrawal Agreement provides, *inter alia*, that competition decisions adopted by Union institutions addressed to the UK or natural or legal persons in the UK 'shall be binding on and in' the UK. Primarily, this provision is arguably meant to ensure the binding effect for *public enforcement* purposes. Nevertheless, the binding effect 'in' the UK arguably extends to the prohibition to take decisions in the UK that run counter to a Commission decision, as developed in *Factortame* and as codified in Article 16 Regulation 1/2003, so that follow-on actions would remain possible for all decisions taken in a procedure that was initiated under Article 2(1) of Regulation 773/2004 before the end of the transition period.[148]

IX. CONCLUSION

The uncertainty of Brexit, in particular as to the relevant rules on jurisdiction and the possible inability to enforce judgments of UK courts and tribunals across the EU27, and the inability to bring follow-on actions based on Commission decisions at some point after Brexit are likely to constitute not insignificant drawbacks for the future of private enforcement in the UK. If it were not for Brexit, the new rules on collective proceedings - especially if the UK Supreme Court should affirm the Court of Appeal's liberal approach to CPOs in *Merricks v Mastercard* - could arguably make the UK the most attractive European jurisdiction for claimants. It will remain to be seen whether the otherwise not insubstantial advantages that facilitate private enforcement in the UK will be able to offset the burden of Brexit.

148. Article 95(1) with Article 92(1), (3)(b) of the Withdrawal Agreement.

Part II Private Enforcement of EU State Aid Law

CHAPTER 9

The European Perspective

Fernando Pastor-Merchante

I. Introduction
II. The public enforcement of State aid law
III. The role of national courts in the enforcement of State aid law
IV. Stand-alone actions based on the direct effect of the standstill clause
V. Follow-on actions based on the direct effect of Commission decisions
VI. The interplay between the public and the private enforcement of State aid law
VII. Conclusion

I. INTRODUCTION

The purpose of this chapter is to lay out the general framework that governs the 'private enforcement of EU State aid law', serving as a prelude to the national studies presented below. The term 'private enforcement' is a buzzword, one whose precise meaning in the State aid context is not always clear. Hence the need to elucidate the sense in which the expression is used in this chapter.

Under EU law, the concept of 'State aid' encompasses a broad range of state measures of financial support to firms, including subsidies, tax breaks, public procurement decisions, underpriced sales of public assets, overpriced purchases of private assets, privileged guarantees and many others.[1] What all these measures have in common is that they represent a financial advantage granted by the state upon their

1. Commission Notice on the notion of State aid as referred to in Article 107(1) of the Treaty on the Functioning of the European Union [2016], OJ C 262/1. *See also* J. Jorge Piernas López, *The Concept of State Aid under EU Law. From Internal Market to Competition and Beyond* (OUP 2015).

beneficiary undertakings. Indeed, the main rationale behind the legal regime on State aid is the concern for the distortionary effects that this advantage may have upon competition and trade within the internal market.[2]

It is therefore possible to think of the implementation of State aid measures as an action that gives rise to a triangular relationship, with the *granting authority* at the apex (i.e., the state organ which decides on and funds the measure), the *beneficiary undertaking(s)* at one vertex (i.e., the firm which receives the advantage) and affected *third parties* on the other (i.e., the stakeholders on which the State aid inflicts some form of harm or loss, such as competitors and taxpayers). Thus, the term 'private enforcement' refers to the legal actions that third parties may bring, before national courts, in order to fight the approval or implementation of State aid measures.

This definition calls for a couple of further clarifications. First of all, as used in this chapter, the term 'private enforcement' does not encompass actions brought by the granting authority or by the beneficiary undertakings in the State aid context (e.g., judicial actions triggered by national authorities to recover State aid or actions triggered by State aid beneficiaries to resist recovery). Although some of the problems raised by these actions are similar to the problems raised by third-party actions, they are normally motivated by a completely different concern, if only because of the different incentive bias of these a priori pro-State aid actors. This not to say that the 'third-party' label cannot include public actors other than the granting authority. Indeed, it is entirely possible that a third-party public authority takes issue with a measure of State aid granted by a different organ or level of government.[3] Although it is hard to see what is 'private' about these types of disputes, they are subject to the same legal regime as disputes initiated by private actors (at least from an EU law perspective, which is the one that matters in this chapter).

Second, the term 'private enforcement' captures all third-party actions, irrespective of their target (i.e., granting authorities or beneficiary undertakings). This may seem paradoxical, given the public nature of the former. However, granting authorities are actually the standard target of the legal actions that State aid law places in the hands of affected third parties: because the formal addressees of the EU rules on State aid are Member States (and not private firms), EU law only provides a legal basis to sue granting authorities (and not the beneficiary undertakings).[4] Thus, the 'private enforcement of State aid law' often takes place through judicial proceedings for the review of administrative actions (and, in the Member States which have a specific set of courts for administrative and/or tax law matters, before those specialised 'public law' organs).

In order to describe the main rules and principles that frame the private enforcement of State aid law, the chapter unfolds as follows. Section II describes the overall institutional design of the system of State aid control, which heavily relies on

2. I discuss the theory of harm that informs EU State aid law in Fernando Pastor-Merchante, *The Role of Competitors in the Enforcement of State Aid Law,* 15–33 (Hart 2017).
3. For example, ECJ, Case C-71/04 *Administración del Estado v Xunta de Galicia* [2005] ECR I-7419.
4. ECJ, Case C-39/94 *Syndicat Français de l'Express International (SFEI) v La Poste* [1996] ECR I-3547, para. 74.

the centralised control exercised by the Commission. Although this design seems to leave very little room for private enforcement, section III identifies the legal provisions on the basis of which third parties may litigate before national courts. These provisions basically allow two types of private enforcement actions: 'stand-alone actions' (based on the direct effect of the standstill clause laid down by Article 108(3) TFEU) and 'follow-on' actions (based on a previous Commission decision). Sections IV and V analyse their respective legal regimes. Finally, section VI reflects upon the way in which public and private enforcement mechanisms interact in this area.

II. THE PUBLIC ENFORCEMENT OF STATE AID LAW

In order to understand the legal framework that governs the private enforcement of State aid law, it is necessary to zoom out and to discuss, as a preliminary point, the institutional design of the system of State aid control as a whole.

As is well known, the system revolves around the general prohibition on State aid laid down by Article 107(1) TFEU, which prevents Member States from putting into place state measures of financial support to firms that meet certain conditions (imputability to the state, use of state resources, selectivity, distortion of competition and effect on trade).[5] However, the general prohibition on State aid is not absolute because its scope is limited by the exceptions listed in sections (2) and (3) of Article 107 TFEU, which exclude from the ban State aid measures that serve certain public interest goals.

From an institutional perspective, the main peculiarity of the system of State aid control is that the administration of these exceptions is reserved to the European Commission.[6] Indeed, as a general rule, Member States are allowed to implement State aid measures only if they have previously secured the formal authorisation of the Commission. This authorisation must be embodied in a formal decision declaring that the State aid in question falls under one of the exceptions and is therefore 'compatible' with the internal market. Without such a decision, the implementation of State aid measures is in principle 'unlawful', even if they actually fit within one of the exceptions - and this notwithstanding the fact that the Commission enjoys no discretion whatsoever in the application of the exceptions of Article 107(2) TFEU[7] and that its discretion under Article 107(3) TFEU has shrunk considerably as a result of the 'juridification' process undergone by this provision.[8]

5. Commission Notice on the notion of State aid, *supra* n. 1.
6. ECJ, Case C-78/76 *Steinike & Weinlig v Germany* [1977] ECR I-595, para. 9; ECJ, Case C-354/90 *Fédération Nationale du Commerce Extérieur des Produits Alimentaires (FNCEPA) and Syndicat National des Négociants et Transformateurs de Saumon v France* [1991] ECR I-5505, para. 14.
7. Article 107(2) TFEU provides that State aid defined therein 'shall' be compatible with the internal market.
8. Article 107(3) TFEU provides that State aid defined therein 'may' be declared compatible with the internal market. However, the Commission has considerably tied its own hands as a result of the progressive development of a dense web of soft-law instruments on the interpretation of this provision, as documented by Mitchell P. Smith, *Autonomy by the Rules: The European Commission and the Development of State Aid Policy* (1998) 36 Journal of Common market

In order to ensure that the Commission is in a position to exercise its prerogatives, Article 108(3) TFEU imposes upon Member States the so-called standstill and notification obligations: before they implement State aid measures, Member States must give notice of their plans and refrain from putting them into place unless and until they receive the green light of the Commission.[9]

Once notified of a State aid plan, the Commission must follow the steps laid down by the so-called Procedural Regulation, which codifies prior case law.[10] The Commission must first carry out a 'preliminary examination' of the plan.[11] If this perfunctory examination allows the Commission to conclude that the notified measure does not actually meet the definition of State aid or that its compatibility with the internal market raises no doubts, it is to record these findings by way of a clearing decision, which brings the procedure to an end ('decision that there is no aid' or 'decision not to raise objections').[12]

Conversely, if this brief examination is not sufficient to dispel all doubts, the Commission must open the 'formal investigation' phase.[13] After consulting with interested parties and hearing the affected Member State, the Commission must basically decide whether to block the plan ('negative decision')[14] or to clear it ('positive decision').[15] It may also decide to approve it, albeit subject to certain restrictions ('conditional decision').[16] If the Member State has already implemented the measure under scrutiny, in violation of its standstill obligation, the Commission may also order its withdrawal ('recovery decision').[17]

Granted, the description offered so far has overlooked some of the intricacies of the system of State aid control. To begin with, the third paragraph of Article 108(3) TFEU contains a 'safeguard clause' which empowers the Council to overrule the Commission when the latter refuses to clear a State aid measure. However, the use of this clause is so rare that it seems unnecessary to dwell upon it.[18]

More importantly, there are certain circumstances where Member States may lawfully implement State aid measures without the prior consent of the Commission. This is the case when the measures of financial support extended to firms constitute 'existing State aid' (e.g., if they are part of a broader scheme that has previously been

Studies, 55; Michael Blauberger, *Of 'Good' and 'Bad' Subsidies: European State Aid Control through Soft and Hard Law* (2009) 32 West European Politics, 719.

9. ECJ, Case 120/73 *Gebrüder Lorenz GmbH v Germany* [1973] ECR 1471, para. 8.
10. Regulation 2015/1589/EU of the Council of 13 July 2015 laying down detailed rules for the application of Article 108 of the Treaty on the Functioning of the European Union [2015] OJ L 248/9, which replaces Regulation 659/1999/EG of the Council of 22 March 1999 laying down detailed rules for the application of Article 108 of the Treaty on the Functioning of the European Union [1999] OJ L 83/1, as amended ('Procedural Regulation').
11. Article 4 of the Procedural Regulation, *supra* n. 10.
12. Article 4(2) and (3) of the Procedural Regulation, *supra* n. 10.
13. Article 4(4) of the Procedural Regulation, *supra* n. 10.
14. Article 9(5) of the Procedural Regulation, *supra* n. 10.
15. Article 9(3) of the Procedural Regulation, *supra* n. 10.
16. Article 9(4) of the Procedural Regulation, *supra* n. 10.
17. Article 16(1) of the Procedural Regulation, *supra* n. 10.
18. Claus Dieter Ehlermann, *State Aid Control in the European Union: Success or Failure* (1995) 18 Fordham International Law Journal 1212, 1216.

approved by the Commission)[19] or if they are covered by the General Block Exemption Regulation (which gives a green light to State aid measures that serve certain objectives, provided their design and implementation conforms to the prescriptions laid down by that regulation).[20] It is also the case if the measures in question fail to reach the threshold defined by the *de minimis* Regulation, which is currently set at EUR 200,000 for a period of three years – although, technically speaking, such measures do not constitute State aid in the first place.[21]

These important qualifications notwithstanding, the point to note is that, as a general rule, the Commission has a monopoly over the administration of the prohibition on State aid and its exceptions. From an institutional perspective, this observation is crucial because it implies that the right forum to fight over the compatibility of State aid measures is the EU institutional layer (i.e., the Commission and the EU Courts, which are the only fora that have jurisdiction to review the legality of State aid decisions)[22] rather than the national one.

Granted, the State aid control procedure outlined above is mostly a matter for the Commission and Member States, with hardly any space for third-party input. However, there are certain avenues through which third parties can try to affect the outcome of the procedure at the EU level.[23] To begin with, they may lodge complaints as a means of bringing to the Commission's attention unlawful State aid measures.[24] They may also submit comments in the course of the public consultation that the Commission must carry out if the procedure reaches the formal investigation stage[25] (something to which third parties are entitled if the compatibility of the contested measure raises 'serious difficulties').[26] Finally, they may challenge the decisions adopted by the Commission at the end of the procedure if they manage to satisfy the stringent standing requirements that Article 263 imposes upon individuals seeking access to the Court of Justice of the European Union.[27]

The other side of the coin is that national courts cannot apply *in full* the rules on State aid. National courts have the power to apply the definition of Article 107(1) TFEU and the *de minimis* Regulation in order to decide whether contested measures constitute State aid and, hence, whether they are subject to the standstill and notification obligations.[28] They are also empowered to declare that State aid measures

19. Article 108(1) TFEU and Articles 21 to 23 of the Procedural Regulation, *supra* n. 10.
20. Commission Regulation (EU) No. 651/2014 of 17 June 2014 declaring certain categories of aid compatible with the internal market in application of Articles 107 and 108 of the Treaty [2014] OJ L 187/1 ('General Block Exemption Regulation').
21. Commission Regulation (EU) No. 1407/2013 of 18 December 2013 on the application of Articles 107 and 108 of the Treaty on the Functioning of the European Union to de minimis aid [2013] OJ L 352/1.
22. ECJ, Case 314/85 *Foto-Frost v Hauptzollamt Lübeck-Ost* [1987] ECR 4199.
23. For a broader take on this topic, *see* Pastor-Merchante, *supra* n. 2.
24. Article 24(2) of the Procedural Regulation, *supra* n. 10.
25. Article 108(2) TFEU and Article 24(1) of the Procedural Regulation, *supra* n. 10.
26. ECJ, Case C-198/91 *Cook v Commission* [1993] ECR I-2487, para. 23.
27. ECJ, Case C-169/84 *Compagnie française de l'azote (Cofaz) v Commission* [1990] ECR I-3083.
28. Case C-78/76 *Steinike*, *supra* n. 6, at para. 14.

covered by a previously approved State aid scheme[29] or by the General Block Exemption Regulation[30] are compatible with the internal market. However, neither of these powers gives them the authority to quash State aid measures on the ground that they are *incompatible* with the internal market.[31] Indeed, the finding that a measure constitutes State aid under Article 107(1) TFEU and that it is not covered by a previously approved State aid scheme or by the General Block Exemption Regulation does not imply that it is incompatible with the internal market. It only implies that the State aid measure in question may not be implemented unless, until and to the extent that it is authorised by the Commission, on the basis of the exceptions of Article 107(2) and (3) TFEU.

The upshot is that the prohibition on State aid laid down by Article 107 TFEU lacks direct effect, in the sense that it is not a source of actionable rights for third parties.[32] To be more precise, it means that third parties do not derive from that provision a general right against State aid and, hence, they may not rely on the general prohibition of Article 107 TFEU as a basis to initiate judicial proceedings before national courts. This is obviously an important limitation from the perspective of the private enforcement of State aid law. Yet, as the following section shows, it does not imply that private enforcement actions are completely foreign to the system of State aid control.

III. THE ROLE OF NATIONAL COURTS IN THE ENFORCEMENT OF STATE AID LAW

In order to understand the role of private enforcement and national courts in the area of State aid law, it is necessary to observe that the system of State aid control designed by the Treaty relies on the willingness of Member States to collaborate with the Commission. This collaboration is necessary throughout the procedure because national authorities are the main source of information for the Commission when it comes to assessing the effects of their State aid plans. However, their collaboration is particularly important at two crucial nodes of the procedure: at the initiation stage (since the standard procedure is designed on the premise that national authorities are going to abide by the standstill and notification obligations)[33] and at the termination stage (since the decisions adopted by the Commission would be dead letters if, faced with a negative decision, national authorities decided to go ahead with their plans).

Needless to say, this collaboration is sometimes missing. When this is the case, the Commission has certain tools at its disposal to protect its own prerogatives and to ensure compliance with the rules on State aid. On the one hand, the Commission may initiate on its own motion an investigation into national measures of State aid, even if

29. ECJ, Case C-44/93 *Namur-Les Assurances du Crédit SA v Office National du Ducroire and Belgium* [1994] ECR I-3829, para. 18.
30. Article 3 of the General Block Exemption Regulation, *supra* n. 20.
31. Case C-354/90 *Fédération Nationale du Commerce, supra* n. 6, at para. 14.
32. Case C-78/76 *Steinike, supra* n. 6, at para. 10.
33. Articles 2 to 11 of the Procedural Regulation, *supra* n. 10.

they have not been notified by the responsible Member States, and order their recovery, if they turn out to be incompatible with the internal market.[34] On the other hand, where the Member States concerned do not comply with conditional, negative or recovery decisions, the Commission may refer the matter to the Court of Justice directly[35] and eventually apply for the imposition of a pecuniary sanction on them.[36]

However, the powers of the Commission are conditioned by its limited administrative capacity, which is inevitably insufficient to spot and take action against *all* attempts by national authorities to sidestep its control or to resist compliance with its decisions. This problem is not specific to the realm of State aid but is rather a transversal feature of EU governance. So, not surprisingly, the response given to this problem in the State aid context has been the same as in other areas of EU law[37] – namely, the 'private enforcement' solution. To put it simply, the 'private enforcement' solution consists in contracting out to national courts the task of ensuring that national authorities comply with EU law. Since national courts act upon application, this strategy requires, as a precondition, the recognition of certain 'subjective rights' in favour of those private actors who are in the best position (information- and incentive-wise) to play the game and to take action against non-complying authorities.

In the State aid context, the 'private enforcement' solution has targeted the two nodes of the procedure where the collaboration of Member States is most crucial. On the one hand, the case law of the Court of Justice has recognised the direct effect of the last sentence of Article 108(3) TFEU, which is precisely the clause that lays down the obligation of Member States to refrain from implementing State aid measures unless and until authorised by the Commission.[38] In so doing, the Court of Justice has conferred upon third parties the right to enforce the standstill obligation against any attempt by national authorities to put in place a measure of State aid without securing the prior authorisation of the Commission. The instrumental value of this move is obvious, for it transforms third parties and national courts into the Commission's 'best allies' in the task of detecting unlawful State aid.[39]

On the other hand, it is also a standard principle of EU law that the decisions adopted by the Commission have direct effect.[40] It follows that third parties are entitled to seek the protection of national courts against any attempt by Member States to resist compliance with the obligations that derive from the decisions adopted by the Commission in this area.[41] Again, from the perspective of the system, this move may

34. Article 12 of the Procedural Regulation, *supra* n. 10.
35. Article 108(2) TFEU and Article 28(1) of the Procedural Regulation, *supra* n. 10.
36. Article 260 TFEU and Article 28(2) of the Procedural Regulation, *supra* n. 10.
37. On this issue, more broadly, *see* literature on the so-called constitutionalisation of the EU legal order: Joseph Weiler, *The Transformation of Europe* (1991) 100 Yale Law Journal, 2403; Bruno de Witte, *'Direct Effect, Primacy and the Nature of the Legal Order'* in Paul P Craig and Gráinne de Búrca (eds), *The Evolution of EU Law* (OUP 2011); Norbert Reich, *'System Der Subjectiven Öffentlichen Rechte' in the Union: A European Constitution of Bits and Pieces* (1995) Collected Courses of the Academy of European Law, VI.
38. Case C-120/73 *Gebrüder Lorenz, supra* n. 9, at para. 8.
39. Discourse delivered by Commissioner Kroes at the University of Leiden, 2005.
40. Article 288 TFEU.
41. Case C-78/76 *Steinike, supra* n. 6, at para. 10.

also be explained in instrumental terms, for it means that third parties are entitled to trigger the judicial enforcement of negative and recovery decisions if their national authorities do not spontaneously comply with them.

In State aid – as in antitrust – it is therefore possible to distinguish two different types of private enforcement actions: 'stand-alone actions' based on the direct effect of the standstill clause of Article 108(3) TFEU and 'follow-on actions' based on the direct effect of the decisions adopted by the Commission in the exercise of its State aid prerogatives. The following two sections analyse the legal regime that governs each of these types of actions.

IV. STAND-ALONE ACTIONS BASED ON THE DIRECT EFFECT OF THE STANDSTILL CLAUSE

The first weapon that third parties have at their disposal in their fight against State aid is the standstill clause of Article 108(3) TFEU. As noted earlier, the direct effect of this provision implies that third parties have the right, as a matter of EU law, not to endure State aid measures, unless, until and to the extent that they have been authorised by the Commission. The other side of the coin is that national courts are under a duty 'to safeguard the rights of individuals against possible disregard, by the national authorities, of the prohibition on putting aid into effect before the Commission has adopted a decision authorising that aid'.[42] The right that third parties derive from the standstill clause and the correlative obligations that it imposes on national courts are the first pillar of the private enforcement of State aid law.

The right that individuals derive from the last sentence of Article 108(3) TFEU mirrors the scope of the obligation that this article imposes upon Member States. As noted earlier, the standstill and notification obligations know certain exceptions because they do not operate in connection to *de minimis*, existing or exempted State aid. Since the implementation of state measures of financial support to firms in these scenarios does not represent a violation of Article 108(3) TFEU, it cannot represent either a violation of the right that third parties derive from that provision.

So, in order to substantiate their claims under Article 108(3) TFEU, third parties must first establish that two premises are met. The first premise is that the contested measures constitute State aid because the only measures that trigger the standstill obligation are the ones that meet the definition laid down by Article 107(1) TFEU.[43] Given the complexity of this definition, this may be a contentious point. Of course, the last word lies with national courts, which are bound by the 'objective' character of the definition, as interpreted by the case law of the Court of Justice.[44]

The second premise is the unlawfulness of the contested measure. Since the direct implementation of State aid measures, without the prior consent of the Commission, is lawful in certain cases, third parties must also establish that the measure that

42. ECJ, Case C-384/04 *Transalpine Ölleitung in Österreich GmbH and others v Finanzlandesdirektion für Tirol and others* [2006] ECR I-4191, para. 44.
43. Case C-78/76 *Steinike, supra* n. 6, at para. 14.
44. ECJ, Case C-487/06 P *British Aggregates v Commission* [2008] ECR I-10515, para. 111.

they target is not covered by a previously authorised State aid scheme, by the *de minimis* Regulation or by the Block Exemption Regulation. In practice, it is the defendant granting authorities (or the beneficiaries, if they act as co-defendants) who normally invoke these exceptions as a shield against the pleas made by appellant third parties. When this is the case, national courts must decide this issue too.

Should national courts conclude that both premises are met (i.e., that the contested measure constitutes 'unlawful State aid'), their duty, under EU State aid law, is to take the appropriate remedial measures in light of their domestic law.[45] Indeed, the lack of harmonisation of the private enforcement of State aid law implies that the procedural regime of these actions is governed by the national laws of Member States, which are therefore the ones which determine the courts having jurisdiction over these claims, the rules on *locus standi*, the statute of limitations and, in general, the procedural rules that frame State aid litigation.[46] As is always the case in EU law, though, the procedural autonomy of Member States is subject to the proviso 'firstly, that those rules are not less favourable than those governing rights which originate in domestic law (principle of equivalence) and, secondly, that they do not render impossible or excessively difficult in practice the exercise of rights conferred by the Community legal order (principle of effectiveness)'.[47]

In principle, the national laws of Member States also govern the remedies that third parties may request and that national courts must grant when the contested measures constitute unlawful State aid.[48] This is the reason why, even though their actions are substantively based on the rights that they derive from an EU law provision such as 108(3) TFEU, third parties must shape their claims in light of the remedial possibilities offered by their national laws. Since Member States normally lack a specific and comprehensive legal regime for State aid measures, these possibilities are normally a function of the nature of the precise measure being challenged – in the sense that the procedural and remedial rules governing third-party actions may be different depending on the form adopted by the contested State aid, which may be a subsidy, a fiscal measure, a decision adopted in a public procurement or commercial context, etc.

However, as far as remedies are concerned, the case law of the Court of Justice actually contains a rather specific set of rules regarding the type of redress to which third parties are entitled in the context of the private enforcement of State aid law. Certainly, these rules do not supersede the rules on remedies laid down by the national laws of Member States. However, they do constrain rather tightly the outcomes that national courts must achieve in these cases in order to live up to the standards imposed on them by virtue of the principle of effectiveness. In other words, EU State aid law, as interpreted by the European jurisprudence, is rather specific when it comes to defining the way in which national courts ought to protect the rights of third parties under

45. Case C-354/90 *Fédération Nationale du Commerce*, *supra* n. 6, at para. 12; ECJ, Case C-672/13 *OTP Bank Nyrt v Magyar Állam* [2015] ECLI:EU:C:2015:185, para. 69.
46. Case C-384/04 *Transalpine Ölleitung*, *supra* n. 42, at para. 45.
47. *Ibid.*
48. *Ibid.*, at para. 46.

Article 108(3) TFEU. Thus, the task of national courts is to pick the right remedies available under their domestic law in order to achieve the result mandated by EU law.

In essence, the result mandated by EU law is the neutralisation of the effects produced by State aid measures unless and until they receive the green light of the Commission. In order to achieve this result, national courts may have to fulfil two different functions.[49] The first function is 'prophylactic': if seized in a timely fashion, national courts must prevent unlawful State aid measures from actually reaching their beneficiaries and, hence, from causing any distortion in the market. It should be noted that the result mandated by EU State aid law is the non-implementation of unlawful State aid measures, irrespective of their formal approval. So, even if seized after the formal approval and entry into force of the legal instrument that puts in place a certain measure of State aid (e.g., the legislative or administrative provisions laying down a subsidy program, a tax exemption, etc.), national courts may still achieve this result if they manage to block its actual entry into operation (e.g., the payment of subsidies to their intended recipients, the recognition of an exemption for individual tax payers, etc.). From the perspective of EU law, the tool used in order to achieve that result is irrelevant: interim or final suspension orders are particularly apt in this context, but other remedies may serve too (e.g., the outright annulment of the legal instrument setting in place the unlawful State aid measure where the infringement of a procedural requirement, such as the prior consultation of the Commission, warrants this solution under national administrative law).[50]

It is often the case, though, that national courts are seized after the contested State aid measures have already been implemented. In this second scenario, national courts are called to fulfil a 'restorative function', which consists in taking 'any steps which appear necessary in the circumstances to nullify the effects of the breach' of Article 108(3) TFEU.[51] Again, the exact remedies used to achieve that result depend on the national laws of Member States. However, EU State aid law and the case law developed by the Court of Justice provide national courts with clear guidelines on the effects that they are expected to eliminate and the manner in which they ought to do so.

The task that lies at the core of their restorative mission is the 'recovery' of unlawful State aid measures, which is how EU State aid law refers to the process through which these measures are removed from the market.[52] Recovery means different things in different contexts given that the steps that need to be taken in order

49. Fernando Pastor-Merchante and Giorgio Monti, '*The Functions of National Courts in the Private Enforcement of State Aid Law*', in Pier Luigi Parcu, Giorgio Monti and Marco Botta (eds), *EU State Aid Law: Emerging Trends at the National and EU Level* (Edward Elgar, 2020).

50. Case C-354/90 *Fédération Nationale du Commerce, supra* n. 6, at para. 12; Case C-39/94 *Syndicat Français, supra* n. 4, at para. 52; Case C-384/04 *Transalpine Ölleitung, supra* n. 42, at para. 46; Case C-672/13 *OTP Bank, supra* n. 45, at para. 69.

51. ECJ, C-354/90 *Fédération Nationale du Commerce Extérieur des Produits Alimentaires (FNCEPA) and Syndicat National des Négociants et Transformateurs de Saumon v France* [1991] ECR I-5505, Opinion of AG Jacobs.

52. Case C-39/94 *Syndicat Français, supra* n. 4, at para. 68; Case C-384/04 *Transalpine Ölleitung, supra* n. 42, at para. 56.

to undo the implementation of a State aid measure obviously depend on its nature.[53] Indeed, it may consist of the repayment by the beneficiaries of the sums received in the form of subsidies or in the payment of the value of the taxes foregone as a result of their unlawful fiscal benefits, to give but a few examples. However, a fundamental principle of the discipline is that it is never acceptable to extend the scope of State aid measures (so as to bring within their scope all potentially affected third parties) instead of ordering their recovery (which implies retrieving the benefits received by those falling with their scope).[54] Thus, even if third parties would often prefer to avail themselves of the financial advantage granted to their competitors (rather than having it eliminated altogether), national courts are banned from granting this kind of remedy.

Its centrality notwithstanding, it is important to observe that recovery is not always necessary and that it is not the only remedy available in State aid cases. It is not a *necessary* remedy because there are certain instances where third parties are not entitled to request recovery of unlawful State aid measures (or, to put it differently, where national courts are not bound to order recovery even if satisfied that the contested measure has been unlawfully implemented). This is the case, in particular, where a Commission decision declares that the contested State aid measure is compatible with the internal market on the basis of the exemptions foreseen in Article 107(2) and (3) TFEU – a possibility analysed in the last section of this chapter.[55]

Furthermore, recovery is not the *only* restorative action that national courts must undertake in order to wipe out the effects produced by the unlawful implementation of State aid measures.[56] To begin with, recovery of unlawful State aid measures always goes hand in hand with the collection of the so-called illegality interest.[57] National courts must see to it that beneficiaries give back not only the nominal value of the financial advantage granted to them but also the value of the additional economic advantage represented by the premature availability of the unlawful State aid measure. The rationale behind this rule is that this is the only way of totally cancelling out the advantageous effects bestowed by unlawful State aid measures upon their beneficiaries, which is a necessary but not sufficient condition to re-establish the level playing field.

Indeed, unlawful State aid measures may produce other side effects, which national courts must neutralise too if asked to do so by third-party applicants. The first type of such side effects is the repercussions felt by other market actors and, in particular, by the beneficiaries' competitors. Competitors and third parties are entitled, as a matter of EU law, to obtain compensation for any loss suffered as a result of the

53. Notice from the Commission – Towards an effective implementation of Commission decisions ordering Member States to recover unlawful and incompatible State aid [2007] OJ C 272/4, para. 51.
54. ECJ, Joined Cases C-393/04 and 41/05 *Air Liquide Industries Belgium SA v Ville de Seraing* [2006] ECR I-5293, para. 45; Case C-384/04 *Transalpine Ölleitung, supra* n. 42, at para. 49.
55. ECJ, Case C-199/06 *Centre d'exportation du livre Français (CELF) v Société internationale de diffusion et d'édition (SIDE)* [2008] ECR I-469, para. 52.
56. Commission notice on the enforcement of State aid law by national courts [2009], OJ C 85/1, paras 30 et seq.
57. Case C-199/06 *Centre d'exportation du livre, supra* n. 55, at paras 50–55.

unlawful implementation of State aid measures.[58] National courts are bound to grant this remedy if the application meets the standard conditions that trigger the extracontractual liability of the State under EU law: 'the rule of law infringed must be intended to confer rights on individuals; the breach must be sufficiently serious; and there must be a direct causal link between the breach of the obligation resting on the State and the damage sustained by the injured parties'.[59] However, the first two conditions are considered to be met, *ex lege*, by claims related to the infringement of Article 108(3) TFEU.[60] Thus, the real challenge for third parties is to prove that they have suffered harm and that such harm has been caused by the unlawful implementation of the contested State aid measure.[61]

The second type of side effects that national courts may need to tackle are those felt by taxpayers, who bear upon their shoulders the cost of financing unlawful State aid measures. Since taxes are rarely earmarked to a specific goal, if taken to an extreme, this could mean that all taxpayers are entitled to a refund whenever public authorities implement unlawful State aid measures. Of course, the impact of State aid measures upon taxpayers is necessarily so diffuse that such a rule would simply be unworkable. This is the reason why, under EU State aid law, taxpayers are only entitled to a refund when a specific tax forms 'an integral part' of an unlawful State aid measure – or, to put it differently, when it is possible to establish such a strong link between the tax and the State aid measure that there is no doubt that the former was earmarked to the funding of the latter.[62]

So, to sum up, in the context of stand-alone actions based on the direct effect of the standstill clause of Article 108(3) TFEU, the first mission of national courts is to impede the implementation of unlawful State aid measures. When this is no longer possible, their second mission is to withdraw unlawful State aid measures (recovery) and to eliminate their side effects upon beneficiaries (illegality interest), competitors (damages) and taxpayers (restitution of taxes). As a matter of fact, though, national courts are often faced with third-party actions against partially implemented State aid measures. When this is the case, their duty is to simultaneously discharge both functions: to block any further implementation of the State aid plan (prophylactic function), while ordering recovery and the elimination of any side effects already produced by its partial implementation (restorative function).

58. Case C-39/94 *Syndicat Français, supra* n. 4, at para. 75.
59. ECJ, Joined Cases C-6/90 and 9/90 *Andrea Francovich and others v Italy* [1991] ECR I-5357; ECJ, Joined Cases C-46/93 and 48/93 *Brasserie du Pêcheur SA v Germany and others* [1996] ECR I-1029.
60. Commission notice on the enforcement of State aid law by national courts, *supra* n. 56, at paras 46–47.
61. Barbara Brandtner, Thierry Beranger and Christof Lessenich, *Private State Aid Enforcement* (2010) 9 EStAL 23, 26; James Flynn, *'The Role of National Courts'* in Andrea Biondi, Piete Eekhout and James Flynn (eds), *The Law of the State Aid in the European Union* 323, 332 (OUP, 2004); Jacques Derenn and Cédric Kaczmarek, *La récupération des Aides illegals: le role du juge national dans le private enforcement du droit des aides d'état* (2009) 10 ERA Forum 251, 259.
62. ECJ, Case C-174/02 *Streekgewest Westelijk Noord-Brabant v Staatssecretaris van Financiën* [2005] ECR I-85, para. 26; Joined Cases C-393/04 and 41/05 *Air Liquide Industries, supra* n. 54, at para. 45.

V. FOLLOW-ON ACTIONS BASED ON THE DIRECT EFFECT OF COMMISSION DECISIONS

Once the Commission has made up its mind regarding the compatibility or incompatibility of State aid measures with the internal market, third parties may also use its final decisions to ground and back their judicial actions before national courts. Armed with a 'negative decision' (one that declares that the contested State aid measure 'shall not be put into effect')[63] or with a 'recovery decision' (one that additionally censures the premature implementation of State aid measures, ordering 'that the Member State concerned shall take all necessary measures to recover the aid from the beneficiary'),[64] third parties may challenge before national courts any attempt by national authorities to act (or to refrain from acting) in violation of these decisions.

Indeed, 'negative decisions' empower third parties to challenge any attempt by national authorities to go ahead with their initial State aid plans. For their part, 'recovery decisions' empower third parties to attack the passivity of national authorities, should they fail to spontaneously and immediately take the appropriate measures to recover unlawfully implemented State aid measures. Albeit to a lesser degree, 'conditional decisions' may also back the judicial endeavours of third parties, insofar as they open the door to challenges based on the allegation that national authorities are not complying with the restrictions stemming from those decisions.

As a matter of fact, though, these 'follow-on' actions are not that different from the 'stand-alone' actions analysed above. On the one hand, their ultimate legal basis also lies in the right that third parties derive from Article 108(3) TFEU. Indeed, although formally grounded on a Commission decision, 'follow-on actions' are also fuelled by the right of third parties not to endure with State aid measures unless, until and to the extent that they have been authorised by the Commission. Not in vain, the main effect of negative and recovery decisions is to confirm that a certain State aid measure is captured by the prohibition of Article 107(1) TFEU and that it may not be implemented on the basis of any of the exceptions of Article 107(2) and (3) TFEU. It is therefore possible to argue that these decisions eliminate any possible uncertainty surrounding the legal regime of State aid measures (because they dispel any remaining doubts regarding their eligibility for an exemption), but that they do not actually alter that regime (because they simply confirm the ban to which they were anyway subject, in the absence of an authorisation by the Commission). Conditional decisions, on their part, are a combination of the other two types of decisions, since they allow the implementation of State aid measures (like positive decisions do) while imposing certain limitations on them (which makes them, to that extent, akin to negative decisions).

On the other hand, and as a consequence of their similar legal basis, 'follow-on' actions are also similar to 'stand-alone' actions from the perspective of the judicial remedies to which they may give rise. As far as 'negative decisions' are concerned, third parties may use them to apply for the same kind of prophylactic measures

---

63. Article 9(5) of the Procedural Regulation, *supra* n. 10.
64. Article 16(1) of the Procedural Regulation, *supra* n. 10.

mentioned earlier. After all, negative decisions impose on Member States a (negative) obligation not to implement the State aid measure in question, which is identical to the standstill obligation derived from Article 108(3) TFEU.[65] Thus, national courts must ensure that the measures targeted by negative decisions never reach their intended beneficiaries. Should granting authorities ignore the ban and go ahead with their implementation, third parties may also use negative decisions to apply for their recovery and for any other applicable restorative remedy. It goes without saying that 'recovery decisions', insofar as they specifically impose a recovery mandate upon national authorities, also empower third parties to apply for that remedy. However, they do not restrict in any way their capacity to apply for other restorative remedies too.

Does this mean that the stand-alone and the follow-on scenarios are completely identical in the State aid context? In reality, the fundamental distinction between both scenarios lies in the different degree of autonomy that national courts enjoy in each of them. In the first scenario, national courts must autonomously decide on their own whether the contested measures constitute State aid for the purpose of Article 107(1) TFEU and, if so, whether their implementation was unlawful. Of course, national courts must discharge this task in light of EU law and, in particular, in light of the objective character of the definition of State aid. Furthermore, they may use the collaboration tools that the Procedural Regulation places in their hands and request the assistance of the Commission.[66] However, their assessment is not constrained by any prior, authoritative determination of the Commission.

In the follow-on scenario, the margin of autonomy of national courts is considerably reduced because they are bound by the determinations recorded by the Commission in its decisions. Indeed, national courts are under a duty to comply with these decisions, from which they can escape only through the preliminary request procedure (if they identify a flaw that compromises the validity of the decision and the Court of Justice endorses their view).[67] Because both 'negative' and 'recovery' decisions contain, by definition, a finding that the measure under scrutiny constitutes State aid, they remove from national courts the capacity to carry out their own assessment of that issue. Furthermore, the finding of incompatibility embodied in both types of decisions also implies that granting authorities must refrain from implementing those measures, which implies the unlawfulness of any move in that direction.

It would be wrong to conclude that follow-on litigation, in the State aid context, is always an easy walkover for third parties. Even if backed up by a negative or recovery decision, third parties may still come across significant obstacles in their fight against State aid. For one thing, the dispute may actually turn on whether the contested measure is actually targeted by a negative or recovery decision. Indeed, this type of dispute often turns on thorny issues, such as the identification of the beneficiary undertakings from whom recovery must be sought and the quantification of their

65. Pastor-Merchante, *supra* n. 2, at 39.
66. Article 29 of the Procedural Regulation, *supra* n. 10.
67. Article 267 TFEU.

respective repayment obligations (two issues that are often left open by the Commission in its decisions).[68] On the other hand, third parties may run into other problems, such as the need to establish loss and causality in the context of tort actions or the need to prove that the taxes whose reimbursement they seek were hypothecated to the State aid measure in question.[69]

In any event, the possibility to buttress their fight against State aid with a negative or recovery decision (or even a conditional decision whose restrictions have allegedly been ignored) represents an important asset for third parties. In this scenario, third parties are relieved from the burden of proving that the contested measures meet the definition of State aid and that their implementation is unlawful. Of course, granting authorities and State aid beneficiaries may take issue with these findings, but their chances of successfully doing so are considerably reduced, once recorded in a formal decision. At the national level, they can only do so indirectly, if they manage to convince the court that a preliminary reference on the validity of the Commission decision is warranted.

VI. THE INTERPLAY BETWEEN THE PUBLIC AND THE PRIVATE ENFORCEMENT OF STATE AID LAW

The analysis developed so far is based on the assumption that State aid litigation always fits into one (and only one) of the two scenarios identified earlier, i.e., that third-party actions are based either on the direct effect of Article 108(3) TFEU or on the decisions adopted by the Commission at the end of its procedures. It turns out, though, that this distinction does not fully capture the whole range of situations where national courts may be called on to intervene in the State aid context. In order to get a broader picture, it is necessary to make two additional observations.

The first observation is that the judicial proceedings taking place before national courts may run in parallel to the administrative procedure taking place before the European Commission, even if they both target the exact same measure. Indeed, unlike in antitrust, there is no rule in the State aid context providing for the suspension of judicial proceedings that have as their object a measure that the Commission has decided to investigate.[70] The rule is actually the exact opposite: namely, that national courts 'may not' stay proceedings on the ground that there is an overlap with an undergoing Commission investigation.[71] The upshot is that, in the State aid context, 'private' and 'public' enforcement trails may cross paths. It is therefore necessary to reflect upon the impact that intervening Commission decisions may have upon national proceedings.

68. ECJ, Case C-310/99 *Italy v Commission* [2002] ECR I-2289, paras 89 and 91.
69. *See* above.
70. Case C-39/94 *Syndicat Français, supra* n. 4, at para. 44; ECJ, Case C-284/12 *Deutsche Lufthansa AG v Flughafen Frankfurt-Hahn GmbH* [2013] ECLI:EU:C:2013:755, para. 32.
71. ECJ, Case C-1/09 *Centre de l'exportation du livre Français (CELF) v Société international de diffusion et d'édition (SIDE)* [2010] ECR I-2099, para. 40.

Their impact is a function of their content. Negative and recovery decisions do not contradict in any manner the claims that fuel stand-alone actions because – as noted earlier– the effect of this type of decision is to confirm that contested measures are subject to the prohibition of Article 107(1) TFEU and, hence, to convey permanent status to the ban on implementation derived from the standstill clause of Article 108(3) TFEU. So, in a way, negative and recovery decisions adopted in the course of a 'stand-alone action' initiated on the basis of Article 108(3) TFEU simply transform such an action into a 'follow-on action', one supported by the determinations made by the Commission in its decision.

The impact of positive and conditional decisions upon ongoing judicial proceedings is trickier because their main legal effect is to relieve contested measures from the implementation ban to which they would otherwise be subject. However, it is settled case law that these decisions do not have the effect of curing retroactively the irregularity derived from the premature implementation of unlawful State aid measures.[72] What this means, in practice, is that the declaration that an unlawfully implemented State aid measure is compatible with the internal market does not relieve national courts from their duty to eliminate the effects produced by that measure before its clearance by the Commission. Thus, national courts may have cause to order recovery of the illegality interest (to make up for the advantage represented by the untimely availability of the contested State aid measure) and to grant some of the additional restorative remedies analysed earlier (if the conditions for compensating the damages suffered by third parties or for reimbursing the sums levied upon taxpayers are met). However, the adoption of a subsequent positive or conditional decision by the Commission does exempt national courts from the duty to order recovery[73] – which could be a futile move, since national authorities would be in a position to re-implement the State aid measure in question immediately after its recovery.

The second observation is connected to the two-phase structure of the Commission's State aid procedure. As noted earlier, the State aid procedure is divided into two phases: the 'preliminary' and the 'formal investigation' stages. So far, the analysis carried out in this chapter has assumed that the follow-on, private enforcement of State aid law is based on the decisions adopted by the Commission at the very end of the procedure. This is a sensible assumption because the Commission may adopt the decisions that normally fuel third-party actions only after going through both phases of the procedure. Indeed, the Commission may close the file at the preliminary stage of the procedure with a clearing decision ('decision that there is no State aid' or 'decision not to raise objections'),[74] but not with a negative decision in any of its variants ('negative', 'recovery' or 'conditional decision').[75] Before adopting any of these decisions, the Commission is bound to investigate the matter in depth, which is the purpose behind the formalities of the second stage of the procedure.

72. Case C-354/90 *Fédération Nationale du Commerce, supra* n. 6, at para. 16.
73. Case C-199/06 *Centre d'exportation du livre, supra* n. 55, at para. 52.
74. Article 4(2) and (3) of the Procedural Regulation, *supra* n. 10.
75. Articles 9(5), 16(1) and 9(4) of the Procedural Regulation, *supra* n. 10.

However, third parties can also seek some support for their judicial endeavours in the interlocutory decisions adopted by the Commission in order to move from the preliminary to the formal investigation stage ('decision to initiate the formal investigation procedure').[76] Their interlocutory appearance notwithstanding, these types of decisions have a certain substantive content of their own, if only because they are motivated by the tentative observation that the measures under scrutiny constitute State aid and that their compatibility with the internal market raises some doubts.

In a recent line of cases, the Court of Justice has held that these types of decisions embody a provisional finding that the measures under scrutiny meet the definition of State aid and that this finding binds national courts, even if it is provisional in nature.[77] This doctrine is very controversial,[78] but its meaning is clear: it implies that national courts must take for granted the State aid nature of any measure targeted by a Commission decision to open the formal investigation phase. In a way, this creates a third scenario, one which shares some traits with the follow-on scenario (insofar as national courts are bound by the assessments made by the Commission with regard to the characterisation of the contested measure as State aid) but also with the stand-alone scenario (insofar as this characterisation is provisional because the Commission may later reach a different conclusion on the basis of the information compiled throughout the procedure).

In any event, the point to note is that the doctrine of the Court of Justice on the binding character of decisions to open the formal investigation phase gives an important edge to third parties in their fight against State aid since it relieves them of the burden of proving that the contested measures satisfy the definition of State aid. It reduces the scope of the controversy to the 'lawful' character of the contested measures (i.e., whether their implementation may be justified on the basis of a previous State aid scheme, the *de minimis* Regulation or the General Block Exemption Regulation), thereby restricting the pleas available to the defendant granting authority.

VII. CONCLUSION

To sum up, one of the peculiarities of the EU legal regime on State aid is the lack of direct effect of its central prohibition, which does not provide third parties with a sufficient legal basis to bring national, judicial proceedings against State aid plans. Indeed, third parties may not invoke before national courts an alleged right against State aid, for such a right cannot be read into Article 107(1) TFEU. However, they do derive from EU law a right not to endure with State aid measures unless, until and to the extent they have been authorised by the Commission (or by a previously approved State aid scheme or by the Block Exemption Regulation). This right is the cornerstone

76. Article 4(4) of the Procedural Regulation, *supra* n. 10.
77. Case C-284/12 *Deutsche Lufthansa AG*, *supra* n. 70, at paras 40–41; Order of ECJ, Case C-27/13 *Flughafen Lübeck GmbH v Air Berlin plc & Co. Luftverkehrs KG* [2014] ECLI:EU:C:2014:240.
78. Thomas Lübbig and Tom Morgan, *State Aid, National Courts and the Separation of Powers: Should Judges be Bound to the European Commission's Unfinished State Aid Business?* (2014) 5 Journal of European Competition Law & Practice 256; Pierre de Brandt, *Lufthansa: A New Era for State Aid Enforcement?* (2014) 5 Journal of European Competition Law & Practice 206.

of the private enforcement of State aid law, for it means that third parties may bring judicial proceedings before national courts in order to enforce the standstill clause of Article 108(3) TFEU ('stand-alone actions') as well as decisions adopted by the Commission in this area ('follow-on actions').

Besides reviewing their respective legal regimes, this chapter has shown that this distinction does not fully capture the different scenarios where the private enforcement of State aid law may take place. On the one hand, the lack of a rule providing for the suspension of judicial proceedings that have as their object a measure that the Commission has decided to investigate means that there may be a convergence between the (public enforcement) procedures unfolding at the EU level and the (private enforcement) proceedings unfolding before national courts. On the other hand, the recognition that certain interlocutory decisions adopted by the Commission in the course of the procedure are binding upon national courts has created an additional scenario, one where third parties may rely on the determinations made by the Commission in its decisions to open the formal investigation phase, despite the provisional character of these determinations.

CHAPTER 10

The Role of the European Commission and the Cooperation with National Courts

*Simone Donzelli**

I. Introduction
II. Legal framework: the roles of the Commission and the national courts in supervising State aid
III. The cooperation tools
  A. From their origins to their codification
  B. The cooperation tools in practice
  C. The use of cooperation tools
IV. The enforcement of State aid rules by national courts in relation to the cooperation tools
V. Gathering information and outlook on enforcement: the 2019 Study
VI. Concluding remarks

I. INTRODUCTION

Since the Schuman Declaration of 9 May 1950[1] and throughout the history of the integration process of the European States, the creation of an internal market has been the key means for promoting peace and well-being. The Treaty on the European Union (TEU)[2] confirms the crucial role of the internal market for the European Union (EU): following the provisions on the fundamental values of the EU and its purpose, its Article 3(3) plainly states that 'the Union shall establish an internal market'.

---

* The views expressed may not be regarded as stating an official position of the European Commission.

1. *See* https://europa.eu/european-union/about-eu/symbols/europe-day/schuman-declaration_en (accessed 2 March 2019).
2. Consolidated version of the Treaty on European Union [2012] OJ C 326/13.

For the internal market to function, Article 3(1)(b) of the Treaty on the Functioning of the European Union (TFEU)[3] gives the EU exclusive competence to establish competition rules. More specifically, Protocol 27 to both the TEU and TFEU spells out that the existence of the internal market requires a 'system ensuring that competition is not distorted'. That system, for what concerns State measures granting financial support to undertakings, is shaped mainly in section 2, Title VII, TFEU, titled 'Aids Granted by States'.

At a glance, in principle, Member States cannot give State aid to undertakings, as that is incompatible with the functioning of the internal market. However, aid is or may be considered compatible with the internal market provided it pursues a prevailing interest of the EU. For example, aid may address market failures, ensure the operation of services of general economic interest or make good the damage caused by natural disasters. The Member States must notify any plans to grant aid to the European Commission (Commission), so that the latter can assess the compatibility of the planned aid with the internal market.

From the outset, the structure of the TEU and the TFEU and the general features of the system of supervision of State aid would suggest that the enforcement of State aid rules is a matter reserved to the Commission, on the one hand, and to Member States (including their authorities and judiciary), on the other hand. As such, the enforcement of State aid rules would have a purely public nature. However, the system is more refined than that, and private enforcement has an important role to play.

The following section describes the legal framework for the system of supervision of State aid and the tasks and responsibilities of the Commission and national courts; section III presents the history of the tools for cooperation between national courts and the Commission, their content and how they function in practice; section IV critically examines the state of play of enforcement, with a focus on private enforcement of State aid rules by national courts based on the evidence provided by the use of the cooperation tools; section V shows how the Commission intends to gather information to reflect on and determine possible future actions. The last section reviews the current state of play of enforcement of State aid rules by national courts, as known by the Commission through the cooperation tools. It is hoped that the new study tendered by the Commission will provide a clear picture about the state of the art of cooperation between the Commission and national courts and promote further the private enforcement of State aid rules.

II. LEGAL FRAMEWORK: THE ROLES OF THE COMMISSION AND THE NATIONAL COURTS IN SUPERVISING STATE AID

Article 107(1) TFEU sets the general prohibition against Member States granting aid by establishing that 'save as otherwise provided in the Treaties, any aid granted by a Member State or through State resources in any form whatsoever which distorts or threatens to distort competition by favouring certain undertakings or the production of

3. Consolidated version of the Treaty on the Functioning of the European Union [2012] OJ C 326/47.

certain goods shall, in so far as it affects trade between Member States, be incompatible with the internal market'.

While establishing this general prohibition, Article 107(1) TFEU also defines the notion of State aid, based on the following criteria:

(i) a direct support by the State, or through its resources, irrespective of its form (e.g., a grant, a loan and a reduced tax burden), that
(ii) confers an advantage in favour of selected undertakings or activities, provided it
(iii) distorts or may distort competition, and
(iv) affects trade between Member States.

The compatibility of State aid with the internal market must be assessed against the rules 'provided in the Treaties'. In particular, paragraphs 2 and 3 of Article 107 TFEU establish categories of State aid that, respectively, are compatible or may be considered to be compatible with the internal market. In addition to those provisions, Article 93 TFEU contains specific provisions relating to transport, Article 106 TFEU concerns aid for the operation of services of general economic interest and Article 109 TFEU contains a kind of residual clause allowing Council regulations on the matter, which can be complemented by Commission regulations under Article 108(4) TFEU. Based on this latter provision, the Commission adopted so-called General Block Exemption Regulations (GBER), declaring certain categories of aid compatible with the internal market,[4] and *de minimis* regulations,[5] concerning aid not deemed to meet the criteria laid down in Article 107(1) TFEU.

Article 108 TFEU defines the framework to prevent grants of aid incompatible with the internal market. Pursuant to its first paragraph, in cooperation with the Member States, the Commission has to keep under constant review all systems of existing aid. In broad terms, as defined by the State aid Procedural Regulation,[6] that concerns State aid previously approved by the Commission or aid predating the accession of a Member State to the Union or the entry into force of the TFEU for that Member State.[7] Under the second paragraph, the Commission has exclusive competence to assess whether any new aid or (substantial) alteration to existing aid is compatible with the internal market, following a preliminary examination or a formal investigation, as defined by the Procedural Regulation.[8]

The supervision of State aid, however, is not limited to the exclusive competence attributed to the Commission. Instead, it relies on the cooperation with Member States

4. *See* Commission Regulation (EU) No 651/2014 of 17 June 2014 declaring certain categories of aid compatible with the internal market in application of Articles 107 and 108 of the Treaty [2014] OJ L 187/1.
5. *See*, for example, Commission Regulation (EU) No 1407/2013 of 18 December 2013 on the application of Articles 107 and 108 of the Treaty on the Functioning of the European Union to *de minimis* aid [2013] OJ L 352/1.
6. Council Regulation (EU) 2015/1589 of 13 July 2015 laying down detailed rules for the application of Article 108 of the Treaty on the Functioning of the European Union (consolidation) [2015] OJ L 248/9 (Procedural Regulation).
7. Procedural Regulation, *supra* n. 6, Article 1(b).
8. *See* Procedural Regulation, *supra* n. 6, respectively, Articles 4 and 6.

and, most importantly, on the judicial review and protection afforded by national courts. This complementarity derives from the provisions of the TFEU and the TEU, as construed by the case law of the Court of Justice of the European Union (CJEU).

Under Article 108(3) TFEU, Member States must notify the Commission of any plans to grant new aid or alter existing aid. In particular, the last sentence of Article 108(3) TFEU establishes what is known as the 'standstill obligation', by which 'the Member State concerned shall not put its proposed measures into effect until [the investigation of the Commission] has resulted in a final decision'. By imposing this obligation, the TFEU ensures that during the time needed by the Commission to conclude its assessment, 'an incompatible aid will never be implemented'.[9]

As the standstill obligation has direct effect,[10] interested parties may bring its infringement to a national court[11] during the assessment by the Commission. Each Member State may provide for a different procedure to ensure compliance with the standstill obligation;[12] however, national courts cannot refrain from acting, as the CJEU has established that they must draw all the consequences from any such infringement.[13]

National courts also play a key role *after* the Commission has adopted a final decision. If the Commission concludes that certain aid is incompatible with the internal market, it has no discretion and must,[14] unless contrary to a general principle of Union law,[15] order the Member State concerned to recover it. To forfeit the undue advantage and restore the situation existing in the internal market prior to the grant of the aid,[16] aid must be recovered with interest.[17] In the absence of uniform rules at EU level, the CJEU has established that recovery of aid is governed by national rules and procedures;[18] Article 16 of the Procedural Regulation has codified these principles. Clearly, any act adopted by the authorities of a Member State to implement the recovery obligation is subject to the judicial review of national courts.

Article 108(3) TFEU, its interpretation by the CJEU, and the Procedural Regulation shed light on the fundamental roles of the Commission and the national courts. These roles, relating to both the private and the public enforcement of State aid rules,

9. ECJ, Case C-199/06 *Centre d'exportation du livre Français (CELF) v Société internationale de diffusion et d'édition (SIDE)* [2008] ECR I-469, para. 47.
10. ECJ, Case C-6/64 *Costa v ENEL* [1964] ECR 1141; ECJ, Case C-120/73 *Lorenz* [1973] ECR 171, para. 8; ECJ, Case C-354/90 *Fédération nationale du commerce extérieur des produits alimentaires ('FNCE')* [1991] ECR I-5505, para. 11; ECJ, Case C-39/94 *SFEI* [1996] ECR I-3547, para. 39.
11. Case C-354/90 *FNCE, supra* n. 10, at para. 14.
12. Case C-120/73 *Lorenz, supra* n. 10, at para. 9.
13. Case C-39/94 *SFEI, supra* n. 10, at para. 40.
14. ECJ, Case C-310/99 *Italy v Commission* [2002] ECR I-2289, para. 99 and case law cited.
15. Procedural Regulation, *supra* n. 6, Article 16(1).
16. ECJ, Case C-142/87 *Belgium v Commission ('Tubemeuse')* [1990] ECR I-959, para. 66; ECJ, Case C-75/97 *Belgium v Commission ('Maribel bis/ter')* [1999] ECR I-3671, paras 64–66; ECJ, Case C-277/00 *Germany v Commission* [2004] ECR I-3925, para. 74; ECJ, Case C-454/09 *Commission v Italy ('New Interline')* [2011] ECR I-150, paras 30, 35 and 37.
17. T-459/93 *Siemens v Commission* [1995] ECR II-1675, paras 97–101; T-415/05, T-416/05 and T 423/05 *Greece and others v Commission* [2010] ECR II-4749, paras 415 and 416; T-303/10 *Wam industriale v Commission* [2012] ECLI:EU:T:2012:505, para. 203.
18. ECJ, Case C-382/99 *Netherlands v Commission ('Service stations')* [2002] ECR I-5163, para. 90 and case law cited.

are complementary but separate.[19] In practice, national courts are called on to perform a series of important and often complex legal and economic analyses and assessments.

In the event of an alleged infringement of the standstill obligation, a competitor of an aid recipient may request a national court to suspend the implementation of an aid measure or to order recovery of the aid put into effect before the Commission's authorisation. In addition, a competitor may request the award of damages in a case brought against the authorities of the Member State concerned or against the aid recipient, if that is allowed under national law. In principle, a prospective aid recipient may also seek legal certainty regarding its right to aid, and national authorities may refer to court a conflict regarding their power to grant aid. To rule on these matters, a national court should examine: (i) whether the contested measure grants aid in the sense of Article 107(1) TFEU or (ii) if the public support falls within the requirements of a *de minimis* Regulation; (iii) whether the aid is existing or new; (iv) whether it is exempt from notification to the Commission, in application of the Commission Decision on the Services of General Economic Interest,[20] of the GBER, or of any other regulation adopted pursuant to Article 109 TFEU; (v) whether the Member State notified the Commission of the measure and (vi) whether the measure has been put into effect prior to the Commission's authorisation. Further, in cases involving a request for damages, the court needs to consider (vii) whether there is a causal link between the infringement and the harm and (viii) how to quantify that harm. These points are all the more important when considering that a Commission decision declaring aid compatible with the internal market is without prejudice to the possible infringement of the standstill obligation.[21]

In the event of an implementation of the recovery obligation, aid recipients may apply to a national court to obtain interim measures, the annulment of a national recovery order or a reduction of the amount to be recovered. An aid recipient may also claim damages or compensation from the Member State concerned; similarly, competitors may lodge a request for damages against the Member State and/or the aid recipient. Here, the national court is required to examine a wide range of EU principles and rules, including: (i) the Union Courts' case law on interim measures granted by national courts;[22] (ii) the principles of primacy and effectiveness of EU law and the principle of equivalence, implying that recovery of State aid should not follow rules different from those applicable to the recovery of a similar claim under national law;[23]

19. ECJ, Case C-284/12 *Deutsche Lufthansa* [2013] ECLI:EU:C:2013:755, para. 27 and case law cited.
20. Commission Decision 2012/21/EU of 20 December 2011 on the application of Article 106(2) of the Treaty on the Functioning of the European Union to State aid in the form of public service compensation granted to certain undertakings entrusted with the operation of services of general economic interest (notified under document C(2011) 9380) [2012] OJ L 7/3.
21. Case C-199/06 *CELF I, supra* n. 9, at paras 45 and 46.
22. The CJEU set four cumulative conditions for a national court to order interim relief from recovery of State aid: *see* ECJ, Joined Cases C-143/88 and C-92/88 *Zuckerfabrik* [1991] ECR I-415, paras 23 and following; ECJ, Case C-465/93 *Atlanta*, [1995] ECR I-3761, para. 51.
23. Case C-6/64 *Costa v ENEL, supra* n. 10; ECJ, Case C-505/14 *Klausner Holz* [2015] ECLI:EU:C:2015:742, paras 40 and 41.

(iii) the applicable set of rules to quantify the element of aid, particularly where the Member State gave aid in a form different from a grant.[24]

In the light of these characteristics, cooperation is paramount to ensure the proper functioning of the system of supervision of State aid. As a national court may be concerned by a case: (i) absent any involvement of the Commission, (ii) while the Commission is investigating or (iii) following a Commission decision, it may prove key for the national court concerned to know whether proceedings before the Commission exist or at what stage they are. To add complexity, national courts 'must [...] refrain from taking decisions which conflict with a decision of the Commission, even if it is provisional'.[25]

It follows that the Commission and the Member States should fulfil their roles in line with the principle of sincere cooperation enshrined in Article 4(3) TEU, by which 'the Union and the Member States shall, in full mutual respect, assist each other in carrying out tasks which flow from the Treaties'. In this context, cooperation with national courts is particularly crucial, as recognised by the CJEU.[26]

Article 29 of the Procedural Regulation provides for three tools by which the Commission and the national courts can cooperate in a spirit of sincere cooperation, namely the possibility for a national court to: (i) request information or (ii) request an opinion and (iii) the Commission's power to submit observations in writing (and orally) to a national court (amicus curiae observations).

III. THE COOPERATION TOOLS

A. From their origins to their codification

While the system of supervision of State aid has remained substantially unchanged since its creation, the systematisation of the cooperation tools between the Commission and the national courts has a more recent history. Based on the principle of sincere cooperation and following a number of judgments of the CJEU,[27] the Commission outlined means of cooperation for the first time in the 1990s.

Taking inspiration from a similar notice applicable to antitrust matters,[28] the 1995 Notice on cooperation between national courts and the Commission in the State aid field[29] (the '1995 Notice on cooperation') contained for the first time embryonic

24. The Commission has adopted several notices relating to the qualification and quantification of the aid element when the public support is granted in a form other than a grant. *See*, for example, the Commission Notice on the application of Articles 87 and 88 of the EC Treaty to State aid in the form of guarantees [2008] OJ C 155/10.
25. Case C-284/12 *Deutsche Lufthansa*, *supra* n. 19, at para. 41.
26. *See*, in this sense, ECJ, Case C-2/88 *Zwartveld* [1990] ECR I-3365, paras 17 and 18.
27. Notably Case C-354/90 *FNCE*, *supra* n. 10.
28. Notice on cooperation between national courts and the Commission in applying Articles 85 and 86 of the EEC Treaty [1993] OJ C 39/6.
29. Notice on cooperation between national courts and the Commission in the State aid field [1995] OJ C 312/8.

cooperation mechanisms for national courts to request procedural and factual information or opinions on substance.[30] The Commission also clarified the scope of its support by specifying that: (i) it could not offer guidance on the merits of the case or deal in its answer with the compatibility of the aid concerned, (ii) its reply was not final or binding and (iii) the national court maintained its right to refer the matter to the CJEU for a preliminary ruling pursuant to Article 267 TFEU.[31] Notwithstanding the positive premises, the 1995 Notice on cooperation was quite generic and did not contain practical instructions about how to request the cooperation of the Commission. In practice, it did not generate a cooperation culture between national courts and the Commission.

To better understand how national courts were playing their role in the enforcement of State aid rules, the Commission tendered the study 'Application of EC State Aid Law by Member State Courts', delivered by the *Association des Avocats Européens* in 1999 (the '1999 Study'). That same year, the first regulation establishing State aid procedures entered into force (the '1999 Procedural Regulation'),[32] without any provision about the cooperation tools.

For around ten years, the purpose and scope of the 1995 Notice on cooperation remained unquestioned, until a major review of the Commission policy on State aid.

Following, among other factors, the enlargement of 2004[33] and the multiplication of legal acts on State aid at EU level, the Commission proposed in 2005 an ambitious State Aid Action Plan (SAAP).[34] In particular, with a view towards focusing on 'less and better targeted State aid; a refined economic approach; more effective procedures [and] better enforcement', the Commission highlighted that the supervision of State aid in the internal market is 'a shared responsibility between the Commission and Member States'.[35] On that basis, the SAAP recognised the importance of private litigation before national courts as a means to 'provide increased discipline in the field of State aid'[36] and announced the review of the 1995 Notice on cooperation.

Following that announcement, the Commission tendered an update to the 1999 Study, delivered in 2006 (the '2006 Study').[37] The 2006 Study presented the enforcement of State aid rules by the national courts of the Member States preceding the 2004

30. *Ibid.*, respectively, paras 28 and 29.
31. *Ibid.*, para. 30.
32. Council Regulation (EC) No 659/1999 of 22 March 1999 laying down detailed rules for the application of Article 93 of the EC Treaty [1999] OJ L 83/1.
33. On 1 May 2004, Cyprus, the Czech Republic, Estonia, Hungary, Latvia, Lithuania, Malta, Poland, Slovakia and Slovenia joined the EU.
34. State aid action plan – Less and better targeted State aid: a roadmap for State aid reform 2005–2009 (Consultation document), COM(2005) 107 final (SAAP).
35. *Ibid.*, para. 18.
36. *Ibid.*, para. 55.
37. Thomas Jestaedt, Jacques Derenne and Tom R. Ottervanger (eds), *Study on the enforcement of State aid law at national level* (2006 European Commission).

enlargement[38] and more particularly the enforcement of Commission decisions concerning incompatible aid, based on a sample of five Member States.[39] Not surprisingly, it revealed an increase in the number of cases brought before national courts, but it also showed difficulties and a lack of uniform rules or remedies.[40]

Drawing from the conclusions of the 2006 Study, the Commission adopted in 2009 a new notice (the '2009 Enforcement Notice')[41] describing the scenarios national courts may be confronted with when enforcing State aid rules. The 2009 Enforcement Notice, which is still in force, provides examples and the applicable case law or practice of the Commission, significantly expanding the scope of the 1995 Notice on cooperation.

More importantly, for the purpose of this chapter, the 2009 Enforcement Notice presents in an entire section the 'Commission support for national courts', consisting in replies to the requests for information or opinion submitted by national courts. In preparing the 2009 Enforcement Notice, the Commission again took inspiration from the 2004 Notice on cooperation in the antitrust domain,[42] with the exception of amicus curiae observations.

In fact, while Council Regulation (EC) No 1/2003[43] had introduced the possibility for the Commission, on its own initiative, to submit observations to the national courts dealing with antitrust matters – a cooperation tool also cited in the 2004 Notice on cooperation in the antitrust domain – neither the 1999 Procedural Regulation nor the 2009 Enforcement Notice contained provisions in that sense.

Just a few years following the adoption of the 2009 Enforcement Notice, the new Europe 2020 strategy for growth, on the one hand, and the economic and financial crisis, on the other hand, led the Commission to launch a new reform of State aid control, the State Aid Modernisation (SAM).[44] Among its objectives, the SAM required the Commission to focus its *ex ante* scrutiny on cases having the biggest impact on the internal market; for their part, Member States were given more responsibilities. To attain this objective, a number of legal texts were amended, including the 1999 Procedural Regulation. With this recalibration of responsibilities, cooperation between the Commission and Member States, including the latter's judiciary, was to strengthen and preserve the effectiveness of the supervision of State aid.

38. The Member States preceding the 2004 enlargement were Austria, Belgium, Denmark, Finland, France, Germany, Greece, Ireland, Italy, Luxembourg, the Netherlands, Portugal, Spain, Sweden and United Kingdom.
39. The five Member States chosen were Belgium, France, Germany, Italy and Spain.
40. A 2009 update of the study, extending the scope of analysis to the 27 Member States, confirmed the trend. *See* Jacques Derene, Cédric Kaczmakrek and Jonathan Clovin (eds) *2009 update of the 2006 Study on the enforcement of State aid rules at national level* (2009 European Commission).
41. Commission notice on the enforcement of State aid law by national courts [2009] OJ C 85/1.
42. Commission Notice on the co-operation between the Commission and the courts of the EU Member States in the application of Articles 81 and 82 EC [2001] OJ C 101/54.
43. Regulation (EC) No 1/2003 of the Council of 16 December 2002 on the implementation of the rules on competition laid down in Articles 81 and 82 of the Treaty [2003] OJ L 1/1 (Regulation 1/2003).
44. Communication from the Commission to the European Parliament, the Council, the European Economic and Social Committee and the Committee of the Regions – EU State Aid Modernisation (SAM), COM(2012) 209 final.

In that context, the regulation adopted in 2013 to amend the 1999 Procedural Regulation[45] recalled in its first recital that 'Article 107 of the [TFEU] should be applied effectively and uniformly throughout the Union.' Concretely, the current Chapter X of the Procedural Regulation (following codification of the 1999 and 2013 regulations) implements this principle by establishing provisions for the cooperation with national courts.

As a result of the SAM, the cooperation tools have been codified in a legislative act. In addition, the Procedural Regulation introduced, for the first time, the Commission's power to submit amicus curiae observations also regarding State aid matters. While this aligns the State aid means of cooperation to those established in the antitrust domain, the Procedural Regulation does not contain any provision to prevent conflicts between the conclusions of a national court and the investigation of the Commission, differently from Council Regulation (EC) 1/2003.[46]

This difference is particularly significant because it highlights the complementarity of the roles of the Commission and national courts in the supervision of State aid. In fact, it derives from the very purpose of the standstill obligation (i.e., to ensure that the Commission may assess planned aid before it is implemented) that a national court is 'not required to declare that it has no jurisdiction or to stay proceedings until such time as the Commission has adopted a position on how the measures in question are to be categorized'.[47] It follows that due to specific features of the system of supervision of State aid, cooperation is even more important than in other domains of competition law.

B. The cooperation tools in practice

Before describing the content and functioning of the cooperation tools, it is necessary to define the concept of 'national court' because neither the Procedural Regulation nor the 2009 Enforcement Notice defines the notion of a 'national court'. In principle, one could refer by analogy to the definition contained in the 2004 Notice on cooperation in the antitrust domain, by which national courts are 'courts and tribunals within an EU Member State that can apply Articles [101] and [102 TFEU] and that are authorised to ask a preliminary question to the Court of Justice [...] pursuant to Article [267 TFEU]'.[48]

This is complemented by the case law of the CJEU on the right to refer questions for preliminary ruling; in that context, several factors must be taken into account, namely 'whether the body is established by law, whether it is permanent, whether its

45. Regulation 734/2013/EU of the Council of 22 July 2013 amending Regulation (EC) No 659/1999 laying down detailed rules for the application of Article 93 of the EC Treaty [2013] OJ L 204/15.
46. *See* Regulation (EC) No 1/2003, *supra* n. 43, Article 16.
47. Case C-39/94 *SFEI*, *supra* n. 10, at para. 53.
48. Commission Notice on cooperation within the Network of Competition Authorities [2004] OJ C 101/43, para. 1.

jurisdiction is compulsory, whether its procedure is *inter partes*, whether it applies rules of law and whether it is independent'.[49]

It follows that any natural or legal person, undertaking, body, etc. not meeting these requirements is a third party for the purpose of the cooperation tools. This is not surprising because the Commission has a duty of sincere cooperation only vis-à-vis Member States, and more in particular vis-à-vis national courts.

At the same time, the Commission is aware that private enforcement contributes to the effectiveness of the system of supervision of State aid.[50] For example, the Staff Working Document accompanying the Report on Competition Policy 2015[51] reports that third parties requested the Commission to submit amicus curiae observations during that year. In recalling that the Commission must only reply to requests made by national courts, the Staff Working Document recognises that requests made by third parties represent a 'useful tool to inform the Commission about ongoing cases where the submission of observations *ex officio* can be presented'.[52] And as a matter of fact, the Commission has already replied to questions from public prosecutors and submitted amicus curiae observations to arbitration tribunals.

Article 29(1) of the Procedural Regulation states that 'for the application of Article 107(1) and Article 108 TFEU, the courts of the Member States may ask the Commission to transmit to them information in its possession or its opinion on questions concerning the application of State aid rules'. Sections 3.1 and 3.2 of the 2009 Enforcement Notice describe examples of these two cooperation tools.

As regards requests for information, the Commission is under the obligation to transmit the information in its possession.[53] The information may be of a procedural nature, that is to say, whether an aid measure was notified under Article 108(3) TFEU and whether the Commission has initiated a formal investigation or adopted a decision or when it intends do so. The request may also concern the transmission of documents, information on facts, statistics, studies, etc.

The Commission endeavours to transmit the information requested within one month of receipt of the request provided that is complete and no clarifications or consultations are needed.[54] In replying, the Commission must comply with the obligation of professional secrecy pursuant to Article 339 TFEU and cannot disclose confidential information that the national court concerned cannot protect. In addition, the Commission protects its internal 'thinking space' by reserving its right to refuse transmitting information where that would 'interfere with the functioning and independence of the [Union]. This would be the case where disclosure would jeopardise the accomplishment of the tasks entrusted to the Commission'.[55]

49. ECJ, Joined Cases C-58/13 and 59/13 *Torresi* [2014] ECLI:EU:C:2014:2088, para. 17.
50. As stated above, the SAAP, *supra* n. 34, para. 55, stressed the importance of private litigation. *See also* the 2009 Enforcement Notice, *supra* n. 41, para. 5, and the SAM, *supra* n. 44, para. 21.
51. SWD (2016) 198 final, https://eur-lex.europa.eu/legal-content/it/TXT/?uri=CELEX:52016SC0198, pages 12 and 13 (accessed 2 March 2019).
52. *Ibid.*, pages 12 and 13.
53. This obligation derives from the seminal order in Case C-2/88 *Zwartveld*, *supra* n. 26, at paras 17 and 18.
54. 2009 Enforcement Notice, *supra* n. 41, para. 84.
55. *Ibid.*, para. 88.

As regards requests for an opinion, national courts can submit any matter concerning the application of the State aid rules as the 2009 Enforcement Notice refers to 'all economic, factual or legal matters which arise in the context of the national proceedings'[56] and provides an open list of examples. Significantly, most of those examples, if not all, concern private enforcement: for example: (i) whether a certain public support qualifies as State aid, (ii) whether specific aid falls within the scope of application of the GBER or whether it is not subject to notification based on other conditions, (iii) whether the national court should order recovery of the aid and how to calculate interest, (iv) whether the legal prerequisites for damages claims under Union law and issues concerning the calculation of the damage incurred. To preserve its exclusive competence, the Commission does not give opinions on the compatibility of State aid with the internal market.[57] The Commission respects the autonomy and independence of the national court and does not hear the parties, nor will it in the reply consider the merits of the case.[58]

As preparing an opinion requires additional analysis and assessment, as compared to providing information, the Commission endeavours to reply within four months from a complete request.[59] Furthermore, the opinion is not binding on the requesting national court[60] and – clearly – it does not replace the right or duty of the national court concerned to refer a question to the CJEU for preliminary ruling under Article 267 TFEU.

The 2009 Enforcement Notice also establishes a postal address, a single phone number and the e-mail address 'ec-amicus-state-aid@ec.europa.eu' for all the requests for information or opinion that national courts may have – plus 'any other written or oral questions about State aid policy that may arise in their daily work'.[61]

To guarantee the coherent application of Article 107(1) or Article 108 TFEU, Article 29(2) of the Procedural Regulation provides for the power of the Commission to 'submit written observations to the courts of the Member States that are responsible for applying the State aid rules'. The Commission acts on its own initiative but must inform the Member State concerned before submitting its observations. To prepare its observations, the Commission can request that the national court transmit the documents necessary to form its assessment. The Commission may also, with the permission of the court, make oral observations.

While the 2009 Enforcement Notice could not provide for specific information about the amicus curiae observations, some of its provisions should be considered to apply horizontally to all the cooperation tools. In particular, the Commission serves the public interest and therefore does not hear the parties, nor does it intervene in their favour.[62]

56. *Ibid.*, para. 90.
57. *Ibid.*, para. 92.
58. *Ibid.*, para. 93.
59. *Ibid.*, para. 94.
60. *Ibid.*, para. 93.
61. *Ibid.*, para. 97.
62. *Ibid.*, para. 80.

Similarly, even if the 2009 Enforcement Notice refers to the obligation of professional secrecy only in the context of requests for information, that obligation is recalled and spelled out by Article 30 of the Procedural Regulation and must therefore apply to the information encompassed by all three of the cooperation tools.

C. The use of cooperation tools

Paragraph 98 of the 2009 Enforcement Notice states that 'the Commission will publish a summary concerning its cooperation with national courts pursuant to this Notice in its annual Report on Competition Policy. It may also make its opinions and observations available on its website'.

In practice, the Commission has been reporting on its cooperation with national courts in each of the Commission Staff Working Documents accompanying its annual reports on Competition Policy, starting from 2009.[63] For its part, the website of DG Competition posts replies to requests for an opinion[64] and amicus curiae observations.[65]

The information provided by these two sources is a good indication of the cooperation, but it is not necessarily complete. In fact, the early Commission Staff Working Documents contain generic statements about the use of the cooperation tools, while the website of DG Competition contains replies whose publication was authorised by the national courts concerned.

For the purpose of this chapter, reference is made to the data presented during the conference 'Private Enforcement of European Competition and State Aid Law: Current Challenges and the Way Forward', which took place in Augsburg, on 22 and 23 November 2018.[66]

Since the adoption of the 2009 Enforcement Notice, national courts submitted more requests for information (23) than requests for opinion (17). For its part, since the introduction of the power to submit amicus curiae observations (summer 2013), the Commission employed that cooperation tool twenty-one times.

From a procedural point of view, national courts submitted their requests for cooperation by all possible means: e-mails, letters or court orders formally requesting the Commission to submit a reply. The aggregated information contained in the Commission Staff Working Documents shows that the Commission, irrespective of the way the cooperation was sought, has replied within the periods set out in the 2009 Enforcement Notice, with a very small number of exceptions occasioned by the complexity of the case concerned or the need to assess national rules.

63. All the reports on Competition Policy are published on the Commission's DG Competition website, http://ec.europa.eu/competition/publications/annual_report/index.html (accessed 2 March 2019).
64. *See* http://ec.europa.eu/competition/court/opinions.html (accessed 2 March 2019).
65. *See* http://ec.europa.eu/competition/court/amicus_curiae_interventions.html (accessed 2 March 2019).
66. Figures 10.1 to 10.3 are reproduced from Presentation of Mr Luca Rossi, Deputy Head of Unit H4, State aid: Enforcement and monitoring, European Commission, DG Competition.

The requests for cooperation came from eleven Member States,[67] with Germany, Italy and the Netherlands accounting together for 65% of all the requests for information and opinion.

As regards requests for information (Figure 10.1), first instance courts accounted for around half of the requests, and second and last instance courts together took almost all the remaining share. A negligible number of requests came from prosecutor offices. The distribution in terms of court competence shows that around five-sixths of the requests were evenly divided between civil and administrative courts, while criminal courts submitted around one-sixth of the requests.

Figure 10.1 Requests for Information: Distribution and Type of Requesting Courts

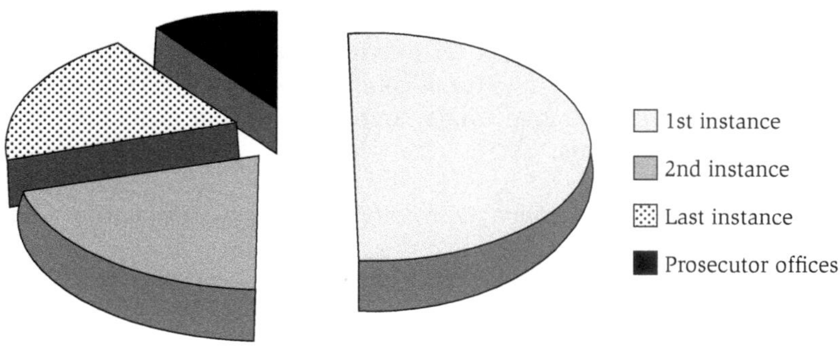

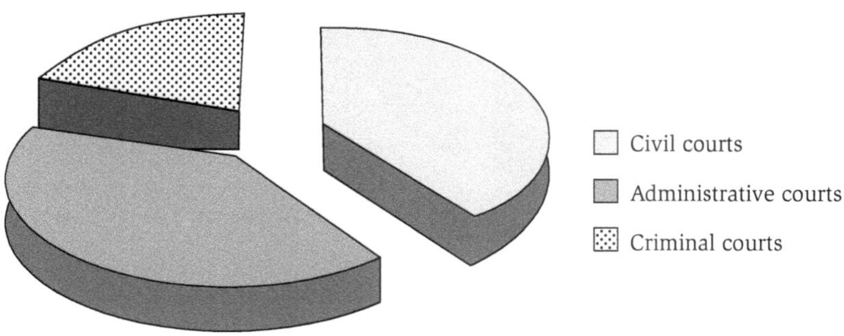

The requests for information tended to seek (Figure 10.2) insights or updates about proceedings by the Commission (about 60%), focused on compliance with the standstill obligation (25%) or sought to verify whether a complaint was submitted to the Commission regarding the matter the court was dealing with (about 15%).

67. Germany, Italy, the Netherlands, Finland, Spain, Austria, Estonia, France, United Kingdom, Greece and Hungary.

Figure 10.2 Requests for Information: Content of the Requests

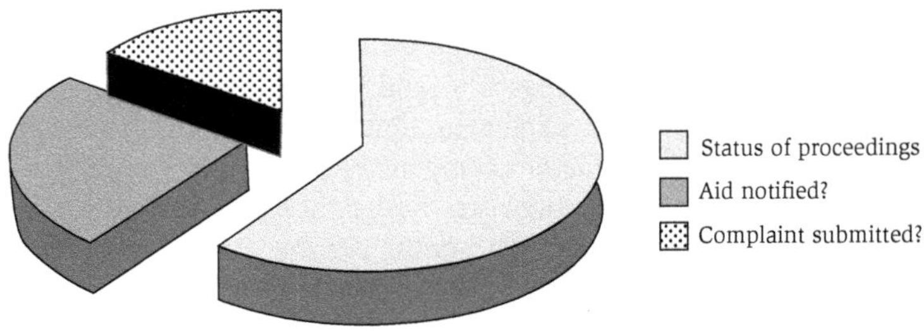

As regards requests for opinion (Figure 10.3), second instance courts accounted for half of the requests, and first and last instance courts together took almost all the remaining share. As for the requests for information, prosecutor offices played a negligible role. The distribution in terms of court competence shows that half of the requests came from administrative courts, around 40% from civil courts and the remainder from criminal courts.

Figure 10.3 Requests for Opinion: Distribution and Type of Requesting Courts

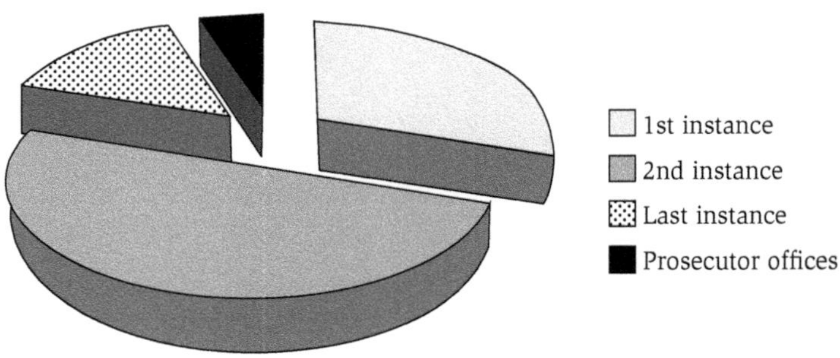

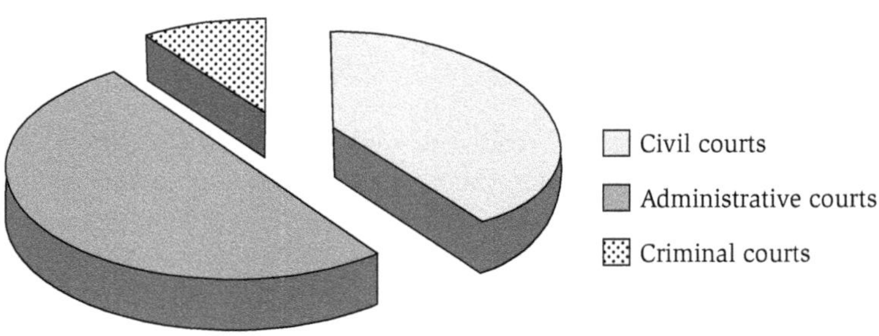

By cross-checking the information contained in the Commission Staff Working Documents and the website of DG Competition, it emerges that the requests for an opinion revolve around a wide range of matters: interpretation of the concept of State aid, the scope of the standstill obligation, rules applicable to services of general economic interest, the quantification of aid, etc.

As regards amicus curiae observations, the Commission submitted more than half of its observations to courts of first instance and the remainder to second or last instance courts. However, many of the observations submitted to first instance courts relate to the same case.[68] Once observations relating to that case are excluded, it emerges that the Commission has tended to submit observations to second or last instance courts on matters that are particularly relevant for the uniform application of Articles 107(1) and 108 TFEU.

IV. THE ENFORCEMENT OF STATE AID RULES BY NATIONAL COURTS IN RELATION TO THE COOPERATION TOOLS

The 2006 Study preceding the 2009 Enforcement Notice stated that 'private enforcement of EC State aid law at Member State level is still in its infancy'. In particular, the authors noted that they had 'found no decisions where private parties were awarded monetary damages based on the grant of illegal aid to a competitor'.

The systematisation, by the 2009 Enforcement Notice, of the existing cooperation tools aimed at facilitating the cooperation with national courts and promoting private enforcement. While the data presented above reflects some developments, the picture appears still quite complex and fragmented.

Thus, as regards requests for an opinion from the lower courts, one may find that the courts lack or are not aware of national precedents, or that they simply prefer to seek an 'authentic interpretation' of the rules they are called on to apply. It also seems that national courts tend not to use the possibility of performing a preliminary assessment of the case and asking the Commission for *information* on previous practice, e.g. a list of Commission decisions assessing whether a specific category or form of public support fulfils the criteria of Article 107(1) TFEU. That practice would allow the court to reach a decision faster, not only because the Commission should provide the information – and could easily gather it – within one month of the request but also because in some instances the fact that the *opinion* of the Commission is not binding may open the way to additional claims by the parties of the case pending before the national court, whereas the *information* given by the Commission is a fact whose assessment is reserved to the national court concerned.

However, it is also true that national courts may prefer referring a question to the CJEU for preliminary ruling pursuant to Article 267 TFEU. Still, the CJEU may dismiss a request, and its ruling requires an amount of time significantly higher than the one- or four-month period associated with the cooperation tools.

It also seems that the courts of some Member States are relatively more aware of the existence of the cooperation tools or are keener on using them.

68. The matter in question, broadly speaking, has an impact on the relationship between EU and international law. *See* http://europa.eu/rapid/press-release_IP-18-6723_en.htm (accessed 2 March 2019).

For example, Germany ranks first among Member States in terms of requests and that may reflect the fact that State aid expenditure has traditionally been significant.[69] However, based on the same benchmark, one may then wonder why French or Hungarian courts made so little use of the cooperation tools.[70] While the legal system of each of the Member States has its own procedures and peculiarities, it is difficult to believe that the application of State aid rules poses no or few issues.

This is particularly true in the post-SAM environment, where, continually since 2015, more than 96% of new aid measures have been exempted from notification by virtue of the GBER.[71] This fact alone, coupled with the transparency obligations,[72] should have provoked a significant increase of private enforcement of State aid rules and, in turn, more cooperation between the national courts and the Commission.

Now, it may be possible that the streamlining of guidelines and the 2016 Guidance on the notion of State aid[73] have eased the task of national courts, to the point where little cooperation is sought. However, as State aid law is made up of rules and exceptions, not to mention the large volume of Commission decisions or case law, it is difficult to believe that national courts are fully confident as regards the regulatory framework.

Significantly, the use thus far of the cooperation tools signals that little support is sought regarding public enforcement. For example, it appears that national courts do not request support in quantifying the aid to be recovered from an aid beneficiary or in determining whether there is economic continuity between the original aid beneficiary and a separate undertaking. However, it is quite certain that these questions arise in the context of recovery proceedings, especially when considering that from 2010 to 2017 Member States recovered around EUR 1.2 billion of aid that the Commission found incompatible with the internal market.[74] Cooperation may be particularly useful in that domain. In 2015, the Commission submitted amicus curiae observations to a Court of Appeal to indicate that some rules under national law impeding the immediate and effective recovery of State aid were to be left unapplied to preserve the primacy and effectiveness of EU law. To ensure the implementation of the recovery decision, the

---

69. *See* European Commission, DG Competition *State Aid Scoreboard 2018* http://ec.europa.eu/competition/state_aid/scoreboard/index_en.html (accessed 2 March 2019). For example, in 2017 Germany spent 1.31% of its GDP on State aid, excluding aid to railways. In that year, Germany had the highest GDP of the European Union, accounting alone for 21.3% of the EU28. Source: Eurostat, 'Share of Member States in EU GDP' https://ec.europa.eu/eurostat/web/products-eurostat-news/-/DDN-20180511-1 (accessed 2 March 2019).
70. *Ibid.* For example, in 2017 France spent 0.76% of its GDP on State aid, excluding aid to railways. In that year, according to Eurostat, France had the third highest GDP of the European Union, accounting alone for 14.9% of the EU28. In 2017, Hungary spent 2.67% of its GDP on State aid, excluding aid to railways, the highest share across all of the Member States.
71. *See* the State aid Scoreboard 2018.
72. *See* http://ec.europa.eu/competition/state_aid/overview/transparency_and_evaluation.html (accessed 2 March 2019).
73. Commission Notice on the notion of State aid as referred to in Article 107(1) of the Treaty on the Functioning of the European Union [2016] OJ C 262/1.
74. Author calculation based on data from the European Commission, DG Competition, *Information on recovery of unlawful aid* http://ec.europa.eu/competition/state_aid/studies_reports/recovery_statistics.xlsx (accessed 2 March 2019).

national court decided to make an innovative use of the interim request for payment as available under French civil procedural law.[75]

More importantly, for the purpose of this chapter, the use of cooperation tools shows to the same degree that there is some progress in private enforcement, as compared to the 'infancy' observed by the 2006 Study. In particular, in the context of their cases, national courts do seek information about investigations by the Commission and opinions about the concept of aid, how to qualify specific measures and the application of the standstill obligation. While this may certainly be encouraging, it is also striking that little cooperation concerns issues relating to the protection of competitors and the award of damages, both matters that are intrinsically linked to the enforcement of the standstill obligation.

In reality, the use of cooperation tools gives only a partial picture about the enforcement - be it public or private - of State aid rules by national courts. For example, in 2018 a French first instance court ordered the seizure of an aircraft pending the reimbursement by an airline of aid found by the Commission to be incompatible with the internal market, showing that use of the cooperation tools is by no means a prerequisite for aggressive enforcement of State aid rules.[76]

With specific regard to claims for damages, recent French judgments show that national courts are in principle well equipped to decide on the consequences of an infringement of the standstill obligation. In particular, the maritime company Corsica Ferries claimed damages from the Corsican administration for the grant of compensation to the competitor SNCM-CNM, in breach of the standstill obligation. The unlawfulness of the aid had been confirmed by a previous judgment by a national court, and the Commission had found that the aid was incompatible with the internal market.[77] In 2017, the first instance court of Bastia ordered the Corsican administration to pay EUR 84 million in damages, this based on the infringement of the standstill obligation, its link with the damage suffered by Corsica Ferries and the evidence supplied by that same party.[78] The judgment was partly annulled in 2018 to permit a new quantification

75. Cour administrative d'appel de Bordeaux, 10 December 2015, no. 15BX01807 *Société Ryanair*. Both the amicus curiae observations and the judgment are available at http://ec.europa.eu/competition/court/amicus_curiae.html (accessed 2 March 2019). Under the French *référé-provision*, a national court can order a provisional payment if the amount owed cannot be seriously called into question. This is the first use of this provision based on a recovery obligation established by a Commission recovery decision.
76. *See* https://fr.reuters.com/article/topNews/idFRKCN1NE10Z-OFRTP (accessed 2 March 2019).
77. Commission Decision 2014/882/EU of 20 November 2013 concerning the State aid SA.16237 (C58/02) (ex N118/02) implemented by France in favour of SNCM (notified under document C(2013) 7066) [2014] OJ L 357/1.
78. Judgment of 23 February 2017 of the *Tribunal administratif de Bastia*, available at http://bastia.tribunal-administratif.fr/content/download/91226/875028/version/1/file/1500375Corsica Ferries.pdf (accessed 2 March 2019). *See also* Bernadette Willemot-Nieuwenhuys, Federico Macchi, *Droit à l'indemnisation suite à la violation par l'état de l'obligation de notification d'une aide d'État – une application concrète par le juge du Tribunal administratif de Bastia* (2017) 2-3 Revue du droit des industries de réseau 189.

of the damages, without prejudice to Corsica Ferries' right to receive damages due to the infringement of the standstill obligation.[79]

V. GATHERING INFORMATION AND OUTLOOK ON ENFORCEMENT: THE 2019 STUDY

The analysis of the use of the cooperation tools shows some progress regarding both the cooperation between national courts and the Commission and the private enforcement of State aid rules. However, that analysis alone is not sufficient because it is clear that national courts apply State aid rules without having recourse to the cooperation tools, as the French examples show.

Due to the very features of the system of supervision of State aid, the Commission can hardly have a thorough overview of the application of State aid rules by national courts. While, on the one hand, it may be aware of concrete matters that arise in the context of recovery proceedings or issues submitted by third parties, there are, on the other hand, virtually no means, besides the cooperation tools, for it to learn about the state of play of private enforcement.

Against this background, the post-SAM environment and the increased *ex ante* responsibilities for Member States - and, consequently, for their courts - require effective private enforcement.

With this objective, in February 2018 the Commission published a call for tenders for a study on the enforcement of State aid rules and decisions by national courts (the 2019 Study).[80] According to the tender specifications, the Study must present in a systematic manner the state of play as regards the enforcement of State aid rules by the national courts of the twenty-eight Member States, starting from 2007.[81] In particular, it has to identify a series of relevant State aid rulings for each of the Member States and present the most significant of them, together with country reports and '[identify] best practices regarding State aid enforcement that can be shared EU-wide' and assess 'to what extent the cooperation tools provided for by Article 29 of the Procedural Regulation are being used and what could be done to render them more efficient if needed, both at EU and at individual Member State level'.[82]

The Commission published the 2019 Study in July 2019.[83] In line with the requirement to offer 'interactive methods to exploit the data supporting the Study',[84]

79. Cour d'appel de Marseille, 12 February 2018, nos 17MA01582-17MA01583, *Collective territoriale de Corse*. Available at http://marseille.cour-administrative-appel.fr/content/download/127127/1286775/version/1/file/17MA01582-17MA01583.pdf (accessed 2 March 2019).
80. *See* the Tender Specifications, https://etendering.ted.europa.eu/cft/cft-display.html?cftId=3191 (accessed 2 March 2019).
81. Thus, the 2019 Study will regard all Member States, moving forward from the end of the period covered by the 2006 Study.
82. Tender Specifications, *supra* n. 80, at 6.
83. *See* Study on the enforcement of State aid rules and decisions by national courts - Final study, available at https://ec.europa.eu/competition/state_aid/studies_reports/studies_reports.html (accessed 28 August 2019).
84. Tender Specifications, *supra* n. 80, at 9.

the authors published an interactive database containing country and case summaries, as well as full text of rulings, where available.[85]

While it is not the object of this chapter to present the content of the 2019 Study, it is certain that the 2019 Study confirms most of the trends identified in these pages. It also shed light in a comprehensive way on the current state of play in terms of the enforcement of State aid rules by national courts and has the potential to have a multiplier effect, prompting further studies and allowing best practices to spread across the Union.

Without speculating about further policy developments, it is not a mystery that the final goal of the Commission was 'to share the information collected and propos[e] best practices to national courts through a revised enforcement notice',[86] to replace the 2009 Enforcement Notice.

VI. CONCLUDING REMARKS

The system of supervision of State aid assigns distinct but complementary roles to the Commission and the national courts. Far from being concerned only by the public enforcement of State aid rules, national courts play a crucial role in ensuring the functioning of the internal market. In fact, the direct effect of the standstill obligation is the source of private enforcement of State aid rules; moreover, based on the case law of the Union Courts, national courts must draw all consequences from its infringement. The responsibility of national courts has also expanded, as following the SAM almost all of the new aid measures are implemented without prior notification being given to the Commission.

In performing its tasks, a national court may be called on to perform complex analyses and assessments and may overlap the work of the Commission. Therefore, a cooperation culture becomes crucial to avoid conflicts and to maintain complementary roles. To this extent, the cooperation tools offer a means for the national courts and the Commission to communicate and, within their respective roles, contribute to the functioning of the internal market.

However, evidence shows that the potential of the cooperation tools has not been fully exploited. On the one hand, the courts of some Member States make more use of the cooperation tools and submit requests concerning, broadly speaking, private and, to a lesser extent, public enforcement. On the other hand, the majority of the national courts do not use the cooperation tools, and it is difficult for the Commission, in light of its role in supervising State aid and the autonomy of national courts, to understand whether that is voluntary or not.

Certainly, the Commission has tried to acquire and share more knowledge: since 2002, DG Competition has invested in training – financing workshops, seminars and

85. *See* https://state-aid.caselex.eu/home (accessed 28 August 2019).
86. *Ibid.*, at 5.

judicial cooperation between national judges applying Union competition law. According to the website of DG Competition, approximately 120 projects have been co-financed as of mid-2018, involving more than 7,000 national judges.[87] However, a recent study shows that the number of judges who may potentially have to deal with State aid rules totals around 16,000 in first instance courts, 5,000 in intermediate instance courts (if applicable) and about 1,200 in last instance courts.[88]

The fact that the Commission has no first-hand views on the private enforcement of State aid rules, as well as the virtual impossibility of reaching every single judge in charge of State aid cases, does not mean that private enforcement is ineffective. The recent judgments of the French courts show that national courts stand ready and are equipped to fulfil their role in the supervision of State aid.

The 2019 Study sheds more light on the current state of play of the application of State aid rules by national courts, including their private enforcement. It highlights best practices and provides insights about the national courts' appreciation of the cooperation tools. While the preparation of the 2019 Study, especially the interviews with judges, may have already proved useful in stimulating a debate at national level about practitioners and judges, its result should help in defining the base for all initiatives designed to improve the recourse to private enforcement and its effectiveness, starting, if necessary, from a revised Commission enforcement notice.

87. *See* http://ec.europa.eu/competition/court/training.html (accessed 2 March 2019).
88. John Coughlan, Wolfgang Heusel et al., *Study on judges' training needs in the field of European competition law* (European Commission 2016), http://ec.europa.eu/competition/publications/reports/kd0416407enn.pdf (accessed 2 March 2019).

CHAPTER 11

Private Enforcement in France

François Lichère

I. Figures and presentation of the French framework for private enforcement of state aid rules
   A. Figures
II. Presentation of the French private enforcement system and its framework
III. Efficiency of the French private enforcement system
   A. Efficient remedies
      1. Standing
      2. Timing of actions
      3. Legal arguments which can be invoked
      4. Power of the courts
      5. Efficiency of recovery actions
      6. Recovery of illegal state aid
   B. Inefficient remedies
      1. Interim measures: conditions and pitfalls
      2. Damages: conditions and practical difficulties
IV. Conclusion

Interestingly, the word 'enforcement', whether being public or private, does not exist in the French language, i.e. no translation is commonly used.[1] Four well-known authors have even used the English phrase 'private enforcement' in three articles written in French.[2] However, the absence of an equivalent French term for private

1. 'Application' or 'execution' are mentioned in dictionaries, but both terms lack legal meanings.
2. M. Karpenschif, *Private enforcement et droit des aides d'État* (2017) 47 La Semaine Juridique Administrations et Collectivités territoriales 2285; *see* also J. Derenne and K. Kaczmare, *La récupération des aides illégales: le rôle du juge national dans le private enforcement du droit des*

enforcement does not imply, in this case,[3] that the concept or the mechanism does not exist. Quite to the contrary, the French system may on its face appear to be quite efficient and maybe even more efficient than other European systems. Yet the question of whether private enforcement is efficient *enough* remains, and this article aims at assessing this efficiency. In the first section, a few figures are given along with the presentation of the framework of the French private enforcement system. In the second section, we will try to assess the efficiency of the different remedies available, including a comparison of the remedies available for competition law where comparison is relevant. Finally, in the conclusion we will assess the combination of all remedies available and briefly consider ways of improving the enforcement of State aid rules in France.

I. FIGURES AND PRESENTATION OF THE FRENCH FRAMEWORK FOR PRIVATE ENFORCEMENT OF STATE AID RULES

A. Figures

In June 2015, the 'Inspection Générale des Finances' – one of the highest civil servant bodies at the government level – issued a quite comprehensive report on the French system of 'contrôle' of State aid, as it is called in French.[4]

The figures were derived from data collected in the year 2013. The data was collected through declarations made by French public authorities in the 'Sari' software program and thanks to the 2013-M-0-16 report made by Demaël Jurgensen and Queyranne in 2013. In 2013, the total amount of State aid reached 110 billion euros, including the 6.5 billion awarded by local authorities; non-selective State aid amounted to 79 billion euros while selective aid reached 31 billion euros. The 31 billion euros were split as follows: 4 billion were awarded to services of general economic interest, 1.3 billion to the agriculture and fishing sectors and 14 billion to railway industries (facilities – 'SNCF reseaux'; and operator – 'SNCF Mobilités'); the rest, i.e. roughly 11 billion euros, was mainly used for overseas programs or postal and telecom pensions. Quite interestingly, the main type of aid consisted of tax reductions.

The 2015 report also evaluates the notifications made to the European Commission between 2000 and 2013: Out of the 476 notifications during this period – which are said to fall within the EU average – only six instances of State aid were declared incompatible with the internal market, representing slightly more than a 1% refusal rate. Amid the six refusals, five concerned aid for undertakings in difficulty. However,

---

aides d'État (2009) 10 ERA Forum 251–268; C. Grynfogel, *Aides d'État – Private enforcement pour les aides d'État, mode d'emploi?* [2018] Contrats Concurrence Consommation no. 5 étude 7.

3. Some argue that the absence of a French equivalent to 'accountability' may imply that French public authorities and French civil servants cannot really be held accountable, despite the existence of Article 15 of the Declaration of the Rights of Man and of the Citizen, which states that '[t]he society has the right of requesting an account from any public agent of its administration'.
4. T. Wahl, J. Thomas, D. Krieff, G. Vanderheyden, Les aides d'Etat, Inspection Générale des Finances, June 2015, www.igf.finances.gouv.fr/files/live/sites/igf/files/contributed/IGF%20 internet/2.RapportsPublics/2015/2014-M-094.pdf (accessed 13 June 2019).

twenty-nine instances of non-notified State aid were declared incompatible out of ninety-three eventually reviewed by the European Commission, equalling approximately a 25% refusal rate for non-notified State aid.

More importantly, the 2015 report evaluates the French system, pointing out some shortcomings. The main one was the quasi non-use of block exemptions: Only five measures per year on average, which is very few compared to the eighty measures implemented in Germany and eighty-nine in Italy. This reluctance of French authorities to use block exemptions is explained by the desire of legal certainty. The report also stressed some internal control deficiencies within the government: insufficient information on State aid rules within ministries and internal expertise disseminated or requested too late. At the local level, the State representatives in charge of overseeing government aid do not seem to consider this control as a priority, their having to check the legality of roughly five million administrative deeds each year.[5] One may also wonder whether State representatives do not face indirect conflicts of interests since they are often in the frontline for finding solutions to avoid bankruptcy or the closing down of important firms.

The report subsequently offers recommendations to the government in order to improve internal public 'control', but it says nothing on private enforcement, either as a solution or as a problem.

These figures have a particular echo in a European context that has been described as not sufficiently efficient in a document titled 'Study on the Enforcement of State aid law at national level', authored in 2006 under the auspices of the European Commission. As stated in the 'Commission notice on the enforcement of State aid law by national courts 2009/C 85/01' that followed it, 'this study was aimed at providing a detailed analysis of private State aid enforcement in different Member States. The Enforcement Study concluded that, in the period between 1999 and 2006, State aid litigation at Member State level had increased significantly. However, the Enforcement Study also revealed that a large number of the legal proceedings at Member State level were not aimed at reducing the anticompetitive effect of the underlying State aid measures. This was because almost two-thirds of the judgments analysed concerned actions brought by taxpayers who sought relief from the allegedly discriminatory imposition of a (tax) burden and actions brought by beneficiaries to challenge the recovery of unlawful and incompatible State aid'.

A personal data search shows that the number of case law decisions at the French level is relatively limited, especially if compared to public procurement awards, this comparison being, in our view, more relevant than in respect of antitrust law. Indeed, there is no public enforcement of State aid rules at the national level, and decisions made by public authorities do not deal with companies' behaviours. The following figures may not be seen as comprehensive since they concern only the administrative

5. The number of administrative deeds sent to the State representative (Préfet) is above five million, divided by 100 State representatives, including overseas, which means that each State representative has on average 50 000 deeds a year to check. *See* https://www.collectivites-locales.gouv.fr/files/files/dgcl_v2/actes/ACTES-EN-CHIFFRES/30-evolutionannuellenbeactestransmisettele transmis_2004-2017.pdf (accessed 13 June 2019).

Supreme Court ('Conseil d'Etat') and include neither the litigation taking place in the administrative courts of first instance (and appeal) nor the cases dealt with by civil courts. Still, the numbers give an idea of the relatively low importance of State aid litigation in quantitative terms: Between 1997 and 2018, 187 cases on State aid reached the administrative Supreme Court, while the latter had to deal with public procurement awards in 740 cases.

The difference is nonetheless easily explainable. As everyone knows, national courts mainly deal with the question of the 'legality' of State aid, i.e. whether a measure is to be classified as new State aid and, as such, whether it should have been notified to the European Commission before being awarded. National courts are not competent to assess the compatibility of State aid with EU law. Moreover, the number of administrative decisions - i.e. decisions taken by public authorities regarding State aid certainly does not amount to the number of public procurement awards decisions, although no data is available. Therefore, the comparison of data regarding the number of litigations in public procurement and state aids may be misleading. Finally, there might also be a less objective reason. Some people may argue that State aids rules - perhaps because compatibility is only assessed at the EU level - are not well known by lawyers, or are at least less known than public procurement rules.

We tend to think that it may also be that private enforcement is structurally insufficient, an idea we hope to demonstrate in the next section.

II. PRESENTATION OF THE FRENCH PRIVATE ENFORCEMENT SYSTEM AND ITS FRAMEWORK

In principle, the private enforcement system on State aid is based on the general rules of national law, as regards both substantive and procedural law. One may notice on the substance that State aid measures undertaken by local authorities are also subject to an additional set of legal rules in order to safeguard national economic interests and, to some extent, to ensure regional leadership as opposed to vesting it in other local authorities ('Départements' and 'Communes').

State aid litigation is brought before administrative courts in principle. However, civil courts may be competent when the aid is awarded by a private body or through certain indirect tax reductions or when a competitor seeks the liability of the beneficiary, all of these situations being quite rare.[6] Consequently, the present report relies mainly on administrative court remedies.

Here are the remedies available before administrative courts:

- Judicial review of unilateral administrative deeds or direct action against public contracts as brought by third parties which can lead to the nullity of both with retroactive effect; both remedies may be accompanied by an order for recovery.
- Possibility of suspension of unilateral deeds or public contracts.

6. *See infra* n. 27 on the *Ducros* case on the unsuccessful damages actions brought by competitors in respect of beneficiaries.

- Damages.

State aid is generally granted through a unilateral deed but sometimes through public contracts which, when signed by public authorities, are usually said to be administrative contracts, i.e. contracts involving the competence of the administrative courts. Most public contracts have such a nature, either by way of legislation – as is the case for public procurement contracts or concession contracts signed by public authorities – or by application of criteria set by the case law of the Conseil d'Etat.

III. EFFICIENCY OF THE FRENCH PRIVATE ENFORCEMENT SYSTEM

The remedies available must be assessed in terms of efficiency notwithstanding the subjective character of this assessment. Some remedies appear to be quite efficient; others much less efficient as will be subsequently seen.

A. Efficient remedies

The first role of national public authorities and more particularly of national courts lies in the classification of actions or measures – or whatever they may be called in practice – which could be deemed as new State aid. The second role lies in the possibility to force public authorities to recover illegal State aid.

Both roles in terms of effectiveness largely depend, by essence through private enforcement, on the ease with which competitors and more generally any third party can challenge a unilateral deed or contract which encapsulates State aid (concession contracts, for instance, may be a source of illegal State aid, especially when the requirements of the *Altmark* case are not met) or challenge refusals of public authorities to recover illegal State aid. One may also notice that public authorities can at any time spontaneously withdraw illegal State aid, i.e. without any challenge.[7]

The fact that no specific remedies have been put in place for administrative courts presents some advantages. Two remedies have proved efficient in responding to illegal State aid: judicial review of unilateral administrative deeds and the direct challenge of administrative contracts. The efficiency of both remedies will be assessed through the issues of standing to bring actions, the timing of actions, the legal arguments which can be invoked, powers of the courts and recovery actions.

1. Standing

Judicial review against unilateral administrative deeds is, for historical reasons, largely open to any parties having an interest, and actions can be brought against almost any deed. Regarding the latter notion, case law permits the challenge of State aid award

7. CAA, 5 October 2004, no. 01PA02717, *Ministre de la Culture-DGA, Société internationale de diffusion et d'édition*; all the case law quoted in this article are available on www.legfirance.gouv.fr (accessed 13 June 2019).

decisions or refusals of recovery or even refusals of notification.[8] Regarding the former, as it is the case for any judicial review, the case law sets a low standard in terms of standing to bring an action seeking judicial review of State aid. In other words, standing rarely represents an obstacle to challenging a unilateral deed comprising State aid. Of course, competitors of the State aid beneficiary always have standing, as the *Ryanair* case has shown, where the Irish airline company and the Strasbourg airport operator, following a claim brought by a competitor, failed to prove that the advantages implemented for Ryanair were the counterpart of 'services' allegedly performed by Ryanair.[9] Of course, the taxpayers responsible for paying a tax funding illegal State aid regimes have standing, and the Conseil d'Etat even ruled in their favour in the famous *GEMO* case after a preliminary ruling from the ECJ.[10] However, the next claim on the same issue, after the relevant French law was changed, was dismissed on the grounds that the new tax was then contributing to the general budget of the French State, which had no link to the illegal State aid awarded to farmers, the 'victims' of the mad cow disease. Interestingly, the Conseil d'Etat went further than the European Court of Justice requirements, making sure that there was no actual link between the tax and the State aid, observing in the process that the amount of taxes did not correspond to the amount of State aid. Had the Conseil d'Etat ruled the opposite, the taxpayers would have had standing to bring an action.[11]

Other interested parties, such as non-governmental organisations, have standing as long as the purpose set in their company articles is related to the activities illegally subsidised or benefiting illegally from any other form of aid.[12]

Moreover, local State representatives always have standing to bring an action to challenge administrative deeds - both unilateral administrative deeds and administrative contracts - before administrative courts as long as they claim they are illegal, as provided by a statute of 2 March 1982.

As for administrative contracts, the Conseil d'Etat created in 2007 a direct remedy opened to competitors, and it extended it in 2014, in the 'Tarn-et-Garonne' case, to any interested third parties having sufficient interest; by doing so the Conseil d'Etat significantly increased the possibility of challenging administrative contracts which include illegal State aid. It remains uncertain whether the standing test for this new remedy is more demanding than for judicial review against unilateral administrative acts, but it does not seem to be very demanding.

8. CE Ass., 7 November 2008, no. 282920, *Comité national des interprofessions des vins à appellation d'origine.*
9. CE, 27 February 2006, no. 264406, *Compagnie Ryanair Limited et CCI de Strasbourg et du Bas-Rhin*, Rec. Leb., 95; Karpenshif, *note* [2006] JCP A no. 1072; Olleon, *concl.* [2006] BJCL no. 6, 407; Eckert, *obs.* [2006] Dr adm., comm. no. 118; Cheynel, *note* [2005] RLC no. 7, comm no. 524; Chérot, *note* [2006] Concurrences no. 2, 130.
10. ECJ, C-126/01 *GEMO SA* [2003] ECR I-13761.
11. CE, 27 July 2009, no. 312098, *Société Boucheries du marché*, with my case law comment: François Lichère, *Aide d'Etat, vache folle et taxe d'équarrissage: la traçabilité s'étend aux circuits de financement* [2009] AJDA 2071.
12. CE, 15 May 2012, no. 324852, *Association 'Vent de colère'*.

2. *Timing of actions*

Regarding the timing of actions, as a general rule claimants must bring their case before administrative courts within a two-month timeframe after the challenged deed has been made public - whether a unilateral deed or an administrative contract. Where publicity was not properly made, challenges were previously not time barred; subsequently, however, the Conseil d'Etat ruled in 2016 that, in order to ensure legal certainty, the challenge must be brought before courts within one year - in principle - following the adoption of the challengeable administrative deed.[13]

3. *Legal arguments which can be invoked*

When it comes to judicial review, any legal arguments can be invoked by the claimant as standing is in effect assessed with regard to the purpose of the challenge and not with regard to the legal arguments put forward. For instance, an environmental association opposed to wind energy managed to have a ruling - stemming from a minister and promoting subsidised renewable energy - nullified by successfully arguing it constituted illegal State aid, this despite the fact that neither the association nor its members would suffer any harm from the illegal State aid award per se.[14]

The situation is slightly different regarding the direct challenge of administrative contracts. If the challenge comes from the local State representative against local administrative contracts or from a member of a local assembly, any legal arguments can be invoked. Other third parties, by contrast, can invoke only breaches from which they have suffered or serious breaches. This is due to the 'sanctity of contract' principle, which is not a so strong a principle but which still has some legal effects. In other words, in order to prevent that a contract is too easily challenged by third parties (apart from the two categories cited above), claimants need to prove the breach results in a specific harm being inflicted on them. Applying this principle to illegal State aid included in an administrative contract means that only competitors are in a position to prove harm from such illegal State aid. For other third parties, they will need to prove that it is a 'serious breach', i.e. one that a court can put forward even if the claimant did not raise the matter.

This brings us to the question, also important for judicial review, of whether the presence of illegal State aid should be considered as a question of 'ordre public', i.e. a question a court must raise on its own even if parties do not raise it. This issue has, to our knowledge, not been ruled on, and it is not yet certain if illegal state aids would be considered as such since it would have probably already said so if it were the case.

13. CE Ass. 13 July 2016, no. 387763, *M. Czabaj*, [2016] Lebon 340; O. Henrard, *concl.*, *ibid.*; Eveillard, *note* [2016] Dr adm., comm. 63; S. Deygas, *comm.* [2016] Procédures, no. 312; Le Bot, *chron.* [2017] JCP A, 2053; Pauliat *note* [2016] JCP A 2238; Xavier Souvignet, *note* [2016] JCP G 1396; Louis Dutheillet de Lamothe, Guillaume Odinet, *Délai de recours: point trop n'en faut* [2016] AJDA, 1629; François Julien-Laferrière, *Le juge n'est pas le législateur* [2016] AJDA 1769.
14. CE, 15 May 2012, no. 324852, *Association 'Vent de colère'*.

There is also no case law which allows a court to reinterpret an Article 107 claim as a 108(3) claim; therefore, such a claim is likely to be dismissed.

4. *Power of the courts*

Regarding judicial review, illegal State aid is likely to be annulled with, as in any annulment by a court, a retroactive effect. Thus, the deed is considered as not having ever existed. Since 2004, administrative courts have been authorised, under exceptional considerations of general interest, to delay the effect of the annulment, which can lead to retroactive effects being avoided.[15] However, it is unlikely that such a power could be used when it comes to illegal State aid, unless the court faces a situation where the ECJ allows it, as in the *CELF* case.[16]

Regarding direct challenge of administrative contracts, the powers of the court are in theory much wider: depending on the nature of the breach, the court can leave the contract as such, invite parties to redress the illegality when possible, terminate the contract or annul it. If the illegality cannot be redressed and the illegality is deemed incompatible with the existence of the contract, the court must terminate the contract, but only if there is no general interest that justifies maintaining the contract. Finally, the contract has to be annulled where its subject matter is illicit or in the event of serious breaches. In addition, damages may be awarded. There is no example thus far of a contract whose object is to award State aid. Regarding contracts with a State aid side-effect, as in concession contracts, two examples are known which led to the annulment of the contract[17] or its termination,[18] thus proving that the clauses at stake were not separable from the rest of the contract.

5. *Efficiency of recovery actions*

One may also assess the efficiency of judicial review or the direct challenge of administrative contracts by taking into account the possibility of order that a court can deliver against public authorities in order to ensure recovery of the illegal State aid. Such orders are widely open to the administrative courts – thanks to the Act of 8 February 1995 – for any administrative court ruling which implies a positive action from a public authority. If the public authority does not abide by the order, the court may also add penalties.

Regarding orders to recover illegal State aid, an interesting example is provided by the follow up to the challenge brought against the French measure of subsidised wind energy as discussed above. In its 2012 ruling, the Conseil d'Etat sent a request for preliminary ruling to the ECJ, which, on 19 December 2013, declared it to be illegal State aid (C-262/12); this ruling was endorsed by the Conseil d'Etat in 2014. The very

15. CE Ass., 11 May 2004, no. 255886, *Association AC !*.
16. ECJ, Case C-1/09 *Centre de l'exportation du livre Français (CELF) v Société international de diffusion et d'édition (SIDE)* [2010] ECR I-2099.
17. CAA Nancy, 13 September 2013, no. 12NC00735, *France telecom*.
18. CE, 25 October 2017, no. 403335, *Corsica ferries*.

same year, the European Commission then ruled in favour of the compatibility of the system. Nonetheless, the Conseil d'Etat issued in 2016 an order to the government to recover the loan-interest costs the beneficiaries of the aid would have incurred had the aid not been awarded (which was in fact awarded through the implementation of the non-notified measure). Not only was the order issued but a penalty of 10,000 euros per day would have to be paid by the government if the recovery was not made in the following six months.

6. *Recovery of illegal state aid*

Regarding the actual recovery of illegal State aid by public authorities, the French system appears to be quite efficient in this regard as well since it does not require the public authority to obtain an order from a court. The public authority has to issue a direct order to the beneficiary of the illegal State aid. Of course, the beneficiary can challenge the order in front of an administrative court, and this challenge used to have suspensive effect. However, this suspensive effect has been excluded by the ECJ as contrary to the effectiveness principle.[19] In another case, the ECJ ruled that 'Article 14(3) of Council Regulation (EC) no. 659/1999 of 22 March 1999 laying down detailed rules for the application of Article [88] of the EC Treaty is to be interpreted as not precluding, in circumstances in which amounts corresponding to the aid in question have already been recovered, annulment by the national court of assessments issued in order to recover the unlawful State aid on grounds of there being a procedural defect, where it is possible to rectify that procedural defect under national law. That provision does, however, preclude those amounts being paid once again, even provisionally, to the beneficiary of that aid.'[20]

If the firm does not make reimbursement, the public authority can seek a court order to seize assets. In November 2018, an airplane of the Ryanair company was seized by the police, and the 526,000 euros Ryanair had refused to reimburse up to that point were paid the following day, resulting in the airplane being promptly released.[21]

The last example, despite its immediate effect, can also be seen as a limit of the system of private enforcement through judicial review or direct challenge of administrative contracts. The low-cost business model of Ryanair relies on contract agreements that are signed with airports operators, usually of modest size, and that feature many advantages secured for the company, these quite obviously constituting illegal State aid, as determined by the Conseil d'Etat in the 2006 case cited above. Nonetheless, since it is in practice mostly only competitors that contest such agreements, some contracts likely go unchallenged because of the sheer number of contracts at stake. A recent case shows that private enforcement may not be efficient enough: The European Commission decided to challenge the same type of agreement put in place for the

19. ECJ, Case C-232/05 *Comission v France* [2006] ECR I-10071.
20. ECJ, Case C-210/09 *Scott SA and Kimberly Clark SAS v Ville d'Orléans* [2010] ECR I-4613.
21. Bruno Trevidic, *Un avion de Ryanair saisi à Bordeaux*, LesEchos, 9 November 2018, https://www.lesechos.fr/09/11/2018/lesechos.fr/0600117045311_un-avion-de-ryanair-saisi-a-bordeaux.htm (accessed 13 June 2019).

Nimes-Garons (south of France) airport years after the agreement was signed.[22] The wide dissemination of such illegalities, through many contracts signed in France and Europe, makes it difficult for private competitors to challenge them, even more so given that challenging illegal State aid is not their core business. More importantly, their knowledge of the existence of such illegal measures may be uncertain, this in spite of the legal requirement to publish aid above EUR 500,000. Indeed, that obligation, implies that public authorities consider the measures as State aid, which is usually not the case regarding illegal State aid.

Another limit to the system efficiency is the recovery of illegal taxes: When taxpayers seek relief from the allegedly illegal tax, they will not seek an order against the public authority to recover the illegal State aid; rather, they will merely ask for the tax to be refunded.

Most importantly, two remedies do not appear to be sufficiently efficient: interim measures and damages.

B. Inefficient remedies

1. Interim measures: conditions and pitfalls

As a general rule, the judicial review (i.e. the challenge of) administrative acts has no suspensive effect. But this shortcoming is somewhat compensated by the possibility of having an administrative court suspend the effect of any administrative deed provided that two conditions are met:

- The court has serious doubt about the legality of the administrative deed.
- There is an urgent need to suspend the effect. This condition is met if the act is seriously harming the interest of the claimant or harming public interest.

There are no other constraints, and in particular, there is no requirement that interim measures be granted only if there is no likelihood that damages will be granted, as is the case in English law.

The question here lies rather in the court's assessment of the two above-described conditions when illegal State aid is at stake.

The 'serious doubt' test is often present in cases of non-notification: Judges can quite easily assess whether there exists a new and unnotified aid even in emergency where the claimant seeks interim relief (called 'référé suspension') which is a procedure which, in practice, takes one to two months of proceedings before the administrative Court of First Instance.

However, the 'urgency' test is problematic: The Conseil d'Etat ruled that non-notification is not per se a matter of urgency;[23] therefore, claimants have to prove either a harm to the public interest or a serious harm to their own interest, which would

22. GC, Case T-53/16, *Ryanair and Airport Marketing Services v Commission* [2018] ECLI: EU:T:2018:943.
23. CE, 2 July 2010, no. 340699, *Société Régional.*

happen only when competitors can prove that State aid compromises their own viability. To our knowledge, this has never been the case. In only one case did the Conseil d'Etat find such an urgency; this was based on a quite unusual situation regarding a decision of an airport operator to grant advantages to low-cost airlines companies after several similar decisions had been quashed. The accumulation of illegal measures led the Conseil d'Etat to rule there was an urgent need to suspend the measures due to the harm posed for the normal effects of competition ('jeu normal de la concurrence').[24] It is the only example of illegal State aid being suspended.

2. *Damages: conditions and practical difficulties*

The award of damages could, in theory, be a good incentive for enforcing State aid rules because of both the potential claim of the beneficiary against the public authorities in the event the aids are declared illegal and the potential claim of competitors against the beneficiary or against the public authority.

However, one may spot practical difficulties for all types of damages claims.

Regarding the claim of the beneficiary against a public authority which illegally granted aid that the beneficiary later had to reimburse, the case law holds that there is in principle no prejudice suffered by the beneficiary for the lost aid and, in particular, that the beneficiary cannot be compensated for the amount it had to reimburse without compromising the rule itself.[25] The only prejudice the illegal beneficiary can claim from the public authority that granted the illegal aid is the cost of a loan made in order to the reimburse the illegal State aid. But even in this case the plaintiff may have to assume part of the cost: In one case, a court let 25% of the costs fall upon the beneficiary for lack of precaution.[26]

Regarding the claim of competitors against beneficiaries, although the Cour de cassation has ruled on this issue on only one occasion, it decided in favour of dismissing the claim on the grounds there was no evidence that the illegal measure was linked to any prejudice.[27] One author recently observed that there have been no positive applications so far.[28]

Finally, regarding damages claim of competitors brought against public authorities, there are also practical difficulties. As in any case of damages based on fault, the evidence of a causal link between the illegal State aid – essentially a fault – and the loss of the competitor is the cornerstone of the action.

When it comes to existing aid later declared incompatible with the internal market by the Commission, the Conseil d'Etat recently ruled that the starting date for

24. CE, 28 July 2009, no. 329819, *Société Air France*.
25. CE, 7 June 2017, no. 386627, *Sté Le Muselet Valentin*.
26. CAA Paris, 23 January 2006, no. 04PA01092, *Société Groupe Salmon Arc-en-ciel;* Pouyaud, *obs.* [2006] JCP A no. 1144; L. Helmlinger, *concl.* [2006] AJDA 766 et Richer, Jeanneney et Charbit, *chron.* [2006] AJDA 1142; M. Disant, *étude* [2007] RFDA 547.
27. Cass. com., 15 June 1999, *Établissements J. Richard Ducros c/ Société Métallique Finsider Sud;* Leclerc, *obs.* [2000] D. 322; [1999] RJDA 818; Europe, January 2000, comm. no. 5, 20.
28. C. Grynfogel, *supra* n. 2.

prejudice is the issuance of the decision of incompatibility by the Commission and not prior to it, which conforms with the presumption that existing aid is compatible.[29]

Regarding illegal State aid, there are many obstacles to or constraints on obtaining damages:

- First, the length of the proceedings: Any damages action – which has to be brought within a four-year time limit – should start with a request for damages sent to the public authority. If the latter explicitly refuses or implicitly refuses (after two months of silence), the petitioner has two months to file a complaint.
- Second, proving harm has been suffered: This generally implies the competitor having to establish that it has had less business than it would normally have experienced in the absence of the illegal State aid. One may argue that business was just decreasing or had simply stopped increasing.
- Last but not least, a claimant has to establish the existence of a link between the prejudice and the illegal State aid.

At first sight, French law may appear as a presenting a desirable model since two ongoing cases have demonstrated that such a link can or may be proved. In the first one, being the consequence of the famous *CELF* case described above, the evidence has not yet been finalised, but the Conseil has foreclosed a Court of Appeal judgment on the grounds that the court had no other alternative than to obtain an expert opinion on the issue in question, administrative courts being based on inquisitorial procedures. The case is still pending before the administrative Court of Appeal of Paris.[30]

The second case – also famous because of the many proceedings before French and European courts (*see* in particular T-454/13) – deals with illegal State aid extended to the SNCM company and challenged by Corsica ferries regarding the sea routes between France and Corsica; it has resulted in the administrative Court of First Instance of Bastia granting damages to Corsica ferries in the amount of 84 million euros. The Marseille court upheld most components of the judgment: on the substitutability of the boat services of the two companies; on the likelihood of customers transferring to Corsica ferries had the illegal subsidies not been granted to SNCF; on the absence of evidence regarding the incapability of Corsica ferries to fill customer needs; on the expert opinion regarding the proportion of customers who would transfer to the competitor and the potential increase in fixed costs in the event of transfer. However, a new review has been ordered to assess the prejudice; the case is still pending and may be brought before the Conseil d'Etat.

In other words, there has been no definitive judgment granting damages on this basis so far. Furthermore, we hold the view that such damages can only be granted in cases of duopolies – as in the case of *CELF* and Corsica ferries. It is only in such a case that a court may be able to assess the likelihood of customers transferring to the claimant, a finding which is difficult to assess when several competitors are involved.

29. CE, 25 October 2018, no. 408789, *Ryanair*.
30. CE, 13 January 2017, no. 382427, *Société internationale de diffusion et d'édition*.

In the case of a company receiving illegal State aid and being awarded a public contract, such as a concession contract or a public procurement contract, it is even more difficult as there are several award criteria at stake: Would the competitor have won the award without the illegal aid, provided that there are usually several award criteria? Interestingly, the Cour de cassation rejected, for this very reason, the damages claim of a competitor brought against the public procurement awardee in the 1999 Ducros case described above.

Even if the courts were to apply the serious chance theory, under which there is a certain margin of uncertainty about the actual link between the fault and the prejudice, it remains uncertain that they would grant damages on a balance of probability since they may lack a minimally (sufficiently) likely link between illegal state aid and prejudice.

Finally, one may wonder if the new Directive 2014/104/EU of 26 November 2014 on certain rules governing actions for damages under national law for infringements of the competition law, provisions of the Member States and of the European Union may be used as a model since it is applicable only for anticompetitive conduct.

This a very unlikely since, as a general principle, administrative judges would not necessarily look at private enforcement in the antitrust law which is applicable before civil courts. This is also confirmed by the CAA Marseille case on Corsica ferries described above: no reference was made to Directive 2014/24 in either the pleadings of the 'rapporteur public' – the equivalent of the advocate general before the ECJ – or even in the lawyers' submissions (from what we have heard). There might be cultural reluctance, but there might also be legal hesitance to extend the new rules set in this directive without a statute saying so – see the examples of a suspension of limitation periods for bringing an action for damages or the presumption of prejudice.

Finally, one may wonder if a grant of damages is impermissible unless there is a decision of incompatibility made by the Commission and not merely a situation of non-notified State aid.

Even if the latter were ruled out, there would remain many obstacles to obtaining damages.

IV. CONCLUSION

Some conclusions may be drawn from the previous sections as a general assessment of private enforcement of State aid in France. Despite the existence of some efficient remedies, as long as interim measures and damages stay as they are, recovery orders occur too late compared to the harm caused to the market. In other words, there is no way to redress the harm inflicted on the competitors since it will take years to have the aid recovered and since competitors are very unlikely to secure damages. It is questionable whether changes to interim measures and damages could be made by a European directive without breaching procedural autonomy. And even if it were so, questions regarding the insufficient publicity of State aids award and the likelihood of competitors being willing to challenge illegal State aid raise some concerns.

The question remains as to whether there is a need for public enforcement at the national level. One may argue that national competition authorities should be competent for assessing the existence of State aids, for block exemptions and for declarations of incompatibility - with powers to investigate - whereas the European Commission could still be competent for assessing compatibility. Such a semi-decentralised system would be compatible with both the principle of procedural autonomy and with the principle of incompatibility of State aid, with the internal market and would be certainly be more efficient than the current system mainly based on private enforcement.

CHAPTER 12
Private Enforcement in Germany

Sebastian Unger & David Hug

I. Introduction: Germany as a late developer in private enforcement
II. Private enforcement of the standstill obligation in Germany
    A. Private enforcement and the dualistic court system
    B. Violation of a subjective right as the procedural bottleneck
    C. Claims for recovery of state aid in typical constellations
        1. State aid granted by administrative acts
        2. State aid granted by private or public law contracts
        3. State aid granted in two stages
    D. Interim measures to safeguard competitors' rights
III. The competitors' information deficit
    A. Transparency obligations under EU law
    B. Rights to information under national law
IV. Competitors' claims for damages
    A. Legal basis under national law
    B. Burden of proof on the claimant
    C. Potential facilitation of evidence
V. Cooperation between the National Courts and the Commission
    A. Deutsche Lufthansa and its general reception in Germany
    B. Coming to terms with Deutsche Lufthansa: the German courts
VI. Conclusion

I. INTRODUCTION: GERMANY AS A LATE DEVELOPER IN PRIVATE ENFORCEMENT

In the field of private enforcement of EU state aid law, Germany is a late developer. For a long time, especially the lower civil courts considered the standstill obligation laid down in Article 108(3) sentence 3 TFEU as not being addressed to individual competitors but only the Member States.[1] It was merely acknowledged that an infringement of the standstill obligation should lead to the invalidity of both private and public law contracts granting state aid.[2] Consequently, competitors could not invoke and, therefore, were unable to enforce the standstill obligation in the national courts by filing a claim for the recovery of state aid or for damages caused by its premature granting. Rather - and in obvious contradiction to the principles laid down especially in the jurisprudence of the European Court of Justice[3] and the Commission's State Aid Action Plan[4] - competitors were explicitly directed to the mere possibility of submitting a complaint to the Commission.[5]

This situation has changed fundamentally. In two landmark decisions handed down in 2011, the Bundesgerichtshof (Federal Court of Justice) has allowed competitors of the beneficiary to invoke an infringement of the standstill obligation in order to claim the recovery of state aid, including interest.[6] Both decisions are widely considered a 'paradigm shift'[7] in private enforcement of EU state aid law in Germany. Indeed, in the wake of the decisions, both the German civil courts and the German administrative courts (which were far less reluctant to support private enforcement from the beginning) have gradually embraced their role in EU state aid law. At the same time, private enforcement in Germany has remained limited to competitors' actions against the granting authority. Every now and then, the Bundesgerichtshof has entertained the idea of the standstill obligation addressing not only the granting authority but also the beneficiary.[8] However, this has not yet led to the actual recognition of competitors' claims against the beneficiaries of unlawful state aid. Indeed, an extension of the standstill obligation's scope to beneficiaries would further intensify the controversial consequences of their failure to verify that state aid was duly notified to the Commission.[9]

1. Oberlandesgericht (OLG) Schleswig, 20 May 2008, 6 U 54/06 [2009] BeckRS, 1231; *see also* OLG Koblenz, 25 February 2009, 4 U 759/07 [2009] BeckRS, 6411.
2. OLG Schleswig, 6 U 54/06, *supra* n. 1.
3. ECJ, Case 120/73 *Lorenz GmbH v Bundesrepublik Deutschland and Others* [1973] ECR 1471, paras 7 et seq.; ECJ, Case 354/90 *Fédération nationale du commerce extérieur des produits alimentaires (FNCE) and Others v France* [1991] ECR I-5505, paras 11 et seq.; ECJ, Case 39/94 *Syndicat français de l'Express international (SFEI) and Others v La Poste and Others* [1996] ECR I-3547, paras 39 et seq.
4. State aid action plan - Less and better targeted state aid: a roadmap for state aid reform 2005–2009 (Consultation document), COM(2005) 107 final (SAAP), para. 55: 'Private litigation in front of national courts could therefore provide increased discipline in the field of state aid'.
5. OLG Koblenz, 4 U 759/07, *supra* n. 1.
6. Bundesgerichtshof (BGH), 10 February 2011, I ZR 136/09 [2011] EuZW 440; BGH, 10 February 2011, I ZR 213/08 [2011] BeckRS, 5517.
7. Andrés Martin-Ehlers, *Drittschutz im Beihilfenrecht – Paradigmenwechsel in der deutschen Rechtsprechung* [2011] EuZW 583, 584 ff.; *see also* Sebastian Unger, '*Subventions- und Beihilfenrecht*' in Reiner Schmidt and Ferdinand Wollenschläger (eds), *Kompendium Öffentliches Wirtschaftsrecht* § 8 para. 96 (5th ed., Springer 2019).
8. BGH, 4 April 2003, V ZR 314/02 [2003] EuZW 444, 445.
9. Under EU law, this does not raise any objections, ECJ, Case 39/94, *SFEI and Others v La Poste and Others*, *supra* n. 3, at para. 75; Klaus Rennert, *Beihilferechtliche Konkurrentenklagen vor deutschen Verwaltungsgerichten* [2011] EuZW 576, 582.

This short historical account of private enforcement of EU state aid law in Germany sounds like a success story. However, the euphoria that followed the 2011 decisions of the Bundesgerichtshof has not led to a private enforcement boom in Germany.[10] This is especially true for damages claims: There is not one reported German case dealing with a competitor's claim for damages. This leads to the question of whether there is room for improvement. Against this background, the national report outlines the legal framework for the private enforcement of the standstill obligation in Germany (II.).[11] Subsequently, it will have a closer look at three major problem areas: the competitors' information deficit (III.), claims for damages (IV.) and the cooperation between the national courts and the Commission (V.).

II. PRIVATE ENFORCEMENT OF THE STANDSTILL OBLIGATION IN GERMANY

A. Private enforcement and the dualistic court system

Germany has a dualistic court system.[12] Consequently, both the civil and the administrative courts are faced with the task of protecting competitors if public authorities grant state aid without duly notifying it to the Commission and, in doing so, infringe the standstill obligation laid down in Article 108(3) sentence 3 TFEU. Jurisdiction largely depends on the design of the aid: If state aid is granted in private law forms, the civil courts decide on the basis of civil law remedies. If state aid is granted in public law forms, it is dealt with by the administrative courts on the basis of public law remedies.[13] However, this is true only for the recovery of unlawful state aid. If the competitor claims damages,[14] jurisdiction always lies with the civil courts, irrespective of whether state aid was granted in private or in public law forms.[15]

---

10. Rennert, *supra* n. 9, at 576; Ulrich Soltész, *Ryanair und Tierkörperbeseitigung – Wendepunkt für beihilferechtliche Konkurrentenklagen?* [2012] EuR 60, 64 et seq.; Ulrich Soltész, *Private Enforcement im EU-Beihilferecht – Noch immer in den Kinderschuhen* [2018] NZKart 553, 553 et seq.
11. This report concentrates on the enforcement of the standstill obligation. However, this is only one (albeit the most important) scenario of private enforcement of EU state aid law. If the Commission's procedure results in a final decision that state aid is incompatible with the internal market and has to be recovered, the competitor's interest shifts from the enforcement of the standstill obligation to the enforcement of the negative decision and the recovery order. Both can be enforced in German courts, *see* OLG Koblenz, 10 June 2013, 6 B 10351/13 [2013] EuZW 677.
12. Peter M. Huber and Michael Guttner, '*§ 127. Zur verfassungsrechtlichen Prägung des Verwaltungsrechtsschutzes im europäischen Rechtsraum*', in Armin von Bogdandy et al. (eds), *Handbuch Ius Publicum Europaeum* para. 9 (vol. 8, C.F. Müller 2019).
13. Neither private nor public law provides specific legislation dealing with private enforcement of EU state aid law. Consequently, competitors are referred to the general legal rules. For an exception, *see* BGH, V ZR 314/02, *supra* n. 8.
14. Below IV.
15. *See* Article 34 of the Basic Law for the Federal Republic of Germany: 'If any person, in the exercise of a public office entrusted to him, violates his official duty to a third party, liability shall rest principally with the state or public body that employs him. In the event of intentional wrongdoing or gross negligence, the right of recourse against the individual officer shall be preserved. The ordinary courts shall not be closed to claims for compensation or indemnity'.

B. Violation of a subjective right as the procedural bottleneck

It is a fundamental principle of German law that individuals can bring an action against unlawful public measures only if they can claim a violation of their rights.[16] Therefore, in order to enforce the standstill obligation in German courts, plaintiffs do not solely have to allege that it confers an individual right on competitors of the beneficiary; they also have to convince the court that they can be qualified as competitors of the beneficiary affected by the state aid.[17] As a consequence, not everyone can claim an infringement of the standstill obligation in court. Rather, this right is limited to competitors of beneficiaries of unlawful state aid.

Against this background, the notion of competitor is of great significance for the scope of private enforcement of EU state aid law. However, the German courts have not yet developed a coherent concept in order to determine the competitors of a beneficiary of state aid. Whereas the Oberlandesgericht (Higher Regional Court) follows a rather restrictive approach and requires competitors to be directly affected by the state aid,[18] the Oberverwaltungsgericht (Higher Administrative Court) Koblenz[19] and the Bundesgerichtshof[20] consider it sufficient if the competitor and the beneficiary share the same group of customers.[21] Therefore, in most cases, competitors will hardly have any problems claiming a potential violation of their rights by the premature granting of state aid not duly notified to the Commission.

C. Claims for recovery of state aid in typical constellations

The legal framework for the recovery of state aid and its private enforcement depend on the nature of the aid, which can be granted in three ways. First and most prominently, it can be granted by an administrative act (1). Second, it can be granted by a private or public law contract (2). In both of these scenarios, the aid is granted in a one-stage procedure. However, it can also be granted in two stages. In this third scenario, an initial administrative act is followed by a contract (3).

16. Wolfgang Kahl, '*§ 74. Grundzüge des Verwaltungsrechts in gemeineuropäischer Perspektive: Deutschland*', in Armin von Bogdandy et al. (eds), *Handbuch Ius Publicum Europaeum* paras 121 et seq. (vol. 5, C.F. Müller 2014).
17. Thomas Schmidt-Kötters, '§ 57. *Rechtsschutz der Wettbewerber des Beihilfeempfängers im Verwaltungsverfahren und vor den Verwaltungsgerichten*', in Martin Heidenhain (ed), *Handbuch des Europäischen Beihilfenrechts* paras 18 et seq. (C.H. Beck 2003).
18. OLG Brandenburg, 21 July 2009, Kart U 1/07 [2010] NJOZ, 208.
19. Oberverwaltungsgericht (OVG) Koblenz, 24 November 2009, 6 A 10113/09 [2010] EuZW 274, 275.
20. BGH, I ZR 136/09, *supra* n. 6, at 442 et seq.; *see* also OLG Frankfurt am Main, 7 February 2018, 4 U 207/17 [2018] BeckRS, 18922.
21. Marc Bungenberg and Matthias Motzkus, *Die Praxis des Subventions- und Beihilfenrechts in Deutschland* [2013] WiVerw 76, 124; Annika Schuhmacher, *Die zunehmende Bedeutung der Rechtsdurchsetzung durch Wettbewerber im Bereich des EU-Beihilfenrechts* [2012] KommJur 179, 182.

1. *State aid granted by administrative acts*

If state aid within the meaning of Article 107(1) TFEU is granted by an administrative act, jurisdiction lies with the administrative courts (section 40(1) sentence 1 of the Code of Administrative Court Procedure). The administrative act violates the standstill obligation if it is issued before the Commission has reached a final decision. Therefore, it is unlawful. However, according to German administrative law, it is not void.[22] Rather, it has to be rescinded by the courts (section 113(1) sentence 1 of the Code of Administrative Court Procedure). Therefore, the competitor has to request the rescission by means of a rescissory action (section 42(1) of the Code of Administrative Court Procedure). As stated above, the action is admissible only if the competitor claims that his rights have been violated by the administrative act (section 42(2) of the Code of Administrative Court Procedure). As the administrative courts (1) consider the standstill obligation as safeguarding not only competition in general but also the individual competitors[23] and (2) follow a rather broad concept of competitor,[24] in most cases this hardly proves to be an obstacle. In principle, rescissory actions have to be lodged within one month (section 74(1) of the Code of Administrative Court Procedure). However, this applies only if the administrative act has been notified to the plaintiff. Otherwise, the deadline period is not initiated. Administrative acts granting state aid are regularly notified only to the beneficiary. Therefore, in principle, there is no deadline period for competitors' actions. A ruling of the Bundesverwaltungsgericht (Federal Administrative Court) which, nonetheless, allowed competitors to lodge actions only within one year,[25] was overturned by the Bundesverfassungsgericht (Federal Constitutional Court), according to which forfeiture of the competitors' right to lodge an action against the granting of unlawful state aid does not follow a rigid time table.[26]

If the administrative court rescinds the administrative act (section 113(1) sentence 1 of the Code of Administrative Court Procedure), the implemented state aid is without legal grounds and, therefore, can be recovered by the granting authority. The competitor can claim this recovery.[27] Procedurally, it can be enforced together with the rescissory claim: If an administrative act has already been executed, the Code of Administrative Court Procedure allows the court to 'state on request that and how the administrative authority has to countermand execution' section 113(1) sentence 2 of the Code of Administrative Court Procedure).

As to objections raised by the beneficiary of state aid against its recovery, the European Court of Justice acknowledges that 'there may be exceptional circumstances in which it would be inappropriate to order repayment of the aid' and points to 'circumstances on the basis of which [the beneficiary] had legitimately assumed the aid

22. Unger, *supra* n. 7, at § 8 para. 72.
23. Above I.
24. Above II.B.
25. Bundesverwaltungsgericht (BVerwG), 16 December 2010, 3 C 44/09 [2011] EuZW 269, 270 et seq.
26. Bundesverfassungsgericht (BVerfG), 29 October 2015, 2 BvR 1493/11 [2016] NVwZ 238, 241.
27. OVG Koblenz, 6 A 10113/09, *supra* n. 19, at 277.

to be lawful' and, therefore, 'is not precluded [...] from declining to refund that aid'.[28] However, the scope of this objection is rather limited, as the European Court of Justice considers the beneficiary to be obliged to inform himself about the Member State having duly notified the aid to the Commission. If he fails to do so, he cannot legitimately assume the aid to be lawful.[29] Against this background, the European Court of Justice's reference to 'exceptional circumstances' is clearly overstretched by the administrative courts if they refrain from ordering the recovery of unlawful state aid because it 'has not significantly affected the market situation in favour of the beneficiary' and, therefore, its recovery 'would not have an effect on competition'.[30] Moreover, this is hardly in line with the Procedural Regulation, which limits the Commission's power to adopt 'recovery injunctions' to cases in which (1) 'there is a serious risk of substantial and irreparable damage to a competitor' and, therefore, (2) there is 'an urgency to act' (Article 13(2) of the Procedural Regulation), but which does not limit the national courts' power to recover state aid implemented in breach of the standstill obligation.[31] In fact, according to the Commission and the European Court of Justice '[t]he essential role played by national courts [...] also stems from the fact that the Commission's own powers to protect competitors [...] against unlawful aid are limited'. It is therefore up to the national courts to compensate for the Commission's limited power to enforce the standstill obligation. This implies little room for manoeuvre.

2. *State aid granted by private or public law contracts*

If state aid within the meaning of Article 107(1) TFEU is granted by a contract – a prominent example is the sale of property below market value – without having been duly notified to the Commission, the courts and most scholars[32] consider the contract void as it violates the standstill obligation laid down in Article 108(3) sentence 3 TFEU (section 134 of the Civil Code, which according to section 59(1) of the Administrative Procedure Act applies mutatis mutandis to public law contracts).[33] As a consequence, the implemented state aid is without legal grounds and, therefore, can be recovered by the granting authority. The competitor can claim this recovery and can enforce the

28. ECJ, Case 199/06 *Centre d'exportation du livre français (CELF) and Ministre de la Culture et de la Communication v Société internationale de diffusion et d'édition (SIDE) I* [2008] ECR I-469, paras 42 et seq.; *see* also Gerhard Wagner, *'Die zivilrechtliche Durchsetzung des Europäischen Beihilferechts – Enforcement außer Rand und Band?'* in Thomas Ackermann and Johannes Köndgen (eds), *Privat- und Wirtschaftsrecht in Europa. Festschrift für Wulf-Henning Roth zum 70. Geburtstag* 665, 672 et seq. (C.H. Beck 2015).
29. Unger, *supra* n. 7, at § 8 para. 74; Wagner, *supra* n. 28, at 672 et seq.
30. OVG Koblenz, 6 A 10113/09, *supra* n. 19, at 277 et seq.
31. Rennert, *supra* n. 9, at 583.
32. Other scholars consider the contract to be merely transitorily invalid and to become valid as soon as the Commission has reached a positive decision. For this approach, *see* Wolfgang Kahl, *35 Jahre Verwaltungsverfahrensgesetz – 35 Jahre Europäisierung des Verwaltungsverfahrensrechts* [2011] NVwZ 449, 453; Unger, *supra* n. 7, at § 8 para. 75.
33. BGH, V ZR 314/02, *supra* n. 8, at 444 et seq.; OVG Berlin-Brandenburg, 18 February 2015, OVG 6 B 24/14 [2015] BeckRS, 43054; OVG Berlin-Brandenburg, 18 December 2017, OVG 6 B 3/17 [2018] EuZW 323, 324.

claim in the national courts. In the case of a private law contract, the claim is based on private law (section 823(2) and section 1004(1) of the Civil Code),[34] and jurisdiction lies with the civil courts.[35] In the case of a public law contract, the claim is based on public law, and jurisdiction lies with the administrative courts. In both cases there is no procedural time limit for bringing the claim to court. However, the standard limitation period of three years applies (section 195 of the Civil Code).[36]

As the beneficiary can only raise objections against the recovery of state aid in the rare and rather exceptional case that he had legitimately assumed the aid to be lawful,[37] the granting authority will usually not be in a position to defend itself against a competitor's claim for the recovery of state aid by pointing to its actual or legal impossibility. Whereas the administrative courts tend to overstretch the possibility of 'exceptional circumstances' mentioned by the European Court of Justice,[38] the civil courts follow a rather narrow approach.[39]

3. *State aid granted in two stages*

The legal situation becomes more complex if state aid is granted in two stages. In these cases, the granting authority first issues an administrative act in which it decides to grant state aid. Subsequently, the granting authority itself or an intermediary third party, such as a bank, implements the aid by concluding a private or public law contract with the beneficiary.[40] If this happens in violation of the standstill obligation, the administrative act is unlawful and can be rescinded by the administrative courts following a competitor's rescissory action (section 113(1) sentence 1 of the Code of Administrative Court Procedure). However, this does not automatically affect the validity of the contract (at the second stage), which makes it difficult for a competitor to claim the recovery of the aid as the contract still provides a legal basis for the aid. Moreover, if the administrative act (at the first stage) is followed by a private law contract (at the second stage), jurisdiction for the rescission of the administrative act and for the order of recovery is divided between the administrative and the civil courts. Against this background, scholars have put forward the idea of a closer legal link between the administrative act and the contract. As a consequence, the rescission of

34. Section 823(2) of the Civil Code requires 'a breach of a statute that is intended to protect another person'. This statute is Article 108(3) sentence 3 TFEU, which is infringed if state aid is granted without having been notified to the Commission or before the Commission has reached a final decision, *see* BGH, I ZR 136/09, *supra* n. 6; BGH, I ZR 213/08, *supra* n. 6.
35. Wagner, *supra* n. 28, at 674 et seq.
36. BGH, I ZR 136/09, *supra* n. 6, at 444; BGH, I ZR 213/08, *supra* n. 6, at para. 47; Martin Kellner, *Auswirkungen der Schuldrechtsreform auf die Verjährung im Staatshaftungsrecht* [2002] NVwZ 395, 396 et seq.
37. Above II.C.1; BGH, I ZR 136/09, *supra* n. 6, at 444; BGH, V ZR 314/02, *supra* n. 8, at 446; BGH, 20 January 2004, XI ZR 53/03 [2004] EuZW 252, 253 et seq.; Wagner, *supra* n. 28, at 672 et seq.
38. Above II.C.1.
39. BGH, I ZR 213/08, *supra* n. 6, at para. 45.
40. Bungenberg and Motzkus, *supra* n. 21, at 98.

the administrative act would (as a condition subsequent) lead to the invalidity of the contract and enable the competitor to claim the recovery of the aid.[41]

D. Interim measures to safeguard competitors' rights

The European Court of Justice requires national courts 'to adopt safeguard measures' if 'there is no doubt regarding the classification as State aid, [...] the aid is about to be, or has been, implemented, and [...] no exceptional circumstances have been found which would make recovery inappropriate'.[42] In doing so, the courts 'may order either the repayment of the aid with interest or [...] the placement of the funds on a blocked account so that they do not remain at the disposal of the recipient, without prejudice to the payment of interest for the period between the expected implementation of the aid and its placement on that blocked account'.[43]

Although the German courts have repeatedly pointed to the possibility of interim measures to safeguard competitors' rights in view of an infringement of the standstill obligation,[44] and both German private law (in sections 935 et seq. of the Code of Civil Procedure) and German public law (in sections 80 et seq. and 123 of the Code of Administrative Court Procedure) provide a sound legal basis to grant such measures,[45] there are hardly any cases in which a party has even applied for interim measures. Therefore, there is no case law on the issue.[46] One of the reasons for this might be section 945 of the Code of Civil Procedure,[47] according to which the party that has obtained the order for an interim measure has to compensate the opponent for the damages that he has suffered as a result of the measure if the order proves to have been unfounded from the start or is repealed.[48] However, the greater impediment for an effective use of interim measures seems to be the competitors' information deficit: If competitors learn of Member State measures that might constitute unlawful state aid under Article 107(1) TFEU at all, they often do so only after their implementation and therefore at a stage too late for interim measures.

41. Rennert, *supra* n. 9, at 579 et seq.
42. ECJ, Case 1/09, *Centre de l'exportation du livre français (CELF) and Ministre de la Culture et de la Communication v Société international de diffusion et d'édition (SIDE) II* [2010] ECR I-2099, para. 36.
43. ECJ, Case 1/09, *CELF and Ministre de la Culture et de la Communication v SIDE II*, *supra* n. 42, at para. 37.
44. BVerwG, 3 C 44/09, *supra* n. 25, at 270; BGH, XI ZR 53/03, *supra* n. 37, at 253.
45. Marc Bungenberg, '*Rechtsschutz im Beihilfenrecht*', in Ulrich Immenga and Ernst-Joachim Mestmäcker (eds), *Wettbewerbsrecht* paras 66 et seq. (vol. 3, 5th ed., C.H. Beck 2016).
46. For a rare example, *see* Verwaltungsgericht (VG) Berlin, 26 April 2012, VG 20 L 91/12 [2012] BeckRS, 50876; for interim measures in order to safeguard competitors' rights in view of a negative decision and a parallel recovery order, *see* also OLG Koblenz, 6 B 10351/13, *supra* n. 11.
47. Section 123(3) of the Code of Administrative Court Procedure refers to the provision.
48. Ulrich Soltész, *Private Rechtsdurchsetzung durch Wettbewerber im europäischen Beihilferecht – Vision oder Illusion?* [2006] ZWeR 388, 392 et seq.

III. THE COMPETITORS' INFORMATION DEFICIT

The competitors' information deficit is a major impediment to private enforcement of competition law in general.[49] State aid law is no exception in this respect.[50] In order to enforce the standstill obligation in front of national courts (and – before that – in order to decide to do so), competitors need sufficient information on Member State measures that might constitute unlawful state aid under Article 107(1) TFEU. The reluctance of the Commission (and the European Court of Justice) to grant a right of access to documents in the hands of the Commission[51] increases the pressure on the Member States to ensure a sufficient level of information.[52]

A closer look at the competitors' information deficit reveals that access to information on the concrete design of measures that might constitute unlawful state aid plays a secondary role. The competitors' primary objective is to find out about the sheer existence of such measures.[53] Therefore, the Member States' subsidisation practice needs to be sufficiently transparent. This leads to transparency obligations under EU law (A) and to rights to information under national law (B).

A. Transparency obligations under EU law

EU law already provides for transparency in Article 9 of the General Block Exemption Regulation and – more importantly – in the Commission's transparency communication from 2014.[54] According to this communication 'Member States shall, as a condition for granting aid in line with the relevant guidelines, establish comprehensive State aid websites, at regional or national level, for the publication of information on aid measures and their beneficiaries. [...] The transparency requirement applies in general to all State aid, except for smaller aid awards of less than EUR 500,000'.[55] Article 9 of the Block Exemption Regulation contains a corresponding publication requirement for state aid exempted from the notification requirement.

49. On the competitors' information deficit in general, *see* Michael Bakowitz, *Informationsherrschaft im Kartellrecht*, 29 et seq. (Nomos 2018); Wolfgang Mederer, *Richtlinienvorschlag über Schadensersatzklagen im Bereich des Wettbewerbsrechts* [2013] EuZW 847, 849 et seq.
50. Marc Bungenberg and Matthias Motzkus, '*Länderbericht Bundesrepublik Deutschland*', in Alexander Birnstiel et al. (eds), *Europäisches Beihilfenrecht* para. 149 (Nomos 2013); Fernando Pastor-Merchante, *The Role of Competitors in the Enforcement of State Aid Law*, 75 (Hart 2017); Soltész, *supra* n. 48, at 392 et seq.
51. ECJ, Case 139/07 P, *Commission v Technische Glaswerke Ilmenau GmbH* [2010] ECR I-5885, para. 58.
52. Ulrich Soltész, *Die Rechtsprechung der Unionsgerichte zum Beihilferecht im Jahre 2010* [2011] EuZW 541, 546.
53. Bungenberg and Motzkus, *supra* n. 21, at 132.
54. Communication from the Commission amending the Communications from the Commission on EU Guidelines for the application of State aid rules in relation to the rapid deployment of broadband networks, on Guidelines on regional State aid for 2014–2020, on State aid for films and other audiovisual works, on Guidelines on State aid to promote risk finance investments and on Guidelines on State aid to airports and airlines (Transparency Communication) [2014] OJ C 198/30.
55. Transparency Communication, *supra* n. 54, at 31.

In view of these transparency obligations, competitors can search a database[56] for notifiable and exempted state aid in certain regions, certain economic sectors and for certain enterprises, provided of course that the Member States do not refrain from publicising a measure because they incorrectly do not consider it to be state aid within the meaning of Article 107(1) TFEU. This is the blind spot of any transparency obligation under EU law. It can be remedied by additional transparency obligations under national law which are not limited to state aid within the meaning of Article 107(1) TFEU but apply also to other aid measures.[57]

B. Rights to information under national law

If a competitor has found out about the existence of a measure he believes to constitute unlawful state aid, he can invoke rights to information under national law against the granting authority in order to gain information on the nature and legal basis of the measure and to prepare a claim for recovery or even damages. German law offers a variety of legal instruments to do so.

First, freedom of information legislation on the federal level and in thirteen of the sixteen Länder grants an unconditional right to access official information from all public authorities performing administrative tasks under public or private law.[58] This right extends to the granting of state aid.[59] Although, with regard to business secrets,[60] the right to access official information exists only 'to the extent that the concerned party has consented', this limitation is hardly a legal basis for refusing access to information: First, the key data of state aid does not allow any direct conclusions on the economic situation of the beneficiary.[61] And second, the data has to be publicised under the transparency obligations laid down in EU law anyway.

With the rise of the freedom of information legislation, the rather conventional right to inspect files has become less important. It remains relevant where, as it is the case in three of the sixteen Länder (Bavaria, Lower Saxony and Saxony), there is no freedom of information legislation.[62] However, the right to inspect files is subject to strict conditions: According to the Administrative Procedure Acts, it applies only to administrative procedures (and, therefore, not to constellations in which state aid is

56. Available at https://webgate.ec.europa.eu/competition/transparency/public?lang=de (accessed 15 November 2019).
57. *See* section 3(1)(No. 14) of the Hamburg Transparency Act, according to which the Hamburg authorities are required to publish information on the granting of subsidies and allowances.
58. Elke Gurlit, *Informationsfreiheit in Deutschland* [2007] Die Verwaltung 441, 441 et seq.; Friedrich Schoch, *Informationsfreiheitsgesetz,* 88 et seq. and 113 et seq. (2nd ed., C.H. Beck 2016).
59. Soltész, *supra* n. 52, at 546.
60. Friedrich Schoch, *Aktuelle Entwicklungen im Informationsfreiheitsrecht nach dem IFG des Bundes* [2013] NVwZ 1033, 1039.
61. Bungenberg and Motzkus, *supra* n. 50, at para. 149.
62. On the relationship between the right to access information under freedom of information law and the right to inspect files under general administrative law, *see* Dieter Kallerhoff and Thomas Mayen, in Paul Stelkens et al. (eds), *Verwaltungsverfahrensgesetz* § 29 VwVfG paras 21 et seq. (9th ed., C.H. Beck 2018).

granted under private law), expires with the conclusion of the procedure and can only be invoked by participants in the procedure.[63]

In addition to these written rights to information (which are independent from a competitors' action), at least the civil courts consider competitors to be entitled to obtain information from the granting authority in order to substantiate a parallel claim for recovery or damages.[64]

Against this background, it can be stated that – at least in theory – the competitors have sufficient rights to information at hand. However, practitioners see room for improvement.

IV. COMPETITORS' CLAIMS FOR DAMAGES

In EU law and particularly in EU competition law, individuals' claims for damages and, subsequently, the award of damages by national courts are well-established instruments to ensure that EU law takes full effect and that the rights it confers on individuals are protected.[65]

In *Courage* the European Court of Justice stressed that '[t]he full effectiveness of Article 85 of the Treaty [...] would be put at risk if it were not open to any individual to claim damages for loss caused to him by a contract or by conduct liable to restrict or distort competition. Indeed, the existence of such a right strengthens the working of the Community competition rules and discourages agreements or practices, [...] which are liable to restrict or distort competition. From that point of view, actions for damages before the national courts can make a significant contribution to the maintenance of effective competition in the Community'.[66] This applies not only to antitrust law but also to state aid law.[67] Accordingly, the European Court of Justice[68] and the Commission have repeatedly pointed competitors to the possibility of claiming 'compensation for damage caused [...] by [...] unlawful state aid [...] under national law'.[69]

Contrary to these stipulations, claims for damages are of no relevance in the German private enforcement regime.[70] There is not a single reported case in which a competitor of a beneficiary tried to claim compensation for harm caused by a breach of the standstill obligation or for unlawful state aid in general. This is not because there

63. Kallerhoff and Mayen, *supra* n. 62, at § 29 VwVfG para. 1.
64. BGH, I ZR 136/09, *supra* n. 6, at 445; BGH, 21 July 2011, I ZR 209/09 [2012] GRUR-RR 157, 160; OLG Schleswig, 8 April 2015, 6 U 54/06 [2015] BeckRS, 9177.
65. Jens-Uwe Franck, *Marktordnung durch Haftung* 1 et seq. (Mohr Siebeck 2016); on the individual's role in law enforcement in general, *see* Johannes Masing, *Die Mobilisierung des Bürgers für die Durchsetzung des Rechts* 13 et seq. (Duncker & Humblot 1997).
66. ECJ, Case 453/99, *Courage Ltd and Crehan* [2001] ECR-I, 6297, paras 26 et seq.
67. Pastor-Merchante, *supra* n. 50, at 75 et seq.
68. ECJ, Case 199/06, *CELF and Ministre de la Culture et de la Communication v SIDE I, supra* n. 28, at paras 53 and 55.
69. Commission notice on the enforcement of State aid law by national courts [2009] OJ C 85/1, at paras 43 et seq.
70. Martin Ebers, *Rechte, Rechtsbehelfe und Sanktionen im Unionsprivatrecht,* 684 (Mohr Siebeck 2016); Ulrich Soltész, *Private Enforcement im EU-Beihilferecht – Noch immer in den Kinderschuhen* [2018] NZKart 553, 553.

is no legal basis for such claims (A). Rather, the problem of proving harm remains unresolved and seems to deter competitors (B and C).

A. Legal basis under national law

In its notice on the enforcement of state aid law by national courts, the Commission points to 'the "*Francovich*" and "*Brasserie du Pecheur*" jurisprudence' of the European Court of Justice which 'confirms that Member States are required to compensate for loss and damage caused to individuals as a result of breaches of Community law for which the state is responsible'.[71] Against this background, the national courts are required to award damages under national law where (1) the rule of EU law infringed is intended to confer rights on individuals, (2) the breach is sufficiently serious and (3) there is a direct causal link between the breach and the damage suffered. Accordingly, the Bundesgerichtshof acknowledges a claim for damages caused by a sufficiently serious breach of EU law intended to confer rights on individuals.[72] As the German civil courts – after initial reluctance – consider the standstill obligation as conferring rights on competitors, there is no doubt that this claim (which pursuant to German procedural law can be asserted in the civil courts only) covers harm caused by unapproved state aid.

B. Burden of proof on the claimant

However, according to German procedural law, the burden of proof is on the claimant.[73] Therefore, the competitor has to prove that the violation of the standstill obligation is sufficiently serious and that it has caused financial damage. Usually, this requires the judge to be fully convinced of a breach of the standstill obligation and a causal relationship between the implementation of state aid prior to its approval and the competitor's financial loss. It is not sufficient that the judge considers this only to be probable.[74]

Whereas in most cases competitors will easily be able to prove a sufficiently serious breach of the standstill obligation[75] (which does not vest the granting authority with any discretion as to whether state aid has to be notified or not), it is widely considered practically impossible to convince the judge that a financial loss was caused by the violation of the standstill obligation and not by other factors such as, in

71. 2009 Enforcement Notice, *supra* n. 69, at para. 45.
72. BGH, 24 October 1996, III ZR 127/91 [1997] NJW 123, 124; BGH, 4 June 2009, III ZR 144/05 [2009] EuZW 865, 866 et seq.
73. Natascha Sasserath, *Schadensersatzansprüche von Konkurrenten zur Effektivierung der Beihilfenkontrolle?*, 192 (Duncker & Humblot 2001).
74. Hanns Prütting, in Thomas Rauscher and Wolfgang Krüger (eds), *Münchener Kommentar zur Zivilprozessordnung mit Gerichtsverfassungsgesetz und Nebengesetzen* § 286 ZPO paras 35 et seq. (vol. 1, 5th ed., C.H. Beck 2016).
75. Bungenberg, *supra* n. 45, at para. 89; Schuhmacher, *supra* n. 21, at 182.

particular, a general lack of competitiveness.[76] In its notice on the enforcement of state aid law by the national courts, even the Commission admits that 'damage assessments' are 'complicated [...] where [– and this is the typical case –] the aid merely leads to an overall loss of market share'.[77] And even if the beneficiary has 'w[o]n over a contract or a specific business opportunity from the claimant',[78] it usually remains unclear whether the unlawful aid or the quality of his offer enabled him to do so.

C. Potential facilitation of evidence

This leads to the question of whether the proving of harm can be facilitated. In its notice on the enforcement of state aid law by the national courts, the Commission points to 'national procedural rules'.[79] Indeed, German procedural law facilitates proof if 'the issue of whether or not damages have occurred, and the amount of the damage [...] to be reimbursed, [is] in dispute among the parties'.[80] The Bundesgerichtshof has generously resorted to this facilitation in order to award damages in antitrust cases and – thereby – to refrain from putting the full effectiveness of EU antitrust law at risk.[81] In addition to this, the civil courts have allowed prima facie evidence to prove harm resulting from infringements of antitrust law.[82] This prima facie evidence is based on the economic assumption that infringements of antitrust law typically lead to higher market prices and, therefore, inflict financial harm upon direct purchasers.[83] The infringer can rebut the evidence only by fully convincing the judge of an atypical course of events.[84]

The interesting question is whether this facilitation of proof established under national law should be transferred to state aid law in order to enhance the effectiveness of competitors' claims for damages. This doctrinal question is linked to the political question of whether state aid law – in analogy to Article 17(2) of the Cartel Damages Directive – requires a rebuttable presumption of harm caused by a breach of the standstill obligation. Under such a presumption a claimant would only have to prove that he is a competitor of the beneficiary in order to substantiate his claim for damages.

However, a rebuttable presumption of harm (and even a mere facilitation of proof) is justified only if, on the basis of empirical data, state aid not only regularly but nearly always inflicts financial harm upon the beneficiary's competitors. This is highly questionable. According to Article 107(1) TFEU, state aid granted by a Member State is 'incompatible with the internal market' also where it merely 'threatens to distort

76. Ulrich Soltész, *Der Rechtsschutz des Konkurrenten gegen gemeinschaftsrechtswidrige Beihilfen vor nationalen Gerichten* [2001] EuZW 202, 206; Unger, *supra* n. 7, at § 8 para. 97.
77. 2009 Enforcement Notice, *supra* n. 69, at para. 49.
78. 2009 Enforcement Notice, *supra* n. 69, at para. 49.
79. 2009 Enforcement Notice, *supra* n. 69, at para. 51.
80. Section 287(1) sentence 1 of the German Code of Civil Procedure.
81. BGH, 12 July 2016, KZR 25/14 [2016] NZKart 436, 440.
82. René Galle, *Der Anscheinsbeweis in Schadensersatzfolgeklagen – Stand und Perspektiven* [2016] NZKart 214, 214; Thomas Thiede and Tim Träbing, *Praxis des Anscheinsbeweises im Kartellschadensersatzrecht – ein Rechtsprechungsbericht* [2016] NZKart 422, 422.
83. OLG Karlsruhe, 31 July 2013, 6 U 51/12 (Kart.) [2014] NZKart 366, 367.
84. Galle, *supra* n. 82, at 218.

competition' but has not yet actually distorted it. Against this background, the Commission and the European courts have largely isolated the notion of state aid from an actual impairment of competitors.[85] Consequently, the mere finding of state aid under Article 107(1) TFEU hardly provides a sustainable basis to conclude that competitors of the beneficiary have suffered harm.[86] A statutory presumption of harm is therefore not justified. In any case, such a presumption would have to be carefully tailored to situations in which a causal relationship between the implementation of state aid and financial harm to competitors is established. This shows that one cannot simultaneously have both a wide notion of state aid and a presumption of harm caused by it. Apart from this, the total lack of even attempts to claim damages caused by unapproved state aid raises the question whether claims for damages are actually a suitable instrument to ensure the full effectiveness of EU state aid law.

V. COOPERATION BETWEEN THE NATIONAL COURTS AND THE COMMISSION

The standstill obligation is violated only if the contested measure constitutes state aid within the meaning of Article 107(1) TFEU. Therefore, the idea of the enforcement of the standstill obligation by the national courts implies that they have the power to interpret the notion of state aid. Accordingly, the German courts consider themselves entitled (and obligated) to decide autonomously whether a measure falls within the scope of Article 107(1) TFEU or not.[87]

In doing so, they have displayed a certain reluctance to admit the Commission to their proceedings beyond the Commission's statutory right to submit written observations to the court. Only recently, a lower civil court refused to subpoena the Commission as the court considered its decision not to affect the legal interests of the Commission.[88] In the light of the principle of effectiveness (and the idea of a mutual duty of loyal cooperation as entertained in the Procedural Regulation) this reservedness is not necessarily convincing. It displays a general unease among German courts about the idea of cooperating with an administrative body when reaching a judicial decision.[89] This unease comes to light in the discussion about the effect that Commission decisions after a preliminary examination have on national court proceedings.

A. Deutsche Lufthansa and its general reception in Germany

Both German scholars and courts have for a long time rejected a binding effect of decisions under Article 4 of the Procedural Regulation. They mainly put forward three

85. Ernst-Joachim Mestmäcker and Heike Schweitzer, in Ulrich Immenga and Ernst-Joachim Mestmäcker (eds), *Wettbewerbsrecht* Article 107 Abs. 1 AEUV paras 306 et seq. (vol. 3, 5th ed., C.H. Beck 2016).
86. For a different notion, *see* Schuhmacher, *supra* n. 21, at 182 et seq.
87. BVerwG, 26 October 2016, 10 C 3/15 [2017] EuZW 355, 357; BGH, I ZR 136/09, *supra* n. 6, at 445 et seq.
88. OVG Berlin-Brandenburg, 7 August 2017, OVG 6 B 3/17.
89. *See* BGH, 9 February 2017, I ZR 91/15 [2017] EuZW 312, 314.

arguments: (1) the provisional nature of decisions after a merely preliminary examination, (2) the limited procedural and judicial rights of the beneficiary and (3) the independence of the judiciary from the executive.[90] Against the background of the decision handed down by the European Court of Justice in the case *Deutsche Lufthansa* in 2013, this understanding of preliminary Commission decisions and its effect on national court proceedings is no longer an option.

In *Deutsche Lufthansa*, the European Court of Justice does not explicitly hold that Commission decisions after a preliminary examination are binding on national courts. However, it requires the courts to duly taken them into account: 'Where they entertain doubts as to whether the measure at issue constitutes state aid [...] or as to the validity or interpretation of the decision to initiate the formal examination procedure, national courts may seek clarification from the Commission and [...] they may or must refer a question to the Court for a preliminary ruling'.[91] The German courts have considerable problems coming to terms with these instructions. Recently, both the Bundesverwaltungsgericht[92] and the Bundesgerichtshof[93] were given the chance to adjust their approach to the European Court of Justice's jurisprudence.

B. Coming to terms with Deutsche Lufthansa: the German courts

Whereas the Bundesgerichtshof was faced with a 'decision to open the formal investigation procedure', the Bundesverwaltungsgericht had to deal with a 'decision not to raise objections'. Both courts consider themselves not to be absolutely and unconditionally bound by the Commission's decision. In line with the European Court of Justice pointing them to the possibility of seeking clarification from the Commission and – subsequently – the European Court of Justice if they are in doubt as to whether a measure constitutes state aid, they claim a right to assess themselves whether this is the case or not. This right is not disputed by the European Court of Justice. Even the validity of a 'positive decision' after a formal investigation procedure can be questioned by the national courts in order to refer it to the European Court of Justice for a preliminary ruling. The interesting question, therefore, is not whether the national courts have the power to interpret the notion of state aid but rather how to proceed if their assessment deviates from that of the Commission under Article 4 of the Procedural Regulation.

The Bundesverwaltungsgericht points to the usually 'obvious' and (even in the case of new findings) 'not excluded' possibility of referring the case back to the

90. BGH, I ZR 91/15, *supra* n. 89, at 314; BVerwG, 10 C 3/15, *supra* n. 87, at 357 et seq.; *see* also Andrés Martin-Ehlers, *Die Bindungswirkung einer Eröffnungsentscheidung der Kommission im Beihilferecht* [2014] EuZW 247; Ulrich Soltész, *Die Entwicklung des europäischen Beihilferechts im Jahr 2013* [2014] EuZW 89; Georg M Berrisch, *Mehr Fragen als Antworten – Keine Klärung der 'Bindungswirkung' von beihilferechtlichen Eröffnungsentscheidungen der Kommission* [2014] EuZW 253; Tobias Traupel and Carsten Jennert, *Der EuGH überdehnt die Bindungswirkung der Verfahrenseröffnung im Beihilferecht: Wo die Kommission keinen Verstoß festgestellt hat, kann das nationale Gericht auch nicht gebunden sein* [2014] EWS 1.
91. ECJ, Case 284/12 *Deutsche Lufthansa* [2013] ECLI:EU:C:2013:755, para. 44.
92. BVerwG, 10 C 3/15, *supra* n. 87.
93. BGH, I ZR 91/15, *supra* n. 89.

Commission for clarification and – subsequently – the European Court of Justice for a preliminary ruling. However, it does not consider itself obligated to do so before deviating from the Commission's preliminary assessment of a measure.[94] This reduces the 'decision to open the formal investigation procedure' to one aspect among others, which is not in line with *Deutsche Lufthansa*. This is especially true for a 'decision not to raise objections'. Such a decision is not provisional. Rather, it closes the investigation procedure. Therefore, the national courts put the coherence of EU state aid law at risk if they deviate from the Commission's assessment without referring the case to the European Court of Justice for a preliminary ruling.

The Bundesgerichtshof – just like the Bundesverwaltungsgericht – claims the right to assess autonomously whether a measure constitutes state aid, even in the face of a Commission 'decision to open the formal investigation procedure' (which implies that this is the case). Different from the Bundesverwaltungsgericht, however, the Bundesgerichtshof considers itself not only entitled but also obligated to seek clarification from the Commission and the European Court of Justice before being in a position to deviate from the Commission's preliminary assessment.[95] This approach is in line with the instructions set out by the European Court of Justice in *Deutsche Lufthansa*. However, the Bundesgerichtshof undermines these instructions when, in a first step, it follows the Commission's preliminary assessment but then, in a second step, refrains from recovering unlawful state aid if it considers this recovery not to be in line with the principle of proportionality.[96] Explicitly referring to this principle, the Bundesgerichtshof has indeed entertained the idea of not ordering the recovery of state aid 'merely on the basis of a decision to initiate the formal investigation procedure' if (1) it is highly probable that ultimately the aid will be declared compatible with the internal market and (2) the recovery of the aid would seriously threaten the existence of the beneficiary.[97]

Neither the approach of the Bundesverwaltungsgericht nor the approach of the Bundesgerichtshof is convincing. The basis for the recovery of state aid is not the Commission's decision to initiate the formal investigation procedure but the infringement of the standstill obligation. Therefore, the national courts are required to assess whether the standstill obligation has been infringed or not. This assessment (which implies a decision about the aid character of the implemented measure) is not preliminary but final. Either there is a breach of the standstill obligation (in which case the court has to order the recovery) or there is no breach of the standstill obligation (in which case – and usually only in this case – the court can and must refrain from ordering the recovery). Although the European Court of Justice acknowledges that the

94. BVerwG, 10 C 3/15, *supra* n. 87, at 358 et seq.
95. BGH, I ZR 91/15, *supra* n. 89, at 315.
96. Andrés Martin-Ehlers, *Anmerkung zu BGH, 9.2.2017 – I ZR 91/15* [2017] EuZW 316, 316 et seq.; for a positive assessment of the decision, *see* Ulrich Karpenstein and Jenny K Dorn, *Zwischen Bindungsgebot und Abweichungsverbot – BGH und BVerwG auf neuen Wegen im Beihilfenrecht* [2017] EuZW 337, 339 et seq.; Klaus Rennert, *Bedeutung von Kommissionsentscheidungen im Beihilfeprüfverfahren für die nationalen Gerichte* [2017] EuZW 567, 568 et seq.
97. BGH, I ZR 91/15, *supra* n. 89, at 315 et seq.

recovery of unlawful state aid may not be 'appropriate' under 'exceptional circumstances', this exception is clearly overstretched if it is interpreted as a general reference to the principle of proportionality. Article 13 of the Procedural Regulation limits the Commission's power to adopt 'recovery injunctions' to cases in which (1) 'there is a serious risk of substantial and irreparable damage to a competitor' and, therefore, (2) 'an urgency to act'. However, there is no such limitation of the national courts' power to recover state aid implemented in breach of the standstill obligation. In fact, according to the Commission, '[t]he essential role played by national courts [...] also stems from the fact that the Commission's own powers to protect competitors [...] against unlawful aid are limited'.[98] It is therefore up to the national courts to compensate for the Commission's limited power to enforce the standstill obligation. This implies little room for manoeuvre and is different only in the case of interim measures. Therefore, in sum, it has to be stated that – albeit in different ways – both the Bundesgerichtshof and the Bundesverwaltungsgericht do not comply with the instructions laid down by the European Court of Justice in *Deutsche Lufthansa*.

VI. CONCLUSION

Following two decisions handed down by the Bundesgerichtshof in 2011, both the German civil and administrative courts have taken on the role in EU state aid law assigned to them by the European Court of Justice and the Commission. In doing so, they have permitted competitors' claims for the recovery of state aid granted in violation of the standstill obligation laid down in Article 108(3) sentence 3 TFEU. However, this has not led to a boom in private enforcement of EU state aid law. This is especially true for damage claims which are of no practical relevance. The situation, therefore, is considerably different from that in EU antitrust law.

One reason for this is the competitors' information deficit. An effective private enforcement regime depends on the competitors' knowledge of potentially unlawful aid measures. Transparency obligations requiring the Member States to disclose information about state aid and its beneficiaries are not likely to lead to significant improvements as Member States regularly consider controversial measures not to constitute state aid within the meaning of Article 107(1) TFEU and therefore refrain from publishing information. Furthermore, where the Commission has not yet reached a decision to initiate the formal investigation procedure, competitors claiming the recovery of unlawful state aid face the problem of proving that measures constitute state aid within the meaning of Article 107(1) TFEU. The problem is aggravated by the 'more economic approach' to EU state aid law, which has led to a rise of economic analysis in the assessment of potential aid measures.[99] Against this background, a competitor will hardly be in a position to carry out a solid 'private investor test'. Therefore, private enforcement comes with considerable risks in the light of which a

98. 2009 Enforcement Notice, *supra* n. 69, at para. 25.
99. Soltész, *supra* n. 70, at 553.

complaint to the Commission (section 24(2) of the Procedural Regulation) will often be preferred to bringing a claim for recovery in the national courts.[100]

It is questionable whether these problems could be solved by harmonising the national private enforcement regimes. Facilitation of proof might help. However, the problems competitors face rarely originate from deficiencies of national law. Rather, they can be traced back to structural differences between the antitrust regime and the state aid law regime. Against this background, the question remains whether private enforcement of EU state aid law can ever play the role assigned to it by the European Court of Justice and the Commission.

100. Soltész, *supra* n. 70, at 553 et seq.

CHAPTER 13

Private Enforcement in Italy

Roberto Caranta & Benedetta Biancardi[*]

I. Introduction: the development of private enforcement in Italy
II. Legal framework
  A. An asymmetric dual jurisdiction system
  B. Standing
III. Substantive prohibition of state aid (Article 107 TFEU)
IV. Enforcement of the standstill obligation (Article 108(3) section 3 TFEU) and interim relief
V. Transparency and right of access
VI. Damages
VII. Cooperation and coordination between national courts and the European Commission and the CJEU
VIII. A digression on public procurement and concessions
IX. Private enforcement of EU competition and state aid law: the way forward

I. INTRODUCTION: THE DEVELOPMENT OF PRIVATE ENFORCEMENT IN ITALY

Public enforcement of State aid law is still dominant in Italy. Taking litigation as the yardstick, a large number of cases concern challenges to the recovery of illegally granted State aid, including State aid schemes of a fiscal nature involving hundreds if

* Roberto Caranta has written sections I., II., IV. and V; the authors have contributed jointly to the conclusions. Benedetta Biancardi has written sections III., VI., VII., VIII., and IX.; the authors have contributed jointly to the conclusions.

not thousands of undertakings.[1] A more particular and recent case of public enforcement revolved around the withdrawal of a concession for services of general economic interest (SGEI) ferry services from Sicily. The concession had been awarded following an open tender procedure that was, however, designed and managed in breach of State aid rules. More specifically, the transaction was not in conformity with market conditions, notwithstanding the tender procedure, because: (a) the cost for the public service obligation had been overestimated because of criminal cooperation between the responsible public servant and the tenderer, and (b) the overestimate had not been corrected through the award procedure because only one tenderer had taken part to it. The Sicilian regional government had withdrawn the concession, but the decision was challenged - unsuccessfully - by the beneficiary.[2]

Still, private enforcement is starting to make a dent against unfair public support for industry practices. Even if the number of cases is still limited, the trend clearly points upwards and most cases, as it will be further illustrated in this chapter, are very relevant both for their economic value and for the societal impact that the application of EU State aid rules may have. From the latter point of view, most of the cases discussed here serve to create an overall picture of Italy and its institutions as still very much fitting the patterns of paternalistic State intervention that have been a *fil rouge* of (united) Italian history. The same cases, however, bear witness to an increasing readiness of market participants to challenge the status quo. At least to a certain extent, these actions do not fall on deaf ears. Some courts, and especially the *Consiglio di Stato*, the highest administrative court in the country, are capable of issuing rigorous pro-competitive judgments.

This quite recent development is of course expected to encourage more private enforcement actions even if the picture is not all rosy, and indeed some judgments may be considered backwards when not plainly wrong.

II. LEGAL FRAMEWORK

A. An asymmetric dual jurisdiction system

Because of the requirement that aid be 'granted by a Member State or through State resources' (Article 107(1) TFEU), the decision granting aid will often be characterised as an 'administrative act' (*provvedimento amministrativo*) done by a public authority. It is however, possible that aid is provided by public or private, undertakings,

1. For example concerning fiscal benefits for undertakings which had suffered damages due to natural disasters, as foreseen by Decreto-Legge, 24 December 2002, no. 282, *Disposizioni urgenti in materia di adempimenti comunitari e fiscali, di riscossione e di procedure di contabilità*. Cass., Sez. V Ord., 10 October 2018, no. 24986, recently reiterated that aid should be limited to actual damage suffered, in so far as not already covered under insurance or other forms of coverage; *see also* Cass., Sez. V Ord., 24 July 2018, no. 19577. The relevance of tax benefits for State aid law goes well beyond Italy: R.H.C. Luja, *'Defining the Scope of State Aid. How Tax Cases Affect the State Aid Framework'* in S. Schoenmaekers, W. Devroe and N. Philipsen (eds), *State Aid and Public Procurement in the European Union* 19 et seq. (Intersentia 2014).
2. Cons. Giustizia Amm. Reg. Sicilia, 30 July 2018, no. 459 (the full text of all decisions by administrative courts is available at www.giustizia-amministrativa.it – in Italian only).

disbursing what are State resources. The Court of Justice has early on affirmed that 'there is no necessity to draw any distinction between cases where the aid is granted by the State and cases where it is granted by public or private bodies established or appointed by the State to administer the aid'.[3] In its seminal *Stardust Marine* judgment, the Court further ruled that for a measure to be regarded as State aid, two cumulative conditions must be fulfilled: the measure must involve public funds and it must be imputable to the State.[4]

Generally speaking, Italy has a dual jurisdiction system. To make a complex issue simple, the general 'ordinary' courts are competent when rights are at stake, including the right not to pay taxes in excess of what is required by the law. In the latter case, the specialised tax courts are in principle competent. However, concerning specifically State aid, under Article 133(1)(z-*sexies*) of D.lgs. 2 July 2010 no. 104 (the Code of Judicial Administrative Procedure), as amended by Article 49 of L. 24 December 2012, no. 234, administrative courts are now the only courts competent to hear actions (a) brought against decisions granting aid or (b) challenging follow-on recovery actions. This is so irrespective of the nature of the aid involved and the entity granting it.[5] Ordinary courts, including specialised tax courts, are no longer competent in this area, and this should in principle extend to the illegal refusal of aid.[6] Furthermore, under Article 119 of the Code of Judicial Administrative Procedure, follow-on actions are subject to a special procedural regime, with shortened deadlines (*rito abbreviato*), in order to speed up litigation regarding the recovery of illegal aid.[7]

Concerning specifically private enforcement, either civil or administrative courts have competence to entertain claims for breach of EU rules. An easy rule of the thumb applies: If the (damages) action is brought against the beneficiary of the aid, the civil courts have jurisdiction; if it is brought against the entity (public or private) granting the aid, administrative courts are competent.

As is well known, the power and duty of national courts to safeguard private enforcement of State aid rules is the consequence of the direct effect attributed to Article 108(3) TFEU.[8] Article 50 of L. 24 December 2012, no. 234, further hammered on

3. Joined Cases 67, 68 and 79/85 *Gebroeders Van der Kooy et al v Commission* [1988] ECR 219, para. 35.
4. Leading cases: Case C-482/99 *Stardust Marine* [2002] ECR I-4397; Case C-379/98 *Preussen Elektra* [2001] ECR I-2099; *see* for discussion G. S. Ølykke, *Public Undertakings and Imputability – The Case of DSBFirst* [2013] EStAL 341.
5. The situation is somewhat more complex for actions brought by a beneficiary or an aspiring beneficiary: refusal of aids must be challenged in front of an administrative court; decisions to withdraw aid still fall under the competence of administrative courts if adopted because of the illegality of the aid; if withdrawal decision were motivated by breaches of conditionality rules, then civil courts are competent: e.g., Cass., Sez. Un., 23 September 2010, no. 20076; Cons. Stato, Sez. VI, 24 January 2011, no. 465; T.A.R. Sicilia, Sez. I, 3 July 2018, no. 1541; T.A.R. Toscana, Sez. II, 24 May 2018, no. 737. *See* for analysis P. Vella, in L. Costato, L.S. Rossi, P. Borghi (eds), *Commentario alla legge no. 234,* Article 49, (Editoriale Scientifica 2015).
6. A recent case is Cons. Stato, Sez. III, 22 February 2019, no. 1236.
7. The application of this special procedural regime to follow-on actions was established in Article 49(1) of L 24 December 2012, no. 234.
8. In its seminal judgment *Lorenz,* the Court established that: 'the prohibition on implementation referred to in the last sentence of Article 93 (3) [now Article 108.3] has a direct effect and gives rise to rights in favour of individuals, which national courts are bound to safeguard. The

the concept by providing that 'the decisions ("provvedimenti") granting State aid in violation of Article 108 paragraph 3 of the Treaty on the Functioning of the European Union can be challenged before the competent regional administrative court'.[9]

When reading through the distinction between prophylactic and restorative actions,[10] administrative courts are basically the only ones competent to stop a measure of State aid from being granted and therefore to uphold the standstill obligation. Administrative courts have the power to stay the decision to grant aid, thus effectively stopping the grantor from disbursing the aid. While civil courts may, in theory, forbid a prospective beneficiary from accepting or spending a grant of State aid, this has not happened so far.[11]

Generally speaking, restorative actions aiming at nullifying the effects of illegally granted aid are much more common, not least because too often competitors become aware of these aids only after they have been decided upon and disbursed. The *Arriva Italia* and the *Cineca* cases, which will be discussed below, are good demonstrations of the kind of restorative actions which are brought in front of the administrative courts.[12] As will be illustrated later on in this contribution, administrative courts are also competent for damages actions against the entities having granted illegal State aid.[13]

Following an annulment action, the entity having disbursed the aid must recover it. Under Articles 112 and following the Code of Judicial Administrative Procedure, the administrative courts are generally competent to order that follow-up action is taken, and they may also name an official responsible for taking the necessary measures in case of inaction of a State organ.

Civil courts will instead be competent where an action is brought against the recipient of the aid or when the nullity of a contract tainted by State aid is raised as an exception in litigation among private parties.[14] Civil courts, as will be shown with reference to the *Saremar* cases, are also competent with reference to damages actions against the beneficiaries of State aid.[15]

B. Standing

The starting point is that an *actio popularis* is not allowed in Italy; therefore, those who are able to demonstrate that they have suffered a prejudice from the violation of the

immediately applicable nature of this prohibition extends to the whole of the period to which it applies' (Case C-120/73, *Lorenz* [1973] ECR 1471, para. 8); *see also* C-354/90, *FNCE* [1991] ECR I-5505, para. 11; C-39/94, *SFEI* [1996] ECR I-3547, para. 39.

9. Our translation.
10. *See* for discussion F. Pastor-Merchante, *The Role of Competitors in the Enforcement of State Aid Law*, 45 et seq. (Hart 2017).
11. *See* further below section V.
12. Below section IV.
13. Below section VII.
14. For example Cass, Sez. I, 15 September 2017, no. 21481 (ord.) and Cass, Sez. I, 27 April 2018, no. 10303 (ord.), both discussed below.
15. Below section VII.

Article 108(3) TFEU obligation only may avail themselves of the provision on private enforcement.[16]

Unlike in antitrust law, consumers may hardly be said to be harmed by the grant of allegedly illegal aid. Unsurprisingly, we could not find State aid cases brought by consumers or their associations.[17]

Taxpayers have standing only to challenge decisions directly affecting what they have to pay.[18] For instance, the *Consiglio di Stato* granted standing to a body representing corporate interests, thereby allowing it to challenge the decision of a municipality to exempt itself from the payment of a local levy since the exemption translated to higher taxes for (among others) the local industry.[19] In principle, this should also apply in case of State aid granted based on levying specific taxes on some economic activity, but there are no such cases reported.

This leaves competitors. Their standing to challenge contract award decisions was traditionally recognised by Italian administrative courts, and it was later extended to the case of direct awards.[20] Their standing to challenge decisions by the Competition Authority seen as favourable to other market participants (e.g., green lighting a proposed merger) has been clearly recognised in the case law.[21] Standing to bring judicial review proceedings against a decision granting State aid has not normally been challenged.[22] Standing was, however, litigated in the recent *Cineca* case,[23] whose substantive law aspects will be analysed later on in this contribution.[24] Cineca is public consortium participated in by the State and by State universities and research centres. It is entrusted with providing data analysis and management, statistics and IT services for its members. It also offers IT services on the market. The standing of a competitor to challenge State aid allegedly granted to Cineca was granted by the *Consiglio di Stato*, holding (a) the State support Cineca benefits from is susceptible to alter competition to the detriment of its competitors, and (b) supervening rules changing the governance of Cineca and making it an in-house entity under Article 12 of Directive 2014/24/EU[25] do not change the fact that Cineca still offers its services on the market competing with commercial companies.[26]

16. Case C-174/02 *Streekgewest Westelijk Noord-Brabant v Staatssecretaris van Financiën* [2005] ECR I-00085, para. 19. *See* in general L. Salvi, '*Articolo 50, Ricorso giurisdizionale per violazione dell'Articolo 108, paragrafo 3, del Trattato sul funzionamento dell'Unione Europea*' in L. Costato, L.S. Rossi, P. Borghi (eds), *Commentario alla legge no. 234* (Editoriale Scientifica 2015).
17. Although, in principle, they could have standing, *see ibid.*, at 453, 462.
18. Cons. Stato Sez. V, 14 June 1996, no. 693.
19. Cons. Stato Sez. V, 19 September 1995, no. 1314, in Dir. e Prat. Tributaria (1996) II, 752, note R. Damonte.
20. Among the earlier cases Cons. Stato Sez. V, 10 May 1999, no. 546.
21. Leading case: Cons. Stato, Sez. VI, 14 June 2004, no. 3865.
22. For example Cons. Stato, Sez. V, 24 May 2018, no. 3123.
23. Cons. Stato, Sez. VI, 22 October 2018, no. 6009.
24. Section VI.
25. M. Burgi, '*Contracting authorities, in-house services and public authorities cooperation*' in F. Lichère, R. Caranta and S. Treumer (eds), *Modernising Public Procurement: The New Directive* 54 et seq. (DJØF 2014).
26. Cons. Stato, Sez. VI, 22 October 2018, n. 6009, paras 3.3. et seq.

Italian competition law gives the *Autorità garante della concorrenza e del mercato* (AGCM), the Italian Competition Authority, standing to challenge both general and individual measures and decisions breaching competition rules.[27] In one recent case, discussed further below, the provision on standing was applied to give the Authority standing to challenge a direct award of a local railways transport service.[28] This claim was joined with one brought by a competitor, and, of course, it is a matter for debate whether judicial action initiated by public authorities is covered under the notion of 'private enforcement'. One element pointing towards a positive answer would be that this applies to authorities not given official powers to adopt binding decisions in this area and which, as such, must have recourse to judicial remedies on the same footing as individuals and companies.[29]

III. SUBSTANTIVE PROHIBITION OF STATE AID (ARTICLE 107 TFEU)

As the Court of Justice held in *Transalpine Ölleitung in Österreich*, '[a] national court may have cause to interpret the concept of aid contained in Article [107 TFEU] in order to determine whether a State measure has been introduced in disregard of Article [108(3) TFEU]. Thus it is for that court to verify, inter alia, whether the measure at issue constitutes an advantage and whether it is selective, that is to say, whether it favours certain undertakings or certain producers within the meaning of Article [107(1) TFEU]'.[30]

Two recent cases illustrate the struggle the Italian *Consiglio di Stato* may face in characterising a given measure as State aid (or not). The first is *Arriva Italia*.[31] A relatively small train and bus service operator in the South of Italy, Ferrovie del Sud Est e Servizi Automobilistici s.r.l. (henceforth FSE), was on the brink of bankruptcy. Some facts are still shrouded by mist even after the case has been sent to the Court of Justice. Basically, the Italian State, which owned 100% of the company, enacted legislative provisions enabling the competent minister to give the company EUR 70 million in emergency aid and to transfer the ownership of the company to Ferrovie dello Stato Italiane s.p.a. (henceforth FSI). FSI was the old monopolist and is now the – still wholly State-owned – holding for the companies providing most railway services in Italy,

27. Under Article 21-*bis*, para. 1 of Law no. 287, 10 October 1990, the Competition Authority is expressly entitled to challenge measures unlawfully granting State aid insofar as it determines a violation of competition rules.
28. T.A.R. Sardegna, Sez. Cagliari, 25 July 2018, no. 682.
29. *See* for analysis R. Giovagnoli, *Atti amministrativi e tutela della concorrenza. Il potere di legittimazione a ricorrere dell'AGCM nell'art. 21-bis legge n. 287/1990, Relazione al convegno tenutosi presso l'Università degli studi di Milano il 27 settembre 2012*, in Giustamm.it no. 10/2012; F. Cintioli, *Osservazioni sul ricorso giurisdizionale dell'Autorità garante della concorrenza e del mercato (art. 21 bis della legge n. 287 del 1990)*, in Federalismi.it no. 12/2012, 13 June 2012, https://www.federalismi.it/nv14/articolo-documento.cfm?artid=20213 (accessed 6 June 2012).
30. ECJ, Case C-368/04 *Transalpine Ölleitung in Österreich GmbH and others v Finanzlandesdirektion für Tirol and others* [2006] ECR I-9957, para. 39 (references have been update to the TFEU); the Court refers to Case C-345/02 *Pearle and Others* [2004] ECR I-7139, para. 31.
31. ECJ, Case C-385/18 *Arriva Italia and Others*, pending; the reference order is the already mentioned case Cons. Stato, Sez. V, 24 May 2018, no. 3123.

including the management of the rail network. The emergency aid was re-qualified as contributions to the management of the network in a subsequent piece of legislation. The relevant minister authorised the transfer with a decree and signed the contract with FSI, without asking any payment for it to FSI. The decision was challenged by Arriva Italia and by other undertakings, which had previously signalled to the minister their interest in buying FSE. At first instance, the claimants put more emphasis on the breach of national rules for privatisations that generally require a competitive procedure for the sale of State holdings. On appeal, however, the focus was squarely set on State aid rules.

A number of different aspects were litigated in *Arriva Italia*. One point considerably stressed by the *Consiglio di Stato* is that the effects of the measure challenged were fully confined to the State holdings system, one fully State-owned company being acquired by another fully State-owned company. However, as already recalled, FSI is the holding company of the companies today providing most railway services in Italy, including passenger transport and management of the rail network, and the action taken by the Italian government actually forecloses a local market to potential competitors without FSI having to pay any costs. Since rail services are part of the SGEI for whose provision the State is responsible, granting the subsidy might be covered by the exception under Article 106(2) TFEU as the (only) way to ensure the continuation of the service to the benefit of users. Alternatively, according to the *Consiglio di Stato*, given the dire situation in which FSE found itself, acquisition by FSI might have been seen as the (only) way for the State, acting as a market operator, to save and restructure its holdings. Somewhat contradictorily, referring to the old *Lanerossi I* case, the *Consiglio di Stato* adds that the transfer of ownership and the financial contribution given might be justified by the decision not to privatise the service, using the discretion left to the Member States by Article 345 TFEU. Also, since it is unclear whether the aid was actually disbursed, the measure possibly having being carried out by simply moving the money between different segments of the State budget, the *Consiglio di Stato* argues that ultimately State aid can be ruled out because there was no transfer of State resources to a market operator.[32] Finally, since Arriva Italia was already established and operating in Italy, the *Consiglio di Stato* doubted whether the aid could affect trade between the Member States. The fact that the acquisition concerned a small regional train operator had motivated the Italian Competition Authority to conclude that the merger would not hinder competition on the national market.[33]

The *Consiglio di Stato* amassed arguments shedding doubt on whether the whole operation could amount to a State aid measure, but it decided to refer the case to the Court of Justice anyway.[34] It is worth noting that the Court of Justice has been recently seized of another railway case opposing Trenitalia s.p.a. (the subsidiary of FSI actually providing train services) against Arriva Italia Rail concerning the direct award of train

32. Cons. Stato, Sez. V, 24 May 2018, no. 3123, para. VI.1.
33. Cons. Stato, Sez. V, 24 May 2018, no. 3123, para. VI.4.
34. The case was referred to the Court of Justice by the Consiglio di Stato, Sez. V, 24 May 2018, no. 3123.

services.[35] This case is relevant for both standing and access to information, but the preliminary questions sent to the Court focus on the interpretation of Regulation (EC) no. 1370/2007 on railway services and not on State aid.[36]

A second case concerned *Cineca.*[37] As already described, Cineca is a public consortium participated in by the State and by State universities and research centres. It is entrusted with providing data analysis and management, statistics and IT services for its members. It also offers IT services on the market. The Ministry considered that the consortium provided 'instrumental services' to universities as an in-house provider and, consequently, regularly financed the consortium for such services. Be Smart s.r.l., a competitor operating in the IT services market, challenged the most recent ministerial decree providing what was alleged to be State aid for (a) the above-mentioned services and (b) high-performance computing. The first instance court annulled the decree in so far as it concerned services under (a) and upheld the rest. The judgment was appealed and cross-appealed. Counsel for Cineca argued that it was for the Commission (to which Be Smart s.r.l. had also addressed a complaint) and not for the national court to declare that the measure at issue constituted a State aid incompatible with the Treaty. The reasoning of the *Consiglio di Stato* impeccably follows the case law of the Court of Justice and guidance from the Commission by recalling that, as held by the Court in *Transalpine Ölleitung in Österreich,* the national courts have indeed a role to play in enforcing EU State aid rules. More specifically, consistent with *SFEI,* the *Consiglio di Stato* stressed that the fact that the Commission has initiated proceedings does not deprive national courts of the duty to enforce State aid law.[38] In any event, even if the Commission were to hold the aid compatible with the Treaty, the breach of the duty of prior notification could not be without consequences.[39]

On the substance, Cineca argued that its activities pursued an essential State function not having economic value and that, in any event, the contribution it received from its participants only covered its costs. These arguments were rebuffed by the *Consiglio di Stato,* holding that the services provided by Cineca, far from discharging essential public law activities of the State, were simply tools for State activities that market participants could have easily provided.[40] Also, it was irrelevant that Cineca was not working for profit. Applying the market investor test, the *Consiglio di Stato* held that the State contribution was covering costs that under normal market conditions should have been borne by the company.[41] The first instance judgment was affirmed also concerning high-performance computing. According to the *Consiglio di Stato,* funds granted to Cineca under this heading qualify as lawful State aid in the light

35. ECJ, Case C-515/18, *Autorità Garante della Concorrenza e del Mercato,* pending.
36. Regulation (EC) no. 1370/2007 of the European Parliament and of the Council of 23 October 2007 on public passenger transport services by rail and by road and repealing Council Regulations (EEC) Nos 1191/69 and 1107/70 [2007] OJ L 315/1.
37. Cons. Stato, Sez. VI, 22 October 2018, no. 6009.
38. *Ibid.,* para. 4.3; Case C-39/94 *SFEI, supra* n. 8, at paras 44 and 50–53, is referred to.
39. *Ibid.*; ECJ, Case C-354/90 *Fédération Nationale du Commerce Extérieur des Produits Alimentaires (FNCEPA) and Syndicat National des Négociants et Transformateurs de Saumon v France* [1991] ECR I-5505, para. 16 is referred to.
40. *Ibid.,* paras 6.2. et seq.
41. *Ibid.,* paras 7.2. et seq.

of the Commission Communication on Framework for State aid for research and development and innovation[42] because the subsidy goes to a research organisation putting a research infrastructure at the disposal of the research community.[43] Alternatively, the aid need not be notified since the conditions laid down in Article 26 of Commission Regulation (EU) no. 651/2014 declaring certain categories of aid compatible with the internal market in application of Articles 107 and 108 of the Treaty are met. The commercial activity of Cineca was found to be below 20% of the total turnover of the company, and the costs and revenues for the commercial activity (and for all of Cineca's activities) are 'accounted for separately on the basis of consistently applied and objectively justifiable cost accounting principles'.[44]

Even if it did not feel the need to raise questions for preliminary reference, in *Cineca* the *Consiglio di Stato* did indeed displayed full knowledge of the relevant EU rules on State aids as interpreted by the Commission and the Court of Justice.

Even more recent cases focus on the recovery of misused[45] or conditional aids.[46]

IV. ENFORCEMENT OF THE STANDSTILL OBLIGATION (ARTICLE 108(3) SECTION 3 TFEU) AND INTERIM RELIEF

In *Transalpine Ölleitung in Österreich*, the Court of Justice held that, '[w]hilst assessment of the compatibility of aid measures with the common market falls within the exclusive competence of the Commission, subject to review by the Community Courts, it is for the national courts to ensure that the rights of individuals are safeguarded where the obligation to give prior notification of State aid to the Commission pursuant to Article [108(3) TFEU] is infringed'.[47]

The standstill obligation comes into play once a measure is classified as State aid. As discussed above, restorative actions are much more frequent than prophylactic ones, meaning that the obligation to give prior notification has already been breached. Most of the cases analysed in this contribution are fully representative of this pattern. One somewhat special case is *Arriva Italia*. As already discussed, it is uncertain on the facts of the case whether the contribution has already been paid to the beneficiary or whether only changes were made to the State budget which would allow the transfer (which, in any case, already represents a violation of the standstill principle set by Article 108(3) TFEU).[48]

42. Communication from the Commission – Framework for State aid for research and development and innovation [2014] OJ C 198/1.
43. Cons. Stato, Sez. VI, 22 October 2018, no. 6009, para. 11.2.
44. *Ibid.*, paras 11.2. et seq.
45. Cons. Stato, Sez. III, 25 March 2019, no. 1932.
46. T.A.R. Sardegna, Sez. I, 17 April 2019, no. 353.
47. ECJ, Case C-384/04 *Transalpine Ölleitung in Österreich GmbH and others v Finanzlandesdirektion für Tirol and others* [2006] ECLI:EU:C:2006:644, para. 38; the Court refers to Joined Cases C-261/01 and C-262/01 *Van Calster and Others* [2003] ECLI:EU:C:2003:571, para. 75. On the complementary but separate roles of the Commission and the national courts, *see also* ECJ, Case C-284/12 *Deutsche Lufthansa AG v Flughafen Frankfurt-Hahn GmbH* [2013] ECLI:EU:C:2013:755, para. 27 and the case law cited.
48. Cons. Stato, Sez. III, 24 March 2019, no. 1932.

Interim measures available from the administrative courts would in principle afford some temporary remedy whether the aid has already been disbursed or not. In Italy, interim relief is conditioned on there being established strong prima facie evidence of illegality and (concurrently) of the risk that a belated annulment of the challenged measure allegedly granting a State aid would be pointless. Assuming that the measure brought in front of the court has not been notified, which is easy to ascertain, the first requirement in State aid litigation translates into the question of whether the measure itself may be prima facie qualified as State aid. Provided that illegal aid must be recovered, assessment of the second requirement very much depends on whether there is a risk that the beneficiary might not in the future be able to return the aid received.[49] Another relevant consideration might be whether the aid could irremediably alter the market.[50] It is submitted, however, that the latter assessment would not be easily fit into the short timeframes and limited possibilities for the parties to develop their arguments that characterise interim procedures. Concerning the interim measures that may be taken, they are different depending on whether the aid has been disbursed yet. If not, then the administrative court seized might order a suspension of the disbursement. If, instead, the aid has already been disbursed, the claimant could ask for a (temporary) recovery of the measure as a consequence of the decision to suspend the effects of the measure challenged.

Remarkably, interim relief was not sought in the recent cases analysed in this contribution. It is true that in two of them the beneficiary was the State-owned primary provider of rail services in the country, and in the other case, it was a State-owned consortium. Future recovery was all but certain in all cases so that the second condition for interim relief was clearly missing. Additionally, in *Arriva Italia* the *Consiglio di Stato* was clearly of the view that, for a number of reasons, the measure at stake could not be treated as State aid. It referred the case to the Court of Justice because it felt it was its duty to do so, but if asked for interim relief the top administrative court would certainly not have considered the applicant's case strong enough to warrant a stay of the payment or a provisional recovery of any sum disbursed.

V. TRANSPARENCY AND RIGHT OF ACCESS

The European Union has early on laid down a set of transparency obligations, which are complementary but fundamental to ensure proper enforcement of State aid rules.

49. In general terms, such risk is considered not to occur when the allegedly unlawful measure is granted to public entities or enterprises, since it would always be possible, and relatively easy, for the State to then recover the aid. However, the conclusion of the recent *SEA-Airport Handling* case has proven that recovery might not take place if the public company benefitting from the aid is meanwhile extinguished and 'replaced' with a new and different enterprise. This is so because the new enterprise does not inherit, at least in principle, the measures addressed to the extinguished operator. *See* Case T-167/13, *Comune di Milano v Commission* [2018] ECLI:EU: T:2013:331.
50. Maintaining unlawful subsidies in certain specific markets might have a huge impact on competitors, up to the point of determining their exit from the relevant market and even their complete bankruptcy. *See* in that regard the *Traghetti del Mediterraneo* saga analysed in section VII.

The main piece of legislation is Directive 2006/111/EC on the transparency of financial relations between Member States and public undertakings as well as on financial transparency within certain undertakings.[51] Article 2 of the Transparency Directive, as it is known, imposes, in particular, an obligation to maintain separate accounts on any undertaking that (i) enjoys a special or exclusive right granted by a Member State or is entrusted with the operation of a service of general economic interest, (ii) receives public service obligations compensation[52] in any form in relation to such service and (iii) carries on other activities.[53]

The obligation to maintain separate accounts has been transposed at national level, although the applicable legal framework is somewhat unclear. In sum, entities involved in mixed activities (as generally identified by Article 2 of the Transparency Directive) are required to either, under certain circumstances, keep separate accounts or to set up different bodies to perform activities on the market.[54] Furthermore, the 'National Record on State Aid' has recently been set up with the purpose of helping public authorities verify the *de minimis* thresholds have been respected when disbursing new aid. In essence, the Record will also help public authorities - including contracting authorities - to identify what aid has been granted to what enterprises.[55]

From a private enforcement point of view, transparency rules constitute a precious tool for challenging an unlawful State aid scheme. The (lack of) compliance with the obligation of separation of accounts might represent the decisive element in establishing the breach of State aid rules. This is probably the reason why both national courts and economic operators are becoming much more aware of this set of transparency obligations in State aid cases. For instance, in the aforementioned *Cineca* case, the

51. Commission Directive 2006/111/EC of 16 November 2006 on the transparency of financial relations between Member States and public undertakings as well as on financial transparency within certain undertakings [2006] OJ L 318/17.
52. *See* generally P. Nicolaides, '*Compensation for Net Extra Costs of Public Service Obligations*' in S. Schoenmaekers, W. Devroe and N. Philipsen (eds), *State Aid and Public Procurement in the European Union* 77 et seq. (Intersentia 2014).
53. Separation of accounts is relevant for the application of a number of State aid rules and exceptions, such as Article 26 of Commission Regulation (EU) no. 651/2014, discussed above with reference to the *Cineca* case: *see* Cons. Stato, Sez. VI, 22 October 2018, no. 6009, at para. 11.4.
54. A detailed analysis of the internal rules transposing the transparency obligations set by the European Transparency Directive - and their scope of application - goes beyond the purpose of the present contribution. To summarise, Legislative Decree 11 November 2003, no. 333 has cloned at national level the obligations set by the Transparency Directive (also in terms of thresholds and limits of scope). This piece of legislation has to be coordinated with (1) Article 8 of Law 10 October 1990 no. 287, which imposes a general obligation to act 'by means of separate entities' upon all undertakings, public or private, which are entrusted with a special or exclusive right or with the provision of a SGEI and which, at the same time, operate in the market under competitive terms and (2) Article 6(1) of Legislative Decree 19 October 2016, no. 175 (the newly released 'Code of State-owned enterprises'), which has introduced a privileged regime for 'undertakings subject to public control' that carry out at the same time exclusive or special rights and other economic activities in the market. Article 6 requires that they are to maintain separate accounts in relation to the different activities, instead of setting up a different legal entity. *See* for general analysis F. Guerrera, '*Articolo 6, principi fondamentali sull'organizzazione e sulla gestione delle società a controllo pubblico*' in G. Morbidelli (ed.) *Codice delle Società a partecipazione pubblica* (Giuffrè 2018).
55. The Record has been established by Law 29 July 2015, no. 115.

Consiglio di Stato specifically looked at the separation of accounts between the different activities of the public operator in order to acknowledge the presence of potential cross-subsidisation.[56] Also in the *Arriva Italia* case, the *Consiglio* referred to the financial separation of accounts (or rather in that case financial separation of entities), though arguably in a less clear and efficient way.

In principle, transparency rules seem the solution to all evils; however, in practice, this might not be so if they are not coupled with adequate rules on a right of access. Put otherwise, substantive transparency rules remain almost useless – at least from a private enforcement viewpoint – if the private competitor cannot have access to information regarding the financial and organisational structure of the contested beneficiary so as to trigger the violation of separation of accounts and thus the breach of State aid rules. Moreover, access to information regarding the subsidies disbursed to certain beneficiaries might as well allow their competitors to challenge possible overcompensation, thus a breach of State aid rules.

This issue is illustrated in a recent national 'saga' where, once again, Arriva Italia Rail and Trenitalia (the commercial company of the FSI group) crossed swords.[57] In this case, Arriva Italia Rail contended that Sardinian regional government's direct award of the regional railway service to Trenitalia was in breach of Regulation EU no. 1370/2007 on railway services. More specifically, it was contested that the Region did not properly comply with the transparency obligations set by Article 7 of the Regulation and that, in light of Arriva Italia Rail having submitted a more economically advantageous offer, the regional authority should have launched an open tender instead of directly awarding the service to the incumbent Trenitalia for a higher price. The potential breach of State aid rules here lies in the risk of overcompensation for the service: If another economic operator was able to offer a lower price and the local authority still directly awarded the service to the incumbent for a higher price, then the whole operation might result in a violation of *Altmark* rules on overcompensation.[58] To support its claim, Arriva Italia Rail requested access to a series of documents regarding both the offer presented by Trenitalia – especially in terms of compensation for the public service discharged – and, in general, its financial and organisational structure. The regional authority only partially disclosed the information, and Arriva Italia Rail contested the measure before the competent administrative court in a parallel litigation. Eventually, the *Consiglio di Stato* considered that Arriva Italia Rail had not sufficiently proved its 'instrumental interest' in having access to this information in order to challenge the absence of an open tendering procedure and considered that the interest of the incumbent in protecting its commercial and industrial secrets prevailed. The *Consiglio di Stato* affirmed that the standing of Arriva Italia Rail to contest the lack of a competitive procedure did not automatically entail full access to the relevant information regarding the opponent incumbent. The court very much based its

56. Cons. Stato, Sez. VI, 22 October 2018, no. 6009, para. 11.4.
57. Cons. Stato, Sez. V, 24 May 2018, no. 3122.
58. Case C- 280/00, *Altmark* [2003] ECR I-7747, *see* generally W. Devroe and D. Gabathuler, '*The Evolving Treatment of Services of General Economic Interest under EU Law*' in S. Schoenmaekers, W. Devroe and N. Philipsen (eds), *State Aid and Public Procurement in the European Union* 47 et seq. (Intersentia 2014).

reasoning on Article 7 of Regulation EU no. 1370/2007, holding that all the information foreseen therein had been disclosed so that all the remaining information should be considered as covered by the rules on industrial and commercial secrets.[59]

In a parallel procedure, the Antitrust Authority, which is as mentioned entitled to claim breaches of State aid and competition rules (*see* above), challenged the direct award to Trenitalia before the competent administrative court. The first instance regional administrative court (TAR) decided to stay proceedings and submit a preliminary reference to the Court of Justice, asking to clarify the meaning and the implications – also in terms of the relevant activity being opened up to competition – of the transparency obligations set by Article 7 of Regulation EU no. 1370/2007.[60] The case is currently pending before the Court of Justice, which hopefully will shed some light on whether the direct award was compliant with the Regulation.[61]

Some conclusions, however, might already be drawn from the cases discussed above. Indeed, although it remains somewhat unclear whether the Region had actually revealed all (and only) the relevant documents, it emerges how the right of access to the 'economic and financial information' of economic operators plays in principle an important role in the private enforcement of State aid rules. Thus, it is important to strike an adequate balance between the interest of the entity challenging the breach of State aid rules and the interest of the alleged beneficiary in protecting its industrial and commercial privacy. The approach adopted by the case law on the matter will have a decisive impact on the application of this tool in State aid cases. Arguably, the balance struck by the *Consiglio di Stato* in the aforementioned case did not ease the way for private enforcers.

VI. DAMAGES

In principle, when it comes to damages, private competitors have two options: either they address the claim against the State granting the aid or they address it against the beneficiary of the unlawful State aid measure.

With the first option, competitors are in essence contending the liability of the State (or one of its institutions) according to *Francovich*, and administrative courts are the ones competent to hear the matter.[62] The *Traghetti del Mediterraneo* saga analysed below is the first and so far only case of this kind.

When the competitor brings an action against the beneficiary, civil courts are instead competent. On a substantive level, the Court of Justice has early on established in *SFEI* that the EU State aid enforcement system does not impose any specific

59. *Ibid.*, para. 16.
60. TAR Sardegna, Sez. I, 25 July 2018, no. 682.
61. ECJ, Case C-515/18, *Autorità Garante della Concorrenza e del Mercato*, pending.
62. Joined Cases C-6 and C-9/90 *Francovich* [1991] ECR I-5357. Further developed in Joined Cases C-46 and C-48/93 *Brasserie du Pecheur and Factortame III* [1996] ECR I-1029; Case C-224/01 *Köbler* [2003] ECR I-10239. *See* for general analysis J Goyder and M Dons, *Damages claims based on State aid law infringements* (2017) 3 EStAL 418. The present contribution focuses on private enforcement, thus it does not analyse the – rather controversial – possibility for the beneficiary to seek damages from the granting State.

obligations upon the beneficiary; however it did not preclude the possibility for Member States to do so, stating that 'if, according to national law, the acceptance by an economic operator of unlawful assistance of a nature such as to occasion damage to other economic operators may in certain circumstances cause him to incur liability, the principle of non-discrimination may lead the national court to find the recipient of aid paid in breach of Article [108(3)] of the Treaty liable'.[63]

In Italy, receiving State aid might amount to unfair competition, which is a tort under Article 2598(3) of the Civil Code.[64] Under this provision, which complements the rules protecting industrial design and trademarks, a party who behaves inconsistently with professional integrity and harms the business of a competitor is liable for unfair competition. The burden of proof as to both the casual link between the illegally received State aid and the damage suffered squarely rests on the plaintiff following the Italian default rules on tort liability. With specific regard to State aid breaches, however, the case law is still ambiguous as to whether the mere receipt of the aid amounts to unfair competition or whether there is required a further misconduct of the beneficiary, which consists in taking advantage – in an abusive manner – of the unlawful benefit received.[65] Furthermore, according to Article 2600 of the Civil Code, unfair competition can lead to damages only if the claimant also proves the subjective element of the beneficiary's intent or negligence in its anticompetitive conduct.

The situation is well-illustrated in the two *Saremar* cases. The State wholly owned a large ferry company also holding the entire capital of the regional companies. The holding was on the brink of bankruptcy and finally became insolvent. Before that, however, the State 'privatised' the holding company and transferred to the competent regional authorities some of the subsidiaries, including Sardegna Regionale Marittima (henceforth *Saremar*) with a view to privatise them. The private commercial companies managing most of the sea routes with Sardinia considerably raised the ticket prices for the 2011 and 2012 summer seasons. The Sardinian regional government (a) instructed *Saremar*, which was still totally owned by the Region, to open new routes offering low ticket prices and (b) gave the same company EUR 3 million in order to promote Sardinia's overall tourist services, a bank guarantee for a EUR 3 million loan, and about EUR 1 million as capital hike. The all-ferry-services 'privatisation' was also investigated by the EU Commission for breach of State aid rules, and a decision was adopted specifically targeting the aid granted to *Saremar*.[66] In the meantime, two

63. Case C-39/94, *SFEI, supra* n. 8, at paras 73 and 74.
64. The competence of civil courts regarding damage claims for unfair competition was established for the first time by the Court of Cassation in its judgment of 23 May 1980, no. 3397.
65. For an interesting analysis on national case law *see* C. Cellerino, *Le azioni nei confronti del beneficiario di aiuti di Stato e i limiti all'«effetto diretto orizzontale» dell'art. 108.3. TFUE: problemi e spunti dalla recente giurisprudenza nazionale* (2015) 4 Dir. Comm. Int. 1124.
66. Commission decision on the measures SA.32014 (2011/C), SA.32015 (2011/C), SA.32016 (2011/C) implemented by the Region of Sardinia in favour of Saremar, 22 January 2014, C(2013) 9101 final.

commercial companies brought damages actions for unfair competition against *Saremar*, claiming it had practised predatory pricing thanks to the allegedly illegal State aid received. The courts seized were in Genoa.[67]

In both judgments, no damages were awarded to the claimants. However, the two courts followed two different lines of reasoning. In *Grandi Navi Veloci,* the Genoa court considered the evidence sufficient to prove a *risk* of unfair competition resulting from the use of the unlawful aid, and the claim was dismissed mostly because the harm alleged by the competitor actually referred to a period prior to the granting of the unlawful measure.[68] In *Moby*, by contrast, the court went so far as rejecting any intention to harm competitors, holding that the pricing policy was intended to provide affordable prices rather than hurt competitors. Thus, the conduct of the beneficiary was not sufficient to award damage according to the Article 2600 standard.[69] It probably did not help the claimant that it had refused to disclose any documents relating to its own pricing policy (itself under the scrutiny of the Italian Competition Authority).

Finally, the *Traghetti del Mediterraneo* saga seems to sum up all the shortcomings of the current system of damages, proving how difficult it might be, in practice, to secure an award of damages from the State or from the aid beneficiary.

The controversy originated between Tirrenia and Traghetti del Mediterraneo (henceforth TDM), two shipping companies which in the 1970s provided regular ferry services between mainland Italy and the islands of Sardinia and Sicily. TDM contended that Tirrenia was able to adopt a low-price policy because of the subsidies received from the State, which were in breach of European State aid rules (the subsidy scheme had been established by national law no. 684/1975). Thus, TDM brought an action for damages *against Tirrenia* before the District Court of Naples. The application brought by TDM was dismissed both at first instance and on appeal. The case landed before the Supreme Court of Cassation, which refused to make a preliminary reference to the Court of Justice in relation to the interpretation of State aid rules and case law, considering that the subsidy scheme was fully compliant with both the national provisions and the principles established at EU level; consequently, it dismissed the application. TDM, which has meanwhile gone bankrupt and become known as FTDM, filed a new damage application *against the State* before the District Court of Genoa, holding that the State was in breach of *Francovich* on several grounds and in particular for having failed to comply with obligations set by Article 267(3) TFEU. The District Court referred the case to the Court of Justice, giving rise to the well-known 2006 judgment of *Traghetti del Mediterraneo.*[70] Following the principles established by the ECJ, the District Court found that the State judiciary had acted unlawfully, and, in parallel, it 'reopened' the action for damages brought by FTDM. In order to rule on this latter proceeding, the District Court made another preliminary reference to the Court of

67. Trib. Milano, 22 April 2015, *Moby spa v Sardegna Regionale Marittima spa* and Trib. Genova, 11 August 2014, no. 2919 *Grandi Navi Veloci spa v Sardegna Regionale Marittima spa.*
68. Trib. Genova, no. 2919, *supra* n. 67.
69. *Ibid.*
70. ECJ, Case C-173/03 *Traghetti del Mediterraneo* [2006] ECR I-5177.

Justice (the one that the Court of Cassation had failed to send), seeking clarification on the interpretation of the notion of State aid in the controversy at hand. The result was the 2010 judgment *Fallimento Traghetti del mediterraneo,* in which the European Court stated that the subsidies at issue would constitute State aid if they were able to affect trade between Member States or distort competition, which was for the national court to determine.[71] Consequently, the District Court *ordered the State to pay damages* to FTDM as a result of the unlawful conduct of the State as regards the use of its judicial function. The State appealed before the Court of Appeal, which reached a different conclusion on the merits of the case: It excluded damages for the conduct of the State judge because it considered that the result in the main proceeding (the damage claim *against Tirrenia*) would have not been different had the Court of Cassation made a reference to the Court of Justice. In particular, it was not proved that the beneficiary had used the unlawful subsidy scheme to practice predatory pricing; what was missing was the necessary subjective element under Article 2600 of the Civil Code, which consists of the 'beneficiary's awareness of excluding competitors from the market'.[72] However, the Court of Appeal held the State liable in its legislative capacity, stating that Law no. 684 granting the subsidies was in breach of State aid rules; thus, it *ordered the State* to pay more than EUR 2 million of damages in favour of FTDM. The State appealed, however, before the Court of Cassation, contesting the qualification of the subsidy (and the subsequent duty to award damages) as new aid instead of as existing aid. This time the Court of Cassation decided to stay proceedings, making, for the third time, a preliminary reference. The Court of Justice in its most recent judgment of 23 January 2019[73] confirmed the overall breach of State aid rules[74] and the qualification of the measure as new aid. Furthermore, the Court felt it important to stress two important aspects in this apparently never-ending judicial saga. First, in the context of private enforcement, national courts enjoy a certain level of independence when hearing an action for damages in the absence of a Commission decision.[75] Secondly, State entities cannot rely on the principle of legitimate expectations as far as it is established that the State aid was granted in violation of the standstill notification; nor can they impose a more restrictive limitation period for the damages action of competitors, since this would amount to a breach of both the principle of legal certainty and the principle of sincere cooperation.[76]

71. ECJ, Case C-140/09 *Fallimento Traghetti del Mediterraneo* [2010] ECR I-5243.
72. Corte d'Appello di Genova, 2 July 2014, *Presidenza del Consiglio dei Ministri v Fallimento Traghetti del Mediterraneo.*
73. ECJ, Case C-387/17 *Presidenza del Consiglio dei Ministri v Fallimento Traghetti del Mediterraneo spa* [2019] ECLI:EU:C:2019:51.
74. Case C-387/17 *Presidenza, supra* n. 73, at para. 42.
75. More specifically, the Court held that 'when an applicant is able to demonstrate before the national court that he has suffered loss caused by the premature implementation of State aid and, more specifically, as a result of the illegal time advantage which the beneficiary gained from such an implementation, the action for damages can, in principle, be upheld even though the Commission has already approved the aid in question by the time the national court decides on the application' (para. 60).
76. Paragraphs 70, 74 and 77.

To conclude, it is worth noting how, in all the recent aforementioned cases before the administrative courts, the competitors 'solely' requested that the State annul the unlawful scheme/measure and, eventually, recover what it had already disbursed, but they did not submit damages claims. This result might be because the main aim for private competitors operating in the same market is to deprive the subsidised undertakings of their unlawful advantage or – when the operators are involved in the same procurement procedure – to exclude the competing tenderer; thus, the result is mainly achieved already through the annulment of the measure (or the exclusion of the tenderer) and the recovery action. However, arguably, the main reason for this situation is the stringent, almost impossible, burden of proof that private competitors have to bear in order to demonstrate actual and direct damage having been suffered.

VII. COOPERATION AND COORDINATION BETWEEN NATIONAL COURTS AND THE EUROPEAN COMMISSION AND THE CJEU

Italian courts tend not to address questions or requests for collaboration to the Commission. However, they normally pay due regard to the decisions taken by the Commission on the matter of State aid. The two judgments in the *Saremar* litigation provide good examples of this. The tribunals adhered to the Commission's decision in finding (a) that the promotional activities had been fairly paid, and (b) that the bank 'guarantee' was not really a State aid, the Region having contented itself with reassuring the loan provider that it would be informed of changes in the property structure of *Saremar*. Moreover, based on the same reasoning of the Commission, the two courts (c) ruled that an additional capital injection (EUR 824,309.69) constituted an illegal State aid.

The *Arriva Italia* case provides another example of close cooperation of an Italian court with the Commission. In that case the *Consiglio di Stato* referred to an interlocutory decision by the Commission as a ground to doubt that the aid was compatible with the Treaty.[77]

Concerning the referral of preliminary questions to the Court of Justice, the practice is mixed, with administrative courts frequently making references to the Court and civil courts often apparently oblivious of their duties under Article 267 TFEU.

As already recalled in *Arriva Italia*, the *Consiglio di Stato*, faced with uncertainty as to whether the transfer of the FSE amounted to State aid, called on the Court of Justice for help.[78] In *Cineca*, the *Consiglio di Stato* instead referred to *Cilfit* and the doctrine of *acte clair* since the State aid nature of the measure at issue in the case was plain.[79]

77. Cons. Stato, Sez. VI, 24 May 2018, no. 3123, point VI.2., referring to decision C(2014) 1824 *Rete Ferroviaria Trenitalia*.
78. Cons. Stato, Sez. VI, 24 May 2018, no. 3123, point VI; as already pointed out, questions focusing on Regulation (EC) no. 1370/2007, *supra* n. 36, were instead raised by ECJ, Case C-515/18, *Autorità Garante della Concorrenza e del Mercato*, pending.
79. Cons. Stato, Sez. VI, 22 October 2018, no. 6009, para. 10.

Italian courts, and especially civil ones, have refrained from referring preliminary questions to the Court of Justice in a number of other cases. The results do not always deserve praise. One reasonably straightforward case concerned two persons linked (probably as wife/daughter and/or son, the frustrating application of privacy rules in Italy does not allow us to know) to a bankrupt man who, in the year prior to bankruptcy, had 'sold' them the house where they lived. This falls under special rules providing for the restitution/reintegration of assets (clawback) of a bankrupt party – which were disposed of in the two years preceding bankruptcy – to pay creditors. The claimants maintained that these rules, and the fact that money or goods recovered might be used to continue the business, amounted to illegal State aid. The Italian Court of Cassation gave short shrift to these arguments. It recalled that the Court of Justice had already found parts of the old Italian bankruptcy law in contradiction with EU State aid rules, and those parts had been repealed. The Court of Justice had instead left standing the remainder of the bankruptcy law, including the rules on restitution/reintegration. The Court of Justice had assumed that any extant conflict, not relevant on the facts of the case referred to it, could in any event be managed by national courts setting aside the relevant rules.[80]

Another recent decision by the Court of Cassation is more troubling. A bank alleged that its credits in relation to a bankruptcy procedure (namely loans that had been extended to a subsequently bankrupt debtor) had not been considered as being covered by priority rights. Normally such credits take priority over other credits. The reason for that qualification was that the loan had benefited from a guarantee from a Region-owned financing institution, which, according to the lower courts, amounted to State aid. The Court of Cassation quashed the appeal judgment by holding that the courts below had been wrong in finding (i) that the guarantee was a nullity because it had been given in breach of Article 107 TFEU and (ii) that the nullity affected the guaranteed loan. According to the court, nullity flowing from breach of mandatory rules may be waived by specific rules applying to special circumstances. Unlike Article 101(2) TFEU, Article 107 does not expressly declare decisions tainted by State aid a nullity and, anyway, it is solely directed to the Member States. Member States, the court reasoned, can only recover aid, which in this case was the guarantee and not the guaranteed loan.[81]

The 'reasoning' is logically inconsistent. The Court of Cassation equated an EU provision not explicitly providing for nullity as a consequence for its breach to an explicit provision derogating from the general rule in Italian law making nullity the consequence of the breach of a mandatory provision. It is troubling that the Court of Cassation not only failed to consider whether to refer the case to the CJEU but was also totally oblivious of the duties binding national courts not to give effects to measures possibly tainted by State aid rules.

80. Cass, Sez. I, 15 September 2017, no. 21481 (ord.).
81. Cass, Sez. I, 27 April 2018, no. 10303 (ord.).

VIII. A DIGRESSION ON PUBLIC PROCUREMENT AND CONCESSIONS

A *fil rouge* links most of the cases analysed in this contribution. They concern the award and management of public contracts and specifically concessions awarding SGEI – and even more specifically transport cases.[82] In some cases, litigation springs from State aid afforded to the incumbent provider of ferry services (*Saremar*), including through misuse of an award procedure (*Liberty Lines*). Other cases, including two preliminary references, concern railway services. Italian public authorities might be seen as going out of their way to protect the incumbent former State monopolist from an international competitor (*FSI*, *Arriva Italia Rail*). A more 'classical' public procurement case is *Cineca*, but here again the State is seen as shielding a company it owns from competition.

This 'density' of public procurements and concessions among private enforcement of State aid cases cannot be explained away as a coincidence. At least two reasons spring to our minds. The first is that aid in this area is ultra-selective. In case of industry-wide schemes, aid benefits all (national) industry participants. No one is left behind, so that more often than not there is no (domestic) competitor having an interest in challenging the measure. These aids are selective in the old protectionist way as they target foreigner undertakings. Aid in the public contracts domain is, by contrast, ultra-selective in that only one market participant benefits from the aid to the direct detriment of all other undertakings operating on the same relevant market, including domestic ones. Moreover, concessions markets, and especially SGEI, have very few participants, and contracts are few and of high value. Especially new entrants trying to claim some ground from the old State-owned monopolist will have strong incentives to litigate. In most 'classic' public procurement markets, however, incentives are lower since the large number of market participants renders less obvious which one of them is affected in a direct and significant way by aid given to another company. Therefore, *Cineca* is somewhat exceptional in that the aid has been challenged by one of the very many IT service providers on the Italian market.

Market structure considerations go some ways in explaining why State aid issues are not more frequently litigated in 'classic' public procurement markets,[83] this notwithstanding the fact that State aid is expressly mentioned in Directive 2014/24/EU on the award of public procurement as a ground to exclude an abnormally low tender. Under Article 69(4) of the Directive, '[w]here a contracting authority establishes that a tender is abnormally low because the tenderer has obtained State aid, the tender may be rejected on that ground alone only after consultation with the tenderer where the latter is unable to prove, within a sufficient time limit fixed by the contracting authority, that the aid in question was compatible with the internal market within the

82. *See* more generally the analysis by P. Nicolaides and S. Schoenmaeker, *Public Procurement, Public Private Partnerships and State Aid Rules: A Symbiotic Relationship* (2014) 1 EPPPL, 13 et seq.
83. *See* the analysis by A. Sanchez Graells, *Enforcement of State Aid Rules for Services of General Economic Interest before Public Procurement Review Bodies and Courts* (2014) 10 Competition Law Review 3.

meaning of Article 107 TFEU. Where the contracting authority rejects a tender in those circumstances, it shall inform the Commission thereof'.[84]

Abnormally low tenders are very often litigated in Italy. In these cases, the competitor bringing the action is another economic operator which is interested in being awarded the contract. Often the economic operator whose tender was ranked second is the one challenging the award, and it obviously has strong incentives to have the winner excluded and to obtain the contract in its place. However, despite the high amount of litigation regarding abnormally low tenders, we could find only very few cases in which the national provision implementing Article 69(4) of Directive 2014/24/EU was invoked in front of Italian administrative courts, none of which was successful for the competitors.[85]

Arguably, this might be due, on the one hand, to the lack of awareness as to the State aid rules applicable in 'classic' procurement procedures and, on the other hand, to the competing tenderers' lack of access to adequate information needed to first identify the presence of the subsidy and to then challenge it in order to obtain damages.[86]

Indeed, unlike in the recent cases discussed above (where State aid rules are mostly used as a way to achieve the opening of a certain market), there seems to be still little use of rules regarding transparency and separation of accounts in case of abnormally law tenders. As discussed, reference to this set of rules could facilitate the verification procedure of contracting authorities and national courts and would be extremely useful for the competitors. Yet the contracting authorities confronted with an abnormally low offer seem reluctant to investigate possible violations of State aid rules, and, in turn, private enforcers seem willing to base their challenge of the anomaly on any ground but the breach of State aid and transparency rules.

The second reason for which private enforcement is still under-used in these types of procedures is that private competitors need to prove the 'direct causal link' between the breach of State aid rules and the damage suffered.

In principle, it could be easier to comply with this standard of proof in a procurement procedure, where the selective impact of the award is evident. In general, an economic operator can fulfil the 'direct causal link' requirement as long as it proves that the existence of an illegal aid in favour of a competitor has prevented his being awarded the tender. In case of abnormally low tenders, private competitors can challenge the award when they do not agree with the evaluation of the contracting authority and consider the anomaly to be the result of an aid incompatible with the

84. *See* generally T. Indén, *'Article 69. Abnormally low tenders'* in M. Steinicke and P.L. Vesterdorf, *EU Public Procurement Law* 751 et seq. (Nomos 2018).
85. Notably, in its request for preliminary ruling to the ECJ in the *Data Medica Service* case, the Consiglio di Stato considered that the abnormally low tender mechanism was not sufficient to identify possible breaches of State aid rules in the procurement context when public economic operators are involved (ECJ, Case C-568/13 *Azienda Ospedaliero-Universitaria di Careggi-Firenze v Data medical Service Srl* [2014] ECLI:EU:C:2014:2466, para. 28; *see also* the reasoning of the *Consiglio di Stato* in its reference order, Cons. Stato, Sez. III, 30 October 2013, no. 5241).
86. *See* the analysis by F. Pastor-Merchante, *The Role of Competitors in the Enforcement of State Aid Law*, Chapter 3 (Hart 2017).

TFEU.[87] However, in such cases, the standard of proof becomes again burdensome since the competitor has to prove (i) that the awarded tenderer has benefitted from incompatible aid, (ii) that the incompatible aid has been used to submit the abnormally low offer and (iii) had the abnormally low offer been excluded, he would have won the tender.[88]

Needless to say, this is not an easy task. The possibility for competing tenderers to challenge an award extended to an abnormally low offer raises the aforementioned issue of access to sufficient details about the winning bid.[89] In practice, it indeed remains very hard for a competing undertaking to know – or to have access to information that would prove – whether the awarded tenderer has benefitted *and used* incompatible aid in order to submit the abnormally low offer. Furthermore, the interest of the contesting tenderer has to be balanced with the need to protect the winning tenderer from an excessive disclosure of information regarding its offer and its enterprise in the post-award phase.[90]

IX. PRIVATE ENFORCEMENT OF EU COMPETITION AND STATE AID LAW: THE WAY FORWARD

When discussing the future of private enforcement of EU State aid law, two different types of challenges must be distinguished: structural problems and knowledge problems.

By 'structural' problems we mean the ways State aid litigation is handled from both factual and procedural/remedial points of view. Factually, one must acknowledge that more often than not subsidies benefit an entire national industry, so that only foreign companies are adversely affected. Most probably, no individual foreign company would consider private enforcement as an avenue for redress in parallel with bringing the issue to the Commission's attention. This issue is not specific to Italy. From a policy perspective, it would probably make sense to envisage and promote representative interest litigation that affords standing to foreign institutions like *chambres de commerce* and industry associations. This would not pose problems in Italy since such representative actions are widely allowed by our courts.[91]

---

87. Article 69(4) and its national transposition sets a duty for the contracting authority to verify in the *inter partes* verification phase whether the abnormal character of the offer depends on the existence of incompatible aid. If so, the adjudicating authority is entitled to exclude the tenderer and is obliged to inform the Commission; otherwise it can confirm the award.
88. *See* the analysis in B. Biancardi, *Abnormally Low Tenders of Public Providers, a cross subsidisation issue?* (2018) 4 EPPPL 270, 278 et seq.; *see also* T. Inden, 'Award of the Contract' in M Steinicke and P L Vesterdorf (eds), EU Public Procurement Law (C.H.Beck Hart Nomos Publishing, 2018), 748 et seq.
89. *See* Sanchez Graells, *supra* n. 83.
90. *See* for discussion A. Sanchez Graells, *The difficult balance between transparency and competition in public procurement: Some recent trends in the case law of the European Courts and a look at the new Directives* (2013) University of Leicester School of Law Research Paper no. 13-11.
91. There is a rich case law concerning the standing of professional organisations to challenge administrative measures detrimental to their associates: besides Cons. Stato Sez. V, 19 September 1995, no. 1314, already referred to, *see*, e.g., Cons. Stato, Sez. V, 3 October 2017, no. 4614;

As shown by the public contract cases analysed above, the situation is different for ultra-selective aid, favouring one undertaking over all others, domestic or foreign. The issues here are procedural and/or remedial. The first issue is information about existing aid and more generally about business data relevant to ascertaining the existence of aid. The latter is still limited, and EU secondary law may be read as limiting the right of access, as it was in the *Arriva Italia Rail* case.[92] The second issue is the difficulty for the competitor of the beneficiary of the State aid to prove harm and obtain damages. Some form of punitive damages might go some way in providing incentives for private enforcement actions, but as is well known this option was ruled out by Directive 2014/104/EU on certain rules governing actions for damages under national law for infringements of the competition law provisions of the Member States and of the European Union.[93] The presumption of harm as established under Article 17(1) and (2) of the same Directive might however be useful in the area of State aid as well.[94]

Issues concerning the actual 'knowledge' of Italian courts regarding State aid rules seem now to be less relevant than in the past. The cases discussed in this contribution clearly show that the administrative courts, and the *Consiglio di Stato* on top of them, are fast becoming acquainted with EU State aid law and are ready to refer to the Court of Justice for guidance. This is not true for the *Corte di Cassazione*, but clearly most cases, and the most relevant ones, are today heard by the administrative courts. Based on the learning process concerning the (then) EEC law of public procurement, it is expected that the legal profession will take its cue from the courts and increasingly raise State aid issues in front of the Italian courts, and this even more so if and when the above-mentioned structural problems are addressed.[95]

---

the only limit is that an association cannot take a side in litigation opposing two associates: Cons. Stato, Sez. V, 21 June 2017, no. 3029.

92. Cons. Stato, Sez. V, 24 May 2018, no. 3122, para. 16.
93. *See* Article 3(3): 'Full compensation under this Directive shall not lead to overcompensation, whether by means of punitive, multiple or other types of damages'.
94. '1. Member States shall ensure that neither the burden nor the standard of proof required for the quantification of harm renders the exercise of the right to damages practically impossible or excessively difficult. Member States shall ensure that the national courts are empowered, in accordance with national procedures, to estimate the amount of harm if it is established that a claimant suffered harm but it is practically impossible or excessively difficult precisely to quantify the harm suffered on the basis of the evidence available. 2. It shall be presumed that cartel infringements cause harm. The infringer shall have the right to rebut that presumption'.
95. It was actually a first instance administrative court that precipitated interest in and consequently knowledge of EU public procurement law, this occurring after the court raised on its own motion the question of whether then EEC law had been breached in connection with an abnormally low tender that precipitated interest in and consequently knowledge of EU public procurement law in Italy: T.A.R. Piemonte, Sez. II, 8 February 1989, no. 34, *Giur. Ital.* 1989, III, 1, 148, note R. Caranta.

CHAPTER 14

Private Enforcement in the Netherlands

Jacobine E. van den Brink & Willemien den Ouden

I. Introduction
II. Illegal state aid: which court has jurisdiction?
III. The Dutch administrative courts and state aid claims
- A. Spatial planning
- B. Unlawful advantage for the competitor
- C. Levy decisions
- D. Decisions to reject a request for aid and revocation decisions
- E. Recovery decisions

IV. The Dutch tax courts and state aid claims
V. The Dutch civil courts and state aid claims
- A. Introduction
- B. Types of disputes before the civil courts
  1. Disputes where the government is accused of having granted an advantage to a competitor
  2. Disputes between the alleged beneficiary and another private party
  3. Disputes about levies intended to finance state aid
  4. Disputes concerning expropriation
  5. Disputes on the enforcement of a recovery decision taken by the European Commission
  6. Disputes where the government has revoked a granted benefit or refuses to grant an advantage
- C. Available judgment options for the civil courts
- D. Bottlenecks in state aid cases before the civil courts
  1. Interest requirements and the Schutznorm
  2. Qualification of state aid
  3. Compensation for damages in state aid cases

4. A ray of light: the alleged support conflicts with general principles of sound administration
VI. Taking stock of the private enforcement of state aid law in the Netherlands
VII. Dutch State Aid Recovery Act

I. INTRODUCTION

State aid cases are no rare phenomenon in the Netherlands. A much-discussed recent example concerned the well-known coffee chain Starbucks, which as a result of a fiscal ruling had paid little tax for years. The European Commission regarded this advantage as unlawful State aid. However, tax aid is by no means the most important form of State aid that comes before the Dutch courts. The courts more often deal with alleged support for spatial development projects, subsidy decisions or loans under 'soft' conditions. Competitors of State aid recipients frequently ask the courts to protect them against unfair competition as a result of State aid. This is often referred to as the 'private enforcement' of State aid law. Dutch case law shows, however, that the category of private individuals who invoke State aid law to protect their interests is broader than just competitors. Local residents and insured persons, for instance, also frequently claim a breach of State aid law. In this contribution, we will include these situations in the term private enforcement of State aid law. This decision is based on the idea that the European Commission, wanting to concentrate more on the major issues, leaves less serious cases involving State aid law to the national courts. From the perspective of enforcement, it does not matter much which parties bring alleged violations of State aid law before these courts. We will, therefore, outline how the Dutch judiciary, in ruling on State aid arguments raised by private individuals, contributes to the enforcement of State aid law. What are the most important issues and problems at stake and what best practices can be distinguished in the private enforcement of State aid law in the Netherlands?

To answer these questions, we have studied the Dutch case law that deals with State aid law. For the period from November 2005 up to November 2015, all Dutch case law containing references to the words 'State aid' has already been identified and analysed by Metselaar, who published a study on the enforcement of State aid law in the Netherlands in 2016.[1] In addition, we have analysed the case law in the period from November 2015 up to 1 November 2018. On the basis of this, we can paint a picture of the role that State aid law plays in current Dutch legal practice. This study of case law can, however, only serve as a sketch of the situation. First, www.rechtspraak.nl only publishes a selection of judgments given by the Dutch courts. This makes it impossible to obtain the full picture, but this is a relative limitation since all judgments of the highest courts are made public. Second, examining the case law does not clarify the

1. A.J. Metselaar, *Drie rechters en een norm. Handhaving van de Europese staatssteunregels voor de Nederlandse rechter en de grenzen van de procedurele autonomie (Three judges and one norm. The enforcement of the European State aid rules before Dutch courts and the limits of national procedural autonomy)* (Wolters Kluwer 2016).

number and nature of disputes related to State aid law that are settled outside the courts. To provide more detail and add more colour to this sketch of current Dutch legal practice, the Dutch literature on the private enforcement of State aid law has also been incorporated in our analysis.

On the basis of the acquired data, we will first discuss in section II. the various Dutch courts that offer legal protection in State aid cases. The Netherlands has a complicated division of jurisdiction with regard to government actions, which entails that more than one court may be competent. They all deal with State aid disputes according to the procedural rules applicable in their field of law. We will distinguish mainly between the assessments of State aid cases by, successively, the administrative courts, who have reviewed most of the cases in the aforementioned period, the tax courts, who are rarely confronted with these cases, and the civil courts, who in theory function as ordinary courts, but who nonetheless handle many State aid cases. In sections III., IV. and V., we will discuss how these three courts deal with State aid arguments put forward by private parties. Section VI draws our conclusions – with the thread linking the three Dutch courts being that State aid proceedings by private parties are rarely successful. Finally, in section VII., we will consider the relatively recent State Aid Recovery Act, which entered into force on 1 July 2018. What changes will this legislation bring in Dutch practice dealing with private law enforcement?

II. ILLEGAL STATE AID: WHICH COURT HAS JURISDICTION?

The study of State aid case law referred to above immediately shows that many different Dutch courts can have jurisdiction in State aid disputes. Proceedings are brought before various administrative courts, tax courts and the civil courts. This is due to the division of jurisdiction within the Dutch legal system. Decisive for the jurisdiction of these different courts is the act by which the alleged unlawful State aid was granted. In principle, the administrative courts have jurisdiction in disputes concerning 'decisions':[2] written decisions taken by an administrative authority that involve a unilateral public legal act. If the contested State aid is issued, or partly issued, by such an administrative decision, for example, a subsidy decision or the adoption of a zoning plan, the administrative court is competent. A complicating factor, however, is that there are several last instance administrative courts in the Dutch legal system. The most important of these, with general jurisdiction in appeal, is the Administrative Jurisdiction Division of the Council of State. Another last instance administrative court is the Trade and Industry Appeals Tribunal (*College van Beroep voor het Bedrijfsleven, CBb*): a specialised administrative court that rules on disputes in the area of social-economic administrative law. In addition, this Appeals Tribunal also rules on appeals concerning specific laws, such as the Competition Act and the Telecommunications Act. Due to its specialisation, this court deals with State aid cases on a regular basis. A second specialised highest administrative court is the Central Appeals Tribunal (*Centrale Raad van Beroep, CRvB*): a Court of Appeal which is mainly active in legal areas

2. As defined in Article 1:3 of the General Administrative Law Act (GALA).

concerning social security and public service. It is the highest judicial authority in these areas, only dealing with State aid issues in exceptional cases. Finally, where decisions in the field of tax are concerned, the tax courts are competent, with the Supreme Court sitting in last instance. The judgements of the administrative and tax courts in first instance are the results of an annulment claim that is directed against a decision: a decision is annulled or it remains in force. In appeal, the highest administrative court will review the judgement of the Court of First Instance.

If no possibilities exist to bring a case before the administrative or tax courts, then the civil courts step into the picture. The civil courts function like ordinary courts. This is a somewhat misleading term in this respect. In many cases, alleged State aid was provided by means of a private contract; in these cases, the civil courts have jurisdiction. The same applies to support that is made possible by an Act of Parliament. These Acts do not constitute administrative decisions that can be challenged before the administrative court because they are not drawn up by administrative bodies (as follows from Article 1:1(2) of the General Administrative Law Act (hereinafter: 'GALA')). In these cases, the enforcement of State aid law must therefore also be requested before a civil court.

This finely branched division of jurisdiction means that it can be difficult in general to establish which court should offer legal protection to a private individual against the various forms of government action. This problem also arises in the case of government action that involves unlawful State aid. In the Netherlands, it is often uncertain whether an administrative decision has been made, against which a complaint can be lodged before the administrative court, or whether the administrative authorities acted in a different way, which gives the civil courts jurisdiction. Moreover, the case law on this subject is constantly developing and remains a topic of debate. Specifically in relation to the enforcement of State aid law, it is relevant that private law entities that allocate public funds are sometimes regarded as administrative bodies that take subsidy decisions, thus falling under the jurisdiction of the administrative courts, and that some private law contracts between administrative authorities and private parties are nevertheless regarded as subsidy decisions by the administrative courts. In these cases, it is important to note that, in principle, administrative decisions should be challenged within six weeks. Otherwise, the decision will be given formal legal force (*res iudicata*) and will be presumed to be legal, both by the administrative courts and the civil courts.

A second problem arising from this finely branched jurisdiction on government action is that an aid measure may consist of a set of acts that fall under the jurisdiction of different Dutch courts.[3] The jurisprudence on the company *Eigen Veerdienst Terschelling* illustrates that this is not just a danger in theory. This company has litigated for years, in order to be able to compete for a ferry service between Harlingen, Terschelling and Vlieland. *Eigen Veerdienst Terschelling* took the view that this ferry service was successfully operated by another company because of government action in violation of State aid law. The alleged State aid consisted of all sorts of different

3. Metselaar, *supra* n. 1, at 115.

elements: public service contracts, co-use agreements, lease contracts for the access road to the port area, concession loans, exemptions from sales tax and mooring permits.[4] As a consequence, *Eigen Veerdienst Terschelling* had to litigate in both the administrative as well as in the civil courts.[5] It is obvious that the legal position of *Eigen Veerdienst Terschelling* would have been considerably stronger if one court had assessed whether the various elements combined constituted unlawful State aid. It is also conceivable that the fact that private parties sometimes have to litigate before different courts does not lead to much enthusiasm on their part to enforce State aid law in this way. Private enforcement of State aid law tends to be a complex issue that requires detailed knowledge of the Dutch legal system and a lot of perseverance. Submitting a complaint to the European Commission thus quickly becomes a simple and more attractive alternative.

III. THE DUTCH ADMINISTRATIVE COURTS AND STATE AID CLAIMS

When writing on private enforcement of State aid law in the Netherlands, it is logical to first discuss the disputes settled by the administrative courts. If we consider the published case law, the administrative courts receive the highest proportion of disputes in which State aid law plays a role. The study conducted by Metselaar showed that 271 administrative cases were published throughout the period from 2005 to 2015. The research that we carried out for this contribution showed that seventy-seven judgments were added to this category in the period from 1 November 2015 to 1 November 2018.[6] These recent rulings, however, did not change the overall picture, instead only serving to validate it.

A. Spatial planning

The overall picture starts with the observation that the most extensive group of administrative disputes is not initiated by entrepreneurs complaining about State aid given to their competitors. In more than half of the cases, the plaintiffs are citizens who expect they will be harmed in their interests through an environmental law decision. Their feared damages do not include competitive damages. These local residents usually file many sorts of objections against such a decision, including State aid law arguments. The basic contention in these challenges is often that the contested administrative decision to approve or enact a zoning plan can only be implemented if State aid is provided and that this State aid measure has not been or will not be approved by the European Commission.

4. Metselaar, *supra* n. 1, at 116.
5. *See*, e.g., Rechtbank Den Haag, 31 December 2013, ECLI:NL:RBDHA:2013:18370 and Rechtbank Leeuwarden, 12 December 2012, ECLI:NL:RBLEE:2012:BY5837.
6. In thirty of these judgements the term 'State aid' was mentioned, but the law on State aid was only indirectly relevant.

As of 2004,[7] the Council of State has weighed State aid arguments in such cases within the context of the question whether the zoning plan is 'financially feasible'. According to Dutch spatial planning law, the municipal board must, before enacting a zoning plan, investigate the feasibility of the plan.[8] Where it is not possible to demonstrate that the contested zoning plan could also be implemented if the municipal support required for the plan cannot be granted because of an infringement of State aid law, the Council of State has ruled that the administrative decision to enact the zoning plan was not prepared with due care. This case law led to the initiation of many State aid claims in zoning plan procedures. Some of them were successful, and several zoning plan decisions were annulled on the grounds of State aid law.[9]

In 2011, this approach was refined to include the requirement that in cases where the plaintiff had made a plausible State aid argument, he must also make it plausible that the municipal authorities should in all reasonableness have realised in advance that the plan could not be implemented within the plan period without providing unlawful State aid.[10] When reviewing this aspect, it must considered whether other market parties could possibly have effectuated the plan, instead of the State aid recipient. This line of reasoning in the case law led to a decline in the number of successful claims on the grounds of State aid law in the area of spatial planning from 8% to 2%, according to Aalbers and Jaarsma.[11]

After a relativity requirement (the *Schutznorm*) was introduced in GALA on 1 January 2013,[12] the Council of State decided to limit the possibilities for plaintiffs to successfully invoke State aid law in spatial planning cases even further. In a judgment in 2016,[13] the Council of State stated that before the administrative court is entitled to assess the financial feasibility of the contested zoning plan on the grounds of State aid law, it must first be established whether, in principle, residents who are not affected by competitive interests can invoke the State aid rules in this context. The answer to that question was given in the negative: the Council of State took the view that Article 108(3) Treaty on the Functioning of the European Union (TFEU) is clearly not intended to protect their interests. Since local residents do not derive any rights from Article 108(3) TFEU, the application of the relativity requirement is therefore not in conflict with the requirements imposed by EU law on the application of national procedural law in cases within the realm of EU law, according to the Council of State. This case law is

7. Raad van State, 6 May 2004, ECLI:NL:RVS:2004:AO8853 *Zoning plan Haaksbergen*.
8. *See* Article 3.1.6 Bro.
9. *See*, e.g., Raad van State, 15 February 2012, ECLI:NL:RVS:2012:BV5119 *Zoning plan de Zumpel-Kloosterstraat Julianastraat Grubbenvorst*.
10. Raad van State, 13 April 2011, ECLI:NL:RVS:2011:BQ1077 *Zoning plan Centrum Haaren*.
11. M. Aalbers and M. Jaarsma, *Het beginsel van een marktdeelnemer in de markteconomie: rechtsontwikkelingen en praktische knelpunten in gebiedsontwikkeling. Terug naar de basis?* (*The principle of a trader in the market economy: legal developments and practical bottlenecks in area development. Back to the basics?*) [2015] Tijdschrift voor Staatssteun (*Dutch Journal on State aid*) 104, 108.
12. *See* Article 8:69a GALA.
13. Raad van State, 2 November 2016, ECLI:NL:RVS:2016:2892 *Zoning plan De Hagen Hollum*. *See* for a more recent example, Raad van State, 23 May 2018, ECLI:NL:RVS:2018:1686 *Zoning plan Horst aan de Maas*.

now also seen outside the category of zoning plan cases, appearing for example in a complaint against an airport extension decision.[14]

The introduction of the relativity requirement also turned out to have major consequences for claimants in proceedings against a zoning plan decision that claim to have competitive interests that are threatened by unlawful State aid. Since 2016[15] they stumble on the fact that the State aid argument is only reviewed in an indirect way, namely through the assessment of the financial and economic feasibility of the zoning plan. This standard requirement in Dutch spatial law is aimed at protecting interested parties from being confronted with the adverse spatial consequences of a zoning plan that is not feasible, for example in the form of semi-realised objects. These disadvantages are not suffered by competitors who are not located in the immediate vicinity of the area or plot of land in question. They can therefore no longer invoke this provision, and as a consequence, their State aid argument can no longer be considered. Since the possible distortion of competition due to unlawful State aid can be submitted to a national court by challenging a different government action (for instance the accompanying subsidy decision or the purchase agreement for the land), the Council of State does not see any tension in relation to the requirements imposed by EU law on the application of national procedural law in cases within the scope of EU law.[16]

As a result of these recent rulings, only appellants who can be affected in their competitive interests by decisions concerning zoning plans and who are in the immediate vicinity of the concerned area or plot of land can successfully rely on the rules on State aid law in proceedings against the zoning plan.[17] This means that an enormous potential for the private enforcement of State aid law in administrative law has been cut off. In the last three years, seventeen cases against zoning plan decisions faltered on the relativity requirement.[18] In the period from 1 November 2015 to 1 November 2018, we found no examples of successful claims based on State aid law[19] in the area of spatial planning.

In the meantime, the threshold of the relativity requirement has also been applied by other administrative courts to avoid reviewing State aid arguments from appellants who are not affected in terms of their competitive interests. These cases are in the area

14. Raad van State, 15 November 2017, ECLI:NL:RVS:2017:3126 *Airport Regulatory Enforcement Decision Twente Airport.*
15. Raad van State, 9 November 2016, ECLI:NL:RVS:2016:2975 *Zoning plan Leidsche Rijn*. Previously, the Council of State had applied the relativity requirement to shareholders who challenged the expropriation order of the Minister of Finance concerning SNS REAAL and SNS Bank, with a part of their claim being that the State aid provided in the expropriation decision was unlawful: Raad van State, 25 February 2013, ECLI:NL:RVS:2013:BZ2265.
16. Where the Administrative Jurisdiction Division in particular refers to ECJ judgments Case 33/76 *Rewe* [1976] ECR 1989, para. 5; ECJ, Joined Cases C-317/08, 318/08, 319/08 and 320/08 18 March *Alassini et al.* [2010] ECR I-2213, paras 47–49; ECJ, Case C-432/05 *Unibet* [2007] ECR I-2271, para. 65.
17. Cf. Raad van State, 21 December 2016, ECLI:NL:RVS:2016:3386 *Leeuwarden-Bioscoop Harmonieplein.*
18. Meanwhile the test of a 'financially feasible' zoning plan is also still applied. We found twenty judgments in which an administrative judge applied this test in the period from 1 November 2015 to 1 November 2018.
19. In total we administered forty published judgements that mentioned State aid arguments in this field of law.

of social security. Two examples are the challenge raised against a fine due to the refusal of an unemployed person to sign an employment contract[20] and the challenging of a fine for non-fulfilment of the Dutch insurance obligation which, according to the appellant, led to enforced financing of the pharmaceutical industry and thus to illegal State aid.[21]

This line of jurisprudence has led to a situation wherein a large part of the administrative law cases where State aid arguments are put forward, these arguments are not reviewed due to the relativity requirement. National procedural provisions, in particular, the relativity requirement, make it possible to leave State aid questions unanswered. The administrative courts do not see this as a problem, for in their view it is clear that State aid law is not intended to protect these citizens. No questions were referred to the ECJ on this subject, even though the limits of the scope of protection of State aid law had not been dealt with extensively by the European court.

B. Unlawful advantage for the competitor

The classic situation of private enforcement of State aid law by competitors is also a regular occurrence in the Dutch administrative courts. Metselaar reported forty-two published cases in the period from 2005 to 2015, and we added no relevant cases to that number in the past three years.[22] These cases often concern subsidy decisions,[23] but decisions about the granting of licences that provide a financial advantage without having to pay a market-based compensation also occur.[24] In terms of size, this is a limited category of cases in which competitors directly challenge an administrative decision affecting their competitive interests. They, too, do not seem to be able to successfully invoke State aid law in the Dutch courtroom.

This is partly caused by the fact that such competitors are not always seen as an interested party within the meaning of Article 1:2 GALA. In each case, the administrative court first assesses whether the appellant is directly affected by the decision that is being challenged, before reviewing that decision. According to established case law, litigating competitors are required to be active in the same market segment and service area as the addressee of the (alleged) aid decision. The same market segment is assumed when the products or services offered by the two companies are in competition with each other. The service area of products or services concerns the geographic market in which they are delivered. Generally, the Dutch administrative courts are not very strict in applying these requirements. Broad access to the administrative courts for

20. Centrale Raad van Beroep, 21 February 2017, ECLI:NL:CRVB:2017:607.
21. Centrale Raad van Beroep, 20 June 2018, ECLI:NL:CRVB:2018:1857.
22. Competitors only complained indirectly about State aid for their rivals, for instance in a complaint against the rejection of a subsidy application: Rechtbank Zeeland-West-Brabant, 7 November 2016, ECLI:NL:RBZWB:2016:6944 *subsidie aanvraag peuterspeelzaalwerk*.
23. *See*, e.g., Raad van State, 17 August 2011, ECLI:NL:RVS:2011:BR5195 *Stichting NOB*.
24. *See*, e.g., Raad van State, 6 June 2018, ECLI:NL:RVS:2013BY9933 *Open Universiteit Nederland*.

competitors is in line with low-threshold access for citizens to the administrative courts, something considered desirable in the Netherlands.[25]

It is therefore particularly striking that the interested party test in State aid cases sometimes seems to be carried out more strictly than in other cases involving a competitor challenging an administrative decision. The most widely discussed example of this stricter test concerns the so-called *Vogelaar* case.[26] This case related to financial support provided to certain housing corporations in order to combat problems with living conditions in a few selected disadvantaged neighbourhoods, referred to as the *Vogelaarwijken*. To achieve this, a levy was imposed on all Dutch housing associations. The paying corporations believed this scheme of levying and subsidising to be in conflict with the European State aid rules. They objected to both the levy decision, which was judged legal by the administrative court, and to the subsidy decisions addressed to their competitors. It is striking that although in the proceedings concerning the levy decision the revenues were necessarily allocated to the financing of the aid, the administrative court did not consider this sufficient to automatically consider the payers as also being interested parties in the administrative decisions to grant the subsidies. The Council of State took the position that, under Dutch law, the payers had no direct interest in the subsidy decisions because it was impossible to establish which corporation paid for which supported project. Moreover, the collection of the levy did not automatically lead to the provision of subsidy. The purpose of the collection of the levy was to create financial scope for a subsidy scheme. Which corporations would receive money on the basis of this scheme and which criteria would be applied was a second, separate, issue according to the Council of State. Those parties who are considered to be interested parties in the context of levy decisions are therefore not automatically also interested parties in the subsequent subsidy decisions in the Netherlands. In order to be considered to be an interested party in the administrative decisions on subsidies, parties have to fulfil the requirements of Article 1:2 GALA. It must, therefore, be examined whether the paying parties are active in the same market segment and service area as the subsidy recipients. The levy payers in the *Vogelaar* case seem to comply with this requirement, but interestingly enough this was not deemed sufficient. The Council of State also checked in this case whether the competitors had made a 'reasonable case' that they would indeed suffer a loss of turnover as a result of the alleged State aid. This hurdle was too high for the levy payers, and as a result, their complaint was declared inadmissible.

This unusual interested party test has been criticised in Dutch literature, among other reasons because of the requirement that the principles of effectiveness and equivalence must be respected when applying national procedural law in cases that fall within the scope of EU law. Dutch case law provides more examples of a more stringent assessment by the Dutch administrative courts in relation to the interested party aspect,[27] as well as the requirement of sufficient legal interest.[28] This case law has led

25. *See* J. Wieland, *De bescherming van concurrentiebelangen in het bestuursrecht (The protection of competitors interests in Dutch administrative law)* (Boom Juridische uitgevers 2017).
26. Raad van State, 6 February 2013, ECLI:NL:RVS:2013:BZ0794 *Vogelaarwijken*.
27. *See*, e.g., Raad van State, 29 May 2013, ECLI:NL:RVS:2013:CA1378 *Edufax*.

to some authors stating that procedural autonomy appears to be a serious obstacle for successfully invoking State aid law.[29] Some even suspect that the courts use procedural arguments in some of these cases in order to avoid a substantive assessment of the dispute.[30]

There are, of course, also cases where competitors successfully overcome the obstacles of the interested party test and the relativity requirement. However, in those cases the plaintiff then has to prove that State aid rules were infringed, which is usually not an easy task due to the lack of information that competitors have. The administrative courts are not inclined to use their own investigative powers to establish illegal State aid.[31] Furthermore, if a substantive assessment by an administrative court is carried out, it is sometimes rather indirect in nature.[32] The contested decision is often reviewed in the light of formal principles of good administration. If it cannot be excluded that the contested aid measure has resulted in unlawful State aid, the contested decision will be annulled due to conflict with the requirement that decisions are carefully prepared, known as the principle of due care.[33] In this context, the administrative court created a duty for the administrative authority to ensure and substantiate that no illegal State aid will be granted. The consequence of this approach is that the State aid rules are not directly applied by the court itself.

It must be concluded that in the vast majority of cases in which administrative courts substantively review a decision that might infringe State aid law, it is ruled that no (illegal) State aid is involved, often with no extensive reasoning being given,[34] and in an increasing number of cases this occurs after the Commission has been asked for advice by the courts themselves.[35] However, the number of published cases in which the administrative courts have turned to the Commission can still be counted on two hands. There are many possible explanations for the fact that the annulment of a decision concerning illegal State aid law by the administrative courts is a rarity[36] in the Netherlands, and these are discussed by Metselaar in her comprehensive 2015 study. Are competitors complaining without good reason? Are they being hindered by a lack of information? Are the Dutch administrative courts not inclined to apply complex State aid law or are they just not strict enough when doing so? These may all be relevant

28. College van Beroep voor het bedrijfsleven, 13 September 2012, ECLI:NL:CBB:2012:BX6991 *Thuiszorg Service Nederland*.
29. *See* Metselaar, *supra* n. 1, at 184 and R.J.M. van den Tweel, *Staatssteun en de rol van de nationale rechter, tien jaar verder* [2015] SEW 553 et seq.
30. Metselaar, *supra* n. 1, at 197.
31. Metselaar, *supra* n. 1, at 312 et seq.
32. Metselaar, *supra* n. 1, at 312.
33. Raad van State, 17 December 2003, ECLI:NL:RVS:2003:AO0234 *Martiniplaza*; Raad van State, 6 June 2012, ECLI:NL:RVS:2012:BW7642; Raad van State, 15 February 2012, ECLI:NL:RVS: 2012:BV5119 *Zoning plan de Zumpel-Kloosterstraat Julianastraat Grubbenvorst*.
34. *See* Metselaar, *supra* n. 1, at 288 and 314. *See* for a more recent example: Rechtbank Zeeland-West-Brabant, 7 November 2016, ECLI:NL:RBZWB:2016:6944 *subsidie aanvraag peuterspeelzaalwerk*.
35. *See* for instance Raad van State, 30 January 2013, ECLI:NL:RVS:2013:BY9933 *Open Universiteit*: no State aid involved.
36. Rechtbank Rotterdam, 28 March 2013, ECLI:NL:RBROT:2013:BZ5824 *Veerverbinding Boven Hardinxveld*, is a rare example.

factors but it is not possible to give a final explanation on the basis of the published case law alone. The small chance of a competitor being successful in State aid cases is probably one of the reasons that they lodge very few requests for interim relief. The same goes for requests for compensation of damages by the responsible authorities: the studied case law offers no examples.

C. Levy decisions

As has already been made clear, parties who are obliged to pay levies can also challenge these decisions, as the aforementioned case of the *Vogelaar* neighbourhoods shows. In those cases, the interested party test does not usually lead to problems: the interests of the payers are directly affected as the addressee of the levy decision. However, in such cases, the administrative court does check whether levy decisions fall within the scope of the Treaty provisions on State aid. Taxes do not fall within the scope of the provisions of the Treaty concerning State aid unless they constitute the method of financing an aid measure, thus constituting an integral part of that measure. According to the European Court of Justice (ECJ), a tax or levy can only be regarded as forming an integral part of an aid measure when the revenue is required to be allocated to finance the aid. In several Dutch cases, this connection between revenue and alleged State aid was indeed established. This did not mean, however, that the appellants successfully invoked State aid provisions; it still proved to be very difficult for them to demonstrate unlawful State aid.

In those cases,[37] it is striking that a detailed discussion was held on whether the granting of the subsidies paid from the levies entailed unlawful State aid because the final aid measure had a different design than what had previously been presented to the Commission and had been approved by it.[38] In that context, a discussion arose about the correct interpretation of the relevant Commission decision. Remarkably, the Dutch court did not ask the Commission itself to provide more clarity about its intentions. Despite the fact that the ECJ made it clear that if doubt exists about the correct interpretation of a Commission decision, a request for advice should be put to the Commission or a preliminary question should be sent to the Court,[39] the Council of State gave its own interpretation of the Commission decision. On the basis of that interpretation, it came to the conclusion that no unlawful State aid had been issued. As a result the charged levy decisions were not annulled.

37. Raad van State, 2 November 2011, ECLI:NL:RVS:2011:BU3143 *Vogelaar I*, and Raad van State, 28 September 2016 ECLI:NL:RVS:2016:2568 *Vestia*.
38. This question also appears in the other categories of alleged State aid cases brought before the Dutch administrative courts. The courts have not yet developed a standard approach to deal with this question. *See* Metselaar, *supra* n. 1, at 360–369.
39. ECJ, Case C-574/14 *PGE Górnictwo* [2016] ECLI:EU:C:2016:686, paras 36–40.

D. Decisions to reject a request for aid and revocation decisions

An important category of cases brought before the Dutch administrative courts in which State aid law plays a role is the situation where the national authorities invoke State aid law. In such cases, national authorities argue that the requested support should be refused or granting decisions that have been issued previously should be withdrawn or changed because of the fact that the concerning support or grant has to be qualified as illegal state aid.[40] This category is the second largest after the complaints against decisions on zoning plans by competitors and, more often, local residents. However, this category will not be dealt with here since, strictly speaking, it does not involve private enforcement. After all, it is the government who invokes State aid law, not private parties. It should be noted, however, that the national authorities may request such decisions because private parties have requested enforcement of State aid law. It is, therefore, striking that in our selection there were no cases where this was the case. Metselaar calls this category 'the great absentee' and considers it likely that this is the result of the Dutch law of evidence.[41] When administrative authorities revoke a favourable decision on the basis of State aid law, they are required to prove that unlawful State aid was granted. When reviewing such unfavourable decisions, the Dutch administrative court places strict requirements on the reasoning. This may be an important factor for refraining as much as possible from issuing such decisions, except in cases where it is evident that State aid is involved, and, for example, the discussion is only about whether it falls within the scope of the Commission's approval decision.[42]

E. Recovery decisions

Finally, there is the category of disputes concerning decisions to recover illegal State aid, which can be challenged by the addressee before the Dutch administrative courts. It is striking that only few recovery decisions have been challenged before the administrative courts, but these cases were the source of intense debate on State aid in the Netherlands. This category does not concern private enforcement in the strict sense either since it concerns decisions taken by national authorities. It should be noted, however, that these decisions may constitute the final element of a request for enforcement of State aid law by competitors. This was the case, for example, with the BPM recovery decision.[43] In this classic case, competitors had complained to the European Commission about State aid measures outside the framework of a prior approval decision. The Commission investigated the case and ordered the Dutch State to recover the State aid that had been granted unlawfully. The responsible Dutch minister acted on that order, but it turned out that taking a recovery decision that

40. *See*, e.g., College van Beroep voor het bedrijfsleven, 8 July 2008, ECLI:NL:CBB:2007:BD8217 and College van Beroep voor het bedrijfsleven, 8 July 2008, ECLI:NL:CBB:2008:BD8212 (both on MEP subsidies).
41. Metselaar, *supra* n. 1, at 301.
42. *See*, e.g., Raad van State, 15 April 2015, ECLI:NL:RVS:2015:1152 *Zorg en Zekerheid*.
43. Raad van State, 11 January 2006, ECLI:NL:RVS:2006:AU9415 *BPM*.

complied with EU law requirements was not an easy task within the context of the Dutch legal order. Dutch law did not provide a suitable legal basis.[44] Furthermore, Dutch law required that the recovery of unlawful State aid was laid down in an administrative decision that could be challenged before the administrative courts, while the interest claim had to be filed by the administrative authorities at the civil court. This case ultimately led to the State Aid Recovery Act, which entered into force on 1 July 2018 and is discussed in section VII. of this chapter.

IV. THE DUTCH TAX COURTS AND STATE AID CLAIMS

We can be brief about the possibilities for private parties to lodge a complaint against State aid that is provided to their competitors through tax benefits. In the Netherlands, competitors of tax aid recipients do not have access to the tax courts by virtue of their position as competitors.[45] This follows from Article 26a of the State Taxes Act which states that only parties who are addressed by decisions of tax authorities have access to court. This means that it was not possible for competitors of Starbucks, like Coffee Lovers or Costa, to initiate proceedings before a Dutch tax court. Whether the competitor has a direct interest in the fact that his competitor receives a tax advantage is therefore irrelevant. This means that competitors of tax aid recipients must bring proceedings before the civil courts,[46] something that hardly ever occurs.[47] In this regard, Metselaar gives as a first explanation that the question of when a tax measure qualifies as State aid is, by its very nature, very difficult to answer.[48] It took until 2016 before a Commission Communication on the concept of State aid clarified this issue.[49] A second explanation for the fact that proceedings before the civil courts concerning tax aid hardly ever occur, can be found in the fact that Dutch tax law is subject to a duty of confidentiality pursuant to Article 67 of the State Taxes Act.[50] On the basis of this article, the tax authorities are not required to disclose information regarding persons or the property of another party, insofar as this is not necessary for the implementation of the Tax Code. Tax rulings are also treated confidentially.[51] Levy payers who wish to lodge a complaint against tax decisions addressed to them because unlawful State aid would be financed by the levies are admissible at the tax courts.[52] However, such proceedings are also very rare and rarely lead to success.[53]

Since competitors have no access to the tax courts by virtue of their position as competitors only, there is a risk in the Netherlands that fiscal State aid will remain out of the picture. In most cases, neither party – neither the recipient of fiscal State aid nor

44. Also Raad van State, 15 April 2015, ECLI:NL:RVS:2015:1152 *Zorg en Zekerheid*.
45. *See* also Metselaar, *supra* n. 1, at 166.
46. Metselaar, *supra* n. 1, at 167.
47. Metselaar, *supra* n. 1, at 167.
48. Metselaar, *supra* n. 1, at 134.
49. Commission Notice on the notion of State aid as referred to in Article 107(1) of the Treaty on the Functioning of the European Union [2016] OJ C 262/1.
50. Metselaar, *supra* n. 1, at 134.
51. Metselaar, *supra* n. 1, at 134–135.
52. Metselaar, *supra* n. 1, at 168.
53. *See* Metselaar, *supra* n. 1, at 129–130.

the tax authority involved – has an interest in raising a violation of the European State aid rules.[54] Of course, it is still possible for competitors to lodge a complaint with the European Commission.

V. THE DUTCH CIVIL COURTS AND STATE AID CLAIMS

A. Introduction

In this section, we will take a closer look at the various types of State aid disputes that the civil courts have to deal with in the Netherlands. The research conducted by Metselaar has established that in the period from 1 November 2005 up to and including 31 October 2015, civil courts rendered 142 judgments in which State aid was at issue.[55] In the period from 1 November 2015 to 31 October 2018, another seventy-seven judgments were announced in which the keywords 'State aid' appear.[56] A considerable number of these are cases where State aid is addressed only indirectly; these will be left out of our considerations in the rest of this section. We will discuss the different types of State aid disputes that occur most frequently in section V.B. In section V.C. we will discuss the ensuing issues.

B. Types of disputes before the civil courts

In cases where it is not possible to lodge a complaint against government action before the administrative courts or the tax courts, the civil courts have jurisdiction to hear the dispute. This means that if the State aid is not provided in the form of a decision, but in the form of a private law legal act or State aid that is made possible by an Act of Parliament, the civil courts come into the picture.[57] Here, for example, we find purchase agreements, such as the sale of land or a building, but also service agreements related to, for instance, waste collection or advertising objects.[58] Many legal claims can be brought before the civil courts.[59] For example, pursuant to Article 3:296(1) Dutch Civil Code, it may be requested that further support is stopped, that acts are suspended or suspended until the European Commission has given its approval, that the aid already granted or the consequence of the aid is cancelled and that the aid is recovered, including interest. A ban on anti-competitive activities or a prohibition of future aid may also be requested. Requesting that the granting authority be ordered to notify the European Commission of the agreement granting unlawful State aid is also possible.[60]

54. Metselaar, *supra* n. 1, at 135 and R.H.C. Luja, *De rol van nationale rechters bij de handhaving van de standstill-bepaling in fiscale zaken* [2014] Tijdschrift voor Staatssteun 99, 101.
55. Metselaar, *supra* n. 1, at 117.
56. Searched at www.rechtspraak.nl on the basis of the word 'staatssteun' (State aid).
57. Cf. Adriaanse, *Handhaving van EG-recht in situaties van onrechtmatige staatssteun*, 241 (Wolters Kluwer 2006).
58. Cf. Metselaar, *supra* n. 1, at 117.
59. *See* Adriaanse, *supra* n. 57, at 283–284 and Metselaar, *supra* n. 1, at 417.
60. *See*, e.g., District Court Limburg, 3 August 2016, ECLI:NL:RBLIM:2016:6765 *Maankwartier*, and District Court Noord-Nederland, 1 July 2015, ECLI:NL:RBNNE:2015:3300 *Spaansen Holding*.

Various provisions from the Dutch Civil Code can be used as a basis for these claims: tort (Article 6:162), nullity (Article 3:40), undue payment (Article 6:203), unjustified enrichment (Article 6:212), dissolution (Articles 6:258 and 6:265), standards of reasonableness and fairness (Article 6:2) and general principles of good administration (*see* sections 3:14 Dutch Civil Code and 3:1(2) GALA).[61] It is also possible to claim damages for a breach of the standstill clause in Article 108(3) TFEU, which constitutes a wrongful act (Article 6:162 Dutch Civil Code).[62] Finally, pursuant to Article 3:302 Dutch Civil Code, a declaratory judgment may be requested to have the (partial) nullity of a given legal act – such as an agreement granting State aid – established in court.[63] It is important to note that besides substantive proceedings, interim proceedings can also be brought before the civil courts (Article 254(1), Dutch Judicial Proceedings Act).

Which claim is chosen depends on the type of dispute that is at stake. For example, if a third party is of the opinion that unlawful State aid has been granted to a competitor by means of a private law agreement, a claim for undue payment is not very helpful. After all, no payment has been made in the relationship between the third party and the competitor receiving State aid from the government; it is not the third party, but the granting authority that has performed the act.[64] In such a case, it is more obvious that the granting authority is held liable for unlawful State aid (Article 6:162 Civil Code), or the invalidity of the private law agreement is invoked because of a conflict with a mandatory legal provision, namely Article 108(3) TFEU.[65]

In the remainder of this section, we will deal with the State aid disputes that are brought most frequently before the civil courts.

1. *Disputes where the government is accused of having granted an advantage to a competitor*

Most State aid litigation that comes before the civil courts deals with the situation where a private party takes the government to court because it is deemed to have provided unlawful State aid to a competitor. In the period from 1 November 2005 to 1 November 2015, sixty such judgments were published.[66] For the period from 1 November 2015 to 1 November 2018, we counted another thirteen judgments at www.rechtspraak.nl in which a private party had invoked Article 108(3) TFEU against the government. Enforcing the State aid rules is frequently closely related to the argument that the public procurement rules have been violated.[67] For example, a group of cleaning companies, which had previously been hired to provide cleaning services for government premises, disagreed with the transfer of these cleaning activities to a

61. Metselaar, *supra* n. 1, at 417.
62. Cf. Metselaar, *supra* n. 1, at 417.
63. Metselaar, *supra* n. 1, at 415.
64. Cf. Adriaanse, *supra* n. 57, at 304.
65. Cf. Adriaanse, *supra* n. 57, at 298 et seq.
66. Metselaar, *supra* n. 1, at 117-118.
67. Metselaar, *supra* n. 1, at 118. In the period after 1 November 2015, four out of twelve cases concerned public procurement disputes.

new organisation that had been set up for this purpose.[68] The cleaning companies argued that this was not only in conflict with public procurement law but also with State aid law. Besides a violation of public procurement law, a company can also argue that an agreement concluded between the government and a market party is not consistent with the market, e.g., disputes about agreements concerning the exploitation of car parks or concerning land in the waste sector.[69] A private party may also claim that certain buildings[70] or land[71] have been sold at prices below the market price, thus constituting unlawful State aid. Situations also occur where a company argues that a subsidy scheme involves unlawful State aid because only a few parties are entitled to the subsidy under the scheme or because the eligible activity has been wrongly classified as a service of general and economic interest (SGEI).[72]

2. *Disputes between the alleged beneficiary and another private party*

The most interesting dispute in this category is where a private party claims that its competitor has received unlawful State aid and has therefore acted unlawfully in relation to the claimant. This situation occurred only once during the period from 1 November 2005 to 1 November 2018, namely in the *Baby Dan* case.[73] In this case, Baby Dan, a manufacturer of stair safety gates under the name Danamic, argued that its competitors WeDeKa and De Risse had acted unlawfully towards it by accepting unlawful State aid from the government.

3. *Disputes about levies intended to finance state aid*

Civil courts are also sometimes confronted with cases where it is argued that a levy has been used to finance unlawful State aid. In these cases, it is not the levy decision that is at issue – this decision has to be challenged at the tax courts or administrative courts (*see* section III.C.) – but the Acts of Parliament on the basis of which the levy has been imposed. These disputes are also rare: there have been only five such cases in the period from 1 November 2005 to 1 November 2018.[74]

68. Rechtbank Den Haag, 24 January 2018, ECLI:NL:RBDHA:2018:316.
69. Metselaar, *supra* n. 1, at 118.
70. Rechtbank Den Haag, 30 December 2015, ECLI:NL:RBDHA:2015:15812 *De Stolp* and District Court Limburg, 3 August 2016, ECLI:NL:RBLIM:2016:6765 *Maankwartier*.
71. Rechtbank Midden-Nederland, 7 December 2016, ECLI:NL:RBMNE:2016:6542 *Park Vliegbasis Soesterberg*.
72. Rechtbank Den Haag, 26 April 2017, ECLI:NL:RBDHA:2017:4278 *Non Invasive Prenatal Test*.
73. Gerechtshof Amsterdam, 29 June 2006, ECLI:NL:GHAMS:2006:AZ1425 *Baby Dan*.
74. There are four cases in the period from 1 November 2005 – 1 November 2015. *See* Metselaar, *supra* n. 1, at 120. In the period from 1 November 2015 to 1 November 2018, we found one ruling that looks at this situation, namely Gerechtshof Den Haag, 5 July 2016, ECLI:NL:GHDHA:2016:1951.

4. *Disputes concerning expropriation*

The next category of disputes worth mentioning is that concerning expropriation, where a party relies on the State aid rules to prevent expropriation initiated by the government.[75] In these types of proceedings, it is argued that it is uncertain whether the plan, which the expropriation is intended to benefit, could be realised without unlawful State aid being provided.[76]

5. *Disputes on the enforcement of a recovery decision taken by the European Commission*

Disputes concerning the enforcement of a recovery decision taken by the European Commission usually relate, in practice, to a situation where the government brings proceedings before the civil courts to recover unlawful State aid. The category of disputes discussed in the section below also refers to claims to prevent or recover unlawful State aid. Similar to the refusal and withdrawal decisions that are litigated in the administrative courts (*see* section III.D.), it is tempting not to pay much attention to these categories. After all, these categories do not strictly concern private enforcement; it is the government that invokes State aid law. Nevertheless, both categories merit further discussion, since again it cannot be ruled out that the government initiates these proceedings at the civil courts because individuals have requested enforcement of State aid law. Judgments by the Dutch civil courts concerning the enforcement of recovery decisions taken by the European Commission are very rare. In the period from 1 November 2005 to 1 November 2018 there were only three such judgments. Metselaar clarifies this by stating that apparently there are only few recovery decisions by the European Commission that give rise to questions to be submitted to the civil courts.[77] The underlying disputes relate, for example, to the question of how State aid should be recovered when aid recipients have gone bankrupt.[78]

6. *Disputes where the government has revoked a granted benefit or refuses to grant an advantage*

Even if the European Commission has not taken a recovery decision, it regularly occurs that the government granting authority itself invokes State aid law. This occurred no less than twenty-four times between 1 November 2005 and 1 November 2015.[79] In the period from 1 November 2015 to 1 November 2018, we counted two judgments relating to a situation of this nature.[80] At issue were cases where a municipality relied on the

75. Metselaar, *supra* n. 1, at 120.
76. Hoge Raad *(Supreme Court)*, 30 June 2006, ECLI:NL:HR:2006:AV9441.
77. Metselaar, *supra* n. 1, at 118–119.
78. Rechtbank Rotterdam, 24 August 2011, ECLI:NL:RBROT:2011:BR6507 *Kliq Re-integratie.*
79. Metselaar, *supra* n. 1, at 119.
80. Rechtbank Noord-Nederland, 16 December 2015 ECLI:NL:RBNNE:2015:5815 and Rechtbank Overijssel, 14 March 2018, ECLI:NL:RBOVE:2018:788.

nullity of a concluded guarantee agreement[81] or a purchase agreement[82] because these agreements included unlawful State aid.

C. Available judgment options for the civil courts

The administrative and tax courts deliver their judgments in the context of an annulment procedure that is directed against a decision: a decision is annulled or it remains in force. The civil courts have much more variety in their judgment options.[83] They can impose various prohibitions carrying the consequence that the granting of State aid is prevented or stopped or that State aid must be recovered.[84] The civil courts can also award damages and issue a declaratory judgment, establishing, for example, that contracts in violation of the standstill obligation are null and void.[85] In State aid cases, it can be worthwhile to ask for a declaratory judgment stating that certain services have been unduly paid or that the other party has acted unlawfully, but foremost that certain actions are null and void.[86] Declarations of this nature make it easier to ensure that a claim is made for undue payment, that an agreement is dissolved or that compensation is awarded.

Notwithstanding all these judgment options, this does not mean that the effective enforcement of State aid is guaranteed. The Dutch civil courts are bound to the principle of party autonomy.[87] In other words: the parties act autonomously in what they claim before the court; the civil courts cannot consider anything other than what has been claimed.[88] This means that if a party only claims suspension, dissolution or termination of an agreement which allegedly embodies state aid, the Dutch civil courts cannot order the recovery of the aid that was already granted. This, after all, was not demanded by the parties.[89] Because proceedings in the Dutch civil courts take a long time, it is important to note that interim proceedings can be conducted; this opportunity is gratefully used in practice.[90] Interim proceedings are completely independent proceedings before a preliminary relief judge. They can be started without having to initiate proceedings on the merits of the underlying case.[91] When a case is subsequently initiated on its merits, the interim court order will not be binding on the court hearing the main action.[92] Because the interim court order is provisional in nature, the

81. *See*, e.g., Hoge Raad, 29 March 2013, ECLI:NL:HR:2013:BY6012 *Commerz* and Hoge Raad, 26 April 2013 ECLI:NL:HR:2013:BY0539 *Residex*.
82. Rechtbank Noord-Nederland, 16 December 2015 ECLI:NL:RBNNE:2015:5815.
83. Metselaar, *supra* n. 1, at 414.
84. Adriaanse, *supra* n. 57, at 312. *See* for an extensive discussion on the various ruling options of the civil court, Metselaar, *supra* n. 1, at 458–499.
85. Adriaanse, *supra* n. 57, at 312.
86. Cf. Metselaar, *supra* n. 1, at 417.
87. Metselaar, *supra* n. 1, at 414.
88. Metselaar, *supra* n. 1, at 414.
89. *See* in detail Metselaar, *supra* n. 1, at 482–484.
90. Metselaar, *supra* n. 1, at 415.
91. Metselaar, *supra* n. 1, at 415.
92. Metselaar, *supra* n. 1, at 415.

decision-making possibilities of the preliminary relief court are limited.[93] For example, it cannot issue a declaratory judgment since this would be a binding judgment; nor can it give a constitutive judgment, in the sense that an agreement is dissolved or annulled.[94] However, the preliminary relief judge may be asked to suspend an agreement or draft agreement, as well as its preparation or execution, until the time when the European Commission will be able to decide on the admissibility of the aid.[95]

D. Bottlenecks in state aid cases before the civil courts

The two preceding sections have demonstrated that private parties and government authorities have many opportunities at their disposal before the civil courts when raising the issue of unlawful State aid. The civil courts also have various options when it comes to a judgment: they can award compensation or order the suspension or recovery of unlawful State aid. Adriaanse concluded from this that the civil courts in the Netherlands can comply to a large extent with the requirements set by the ECJ for legal protection at national level.[96] More important, however, is the question about where these proceedings ultimately lead. Do civil courts actually play a significant role in the fight against unlawful State aid? This section will consider the extent to which civil courts impose interest (standing) requirements on the parties who invoke State aid rules (section V.D.1), the problems that arise in the qualification of State aid (section V.D.2) and the possibilities for obtaining compensation when a breach of the State aid rules has been established (section V.D.3). The case law leads to the conclusion that State aid claims brought before the civil courts are rarely successful. In section V.D.4, it will nevertheless be discussed whether we can find some glimmers of light in the case law of the civil courts.

1. *Interest requirements and the Schutznorm*

a) Competitors

Unlike administrative law, no admissibility requirement exists in civil law for competitors comparable to Article 1:2 GALA, which requires that a party is directly affected by the decision that is being challenged.[97] This means that the civil courts do not assess whether litigating competitors are active in the same market segment and service area as the aid recipient. However, under Article 3:303 of the Dutch Civil Code, the competitor should have sufficient interest in the claim. A civil court has never ruled that a claimant does not qualify as a competitor and therefore lacks sufficient interest.[98] To the contrary, from various judgments, it emerges that civil courts take the view that

93. Metselaar, *supra* n. 1, at 415.
94. Metselaar, *supra* n. 1, at 415-416.
95. Cf. Metselaar, *supra* n. 1, at 482.
96. Adriaanse, *supra* n. 57, at 320.
97. Cf. Metselaar, *supra* n. 1, at 199.
98. Metselaar, *supra* n. 1, at 200-201.

finding insufficient interest may not be done too lightly.[99] When a competitor claims to have suffered, to suffer or that it will suffer damage as a result of the actions of the granting authority and the aid recipient, it is quickly assumed that the competitor has sufficient legal interest. It is plausible, however, that the question of whether a competitor is actually materially and individually affected by the actions of the granting authority and the aid recipient may become relevant at a later stage in the proceedings, namely when assessing whether the damage suffered by the competitor was actually caused by unlawful State aid.[100] In that case, a judgment must first have been reached establishing unlawful State aid. As discussed in the next section, competitors who claim that unlawful State aid was granted have never been able to demonstrate a violation of State aid rules before the Dutch civil courts.[101]

b) Other private parties that invoke state aid law

If private parties other than competitors and levy payers claim unlawful State aid, but it is established that an appeal to the State aid rules is not intended to reverse the unlawful State aid, the civil courts assume that sufficient procedural interest is lacking. In the *Accolade/Ludinga* judgment, the Accolade Foundation sought a declaratory judgment stating that a contract by which the municipality of Harlingen had sold certain plots of land to Ludinga Vastgoed was null and void because it conflicted with Article 108(3) TFEU.[102] However, Accolade's motive in this claim was not the reversal of unlawful State aid but the reversal of the sale of land by Ludinga to the Accolade Foundation,[103] as it regretted the purchase of this land. The District Court of Noord-Nederland rejected Accolade's claim for that reason.[104]

In cases where a party wants to prevent expropriation and wishes to argue that the plan which requires the expropriation could not be realised without unlawful State aid being granted, the Supreme Court has ruled that State aid law does not aim to protect private property but rather to promote fair competition in the common market.[105] The possibility that there is unlawful State aid cannot, therefore, affect the

99. *See* Rechtbank Limburg, 3 August 2016, ECLI:NL:RBLIM:2016:6765. *See* also Rechtbank Maastricht, 3 May 2010, ECLI:NL:RBMAA:2010:BM3162 *AZM*, where the court also takes into account the EU law principle of effective judicial protection.
100. *See* Rechtbank Limburg, 3 August 2016, ECLI:NL:RBLIM:2016:6765 and Metselaar, *supra* n. 1, at 201.
101. Metselaar, *supra* n. 1, at 201.
102. Rechtbank Noord-Nederland, 4 June 2014, ECLI:NL:RBNNE:2014:2790.
103. *See* Metselaar, *supra* n. 1, at 489.
104. Although the District Court Noord-Nederland does not explicitly mention Article 3:303 Dutch Civil Code, it can be deduced from the ruling that the District Court is of the opinion that sufficient legal interest is lacking. The court writes as follows: 'Accolade has also not stated what interest it has in State review other than other the (private) interest mentioned above. This implies that there is no reason for an investigation into the question whether the unlawful State aid has actually been involved in the land transaction between the municipality and Ludinga VG'.
105. *See* Hoge Raad, 30 June 2006, ECLI:NL:HR:2006:AV9441 and also Hoge Raad, 23 December 2011, ECLI:NL:HR:2011:BU4934 and the related conclusion of Advocate General IJzerman, Parket bij de Hoge Raad, 23 December 2011 ECLI:NL:PHR:2011:BU4934.

legality of the expropriation order.[106] The reasoning of the Supreme Court is comparable with the *Schutznorm* applied by the administrative judge. It is interesting to note that the Supreme Court did not refer to European Union case law and also did not refer questions for preliminary rulings.[107]

Nevertheless, the above does not mean that parties lacking a competitive interest - like non-government actors or levy payers -[108] never have an interest in bringing proceedings when they invoke State aid rules. Relevant in this context is the case *Stichting Vrijplaats Koppenhinksteeg.*[109] The Koppenhinksteeg Foundation had squatted a building in the municipality of Leiden, which the municipality had previously sold. In interim proceedings, the municipality of Leiden demanded that the Foundation vacate the premises. However, the Foundation believed that the sale of the property had taken place in violation of State aid rules and, in the counterclaim, requested a ban on the further implementation of the purchase agreement. According to the municipality of Leiden, the Foundation could not rely on State aid law because it was not a competitor or levy payer. The District Court of The Hague, however, ruled that the Foundation could invoke the standstill clause. The court reasoned that the purchase agreement would ultimately result in the building Vrijplaats Koppenhinksteeg being vacated and renovated, with all the associated consequences for the Foundation, and that this agreement was the result of a sales procedure in which the Foundation participated and against which it was raising objections.[110] This assessment suggests that private parties that are not competitors and not subject to a levy may also invoke State aid law under certain circumstances, provided they are significantly affected by the alleged State aid in another way.[111] The Court of Appeal in The Hague, however, subsequently left the question of who is protected by State aid law - the *Schutznorm* - in a state of uncertainty. The Court ruled that the Foundation had, in any event, sufficient interest within the meaning of Article 3:303 Dutch Civil Code because it participated in the public procurement procedure that led to the sale of the squatted property. The Foundation was thus still regarded as a competitor, albeit a competitor in the public procurement procedure.[112] The case demonstrates that a party can have sufficient interest in relying on the State aid rules in civil law procedures even if it is not directly affected by the alleged unlawful State aid.[113] The Foundation did not claim that it was adversely affected by its competitive interests. A similar decision of the Court of Appeal of the District Court of Dordrecht also demonstrated that the Polders Graafstroom Foundation, which did not compete with the aid recipient at issue in that case

106. *See* Metselaar, *supra* n. 1, at 207-208.
107. Cf. Metselaar, *supra* n. 1, at 212.
108. Levy payers always have sufficient interest in bringing proceedings before the civil court against an Act of Parliament on the basis of which they have to pay the levy. *See* Metselaar, *supra* n. 1, at 203. However, this is only the case if the levy forms an integral part of an aid measure, which means that the revenues are necessarily allocated to the financing of the aid.
109. *See* Rechtbank's-Gravenhage, 8 January 2010 ECLI:NL:RBSGR:2010:BK8654.
110. Metselaar, *supra* n. 1, at 206.
111. Metselaar, *supra* n. 1, at 206.
112. Metselaar, *supra* n. 1, at 206.
113. Cf. Metselaar, *supra* n. 1, at 206.

but which was active for environmental interests, had standing by virtue of Article 108(3)TFEU.[114]

It follows from this case law that it is not precluded in advance that private parties other than competitors and levy payers can invoke the standstill obligation under Article 108(3) TFEU when they claim to have been otherwise harmed by a violation of the State aid rules.[115] In that respect, the civil courts appear to take a slightly more flexible approach than the administrative courts. It should be noted, however, that this issue - as far as we have been able to ascertain - was dealt with in only a few judgments, coming from lower civil courts. In addition, the Supreme Court in expropriation cases takes a very strict approach: the standstill obligation in Article 108(3) TFEU does not extend to the protection of private property. Moreover, if it is certain that improper use is made of State aid law, the civil courts rule that there can be no valid assertion of a legal interest. Further judgments on this point have yet to be given.

c) *Government interest in bringing proceedings in the civil courts*

The case law of the civil courts shows that the courts have hardly ever concluded that the government has insufficient interest in invoking State aid rules. The point of departure is that the government is free to recover the illegal State aid or invoke the nullity of an agreement concluded by it on the ground that it might involve illegal State aid.[116] There is only one judgment published in which a civil court considered whether the government was obliged under EU law to invoke State aid law in relation to its demand.[117]

2. *Qualification of state aid*

It appears from the previous section that the requirement of sufficient legal interest for competitors who call on the civil courts to enforce State aid law poses few problems. This implies that the claims of competitors that are based on State aid law are usually assessed in terms of content. However, a much bigger problem arises in this phase. To date, no competitor has yet succeeded in convincing the civil courts that the government provided unlawful State aid.[118] The claims of competitors are rejected in many cases because they have not complied with the obligation to furnish facts. Party autonomy and the passivity of the court are two fundamental principles in proceedings before the Dutch civil courts, and in line with this, the civil courts base their judgment on the facts that are established.[119] These facts are mainly determined by the dispute between the parties. Thus, the party who is obliged to furnish facts must state all the

114. Rechtbank Dordrecht, 12 May 2009, ECLI:NL:RBDOR:2009:BI3617.
115. Cf. Metselaar, *supra* n. 1, at 212.
116. *See* Metselaar, *supra* n. 1, at 203–205.
117. Rechtbank Middelburg, 13 August 2010, ECLI:NL:RBMID:2010:BN9817.
118. *See* Metselaar, *supra* n. 1, at 264 for the period from 1 November 2005 - 1 November 2015. Also after this date we have not come across any judgments to the contrary.
119. Article 149(1), Dutch Judicial Proceedings Act. *See* in this regard Metselaar, *supra* n. 1, at 236.

facts necessary for the occurrence of the intended legal consequence.[120] In principle, the obligation to furnish facts and the burden of proof rest on the party who relies on the legal consequences of the facts or rights that it is claiming. For example, the party claiming an agreement null and void by virtue of unlawful State aid must provide all the facts to that effect and must prove them in relation to each of the conditions of Article 107(1) TFEU.[121] In most cases, it is determined that the State aid claims cannot be awarded because those invoking the State aid rules have failed to comply with their duty to furnish facts.[122] Specifically, facts are deemed unsubstantiated or insufficiently substantiated, or they are seen as not leading to the qualification of State aid.[123] The case law shows that it is not easy to substantiate facts sufficiently. In theory, competitors can argue before the civil court that the government or the alleged aid recipients should provide information about the alleged State aid agreements. However, this sort of claim has so far been rejected due to insufficient interest.[124] For example, the District Court of Limburg ruled that the plaintiffs had insufficiently argued and substantiated that the requested information was necessary to provide proof of unlawful State aid,[125] and the District Court of Gelderland concluded that the plaintiff had not sufficiently demonstrated that the municipality had provided benefits to JCDecaux in breach of Article 107(1) TFEU.[126]

Although the claims of competitors in the area of State aid law have little success, the case law shows that the civil courts do in general discuss the arguments, disputes and substantiation of these claims in a thorough manner.[127] In interim proceedings, however, it is a different matter. The preliminary relief judge is usually brief in articulating whether State aid has been established or not.[128] This is not surprising; in these proceedings the formal rules of civil evidence do not apply and the parties have less time to bring their point of view to the fore or to substantiate it.[129] However, there are exceptions, such as the *NIPT* case, where the Court of Appeal in The Hague, after detailed justification and substantiation, came to the conclusion that the contested NIPT Subsidy Scheme was compatible with the internal market and was

120. Beenders, *T&C Rv 2012*, Article 149, note 2.
121. Metselaar, *supra* n. 1, at 263.
122. Metselaar, *supra* n. 1, at 264.
123. Metselaar, *supra* n. 1, at 264.
124. Rechtbank Limburg, 9 December 2015, ECLI:NL:RBLIM:2015:10461 *Stichting Laurentius en Petronella* and Rechtbank Gelderland, 26 April 2018, ECLI:NL:RBGEL:2018:2856.
125. Rechtbank Limburg, 9 December 2015, ECLI:NL:RBLIM:2015:10461 *Stichting Laurentius en Petronella*.
126. Rechtbank Gelderland, 26 April 2018, ECLI:NL:RBGEL:2018:2856. *See* also Gerechtshof Den Haag, 7 March 2017, ECLI:NL:GHDHA:2017:470.
127. Metselaar, *supra* n. 1, at 267. *See*, e.g., for judgments subsequent to 1 November 2015: Rechtbank Limburg, 21 March 2016, ECLI:NL:RBLIM:2016:6765 and Rechtbank Amsterdam, 18 October 2017, ECLI:NL:RBAMS:2017:10553.
128. Metselaar, *supra* n. 1, at 271. *See*, e.g., Rechtbank Amsterdam, 25 June 2016, ECLI:NL:RBAMS:2016:3127, where the provisional relief judge briefly stated that Becton Dickinson insufficiently substantiated its claim that the tender procedure violated the prohibition of State aid, such that the claim was disregarded.
129. Metselaar, *supra* n. 1, at 271–272.

exempted from the requirement to provide notification to the European Commission, as laid down in Article 108(3) TFEU.[130]

In cases where a complaint has also been submitted to the European Commission with regard to alleged State aid, the civil courts are sometimes willing to put questions to the European Commission about the status of the investigation.[131] The answer from the European Commission is, after all, relevant to the assessment of the claim.[132]

Unlike competitors, in a number of cases, the government did succeed in making a reasonable case for the existence of State aid.[133] This can be explained by the fact that the government, which relies on the standstill clause in civil proceedings against an alleged beneficiary, is in a favourable position.[134] First, the government is a party to the agreement in which State aid is deemed to be present; it therefore has knowledge of the relevant facts and circumstances.[135] Second, in this type of dispute the government is usually the defendant in the proceedings at first instance.[136] The government relies on the standstill provision as its defence against the alleged beneficiary's claim to enforce an established right, such as the right to fulfilment of the agreement.[137] As a result, the alleged beneficiary must first make a reasonable case for the government having a certain obligation that it must fulfil.[138] Only when this is successful will State aid come into the picture in the government's defence.[139] In that event, the government must then demonstrate that all elements of the concept of State aid within the meaning of Article 107(1) TFEU are present; the government, therefore, bears the obligation to furnish facts as well as the burden of proof.[140]

3. *Compensation for damages in state aid cases*

Since competitors have not once succeeded in convincing the civil courts that the government provided unlawful State aid, compensation has simply never been included in a judgment.[141] In Dutch literature, it is pointed out that – even if a competitor

130. Rechtbank Den Haag, 26 April 2017 ECLI:NL:RBDHA:2017:4278 *Non Invasive Prenatal Test*. *See* also Rechtbank Limburg, 12 May 2016 ECLI:NL:RBLIM:2016:4033, where the preliminary relief judge discussed extensively whether the cumulative criteria of Article 107(1) TFEU have been met.
131. *See* Rechtbank Limburg, 15 August 2018, ECLI:NL:RBLIM:2018:7705 and Gerechtshof 's-Hertogenbosch, 16 May 2017, ECLI:NL:GHSHE:2017:2127 *Shanks*.
132. Gerechtshof 's-Hertogenbosch, *supra* n. 131.
133. *See* Metselaar, *supra* n. 1, at 278 et seq.
134. Metselaar, *supra* n. 1, at 283.
135. Metselaar, *supra* n. 1, at 283.
136. Metselaar, *supra* n. 1, at 283. This is not always the case. *See*, e.g., Rechtbank Noord-Nederland, 16 December 2015 ECLI:NL:RBNNE:2015:5815, in which the government as claimant argued that unlawful State aid was at stake and that the agreement in question was thus null and void/must be annulled.
137. Metselaar, *supra* n. 1, at 283.
138. Metselaar, *supra* n. 1, at 283.
139. Metselaar, *supra* n. 1, at 283.
140. Metselaar, *supra* n. 1, at 283.
141. Metselaar, *supra* n. 1, at 491. This has also not occurred after 1 November 2015 nor prior to 1 November 2005 (*see* in this respect Adriaanse, *supra* n. 57, at 312).

were to succeed in proving unlawful State aid - the demonstration of a causal link between damage suffered and a violation of the European rules will be problematic.[142]

The *Baby Dan* case shows that it is extremely complicated in the Netherlands to hold the recipient of alleged State aid liable for the receipt of unlawful State aid.[143] The Court of Appeal in Amsterdam for the time being has indeed assumed that the benefits provided to the competitors of Baby Dan - WeDeKa and De Risse - do qualify as State aid within the meaning of Article 87 of the EC Treaty (now Article 107 TFEU) and thus should have been notified to the European Commission.[144] However, this does not lead to the conclusion that WeDeKa and De Risse acted unlawfully and are therefore liable for damages. WeDeKa and De Risse are not obliged to give notification of the State aid; this obligation applies only to the authorities that grant the alleged State aid. It is only if the European Commission were to decide that the State aid is unlawful that this could in certain circumstances result in WeDeKa and De Risse - on the basis of national law - having acted unlawfully in relation to Baby Dan by receiving this support. In that regard, it is relevant whether WeDeKa and De Risse should have understood that there was a real risk that they had received unlawful State aid, according to the Court of Appeal. But even if it must be assumed that WeDeKa and De Risse should have grasped this, it does not automatically lead to a successful claim. The fact is that the European Commission had never given an opinion on the alleged State aid given to WeDeKa and De Risse. Furthermore, on the basis of what Baby Dan had put forward, it could not be established how the European Commission would have assessed the aid in question and what this would then have led to. In short: in order to make the recipient liable for damages suffered, the competitor of an alleged aid recipient must prove that the Commission in the intervening period has ruled that the aid measure is contrary to EU law or make a reasonable case that the Commission would have done so if it had given an opinion on the aid.[145] It is clear that this is a very complicated task, if not an impossible one.

4. *A ray of light: the alleged support conflicts with general principles of sound administration*

The previous sections demonstrate that litigation before the civil courts does little to help competitors in their fight against unlawful State aid. In most cases, it is impossible to make a reasonable case that State aid has been provided. Nevertheless, competitors have achieved small victories in two cases in which their competitive interests were threatened by alleged State aid. Although the Dutch civil court did not rule that unlawful State aid was involved because the criteria of Article 107(1) TFEU had not

142. Metselaar, *supra* n. 1, at 492. This is also affirmed in the case law in the rare judgments where the court did mention the possibility of compensation for damage without it already having established whether unlawful State aid was involved at all. *See* Rechtbank Assen, 30 May 2012, ECLI:NL:RBASS:2012:BW7185.
143. *See* Metselaar, *supra* n. 1, at 493.
144. Gerechtshof Amsterdam, 29 June 2006, ECLI:NL:GHAMS:2006:AZ1425 *Baby Dan*.
145. Metselaar, *supra* n. 1, at 493.

been fulfilled, it did ultimately conclude that the alleged aid was contrary to the general principles of sound administration.

The first case that is relevant in this context is *MuzyQ*. This case concerned a EUR 26-million guarantee issued by the board of the sub-municipality Oost/ Watergraafsmeer (a district of the Amsterdam municipality) to the Orfeus Studios Foundation for the creation of practice rooms for musicians. This resulted in the MuzyQ music centre. Two companies that also rent practice studios to musicians initiated proceedings before the civil court, claiming that the guarantee qualified as unlawful State aid. However, the District Court of Amsterdam found that the two companies had insufficiently substantiated the (potential) effect of the aid on trade. This means the State aid criterion had not been fulfilled. However, the court held that the municipality had breached the principle of due care by not taking into account the interests of the two companies in deciding to stand surety for the Orfeus Studios Foundation. In a later interlocutory judgment, the District Court of Amsterdam ruled that there was a causal link between the careless actions of the municipality and the decline in sales of the two competing companies.[146] Eventually, the municipality was ordered to pay compensation amounting to EUR 195,079.75.[147]

The second case in which the civil court came to the conclusion that favouring a competitor violated the duty of care and Article 3:14 of the Civil Code concerned the sale by the municipality of Krimpenerwaard of a municipal sports hall and activity centre called De Stolp to the foundation *Stichting Stolwijk Ontmoet*.[148] The owner of a restaurant and conference centre in Stolwijk alleged that prohibited state support had been provided and brought proceedings before the civil court. According to the owner, the municipality had sold De Stolp for a price that was too low, had borne costs that a normal salesman would not carry and had provided a loan to *Stichting Stolwijk Ontmoet* which the foundation would not have been able to obtain in the open market. The renting out of reception rooms at De Stolp had led to a drop in turnover for the owner of the restaurant. However, the District Court of The Hague ruled that there was no State aid involved because the criterion that the aid measure should have an effect on trade between Member States was not met. According to the court, the alleged support was granted to a local citizens' initiative, which was set up with the aim of preserving social activities in De Stolp, a village hall in Stolwijk which is located in the middle of the Netherlands and not in the vicinity of the national borders, for the local population. The activities had a purely local character and a limited geographic scope. However, the court subsequently ruled that the municipality nevertheless had acted unlawfully in relation to the owner of the restaurant and therefore had to pay compensation. According to the court, the municipality had violated the principle of due care. The municipality had not shown that it had at any time considered the competitive interests of the owner of the restaurant or that it had weighed these interests against the sale of De Stolp to *Stichting Stolwijk Ontmoet*, this despite the fact that the municipality had provided the foundation with advantages in terms of both the

146. District Court of Amsterdam, 15 October 2014, not published.
147. *See* Rechtbank Amsterdam, 29 April 2015, ECLI:NL:RBAMS:2015:2388.
148. Rechtbank Den Haag, 30 December 2015, ECLI:NL:RBDHA:2015:15812 *De Stolp*.

purchase agreement and the loan that it could not have obtained on the open market. The District Court also considered it plausible that the owner of the complaining restaurant and conference centre had suffered a loss of turnover and had thus suffered damage.

Both judgments demonstrate that competitors - in spite of the fact that State aid is not established because the criteria of Article 107(1) TFEU are not met - are not always left empty-handed. Their interests as competitors are protected by applying a national principle of good administration.

VI. TAKING STOCK OF THE PRIVATE ENFORCEMENT OF STATE AID LAW IN THE NETHERLANDS

We started this contribution with the question of what the most important issues and problems are and which best practices can be distinguished in the private enforcement of State aid law in the Netherlands.

For a good understanding of Dutch practice in the context of State aid law, it is crucial to keep in mind that the Netherlands has a complicated division of jurisdiction with regard to government action, entailing that more than one court may be competent. This finely branched jurisdiction for government action can lead to uncertainty about which court is competent in a dispute concerning alleged State aid and - more often - can mean that when an aid measure consists of a set of acts, private parties sometimes have to litigate before different courts. Submitting a complaint to the European Commission then soon becomes a simple and more attractive alternative.

Nevertheless, private parties do end up in the national courtrooms with disputes concerning State aid. The various courts deal with State aid disputes according to the procedural rules applicable in their field of law. Therefore problems and best practices differ in each field of law.

Looking at the administrative courts those not surprisingly handle the majority of disputes in which State aid law is relevant, a first conclusion must be that national procedural law plays a very important role. Since the introduction of a relativity requirement (the *Schutznorm*) in GALA in 2013, the chances of plaintiffs successfully invoking State aid law in spatial planning disputes (these representing the majority of the cases in which State aid law is invoked in administrative courts) have been seriously reduced. This holds true not only for residents who lack any competitive interests that are affected by the challenged zoning plan decision but also for competitors whose competitive interests could be affected by the unlawful State aid. The *Schutznorm* cut off an enormous potential for the private enforcement of State aid law in administrative law in the Netherlands.

Not only must the *Schutznorm* threshold be passed by competitors, other national procedural rules can hinder them as well, e.g., the requirement that appellants qualify as interested parties. According to established case law, litigating competitors are required to be active in the same market segment and service area as the addressee of the (alleged) aid decision. This interested party test seems to be carried out more strictly in cases invoking State aid law than is customary in Dutch legal practice.

When competitors successfully overcome the obstacles of Dutch administrative procedural law, they have to prove or at least make plausible that State aid rules have been infringed. This turns out to be no easy task due to many competitors lacking information about aid arrangements. The administrative courts are not inclined to use their own investigative powers to establish illegal State aid. Furthermore, if a substantive assessment is made by an administrative court, it is sometimes rather indirect in nature. Most important is the conclusion that in most cases in which administrative courts substantively review a decision that might infringe State aid law, they rule that no (illegal) State aid is involved and often give no extensive reasoning for this decision. All in all, the chances of success are very small for competitors who lodge a State aid complaint at the administrative courts.

When it comes to fiscal state support, competitors do not have access to the tax courts by virtue of their position as competitors. It is therefore almost impossible for them to raise the issue of fiscal state support at the tax courts. Submitting a complaint to the European Commission thus, once again, becomes a simple and more attractive alternative.

State aid that is provided through private law instruments, such as an agreement, must be challenged by competitors before the civil courts. Although there are many possible claims and the civil courts quickly assume that a competitor has an interest in bringing proceedings, in practice, it appears to be very difficult to stop or reverse the provision of State aid. This is caused by the passive approach of the Dutch civil courts. The civil court has never been convinced by a competitor that unlawful State aid has actually been granted. However, in some cases, the civil court concluded that the alleged aid was contrary to general principles of sound administration.

The above leads to the conclusion that competitors are rarely successful when they complain to the Dutch courts about the provision of alleged unlawful State aid. This applies to the administrative courts, the tax courts and the civil courts. It is therefore more attractive for competitors to submit a complaint to the European Commission.

Thus the question arises whether it would help competitors if the EU were to impose rules governing actions for damages under the European State aid rules, comparable to Directive 2014/104. Although the rules laid down in this Directive hardly offer a solution to the problems identified above, it would help competitors if it became easier to gain access to evidence (*see* Chapter II of Directive 2014/104).

VII. DUTCH STATE AID RECOVERY ACT

In the previous section, it was concluded that it is not easy for private parties to successfully raise State aid law before the various Dutch courts. This is mainly caused by Dutch procedural law. The *Schutznorm* and the interested party test form the most important obstacles before the administrative courts. At the tax court, it is not possible at all for competitors to challenge State aid that is granted to their economic rivals through tax law. Finally, at the civil courts, competitors hardly ever succeed in convincing the passive civil court of the fact that there is a situation involving State aid.

The State Aid Recovery Act,[149] which entered into force on 1 July 2018 and is intended to facilitate the implementation of State aid law in the Netherlands, does little to provide a solution to these problems. We therefore do not expect a significant decrease in the procedural obstacles which private parties encounter when they attempt to raise the issue of unlawful State aid at a Dutch court.

The State Aid Recovery Act refers primarily to the recovery of unlawful State aid by governments, in the event the European Commission takes a recovery decision. In view of the background to the State Aid Recovery Act, this is not surprising. The origins of the Act lie in the fact that in 2005 it became clear that it was legally difficult in the Netherlands for the Dutch authorities to recover unlawful State aid pursuant to the requirements of EU law.[150] Indeed, there was no general competence to claim the recovery of interest.[151] Threatened with an infraction procedure by the European Commission, the Dutch legislature set to work on a law that would deal with the recovery of unlawful State aid. It took almost fifteen years before the law eventually came into force.

If the State Aid Recovery Act does not offer a solution to the problems identified in this contribution, what does it achieve? The State Aid Recovery Act, first of all, creates a legal basis for administrative authorities to recover unlawful State aid as a result of a decision by the European Commission, by means of a so-called payment decision. It does not matter whether this concerns State aid that has been provided by means of administrative or private law (legal) acts. The aid to be recovered also includes interest.[152] A special scheme applies to fiscal support; pursuant to Article 2(2), fiscal aid is recovered on the basis of the tax laws themselves.

Second, in cases where no Commission recovery decision is available, Article 7(1) of the State Aid Recovery Act stipulates that the administrative authority concerned is obliged to amend a decision if this decision is in conflict with the European State aid rules. Pursuant to Article 7(2), the relevant administrative authority is also obliged and authorised to claim interest. The law on the recovery of State aid therefore has the effect that administrative bodies always have the power to modify a decision if unlawful State aid is established. Private parties can therefore ask administrative authorities to make use of the obligations and powers laid down in the State Aid

149. This Act has received much attention in Dutch legal literature. *See* J.C. van Haersolte, *Terugvordering van staatssteun vindt zijn plek in de Nederlandse wetgeving (Recovery of State aid finds its way into Dutch legislation)* [2018] INTER 176; A.A. al Khatib, *De wet terugvordering staatssteun: een adequate grondslag voor de terugvordering van staatssteun? (The State Aid Recovery Act: an adequate legal basis for the recovery of State aid?)* [2018/2] De Gemeentestem 2. This includes the legislative proposal. *See* A.J. Metselaar, *Een vogel in de hand: nieuwe regels voor de terugvordering van staatssteun (A bird in the hand: new rules for the recovery of State aid)* [2016] Tijdschrift voor Staatssteun 110.

150. Raad van State, 11 January 2006, ECLI:NL:RVS:2006:AU9416.

151. *See* Raad van State, 11 January 2006, ECLI:NL:RVS:2006:AU9416 and Rechtbank Rotterdam, 4 July 2007, ECLI:NL:RBROT:2007:BB0270.

152. Concerning the recovery of unlawful State aid in response to a recovery decision of the European Commission, this has been laid down in Article 3(1), State Aid Recovery Act. For the recovery of unlawful State aid in the event that there is not (yet) a Commission decision, the claim for interest is established in Article 7(2) and (4) State Aid Recovery Act.

Recovery Act.[153] This also means that competitors can always obtain an opinion from the governing body about the allegedly unlawful State aid; they can thus provoke decisions which they can challenge before the administrative courts. As a result, it can no longer be argued against them that a decision granting the State aid has formal legal force and cannot be revoked. However, the State Aid Recovery Act does not regulate State aid provided through private law instruments in the event a Commission recovery decision is lacking.[154]

Third, the State Aid Recovery Act not only refers to the recovery of unlawful State aid but also partly focuses on preventing it. For example, the Act gives administrative authorities the competence to reject an application for a subsidy if, in the opinion of the administrative authorities, the provision of the subsidy is not compatible with the provisions of Articles 107 and 108 TFEU. This also gives guidance to competitors if they oppose decisions that include State aid aimed at economic rivals.[155] However, this advantage should not be overestimated, as in addition it is already forbidden to take subsidy decisions that are in conflict with EU law. The State Aid Recovery Act merely constitutes a clarification of this point. Nevertheless, this clarification is a positive development; for competitors it becomes clearer that it is possible to ask an administrative body to use this competence to disallow subsidies that constitute unlawful State aid. This also gives guidance to competitors if they oppose decisions that include State aid aimed at economic rivals

Finally, the State Aid Recovery Act contains an important development in terms of legal protection. If an administrative authority takes a payment decision in response to a decision of the European Commission, it must be challenged before a specialised administrative court: the Trade and Industry Appeals Tribunal.[156] This means that a more specialised State aid court will be established in the Netherlands. It should be noted immediately that State aid disputes will continue to have a much wider scope than the payment decision alone. For most State aid disputes, after all, there is no Commission decision available. Private parties will also want to litigate in those cases to prevent or reverse unlawful state support. In such situations, other courts – other administrative courts and the civil courts – are authorised to hear their disputes. In the future, those Dutch courts will thus also be confronted with State aid disputes, in the process facing all the complications that have been outlined above.

153. *See* also Metselaar, *supra* n. 149, at 117.
154. This is currently the case. *See* Raad van State, 17 August 2011, ECLI:NL:RVS:2011:BR5195 *Stichting NOB*.
155. The Recovery of State Aid Act provides for an extension of this in Article 4:35 GALA.
156. Article 9 State Aid Recovery Act.

CHAPTER 15

Private Enforcement in Spain

Luis Arroyo Jiménez & Patricia Pérez Fernández

I. The enforcement of the standstill obligation
  A. General issues
  B. Legal framework
  C. Public law remedies
    1. Preventing the payment of unlawful aid
    2. Recovery of unlawful aid and illegality interest
    3. Damages for competitors and other third parties
    4. Interim measures against unlawful aid
    5. Procedural issues
  D. Private law remedies
II. Cooperation and coordination between national courts and the European Commission
III. The enforcement of European Commission decisions
  A. Recovery of subsidies
  B. Recovery of fiscal state aids
IV. Conclusions

I. THE ENFORCEMENT OF THE STANDSTILL OBLIGATION

A. General issues

Spanish courts often deal with cases related to state measures that have not been notified with the European Commission (hereinafter 'Commission'), allegedly in connection with a violation of Article 108(3) TFEU. In most cases, they are judicial proceedings between different administrative bodies. This is because Spain has a territorially decentralised political structure – the central State, seventeen Autonomous

Regions plus two Autonomous Cities, and more than eight thousand local governments. These judicial proceedings are vehicles for inter-administrative conflicts. Some of them take place amongst bordering Autonomous Regions, as a result of dumping policies implemented in one of them (e.g., ECJ, Case C-428/06 *Unión General de Trabajadores de la Rioja* [2008] ECR I-6747, followed by Judgment of the Supreme Court, 3 April 2012). Others are the result of an action by the central State against regional or municipal measures that had not been notified with the Commission (e.g., ECJ, Case C-71/04 *Xunta de Galicia* [2005] ECR I-7419, followed by Judgment of the Supreme Court, 7 February 2006). Finally, local governments also challenge State or regional measures that provide for local tax exemptions, arguing that they constitute illegal State aid (e.g., ECJ, Case C-387/92 *Banco Exterior de España* [1994] ECR I-877; Case C-522/13 *Navantia* ECLI:EU:C:2014:2262; Case C-74/16 *Congregación de Escuelas Pías Provincia Betania* ECLI:EU:C:2017:496).

Unlike what happened with the private enforcement of competition law thanks to Directive 2014/104/EU, private enforcement of State aid rules has not been harmonised by EU legislators, which makes its enforcement in the different Member States of sizable interest. In Spain, the enforcement of Article 108(3) TFEU based on the initiative of private actors has been very rare.[1] Private parties usually participate as interveners in judicial proceedings that have begun with an action lodged by a public body (e.g., ECJ, Case C-428/06 *Unión General de Trabajadores de la Rioja* [2008] ECR I-6747, followed by Judgment of the Supreme Court, 3 April 2012; Case C-275/13 *Elcogás*, ECLI:EU:C:2014:2314, followed by Judgment of the Supreme Court of 27 February 2015). These cases are very rarely initiated by competitors of State aid beneficiaries (e.g., Judgment of the Supreme Court, 2 January 2008, *Biomasa*; and ECJ, Case C-233/16 *ANGED* ECLI:EU:C:2018:280).[2]

This suggests that private enforcement of Article 108(3) TFEU has huge room for improvement in Spain. It must be underlined that private enforcement of Article 108(3) TFEU in Spain does not face any structural hindrance from a substantive administrative law perspective, nor in terms of procedural law. Neither is the idea of a challenge to State aid being made by the recipient's competitor problematic from the point of view of constitutional principles or the legal tradition. Therefore, the underdevelopment of private enforcement of Article 108(3) TFEU seems to be a consequence of defective incentives derived from EU and domestic legislation.

B. Legal framework

Article 108(3) TFEU obligation is implemented in Spain through general administrative law and procedural law. On the one hand, Article 9(1) LGS establishes that:

1. D. Ordóñez Solís, *Enfoques y desenfoques en la aplicación del regimen europeo de ayudas de Estado por los jueces españoles* (2018) 6 Revista Aranzadi Unión Europea 43.
2. J.J. Piernas López, *Revisiting some fundamentals of fiscal selectivity: the ANGED case (C-233/16)* (2018) 17 EStAL 274.

> When, in accordance with articles 87 to 89 of the Treaty establishing the European Union [current Articles 107 to 109 TFEU], projects for the establishment, granting or modification of a subsidy must be notified, the competent authorities will notify the appropriate projects in accordance with [the specific procedure] with the European Commission. In these cases, a subsidy cannot be paid as long as it is not considered compatible with the common market.

On the other hand, the specific procedure for the notification of State aid - not only subsidies - is regulated by Royal Decree 1755/1987, of 23 December, as well as by an agreement adopted in 1990 by the Sectorial Conference for matters connected with the European Communities, which constitutes an inter-administrative cooperation body. Any public body planning to grant aid subject to Article 108(3) TFEU must give notice of the project, at least three months in advance, to the Secretary of State for EU matters, which belongs to the central administration controlled by the Ministry of Foreign Affairs. The Secretary of State for EU matters is responsible for ultimately notifying the European Commission through the Permanent Representation of Spain before the EU, as well as for the coordination of contact.

The Spanish Competition Authority (CNMC) is not entitled to enforce State aid law. According to Article 11 LDC, the CNMC is only able to assess the conditions for the granting of aid and its potential effects on competition on its own initiative or at the request of any public authorities. It also may issue reports regarding individual state aid frameworks and submit specific recommendations to public authorities in order to ensure the maintenance of effective competition in the market.

Judicial review of administrative decisions follows a dualist system in Spain: administrative decisions can be reviewed by both administrative law courts (when they have been taken under the application of substantive public law) and civil law courts (when they have been taken under the application of private law). In this area, it all depends on the instrument under which the non-notified State aid has been granted:

(i) if it has been conferred by means of administrative rules, administrative acts, administrative contracts or civil contracts concluded in order to implement an administrative act (e.g., land selling contracts subscribed by an administrative authority), public law remedies will apply, and judicial review will take place before the administrative law courts;
(ii) if it has been granted by a private contract that has not been subscribed in order to implement an administrative act (e.g., land selling contracts subscribed by a public owned company), private law remedies may apply and Article 108(3) TFEU enforcement will be in the hands of civil law courts. This only rarely applies, since most contracts concluded by administrative authorities are either administrative contracts or civil contracts that implement an administrative act.

A final situation must be taken into consideration: If the State aid was conferred by a parliamentary statute, judicial review can only take place before the Constitutional Court. The Court will focus only on the constitutional review of the statute and not on its compliance with Article 108(3) TFEU, so it will be necessary to challenge the individual implementing decisions before the ordinary courts.

C. Public law remedies

Within the framework of an action before an administrative law court, the appellant may seek a series of typical remedies that basically cover all means of redress for competitors, as well as for other third parties affected by unlawful State aid which have been identified by the ECJ and the Commission. On the one hand, Article 31 LJCA states that:

(1) The appellant may file a claim seeking a declaration of illegality and, where appropriate, the annulment of the acts and rules that are susceptible of being challenged according to the preceding chapter.
(2) The appellant may also file a claim for recognition of an individualised legal situation and the adoption of appropriate measures for its full restoration, including the compensation of damages, when appropriate.

On the other hand, Article 129(1) LJCA states that:

> Interested parties may request at any stage of the process the adoption of any measure aimed at ensuring the effectiveness of the final judgment.

These two provisions cover all the relevant means of redress in view of the 2009 Commission Notice on the Enforcement of State Aid Law by National Courts:[3] the prevention of the payment of not-yet-paid unlawful aid; the recovery of paid unlawful aid, as well as the illegality interest; damages suffered by competitors and other third parties; and interim measures against unlawful aid.

1. Preventing the payment of unlawful aid

When State aid has already been granted but it has not yet been paid, national courts are obliged to prevent this payment from taking place. Spanish administrative law courts can be asked – within a two-month deadline – to declare that the administrative act or rule that conferred the State aid is unlawful and therefore to annul it, in accordance with Article 31(1) LJCA. The logical consequence of the granting act being invalid as a result of the Member State's breach of Article 108(3) TFEU is the suppression of the payment's legal basis. At this stage, such annulment is the way to prevent the execution of the payment.

A substantive problem that arises here is classifying the kind of invalidity of administrative acts or rules that confer State aid when it has not been notified with the European Commission. According to Spanish general administrative law, procedural

3. Commission notice on the enforcement of State aid law by national courts [2009] OJ C 85/1.

flaws may lead to three legal consequences in terms of the unlawfulness of administrative acts: (i) as a general rule, they lead to the relative invalidity of the administrative act (*anulabilidad*), which could be cured at a later stage, and whose declaration produces *ex nunc*, i.e., non-retroactive, effects (Article 48(1) LPAC); (ii) they can also have no consequences whatsoever for the act's validity (*irregularidad no invalidante*) if, under the specific circumstances at stake, the specific flaw has not been materially relevant in terms of the content of the administrative decision (Article 48(2) LPAC); and finally (iii) they can also lead to the absolute invalidity of the administrative act (*nulidad de pleno Derecho*), which cannot be cured and whose declaration generates *ex tunc*, i.e., retroactive, effects. This happens, *inter alia*, when they have been adopted with 'absolute disregard for the applicable administrative procedure' (Article 47(1) e) LPAC). This third category has been interpreted by the courts as including the infringement of procedural steps that are both compulsory and particularly relevant (Judgments of the Supreme Court, 21 March 1988 and 2 November 2010). The infringement of the standstill obligation should be regarded as a procedural flaw of the third and most serious type of procedural flaws.[4] The same applies to the administrative act that serves as a legal basis for the conclusion of a contract.

Nonetheless, new grants of State aid are usually established by administrative rules. Here the need of choosing between these two forms of invalidity disappears because, according to a rather controversial principle of Spanish public law, administrative rules can suffer only from the third type of unlawfulness – resulting in absolute invalidity (Article 47(2) LPAC). This is the legal effect following the violation of Article 108(3) TFEU, as it can be seen in practice (Judgment of the Supreme Court, 2 January 2008, *Biomasa*; and Judgment of the Supreme Court, 7 February 2006, following ECJ, Case C-71/04 *Xunta de Galicia* [2005] ECR I-7419;[5] and Judgment of the Supreme Court, 24 November 1998, in the fishing ships case[6]).

Therefore, administrative decisions that confer State aid in breach of Article 108(3) TFEU are subject to the most serious type of invalidity, regardless of such aid taking on the form of an administrative act, a contract (Article 47(1) e) LPAC), or a rule (Article 49(2) LPAC).

2. *Recovery of unlawful aid and illegality interest*

When a State aid has not only been granted but already been paid, national courts are still obliged to protect the rights of individuals affected by violations of the standstill obligation. This should occur in two courses of action provided for by Article 31 LJCA, which have to be addressed in the same complaint. First, competitors or third parties

4. J.L. Buendía Sierra, *'Spain'* in Paul F. Nemitz (ed) *The Effective Application of EU State Aid Procedures*, Chapter 20, 367 (Kluwer Competition Law Series 2007).
5. M. Pedraz Calvo *The Validity of National Measures when Implementing Illegal Aid before National Judges: The Xunta de Galicia Judgment* (2017) 17 EStAL 446 et seq.
6. J.A. Rodríguez Miguez, *'La aplicación privada en materia de ayudas de Estado o públicas'* in L. A. Velasco et al (eds), *La aplicación privada del derecho de la competencia*, 501 (Lex Nova 2011).

can seek the annulment of the administrative act or rule (Article 31(1) LJCA). This will take place according to the legal framework that has just been described.

Simultaneously, they may seek the acknowledgement of an individualised legal situation and its full reestablishment (Article 31(2) LJCA). The concept of an individualised legal situation as used by the law is vague by design, since it aims at covering both legitimate interests and subjective rights, in accordance with the constitutional definition of the right to effective judicial protection (Article 24 (1) CE). It is therefore immaterial whether competitors have a subjective right or a simple interest in the fulfilment of the standstill obligation. Alongside the annulment of the administrative decision, they can seek judicial recognition of the legal position according to which the public administration may not confer aid before the Commission grants its authorisation.

Moreover, competitors can also seek the adoption of measures for the full restoration of the situation before the grant of illicit aid. Ordering the full recovery of unlawful aid is the appropriate measure for claimants to see their rights completely reestablished. Therefore, it is part of the national court's obligation to protect the individual rights of the claimant under Article 108(3) TFEU (2009 Commission Notice, section 30). The law expressly provides for this link between annulment and reimbursement in the case of subsidies, as Article 36(4) LGS states that:

> The judicial or administrative declaration of invalidity will include the obligation to return the amounts received.

The need to recover the financial advantage resulting from premature implementation of the aid is part of the national courts' obligation under Article 108(3) TFEU. Spanish administrative law expressly provides for this with respect to subsidies, as Article 37(1) LGS states that:

> The amounts received will be reimbursed, together with the corresponding interest from the date on which the grant was paid until the date on which the refund is ordered.

In view of the 2009 Commission Notice, once the national court has decided that unlawful aid has been disbursed in breach of Article 108(3) TFEU, 'it must quantify the aid in order to determine the amount to be recovered' (paragraph 36). This seems to differ from the practice of Spanish courts, which usually declare a specific amount in terms of financial obligations only if it directly results from the information at their disposal (e.g., from the administrative act granting a subsidy). If quantification requires more or less intricate operations, Spanish courts usually refer the determination them to the subsequent implementation of the ruling by the public administration.

The effectiveness of the recovery obligation depends on both substantive and procedural circumstances. According to the ECJ case law, the national courts' recovery obligation is not absolute (2009 Commission Notice, sections 30 et seq.). Nevertheless, the exceptions to this obligation admitted by EU law are rather strict. According to the 2009 Commission Notice, the legal standard to be applied in this context should be similar to the one applicable under the Procedural Regulation. Article 16(1) of Regulation 2015/1589 states that:

The Commission shall not require recovery of the aid if this would be contrary to a general principle of European Union law.

Despite a rather reluctant administrative practice in 107(1) TFEU cases, where recovery follows Commission Decisions there are no specific Spanish law issues arising with respect to Article 108(3) TFEU. When annulment is decided by a court on the ground of an infringement of Article 108(3) TFEU, there is nothing that hinders the effectiveness of the recovery obligation. Courts have expressly rejected that illegal State aid beneficiaries may claim for damages against the granting authority. In a recent Judgment of 5 September 2018, the Supreme Court has declared that (i) recovery does not cause an actual damage because it is aimed at suppressing a previously conferred illegal competitive advantage; and that (ii) the recipient cannot invoke the principle of legitimate expectations if Article 108(3) TFEU was infringed.

While the reimbursement obligation is directly declared by the court, its fulfilment requires, on a general basis, the implementation of an administrative procedure.[7] In the case of fiscal State aid, the new recovery procedures established in the 2015 amendment of the General Tax Law will apply (these will be tackled later in sub III.2). These procedures have been created in order to facilitate the implementation of Commission Decisions, as well as to comply in a better way with the relevant EU Regulation. Nevertheless, they will also certainly be applicable in the case of aid declared illegal by national courts.

As for subsidies, the reimbursement procedure is regulated in Articles 36 LGS et seq. The procedure begins with an administrative order; the recipient has a right to be heard, and the procedure has to end within twelve months from the administrative order initiating it. The reimbursement obligation can be directly enforced against the State aid recipient. Despite the fact that Article 39 LGS generally provides for a four-year time limit, in EU law cases courts apply the ten-year limitation period established in Article 17(1) of Regulation 2015/1589, following the primacy principle (Judgment of the Supreme Court, 9 May 2013).

These administrative procedures constitute a way of implementing a legal obligation that has been imposed on the public administration by the court. Where the former fails to implement the reimbursement procedure within that period of time, the appellant can seek judicial enforcement of the recovery obligation. According to Article 108(1) LJCA, the court can implement the ruling through its own means or by requiring the collaboration of other administrative authorities.

If the public administration does not refuse to implement the ruling but carries out an activity that may infringe the judgment, Article 108(2) LJCA entitles the court, at the request of the interested parties, to stop the obstructing administrative behaviour and to re-establish the situation according to what the ruling foresees.

7. D. Ordóñez Solís, *La ejecución forzosa de la recuperación y de la devolución de las ayudas de Estado en la UE y en España* (2009) 9 Gaceta Jurídica de la Unión Europea y de la Competencia 16.

3. *Damages for competitors and other third parties*

The third possible remedy is to claim for damages. Public law remedies allow the awarding of damages only where caused by the public administration, i.e., the authority granting the illegal State aid, and not by the State aid recipient, who will have to be sued before a civil law court specialised in commercial law (*Juzgado de lo Mercantil*). The emerging procedural avenues are taking mainly two forms.[8] First, damages can be claimed directly before the administrative authority - within a limitation period of one year. This would be the right way to claim for damages if the aid has already been declared illegal. Second, they can be claimed before an administrative law court in the same action aimed at obtaining the annulment of the administrative act or rule. As has been said, competitors and other third parties may seek the recognition of an individualised legal situation and its full reestablishment. Article 31(2) LJCA expressly proclaims that restoration measures may include compensation for damages 'when appropriate'. This last caveat refers to the requirements that a claim for damages has to comply with an order to be upheld by the courts. The problems arising in such a case may likewise materialise in two ways.

As regards the attribution of liability, Spanish administrative law is aligned with EU law. However, there is a difference between both systems: While the *Francovich* and *Brasserie du Pêcheur* case law of the ECJ requires a breach of community law in order to be 'sufficiently serious', according to Spanish law any type of unlawfulness is sufficient. Nevertheless, a closer analysis shows that the abovementioned gap does not really exist. As the 2009 Notice makes clear, 'where the authority in question has no discretion', as regarding the application of Article 108(3) TFEU, 'the mere infringement of Community law may be sufficient to establish the existence of a sufficiently serious breach'. In sum, although departing from different points, both systems seem to converge in conceiving mere unlawfulness as the foundation of liability.

More serious is the problem of proving causation and the existence of actual damage. Article 32 LRJSP establishes that:

(1) Individuals have a right to be compensated by the corresponding Public Administrations for any injury they suffer in any of their assets and rights, provided that the injury is a consequence of the normal or abnormal functioning of public services except in cases of force majeure, or of damages that an individual has the legal duty to support in accordance with the Law.
(2) The alleged damage must be effective, economically evaluable and individualised in relation to a person or group of people.

According to the ECJ case law, and also Spanish law, there has to be a direct causal link between the breach of the Member State's obligation and the damage suffered by the injured parties. The fact that the public administration confers illegal State aid to an undertaking, to whom it also confers a selective advantage in and of

8. P. Callol García *'Spain'* in T. Jestaedt, J. Derenne and T. Ottervanger, *Study on the enforcement of State aid rules at national level*, 423 (European Communities Publications Office 2006).

itself, certainly inflicts a damage on its competitors, one that can consist of both an emergent damage or a loss of profit. The problem arises when it comes to precisely evaluating this damage, as well as to establishing a cause-effect relation with the granted aid.[9] In this respect, the problematic determination of the damage suffered does not differ from the quantification of damages as a consequence of a violation of Article 101 or 102 TFEU (anticompetitive agreements/abuse of a dominant position). The burden of proving the suffered damage falls on the claimant because acts of the public administration are presumed to be valid (Article 39(1) LPAC). Furthermore, this is also the general rule established in Article 217 of the Code of Civil Procedure (*Ley de Enjuiciamiento Civil*), which also applies to judicial proceedings conducted by administrative law courts. As in general claims for damages cases, different ways or means of proof are acceptable before Spanish courts. These include questioning the parties to the procedure, public or private documents, expert opinions, questioning witnesses, and economic evidence, such as economic reports elaborated by experts that calculate the damage suffered by the claimant (Articles 137 and 299 of the Code of Civil Procedure).

It is rather difficult to accurately evaluate the damage caused to a competitor by the conferral of State aid. Often hypothetical calculations need to take place, which is not always easy. It may be possible that thanks to the aid, the beneficiary has had access to a business opportunity to the detriment of the claimant. As the 2009 Notice makes clear, in such a case the damage evaluation may be easier.

More common will be the situation in which 'the aid merely leads to an overall loss of market share'. In that case, the 2009 Notice recommends that the court 'compare the claimant's actual income situation (based on the profit and loss account) with the hypothetical income situation had the unlawful aid not been granted' (section 49.c). It is doubtful whether this may satisfy the standards applied by Spanish courts in order to accept that an evaluable damage has been caused by the State aid. Indeed, it might be too uncertain or difficult to determine what the hypothetical income situation of the claimant would have been in the event the unlawful aid had not been granted. This uncertainty is probably one of the reasons that explains the lack of incentives for competitors to claim for damages.

A good example of these difficulties is the Judgment of the High Court, 15 February 2005, which rejects a claim for compensation made by a shipping company against the central State in regard to subsidies granted to a competitor:

> [It has not] been proven that the aid received by [Trasmediterránea] was due precisely to the purpose of permitting the reduction of tariffs. Therefore, a linkage of state compensations to this specific purpose of permitting the price reduction has not been established. The complexity of the cost structure of Trasmediterránea, a company that provides various types of maritime services between the islands and that can realize significant economies of scale, determines, in the

9. J.A. Pérez Rivarés, *La aplicación del Derecho de la Unión Europea sobre ayudas estatales por los Tribunales nacionales* (2012) 42 Revista de Derecho Comunitario Europeo, 37 et seq.; F. Pastor-Merchante, *La aplicación privada de la normative europea sobre ayudas de Estado* (2015) 55 Revista Española de Derecho Europeo, 31 et seq.; F. Pastor-Merchante, *The Role of Competitors in the Enforcement of State Aid Law*, 75 et seq. (Hart 2017).

opinion of this Chamber, that it is not possible to directly attribute the reduction of rates to the subsidies (para. 11).

This ruling is problematic from various perspectives. Not only does it show an unconvincing identification of the purpose and the effects of the subsidy, but it also reflects a reluctance to investigate to what extent the price reductions were potentially due to subsidies enjoyed by the beneficiary.

A final point must be clarified. In Spain, primary legal protection (through annulment and recovery) and secondary legal protection (through compensation of damages suffered) are not alternative avenues but different remedies that are conditioned on the satisfaction of their respective requirements. Therefore, they are not reciprocally related under a principal-subsidiary scheme. Indeed, granting damages to the competitor of the recipient or to other parties would require the State aid to be illegal and therefore imply its previous or simultaneous judicial annulment. However, the effectiveness of recovery would have an effect on the damage intensity and therefore on the final amount granted by the court. Indeed, if the public administration does not simply refuse to implement the ruling ordering a recovery of the damages suffered, but proceeds to carry out activity that may infringe the judgment, Article 108(2) LJCA entitles the court, as has been said, to re-establish the situation to the status required by the ruling and also to determine the additional damages that have been caused by the obstructionist administrative behaviour.

4. Interim measures against unlawful aid

According to the case law of the ECJ, the duty of national courts to draw the necessary legal consequences from violations of the standstill obligation comprises the adoption of interim measures where this is appropriate to safeguard the rights of individuals and the effectiveness of Article 108(3) TFEU. As has been mentioned, when State aid has already been granted but has not yet been paid, national courts are obliged to prevent this payment from taking place. This can include ordering the suspension of the effectiveness of the relevant administrative act or rule until the substance of the matter is resolved by the court.

Suspension is not the appropriate interim measure when State aid has not only been granted but has already been paid. In these cases, the court might be forced to order the suspension as well as the provisional recovery of the aid. According to Article 129 LJCA, administrative law courts may not only order a suspension but also any type of positive measure that may be deemed appropriate in order to guarantee the effectiveness of its final ruling, such as an interim recovery order.

This assessment of possible interim measures is carried out in a proceeding that is separate from and incidental to the main one. An oral hearing with the opposing party (defendant) is to take place within ten days of the day on which the interim measures are requested. The decision on the interim measures request is to be taken within the following five days (Article 131 LJCA). Where the requested interim measures are granted, they will be in force until the final judgment is issued (Article

132 LJCA). Nevertheless, they could be modified or revoked during the procedure if the situation has changed.

As regards the necessary conditions for an interim measure to be taken, Article 130 LJCA provides that:

(1) After carefully balancing all the conflicting interests in a specific case, an interim measure may only be ordered when the implementation of the act or provision could cause the action to lose its legitimate purpose.
(2) The interim measure may be denied when, in a reasoned opinion of the court, it could cause a serious disturbance of general public interests or the interests of a third party.

Thus, the court could decide to grant the interim measure in question when the execution of the challenged act, or the application of the challenged provision, could eliminate the legitimate purpose of the action. In any case, the court would need to assess the potential that the effectiveness of the final judgment would be put at risk if the interim relief were not granted, and it would need to weigh the balance of public and private interests involved in the specific case; additionally, the court has to consider judicial protection of the potential outcome and the protection of the claimant's right to be awarded compensation for damage.

At a very first view, this can be problematic. According to the 2009 Notice:

> Where, based on the case law of the Community courts and the practice of the Commission, the national judge has reached a reasonable *prima facie* conviction that the measure at stake involves unlawful State aid, the most expedient remedy will, in the Commission's view and subject to national procedural law, be to order the unlawful aid and the illegality interest to be put on a blocked account until the substance of the matter is resolved (section 61).

In Spain, the principle of *fumus boni iuris* has a minor role in general administrative law. Nevertheless, in cases involving EU law, Spanish courts invariably take this perspective into account when balancing the conflicting interests. Therefore, it would not be a problem for an administrative law court to grant interim protection if the challenged act or rule has apparently conferred non-notified State aid.

Moreover, in a series of Judgments (16 July 2012, 23 November 2012, 30 January 2014, 17 July 2014), the Supreme Court has declared the obligation of lower courts to apply section 62 of the 2009 Notice of the Commission. In the event of an ongoing investigation by the Commission, where the lower court wishes to await the outcome of the Commission's compatibility assessment, it should order the placement of the funds on a blocked account. Despite not having a binding nature in and of itself, the Supreme Court has proclaimed that this Notice is an authoritative source when it comes to analysing the legal consequences of Article 108(3) TFEU. And it has to be mentioned that Article 129 LJCA provides the necessary flexibility in terms of designing the appropriate measure.

Article 133(1) LJCA deals with the problem of damages caused by interim measures and confers upon the court the power to condition the order to the offer of some kind of guarantee by the appellant:

> When damages of any kind could arise from the interim order, the appropriate measures may be agreed to avoid or mitigate them. Likewise, the presentation of a bond or any other sufficient guarantee may be required to respond to them.

A final point should be clarified. Despite Articles 129 LJCA et seq. providing for an appropriate legal framework in terms of complying with EU law requirements, there are only few cases where the claimants challenging non-notified state aid are seeking interim relief. The reason probably lies in the fact that, as mentioned, they are mainly other public bodies whose incentives to immediately obtain legal protection may not be as strong as the incentives of competitors. Therefore, it can be presumed that if competitors made more use of private enforcement possibilities, this would certainly lead to more frequent requests for interim measures.

5. *Procedural issues*

The addressees of the action lodged before the administrative law court will be both the authority that conferred the State aid and its recipient. The action is directly addressed to the former, since, according to Article 21(1)a) LJCA, the defendants will be those administrative authorities whose acts or rules are being challenged. The court is obliged to communicate the complaint to the aid beneficiary, since, according to Article 21(1)b) LJCA, defendants can also be those whose rights and legitimate interests may be affected if the court decides in favour of the appellant. This is not the burden of the appellant but of the court itself (Article 48 LJCA). The failure to communicate the action and to give the beneficiary an opportunity to intervene would lead to an infringement of his or her fundamental right to effective judicial protection (Article 24(1) CE).

In Spain, there is no discussion on whether individuals or firms have a right to lodge an action against administrative measures that provide any kind of benefit to their competitors. Article 24(1) CE proclaims a fundamental right to obtain the effective judicial protection of both subjective rights and legitimate interests. Article 19(1)a) LJCA grants *locus standi* to those holding either a subjective right or a legitimate interest. The concept of legitimate interest is interpreted by the courts very extensively: it can be direct or indirect, individual or collective. But it cannot consist of a mere interest in the implementation of the law. A legitimate interest requires a specific connection of the appellant with the question that is going to be decided by the court. This specific connection can nonetheless be obtaining a specific benefit or preventing a specific harm. There is no doubt that competitors may obtain a specific benefit if State aid that has not been notified to the European Commission is declared illegal by a court and its recovery is ordered. Associations and groups affected by the measure seeking to protect a collective interest also have standing, like public bodies acting within the scope of their competences.

D. Private law remedies

Article 108(3) TFEU enforcement will be in the hands of civil law courts on a rather exceptional basis in Spain. State aid usually has its origin in decisions adopted in the exercise of public law prerogatives, such as a parliamentary statute, an administrative rule, or an administrative act. Even when the aid is granted by an administrative contract, the conclusion of the latter implies the implementation of the award decision, which is contained in an administrative act. In all these cases, the declaration of illegality as a result of the infringement of Article 108(3) TFEU remains in the hands of administrative law courts.

Spanish civil courts have been reluctant to rule in these kinds of cases. They have instead declared that control of the standstill obligation in cases of State aid granted by administrative law instruments - including public contracts - lies beyond their jurisdiction and within the powers of administrative law courts (Judgments of the Supreme Court, 20 May 1996 and 14 November 2002, and of the Madrid Court of Second Instance ('Audiencia Provincial'), 28 December 2012).

If the aid is granted by the State directly through a private contract that is not concluded in the implementation of a previously adopted public law decision, private law remedies may apply and Article 108(3) TFEU enforcement will be open to civil law courts, which will be entitled to verify whether a grant of State aid has not been notified in breach of this provision. In this second scenario, competitors and third parties can seek annulment of the contract (Article 1301 CC), as well as recovery of the aid (Article 1303 CC).

A somewhat different issue is whether, once the illegality of the aid has been declared by the competent administrative court, competitors can sue the beneficiary. On the one hand, Article 15 LCD establishes:

(1) Acquiring a significant competitive advantage through the violation of laws is an act of unfair competition.
(2) The mere infringement of competition rules shall also be considered as an act of unfair competition.

On the other hand, Article 32 LCD establishes that different actions may be exercised against acts of unfair competition. In particular, competitors can seek injunctions and damages.

This avenue has been used in the past in the context of antitrust law (Judgment of Commercial Court Number 5 of Madrid, 11 November 2015 *Conduit/Telefónica*). Early academic literature has suggested that this could be a practicable avenue also in State aid law.[10] Thus, competitors could seek injunctions and damages against the State aid beneficiary, arguing that the defendant had acquired a significant competitive advantage through the violation of Article 108(3) TFEU.

10. J. Massager, *Comentario a la Ley de Competencia Desleal* (Civitas 1999); Callol García, *supra* n. 8, at 422; C. González-Páramo and S. Pérez, *'Spain'* in: *2009 update of the 2006 Study on the enforcement of State aid rules at national level,* 329 (Lovells 2009).

Nevertheless, competitors in Spain have not used Articles 15 and 32 LCD in order to sue the recipient of illegal aid for damages. There are two possible reasons for this. First, it has been argued that in order to consider that unfair competition practices are taking place, Article 15 LCD requires positive conduct on the part of the offending undertaking.[11] In some circumstances, it might be true that the recipient does not need to engage in positive conduct in order to obtain the aid. Nevertheless, asking for the application of a tax exception or subsidy, or even concluding a contract are genuinely forms of positive conduct that should suffice in terms of Article 15 LCD.

A second and more persuasive explanation is the uncertainty of private law remedies that rest on the illegality of State aid, such as those granted by Article 15 LCD, since the violation of Article 108(3) TFEU will usually fall under the competence of administrative law courts. In this dualist context, it is all too risky to sue the recipient before a civil court since the jurisdiction to declare the administrative decision invalid will, on a general basis, belong to administrative law courts. Seeking annulment, recovery and, eventually, damages from the administrative authority before an administrative law court seems a more practicable track. Nevertheless, as it has been already mentioned, this route has been used only occasionally.

II. COOPERATION AND COORDINATION BETWEEN NATIONAL COURTS AND THE EUROPEAN COMMISSION

Article 29 of Regulation 2015/1589 provides for two cooperation instruments amongst national courts and the European Commission. On the one hand, national courts may ask the Commission to transfer to them information in its possession, as well as to voice its opinion on questions concerning the application of State aid rules. Spanish courts have rarely made use of this tool. In view of the underdevelopment of private enforcement of State aid law in Spain, this does not seem to be surprising.

On the other hand, Article 29 of Regulation 2015/1589 also establishes that:

> [T]he Commission, acting on its own initiative, may submit written observations to the courts of the Member States that are responsible for applying the State aid rules. It may, with the permission of the court in question, also make oral observations.
>
> The Commission shall inform the Member State concerned of its intention to submit observations before formally doing so.
>
> For the exclusive purpose of preparing its observations, the Commission may request the relevant court of the Member State to transmit documents at the disposal of the court, necessary for the Commission's assessment of the matter.

From the perspective of national procedural law, this *amicus curiae* intervention could raise some questions. Since the position of *amicus curiae* is not foreseen in Spanish procedural law, the Commission will not be formally considered as a party in the judicial proceeding. If the Commission submits written observations, they would be taken into account only to the extent the parties bring them to the judicial

11. Buendía Sierra, *supra* n. 4, at 361.

proceeding. Otherwise, the court will only be able to bear them in mind after asking the parties about them. In the same terms, a representative of the Commission could be invited to testify as a qualified expert. Finally, the transmission of judicial information to the European Commission - which eventually can try to reuse this information in subsequent procedures - could be problematic from the perspective of the right to a fair trial (Article 24(2) CE) where that information had been originally obtained for judicial purposes.

As regards the Lufthansa case (ECJ, Case C-284/12 *Deutsche Lufthansa* [2013] ECLI:EU:C:2013:755), it has already been said that, in recent times, Spanish courts have been very cooperative in the event of an ongoing investigation being carried out by the Commission. The preliminary assessment contained in the decision to initiate the formal examination procedure will certainly be taken into consideration by the national court since it may trigger the *fumus boni iuris* criterion and therefore lead to ordering the interim recovery of the examined aid. As stated, the Supreme Court has even declared the obligation of lower courts to apply section 62 of the 2009 Notice of the European Commission. Nevertheless, it remains unclear whether this should work as an unconditioned duty to order suspension and recovery or rather as a prima facie obligation qualified by proportionality. Indeed, within the context of Spanish procedural law, interim measures have to be decided 'after carefully balancing all conflicting interests' (Article 130(1) LJCA). The criteria laid down in Article 13(2) of the Regulation 2015/1589 set the adoption of an injunction decision by the Commission within the same framework.

There are some interesting Spanish precedents in Luxembourg. Unfortunately, most of them were samples of a failure to fulfil Member State obligations (ECJ, Case C-499/99 *Commission v Spain* [2002] ECR I-6031; Case C-404/00 *Commission v Spain* [2003] ECR I-6695; Case C-177/06 *Commission v Spain* [2007] ECR I-7689; Case C-529/09 *Commission v Spain* [2013] ECLI:EU:C:2013:31; Case C-184/11 *Commission v Spain* [2014] ECLI:EU:C:2014:316).

In turn, Spanish courts have not made frequent use of preliminary references. A recent survey[12] counts eleven references made by Spanish courts in the area of State aid law, these regarding very different issues ranging from regional tax policies to subsidies conferred in strategic sectors such as banking, broadcasting, energy, or shipyards. Almost all of them were made by administrative law courts; one was a referral by a labour law court. Interestingly enough, civil law courts - with jurisdiction in unfair practices - have not made any references to Luxembourg in connection with State aid law.

III. THE ENFORCEMENT OF EUROPEAN COMMISSION DECISIONS

Administrative enforcement of Commission Decisions declaring State aid incompatible with the internal market have traditionally faced a common difficulty in Spain: neither administrative law nor tax law has provided for a specific administrative recovery

12. Ordóñez, *supra* n. 1.

procedure. This problem has come up under different terms in these two areas of law, where it has been solved in different ways.

A. Recovery of subsidies

The enforcement of Commission Decisions declaring a subsidy granted by an administrative act to be incompatible with the internal market has been problematic because, according to the general view, the administrative act had to first be formally annulled by the administrative authority. According to Spanish administrative law, favourable administrative acts (i.e., acts conferring a right or improving a party's legal or factual situation), can only be annulled by the authority that adopted them (i) in cases of absolute nullity and (ii) after having heard the opinion of the Council of State or the equivalent regional advisory body. These substantive and procedural conditions, aimed at protecting the stability of favourable administrative acts, such as those granting subsidies and other State aid, against an administrative declaration of invalidity have been hindering the effectiveness of Commission Decisions and have been in part responsible for enforcement deficits.[13]

In order to comply with the primacy of Commission Decisions, the law on subsidies was modified to make clear that State aid can be recovered following a Decision of the Commission regardless of the granting act being annulled or not. Article 37(1) LGS states that:

> The amounts received will be reimbursed, together with the corresponding interest from the moment of the payment of the subsidy until the date on which the reimbursement is agreed, in the following cases:
>
> [...] h) The adoption of a recovery order according to the provisions of Articles 87 to 89 of the Treaty on European Union [current Articles 107 to 109 TFEU].

Since 2003, when the LGS was enacted, Spanish courts may apply this specific provision of domestic law in order to recover illegal State aid, particularly, as mentioned, non-fiscal State aid. If there is a Commission Decision declaring the illegality of the subsidy, it is no longer required that the administrative act be annulled. This is an exception to the general rule (Judgment of the Supreme Court, 5 April 2018). While the reimbursement obligation is directly declared by the Commission, its fulfilment requires, on a general basis, the implementation of an administrative procedure. The reimbursement procedure is regulated in Articles 41 LGS et seq. The administrative authority initiates the procedure ex officio – on its own initiative, at the request of other bodies or by a complaint. The recovery procedure can also start as a result of the financial control report issued by the General Intervention of the State Administration. The recipient has a right to be heard (*see* Article 42.3 of the LGS). The procedure has to end within twelve months, calculated from the day the procedure was initiated, by virtue of a declaration of the reimbursement obligation of a certain amount

13. Buendía Sierra, *supra* n. 4, at 366 et seq.; Ordóñez, *supra* n. 7, at 14 et seq.

of money within a certain period of time. In case of non-compliance, the reimbursement obligation can be enforced in a mandatory fashion against the state aid recipient, eventually seizing his or her assets (Royal Decree 939/2005). All these administrative actions can be challenged before an administrative law court, although in some cases a previous administrative complaint (before the administrative superiors) may be required.[14]

According to Article 39 of the LGS, the right of the public administration to seek recovery of the illegally obtained aid is time-barred after four years. This period, foreseen by Spanish national legislation, is shorter than the ten-year period foreseen by Article 17(1) of Council Regulation (EU) 2015/1589. Following the principle of primacy of EU law, the period laid down by the LGS should be in line with the one established by the EU Regulation, consequently, ten years. This is also of clear advantage for the public administration. The Spanish Supreme Court has also clarified that the ten-year period is applicable in this case, following the principle of primacy of EU law (Judgment of the Supreme Court, 9 May 2013).

B. Recovery of fiscal state aids

In a series of rulings (starting with Judgments of 13 May 2013 and 14 October 2013, and reaching as recently as 25 May 2017), the Supreme Court declared that Spanish administrative authorities had violated the right to be heard of fiscal State aid beneficiaries as enshrined in the Constitution (Article 105 CE) as well as in the Charter of Fundamental Rights of the EU (Article 41(2) CFR). In the implementation of Commission Decisions declaring certain aid incompatible with the internal market, national authorities had been ordering reimbursement without giving the aid beneficiaries an opportunity to be heard and to discuss their particular situation. Under these circumstances, an opportunity to be heard was justified because the taxpayers at issue could not ask for the application of other benefits incompatible with the ones initially applied for. Consequently, the court ordered that the administrative procedure be repeated in order to satisfy their right to be heard.

These cases led to the amendment of the General Taxation Act 58/2003, of 17 December (LGT), by means of Act 34/2015, of 21 September. The following reforms were introduced in order to comply with the principles of immediate and effective implementation of Commission Decisions: The first was a specific administrative procedure for recovery of fiscal aid. It is initiated ex officio by the tax authority, followed by a provisional assessment of the tax debt, subject to a ten-day period of time for the taxpayer to submit written allegations, and there is to be a final reasoned decision taken within four months, which can also be enforced in a mandatory way against the state aid recipient. These administrative actions can be challenged, first, before administrative tribunals – external to the judicial branch – those are specialised in tax law (Article 264 LGT), and afterwards before an administrative law court. In order to claim before an ordinary court, the action at stake must have been previously

14. Ordóñez, *supra* n. 7, at 16 et seq.

challenged before the administrative tribunals (Article 249 LGT; Checa González, 2004).

A second important novelty is the possibility of modifying previous administrative acts, even those having the force of res judicata ('*firmeza*'), as established by the ECJ in the *Lucchini* case (ECJ, Case C-119/05 *Lucchini* [2007] ECR I-6199). Despite this doctrine having later been qualified by the ECJ[15] Article 263 LGT makes no distinction in this respect:

> If there is a previous administrative act of the Tax Administration regarding the obligation affected by the State aid recovery Decision, the implementation of the latter will determine the modification of the said act, even if it has acquired the force of *res judicata*.

A third amendment of the General Taxation Act 58/2003, of 17 December (LGT), provided for by Act 34/2015, of 21 September, is the incorporation of the limitation period foreseen in Regulation 2015/1589: ten years from the day when the application of the State aid had legal effects under applicable tax law (Article 262 LGT) instead of the four years established as a general rule according to tax law (Article 66 LGT).

IV. CONCLUSIONS

Private enforcement of State aid rules faces problems of transparency and information deficits. Nevertheless, these are not especially acute in Spain, nor is litigation particularly difficult for companies compared to the situation in other Member States. Unlike what happens in terms of incompatible aid, Spanish administrative law has not created significant obstacles for national courts in terms of declaring aid illegal and ordering its recovery.

In our view, the underdevelopment of private enforcement of Article 108(3) TFEU has to do, essentially, with incentives. Leaving aside the difficulties arising from the structural bifurcation between the substantive and procedural regularity of State aid,[16] national law is partially to blame. Before administrative law courts, competitors face prolonged cases with uncertain outcomes. While the annulment of non-notified measures could be an achievable aim, the recovery of the granted aid remains uncertain because it may be at odds with the reluctance on the part of the granting authority. Moreover, obtaining damages is difficult because of the high standards applied by administrative law courts when it comes to proving the existence of an effective and economically evaluable damage, as well as causation. This same situation was formerly the case with the private enforcement of antitrust rules in Spain, but lately, we are seeing some judgments granting damages in cartels cases. Thus, we may observe in the near future a similar trend in the field of State aid law. Lastly, seeking compensation for damage caused by the State aid recipient before civil law courts

15. ECJ, Case C-507/08 *Commission v Slovakia* [2010] ECR I-13489; Case C-505/14 *Klausner Holz Niedersachsen v Land Nordrhein-Westfalen* [2015] ECLI:EU:C:2015:742.
16. F. Pastor-Merchante, *The Role of Competitors in the Enforcement of State Aid Law*, 76 et seq. (Hart 2017).

under the law on unfair competition practices (Articles 15 and 32 LCD) faces an important obstacle, namely that the declaration of the illegality of the granted aid falls within the competence of administrative law courts.

Cooperation amongst national courts and the Commission has not been particularly fluid. This also might be a consequence of the underdevelopment of private enforcement in connection with Article 108(3) TFEU. Nevertheless, recent Supreme Court judgments show a more receptive attitude in terms of a more efficient implementation of the 2009 Notice.

The implementation of Commission Decisions in Spain has not been easy in the past because of (i) the difficulties in annulling previous favourable administrative decisions and (ii) the lack of specific recovery procedures. This situation has been improved, first, with the modification of specific legislation on subsidies and more recently with the adoption of a specific regulation related to the recovery of fiscal State aid.

CHAPTER 16

Private Enforcement in the UK

Christopher Bovis

I. Introduction
II. The structure of the UK's competition regime
III. The UK state aid compliance system
IV. The UK remedial system of state aid
  A. Locus standi
  B. Judicial review in state aid
  C. Damages in state aid
  D. Recovery of illegal state aid
  E. Private enforcement of state aid rules in the UK
V. Conclusions

The chapter will critically assess the principles of state aid law and its evolving application and control in the UK. It will investigate the role of the legal system in the compliance and enforcement mechanisms by the national competition authority and the national courts respectively. It will examine the recovery procedure for unauthorised or unlawful aid and review third party enforcement and damages actions for anti-trust breaches as a result of state aid law violations. Finally, the chapter will reveal the administrative aspects of cooperation between national competition authorities and the EU Commission in the field of state aid monitoring, compliance and enforcement.

I. INTRODUCTION

EU competition rules have been the exclusive jurisdiction of the European Commission, a regulatory system which is based on public law rules. Within the EU and during the last two decades, a fundamental development has reshaped the application and enforcement of competition law and policy in the EU and resulted in decentralisation and private enforcement. Since 2000, National Competition Authorities (NCA) can enforce EU competition rules in a parallel way, imposing fines, structural or behavioural remedies on companies which restrict, distort or hinder competition.

The EU's state aid control rules aim at instilling a level playing field between EU Member States to facilitate their economic integration. The level playing is directed in an environment of competition in order to control state subsidies to undertakings and limit the ability of states to distort competition and trade through state support of industry.

The UK has been one of the most prolific supporters of the EU state aid acquis.[1] The UK's future state aid regime after its departure from the European Union will focus on the state aid relevance to trading relationships with different parts of the world legal systems. The UK has indicated to enact an independent state aid control which will enhance the basic anti-subsidy regime applicable to all WTO members and replicate to a large effect the EU state aid acquis.

The UK legal system and culture on state aid regards that Articles 107 and 108 TFEU are the cornerstones of regulation of state aid by providing that all aid granted using state resources is subject to ex ante control by the European Commission. The concept of aid is a broad one, covering any advantage conferred on an undertaking by the state or through state resources, whether at a local, regional or national level and whether through expenditure, guarantees, grants or preferential loans or reliefs and exemptions from taxes and charges.

Article 107 TFEU is structured on a prohibition basis for the grant of aid. Nevertheless, it provides that aid granted for certain objectives can, and in some cases must, be approved as being compatible with the internal market and also Article 106 TFEU permits Member States to support undertakings in the provision of services of general economic interest. Many aid measures are now exempt from the requirement for prior approval under a series of block exemptions that cover so-called industrial aid, as well as agricultural and fisheries aid and aid to support services of general economic interest. Aid falling within block exemptions is subject to certain reporting and transparency requirements but can be deployed without prior approval. In addition, low-value aid (*de minimis*) is often exempt from controls.

Aid which does not fit within a block exemption is to be reviewed by the European Commission on a case-by-case basis. This gives rise to a standstill obligation which requires that the aid measure cannot be implemented until approval has been obtained.

The European Commission has issued soft law in the form of guidance in order to assist the process of analysing notifiable aid measures. Guidance includes sectoral guidelines (such as broadband network connectivity) as well as horizontal guidelines (e.g., on rescue and restructuring aid or regional aid).

In areas where no guidelines exist, the European Commission will assess the aid against a set of well-established competition principles, namely i) whether the aid is

1. In the UK legal system, since 2000, there have been only eleven negative decisions in respect of aid measures.

directed at achieving an acceptable policy objective; ii) whether the aid is an appropriate policy instrument to address that policy objective; whether the aid has an incentive effect such that it will change the behaviour of the aid recipient; and iii) whether the aid is proportionate and involves only limited distortions of competition and trade. In cases where the European Commission decides that aid which has come to its attention through a notification or otherwise is not approvable, it can block the aid or (in cases where the standstill obligation has not been observed and the aid has already been granted) order its recovery from the beneficiary.

The EU regime on state aid operates predominately as a bilateral regulatory legal system, involving only the European Commission and the Member States. While the standstill obligation is directly effective and can ground a declaration of illegality in the context of domestic judicial review proceedings, private litigation is rare in the UK.

II. THE STRUCTURE OF THE UK'S COMPETITION REGIME

The key elements of the UK's competition legal framework are contained in the Competition Act 1998, which prohibits anti-competitive agreements and abuses of market dominance, and the Enterprise Act 2002, which contains provisions on merger control.

The Competition and Markets Authority (CMA) is the UK's lead authority for competition and consumers, with responsibilities including:

- investigating mergers which could restrict competition;
- investigating potential breaches of UK or EU prohibitions against anti-competitive agreements and abuses of dominant positions, and suspected breaches of the UK criminal cartel offence;
- conducting market studies and investigations in markets where there may be competition and consumer problems;
- enforcing consumer protection legislation, in particular, to tackle practices and market conditions that make it difficult for consumers to exercise choice; and
- considering regulatory references and appeals.

Under the Competition Act 1998, various UK sector regulators have 'concurrent' competition powers and may take action against anti-competitive behaviour and abuses of dominance in their sectors.

The CMA and sector regulators enforce the prohibitions against anti-competitive conduct of, or agreements between, undertakings under EU and national competition law through a civil (administrative) regime. Decisions on whether an infringement has taken place can result in fines of up to 10% of an undertaking's worldwide turnover and disqualification from directorship of the individuals involved for up for fifteen years. Infringement decisions can also be relied upon in support of follow-on private actions and damages claims.

The CMA also has a criminal enforcement function, focusing on individuals involved in cartels. Under the Enterprise Act 2002, individuals convicted of a criminal cartel offence can be fined, imprisoned for up to five years, have assets confiscated, and be disqualified from directorship for up to fifteen years.

In relation to mergers, under the Enterprise Act 2002, the CMA is tasked with determining whether a relevant merger has or may be expected to result in a substantial 'lessening of competition' within any market or markets in the UK for goods or services. Although the Act establishes the primacy of this competition-based test, it also permits the Secretary of State to intervene in a merger on the specified public interest grounds of national security, media plurality, or maintaining the stability of the UK financial system. Unlike the EU, the UK operates a voluntary merger notification regime, but the CMA does have powers to review mergers which have not been voluntarily notified to it.

The Competition Appeal Tribunal (CAT) is the UK's specialist competition tribunal where by appeal or judicial review, decisions of the CMA and sector regulators relating to mergers and antitrust may be challenged. The CAT also hears private claims for damages or injunctions resulting from infringements of competition law.

In relation to state aid virtually no UK-made rules exist at present. EU law is applied directly, with the European Commission responsible for approving any aid not covered by established block exemptions. The EU's State aid rules are contained in Articles 107–109 TFEU, which prohibit all State aid by Member States unless it is deemed 'compatible' for reasons of general economic development (including regional aid to disadvantaged areas). Member States are required to notify any planned aid to the European Commission, which is then responsible for assessing and issuing a decision on whether the aid meets the compatibility conditions.

The EU Treaty defines State aid as: 'Any aid granted by a Member State or through State resources in any form whatsoever which distorts or threatens to distort competition by favouring certain undertakings or the production of certain goods.'

This definition has been broadly interpreted by the Commission and Court of Justice of the European Union (CJEU) to encompass a wide variety of state measures, including subsidies and measures that are economically equivalent GS – such as access to government assets on favourable terms or favourable tax treatment.

To minimise the burden of State aid notification, a General Block Exemption Regulation (GBER) was adopted in 2008, and revised in 2014, which declares certain categories of aid compatible with EU State rules and exempts Member States from the obligation to notify aid under those categories to the Commission. The GBER applies across a range of sectors and numerous types of aid measures, such as aid to support small and medium-sized enterprises (SMEs). The European Commission's *State Aid Scoreboard 2016* shows that more than 96% of new State aid measures in the EU in 2015 were covered by the GBER.

The European Commission has also issued soft law in the form of guidance and adopted additional Regulations with the aim of further simplifying the process of State aid notification and approval. These include the 2014–2020 regional aid guidelines and the *de minimis* Regulation, which established a threshold for small aids which fall outside the scope of EU State aid control.

The UK has no specific legislation implementing the EU state aid rules. Section 2(1) of the European Communities Act 1972 (ECA) provides that 'rights, powers, liabilities, obligations and restrictions from time to time created or arising by or under the Treaties, and all such remedies and procedures from time to time provided for by or under the Treaties, as in accordance with the Treaties are without further enactment to be given legal effect or used in the United Kingdom shall be recognised and available in law, and be enforced, allowed and followed accordingly'.

Section 3 ECA provides for the courts of the UK to apply the decisions of the EU courts when interpreting EU law. The English court has considered itself bound by the findings of fact contained within Commission state aid decisions.[2]

III. THE UK STATE AID COMPLIANCE SYSTEM

The Department for Business, Energy & Industrial Strategy (BEIS) which replaced the Department of Business, Innovation & Skills is the main public outfit to deal with state aid issues in the UK. BEIS has a state aid unit that acts as the main government department for overseeing state aid notifications and responding to queries in relation to state aid. It is responsible for state aid issues across the whole of the UK government, including local and regional government and the devolved administrations. As part of BEIS's remit, it monitors compliance with state aid rules, publishes guidance on state aid and provides advice to interested parties (including local government) on both the application of the state aid rules and UK government policy regarding state aid.

BEIS monitors centrally and submits any state aid notifications to the European Commission and is the main liaison with the European Commission regarding UK state aid issues. A number of other government departments such as the Department for the Environment, Food and Rural Affairs, the Department for Transport, the Department for Communities and Local Government and Her Majesty's (HM) Treasury) and devolved administrations (the Scottish government, the Welsh government and the Northern Ireland Executive) have their own state aid teams. BEIS acts as a central body to oversee all state aid notifications and coordinate the government capabilities in this area, although aid can be granted by all public bodies capable of granting aid. BEIS provides also guidance on how state-owned entities or public-private joint ventures can operate within the ambit of state aid law when dealing with services of general economic interest (SGEI). The UK public infrastructure encapsulates a number of sectors which the government or state-owned actors participate in market activities.[3]

The most significant national schemes governing the application and the granting of aid, that have been approved by the Commission or that qualify for block exemptions are the following: *The Regional Growth Fund*,[4] The *Enterprise Investment Scheme (EIS) and Venture Capital Trusts Scheme (VCT)*,[5] *The Seed Enterprise Investment*

2. *See Betws Anthracite Limited v DSK Anthrazit Ibbenburen GmbH* [2003] EWHC 2403.
3. In *Stagecoach v Secretary of State for Transport* [2010] 3 CMLR 8, the UK courts applied the *Altmark* criteria to determine the application of SGEI.
4. *The Regional Growth Fund (RGF)* was launched in 2010, the scheme has invested over GBP 2.7 billion to aid the growth of local businesses and help such businesses employ more staff by 2020.
5. *The Enterprise Investment Scheme (EIS) and Venture Capital Trusts Scheme (VCT)* aim to help small but high-risk trading companies to access financing for the period between 2015 and 2025 with £6.5 billion aid.

Scheme,[6] *The Social Investment Tax Relief,*[7] *The Innovate UK (Technology Strategy Board) Research, Development and Innovation Scheme.*[8]

Various schemes focus specifically on the environment, in particular the *Renewable Heat Incentive Scheme,*[9] *the Renewable Obligation Scheme,*[10] and the *Natural England Management Agreement Scheme.*[11]

The UK government has indicated that the CMA will take over the European Commission's responsibility of monitoring compliance with state aid rules in the UK following the transitional period of the exit of the United Kingdom from the European Union. The interaction between the European Commission and the CMA as the UK state aid regulator in the future will be the decided after the transitional period of the UK exit from the European Union.

IV. THE UK REMEDIAL SYSTEM OF STATE AID

A. Locus standi

Articles 107 and 108 TFEU have direct effect and as result any award of unlawful state aid by any UK public authority may be struck down by judicial review. In order to be able to apply for judicial review, the claimant must show a sufficient interest in the matter. Competitors of the recipient of alleged unlawful state aid are regarded as having sufficient standing to challenge state aid decisions.[12]

Applications for judicial review must be brought promptly and in any event no later than three months from the date of the decision awarding the alleged aid.

In parallel to the European Commission's state aid enforcement, judicial review proceedings and also action for damages are directed towards the public authority awarding the aid and not the recipient of the aid itself. The latter has the status of an interested third party.

A competitor does not have *locus standi* with regard to damages from a recipient of unlawful aid.[13] A competitor of an unlawful state aid recipient may have a claim against the Member State that is the addressee of the European Commission decision finding the aid unlawful for damages (state liability *Frankovich* damages) or an injunction compelling the Member State to recover the aid.

6. *The Seed Enterprise Investment Scheme* has been designed to help companies raise money when they are starting to trade.
7. *The Social Investment Tax Relief*: the scheme helps social enterprises (e.g., community benefit societies) to raise finance for qualifying business activities.
8. *The Innovate UK (Technology Strategy Board) Research, Development and Innovation Scheme*: the majority of the support granted is covered by the GBER exempt financial support to encourage business investments in research and development.
9. The *Renewable Heat Incentive* schemes: these consist of two separate schemes, one for the domestic sector and one for the non-domestic sector, which promote the use of renewable heat.
10. The *Renewable Obligation Scheme*: this supports the deployment of large-scale renewable electricity generation in the UK.
11. The *Natural England Management Agreement Scheme*: operated by Natural England, this focuses on Sites of Special Scientific Interest.
12. *See R v Attorney-General ex parte ICI* (1987) 1 CMLR 72.
13. *See Betws Anthracite Limited, supra* n. 2.

In case a competitor brings state aid proceedings to a national court during the period when the European Commission is investigating the same case, UK courts can provide a 'second track' of judicial review process. The value of a second track can, therefore, be seen (i) in cases where the decision being sought does not align precisely with the subject matter under investigation by the Commission; and (ii) potentially, in order to take preparatory steps enforcing the payment of sums that may be owing to a beneficiary pending the outcome of a European Commission investigation or appeal to the European courts with respect to the state aid status of those sums.

Deutsche Lufthansa[14] was interpreted narrowly in the Scottish case *Cloburn Quarry Company Limited* [2013] CSOH in relation to a case concerning the Aggregates Levy, exemptions to which were being reviewed by the European Commission in order to assess their legality under the state aid rules. In this case, the judge concluded that the Commission's investigation into the exemptions did not preclude the court from determining that the Aggregates Levy itself constituted unlawful state aid.

A party raising an argument usually bears the burden of proof. This means that an applicant in a judicial review case or a claimant in a damages case must prove any state aid arguments advanced on the balance of probabilities. A damages claimant must also prove the quantum of damages claimed on the balance of probabilities. Conversely, where a defendant wishes to advance state aid arguments in its defence these must be proved on the balance of probabilities.[15]

In relation to evidence and access to documents, orders for disclosure (which is a statement that a document exists or has existed) are typically made at the first case management conference. The case management conference is essentially an early hearing allowing the court to identify the real issues in dispute and direct how the dispute will be conducted. There are different approaches to disclosure under UK law, and the applicable approach will depend on, for example, whether there are electronic documents to be disclosed and what track the dispute has been allocated to. In fast- and multi-track claims involving personal injury claims, the default order is for standard disclosure which, broadly, requires disclosure of documents that assist or harm the case of any of the parties to the dispute. In multi-track claims not involving personal injury claims, the default position is that the judge will decide the particular order for disclosure (the Civil Procedure Rules provide a number of available options) in light of the overriding objective and the need to limit disclosure to what is necessary to justly deal with the case. Separate disclosure rules apply to small-track claims.

The actual inspection of disclosed documents is different from disclosure, which merely confirms that a document exists or has existed. Inspection usually takes place by the parties exchanging copies of the relevant documents. Some documents, such as those covered by privilege, can be withheld from inspection.

14. *See* ECJ, Case C-284/12 *Deutsche Lufthansa AG v Flughafen Frankfurt-Hahn GmbH* [2013] ECLI:EU:C:2013:442.
15. *See Eventech v Parking Adjudicator* [2012] EWHC 1903.

B. Judicial review in state aid

In the UK judicial review is a remedy which lies against any person or body which performs public duties or public functions, such as the State and local authorities.

An application for judicial review is made to the High Court in England and Wales under section 31 of the Supreme Court Act 1981 ('section 31') in accordance with Part 54 of the Civil Procedure Rules ('CPR'), with the defendant being the UK public authority[16] that made the contested decision. The following remedies in judicial review proceedings may be sought: (i) a declaration that the decision made was unlawful; (ii) an order quashing the decision; (iii) an order prohibiting or compelling an action.

In the UK judicial review is typically based on the ground that the action or inaction of the public authority is incompatible with EU law and therefore unlawful. Claimants may also seek, in addition to or instead of these remedies, a declaration and/or injunction. A claim for damages may be included, but only in addition to a claim for judicial review.

In the context of a judicial review, a successful application declaring a measure as unauthorised and therefore unlawful, the government body which authorised the aid would be required to make the decision again. The High Court of Northern Ireland has maintained[17] that national courts of Member States are empowered to determine whether a measure amounts to state aid and can grant remedies to enforce the obligations of the Member State not to put the state aid into effect without prior notification to the European Commission and a positive decision.

Where the UK courts have ruled in favour of a claimant seeking to establish that the payment of a benefit amounts to unlawful state aid, the remedy granted has been a declaration that the measure is unlawful.[18] The likely result of a state guarantee being held to constitute unlawful state aid will be that the court will refuse to enforce it. Where claimants have attempted to claim a benefit that is being withheld by the UK on the grounds that the benefit constitutes state aid in the absence of an explicit decision of the Commission to the contrary, the courts have taken the likely unlawful state aid nature of the benefit into account when denying the claim.

C. Damages in state aid

Private claims for damages or injunctive relief may be brought: in England and Wales, at the High Court or the County Court; in Scotland, at the Court of Session; and in Northern Ireland, at the High Court of Northern Ireland. In most cases, the appropriate

16. State aid arguments have also been used as a defence in private actions. In *Eventech v Parking Adjudicator, supra* n. 15, the appellant used state aid arguments in order to suggest that the fines imposed were unlawful, as the enforcement of traffic restrictions against one group (private hire taxis) and not another (black cabs) amounted to a grant of state aid to the latter.
17. *See* the Renewable Heat Association Northern Ireland Limited (Renewable Heat Association NI) [2017] NIQB 122.
18. *See Attorney-General, ex parte ICI* (1985) 1 CMLR 588 (Div Ct); (1987) 1 CMLR 72 (CA) *and R v Commissioner for Customs and Excise, ex parte Lunn Poly* [1998] EuLR 438 (Div Ct); [1999] EuLR 653 (CA).

remedy is not to seek damages or injunctive relief but rather a judicial review of the governmental decision that gave rise to the alleged aid. In England and Wales, such a claim is launched in the Administrative Court, a branch of the High Court.

Actions for damages are available in principle for a claimant that has been injured by an award of unlawful state aid.[19] In the UK damages have never been awarded by the courts to a party injured by a decision to grant unlawful state aid.

The conditions for competitors to obtain damages for award of unlawful state aid or a breach of the standstill obligation in Article 108(3) TFEU are related to a breach of duty. While damages stemming from an award of unlawful state aid have not been awarded to a claimant in the English courts, such damages would likely take the form of damages for a breach of statutory duty. Damages for a breach of statutory duty are intended to put the injured party in the position it would have been in had the breach not occurred and, as such, can include a claim for lost profits. Interest (dating from the time that the damage accrued) is also available.

In actions for damages, English courts award costs on a *loser-pays* basis. However, a successful claimant is, in practice, highly unlikely to recover all the costs incurred in bringing the claim. The criteria for awarding damages against the Member State that paid the unlawful aid are those for Francovich damages[20] namely: (i) the rule of law infringed was intended to confer rights on individuals;[21] (ii) the infringement is 'sufficiently serious'; and (iii) there is a direct causal link between the breach and the loss suffered. The cause of action is unlikely to be able to be brought against the beneficiary of aid, but the beneficiary can be added to the claim by the state, or the state can bring an action for contribution in relation to an award. As national courts have not awarded damages, it is hard to determine how they would be calculated, but the courts will usually take a compensatory rather than punitive approach in calculating damages.

D. Recovery of illegal state aid

The European Commission has the exclusive power to declare the compatibility of state aid compatible with the internal market. The Commission can, therefore, require the recovery of that State aid by the government if that State aid has been found incompatible and it was granted before the Commission reached its final decision in the case.

National courts can declare that a measure is a state aid and that the government should recover that aid where it has not been notified on the sole basis that the aid has not been notified. Thus, a claimant can go before a national court and secure a finding

19. *See Francovich v Italy C-6/90 and C-9/90* in *Secretary of State for Employment v Mann* [1997] ICR 209.
20. *See* ECJ, Joined cases C-46/93 and 48/93 *Brasserie du pêcheur v Bundesrepublik Deutschland and The Queen / Secretary of State for Transport, ex parte Factortame and Others* [1996] ECR I-1029.
21. *See* ECJ, Case 120/73 *Lorenz v Germany* [1973] ECR 1973, 1471 which confirms that the Article 108(3) TFEU confer rights on individuals.

that a certain State aid is illegal (unnotified aid). The national court can then order the government to recover the State aid.

In cases where the European Commission has issued a decision finding that certain benefits equivalent to state aid are incompatible with the internal market and illegal, it will be required by the UK Government to ensure that the aid is recovered. In practice, the UK Government will have to bring an action in the High Court against the recipient of the illegal aid. The statement of claim accompanying the recovery action is founded upon the UK Government's duty to comply with the decision of the European Commission, and that duty affords the government the right to seek recovery through the domestic courts for the whole of the illegal state aid. It is clear from the CJEU's jurisprudence that the government is under a duty to ensure that a suitable mechanism is in place which allows recovery of illegal aid.

The UK has not adopted any specific legislation to establish a process for recovering unlawful state aid. The European Commission has not opened infringement procedures before the ECJ against the UK under Article 108(2) TFEU, for alleged non-recovery of aid. In practice, however, local authorities frequently include 'claw-back' provisions in their funding agreements with aid recipients. Such provisions are designed to offer the granting authority a contractual method of recovery (should it become necessary). Clawback provisions are particularly likely to be included in scenarios where it is reasonably clear from the outset that the measure involves state aid, but where the parties have concluded that it is lawful.

In order to ensure the effectiveness of UK state aid rules following the transitional Brexit period, the CMA will likely be given powers enabling it to make recovery orders for incompatible aid. It remains to be seen, however, whether such orders will be directed at the governmental agency that granted the aid (in which case the prevalence of claw-back provisions is likely to continue) or directly to the beneficiary of the aid.

Since there is not a contractual recovery legal right in the UK legal system, the basis of recovery of illegal state aid in the UK is not justiciably established. The first case which was heard before the English courts that involved state aid recovery did not formulate the legal basis on which such recovery could be realised. In the DTI[22] case, the European Commission had previously found that the aid received by British Aerospace to assist with its purchase of Rover constituted illegal state aid. Following the Commission's decision, the UK government brought an action against the aid recipient in the English High Court to recover the aid. The government based its case on the duty to comply with the earlier Commission decision. However, the UK recovery proceedings were stayed pending the outcome of an action for annulment of the Commission's decision. The Commission ultimately made a new recovery order that was effected without a court order.

The DTI case is not the only instance in which the Commission has ordered the UK to recover aid. However, like the DTI case, such cases have not offered any guidance as to the basis for recovery of aid. In the BT Group plc case (ECJ, Case C-55/2007 *British Telecommunications and BT Pension Scheme Trustees* ECLI:

22. *See DTI v British Aerospace and Rover PLC* (1991) 1 CMLR 165.

EU:T:2013:466), an escrow account had already been put in place to hold the disputed funds and to effect recovery in the event that the European Court of Justice (ECJ) would confirm the Commission's initial recovery decision. Therefore, the mechanics for effecting recovery were already established before the recovery order was confirmed.[23] The ECJ confirmed the Commission's decision on 22 October 2014.

In the *British Aggregates Levy*[24] case, the European Commission issued a recovery order in respect of an exemption to the Aggregates Levy (see Commission decision of 27 March 2015). At the time, the UK government stated an intention to cooperate with both the Commission and relevant businesses in order to minimise the impact of the recovery order. However, the exact shape of the recovery process remains unclear and, in particular, it remains to be seen whether it will result in any litigation.

In *Advocate General of Scotland v John Gunn*,[25] the Crown was able to successfully apply to the court for the recovery of unlawful aid, and this was considered to be a valid claim by itself in Scotland.

Aid beneficiaries can seek to resist any proposed recovery of state aid by challenging the UK government's recovery actions before the national courts. Alternatively, rather than waiting for a recovery action that can be challenged before national courts, aid recipients can also attempt to obtain a proactive determination that aid is unrecoverable in one of the following ways: (a) where the state, through a decision, has announced its intention to pursue recovery and where that decision is in itself subject to review, the aid recipient can seek to commence judicial review proceedings in order to obtain a declaration of unlawfulness of the decision; and (b) where both the grant and the subsequent recovery of the aid is based on contractual arrangements, the recipient can bring an action before the national courts to seek a declaration that the UK government lacks adequate contractual rights to recover the aid.

Recipients of aid could use more specialist forums to resist recovery. For example, if the aid takes the form of tax relief, which is subsequently withdrawn by HM Revenue & Customs, it might be possible for the recipient to bring the case before a specialist tax tribunal. Aid beneficiaries can seek to resist any proposed recovery of state aid by challenging the UK government's recovery actions before the national courts. In *Advocate General of Scotland v John Gunn*, the court rejected arguments that the repayment would have been a breach of human rights regarding the protection of property.

There is a possibility to obtain interim relief against a recovery order. Aid recipients can seek to obtain interim injunctions in order to suspend a recovery order. In practice, however, a court is unlikely to grant such interim injunctions unless the

23. *See* Commission Decision 2009/703/EC of 11 February 2009 concerning the State aid C 55/07 (ex NN 63/07, CP 106/06) implemented by the United Kingdom of Great Britain and Northern Ireland – Crown guarantee to BT [2009] OJ L 242/21; GC, Joined Cases T-226/09 and 230/09 *BT v Commission* [2013] ECLI:EU:T:2013:466; ECJ, Case C-620/13P *BT v Commission* [2014] ECLI:EU:C:2014:2309.
24. Commission Decision (EU) 2016/288 of 27 March 2015 on the aid scheme SA.34775 (13/C) (ex 12/NN) implemented by the United Kingdom – Aggregates levy, notified under C(2015) 2141 [2016] OJ L 59/87.
25. *See* case *Advocate General of Scotland v John Gunn* [2018] CSOH 39.

applicant can show that the proposed recovery is without any clear legal basis. In addition to challenging the recovery, an aid recipient can bring a challenge before the European courts in respect of the underlying European Commission decision finding the aid to be unlawful. Such a challenge will typically take the form of an action for annulment.

Interim relief against unlawfully granted aid can be granted subject to certain conditions.[26] English courts have a wide discretion to grant interim injunctive relief. The criteria for deciding whether to grant such relief are:

- whether there is a serious question to be tried;
- whether damages awarded at trial would be an adequate remedy as an alternative to an interim injunction;
- whether on the balance of convenience of each party an injunction should be granted; and
- whether there are any additional relevant factors.

A party seeking an interim injunction will normally be required to give an undertaking to compensate the defendant against which the injunction is sought for any damages incurred as a result of the interim injunction in the event that the party's case fails at trial.

E. Private enforcement of state aid rules in the UK

Private actors businesses do not have any general rights to insist on receiving aid. The granting of aid in the UK falls within the discretion of the relevant authority. In addition, several aid schemes in the UK impose specific eligibility criteria that must be satisfied before a business will qualify to receive aid under the scheme. In cases that an applicant to a state aid programme has been unsuccessful in applying for aid, it might be possible to challenge the public authority's negative decision through judicial review proceedings. Such proceedings essentially involve a challenge to the manner in which a decision has been made, rather than the substance of the decision. If the applicant can prove that it has suffered loss caused by the negative decision, it might, in limited circumstances, be possible to lodge an action for damages against the authority in the civil courts.

There are no national bodies with specific competence to which competitors can address state aid complaints. Any complaints of third party competitors to a recipient of state aid can be addressed to the national courts. However, competitors cannot find easily possible illegal or incompatible aid from official sources. There is no centralised register of aid granted or aid measures. There is no specific legislation that gives competitors access to documents on state aid granted to beneficiaries. Nevertheless, there is a right to information under the Freedom of Information Act 2000, and applicants can submit a Freedom of Information Act Request to obtain specific information from government and public authorities that are subject to the act. A

26. *See* case *American Cyanamid Co v Ethicon Ltd* [1975] AC 396.

similar act, the Freedom of Information (Scotland) Act 2002, applies in Scotland. BEIS has issued guidance covering the principle of transparency and in particular, the implementation of the GBER which obliges Member States to publish details online of any individual aid awards made.

V. CONCLUSIONS

The UK government, as part of the Withdrawal Agreement from the EU, has an implementation period of adjustment beginning in March 2019. The UK will remain within the EU's state aid regime for the duration of the implementation period and the European Commission will continue to receive and assess notifications from UK aid grantors. After the implementation period, the Competition and Markets Authority (CMA) will take on its new role as the enforcer of UK state aid regulation and monitoring authority of state aid rules for the whole of the UK.

Section 6 of the European Union (Withdrawal) Act 2018 provides for the retention of EU law, modified as necessary to take account of the new domestic context. It also provides that EU case law, as it exists on or before exit day, will (or may) continue to be of relevance to the interpretation of retained EU law (whether or not in a modified form). Under the European Union (Withdrawal) Act 2018, the UK government has copied the EU state aid rules, subject to certain technical modifications to ensure that the regime operates effectively in a domestic context. This includes transplanting the existing block exemptions covering all sectors of the economy and also giving effect to existing European Commission approval.

The scope of the jurisdiction of Competition Appeals Tribunal (CAT) as a specialist nature competition tribunal, reveals a forum that in the forthcoming years, could become the central forum for all competition law claims, including state aid private enforcement in the UK as a result of the implementation of the European Union (Withdrawal) Act 2018 and following the exit of the UK from the European Union.

PART III Analysis and Outlook

CHAPTER 17

Private Enforcement of EU Competition and State Aid Law: Comparative Analysis and the Way Forward

Ferdinand Wollenschläger & Wolfgang Wurmnest

I. Private enforcement of EU competition law after Directive 2014/104/EU
  - A. The Damages Directive: standard setting, frictions and (potential) impact
    1. General standards
    2. Frictions with primary law
    3. Fostering private enforcement?
  - B. Harmonising the law of private enforcement
    1. Entity liable for damages
    2. Binding effect of national decisions
    3. Prescription (limitation of actions)
  - C. The role of national courts and legislatures

II. Private enforcement of EU state aid law
  - A. Background: EU law framework for state aid
  - B. Key issues of private enforcement
    1. Enforcement of EU state aid law
    2. Cooperation and coordination between national courts and the European Commission

III. The way forward
  - A. Spill-over effects
  - B. Strengthening private enforcement of EU competition law
    1. Guidance for courts
    2. Improving the law at the national level
    3. Closing gaps at the European level

C. Constructing a proper framework for private enforcement of EU state aid law

I. PRIVATE ENFORCEMENT OF EU COMPETITION LAW AFTER DIRECTIVE 2014/104/EU

A. The Damages Directive: standard setting, frictions and (potential) impact

1. General standards

The *Damages Directive* (Directive 2014/104/EU) marks a very important step in the history of private enforcement of EU competition law. After many years of discussion, the EU legislature has etched general standards of private enforcement into the law which will form the basis of law enforcement over the years to come. When drafting the Directive, the European legislature could build upon solutions developed in other jurisdictions as well as on the case law of the European Court of Justice.

The Directive's key features can be summarised as follows:

First, the European legislature opted for the principle of compensation, and not deterrence, as the general aim of private enforcement. Putting compensation in the limelight distinguishes EU law significantly from the US approach, under which victims of antitrust law violations can, for example, claim treble damages under the Sherman Act.[1] Such an overcompensation should deter potential wrongdoers from infringing the law and give private plaintiffs incentives to sue. During the discussions about the proper model for private enforcement in Europe, the European Commission briefly flirted with the US model,[2] and the German Monopolies Commission called for the introduction of double damages.[3] Double damages (instead of treble damages) were seen as sufficient given that in US law interest runs only from the date of the judgment, whereas in European jurisdictions pre-judgement interest exists. In the end, the idea of overcoming the 'rational apathy' of private plaintiffs by granting them a windfall profit as incentive to sue was rejected by the EU legislature. Article 3(3) Damages Directive makes clear that the Directive allows only for compensation, and not for overcompensation. Given the long debate on the Directive's aims and scope, it is highly unlikely

1. On the US private enforcement system *see* Alison Jones, '*Private Enforcement of EU Competition Law: A Comparison with, and Lessons from the US*' in Maria Bergström, Marios Iacovides & Magnus Strand (eds), *Harmonising EU Competition Litigation: The New Directive and Beyond* 15, 19–26 (Hart 2016) and the contributions to Part II in Albert A. Foer and Jonathan W. Cuneo (eds), *The International Handbook on Private Enforcement of Competition Law* (Edward Elgar 2010). For a comparative perspective *see* Clifford A. Jones, *Private Enforcement of Antitrust Law in the EU, UK and USA* (OUP 1999).
2. For details *see* Wouter Wils, *Private Enforcement of EU Antitrust Law and Its Relationship with Public Enforcement: Past, Present and Future* (2017) 40 World Competition 3, 14–23.
3. Monopolkommission, *Das allgemeine Wettbewerbsrecht in der Siebten GWB-Novelle (Sondergutachten 41)* para. 83 (Nomos 2004) on German competition law; *see also* Jürgen Basedow, *Perspektiven des Kartelldeliktsrechts* [2006] ZWeR 294, 303.

that this standard will be changed in the years to come. It can, therefore, be predicted that this marked difference from the US approach will remain.

The Damages Directive looks to ensure, however, that victims harmed by competition law infringements receive full compensation (Article 3(1) Damages Directive and Recital 12). This important second feature of the Directive was already set out by the European Court of Justice in the seminal judgments of *Courage* and *Manfredi*.[4] Insofar, the Directive reflects the *acquis communautaire*.[5] Given the lack of collective redress mechanisms at the European level and in many Member States (*see* section I.A.3., *infra*), it is, however, doubtful whether that aim can in practice truly be achieved for all victims.

The third characteristic feature of the Damages Directive is the safeguarding of effective public enforcement. Currently, private enforcement in the area of horizontal cartels rests to a large part on follow-on actions brought after a competition authority has sanctioned a cartel. The detection of cartels by competition authorities depends significantly on functioning leniency programmes. To protect these programmes, the EU legislature has limited the possibilities for private plaintiffs to gain access to sensitive information disclosed during a leniency application.[6]

2. Frictions with primary law

The Damages Directive's rules deviate to a certain extent from the case law of the European Court of Justice. The Court had developed certain standards based on the principle of effectiveness, which is a principle of European primary law. For example, in *Courage* the Court held that '[t]he full effectiveness of [Article 101 TFEU] and, in particular, the practical effect of the prohibition laid down in [Article 101(1) TFEU] would be put at risk if it were not open to any individual to claim damages for loss caused to him by a contract or by conduct liable to restrict or distort competition'.[7] Moreover, in *Pfleiderer* and *Donau Chemie* the Court made clear that, with regard to the access of plaintiffs to documents disclosed by cartel members in leniency applications, the right to claim full compensation would be impaired if national courts could not weigh the interests of the plaintiffs to obtain information against the need for protection of that information in each individual case.[8]

The Damages Directive cut back these rights of the plaintiff. First, it limits a plaintiff's right to claim full compensation in order to protect small and medium-sized enterprises (SME) as well as leniency applicants. According to Article 11(2) and (3) Damages Directive, an SME that participated in a cartel is – under certain conditions –

4. ECJ, Case C-453/99 *Courage Ltd v Bernard Crehan and Bernard Crehan v Courage Ltd and Others* [2001] ECR I-6297, para. 25; ECJ, Joined Cases C-295/04 to C-298/04 *Vincenzo Manfredi and Others v Lloyd Adriatico Assicurazioni SpA and Others* [2006] ECR I-6619, para. 61.
5. Wulf-Henning Roth, *The European Perspective* III.A. and V. (note that all references to other contributions to this book refer to the numbering of the headings).
6. On the frictions between private and public enforcement *see* Roth, *supra* n. 5, at IV.A.
7. Case C-453/99 *Courage and Crehan*, *supra* n. 4, at para. 26.
8. ECJ, Case C-360/09 *Pfleiderer AG v Bundeskartellamt* [2011] ECR I-5161, para. 30; ECJ, Case C-536/11 *Bundeswettbewerbsbehörde v Donau Chemie AG* [2013] ECLI:EU:C:2013:366, para. 49.

liable only to its own direct and indirect purchasers. Article 11(4) Damages Directive limits the liability of an immunity recipient to its direct or indirect purchasers/providers and allows other injured parties to claim damages from the immunity recipient only where full compensation cannot be obtained from other cartel members. The most prominent example of a deviation from the case law of the European Court of Justice is, however, Article 6(6) Damages Directive, which prohibits the disclosure of leniency statements without exception, thereby cutting back the interest-balancing approach developed by the Court.[9]

Assessing the legality of the corrections introduced by the EU legislature raises complex issues regarding the separation of powers and the interplay of primary and secondary law. The last word on the constitutionality of the changes introduced by the Damages Directive lies with the European Court of Justice. The European report in this study has argued that the corrections introduced by the Damages Directive are in conformity with the TFEU;[10] other commentators doubt that in part.[11] In the interests of legal certainty, it is therefore essential that national courts initiate preliminary proceedings to give the European Court of Justice the chance to clarify these important issues.

3. *Fostering private enforcement?*

Understandingly, the European Commission is keen to spread the word that the Damages Directive will foster private enforcement in Europe.[12] Indeed, there can be no doubt that over a longer time span such a positive effect will be demonstrated. It is however too early to measure the precise effects of the Directive on private enforcement given that it was only recently transposed by the Member States and given that many of its rules are not applicable *ratione temporae* to the current proceedings that often deal with cartels that were detected years ago.

A welcomed side-effect of the long and intensive discussion leading towards the adoption of the Directive is that private enforcement of competition rules received a significant amount of attention in academia and amongst practitioners. Whereas 15–20 years ago only a few articles on private enforcement were published in European competition law journals,[13] the tide has turned, and matters of private enforcement are discussed regularly today, including the important procedural aspects. At least in some jurisdictions law firms have realised that private enforcement of competition law can be a good 'business model'. Clients harmed by competition law infringements are, as

9. Roth, *supra* n. 5, at V.B.2.
10. *Ibid.*, at V.B.
11. *See* Christian Kersting and Nicola Preuß, *Umsetzung der Kartellschadensersatzrichtlinie (2014/104/EU): Ein Gesetzgebungsvorschlag aus der Wissenschaft* para. 121 (Nomos 2015) (on Article 11(2), (3) Damages Directive); Christian Kersting, *Die neue Richtlinie zur privaten Rechtsdurchsetzung im Kartellrecht* [2014] WuW 564, 566–567 (on Article 6(6) Damages Directive).
12. *See* Johannes Holzwarth, *The Commission's View* II.
13. One of the first was Jürgen Basedow, *Who will Protect Competition in Europe? From Central Enforcement to Authority Networks and Private Litigation* (2001) 2 EBOR 443, 459–468.

a consequence, regularly advised on the possibility to claim damages from infringers. Reported cases are also on the rise.[14]

B. Harmonising the law of private enforcement

It goes without saying that every directive can only partly harmonise the law. This is not different with regard to the Damages Directive for various reasons. It covers only selected issues of private enforcement, and it spares many procedural issues given the limited competence of the European Union to harmonise national rules. Moreover, even within the area of harmonised law, the Directive does not always provide the necessary clarifications,[15] so that a greater degree of harmonisation will be achieved only over time through decisions rendered by the European Court of Justice. This is also so because the Directive often operates with very general clauses, which gives courts some leeway for interpretation. Finally, the Damages Directive follows a mixed approach. Whereas most rules set forth a full harmonisation, selected provisions were submitted to a minimum harmonisation, thereby allowing Member States to enact rules that are more favourable to private plaintiffs. The limited harmonisation effect will be demonstrated by looking at three illustrative issues.

1. Entity liable for damages

An important issue that was not clarified explicitly by the Damages Directive is the question of whom damages for competition law violations can be sought from. There is unanimity that the legal entity whose representatives or staff members directly participated in the infringement (e.g., by attending price-fixing meetings) is liable for damages. In the area of public enforcement, the European Court of Justice has developed the single economic entity doctrine for sanctioning undertakings under Regulation 1/2003.[16]

Put simply, under this doctrine not only the direct infringer can be sanctioned for breach of EU competition rules but also other legal entities of the economic entity to which the direct infringer belongs to. This is so because the EU competition rules are addressed to 'undertakings', i.e., an economic unit (that is determined according to EU

14. *See* the study cited by Holzwarth, *supra* n. 12, at II.; for older empirical data *see* Barry Rodger, '*The Empirical Data Part 1: Methodology, Case-Law, Courts and Process*' and '*The Empirical Data Part 2: Provisions Relied Upon, Remedies and Success*' in Barry Rodger (ed.), Competition Law – Comparative Private Enforcement and Collective Redress across the EU, 73–120 and 121–156 (Wolters Kluwer 2014).
15. Roth, *supra* n. 5, at III.B.
16. For details of this doctrine *see* Dominik Braun and Manuel Kellerbauer, *Das Konzept der gesamtschuldnerischen Verantwortlichkeit von Konzerngesellschaften bei Zuwiderhandlungen gegen das EU-Wettbewerbsrecht* [2015] NZKart 175–181 (Teil 1), [2015] NZKart 211–216 (Teil 2); Okeoghene Odudu and David Bailey, *The Single Economic Entity Doctrine in EU Competition Law* (2014) 51 CMLRev. 1721–1757.

standards) which may consist of different legal persons.[17] It is, however, the 'undertaking' that infringes the law and that must answer for this infringement. For example, a parent company and its subsidiary can form such an economic entity if the 'subsidiary does not decide independently upon its own conduct on the market, but carries out, in all material respects, the instructions given to it by the parent company'.[18] If such an entity exists, the European Commission can, for example, impute the subsidiary's conduct to the parent company and impose the fine on the parent 'without having to establish the personal involvement of the latter in the infringement'.[19] According to the case law, such an influence can be presumed if the parent company holds 100% of the capital of a subsidiary which committed the infringement.[20] Less clear is the issue if and under which conditions subsidiaries and sister corporations are answerable for infringements committed by other companies of a group.[21]

Against this background, the question arises whether the economic entity doctrine also applies when private plaintiffs seek damages for infringements of EU competition law. Applying the economic entity doctrine to antitrust damages actions could flow either from primary law, as Articles 101, 102 TFEU are addressed to 'undertakings', or from the Damages Directive, which also uses this legal term.[22] A glance at the country reports in this study reveals that some jurisdictions had embraced the single economic entity doctrine even before the Damages Directive, whereas in other jurisdiction this doctrine met with much resistance – which did not fade after the Directive's transposition given that it did not provide the necessary clarity. The final push for a transference of the economic entity doctrine to the area of private law enforcement came from the recent *Skanska* judgment of the European Court of Justice, in which the Court decided for restructuring cases that EU primary law determines which entity is liable for damages. The Court held that:

> the concept of 'undertaking', within the meaning of Article 101 TFEU, which constitutes an autonomous concept of EU law, cannot have a different scope with regard to the imposition of fines by the Commission under Article 23(2) of Regulation No 1/2003 as compared with actions for damages for infringement of EU competition rules.[23]

Even though the economic entity doctrine has entered the area of private enforcement, many details of its application are disputed among national courts and commentators.

17. ECJ, Case C-97/08 P *Akzo Nobel NV and Others v Commission of the European Communities* [2009] ECLI:EU:C:2009:536, paras 54–55.
18. Case C-97/08 P *Akzo Nobel and Others v Commission, supra* n. 17, at para. 58.
19. *Ibid.*, at para. 59.
20. *Ibid.*, at para. 60.
21. For details *see* Christian Kersting, *Haftung von Schwester- und Tochtergesellschaften im europäischen Kartellrecht* (2018) 182 ZHR 8–31.
22. Cf. Articles 1(1) and 2(2) Damages Directive.
23. ECJ, Case C-724/17 *Vantaan kaupunki v Skanska Industrial Solutions Oy and Others* [2019] ECLI:EU:C:2019:204, para. 47.

The United Kingdom adopted the single economic entity concept relatively early to establish jurisdiction. Since then it has been undisputed that a parent company with decisive influence over the market conduct of a subsidiary is jointly and severally liable for damages arising from the subsidiary's participation in a competition law infringement.[24] More controversial was the assessment of the reverse situation where a subsidiary was sued for damages flowing from unlawful conduct of the parent company. For such scenarios, courts have introduced a stricter approach. Subsidiaries can be held liable if it can be proven that they 'knowingly implemented' the competition law infringement.[25] The transposition of the Directive seems not to have altered these standards.

In Italy, the reception of the single economic entity doctrine has apparently so far not troubled the courts, but it was subject to dispute amongst scholars. The Italian report argues that at least after implementation of the Directive and the *Skanska* judgment of the European Court of Justice, parent companies are jointly and severally liable for competition law infringements of their subsidiaries if both firms form an economic entity such that no fault of the parent needs to be proven.[26]

In other jurisdictions, the reception went less smoothly. In Germany, lower courts had refused to apply the economic entity doctrine to private enforcement cases prior to the transposition of the Directive.[27] This reluctance seems to be grounded in the fact that German corporate law is based on the doctrine of separation, which usually excludes that a parent company can be held liable for violations of the law committed by a subsidiary. German scholars are divided over the matter, but the view that EU law controls the determination of which legal persons are liable for infringements of EU competition law is gaining more and more traction.[28] The German report points out that at least after the Directive was implemented, 'the legal situation under German law should be considered sufficiently clarified', and courts should, therefore, be ready to apply the economic entity doctrine as shaped by the European Court of Justice to determine the entity liable for damages for infringements of EU competition law.[29]

Also, the Netherlands had difficulties embracing the single economic entity doctrine in the area of tort law. Prior to the Directive's transposition, there was a court decision in the Elevator Cartel in which the court ruled that parent companies are not liable for competition law infringements committed by their subsidiaries unless it can be proven that the parent also actively participated in the cartel.[30] This decision resembles the approach of German courts given that also under Dutch law there is no general 'group liability' of all companies belonging to a corporate group. But the Dutch

24. Florian Wagner-von Papp, *Private Enforcement in the United Kingdom* IV.
25. *Ibid.*
26. Enrico Camilleri, *Private Enforcement in Italy* IV.A.
27. Jens-Uwe Franck, *Private Enforcement in Germany* IV.A.
28. Christian Kersting, '*Kapitel 7: Kartellschadensersatz: Haftungstatbestand – Bindungswirkung – Schadensabwälzung*' in Christian Kersting and Rupprecht Podszun (eds), *Die 9. GWB-Novelle* 115, 124–125 (C.H. Beck 2017) with further references.
29. Franck, *supra* n. 27, at IV.A.
30. Rogier Meijer and Erik-Jan Zippro, *Private Enforcement in the Netherlands* IV.

report also argues that after the *Skanska* judgment of the European Court of Justice, Dutch courts must decide differently in the future.[31]

Under French law, there seems, at least after the transposition of the Directive, to be a consensus that other entities of a group of companies can be held liable for damages. A dispute revolves, however, around the conditions for such a liability. Prior to the transposition of the Directive, French courts held that entities are liable only when it can be proven that they participated in the legal infringement and acted with fault.[32] The French report points out, however, that in light of the recent *Skanska* judgment of the European Court of Justice, it seems likely that the case law needs to be adapted given that the European Court seems to favour tort law liability for those firms which fall under competition law's single economic entity doctrine.[33]

Summing up, the case law at the national level is sparse and the existing judgments were handed down prior to the Directive's transposition. Among scholars there is, however, a trend to embrace the single economic entity doctrine in tort actions. Under this approach, a parent company is jointly liable for competition law infringements committed by a subsidiary provided that the parent company formed an economic entity with the subsidiary. Less clear is the answer regarding the circumstances under which subsidiaries are liable for damages flowing from the participation of the parent company (or other companies of the group) in a cartel.

2. *Binding effect of national decisions*

Whereas the Directive did not clarify the issue as to which entity is liable for damages, the European legislature explicitly incorporated a rule on the binding effect of decisions by national competition law authorities and review courts into the Directive to 'enhance legal certainty, to avoid inconsistency in the application of Articles 101 and 102 TFEU [and] to increase the effectiveness and procedural efficiency of actions for damages' (Recital 34). A similar rule for infringement decisions of the European Commission can be found in Article 16(1) Regulation 1/2003 prohibiting national competition authorities and courts from taking decisions running counter to a prior Commission decision when assessing agreements, decisions, or practices under Articles 101 and 102 TFEU. The binding effect of decisions of national competition authorities helps private plaintiffs to prove a competition law infringement. The Directive distinguishes between decisions rendered by a national competition authority or review court of the same state in which the action for damages is brought ('local cases') and decisions rendered by authorities or review courts of other EU Member States ('cross-border cases').

In 'local cases' a final decision of a national competition authority or review court finding an infringement of competition law is to be deemed irrefutably established for the purposes of an action for damages brought before national courts in that state under Articles 101 and/or 102 TFEU or under national competition law, i.e., under rules

31. Meijer and Zippro, *supra* n. 30, at IV.
32. Rafael Amaro, *Private Enforcement in France* IV.A.2.
33. *Ibid.*

pursuing the same objective as the EU competition rules (Article 9(1) Damages Directive). Moreover, Recital 34 clarifies that the effect of a final decision is not binding in all regards, but only as to 'the nature of the infringement and its material, personal, temporal and territorial scope as determined by the competition authority or review court in the exercise of its jurisdiction'.

In 'cross-border cases' the binding effect of decisions taken in other EU Member States is not as comprehensive. Those decisions may be presented before national courts 'as at least *prima facie* evidence that an infringement of competition law has occurred and, as appropriate, may be assessed along with any other evidence adduced by the parties' (Article 9(2) Damages Directive). This softer approach towards foreign decisions resulted from the fact that national administrative proceedings are not harmonised and a far-reaching binding effect might run counter to the fundamental rights of the defendants, as is particularly guaranteed by Article 47 of the EU Charter of Fundamental Rights.[34] However, the Directive follows in this regard a minimum harmonisation approach ('at least'), which allows Member States to strengthen the binding effect if they so desire. The jurisdictions that formed the basis for the present study were, however, very reluctant to introduce far-reaching changes. In addition, some jurisdictions struggle to combine the binding effect with the autonomy that is constitutionally granted to the courts.

The most sweeping rule can be found in Germany. The German legislature had already introduced a rule on the binding effect of national competition decisions in the 7th amendment of the Competition Act of 2005.[35] This provision was maintained when the Directive was transposed, apart from some minor linguistic changes (and a new section number) that did not alter its content.[36] The German transposition goes further than the Directive. As far as final decision finds a violation of European or German competition rules, this infringement is deemed to be irrefutably established not only in cases in which the decision was rendered by the German competition authority or the European Commission, but also if it was rendered by a competition authority in another Member State. The same holds true for decisions of the respective review courts. Thus, in cross-border cases concerning infringements of Articles 101 and/or 102 TFEU, Germany has extended the binding effect also to final decisions of authorities/review courts of other Member States even though the Directive demands only a prima facie evidence effect.[37] The German transposition is silent on the effect of decisions of competition authorities from other EU Member States which find an infringement of national competition rules that pursue the same aim as Articles 101 and 102 TFEU. The legislative materials reveal that German courts must consider such decisions as prima facie evidence and that the German legislature assumed that no legislative action was necessary given that this approach is already well-established in case law. As private plaintiffs might not be fully aware of their rights, the reluctance of

34. Camilleri, *supra* n. 26, at IV.B.; Franck, *supra* n. 27, at IV.B.1.
35. Franck, *supra* n. 27, at IV.B.
36. Kersting, *supra* n. 28, at 144.
37. Franck, *supra* n. 27, at IV.B.1.

the German legislature to introduce a clear-cut rule on foreign decisions dealing with breaches of national competition law is rightly criticised by the German report.[38]

All other jurisdictions analysed in this study have opted for a more literal transposition of Article 9(2) Damages Directive. In these jurisdictions, foreign decisions in cross-border cases can be presented as (ordinary) *mode de preuve* (France),[39] as (ordinary) means of proof (Italy),[40] or as prima facie evidence (Netherlands[41] and United Kingdom[42]). Under Dutch law, Article 9(2) Damages Directive was not transposed by statute as the concept of prima facie evidence was deemed to be well-established in the case law. This decision is criticised in the Dutch report as it might impair legal clarity.[43]

Details regarding the binding effect have to be clarified by the courts in the years to come. A first issue concerns the question of which parts of a decision can deploy a binding effect. The jurisdictions with 'national precursors' of Article 9(1) Damages Directive have restricted the binding effect to certain parts of the decision, namely the operative part of the decision and those parts of the reasoning that constitute the essential basis for the operative part.[44] It seems likely that this approach will meet with the approval of the European Court of Justice. Moreover, it is generally accepted that issues of causation or damage, even though they are sometimes difficult to prove for plaintiffs, are not covered by the binding effect.[45] More controversial are questions on the general reach of the binding effect under Article 9(1) Damages Directive. As general rule, due process demands that the binding effect can be invoked only against the addressees of the decision who could defend themselves in the prior administrative proceeding.[46] The crucial question is whether courts may – in exceptional cases – refuse to apply the irrebuttable presumption when finding that the concerned decision is manifestly illegal, as it is discussed in Italy.[47]

With regard to the rule enshrined in Article 9(2) Damages Directive, the years to come will show how judges interpret and apply the prima facie evidence rule. It remains to be seen whether those jurisdictions with strong constitutional reservations against rules that bind their courts might deviate from the case law that will develop in other jurisdictions.

Summing up, Article 9 Damages Directive improved the situation for the plaintiffs in that jurisdiction that had no rule on the binding effect of administrative decisions in follow-on antitrust damages actions. As a differentiated rule was necessary in light of constitutional concerns raised by some Member States, the Directive achieves a sound degree of harmonisation. Open issues will have to be clarified by the European Court of Justice in the years to come.

38. *Ibid.*
39. Amaro, *supra* n. 32, at IV.B.1.
40. Camilleri, *supra* n. 26, at IV.B.
41. Meijer and Zippro, *supra* n. 30, at V.
42. Wagner-von Papp, *supra* n. 24, at V.
43. Meijer and Zippro, *supra* n. 30, at V.
44. Wagner-von Papp, *supra* n. 24, at V.
45. Camilleri, *supra* n. 26, at IV.B.; Franck, *supra* n. 27, at IV.B.2.
46. *Ibid.*
47. *See* on this discussion Camilleri, *supra* n. 26, at IV.B.

3. *Prescription (limitation of actions)*

National rules on prescription (limitation of actions) for damages are complex, and often general rules apply. In practice, prescription rules that do not reflect the particularities of competition law violations may restrict the effective enforcement of antitrust damages actions considerably.[48] Against this background, the European legislature was right to enshrine rules on prescription in the Directive. The main rule is laid down in Article 10 Damages Directive, and there are additional rules for the liability of immunity recipients (Article 11(4) Damages Directive) and for the suspensive effects of consensual dispute resolution (Article 18(1) Damages Directive). Whereas most of this provisions are based on the model of full harmonisation, a prescription period of 'at least' five years was designed as a minimum harmonisation rule (Article 10(3) Damages Directive). In addition, Member States are allowed to maintain or introduce absolute limitation periods as far as they do not render the exercise of the right to full compensation practically impossible or excessively difficult (Recital 36 Damages Directive). The harmonisation approach taken by the Directive is sensible. It focuses on crucial issues (commencement of the limitation period, minimum length of this period, selected issues of suspension) and gives Member States sufficient leeway to integrate these rules into the national systems of prescription (limitation of actions).

The national reports of this study agree that the European rules were transposed in conformity with EU law, even though the rules vary in detail. In accordance with Article 10(2) Damages Directive, the short run 'subjective' limitation period is not to begin to run before the following conditions are met: the competition law infringement has come to an end, the injured claimant (understood as the person that was originally harmed by the infringement, which in assignment cases must not necessarily be the actual claimant[49]) knows or can reasonably be expected to know[50] (i) of the relevant behaviour and the fact that it constitutes an infringement of competition law, (ii) that the infringement caused harm, and (iii) the identity of the infringer.[51]

Regarding the length of the subjective period, the adopted solutions vary. France,[52] Italy,[53] and the Netherlands[54] have introduced or maintained a five-year period and the same holds true for Scotland.[55] In Germany, the limitation period is also five years, but it runs from the end of the year in which the claim arose and the

48. *See* Joined Cases C-295/04 to C-298/04 *Manfredi*, *supra* n. 4, at paras 78–82. On the interpretation of the Italian prescription rules by the Italian Supreme Court in the aftermath of this case, *see* Camilleri, *supra* n. 26, at IV.C.
49. Kersting and Preuß, *supra* n. 11, at para. 82.
50. In Germany, a defendant contending that a claimant should reasonably have known of these facts must establish that the claimant demonstrated gross negligence in not learning of the relevant facts, *see* Franck, *supra* n. 27, at IV.C.1.
51. Amaro, *supra* n. 32, at IV.C.4.; Camilleri, *supra* n. 26, at IV.C.; Meijer and Zippro, *supra* n. 30, at VI.
52. Amaro, *supra* n. 32, at IV.C.4.
53. Camilleri, *supra* n. 26, at IV.C.
54. Meijer and Zippro, *supra* n. 30, at VI.
55. Wagner-von Papp, *supra* n. 24, at VI.

conditions mentioned in the preceding paragraph are met (*Ultimoverjährung*). This approach usually discharges parties and courts from the burden of determining the exact date when the requirements for the start of the limitation period are met.[56] In England and Wales, a six-year period applies.[57]

In all jurisdictions analysed in this study, an enforcement action by a competition authority suspends the limitation period in line with Article 10(4) Damages Directive.[58]

Some Member States have maintained or introduced absolute limitation periods according to which a claim/action is time-barred if a very long time has passed after the infringement has come to an end. The Netherlands[59] and France[60] have set forth a period of twenty years. Under German law, there are two absolute limitation periods. A period of ten years applies from the date when the claim arose and the competition law infringement on which the claim is based came to an end. In addition, claims for competition damages become time-barred thirty years from the date when the infringement occurred, irrespective of the knowledge of the plaintiff or whether the infringement has come to an end.[61] Whether the ten-year period is in line with the principle of effectiveness has been called into question. The German report takes the position that the German implementation is in conformity with the principle of effectiveness.[62]

Summing up, the Directive has prolonged the hitherto existing limitation periods in many jurisdictions. It has also shaped the conditions under which the 'subjective' limitation period begins to run, which fosters legal clarity and ensures that plaintiffs can usually recover damages after the infringement has been sanctioned by a competition authority. Thus, the Directive has improved the conditions for plaintiffs considerably.[63] Nonetheless, practical problems do arise with regard to the applicability of certain national provisions *ratione temporae* in cases where the national prescription rules were altered many times over the last years.[64] This problem has, however, to be fixed at the national level.

C. The role of national courts and legislatures

The success of private competition law enforcement is not only a question of European law and its implementation. Given that the Directive only partly harmonises the law (*see* section I.B., *supra*), also national parliaments and courts will remain important

56. Franck, *supra* n. 27, at IV.C.1.
57. Wagner-von Papp, *supra* n. 24, at VI.
58. Amaro, *supra* n. 32, at IV.C.4.; Camilleri, *supra* n. 26, at IV.C.; Franck, *supra* n. 27, at IV.C.3.; Meijer and Zippro, *supra* n. 30, at VI.; Wagner-von Papp, *supra* n. 24, at VI.
59. Meijer and Zippro, *supra* n. 30, at VI.
60. Amaro, *supra* n. 32, at IV.C.4. and 5. (noting doubts on the conformity of that rule with the principle of effectiveness).
61. Franck, *supra* n. 27, at IV.C.2.
62. *Ibid.*
63. This is also the case in other jurisdictions, for example in Sweden, where the Directive's prescription rules were transposed verbatim, *see* Magnus Strand, '*Managing Transposition and Avoiding Fragmentation: The Example of Limitation Periods and Interests*' in Magnus Strand, Vladimir Batistas Venegas & Marios C. Iacovides (eds), *EU Competition Litigation: Transposition and First Experiences of the New Regime* 42, 49–50 (Hart 2019).
64. *See* Amaro, *supra* n. 32, at IV.C.2.

actors in the construction of a sound and effective system of law enforcement.[65] Many possible impediments to private enforcement - such as the lack of specialised courts,[66] high litigation cost,[67] courts with insufficient resources to handle antitrust damages actions,[68] and rules of proof that do not reflect the complexity of competition law claims[69] - must be fixed by national courts or law-makers. Regulatory competition might help to improve the legal framework at the national level.[70]

II. PRIVATE ENFORCEMENT OF EU STATE AID LAW

A. Background: EU law framework for state aid

Establishing an internal market, one of the Union's central aims, implies ensuring that competition within the European Union is not distorted (Article 3(3) TEU and Protocol No 27 on the Internal Market and Competition). To this end, the Member States have agreed on common rules on competition, including, *inter alia*, a prohibition on certain types of state aid (Article 107(1) TFEU). This rule - to which Article 107(2) and (3) formulate exceptions - is procedurally strengthened by an obligation of the Member States to inform the European Commission 'in sufficient time to enable it to submit its comments, of any plans to grant or alter aid'; moreover, '[t]he Member State concerned shall not put its proposed measures into effect until this procedure has resulted in a final decision' (Article 108(3) TFEU).[71]

The aforementioned provision already hints at the main form of enforcing EU state aid law, namely its public enforcement by the European Commission in cooperation with the Member States' administrations according to Article 108 TFEU and Regulation 2015/1589. Yet, in view of limited administrative capacities at the European level and the trend towards a decentralisation of state aid control, private enforcement[72] has become increasingly important.[73] Moreover, in state aid law, private

65. A comparative overview of factors influencing the success of private enforcement is provided by Barry Rodger, '*Institutions and Mechanism to Facilitate Private Enforcement*' in Rodger, *supra* n. 14, at 23-71.
66. That specialised courts, i.e., bodies that decide generally on private competition law disputes or at least on actions for damages for breaches of competition law, usually lead to a better decision practice in competition cases is argued, *inter alia*, by Franck, *supra* n. 27, at III.D.2.; Wagner-von Papp, *supra* n. 24, at III.A.2. This view is, however not universally shared, *see* Rodger, *supra* n. 65, at 23, 24-25 with further references.
67. Wagner-von Papp, *supra* n. 24, at III.B. (for litigation in the UK).
68. Meijer and Zippro, *supra* n. 30, at III. (pointing out that while in the Netherlands courts still possess sufficient resources, there are signs that courts are struggling to handle mass claims effectively).
69. *See* the critique voiced by Camilleri, *supra* n. 26, at V.
70. Jürgen Basedow, *Die kartellrechtliche Schadensersatzhaftung und der Wettbewerb der Justizstandorte* [2016] Basler Juristische Mitteilungen 217, 239.
71. For further details Fernando Pastor-Merchante, *The European Perspective* II. and III.; Simone Donzelli, *The Role of the European Commission and the Cooperation with National Courts* II.
72. For a conceptual clarification Pastor-Merchante, *supra* n. 71, at I.
73. *See* also European Commission, Notice on cooperation between national courts and the Commission in the State aid field [1995] OJ C 312/8, paras 3 (also referring to the possibility to react promptly) and 13 (referring to the possibility to award damages); European Commission,

enforcement may even be considered more important than in the area of competition law since public enforcement suffers from a structural deficit: infringements of EU state aid law do not primarily result from actions taken by private market actors, but from actions of national administrations granting state aid in violation of EU law. This dual role of national administrations may result in a certain reservedness when recovering illegal state aid.

Against this background, the importance of private enforcement for an effective enforcement of EU state aid law has been stressed continuously,[74] and one may also observe a certain increase in the number of cases before national courts, as observed in a 2006 Study of the European Commission.[75] Nonetheless, there is room for improvement both in terms of numbers and efficiency.[76]

One of the challenges to private enforcement in the area of state aid law results from the fact that this body of law has not yet been harmonised, which is also true of

---

State Aid Action Plan – Less and better targeted state aid: a roadmap for state aid reform 2005–2009 (Consultation document), COM(2005) 107 final (SAAP), paras 55 et seq.; Communication from the Commission to the European Parliament, the Council, the European Economic and Social Committee and the Committee of the Regions – EU State Aid Modernisation (SAM), COM(2012) 209 final, para. 21: 'Should the Commission decide to increase the size and scope of aid measures exempt from notification obligation, responsibilities of Member States for ensuring the correct enforcement of State aid rules would increase. With more measures exempt from the notification requirement, Member States will have to ensure the ex ante compliance with State aid rules of de minimis measures and block-exempted schemes and cases, in strict coordination with the Commission which will continue to exercise ex post control of such measures. The Commission will expect better cooperation from Member States in terms of quality and timeliness of submission of information and notifications' preparation, as well as effective national systems (including private enforcement) to ensure that State aid measures exempt from ex ante notification obligation comply with Union law. A lower administrative burden through less notification obligations can only be envisaged if it is accompanied by increased commitment and delivery on the part of the national authorities in terms of compliance. Consequently, ex post control by the Commission will have to be increased, also because the current results of the monitoring of the implementation of block-exempted measures by Member States reveal frequent lack of compliance with State aid rules. In such a way, effectiveness of enforcement can be ensured'.

74. In its Notice on the enforcement of State aid law by national courts of 9 April 2009 ([2009] OJ C 85/1, para. 1), the Commission reaffirmed its assessment of the 2005 State Aid Action Plan, emphasising 'the need for better targeted enforcement and monitoring as regards State aid granted by Member States and stress[ing] that private litigation before national courts could contribute to this aim by ensuring increased discipline in the field of State aid'. *See* further para. 5: 'In spite of the fact that, as highlighted in the Enforcement Study, genuine private enforcement before national courts has played a relatively limited role in State aid to date, the Commission considers that private enforcement actions can offer considerable benefits for State aid policy. Proceedings before national courts give third parties the opportunity to address and resolve many State aid related concerns directly at national level. In addition, based on the jurisprudence of the Court of Justice of the European Communities ('ECJ'), national courts can offer claimants very effective remedies in the event of a breach of the State aid rules. This can in turn contribute to stronger overall State aid discipline.' *See* further 1995 Notice on cooperation, *supra* n. 73, at para. 3; SAAP, *supra* n. 73, at paras 55 et seq.; SAM, *supra* n. 73, at para. 21.
75. Thomas Jestaedt, Jacques Derenne and Tom R. Ottervanger (eds), *Study on the enforcement of State aid law at national level* (2006 European Commission), 33; Jacques Derenne, Cédric Kaczmakrek and Jonathan Clovin (eds), *2009 update of the 2006 Study on the enforcement of State aid rules at national level* (2009 European Commission), 2.
76. 2009 Enforcement Notice, *supra* n. 74, at para. 4; Jestaedt and Derenne and Ottervanger, *supra* n. 75, at 42 et seq.

public enforcement (Article 16 Regulation 2015/1589).[77] Hence, obligations flowing from EU law have to be enforced according to the rules of national law. However, the European principles of effectiveness and non-discrimination apply, as the Court has put it:

> In that regard, and since there is no Community legislation on the subject, it is for the domestic legal system of each Member State to designate the courts having jurisdiction and to determine the detailed procedural rules governing actions at law intended to safeguard the rights which individuals derive from Community law, provided, firstly, that those rules are not less favourable than those governing rights which originate in domestic law (principle of equivalence) and, secondly, that they do not render impossible or excessively difficult in practice the exercise of rights conferred by the Community legal order (principle of effectiveness).[78]

This is why, as stated by the 2006 Study and as still true despite some advances:

> Private enforcement of EC state aid law at Member State level is still in its infancy. This is not due to shortcomings or inefficiencies in the Member States' legal systems or a lack of knowledge of EC law by Member States' judges but is, instead, due to the diversity of Member States' procedural and substantive rules applicable to situations involving the grant of state aid and the uncertainties (cost risks, uncertain outcome) resulting from the absence of uniform procedures with a clear legal basis.[79]

Against this background, a first step to strengthening private enforcement of state aid law is to analyse the mechanisms of enforcement available within the national legal orders. This analysis allows identifying challenges and best practices. On this basis and with regard to the experiences gained in competition law, the need for a harmonisation at the EU level may be explored.

B. Key issues of private enforcement

EU state aid law comprises two central stipulations with regard to the Member States, namely the substantive prohibition against granting aid incompatible with the internal market (Article 107 TFEU) and the procedural obligations to notify the European Commission 'of any plans to grant or alter aid' and not to put measures into effect until the European Commission has reached a final decision (Article 108(3) TFEU). With regard to the private enforcement of these requirements of EU state aid law, adherence to the standstill obligation has to be secured by the national judiciary. As a preliminary question, this requires assessing the compatibility of an aid measure with the internal market, an assessment which must pay due respect to a possible decision of the

77. Cf. ECJ, Case C-368/04 *Transalpine Ölleitung* [2006] ECR I-9957, para. 35: 'Nevertheless, as is clear from the recital 2 in the preamble to Regulation No 659/1999 and its provisions, that regulation codifies and reinforces the Commission's practice in reviewing State aid and does not contain any provision relating to the powers and obligations of the national courts, which continue to be governed by the provisions of the Treaty as interpreted by the Court'.
78. Case C-368/04 *Transalpine, supra* n. 77, at para. 45; further ECJ, Case C-34/01 *Enirisorse* [2003] ECR I-14243, para. 42.
79. Jestaedt and Derenne and Ottervanger, *supra* n. 75, at 34.

European Commission to initiate the formal examination procedure and which thus raises the issue of the extent of the binding effect of that decision, notably in view of its preliminary nature. This explains why the cooperation and coordination between national courts and the European Commission are of relevance for the private enforcement of EU state aid law. In view of a not fully decentralised system of enforcement, the final decision on the compatibility of an aid measure with the internal market falls within the exclusive competence of the European Commission, which is why the role of private enforcement at the national level is limited to securing the implementation of the Commission's decision. Finally, attention should be drawn to the distinction – as emphasised by *Pastor-Merchante* in the European report – between stand-alone actions based on the direct effect of the standstill clause and follow-on actions based on the direct effect of Commission decisions.[80]

1. *Enforcement of EU state aid law*

a) *EU law background*

aa) Standstill obligation (Article 108(3) TFEU)

As early as the groundbreaking case of *Costa v E.N.E.L.*, handed down on 15 July 1964, the European Court of Justice has held the standstill obligation contained in today's Article 108(3) sentence 3 TFEU as directly applicable and as creating individual rights.[81] This has been confirmed in the judgment in the *Lorenz* case.[82] Moreover, by stressing that 'it is for the internal legal system of every Member State to determine the legal procedure leading to this result', the Court has safeguarded the direct applicability of Article 108(3) TFEU.[83] In *SFEI*, the Court has concretised this formula:

> National courts must offer to individuals the certain prospect that all the appropriate conclusions will be drawn from an infringement of the last sentence of Article 93(3) of the Treaty, in accordance with their national law, as regards the

80. *See* Pastor-Merchante, *supra* n. 71, at III., IV. and V.
81. ECJ, Case 6/64 *Costa v E.N.E.L.* [1964] ECR 587, 596: 'By virtue of Article 92, the Member States have acknowledged that such aids are incompatible with the Common Market and have thus implicitly undertaken not to create any more, save as otherwise provided in the Treaty; in Article 93, on the other hand, they have merely agreed to submit themselves to appropriate procedures for the abolition of existing aids and the introduction of new ones. By so expressly undertaking to inform the Commission 'in sufficient time' of any plans for aid, and by accepting the procedures laid down in Article 93, the States have entered into an obligation with the Community, which binds them as States but creates no individual rights except in the case of the final provision of Article 93 (3), which is not in question in the present case.' *See* for further details Pastor-Merchante, *supra* n. 71, at III. and IV.
82. ECJ, Case 120/73 *Lorenz v Germany* [1973] ECR 1471, para. 8; further ECJ, Case C-39/94 *Syndicat Français de l'Express International (SFEI) v La Poste* [1996] ECR I-3547, para. 39; ECJ, Case C-354/90 *FNCEPA v France* [1991] ECR I-5505, para. 11; Case C-34/01 *Enirisorse, supra* n. 78, at para. 42; Case C-284/12 *Deutsche Lufthansa v Flughafen Frankfurt-Hahn* [2013] ECLI:EU:C:2013:755, para. 29; Case C-505/14 *Klausner Holz* [2015] ECLI:EU:C:2015:742, para. 23.
83. Case 120/73, *Lorenz v Germany, supra* n. 82, at para. 9.

validity of measures giving effect to the aid, the recovery of financial support granted in disregard of that provision and possible interim measures.[84]

And further, in the recent *Klausner Holz* judgment, the Court has held:

> The objective of the national courts' tasks is therefore to pronounce measures appropriate to remedy the unlawfulness of the implementation of the aid, in order that the aid does not remain at the free disposal of the recipient during the period remaining until the Commission makes its decision (...).
>
> To that end, when national courts hold that the measure at issue constitutes state aid within the meaning of Article 107(1) TFEU, implemented in breach of the third sentence of Article 108(3) TFEU, they may decide to suspend the implementation of the measure in question and order the recovery of payments already made or to order provisional measures in order to safeguard both the interests of the parties concerned and the effectiveness of the Commission's subsequent decision (...).[85]

The subsequent declaration of an aid as compatible with the internal market does not remedy a breach of the standstill obligation:

> It must be stated in this regard that the Commission's final decision does not have the effect of regularising ex post facto the implementing measures which were invalid because they had been taken in breach of the prohibition laid down by the last sentence of Article 93(3) of the Treaty, since otherwise the direct effect of that prohibition would be impaired and the interests of individuals, which, as stated above, are to be protected by national courts, would be disregarded. Any other interpretation would have the effect of according a favourable outcome to the non-observance by the Member State concerned of the last sentence of Article 93(3) and would deprive that provision of its effectiveness.[86]

More specifically, a variety of remedies has been acknowledged in the European Court of Justice's case law,[87] notably a declaration of the aid as illegal[88] (with the

84. Case C-39/94, *SFEI, supra* n. 82, at para. 40; similarly and from an earlier date Case C-354/90 *FNCEPA v France, supra* n. 82, at para. 12; confirmed in Case C-368/04 *Transalpine, supra* n. 77, at para. 47; Case C-284/12 *Deutsche Lufthansa, supra* n. 82, at para. 30; Case C-505/14, *Klausner Holz, supra* n. 82, at para. 24. Moreover, as Case C-368/04 *Transalpine, supra* n. 77, at para. 50, has underlined, remedies must be 'such as in fact to negate the effects of the aid granted in breach of Article 88(3) EC and not merely to extend it to a further class of beneficiaries.' In tax cases, this excludes an extension of unlawful tax benefits (*see ibid.*, at para. 49): 'With regard to partial rebate of a tax constituting an unlawful aid measure because it was granted in breach of the obligation of notification, it would not be compatible with the interest of the Community to order that such a rebate be applied also in favour of other undertakings if such a decision would have the effect of extending the circle of recipients, thus leading to an increase in the effects of that aid instead of their elimination'.
85. Case C-505/14, *Klausner Holz, supra* n. 82, at paras 25 et seq.
86. Case C-354/90 *FNCEPA v France, supra* n. 82, at para. 16; further Case C-368/04 *Transalpine, supra* n. 77, at paras 41 et seq., 54; ECJ, Case C-199/06 *Centre d'exportation du livre Français (CELF) v Société internationale de diffusion et d'édition (SIDE)* [2008] ECR I-469, para. 40.
87. For a comprehensive overview *see* also the 2009 Enforcement Notice, *supra* n. 74, at paras 24 et seq.
88. Case C-368/04 *Transalpine, supra* n. 77, at para. 40; Case C-672/13 *OTP Bank Nyrt v Magyar Állam* [2015] ECLI:EU:C:2015:185, para. 37.

consequence of nullity or mere illegality?),[89] the prevention of payment,[90] a suspension of the aid,[91] a repayment of the aid[92] – unless exceptional circumstances apply[93] – plus interest[94] and a mere payment of interest, particularly where there is a subsequent positive decision of the European Commission.[95]

Moreover, damages may be awarded.[96] Claims directed against the Member States may be based on the rules on state liability for breaches of EU law.[97] With regard to claims against the beneficiary of the state aid, the Court has held that EU law 'does not provide a sufficient basis for the recipient to incur liability where he has failed to verify that the aid received was duly notified to the Commission.'[98] Nevertheless, in the same case the European Court of Justice went on to stress that this finding 'does not, however, prejudice the possible application of national law concerning non-contractual liability. If, according to national law, the acceptance by an economic operator of unlawful assistance of a nature such as to occasion damage to other economic operators may in certain circumstances cause him to incur liability, the

89. For the latter, Wolfgang Weiß, *Rechtsschutz von Unternehmen im EU-Beihilferecht* (2016) 180 ZHR 80, 113.
90. 2009 Enforcement Notice, *supra* n. 74, at paras 28 et seq.
91. Case C-368/04 *Transalpine*, *supra* n. 77, at para. 46.
92. Case C-39/94, *SFEI*, *supra* n. 82, at paras 63 et seq.; further Case C-368/04 *Transalpine*, *supra* n. 77, at para. 56; Case C-199/06 *CELF*, *supra* n. 86, at para. 53; Case C-284/12 *Deutsche Lufthansa*, *supra* n. 82, at para. 30.
93. This requirement was further fleshed out in CELF I (Case C-199/06 *CELF*, *supra* n. 86, at para. 43. *See* also ECJ, Case C-1/09 *CELF v SIDE II* [2010] ECR I-2099, paras 41 et seq.): 'a recipient of illegally granted aid is not precluded from relying on exceptional circumstances on the basis of which it had legitimately assumed the aid to be lawful and thus declining to refund that aid. If such a case is brought before a national court, it is for that court to assess the circumstances of the case, if necessary after obtaining a preliminary ruling on interpretation from the Court of Justice'.
94. Case C-199/06 *CELF*, *supra* n. 86, at para. 54: 'As regards the aid itself, it must be added that a measure which consisted only in an obligation of recovery without interest would not be appropriate, as a rule, to remedy the consequences of the unlawfulness if the Member State were to re-implement that aid after the Commission's final positive decision. Since the period between the recovery and the reimplementation would be shorter than that between the initial implementation and the final decision, the aid recipient, would bear, if it had to borrow the amount repaid, less interest than it would have paid if, from the outset, it had to borrow the equivalent of the unlawfully granted aid'.
95. *See* Case C-199/06 *CELF*, *supra* n. 86, at paras 45 et seq.: in case of a subsequent positive decision, national courts must 'order the aid recipient to pay interest in respect of the period of unlawfulness'. Before a final decision of the European Commission a mere payment of interest is not sufficient, if the aid remains in the accounts of the undertaking, *see* Case C-1/09 *CELF II*, *supra* n. 93, at para. 38: in that case 'the "standstill" obligation set out in Article 88(3) EC would not be fulfilled ... It is in no way established that an undertaking which has unlawfully received State aid could, were it not for that aid, have obtained an equivalent amount by way of loan from a financial institution under normal market conditions and thus have that amount at its disposal prior to the Commission decision'.
96. Case C-199/06 *CELF*, *supra* n. 86, at para. 53. *See* for more details Pastor-Merchante, *supra* n. 71, at IV.
97. 2009 Enforcement Notice, *supra* n. 74, at para. 45.
98. Case C-39/94, *SFEI*, *supra* n. 82, at para. 74.

principle of non-discrimination may lead the national court to find the recipient of aid paid in breach of [Article 108(3) TFEU] liable'.[99]

Furthermore, national courts are obliged, in particular if referring a case to the European Court of Justice, to consider the need for granting interim measures: 'Where it is likely that some time will elapse before it gives its final judgment, it is for the national court to decide whether it is necessary to order interim relief such as the suspension of the measures at issue in order to safeguard the interests of the parties.'[100] The choice of the remedy depends on the specific situation.[101]

Finally, it has to be noted that if a procedure is pending before the European Commission, national courts are not released from ordering a recovery of the state aid because of violations of Article 108(3) TFEU.[102] This result is not called into question by the fact that 'the Court did not find that the Commission had the power to declare aid illegal solely on the ground that the obligation to notify had not been complied with and without having to investigate whether the aid was compatible with the common market.' For, 'that finding has no effect on the obligations of national courts deriving from the direct effect which the prohibition laid down by the last sentence of Article 93(3) of the Treaty has been held to have.'[103]

bb) Substantive prohibition of state aid (Article 107 TFEU)

Unlike in EU antitrust law, there is no full decentralisation of private enforcement in EU state aid law since national courts are not entitled to declare a state aid measure in breach of Article 107 TFEU.[104] This results from the fact that the prohibition contained in Article 107(1) TFEU 'is neither absolute nor unconditional since [Article 107(2) and

99. Case C-39/94, *SFEI, supra* n. 82, at para. 75. Cf. further Case C-368/04 *Transalpine, supra* n. 77, at para. 56.
100. Case C-39/94, *SFEI, supra* n. 82, at para. 52. Cf. further Case C-368/04 *Transalpine, supra* n. 77, at para. 46; Case C-284/12 *Deutsche Lufthansa, supra* n. 82, at para. 30.
101. *See* Pastor-Merchante, *supra* n. 71, at IV. and V., for more details.
102. Case C-39/94, *SFEI, supra* n. 82, at paras 41 et seq., notably at paras 44 et seq.: 'In those circumstances, the initiation by the Commission of a preliminary examination procedure under [Art. 108 (3) TFEU] or the consultative examination procedure under [Art. 108 (2) TFEU] cannot release national courts from their duty to safeguard the rights of individuals in the event of a breach of the requirement to give prior notification. Any other interpretation would have the effect of encouraging the Member States to disregard the prohibition on implementation of planned aid. Since the Commission can do no more than order further payments to be suspended so long as it has not adopted its final decision on the substance of the matter, the effectiveness of [Art. 108 (3) TFEU] would be weakened if the fact that the Commission was seised of the matter were to prevent the national courts from drawing all the appropriate conclusions from the infringement of that provision'; *see* further Case C-1/09, *CELF II, supra* n. 93, paras 29 et seq.; Case C-284/12 *Deutsche Lufthansa, supra* n. 82, at paras 32 et seq.; ECJ, Case C-27/13 *Flughafen Lübeck* ECLI:EU:C:2014:240, paras 30 et seq.
103. Case C-354/90 *FNCEPA v France, supra* n. 82, at para. 13.
104. ECJ, Case C-78/76 *Steinike & Weinlig v Germany* [1977] ECR I-595, paras 5 et seq.; Case C-368/04 *Transalpine, supra* n. 77, at para. 38; ECJ, Case C-119/05 *Lucchini* [2007] ECR I-6199, paras 51 et seq.; Case C-672/13 *OTP Bank, supra* n. 88, at para. 37; Case C-505/14, *Klausner Holz, supra* n. 82, at paras 20 et seq.

(3) TFEU] give the Commission a wide discretion and the Council extensive power to admit aids in derogation from the general prohibition in [Article 107(1) TFEU].'[105]

Thus, 'the national courts and the Commission fulfil complementary and separate roles.'[106] Or, as the Court has put it:

> In this respect it should be noted, ... that the principal and exclusive role conferred on the Commission by Articles 92 and 93 of the Treaty, which is to hold aid to be incompatible with the common market where this is appropriate, is fundamentally different from the role of national courts in safeguarding rights which individuals enjoy as a result of the direct effect of the prohibition laid down in the last sentence of Article 93(3) of the Treaty. Whilst the Commission must examine the compatibility of the proposed aid with the common market, even where the Member State has acted in breach of the prohibition on giving effect to aid, national courts do no more than preserve, until the final decision of the Commission, the rights of individuals faced with a possible breach by State authorities of the prohibition laid down by the last sentence of Article 93(3) of the Treaty. When those courts make a ruling in such a matter, they do not thereby decide on the compatibility of the aid with the common market, the final determination on that matter being the exclusive responsibility of the Commission, subject to the supervision of the Court of Justice.[107]

Consequently, EU 'law precludes the application of a provision of national law, such as Article 2909 of the Italian Civil Code, which seeks to lay down the principle of res judicata in so far as the application of that provision prevents the recovery of state aid granted in breach of Community law which has been found to be incompatible with the common market in a decision of the Commission which has become final.'[108]

b) Enforcement at the national level

Against this background, the country reports in the section on state aid in this study have analysed the situation in the respective Member States.

aa) General remarks

In terms of general relevance, many national reports have stressed that private enforcement plays only a limited role, such as in France,[109] Germany,[110] Spain,[111] and the United Kingdom.[112] By contrast, in the Netherlands, private enforcement is of a

105. Case 78/76 *Steinike v Germany, supra* n. 104, at para. 8; further Case C-39/94, *SFEI, supra* n. 82, at para. 36.
106. Case C-39/94, *SFEI, supra* n. 82, at para. 41; further Case C-368/04 *Transalpine, supra* n. 77, at para. 37; Case C-284/12 *Deutsche Lufthansa, supra* n. 82, at paras 27 et seq.; Case C-505/14, *Klausner Holz, supra* n. 82, at paras 20 et seq.
107. Case C-354/90 *FNCEPA v France, supra* n. 82, at para. 14.
108. Case C-119/05 *Lucchini, supra* n. 104, at para. 63. *See* also Case C-505/14, *Klausner Holz, supra* n. 82, at paras 27 et seq.
109. François Lichère, *Private Enforcement in France* I.A.
110. Sebastian Unger and David Hug, *Private Enforcement in Germany* I.
111. Luis Arroyo Jiménez and Patricia Pérez, *Private Enforcement in Spain* I.A.
112. Christopher Bovis, *Private Enforcement in the United Kingdom* I.

certain importance:[113] One can count forty-two actions brought by competitors before administrative courts since 2005 and even more before ordinary courts (approx. eighty), but only rarely are they successful.[114] With regard to Spain, it is interesting to note that intra-administrative enforcement has a certain importance, such as between Autonomous Regions because of unfair competition; in this context, also private parties intervene.[115] Moreover, the Italian report notes a certain relevance in public procurement litigation with regard to the duty to reject abnormally low tenders resulting from the involvement of state aid (Article 69 Directive 2014/24/EU),[116] a finding also mentioned in the Dutch report.[117] A positive perspective (increasing importance) is presented in the Italian report.[118] Also, the report from the perspective of the Commission notes some progress despite low numbers.[119]

With regard to the legal framework, it has been generally emphasised that no specific legislation exists; rather, the general rules of national (substantive and procedural) law apply (Germany, France, Italy).[120] This usually entails a split legal regime in terms of the substantive law, meaning that depending on the subject matter, private or public law rules may apply (Germany, Spain, France, Italy).[121] This also extends to jurisdiction (civil courts, administrative courts, or further courts, such as tax courts), depending on the subject matter of the dispute, and thus potentially results in split jurisdiction (Germany, Spain, France, Netherlands).[122] For the Netherlands, two interesting points have been noted. First, splitting jurisdiction may have negative consequences for the claimant in the case of a set of acts being heard by different branches of the judiciary.[123] Second, litigation before civil courts may be disadvantageous for the claimant (vis-à-vis administrative litigation) since it is more difficult to prove the existence of state aid in view of the principle of party autonomy and the obligation to furnish facts resulting from this principle.[124] Moreover, for Italy, a certain consolidation has been observed: Jurisdiction lies with administrative courts when decisions granting aid are challenged or when recovery actions (irrespective of the nature of the aid and the entity granting it) are pursued;[125] jurisdiction for damages depends, however, on the defendant (beneficiary: ordinary courts; granting entity:

113. Jacobine van den Brink and Willemien den Ouden, *Private Enforcement in the Netherlands* I., III.B. and V.B.1.
114. *Ibid.*, at VI.
115. Arroyo Jiménez and Pérez, *supra* n. 111, at I.A.
116. Roberto Caranta and Benedetta Biancardi, *Private Enforcement in Italy* VIII.
117. van den Brink and den Ouden, *supra* n. 113, at V.B.1.
118. Caranta and Biancardi, *supra* n. 116, at I. and III.
119. Donzelli, *supra* n. 71, at IV.
120. Caranta and Biancardi, *supra* n. 116, at II.A.; Lichère, *supra* n. 109, at I.B.; Unger and Hug, *supra* n. 110, at II.A.
121. Arroyo Jiménez and Pérez, *supra* n. 111, at I.B.; Caranta and Biancardi, *supra* n. 116, at II.A.; Lichère, *supra* n. 109, at I.B.; Unger and Hug, *supra* n. 110, at II.A. and II.C.
122. Arroyo Jiménez and Pérez, *supra* n. 111, at I.B.; Lichère, *supra* n. 109, at I.B.; Unger and Hug, *supra* n. 110, at II.A.; van den Brink and den Ouden, *supra* n. 113, at II. and V.
123. van den Brink and den Ouden, *supra* n. 113, at II.
124. *Ibid.*, at V.D.2.
125. Caranta and Biancardi, *supra* n. 116, at II.A.

administrative courts).[126] Moreover, there is a (practically irrelevant) jurisdiction of ordinary courts for actions seeking to prohibit the receipt or expenditure of aid.[127]

bb) Remedies

The country reports observe that a full set of remedies is available in order to deal with private enforcement (Germany, Spain, France, Italy, Netherlands, UK).[128] Nonetheless, specific challenges and obstacles have been pointed out.

The availability of damages constitutes a strong incentive for competitors to embark on the route of private enforcement.[129] The 2006 Study did not identify cases involving damages, though.[130] This picture has changed only to a limited extent. No cases were reported for Germany,[131] the Netherlands,[132] or the United Kingdom,[133] but a limited relevance has been noted for Italy.[134] In France, there was one unsuccessful case,[135] but two promising cases are pending.[136] This finding can be primarily attributed to the difficulties with regard to proving causation and the existence of a damage as well as to the evaluation of the latter, as has been confirmed in the reports for France,[137] Germany,[138] Italy,[139] the Netherlands,[140] and Spain.[141,142] The French report, however, notes that the situation is different in the case of duopolies, which is also confirmed by the case law.[143]

With regard to claims addressed to the beneficiary of the aid (and not the granting authority),[144] the UK report argues that there is no standing in such cases.[145] Moreover, it is disputed whether receiving illegal state aid constitutes unfair competition and thus

126. *Ibid.*, at II.A. and VI.
127. *Ibid.*, at II.A.
128. Unger and Hug, *supra* n. 110, at II.C.2. - overly restrictive conditions for recovery have been noted; Arroyo Jiménez and Pérez, *supra* n. 111, at I.C.; Bovis, *supra* n. 112, at IV.B.; Caranta and Biancardi, *supra* n. 116; Lichère, *supra* n. 109; van den Brink and den Ouden, *supra* n. 113, at V.C.
129. Cf. Fernando Pastor-Merchante, *The Role of Competitors in the Enforcement of State Aid Law*, 15 et seq. (Hart 2017). Affirmed for France (Lichère, *supra* n. 109, at II.B.2.); questioned, though, in the German report in view of the absence of any practical significance (Unger and Hug, *supra* n. 110, at IV.).
130. Jestaedt and Derenne and Ottervanger, *supra* n. 75, at 33 et seq., 48 et seq.; Derenne and Kaczmakrek and Clovin, *supra* n. 75, at 4.
131. Unger and Hug, *supra* n. 110, at I., IV. and VI.
132. van den Brink and den Ouden, *supra* n. 113, at III.C. and V.D.3.
133. Bovis, *supra* n. 112, at IV.C.
134. Caranta and Biancardi, *supra* n. 116, at VI.
135. Lichère, *supra* n. 109, at II.B.2.
136. *Ibid.*, at II.B.2.
137. *Ibid.*
138. Unger and Hug, *supra* n. 110, at IV.B.
139. Caranta and Biancardi, *supra* n. 116, at VI.
140. van den Brink and den Ouden, *supra* n. 113, at V.D.3.
141. Arroyo Jiménez and Pérez, *supra* n. 111, at I.C.3.
142. Cf. Pastor-Merchante, *supra* n. 129, at 75 et seq.; Pastor-Merchante, *supra* n. 71, at IV. and V.
143. Lichère, *supra* n. 109, at II.B.2.
144. Cf. for the limited relevance of an action against the beneficiary Jestaedt and Derenne and Ottervanger, *supra* n. 75, at 34.
145. Bovis, *supra* n. 112, at IV.A.

gives rise to corresponding claims (Spain, Italy);[146] the Dutch report also highlights that the liability of a beneficiary is difficult to establish.[147]

Standing in private enforcement depends on the general requirements formulated in the respective national system.[148] Generally speaking, no significant obstacles have been identified.

It should be noted, though, that in Germany the invocability of a breach of the standstill obligation by competitors has been acknowledged only since 2011.[149] Moreover, access to courts is limited to competitors, with the notion of 'competitor' remaining disputed.[150] In France, no obstacles have been identified; broad access is granted for challenging administrative acts and contracts,[151] whereby in the latter case a specific harm has to be shown as resulting either from being a competitor or from a serious breach.[152] Similarly, no obstacles have been observed for access to courts in Spain since a legitimate interest is sufficient. To meet this requirement, the mere interest in respecting the legality of any state action does not suffice, but a broad understanding applies, according to which it is immaterial whether the interest is direct or indirect, individual or collective. Thus, standing is granted for competitors and also for associations, groups, and public bodies that are affected.[153] In Italy, standing for competitors has been acknowledged;[154] moreover, it is interesting to note that the competition authority has standing.[155] In the Netherlands, private enforcement initially had a certain relevance in spatial planning law because residents were entitled to challenge planning measures by invoking, *inter alia*, that illegal state aid was involved. However, following the introduction of the relativity requirement (*Schutznorm*) in 2013, the standing of local residents is excluded and that of competitors restricted.[156] Moreover, the relativity requirement has also restricted access to courts in other areas, such as social security law.[157] Although certain restrictive tendencies have manifested, a competitor generally has standing if considered an interested party,[158] but not before tax courts in tax matters; proceedings before civil courts are possible, but inexistent.[159] Furthermore, more flexibility in case of litigation before civil courts has been noted.[160]

146. Arroyo Jiménez and Pérez, *supra* n. 111, at I.D.; Caranta and Biancardi, *supra* n. 116, at VI.
147. van den Brink and den Ouden, *supra* n. 113, at V.D.3.
148. Cf. 2009 Enforcement Notice, *supra* n. 74, paras 70 et seq. Cf. on the development in Germany Jenny K. Dorn, *Private und administrative Rechtsdurchsetzung im europäischen Beihilfenrecht. Vom indirekten Vollzug zum Kooperationsprinzip*, 152 et seq. (Nomos 2017).
149. Unger and Hug, *supra* n. 110, at I. On the initial reluctance, *see* also Dorn, *supra* n. 148, at 27 et seq.
150. Unger and Hug, *supra* n. 110, at II.B.
151. Lichère, *supra* n. 109, at II.A.1.
152. *Ibid.*, at II.A.3.
153. Arroyo Jiménez and Pérez, *supra* n. 111, at I.C.2.
154. Caranta and Biancardi, *supra* n. 116, at II.B.
155. *Ibid.*
156. van den Brink and den Ouden, *supra* n. 113, at III.A.
157. *Ibid.*, at III.A.
158. *Ibid.*, at III.B. and VI.
159. *Ibid.*, at IV. and VI.
160. *Ibid.*, at V.D.1.

Finally, in the United Kingdom a sufficient interest is required, which is affirmed for competitors.[161]

With regard to interim measures, certain difficulties have been highlighted. The French report draws attention to the fact that a violation of the notification obligation as such does not establish urgency; rather, a harm to the public interest or a serious harm for the claimant has to be established.[162] A similar finding applies to Italy, which is why interim protection plays only a limited role.[163] For Germany, the absence of any practical relevance is attributed notably to information deficits.[164] The Spanish report also mentions a limited practical relevance, but it is worth noting that the Spanish Supreme Court obliges lower courts to apply the Commission's 2009 notice with regard to interim protection while an investigation by the European Commission is taking place.[165] Finally, in the Netherlands interim protection is of limited relevance before administrative courts in view of limited chances of success,[166] though a different picture is true for litigation before civil courts.[167]

cc) Information deficits

Information deficits constitute a significant obstacle for competitors with regard to pursuing private enforcement.[168] This is confirmed by the national reports drawing attention to the actual relevance of such deficits (Germany, France, Italy, Netherlands, UK).[169] It has to be added, though, that these deficits are mitigated by transparency obligations (*see* Article 9(1) General Block Exemption Regulation; further, Transparency Directive, Article 7 Regulation 1370/2007) and by competitor claims seeking access to information. In this regard, it has however been rightly stressed that, as a matter of principle, transparency obligations do not help if a measure is (incorrectly) not considered state aid within the meaning of EU law (Germany, France).[170] Nevertheless, national law partially provides for broader transparency obligations (Germany).[171] Moreover, rules on access to information are considered important in this context (Germany, UK).[172]

In view of specific difficulties in cross-border cases,[173] the Italian report highlights that cross-border litigation is not attractive vis-à-vis a complaint raised with the

161. Bovis, *supra* n. 112, at IV.A.
162. Lichère, *supra* n. 109, at II.B.1.
163. Caranta and Biancardi, *supra* n. 116, at IV.
164. Unger and Hug, *supra* n. 110, at II.D.
165. Arroyo Jiménez and Pérez, *supra* n. 111, at I.C.4.
166. van den Brink and den Ouden, *supra* n. 113, at III.B.
167. *Ibid.*, at V.C.
168. Cf. Pastor-Merchante, *supra* n. 129, at 75.
169. Bovis, *supra* n. 112, at IV.E.; Caranta and Biancardi, *supra* n. 116, at V., VIII. and IX.; Lichère, *supra* n. 109, at II.A.6. and III.; Unger and Hug, *supra* n. 110, at III.; van den Brink and den Ouden, *supra* n. 113, at VI.
170. Lichère, *supra* n. 109, at II.A.6.; Unger and Hug, *supra* n. 110, at III.A. and VI.
171. Unger and Hug, *supra* n. 110, at III.B.
172. Bovis, *supra* n. 112, at IV.E.; Unger and Hug, *supra* n. 110, at III.B.
173. Cf. Pastor-Merchante, *supra* n. 129, at 75.

European Commission; introducing representative interest litigation might help in this regard, though.[174]

2. *Cooperation and coordination between national courts and the European Commission*

a) *EU law background*

The application of the standstill obligation stipulated in Article 108(3) TFEU implies that national courts must assess whether a measure of a Member State constitutes state aid within the meaning of Article 107(1) TFEU.[175]

In view of the expertise of the European Commission[176] and information available to it, Article 29(1) Regulation 2015/1589 allows national courts to 'ask the Commission to transmit to them information in its possession or its opinion on questions concerning the application of state aid rules'.[177] Moreover, according to Article 29(2) Regulation 2015/1589, the Commission may also submit observations to national courts ex officio (*amicus curiae*).

Furthermore, if the European Commission has decided to initiate a formal examination procedure, the question arises as to whether that decision has a binding effect and if so to what extent.[178] The Court has held in its fairly recent *Lufthansa* judgment handed down on 21 November 2013 that such a decision has to be duly respected in the context of the national court's assessment:

> In a situation where the Commission has already initiated the formal examination procedure under Article 108(2) TFEU, it is necessary to consider which measures have to be taken by the national courts.
>
> While the assessments carried out in the decision to initiate the formal examination procedure are indeed preliminary in nature, that does not mean that the decision lacks legal effects.
>
> It must be pointed out in that regard that, if national courts were able to hold that a measure does not constitute aid within the meaning of Article 107(1) TFEU and, therefore, not to suspend its implementation, even though the Commission had just stated in its decision to initiate the formal examination procedure that that measure was capable of presenting aid elements, the effectiveness of Article 108(3) TFEU would be frustrated.
>
> On the one hand, if the preliminary assessment in the decision to initiate the formal examination procedure is that the measure at issue constitutes aid and that

174. Caranta and Biancardi, *supra* n. 116, at IX.
175. Case 78/76 *Steinike v Germany*, *supra* n. 104, at para. 14; further, Case C-354/90 *FNCEPA v France*, *supra* n. 82, at para. 10; Case C-39/94, *SFEI*, *supra* n. 82, at para. 49; Case C-368/04 *Transalpine*, *supra* n. 77, at para. 39; Case C-119/05 *Lucchini*, *supra* n. 104, at para. 50; Case C-284/12 *Deutsche Lufthansa*, *supra* n. 82, at paras 34 et seq.; Case C-672/13 *OTP Bank*, *supra* n. 88, at para. 37; Case C-505/14, *Klausner Holz*, *supra* n. 82, at para. 22.
176. *See* for more details Donzelli, *supra* n. 71.
177. *See* also http://ec.europa.eu/competition/court/state_aid_requests.html (accessed 11 November 2019).
178. *See* also Pastor-Merchante, *supra* n. 71, at VI.

> assessment is subsequently confirmed in the final decision of the Commission, the national courts would have failed to observe their obligation under Article 108(3) TFEU and Article 3 Regulation 659/1999 to suspend the implementation of any aid proposal until the adoption of the Commission's decision on the compatibility of that proposal with the internal market.
>
> On the other hand, even if in its final decision the Commission were to conclude that there were no aid elements, the preventive aim of the state aid control system established by the TFEU and noted in paragraphs 25 and 26 of the present judgment requires that, following the doubt raised in the decision to initiate the formal examination procedure as to the aid character of that measure and its compatibility with the internal market, its implementation should be deferred until that doubt is resolved by the Commission's final decision.
>
> It is also important to note that the application of the European Union rules on state aid is based on an obligation of sincere cooperation between the national courts, on the one hand, and the Commission and the Courts of the European Union, on the other, in the context of which each acts on the basis of the role assigned to it by the Treaty. In the context of that cooperation, national courts must take all the necessary measures, whether general or specific, to ensure fulfilment of the obligations under European Union law and refrain from those which may jeopardise the attainment of the objectives of the Treaty, as follows from Article 4(3) TEU. Therefore, national courts must, in particular, refrain from taking decisions which conflict with a decision of the Commission, even if it is provisional.
>
> Consequently, where the Commission has initiated the formal examination procedure with regard to a measure which is being implemented, national courts are required to adopt all the necessary measures with a view to drawing the appropriate conclusions from an infringement of the obligation to suspend the implementation of that measure.
>
> To that end, national courts may decide to suspend the implementation of the measure in question and order the recovery of payments already made. They may also decide to order provisional measures in order to safeguard both the interests of the parties concerned and the effectiveness of the Commission's decision to initiate the formal examination procedure.
>
> Where they entertain doubts as to whether the measure at issue constitutes state aid within the meaning of Article 107(1) TFEU or as to the validity or interpretation of the decision to initiate the formal examination procedure, national courts may seek clarification from the Commission and, in accordance with the second and third paragraphs of Article 267 TFEU, as interpreted by the Court, they may or must refer a question to the Court for a preliminary ruling.[179]

Despite this duty to respect a decision of the European Commission to initiate a formal examination procedure when qualifying national measures as state aid, the question remains whether any qualifications or exceptions apply to this duty, as for instance assumed by the German Bundesgerichtshof (Supreme Court in Civil and Commercial Matters) in a judgment handed down on 9 February 2017. For the Commission's assessment is only of a preliminary nature, and the interests of both the recipient of the state aid and the granting authority have to be considered.[180] In

179. Case C-284/12 *Deutsche Lufthansa*, *supra* n. 82, at paras 36 et seq.; further, Case C-27/13 *Flughafen Lübeck*, *supra* n. 102, at paras 19 et seq.
180. *See* BGH, 9 February 2017, I ZR 91/15, [2017] EuZW 312, paras 49 et seq.

particular, the role of the principle of proportionality has to be assessed in view of a possible recovery of the state aid (see for limitations with regard to a decision of the European Commission to provisionally recover aid, Article 13(2) Regulation 2015/1589).[181]

b) *Enforcement at the national level*

With regard to the binding effect of a decision of the European Commission to initiate a formal examination procedure and possible qualifications, a certain reluctance has been noted in the German report despite the *Deutsche Lufthansa* jurisprudence:[182] The Bundesverwaltungsgericht (Supreme Administrative Court) does not consider itself obliged to refer a case to the European Court of Justice when intending to deviate from the Commission's preliminary assessment; the Bundesgerichtshof (Supreme Court for Civil and Commercial Matters) does acknowledge such a duty, but it formulates a reservation with regard to a subsequent recovery of the state aid. In the United Kingdom as well, a narrow interpretation of the European Court of Justice's judgment has been highlighted.[183] Similarly, an ambivalent finding has been made for Spain[184] and for the Netherlands, where the increasing importance that can be observed[185] is nevertheless accompanied by reluctance.[186]

With regard to a cooperation between national courts and the European Commission in terms of requests for information/observations and *amicus curiae* interventions (Article 29 Regulation 2015/1589), a certain reluctance has been noted, which is also attributable to problems with involving administrative bodies in court proceedings (Germany as well as Spain and Italy).[187] The Spanish report draws, moreover, attention to the fact that an *amicus curiae* intervention is not foreseen in Spanish procedural law.[188] This evaluation is also confirmed from the perspective of the European Commission,[189] which since 2009 has counted only twenty-three requests for information and seventeen requests for opinion, as well as twenty-one *amicus curiae* submissions (since 2013).

Finally, with regard to the role of preliminary references to the European Court of Justice, a certain reluctance (Italy)[190] and a limited role (Spain)[191] have been noted.

181. *See* BGH, I ZR 91/15, *supra* n. 180, at paras 49 et seq.
182. Unger and Hug, *supra* n. 110, at V.A.
183. Bovis, *supra* n. 112, at IV.A.
184. Arroyo Jiménez and Pérez, *supra* n. 111, at II.
185. van den Brink and den Ouden, *supra* n. 113, at III.B. and V.D.2.
186. *Ibid.*, at III.C.
187. Unger and Hug, *supra* n. 110, at V.; cf. further Arroyo Jiménez and Pérez, *supra* n. 111, at II.; Caranta and Biancardi, *supra* n. 116, at VII.
188. Arroyo Jiménez and Pérez, *supra* n. 111, at II.
189. Donzelli, *supra* n. 71, at III.C.
190. Caranta and Biancardi, *supra* n. 116, at VII.
191. Arroyo Jiménez and Pérez, *supra* n. 111, at II.

III. THE WAY FORWARD

A. Spill-over effects

So far, there is only a very limited cross-fertilisation between the private enforcement of EU competition and state aid law. The private enforcement of European competition rules has for many years been discussed intensively. The debate on the enforcement of EU state aid law by private actors is of more recent origin. As a consequence, in legal practice there are no spill-over effects from the area of competition law to the area of state aid law.[192] In view of the structural difficulties in obtaining damages, the idea of easing the standards of proof as established under EU competition law regarding the quantification of harm is considered as a solution for state aid law by the Italian report.[193] The German report, however, questions whether competition law may function as a model for state aid law since structural differences between the two areas of law have to be considered.[194] Notably, the application of rules established under competition law to ease a plaintiff's burden of proof is considered as questionable given that different theories of harm might apply in competition and state aid cases.[195]

B. Strengthening private enforcement of EU competition law

1. Guidance for courts

The quality of private competition law enforcement before national courts depends for a good part on the knowledge judges have about competition litigation. Given that the Damages Directive has led in some jurisdictions to significant changes in the law, private enforcement could be strengthened if courts received further guidance so as to better understand the new legal regime. Guidelines issued by the European Commission are a very important tool for providing direction to national courts in competition cases. The recently adopted 'Guidelines for national courts on how to estimate the share of overcharge which was passed on to the indirect purchaser'[196] must therefore be welcomed. These guidelines not only explain basic legal issues but also refer to the underlying economic theory and evidential issues. In addition, the guidelines not only refer to the case law of the European Court of Justice but also take into account national court decisions. These guidelines provide a valuable first step in strengthening legal certainty. Even though they are not binding for courts, they are a valuable 'soft law instrument', as national courts regularly refer to Commission instruments in competition law disputes. Guidelines will, however, not decide questions not previously dealt with by courts or disputed issues, as the Commission does not want to create new

192. Lichère, *supra* n. 109, at II.B.2.
193. Caranta and Biancardi, *supra* n. 116, at IX.
194. Unger and Hug, *supra* n. 110, at VI.
195. *Ibid.*, at IV.C.
196. European Commission, Guidelines for national courts on how to estimate the share of overcharge which was passed on to the indirect purchaser (2019/C 267/07) [2019] OJ C 267/4.

rules.[197] The guiding effect of this document is thus limited. Given that the body of case law on passing-on issues will increase and more and more questions will be clarified by the European Court of Justice in the years to come, the steering effect can be improved if the guidelines are updated and fine-tuned at regular intervals. In addition, the passing-on guidelines must be regarded as a first step. More guidelines on other issues covered by the Directive, for example on the reach of the binding effect of decisions of national competition authorities, should follow.

Given that the Commission will refrain from deciding on disputes in their guidelines, other soft-law devices should be considered. One idea would be to take up a practice that has been established in the area of uniform commercial law. Larger international expert groups could elaborate opinions on how to interpret and apply certain rules. A prominent example from the commercial world is the 'CISG Advisory Council', a private initiative aiming to strengthen the uniform application of the United Nations Convention on Contracts for the International Sale of Goods ('CISG'). It is composed of scholars and (currently) one judge from different jurisdictions. This group sees itself 'as an independent body of experts, ... afforded [with] the luxury of being critical of judicial or arbitral decision and of addressing issues not dealt with previously by adjudicating bodies.'[198] The CISG Advisory Council thus adopts opinions on novel or disputed questions and takes into account legal developments occurring in various jurisdictions. Even though such opinions are not binding, they provide valuable information for courts given that they are usually well-researched and documented. Similar European groups could emerge for matters regarding the private enforcement of competition law. If such a group gained a good reputation in the European competition law community, its opinions on issues not covered by guidelines issued by the European Commission could help courts when judging such questions.

2. *Improving the law at the national level*

A sound private enforcement system cannot be built overnight, and it cannot be only built at the European level (*see* I.C., *supra*). Given that the possibilities of a harmonisation of the law are limited – as are the competences of the European Union – national courts and legislatures also can and must contribute to a better private enforcement system within the framework that is set by EU law. It would go too far to muster all the suggestions that have been made to improve the current legal framework; some short remarks shall suffice to prove the point.

Courts must first and foremost develop a fine-tuned system in terms of the burden of proof. Without such differentiated rules, private enforcement of competition law will be impaired.[199] Moreover, courts should as far as it is possible to adapt the general procedural rules to the needs and the peculiarities of competition litigation.

Legislatures should – as far as not yet done – design specialised courts or chambers to hear damages actions for competition law infringements given that such

197. *See* Holzwarth, *supra* n. 12, at IV.
198. https://www.cisgac.com (accessed 3 September 2019).
199. *See* Camilleri, *supra* n. 26, at III.; Franck, *supra* n. 27, at III.B.1.b).

claims differ considerably from ordinary commercial litigation. The experiences in jurisdictions that have designed specialised bodies show that judges are consequently in a better position to build up solid knowledge in the area of competition law enforcement, including the economic matters that play an important role in competition litigation.[200] In addition, courts that deal with competition litigation must be equipped with the necessary resources for such cases, as they are very fact-specific, usually involve economic evidence for quantifying the harm,[201] and sometimes have the character of mass litigation where plaintiffs pool claims or bring actions against more than one defendant. If courts are not equipped with the necessary resources, a sound administration of such 'mass proceedings' will fail. A quick and effective 'digitisation' of courts will also help to administer such cases.

3. *Closing gaps at the European level*

Also at the European level, the legal framework could be improved. The application of the Damages Directive by Member State courts should be closely monitored and regularly evaluated by the European Commission. Moreover, attention should be given to areas that are not yet harmonised. Given that in these areas national law is a sort of 'comparative legal laboratory',[202] regulatory competition may lead to the result that a solution adopted in one jurisdiction spreads to other EU Member States. This would one day facilitate enlargement of the Damages Directive to further strengthen private enforcement across the entire European Union.

The most pressing need is, however, to introduce functioning collective redress mechanisms. The European Commission had originally planned to include such an instrument in the Damages Directive but did not prevail due to strong opposition from certain Member States, including Germany.[203] Subsequent attempts to create such an instrument have also failed. It was only a recommendation on collective redress that was issued in 2013.[204] Similar rules on collective redress throughout Europe would, however, be desirable. After the 'Diesel-gate scandal', the Commission has made a new attempt to ameliorate the situation, at least for breaches of EU consumer law, and has proposed strengthening representative actions.[205] This proposal is currently under debate.

It is however necessary to ensure that proper means of collective redress are available also in competition cases and especially for damages claims. If such an

---

200. Franck, *supra* n. 27, at III.D.2.; Wagner-von Papp, *supra* n. 24, at III.A.2.
201. Meijer and Zippro, *supra* n. 30, at III.
202. Basedow, *supra* n. 3, at 294, 298 ('*rechtsvergleichendes Laboratorium*').
203. Wolfgang Wurmnest, '*Schadensersatz wegen Verletzung des EU-Kartellrechts. Grundfragen und Entwicklungslinien*', in Oliver Remien (ed.), *Schadensersatz im europäischen Privat- und Wirtschaftsrecht* 27, 37 (Mohr Siebeck 2012).
204. Commission Recommendation of 11 June 2013 on common principles for injunctive and compensatory collective redress mechanisms in the Member States concerning violations of rights granted under Union Law [2013] OJ L 201/60.
205. Proposal of 11 April 2018 for a Directive of the European Parliament and of the Council on representative actions for the protection of the collective interests of consumers, and repealing Directive 2009/22/EC, COM(2018) 184 final.

instrument fitting the needs of parties harmed by competition law infringements cannot be adopted at the European level in the near future, action at the national level will be necessary in many Member States. The country reports of this study have revealed that many of the existing models at the national level either have a structure that does not help private plaintiffs in antitrust damages cases very much (Germany)[206] or limit the possibility to sue to very few associations, which for their part are ill-equipped for this task (France),[207] or the existing mechanisms are seen as sub-optimal for other reasons, mainly because of the opt-in mechanism (Italy).[208] Much more promising are the models that have recently been established in the Netherlands[209] and the United Kingdom,[210] which are based on an opt-out mechanism.

C. Constructing a proper framework for private enforcement of EU state aid law

As noted in the Commission's 2006 Study, it remains true that private enforcement of EU state aid law continues to have much potential to be developed, although in quantitative terms at least some progress has been highlighted in some reports. Nonetheless, it seems questionable whether a general EU-wide harmonisation of standards is the way forward since the availability of remedies as such has not been identified as the key problem. The only significant exception relates to the availability of damages, an incentive for competitors to pursue claims of private enforcement that is not to be underestimated. Here, it remains true that the difficulties with regard to proving causation and the existence of a damage constitute important obstacles to successful claims. Moreover, it is disputed whether and under which circumstances receiving illegal state aid may give rise to liability and constitute unfair competition. However, even if some alleviation of burdens (imposed on claimants) along the lines of EU competition law might help to reduce obstacles, it has also been rightly stressed that excessive liability must be avoided. Another point to be evaluated is the availability of interim measures, an area where some difficulties have been identified. In this regard it has to be carefully assessed, in view of the uncertainties associated with such measures, when and under which conditions they may be granted. Moreover, it may be considered whether standing for representative actions should be generally acknowledged (Italy)[211] and how access to information may be improved. Irrespective of these issues, factual obstacles have been identified, notably information deficits. Thus, increasing transparency by extending access to information and by creating publication obligations should be considered (Netherlands).[212]

When it comes to cooperation and coordination between national courts and the European Commission, room for improvement has been identified. Here, it can be

206. Franck, *supra* n. 27, at III.C.
207. Amaro, *supra* n. 32, at IV.D.4.
208. Camilleri, *supra* n. 26, at IV.D.
209. Meijer and Zippro, *supra* n. 30, at VII.D.
210. Wagner-von Papp, *supra* n. 24, at VII.B.
211. *See* Caranta and Biancardi, *supra* n. 116, at IX.
212. *See* also van den Brink and den Ouden, *supra* n. 113, at VI.

considered whether a certain formalisation would be helpful, to be achieved by means of a binding legal document; the Damages Directive may provide guidance in this regard. Moreover, factual barriers should also be further diminished, especially by fostering an environment beneficial to cooperation and coordination between the national and EU levels.

As private enforcement of state aid law faces many obstacles, the prospect of improving public enforcement has to be considered. In this regard, entrusting national competition authorities with the task of monitoring state aid law has been proposed (France).[213] Standing for the competition authority is already recognised in Italy,[214] but not in Spain.[215] Finally, in the Netherlands, the principle of good administration is relevant if the interests of competitors have not been taken duly into account, even where no state aid is present.[216]

213. Lichère, *supra* n. 109, at III.
214. Caranta and Biancardi, *supra* n. 116, at II.B.
215. Arroyo Jiménez and Pérez, *supra* n. 111, at I.B.
216. van den Brink and den Ouden, *supra* n. 113, at V.D.4.

Index

A

Access to evidence, 167, 174, 316
Acquis communautaire, 20, 30, 36, 357
Akzo Nobel judgment, 125
Altmark judgment, 239, 278
Amicus curiae, 7, 88, 220, 222–226, 229, 230, 332, 379, 381
Ashurst Report, 14, 120, 144

B

Binding effect of national decisions
  local cases, 362
  cross-border cases, 362–364
Burden of proof, 24, 94, 95, 121, 123, 139, 140, 260–261, 283, 311, 312, 345, 382, 383

C

Causation, 49–51, 136–141
CELF judgment, 242, 246
Class action
  opt-in, 135, 158
  opt-out, 158
  pooling of claims, 72–75, 133–136, 155–159, 182–189
Cogeco judgment, 42–46
Compensation (private enforcement of competition law)
  actual loss/damnum emergens, 17, 20, 139
  loss of profit/lucrum cessans, 17, 20, 53, 139
  overcompensation/deterrence, 22, 23, 121, 133, 278, 356
Compensation (private enforcement of state aid law), 355–386
Compensation for damages, 86, 104, 137, 259, 312–313, 326, 329, 336
Competitive interests, 294–296, 309, 313–315
Competitors' information deficit, 251, 256–259, 265
Cooperation
  amicus curiae, 220, 222–226, 229, 230
  Cooperation and coordination between national courts and the European Commission, 7, 283–284, 332–333, 379–381, 385
  Lufthansa/Deutsche Lufthansa judgment, 262–265, 333
  preliminary reference, 40, 42, 43, 46, 47, 50, 53, 211, 275, 279, 281, 282, 285, 333, 381
Courage judgment, 16–17

D

Damages
assessment of, 89, 123, 261
claim for, 22, 23, 30, 114, 143, 151, 152, 155, 157, 250, 251, 258–262, 325–327, 346
evaluation of, 376
Donau-Chemie judgment, 20, 28, 31, 33

E

Economic unit, 46, 66, 79, 103, 105, 106, 110, 125–127, 152, 176–178, 359
Evidence
access to, 167, 174, 316
disclosure, 27–29, 31, 88, 124, 162, 167–172
prima facie, 24, 45, 94–96, 107–110, 128, 131, 153, 180, 181, 192, 261, 276, 363, 364
Exceptional circumstances, 47, 80, 116, 152, 153, 168, 253, 254–256, 265, 372

F

Follow-on actions, 24, 29, 34, 58, 63, 74, 106, 109, 122, 128, 143, 155, 162, 165, 166, 185, 187, 191–193, 199, 204, 209–212, 214, 269, 357, 370
Forum shopping, 2, 5, 122, 131
Francovich judgment, 33, 260, 279, 281, 326, 347

G

General Block Exemption Regulation (GBER), 201, 202, 213, 217, 219, 225, 230, 257, 342, 378, 351

I

Immunity, 29–30, 32, 37, 82, 86, 110, 121, 150, 181, 358, 365
Impediments to private enforcement of competition law
high costs, 162
lack of collective redress mechanism, 357
lack of specialised courts, 367
Information deficit, 6, 7, 251, 256–259, 265, 336, 378–379, 385
Interested party test, 297–299, 315, 316
Interim proceedings, 303, 306, 309, 311
Interim measures
fumus boni iuris, 329, 333
interim proceedings, 303, 306, 309, 311
Intra-administrative enforcement, 375

J

Jurisdiction (enforcement of state aid law)
division of jurisdiction, 291, 292, 315
dualistic court system, 251
dualist system, 321
dual jurisdiction system, 268–270

K

Kone judgment, 18, 50–51
France, 247, 366
Germany, 255
Italy, 131–133, 282
Netherlands, 150, 153–155, 366
United Kingdom, 162, 166, 181, 182

L

Legitimate interest, 324, 330, 377
Limitation periods (enforcement of competition law), 42–46

N

Notification, 111, 192, 200-202, 204, 219, 225, 230, 233, 236, 240, 254, 274, 275, 282, 312, 313, 321, 341-343, 346, 351, 378
Nullity, 56, 238, 270, 284, 303, 306, 310, 334, 372

O

Otis judgment, 49-51

P

Passing-on (defence) 22-23, 148-149
  guidelines, draft of the European Commission, 52-53
Planning (zoning), 291, 293-295, 300, 315
Pfleiderer judgment, 28, 31, 33, 118, 120, 357
Preparatory work for the Directive on Antitrust Damages Actions
  Green Paper, 134
  proposal of the European Commission, 122, 180
  White Paper, 134
Principles of sound administration, 313-316
Private law remedies, 17, 19, 23, 140, 321, 331-332
Procedural Regulation, 200, 210, 217, 218, 220-226, 232, 254, 262, 263, 265, 266, 324
Public law remedies, 251, 321-330
Public procurement, 197, 205, 237-239, 247, 285-288, 303, 304, 309, 375

R

Ratione temporis/temporae, 41, 58, 59, 69, 70, 358, 366
Recovery actions, 239, 242, 269, 283, 348, 349, 375
Recovery of illegal state aid, 243-244, 347-350
Remedies
  declaratory judgment, 306-308
  effectiveness of the recovery obligation, 323-325
  efficiency of recovery actions, 242-243
  interim measures, 244-245, 328-330
  nullity, 56, 238, 270, 284, 303, 306, 310, 334, 372
  payment of interest, 20, 91, 139, 256, 372
  prevention of the payment, 322
  private law remedies, 17, 19, 23, 118, 140, 141, 321, 331-332
  prophylactic, 206, 208, 209, 270, 275
  public law remedies, 17, 19, 23, 140, 321, 331-332
  repayment/repayment obligations, 207, 211, 253, 256, 349, 372
  rescissory action, 253, 255
  restorative, 210, 212
  suspension, 244, 247, 328

S

Services of general economic interest (SGEI), 216, 217, 219, 229, 236, 268, 273, 285, 304, 340, 343
Skanska judgment, 5, 152, 360, 361, 362
Stand-alone actions, 204-208
Standing/locus standi
  actio popularis, 270
  competitive interests, 294-296, 309, 313-315
  Schutznorm, 152, 294, 307-310, 315, 316, 377
Standstill obligation, 251-256, 275-276, 319-332, 370-373
Structural deficits, 2, 368

T

Tax/taxes
tax exemption, 206, 320
tax reduction, 236, 238
Transparency obligations, 257–258, 265, 276–279, 378

INTERNATIONAL COMPETITION LAW SERIES

1. Ignacio De Leon, *Latin American Competition Law and Policy: A Policy in Search of Identity*, 2001 (ISBN 90-411-1542-0).
2. Wim Dejonghe & Wouter Van de Voorde (eds), *M & A in Belgium*, 2001 (ISBN 90-411-1594-3).
3. Yang-Ching Chao, Gee San, Changfa Lo & Jiming Ho (eds), *International and Comparative Competition Law and Policies*, 2001 (ISBN 90-411-1643-5).
4. Martin Mendelsohn & Stephen Rose, *Guide to the EC Block Exemption for Vertical Agreements*, 2002 (ISBN 90-411-9813-X).
5. Clifford A. Jones & Mitsuo Matsushita (eds), *Competition Policy in the Global Trading System: Perspectives from the EU, Japan and the USA*, 2002 (ISBN 90-411-1758-X).
6. Christian Koenig, Andreas Bartosch, Jens-Daniel Braun & Marion Romes (eds), *EC Competition and Telecommunications Law*. Second Edition, 2009 (ISBN 978-90-411-2564-4).
7. Jürgen Basedow (ed.), *Limits and Control of Competition with a View to International Harmonization*, 2002 (ISBN 90-411-1967-1).
8. Maureen Brunt, Economic Essays on Australian and New Zealand Competition Law, 2003 (ISBN 90-411-1991-4).
9. Ky P. Ewing, Jr., *Competition Rules for the 21st Century: Principles from America's Experience*, Second Edition, 2006 (ISBN 90-411-2477-2).
10. Joseph Wilson, *Globalization and the Limits of National Merger Control Laws*, 2003 (ISBN 90-411-1996-5).
11. Peter Verloop & Valérie Landes (eds), *Merger Control in Europe: EU, Member States and Accession States*, Fourth Edition, 2003 (ISBN 90-411-2056-4).
12. Themistoklis K. Giannakopoulos, *Safeguarding Companies' Rights in Competition and Anti-dumping/Anti-subsidies Proceedings*, Second Edition, 2011 (ISBN 978-90-411-3404-2).
13. Marjorie Holmes & Lesley Davey (eds), *A Practical Guide to National Competition Rules across Europe*, Second Edition, 2007 (ISBN 978-90- 411-2607-8).
14. Sigrid Stroux, *US and EU Oligopoly Control*, 2004 (ISBN 90-411-2296-6).
15. Tzong-Leh Hwang and Chiyuan Chen (eds), *The Future Development of Competition Framework*, 2004 (ISBN 90-411-2305-9).

16. Phedon Nicolaides, Mihalis Kekelekis and Maria Kleis, *State Aid Policy in the European Community: Principles and Practice,* Second Edition, 2008 (ISBN 978-90-411-2754-9).
17. Doris Hildebrand, *Economic Analyses of Vertical Agreements: A Self- Assessment*, 2005 (ISBN 90-411-2328-8).
18. Frauke Henning-Bodewig, *Unfair Competition Law: European Union and Member States*, 2005 (ISBN 90-411-2329-6).
19. Duarte Brito & Margarida Catalão-Lopes, *Mergers and Acquisitions: The Industrial Organization Perspective,* 2006 (ISBN 90-411-2451-9).
20. Nikos Th. Nikolinakos, *EU Competition Law and Regulation in the Converging Telecommunications, Media and IT Sectors*, 2006 (ISBN 90-411- 2469-1).
21. Mihalis Kekelekis, *The EC Merger Control Regulation: Rights of Defence. A Critical Analysis of DG COMP Practice and Community Courts' Jurisprudence*, 2006 (ISBN 90-411-2553-1).
22. Mark R. Joelson, *An International Antitrust Primer: A Guide to the Operation of United States, European Union and Other Key Competition Laws in the Global Economy*, Third Edition, 2006 (ISBN 90-411-2468-3).
23. Themistoklis K. Giannakopoulos, *A Concise Guide to the EU Anti-dumping/ Anti-subsidies Procedures*, 2006 (ISBN 90-411-2464-0).
24. George Cumming, Brad Spitz & Ruth Janal, *Civil Procedure Used for Enforcement of EC Competition Law by the English, French and German Civil Courts*, 2007 (ISBN 978-90-411-2471-5).
25. Jürgen Basedow (ed.), *Private Enforcement of EC Competition Law,* 2007 (ISBN 978-90-411-2613-9).
26. Jung Wook Cho, *Innovation and Competition in the Digital Network Economy: A Legal and Economic Assessment on Multi-tying Practices and Network Effects*, 2007 (ISBN 978-90-411-2574-3).
27. Akira Inoue, *Japanese Antitrust Law Manual: Law, Cases and Interpretation of the Japanese Antimonopoly Act*, 2007 (ISBN 978-90-411-2627-6).
28. René Barents, *Directory of EC Case Law on Competition,* 2007 (ISBN 978-90-411-2656-6).
29. Paul F. Nemitz (ed.), *The Effective Application of EU State Aid Procedures: The Role of National Law and Practice*, 2007 (ISBN 978-90-411-2657-3).
30. Jurian Langer, *Tying and Bundling as a Leveraging Concern under EC Competition Law,* 2007 (ISBN 978-90-411-2575-0).
31. Abel M. Mateus & Teresa Moreira (eds), *Competition Law and Economics – Advances in Competition Policy and Antitrust Enforcement*, 2007 (ISBN 978-90-411-2632-0).
32. Alberto Santa Maria, *Competition and State Aid: An Analysis of the EC Practice,* 2007 (ISBN 978-90-411-2617-7).
33. Barry J. Rodger (ed.), *Article 234 and Competition Law: An Analysis,* 2007 (ISBN 978-90-411-2605-4).

34. Alla Pozdnakova, *Liner Shipping and EU Competition Law*, 2008 (ISBN 978-90-411-2717-4).
35. Milena Stoyanova, *Competition Problems in Liberalized Telecommunications: Regulatory Solutions to Promote Effective Competition*, 2008 (ISBN 978-90-411-2736-5).
36. *EC State Aid Law/Le Droit des Aides d'Etat dans la CE. Liber Amicorum Francisco Santaolalla Gadea*, 2008 (ISBN 978-90-411-2774-7).
37. René Barents, *Directory of EU Case Law on State Aids*, Third Edition, 2019 (ISBN 978-94-035-1101-6).
38. Ignacio De Leon, *An Institutional Assessment of Antitrust Policy: The Latin American Experience*, 2009 (ISBN 978-90-411-2478-4).
39. Doris Hildebrand, *The Role of Economic Analysis in EU Competition Law: The European School*, Fourth Edition, 2016 (ISBN 978-90-411-6245-8).
40. Eugène Buttigieg, *Competition Law: Safeguarding the Consumer Interest. A Comparative Analysis of US Antitrust Law and EC Competition Law*, 2009 (ISBN 978-90-411-3119-5).
41. Ioannis Lianos & Ioannis Kokkoris (eds), *The Reform of EC Competition Law: New Challenges*, 2010 (ISBN 978-90-411-2692-4).
42. George Cumming & Mirjam Freudenthal, *Civil Procedure in EU Competition Cases before the English and Dutch Courts*, 2010 (ISBN 978-90-411-3192-8).
43. A.E. Rodriguez & Ashok Menon, *The Limits of Competition Policy: The Shortcomings of Antitrust in Developing and Reforming Economies*, 2010 (ISBN 978-90-411-3177-5).
44. Mika Oinonen, *Does EU Merger Control Discriminate against Small Market Companies? Diagnosing the Argument with Conclusions*, 2010 (ISBN 978-90-411-3261-1).
45. Eirik Østerud, *Identifying Exclusionary Abuses by Dominant Undertakings under EU Competition Law: The Spectrum of Tests*, 2010 (ISBN 978-90-411-3271-0).
46. Marco Botta, *Merger Control Regimes in Emerging Economies: A Case Study on Brazil and Argentina*, 2011 (ISBN 978-90-411-3402-8).
47. Jürgen Basedow & Wolfgang Wurmnest (eds), *Structure and Effects in EU Competition Law: Studies on Exclusionary Conduct and State Aid*, 2011 (ISBN 978-90-411-3174-4).
48. George Cumming (ed.), *Merger Decisions and the Rules of Procedure of the European Community Courts*, 2012 (ISBN 978-90-411-3671-8).
49. Eduardo Molan Gaban & Juliana Oliveira Domingues (eds), *Antitrust Law in Brazil: Fighting Cartels*, 2012 (ISBN 978-90-411-3670-1).
50. Giandonato Caggiano, Gabriella Muscolo & Marina Tavassi (eds), *Competition Law and Intellectual Property: A European Perspective*, 2012 (ISBN 978-90-411-3447-9).
51. Ben Van Rompuy, *Economic Efficiency: The Sole Concern of Modern Antitrust Policy? Non-efficiency Considerations under Article 101 TFEU*, 2012 (ISBN 978-90-411-3870-5).

52. Liyang Hou, *Competition Law and Regulation of the EU Electronic Communications Sector: A Comparative Legal Approach*, 2012 (ISBN 978-90-411-4047-0).
53. Barry Rodger, *Landmark Cases in Competition Law: Around the World in Fourteen Stories*, 2012 (ISBN 978-90-411-3843-9).
54. Andreas Scordamaglia-Tousis, *EU Cartel Enforcement: Reconciling Effective Public Enforcement with Fundamental Rights*, 2013 (ISBN 978-90-411-4758-5).
55. Bernardo Cortese (ed.), *EU Competition Law: Between Public and Private Enforcement*, 2014 (ISBN 978-90-411-4677-9).
56. Barry Rodger (ed.), *Competition Law: Comparative Private Enforcement and Collective Redress across the EU*, 2014 (ISBN 978-90-411-4559-8).
57. Nada Ina Pauer, *The Single Economic Entity Doctrine and Corporate Group Responsibility in European Antitrust Law*, 2014 (ISBN 978-90-411-5262-6).
58. Urška Petrovčič, *Competition Law and Standard Essential Patents: A Transatlantic Perspective*, 2014 (ISBN 978-90-411-4960-2).
59. David Telyas, *The Interface between Competition Law, Patents and Technical Standards*, 2014 (ISBN 978-90-411-5418-7).
60. Katerina Maniadaki, *EU Competition Law, Regulation and the Internet: The Case of Net Neutrality*, 2014 (ISBN 978-90-411-4140-8).
61. Horacio Vedia Jerez, *Competition Law Enforcement and Compliance across the World: A Comparative Review*, 2015 (ISBN 978-90-411-5815-4).
62. Kadir Ba, *The Substantive Appraisal of Joint Ventures under the EU Merger Control Regime*, 2015 (ISBN 978-90-411-5816-1).
63. Alberto Santa Maria, *Competition and State Aid: An Analysis of the EU Practice*, Second Edition, 2015 (ISBN 978-90-411-5818-5).
64. Lúcio Tomé Feteira, *The Interplay between European and National Competition Law after Regulation 1/2003: "United (Should) We Stand?"*, 2016 (ISBN 978-90-411-5663-1).
65. Giovanni Pitruzzella & Gabriella Muscolo (eds), *Competition and Patent Law in the Pharmaceutical Sector: An International Perspective*, 2016 (ISBN 978-90-411-5927-4).
66. Małgorzata Cyndecka, *The Market Economy Investor Test in EU State Aid Law: Applicability and Application*, 2016 (ISBN 978-90-411-6102-4).
67. Damiano Canapa, *Trademarks and Brands in Merger Control: An Analysis of the European and Swiss Legal Orders*, 2016 (ISBN 978-90-411-6717-0).
68. Inge Graef, *EU Competition Law, Data Protection and Online Platforms: Data as Essential Facility*, 2016 (ISBN 978-90-411-8324-8).
69. Anders Jessen, *Exclusionary Abuse after the* Post Danmark I *Case: The Role of the Effects-Based Approach under Article 102 TFEU*, 2017 (ISBN 978-90-411-8996-7).
70. Baskaran Balasingham, *The EU Leniency Policy: Reconciling Effectiveness and Fairness*, 2017 (ISBN 978-90-411-8479-5).
71. Eugene Stuart & Iana Roginska-Green, *Sixty Years of EU State Aid Law and Policy: Analysis and Assessment*, 2018 (ISBN 978-90-411-8869-4).

72. Anna Renata Pisarkiewicz, *Margin Squeeze in the Electronic Communications Sector: Critical Analysis of the Decisional Practice and Case Law*, 2018 (ISBN 978-90-411-6246-5).
73. Ploykaew Porananond, *Competition Law in the ASEAN Countries: Regional Law and National Systems*, 2018 (ISBN 978-90-411-9102-1).
74. Corinne Ruechardt, *EU State Aid Control of Infrastructure Funding*, 2018 (ISBN 978-90-411-9099-4).
75. Amalia Athanasiadou, *Patent Settlements in the Pharmaceutical Industry under US Antitrust and EU Competition Law*, 2018 (ISBN 978-94-035-0113-0).
76. Miroslava Marinova, *Fidelity Rebates in Competition Law: Application of the 'As Efficient Competitor' Test*, 2018 (ISBN 978-94-035-0570-1).
77. Gabriella Muscolo & Marina Tavassi, *The Interplay Between Competition Law and Intellectual Property: An International Perspective*, 2019 (ISBN 978-90-411-8687-4).
78. Fevzi Toksoy, Bahadir Balki & Hanna Stakheyeva, *Merger Control in the EU and Turkey: A Comparative Guide*, 2019 (ISBN 978-94-035-0934-1).
79. Paulo Burnier da Silveira & William Evan Kovacic (eds), *Global Competition Enforcement: New Players, New Challenges*, 2019 (ISBN 978-94-035-0283-0).
80. Giovanna Massarotto, *Antitrust Settlements: How a Simple Agreement Can Drive the Economy*, 2019 (ISBN 978-94-035-1133-7).
81. Marc Veenbrink, *Criminal Law Principles and the Enforcement of EU and National Competition Law: A Silent Takeover?*, 2020 (ISBN 978-94-035-1434-5).
82. Ferdinand Wollenschläger, Wolfgang Wurmnest & Thomas M.J. Möllers (eds), *Private Enforcement of European Competition and State Aid Law: Current Challenges and the Way Forward*, 2020 (ISBN 978-94-035-0281-6).

www.ingramcontent.com/pod-product-compliance
Ingram Content Group UK Ltd.
Pitfield, Milton Keynes, MK11 3LW, UK
UKHW020229290926
15470UKWH00002B/439

9 789403 50281